Mystic River

AREA OF INSET MAP A

CHARLESTOWN

EAST BOSTON

WASHINGTON ST.

NORTHWEST EXPRESSWAY

MSGR. O'BRIEN HIGHWAY

PROSPECT STREET

CAMBRIDGE STREET

CAMBRIDGE

CHARLESTOWN BRIDGE

COMMERCIAL ST.

TUNNEL

LOGAN AIRPORT

BROADWAY

NORTH END

MAIN STREET

CHARLES ST.

CAMBRIDGE ST.

City Hall

CONGRESS ST.

Massachusetts Institute of Technology

LONGFELLOW BRIDGE

DRIVE

State House

BOSTON INNER HARBOR

Charles River

MEMORIAL

HARVARD BRIDGE

STORROW DRIVE BACK BAY

BEACON STREET

CHARLES ST.

BOSTON COMMON

TREMONT ST.

COMMONWEALTH AVENUE

BOYLSTON ST. COPLEY SQUARE

MASSACHUSETTS

PRUDENTIAL CENTER

TURNPIKE

WASHINGTON STREET

FENWAY PARK

SOUTH END

AREA OF INSET MAP B

TREMONT STREET

W. BROOKLINE ST.

BROADWAY

EAST BROADWAY

HUNTINGTON AVENUE

COLUMBUS AVENUE

MASSACHUSETTS AVENUE

LENOX ST.

KENDELL ST.

STERLING ST.

LOWER ROXBURY

SOUTH BOSTON

South Boston High School

B   O   S   T   O   N

COLUMBUS AVENUE

ROXBURY

MORRISSEY BLVD.

SOUTHEAST EXPRESSWAY

Boston Globe

COLUMBIA ROAD

BLUE HILL AVENUE

DORCHESTER AVENUE

DORCHESTER BAY

FRANKLIN PARK

DORCHESTER

Debnam house

CENTRE ST.

Common
Ground

Common Ground

A TURBULENT DECADE IN THE LIVES
OF THREE AMERICAN FAMILIES

J. Anthony Lukas

ALFRED A. KNOPF
NEW YORK 1985

Grateful acknowledgment is made to the following for permission to reprint previously published material:

Almo Publications: excerpts from the lyrics to *We've Only Just Begun*, lyrics by Paul Williams, music by Roger Nichols. Copyright © 1970 Irving Music, Inc. (BMI). All rights reserved. International copyright secured.

The Boston *Globe*: excerpt from "An Open Letter to Senator Kennedy," by Mike Barnicle, Sept. 8, 1974, reprinted courtesy of the Boston *Globe*.

Chappell & Company, Inc.: excerpts from the lyrics to *Carefully Taught* by Richard Rodgers and Oscar Hammerstein II. Copyright 1949 by Richard Rodgers & Oscar Hammerstein II. Copyright renewed, Williamson Music Co., owner of publication and allied rights throughout the Western Hemisphere and Japan. International copyright secured. All rights reserved. Used by permission.

Macmillan Publishing Company: four lines from "A Full Moon in March" are used by permission of Macmillan Publishing Company from *Collected Plays* of W. B. Yeats. Copyright 1934, 1952 by Macmillan Publishing Co., Inc. Copyrights renewed 1962 by Bertha Georgie Yeats and 1980 by Anne Yeats; rights in the world excluding the United States are administered by A. P. Watt Ltd. as agent for Michael B. Yeats and Macmillan London, Ltd.

Mighty Three Music: excerpts from the lyrics to *For the Love of Money* by Kenneth Gamble, Leon Huff, and Anthony Jackson. Copyright © 1974 Mighty Three Music; excerpts from the lyrics to *I'll Always Love My Mama* by Kenneth Gamble, Leon Huff, Gene McFadden, and John Whitehead. Copyright © 1973 Mighty Three Music. Administered by Mighty Three Music Group, 309 S. Broad Street, Philadelphia, PA 19107.

Edwin H. Morris & Company: excerpts from lyrics to *Hello, Dolly!*, lyrics and music by Jerry Herman. Copyright © 1963 Jerry Herman; excerpts from the lyrics to *Before the Parade Passes By*, lyrics and music by Jerry Herman. Copyright © 1964 by Jerry Herman. All rights throughout the world controlled by Edwin H. Morris & Company, a division of MPL Communications, Inc. International copyright secured. All rights reserved.

Newsweek, Inc.: excerpts from the cover story, November 6, 1967. Copyright © 1967 by Newsweek, Inc. All rights reserved. Reprinted by permission.

Harold Ober Associates Incorporated: excerpts from *Ballad of the Landlord* by Langston Hughes. Copyright 1951 by Langston Hughes. Copyright renewed 1979 by George Houston Bass; *The City*-eight line version by Langston Hughes. Copyright © 1958 by Langston Hughes. Reprinted by permission of Harold Ober Associates Incorporated.

Library of Congress Cataloging in Publication Data

Lukas, J. Anthony, [date]
Common ground.
1. Boston (Mass.)—Race relations. 2. Busing for school integration—Massachusetts—Boston. 3. School integration—Massachusetts—Boston. 4. Diver family. 5. Twymon family. 6. McGoff family. I. Title.
F73.9.A1L85   1985   370.19'342   85-127
ISBN 0- 394-41150-1

Manufactured in the United States of America
Published September 18, 1985
Second Printing, September 1985

To Linda
who saw through me
and saw me through

Author's Note

This is a work of non-fiction. All its characters are real, as are
their names, the places where they live, the details of their
personal lives. Nothing has been disguised or embellished. Where
I have used dialogue, it is based on the recollection of at least one
participant.

The three families at the center of my story were not selected
as statistical averages or norms. On the contrary, I was drawn to
them by a special intensity, an engagement with life, which made
them stand out from their social context. At first, I thought I read
clear moral imperatives in the geometry of their intersecting lives,
but the more time I spent with them, the harder it became to
assign easy labels of guilt or virtue. The realities of urban
America, when seen through the lives of actual city dwellers,
proved far more complicated than I had imagined.

J.A.L.

New York City

January 1985

Contents

Common Ground

1

Diver

Sunlight struck the gnarled limbs outside his window, casting a thicket of light and shadow on the white clapboards. From his desk high under the eaves, Colin Diver could watch students strolling the paths of Cambridge Common or playing softball on the neatly trimmed diamond. It was one of those brisk afternoons in early spring, the kind of day which in years past had lured him into the dappled light, rejoicing in his good fortune. But here he lurked in his study, walled in by books, overcome by doubt.

People kept telling him this should be the best time of his life, the moment he'd been slogging toward these past three years. He was about to graduate near the top of his class; he'd won a highly prized position on the *Harvard Law Review,* and even before graduation had a place reserved for him at a distinguished Washington law firm. Altogether his prospects were splendid. But he'd been in the doldrums all that late winter and early spring of 1968.

It wasn't the prospect of leaving Cambridge. He was as susceptible as anyone to the springtime charms of this place: the white steeple of Memorial Church breaking clean above the elms; the band, splendid in their crimson blazers, crashing through "Ten Thousand Men of Harvard" on the steps of Widener Library; the eight-man crews at dusk dipping their oars in the Charles. But such pleasures were largely reserved for undergraduates; most law students were simply too busy. Harried from Tax to Trusts, from Equity to Evidence, they drudged their way through a different Cambridge. Many might have agreed with Oliver Wendell Holmes, Jr., who entered the Law School in 1864 and recalled later: "One found oneself plunged in a thick fog of details— in a black and frozen night, in which were no flowers, no spring, no easy joys."

Colin had no aversion to legal labors, no trouble heeding his professors' admonitions to "think like a lawyer," for he had learned the law at his mother's knee. Ethleen Diver was among the first women to practice law in a major

3

Boston firm, though the stately old house of Choate, Hall & Stewart had made her wait for that privilege. She'd begun there as a legal secretary in 1926, but even after she took her law degree and passed the bar, her employers had kept her passing the Hukwa tea and S.S. Pierce biscuits for a quarter century. Only in 1951, when she threatened to quit, had they reluctantly permitted her to take on cases of her own. Even then she got only the legal scut work—probate, real estate, income taxes—all the stuff nobody else wanted. But Ethleen didn't mind. She was like a spurned lover who, deep into middle age, had been accepted by the object of her affection. It was all she'd ever wanted.

When Colin was young, his mother took him along to county courthouses, where he sat in the dim old courtrooms mesmerized by adoption or divorce proceedings. When he was a little older, she put him to work copying ancient deeds from dusty volumes. Now and again she took him to the firm's State Street offices, where he watched the solemn partners in conference. Colin didn't like the way they'd treated his mother; he resented it more than she did. But somehow, by the time he was a senior at Amherst, he had inherited his mother's passion for the law.

He was very good at it. His first year at Harvard he'd ranked sixth in a class of 550, thereby earning election to the *Law Review*. Later he became Supreme Court Note Editor, the second-ranking position in the journal's hierarchy. Colin spent forty hours a week at the *Review*. His office there was crammed with copies of *U.S. Law Week;* manuscripts; green, pink, and blue galleys; lawbooks; sandwich wrappings, coffee cups, and aspirin. One day his wife, Joan, asked with a wry grin whether he wanted his breakfast served there too.

But such labors were well worth it. For the *Law Review* unrolled a crimson carpet through a lawyer's life—bringing with it prime clerkships, offers from prestigious law firms, and ultimately partnerships worth six figures a year, professorships at the best law schools, judgeships right up to the Supreme Court. The *Review* boasted such alumni as Felix Frankfurter, Dean Acheson, Elliot Richardson, Joseph Califano, and Archibald MacLeish. It was a ticket of admission to the American establishment.

The trouble was, Colin didn't know whether he wanted to join such an establishment, one which had drawn the country into a terrible war, stirring dissent across the land that spring.

He was no radical. Having grown to political consciousness in the Massachusetts of John Fitzgerald Kennedy, he had modeled himself on that young paragon: idealistic and energetic, but cool and ironic. In October 1963, during Colin's junior year at Amherst, Kennedy had come to dedicate the college's new Robert Frost Library, receive an honorary degree, and deliver one of his most stirring addresses: "What good is a great private college unless it serves a great national purpose?" he had asked. "The problems we face are staggering both at home and abroad. We need the services of every educated man and woman."

The President's visit was marred by what for those days was a most unusual incident. Sixty students and junior faculty stood through the speech with placards calling for a "Civil Rights Law in '63." Dressed neatly in ties and jackets, they uttered not a word during the proceedings. But even this most discreet of demonstrations had been widely denounced as "ridiculous" and "unbecoming the dignity of Amherst." Colin Diver shared that view: he couldn't imagine why anyone would want to embarrass America's bold new leader.

A month later, Kennedy was dead in Dallas. Amherst's president, Calvin Plimpton, told reporters, "Four weeks ago he was here. We saw him; we heard him; and we knew him. He was one of us, for he was our most recent alumnus." Colin shared that sense of personal loss. Kennedy had been the bright star at the center of his political universe. For years he would try to navigate by its recollected light.

But by the time he reached Cambridge, student life had changed beyond recognition. Harvard undergraduates in the mid-sixties were no longer drawn to Kennedy's detached and prudent style; they sought authenticity, commitment, and confrontation. Even the younger law students coming on behind Colin reflected this shifting mood. In October 1967, fifty law students from Cambridge had joined the March on the Pentagon, parading behind a large crimson banner emblazoned "Harvard Law."

Colin was sympathetic to the war protesters, if only because of his precarious draft status. For years he'd stayed a step ahead of the mounting monthly calls, relying first on his college ranking and then—as deferments tightened—on marriage, law school, his first child. But he wasn't sure how long he could remain exempt. As the war news nagged at him, he had edged cautiously into Cambridge's anti-war movement.

On November 9, he had been among four hundred students and faculty who filled Langdell Hall for the law school's first Vietnam "teach-in." Professor Paul Bator set the tone for the evening when he warned, "We cannot let the lawyer's cult of effectiveness reduce us to immobility. Martin Luther King's bus boycotters in Montgomery didn't go through a lawyerlike screening process and yet they started a revolution. We have to be a little bold. We have to make waves."

With words like those in their ears, members of the Law School class of 1968 began to make their career decisions. A few years before, choice was scarcely necessary; through the fifties and early sixties, the overwhelming majority of graduates entered private practice, generally with large corporate firms. But the new social activism had rendered such conventional careers less automatic. By 1967, the percentage entering private practice—as opposed to clerkships, research, teaching, legal services, or government—fell below 50 percent for the first time.

Confronted with this new skepticism about establishment careers, the major law firms tried to sweeten the pot. In February 1968, the premium New York firm of Cravath, Swaine & Moore stunned the legal world by raising its starting salary to $15,000. Others quickly followed. But cash alone had little allure for the class of 1968. According to a poll that spring, a majority of Harvard's third-year law students were more attracted by ample opportunities for *pro bono* activities on behalf of worthy causes. That majority rose to 75 percent among Colin's classmates at the *Law Review,* who were polled during a special meeting at the magazine's offices. Only four of the twenty-four editors said they would be greatly influenced by an offer of $15,000. Some said they would flatly refuse to work for most big firms, who "always seem to be representing the giant corporations against the little guy." One of the activists admonished his more traditional colleagues, "Your natural and understandable ambition for illustrious careers seems to be clouding your vision about what is right in this country and what is simply wrong."

Such was the dilemma which had bedeviled Colin all that winter. Ranking near the top of his class, he had many options, but each had its drawbacks. Clerking for some eminent judge meant more legal research, just what he'd been doing for years on the *Review*. Government was more appealing, but none of the low-level jobs for which he qualified captured his imagination. His best route to a responsible government position would be through a private firm specializing in administrative law. But most such firms were heavily involved in lobbying for industry, an activity which Colin didn't find palatable.

For months that winter, he'd agonized over his decision. He'd discussed it for hours with Joan, mulling over the alternatives, weighing one against another. He had similar sessions with his best friend and *Law Review* colleague, David Mann, arguing about "the nature of the law." Harvard seemed to regard the law as a set of scales designed to keep society in eternal equilibrium. Colin and David could no longer accept that traditional notion, but neither could they endorse the radicals' concept of the law as a hammer to smash the barricades of vested interest. Slowly, they came to view it as a lever with which to pry up the mossy rocks of privilege, bringing air and light to the teeming precincts beneath.

Or to use another metaphor of which they were fond, most private law practice was "greasing the wheels of capitalism." Neither David nor Colin wanted to be a wheel greaser. "Somebody's got to do it," David would say. "Perhaps," Colin replied, "but why does it have to be me?"

In the end neither of them found a practical alternative to private practice. In mid-February, David signed on with Dinsmore, Shohl, Coates & Deupree, a corporate firm in his hometown of Cincinnati. A few weeks later, Colin accepted an offer from Wilmer, Cutler & Pickering, a prominent administrative law firm with spacious offices three blocks from the White House. His friends congratulated him, for although it was barely six years old, W, C & P already ranked as one of Washington's most prestigious firms.

Its prominence derived largely from its most active partner, Lloyd Cutler, who was rapidly emerging as the capital's principal power broker. More than any other Washington lawyer, he had learned to straddle the public and private interest. A former New Deal official, Cutler was a 1930s liberal who called himself "a believer in social change." His firm did prodigious *pro bono* work, from fighting a New Orleans expressway to representing black clients in Baltimore. He was the first secretary to the Lawyers' Committee for Civil Rights, later general counsel to President Johnson's Committee on Urban Housing.

But Cutler also specialized in representing industrial giants in their jousts with government. His firm spoke for J. P. Morgan & Co. against banking reform; for J. C. Penney on consumer legislation; for American Airlines and IBM on tax matters. He personally represented the American Automobile Manufacturers' Association in its bitter struggles with Ralph Nader over automobile safety, and the Pharmaceutical Manufacturers' Association in legislative sparring over drug pricing.

Cutler acknowledged no contradiction between his two roles, firmly believing that differences between big business and big government were reconcilable because they were rooted in honest misunderstandings, not malice or greed. His critics were less charitable. Michael Pertschuk, general counsel to the Senate Commerce Committee, called Cutler "a genius, but an evil genius."

Colin's decision to work for W, C & P had been an uneasy compromise at best. The $14,000 salary was handsome, but to him relatively unimportant; the promise of *pro bono* work was appealing, but most attractive of all was the prospect of getting his feet wet in administrative law and, ultimately, in the world of public affairs. Yet his decision continued to disturb him. He felt increasingly uneasy about going to work for a man who had defended some of the seamier aspects of American business.

As the winter wore on, Colin grew more and more depressed. Somehow the future had lost its lure. At the dinner table, he would lapse into prolonged silences, then mope around the apartment all evening. Joan tried occupational therapy. She bought the makings of a rya rug and for hours that March she and Colin would sit silently on the couch, hooking thirteen shades of yarn. Other nights, after working late at the *Law Review*, he would find himself staring moodily over a cup of muddy coffee at the huge Miró mural which dominated the north wall of the Harkness cafeteria and which somehow echoed his mood. Swimming in a bilious green sea were huge, menacing creatures—an octopus, its tentacles extended, and a sea scorpion, searching for prey. Suspended among the monsters was a humanoid face, staring out through expressionless eyes, one orange, the other green.

He was prey as well to migraine headaches which incapacitated him for hours on end. Walking through Harvard Square or reading in Langdell Library, he would suffer a blurring of his eyesight, followed by a stabbing pain in his skull. Doctors ascribed these attacks to dilation of the blood vessels near the ocular nerve, but psychological pressures, particularly in highly controlled and self-disciplined people, were also a factor. Most of Colin's acquaintances regarded him as unemotional, aloof, even cold. Only his closest friends knew what strong emotions ran just beneath the surface. The effort to keep such feelings under control may well have brought on the crippling headaches from which he suffered all that spring.

Now, on the afternoon of April 4, Colin decided that he'd brooded long enough. Closing the corporate tax volume he'd been idly perusing, he stuffed some papers in his briefcase and hurried down the stairs. Walking across the lawn, he glanced as usual at the stone marker which proclaimed: "Here assembled on the night of June 16, 1775, 1200 Continental troops under the command of Colonel Prescott. After prayer by President Langdon they marched to Bunker Hill." General William Prescott, who commanded the colonial troops at Bunker Hill and admonished them not to shoot until they saw the whites of their enemy's eyes, was one of his wife's ancestors.

His daily walk through Harvard Yard deepened Colin's sense of connection to a significant past. Something about the way the sidewalks sliced the lush lawns into neat geometric shapes satisfied his sense of order. The sharp-edged New England purity—kiln-red bricks, black shutters, gleaming white trim—touched him deeply.

Then he was out again in the dash and hustle of Massachusetts Avenue, past the bicycle exchange, down Mount Auburn Street to the apartment on Flagg Street. Joan was there, feeding one-year-old Brad. Colin stretched out on the bed, picked up the morning *Globe,* and flicked on the clock radio. For half an hour, a Haydn string quartet mixed with the clatter of pans.

At 7:16 p.m., a somber voice interrupted the music: "Dr. Martin Luther King, Jr., was shot outside a Memphis motel this afternoon. His condition was not immediately known."

At 8:19, the voice broke in again: "Dr. Martin Luther King, the civil rights leader and Nobel laureate, was shot and killed late today as he stood alone on the balcony of his motel."

Until well past midnight, Colin and Joan sat on their bed, listening to updates from Memphis and other cities—including Boston—which had begun to burn.

Nothing in Colin's experience had quite prepared him for what he now felt. King hadn't been one of his special heroes; he regarded him as a courageous man who had endured terrible hardships to achieve equality for his people, but he felt little for him personally. Colin had followed the Southern civil rights movement closely and sympathetically but, unlike some of his classmates, he hadn't been impelled to participate in those events. He hadn't joined Amherst Students for Racial Equality, which sent its members South to help integrate public beaches in Florida or register voters in North Carolina. Bizarre and exotic, those events had seemed remote from his own time and place.

Yet King's assassination tapped some secret well of feeling. Perhaps that was because it evoked memories of John Kennedy's death. It seemed to Colin as if every great man who tried to change this country through personal leadership was going to pay with his life.

Or perhaps it was because King's killing echoed the Kerner Commission report, issued only two months before, which had warned: "Our nation is moving toward two societies, one black, one white—separate and unequal." A paperback edition of the report by the National Advisory Commission on

Civil Disorders was selling briskly at bookstores in Harvard Square. Colin and Joan had been shocked by the eruptions of the Newark and Detroit ghettos the summer before and, like many of their friends in Cambridge, were reading the Kerner Report to understand what had gone wrong. Their dog-eared copy was underlined in pencil where they had found telling conclusions. One heavily marked passage said, "In the riot cities we surveyed, we found that Negroes are severely disadvantaged, especially as compared with whites; that local government is often unresponsive to this fact; that federal programs have not yet reached a significantly large proportion of those in need; and that the result is a reservoir of unredressed grievances and frustrations in the ghetto."

They had underlined the section that warned: "What white Americans have never fully understood—but what the Negro can never forget—is that white society is deeply implicated in the ghetto. White institutions created it, white institutions maintain it, white society condones it."

And they had put a star in the margin by the section that went: "White racism is essentially responsible for the explosive mixture which has been accumulating in our cities since the end of World War II."

The Divers knew few Negroes—the notable exception being Howard Thurman, an eminent theologian and spellbinding preacher, long a friend of Joan's family. Colin had come to know and revere Thurman. When he and Joan were married, they had chosen the black minister to perform the ceremony.

Thurman was a friend and confidant of Martin Luther King. After the assassination, he delivered a stirring eulogy for his lost colleague. "Tonight," he said, "there is a vast temptation to strike out in pain, horror, and anger; riding just under the surface are all the pent-up furies, the accumulation of generations of cruelty and brutality. A way must be found to honor our feelings without dishonoring him whose sudden and meaningless end has called them forth. May we harness the energy of our bitterness and make it available to the unfinished work which Martin has left behind."

Sitting cross-legged on their bedroom floor the next afternoon, Colin and Joan heard Thurman's words on WILD, Boston's "soul" station, to which they had tuned because they wanted to hear what blacks were saying about King's death. The station had suspended its normal rhythm-and-blues format and was devoting hour after hour to news and commentary on the assassination and on the violence even then rippling through Boston's streets. The night before along Blue Hill Avenue in the heart of the black community, angry crowds had pelted store windows and cars with rocks and bricks. Nine persons had been injured. The police were out in force. Black ministers and politicians were using WILD's airwaves to "cool" things while, at the same time, expressing indignation at their leader's murder.

Late that afternoon, the station broadcast an impromptu discussion among black spokesmen, chaired by City Councilman Tom Atkins, Boston's only elected black official. Colin paid particular attention because he knew Atkins, who was then completing his second year at the Law School. Like other black leaders, Atkins had been out in the streets most of the night trying to quiet the crowds. Now his voice was drained and weary as he fielded telephoned questions.

Much of his audience was still very angry. "You been tellin' us to do this and do that," cried one young man, "and it didn't make any difference. They killed him anyway. Now what you got to say?"

"Not much," Atkins said. "Not much, my man. Except stay cool for now and hang in there. We'll get over somehow."

The next caller was a woman from Lexington, the suburban community in which Colin and Joan had both grown up. Hers was a smooth, cultivated voice with that waft of extra breath characteristic of Yankee Massachusetts. But this afternoon it was an agonized voice as well. "Everyone out here feels terrible about this," she said. "Please, tell us, Mr. Atkins, what can we do to help you? What can we do for the Negro community?"

For a moment there was silence. Then, his voice rumbling in the lower registers, choosing his words carefully, Atkins began: "Right now, there's nothing you can do for us. Right now, it isn't even safe for you to come in here. Right now, the best thing you can do is to leave us alone and let us try to get our act together. If I may say so, what you ought to do is to go back to your own community and try to get your people together. Try to get them to start caring, to start responding, to start looking at themselves, at their own motivations and attitudes on the matter of race. Before you can do anything for us, you have to look into your own souls."

As Atkins spoke, Colin felt a terrible anguish for his country. Atkins was saying that America was already two societies—separate and unequal, and already so far apart they couldn't reach out to each other in this terrible moment.

Colin contemplated these circumstances all through a weekend marked by further violence in Boston and other cities. On Monday, the Law School's acting dean canceled classes for the next two days so that "each student may have a full opportunity for uninterrupted reflection on recent events and his position in regard to them." Later, it was revealed that the dean had acted after threats from the Law School's Association of African and Afro-American Students that they would picket the school unless it was closed. In any case, Colin took the dean literally: all Monday he remained at home, reconsidering his position.

At 1:00 p.m. Tuesday—as King's funeral cortege wound through Atlanta's streets toward Morehouse College—Colin joined 1,200 Harvard students and faculty in Memorial Church for the university's own memorial service. High in the pulpit, John L. Burkholder, a professor of divinity, declared, "Dr. King's death has challenged us to positive action. We must find new, radical approaches to justice and brotherhood." But it was Charles P. Price, preacher to the university, who pointed out a simple reality that Colin had already noticed but nobody had dared to mention: virtually the entire throng in the church was white, for blacks were holding their own service on the steps outside. The separate services were "a mark of the estrangement between white man and black man that exists today," Price said. "We meet in sorrow and repentance for what we have done to create a situation and sustain such a gap that we cannot even mourn together." Then he led the congregation in singing "We Shall Overcome," and when they reached the words "black and white together," Colin found himself wondering: will we ever be together?

As the strains of the hymn filtered through the tall windows, some of the eighty blacks gathered on the church steps jeered. Jeffrey P. Howard, president of the university's Afro-American Society, told them, "Martin Luther King would have called these people in there hypocrites. If they come out of there with tears in their eyes we want it to be plain we don't want tears. We want black people to have a place here at Harvard. On this campus there is as much racism as anywhere."

After the service, black law students filed across the street to the Ames courtroom at the Law School for a panel on "The Black Man's View" of the assassination. Colin, still brooding over the day's divisions, tagged along and took a seat in the back of the courtroom with a few other whites. There he listened as Bishop Hollifield, president of the black law students' association, told them, "If racism and repression don't give way to justice and hope, America in a little while will be just a page in a history book. The next time the white man slaps us in the face, black people are going to kick the hell out of him. In the meantime, we here in the cloistered world of the university, we students of the law, must pay closer attention to the condition of the black masses, to the agonized voices of our brothers in the street."

2
Twymon

An hour after the transistor radios in the project blared the news of King's death, Snake and Sly were out on Eustis Street slinging rocks at the police. Around the corner on Dearborn Street, someone had thrown a brick through a grocery window and every few minutes a kid would scamper across, grab a juicy grapefruit or a handful of plums, then dash to safety in the jiving black crowd.

But soon the frolic turned serious. The Orchard Park housing project, three square blocks of dingy barracks and barren courtyards, squatted on the edge of Roxbury, Boston's black heartland, but several neighboring streets were still white. Shortly past eleven, John McLaughlin, a twenty-six-year-old white man, rounded the corner in his maroon convertible, with twenty-five-year-old Carolyn MacElroy at his side, their radio blaring a hit tune, oblivious to the turmoil around them. As the car screeched to a halt in the intersection, a brick smashed the windshield. "Get out!" ordered a black kid in overalls. Carolyn MacElroy opened her door and ran back onto Dudley Street, unmolested. But when McLaughlin tried to follow, several teenagers knocked him to the street, blood streaming from his forehead. Policemen quickly pulled him to safety, but soon the crowd had surrounded the convertible, and lifting it by the fenders, they heaved it onto its side. The fuel tank burst into a fierce blaze. At this, a long sibilant sigh issued from the crowd, as if the fire had released hours, perhaps years, of pent-up feeling.

George, whose street name was Sly, and his brother Richard, known as Snake, had been out on Prescott Street, playing stickball against the factory wall, when a little kid had come by with a transistor radio, chanting in a monotone, "Dr. King is dead, Dr. King is dead." At first the brothers jeered, "Get out of here, you little bugger," and lashed the ball harder and higher against the concrete. But when the kid stuck the radio in their faces they heard it too. Although they were only twelve and fourteen, they knew enough about Martin Luther King to feel an acute sense of loss.

Their mother, Rachel Twymon, wept when she heard the news in her apartment on Prescott Street in Orchard Park. When her eight-year-old daughter, Cassandra, said, "Ma, he wasn't a member of our family, so why are you crying?" she replied, "Because, Cassandra, what he got killed for makes him my big brother, because he wanted all of us to be equal." She started to tell Cassandra that there were other reasons why she felt particularly close to King, reasons that went back fifteen years to the days she had known the young theological student they called Martin. But her recollections were interrupted by a knock on the door as two policemen from District 9 appeared to tell her, "They're breaking into your store, Mrs. Twymon. You better get on down there."

Rachel's Specialty Shop, a women's ready-to-wear clothing store, stood at the corner of Washington Street and Warren Avenue, in the heart of the area roiled that night by roving gangs of black youths. The rock thrown through one of Rachel Twymon's display windows had set off a burglar alarm, which rang at the police station. When the police tried to call her at home the line was busy, so they sent a patrol car to alert her. But by then all the buses in the area were halted, as were the Orange Line trains which normally clattered along the elevated trestle over Washington Street, so the police offered to drop her at the store.

Though they skirted the riot area, Rachel could see fires burning and cars with their windshields shattered on several side streets. Once a group of about fifteen youths with sticks in their hands loped across an empty lot. Rachel knew her children had to be mixed up in this somehow; she only hoped they wouldn't get hurt. When the police car pulled up in front of the store, she found to her relief that the grate she'd installed inside the plate glass was still intact and the racks of blouses and hot pants were untouched. But she noticed that the windows at Blair's Foodland down the street had been smashed and that items from a nearby variety store were strewn across the sidewalk. So she decided to spend the night on the cot in the back room. For hours she lay awake staring at the ceiling, listening to the sirens wailing in the night.

The next morning, Washington Street and Blue Hill Avenue—the black community's two principal thoroughfares—were pocked with smashed windows and burned-out stores. Police cars prowled the rubble and only a few pedestrians scuffed along the sidewalks examining the damage. By 1:00 p.m., things were heating up again. Several hundred youths began marching down the major shopping streets telling store owners to close up. On the door or window of each shop they pasted a flyer proclaiming, "This store is closed until further notice in honor of Dr. Martin Luther King, the fallen martyr of the black revolution."

Rachel saw the marchers coming down Washington Street and at first she determined to defy them. The stores on either side of her had long since closed up: Carroll's Cut-Rate Drugs, where her brother Arnold worked as a clerk, and Kim's Kaps, which sold hats, Afro wigs, and costume jewelry. But they were both run by Jews, old-style ghetto merchants who weren't very popular. Rachel's was one of only two black-owned stores in the neighborhood. She felt sure the kids wouldn't molest a "soul sister." If they gave her an argument, she'd explain that she'd been on welfare until she opened the store a few months before, that she had six kids to feed and simply couldn't afford to close up. But then the marchers were on her shouting, "Lock up the doors, sister, this is no time to be doin' business!" Quickly she realized it was no use, so she placed some cardboard over the hole in her window, locked the door, and went home.

Rachel didn't notice that Richard, George, and two of her younger sons— ten-year-old Freddie and nine-year-old Wayne—were tagging along behind the marchers, who then numbered nearly a thousand. When they reached the Jeremiah Burke High School they burned a flag flying at half-staff outside, then forced their way into the school and burned another flag. From there they marched to a Stop & Shop supermarket on Columbia Road which was still open. The white manager took one look at the vast throng building up outside his plate-glass windows, then called it a day. By 4:30, the crowd had broken up into roving gangs which began heaving rocks through store windows and car windshields. Back in the Orchard Park project, a light-skinned Negro was riding his motorcycle through one of the courts when a gang of young blacks knocked him off and beat him, stopping only when Bill Wimberly, director of the Roxbury YMCA, persuaded them the man was black. "It isn't safe to be a white man in Roxbury today," Wimberly told reporters.

The mood in Roxbury that afternoon would not have pleased the apostle of non-violence whose memory the demonstrators sought to honor. A leaflet distributed by the Black United Front said flatly, "Non-violence Is Dead. The Black Community Faces Disaster." Another, issued by two black community groups, warned, "When the riot starts, you can expect martial law which will confine you to your home for as long as a month or more. Start your survival plans now. We must unite for the attacks upon our communities from the police, armed forces, and the white communities. Have a gun and plenty of ammunition. Nothing wrong with a bow and arrow . . ."

Others counseled caution. The Roxbury Youth Patrol passed out leaflets that afternoon saying, "Cool it. The riot squad has M-16 rifles—Mace—a machine so high-pitched it will make you deaf. They're not playing. Keep off the streets. Defend your home and family. Don't start anything." Youth patrol members circulated in the crowds shouting the same message through bullhorns.

They urged young people to stay home that night and watch rhythm-and-blues star James Brown on television. "Don't go downtown, brothers," the patrol said. "Stay home. Put on the TV and watch cool James do his thing." Snake and Sly wouldn't miss James Brown, so they stayed home, huddled around the tube, pounding their feet as James wailed "Please, Please, Please."

On Sunday morning, Rachel and several of her children walked through muted streets to Union Methodist Church, where the Reverend Gilbert Caldwell admonished the congregation, "Don't give way to anger. Don't destroy your own community." Rachel picked up the same theme, telling her children at home that night, "Who do you think you're hurting with all this stuff? Your friends and neighbors, that's who. You can't burn yourself up."

Partly as a result of such efforts, Boston began to cool off that weekend. By early the next week peace had been restored at relatively little cost—21 injured, 30 arrested, barely $50,000 in damage. This was mild in comparison with what happened in many of the 197 other towns and cities where riots broke out in the aftermath of King's assassination: in Washington, for example, where 11 were killed, 1,113 were injured, and $24 million worth of property was destroyed; or Chicago, with 9 killed, 500 injured, and $11 million in damage.

On Tuesday afternoon, as King was buried in Atlanta, black Boston paused to watch the televised services from the Ebenezer Baptist Church, the sweltering three-and-a-half-hour march through Atlanta's streets, and, finally, the interment under a marble monument inscribed: "Free At Last, Free At Last, Thank God Almighty I'm Free At Last." Coretta King's haunted eyes, Daddy King's bowed gray head, Ralph Abernathy's cracked voice brought tears to Rachel's eyes. And once stirred up, those feelings wouldn't die, bringing with them memories of soft Sunday evenings years before when, after the Methodist Youth Fellowship meetings at Union Methodist, she and her girlfriends would stroll up Shawmut Avenue to the Twelfth Baptist Church.

They weren't all that religious. What drove them up the avenue was gospel—those throbbing hymns which blended a heavy dose of spirituality with more than a pinch of sensuality. They couldn't get gospel at Union Methodist, an outpost of staid respectability, so they sought it instead at the more soulful Baptist church.

Usually they had to sit through a boring anthem or two by Coretta Scott, an earnest soprano from the New England Conservatory of Music, who was often on the program because she was the fiancée of the young student minister who preached at Twelfth Baptist through most of 1952 and 1953. When Martin King had come to Boston University's School of Theology in September 1951, his father told him to look up his old friend and Baptist colleague Dr. William Hester, and soon Martin was preaching most of the Sunday-evening sermons at Dr. Hester's church.

Even then, Martin was a commanding figure in the pulpit. The Reverend Mike Haynes, Dr. Hester's assistant, would normally have delivered those Sunday-evening sermons. For a time he was miffed at the preference given King, but soon he recognized that "Martin was completely out of my league."

Rachel too was a bit awed by the young student minister. She didn't talk to him much—he was twenty-three in 1952 and she was only fifteen—but she found his preaching "spellbinding," his cool assurance "impressive." She and her friends agreed he was a real "Bougie," a middle-class boy destined for great things. When those great things came to pass, she identified even further with King. Every time he came back to Boston, she went to hear him. Several times he appeared at Union Methodist seeking funds for his activities and on each occasion Rachel gave more than she could really afford, partly out of nostalgia for those evenings on Shawmut Avenue, partly out of pride in her association with this great man. She followed his career closely in the papers and on TV, and told her friends he was the greatest black man of his generation (just as Jack Kennedy was the greatest white man). After his death, she kept his memory alive in her apartment.

Rachel's walls were covered with inspirational messages: "There are no limits on God's ability to make things right in my life," "Grant that I may not criticize my neighbor until I have walked a mile in his moccasins," "As for me and my house, we will serve the Lord," interspersed with less reverent slogans, such as "God bless this lousy apartment." But now King became a principal theme in this display. On one wall was a bronze plaque of the dead prophet, on another a four-color portrait of him, and on her coffee table a memorial candle bearing on its circular shade an excerpt from his "I Have a Dream" speech.

Not everyone in the family shared Rachel's admiration for King. One of the skeptics was her younger brother Arnold Walker, who shared many of the reservations then common among Northern blacks. The Black Panthers had denounced King as a "bootlicker," Adam Clayton Powell called him Martin "Loser" King, and young ghetto dwellers dismissed him, with heavy irony, as "De Lawd." It was the migration from South to North which, more than anything else, had eroded his constituency. In the settled black communities of Georgia and Alabama, his special amalgam of evangelical rhetoric and middle-class respectability provided the right chemistry for explosive change. But in the bleak ghettos of Chicago and Detroit, these same qualities—and particularly his relentless emphasis on non-violence and integration—proved less effective. When King delivered his "I Have a Dream" speech at the Lincoln Memorial, an angry black voice cried out, "Fuck that dream, Martin! Now, goddamnit, now!"

Arnold Walker had formed his own judgment of "De Lawd" up close. He owed that opportunity to Mike Haynes, the former assistant minister at Twelfth Baptist, who over the years had remained close to King. King had once asked Haynes to be his assistant in Montgomery, but the young minister had stayed on in Boston and eventually succeeded Dr. Hester at Twelfth Baptist. Whenever King came to Boston, Mike Haynes handled the logistics—meeting him at the airport, driving him around town, scheduling his time.

Arnold had known Haynes for years, and when Haynes was elected to the state legislature, Arnold—six years his junior—became a member of his entourage. So he wasn't surprised one morning in April 1965 when Haynes wandered into Carroll's Cut-Rate and asked whether he would like to be a driver for King during his visit to Boston later that month.

It was an extraordinary moment in the civil rights struggle—both for

America in general and for Boston in particular. Only six weeks before, the nation had witnessed King's double confrontation in Selma, Alabama—the first on March 9, when state troopers doused the marchers with tear gas, then waded into their ranks swinging clubs and cattle prods; the second on March 11, when a much larger group of marchers—including five hundred from Greater Boston—finally succeeded in crossing the Pettus Bridge. Later that evening, one of the white Bostonians, a Unitarian minister named Jim Reeb, was badly beaten as he emerged from a black restaurant. Two days later, he died of a fractured skull, and for nearly a week the story of Reeb's death ran side by side with the Selma story on the front pages of Boston's newspapers, giving Bostonians an acute sense of their stake in those events.

The movement for racial equality in Boston was gaining velocity at precisely the same moment. On April 14, a committee of distinguished Massachusetts citizens released a long-awaited report on racial imbalance in the state's public schools. Defining imbalanced schools as those with more than 50 percent black enrollment, the committee found fifty-five such schools in the state, forty-five of them in Boston. It concluded that "racial imbalance is educationally harmful to all children, white and non-white, because separation from others leads to ignorance of others and ignorance breeds fear and prejudice." Among the remedies which the committee recommended was busing—the first time such a step had been proposed by any public body in Massachusetts. The report stirred predictable protest, with Louise Day Hicks, chairwoman of Boston's School Committee, calling the busing proposal "undemocratic" and "un-American." But on April 20, the Boston branch of the NAACP—which had engaged in a steadily escalating confrontation with the School Committee—filed suit in Federal District Court seeking desegregation of Boston's schools.

Boston blacks had been in touch with King all that winter, seeking his aid in their hour of need. King felt a large debt to the birthplace of abolitionism, which had supported his Southern campaigns with hundreds of volunteers and thousands of dollars. Besides, he had long wanted to carry his campaign into the North, where racial discrimination, he felt, was as deeply rooted as it was in the South. In that spring of 1965, Boston seemed the logical target for his first Northern venture.

When King arrived at Logan Airport on the morning of April 22, he wasted no time in reminding Bostonians of the bonds which united him and their city. "I was educated here and it is one of the cities which I call home," he told reporters at the airport. Then they were off, with Arnold Walker driving the borrowed Lincoln Continental, on a day-long tour of the city, including a call on Governor John Volpe, an address to a joint session of the state legislature, an inspection of slum housing and overcrowded schools in black Roxbury, a news conference, a fund-raising reception at a downtown hotel, and finally, a Passover service at Temple Israel.

The next morning, when King arrived at Roxbury's Carter Playground, the crowds were so thick that it took the marshals nearly an hour and a half to herd them into a procession headed toward the Boston Common. It began eight abreast, but soon thousands of spectators joined in, swelling the lines to twenty-five and thirty across. Arnold marched with Mike Haynes in the second rank, just behind King and Ralph Abernathy, and when he turned in Copley Square he saw an awesome stream of determined faces, mixed in nearly equal parts of black and white, some shouldering placards which read: "We Need Better Schools" or "All Men Are Created Equal" or simply "Love," and one group from the Catholic Interracial Council making a particularly dramatic demonstration of their faith in integration, with the black women carrying white babies and the white women carrying black babies.

On the flanks of Boston Common, fresh with new grass, the 22,000 marchers converged on the Parkman Bandstand. Gil Caldwell of Union Methodist got the Freedom Rally started with a mass sing-along, black welfare mothers and suburban stockholders, teenage dropouts and Wellesley college girls raising their voices together in the anthem which made each of them feel a bit stronger and more virtuous:

> We shall overcome, we shall overcome,
> We shall overcome some day.
> Oh, deep in my heart I do believe
> We shall overcome some day.

Then, after a spate of warm-up speeches, the man whom some that day had called "the Black Moses" advanced to the microphone. It had begun to rain, so Arnold unfurled a large black umbrella which he held over King's head as the preacher exhorted his flock:

"I come here not to condemn but to encourage. I would be dishonest to say Boston is Birmingham or that Massachusetts is Mississippi. But it would be irresponsible for me to deny the crippling poverty and the injustice that exist in some sections of this community. The vision of the New Boston must extend into the heart of Roxbury. Boston must become a testing ground for the ideals of freedom. . . . We must not become a nation of onlookers. This fight is not for the sake of the Negro alone, but rather for the aspirations of America itself. All Americans must take a stand against evil."

Standing there next to the prophet, holding the umbrella until his arm ached, Arnold looked out over the crowd, noting in particular the suburban white men in their alligator polo shirts and chino pants, their wives in Lily Pulitzer shifts and silk scarves. As King's voice soared to a crescendo, the whites looked up at him with rapt faces. Sure, Arnold thought, they just love old Black Moses, just love all us *Neeegroes* because he's our leader and he's so non-violent and peaceful and all. But just let us push to get something of *theirs*, and you'll see how they'll act. Then there'll be a different look on those well-fed faces. And these are the people King tells us we should treat like brothers and sisters.

After his thirty-six hours with King, Arnold was more ambivalent than ever about the great man. He made mayors and governors listen when he spoke; he made people on the street straighten up and look as he whipped by in his long black limousine. Arnold was impressed by all that. And he had to admit the man was a powerful speaker; he knew how to grab these people, how to get them fired up.

But Arnold didn't care for *what* the man was saying. He'd never been that hot for non-violence. A few months before, the Southern Christian Leadership Conference had been recruiting people to go down South for the sit-ins. Arnold had gone for an interview, but he'd been rejected because they didn't think he was non-violent enough. And they were right. Arnold would prefer to be the person doing the crackin' rather than the one taking the crackin'. He wouldn't let people beat him with a hose, and prod him with sticks, and hit him over the head with a Georgia toothpick while he just sat there singing "We Shall Overcome."

But then King was a Christian preacher man, and Arnold had always had his doubts about them. His mother was a real Christian lady, a pillar of Union Methodist Church who went to church every chance she got, and so did his sister, Rachel. But Arnold's father had regarded preachers as Father Divines who robbed their own people blind. Growing up in rural Georgia, he'd seen poor sharecroppers giving preachers the choice morsels off their tables while their own kids went hungry. When he married his pious Methodist wife in Boston, he'd laid down the law: He didn't want no ministers with their feet under his table. And he wasn't sticking his feet in any minister's pew.

Arnold respected his mother as he respected many Christians who used the church to get ahead in the white man's world. But he saw how two-faced some of those Christians were—preaching piously about "do unto others as you would have them do unto you," then looking out for themselves at the expense of everybody else. The Christians had never done much for him. Gradually, he began slacking off in attendance at Union Methodist—hittin' and missin', as he put it, but doing more missin' than hittin'.

Instead, he began drifting over to Muhammad's Temple #11 on Intervale Street for the Sunday-afternoon services. Although he could never quite bring himself to become a Muslim, he was getting a lot more out of temple in the afternoon than he got out of his mother's church in the morning.

After all, he knew the minister over there as well as he knew Mike Haynes. Louis X, or Louis Farrakhan as he was later known, was actually Gene Walcott, who had grown up on Sterling Street, right around the corner from the Walkers'. As early as Arnold could remember, Gene had been a star. People said he was prettier than Cassius Clay, a better singer than Harry Belafonte, a better actor than Sidney Poitier, a better talker than Martin Luther King.

But then Gene went to Winston-Salem State Teachers College in North Carolina and two things happened. First, this slick, self-confident son of West Indian parents encountered Southern Jim Crow, which was unlike anything he'd experienced in Boston. He started fighting it, using the "white" toilets in Woolworth's and drinking from the "white" fountains at the bus station, challenging any white man to say him nay. But all that might not have mattered so much had he not been turned down for Belafonte's spot at a New York night-club. When white folks rejected him for the New York gig, he quit Winston-Salem and joined the Black Muslims. Putting his talents to the service of his new faith, he composed its most popular song, "White Man's Heaven Is Black Man's Hell."

Soon he became a disciple of Malcolm X, who had also grown up on Boston's streets. Malcolm "Red" Little had worked for a time as a rest-room attendant at the Roseland State Ballroom and a busboy at the Parker House before operating a burglary ring out of Harvard Square. Sentenced to the Massachusetts State Prison in Charlestown, he paced his cell for hours denouncing God so vehemently that he became known to fellow inmates as "Satan." Then he met a veteran con who converted him to Islam. Staring out his barred window at "the white world" of Charlestown, which rose in bleak three-deckers up Bunker Hill, Red Little became Malcolm X.

By 1958 Malcolm was Islam's minister in New York and it was Gene Walcott—now Louis X—who founded the temple on Boston's Intervale Street. When Arnold Walker heard what his old friend was up to, he came by the temple out of sheer curiosity; when he heard Gene preach, he was electrified. He took special pleasure in Gene's gibes at Christianity as "the white man's religion," and at Christian preachers, symbolized by "the Right Reverend Bishop T. Chickenwing." Through Gene, Arnold was drawn to Malcolm, regularly going to hear him whenever he was in Boston. He was at the Boston Arena on August 18, 1963, when Malcolm derided King's forthcoming "March on Washington," calling it "the Farce on Washington." He applauded as Malcolm condemned "white liberals who denounce what the white man has done to us in the South while they do the same thing in the North—the Northern Fox is more vicious than the Southern Wolf because he poses as your friend." He cheered three months later when Malcolm told the Ford Hall Forum, "We want no part of integration with the wicked race which enslaved us." And when Malcolm was gunned down by three black assassins in Harlem's Audubon Ballroom in February 1965, Arnold remained convinced that whites had somehow contrived the death of the prophet of black pride and self-reliance.

So when Martin Luther King was assassinated three years later, Arnold Walker and his sister Rachel Twymon saw the event from different perspectives. To Arnold, King was a great man, but also a great temporizer, a timid reformer who had long kept his finger in the dike, restraining the torrent of black rage. His death, Arnold hoped, would free blacks to make a clean break with whites and achieve a substantial degree of autonomy. To Rachel, such hopes were misguided. Boston was a primarily white city, America a primarily white nation. Whether they liked it or not, blacks had to learn to live with whites. If King's death served any useful purpose, she thought, perhaps it would persuade a guilt-ridden white America to grant a genuine measure of integration.

3
McGoff

It was the moment she liked best, the vegetables spread out before her in voluptuous profusion: squeaky stalks of celery, damp lettuce, succulent tomatoes, chilled radishes. From the sink rose the earthy smells of wet roots and peels, and from all about her the clamor and fracas of a busy kitchen, gearing up for dinner only minutes away.

Three nights a week, Alice McGoff served as salad chef at the Officers Club of the Charlestown Navy Yard, a break from her usual job as the club's hatcheck girl. Taking coats and hats was more rewarding—tips could run nearly $200 a week—but Alice liked the sounds and smells and breezy camaraderie of the kitchen. That April night she was cheerfully tossing her greens when she noticed a commotion across the room. A black busboy was in tears. Eventually someone told her that Martin Luther King had been killed in a Southern city.

Through her mind flashed a memory five years old, a solemn television announcer reporting the President's assassination in another Southern city. She'd mourned that night as never before, an anguish so acute it might have been for her husband or brother.

She didn't feel that way about Martin Luther King. You had to admit he'd done one hell of a job for his people; if she were black, she would have been the first one in line behind him. And you had to support his crusade down South. No right-minded person wanted blacks to sit in the back of the bus, eat at separate lunch counters, or use different toilets. That sort of thing was just plain wrong. But when King turned northward, Alice had grown skeptical. When King held his big rally on the Boston Common, Alice had asked, "What the hell is he doing up here?" As far as she could see, Boston wasn't prejudiced against blacks—nobody rode the back of the bus, nobody was kept out of restaurants; Boston wasn't Birmingham or Selma. King was getting a bit above himself. So while his assassination was a terrible thing, she couldn't bring herself to grieve for him.

When dinner at the Officers Club was over and the kitchen had been scoured clean, Alice walked up Decatur Street to her apartment in the Bunker Hill housing project. Her husband, Danny, was still tending bar at the Point Tavern, but their seven children were home, huddled around the television set, watching the riots that had broken out in dozens of American cities. For more than an hour, Alice and her kids watched young blacks racing through the nation's streets—burning, looting, battling the police. Her daughters, Lisa and Robin, seemed terrified by the violent images flickering across the screen, but her sons, Danny Jr., Billy, Kevin, Tommy, and Bobby, sat openmouthed, absorbing the action as avidly as they did their weekly police dramas. Well past midnight, Billy took her outside and pointed toward the horizon, where the fires of Blue Hill Avenue cast a dull red glow.

What did the blacks think they were doing? Alice wondered. They acted as though they were the only people who'd ever had it tough in this world. Poor was poor, hungry was hungry. The housing project where the McGoffs lived wasn't any better than those across town in the ghetto. The widow upstairs who had to get by on social security and food stamps didn't have any more than those black welfare mothers the newspapers were always writing about. The discrimination which blacks had confronted over the years was no worse than the arrogance and indifference which the Irish had faced when they came to this country.

The difference between the blacks and the Irish, she thought, was that the blacks had tried to advance through the civil rights movement—sit-ins, marches, demonstrations, ultimately riots—while the Irish had used politics. Alice believed in politics—it was the American way of getting ahead. And for a long while it had paid off. No district in the country had produced a more potent roster of pols than the storied "Old Eleventh," of which Charlestown was part.

As early as 1894, in a race marked by bogus "mattress" voters, street brawls, and bully-boy raids on polling places, a tough little mick named John Francis Fitzgerald had won election to Congress from the Eleventh. "Honey Fitz" promptly repaid Charlestown's support by getting the Navy Yard reopened, bringing hundreds of jobs back to town. But his stock in trade was an appeal to Irish rage against the "blue-nosed Yankee bigots." In 1905, he rode that anger into the Mayor's office.

Eventually, Fitzgerald's old congressional seat passed to an even more aggressive young Irishman, James Michael Curley, who also exploited Irish resentments against the Yankee nabobs. The very term "codfish aristocracy," he once said, was "an insult to the fish." His style was flamboyant, even demagogic, but both as congressman and later as Boston's mayor he appealed less to narrow Irish ethnocentrism than to the poor of all races. Nowhere was he more popular than in Charlestown and no neighborhood received more of his largesse. One of the most consistently Democratic wards in the nation—Democrats routinely defeated Republicans there by margins of five or six to one—Charlestown did well under the New Deal, receiving one of the country's first public housing projects (the very one where the McGoffs now lived), relief assistance for 1,200 of its 30,000 residents, and a staggering 400 federal jobs.

As late as 1942, at age sixty-eight, Jim Curley was returned to Congress from the Eleventh District. Even his subsequent indictment by a federal grand jury for mail fraud didn't dampen Charlestown's enthusiasm for the old scoundrel. Reelected in 1944, he withdrew only after winning his fourth term as mayor. That left his congressional seat to be filled by special election in 1946. One of the candidates was Honey Fitz's grandson—John Fitzgerald Kennedy.

At first, the notion seemed preposterous. Kennedy was virtually a stranger to Boston, having spent the best part of his twenty-nine years in New York, Hyannis Port, and the South Pacific. His "residence" in the district was the Bellevue Hotel on Beacon Hill. "You're a carpetbagger," one politician in the district told him bitterly. "You don't belong here." Moreover, his patrician gloss, the elegant ease acquired at Choate and Harvard and cultivated in London and Palm Beach, was not calculated to go down well in the waterfront saloons of Charlestown, the clammy tenements of the North End, or the bleak three-deckers of East Boston, Brighton, Somerville, and Cambridge. True, his family's roots went deep in the district: not only had Honey Fitz represented it in Congress for six years, but Jack's paternal grandfather, Patrick J. Kennedy, had been born and raised in East Boston and served as its Democratic ward leader for many years. But those roots could be as much a hindrance as an asset. Boston's Irish were notoriously resentful of the "two toilet" Irish who had betrayed their heritage by moving to the suburbs and sending their sons to Harvard.

One who shared those feelings was Alice McGoff's father, Bernie Kirk. A second-generation Irish-American, Bernie had worked for decades at a South End ink factory, where he served as a union shop steward. "The little man has to unite to get anyplace," he would tell his daughter Alice, and that turn of mind was reflected in his stalwart Democratic politics, his unwavering support for Al Smith, David I. Walsh, and Franklin Roosevelt. But he had no use whatsoever for Joe Kennedy, the patriarch of the Kennedy clan, whom he regarded as a womanizer, a high liver, an incurable conniver. "That man's forgotten where he came from," he'd tell Alice, "he's no longer one of us." Moreover, Kennedy was simply too close to Richard Cardinal Cushing, Boston's venerable archbishop. There was a touch of the anticlerical in Bernie; priests were okay when they stuck to the Church's business, he thought, but their writ didn't extend to public life. Cushing and Kennedy were both overreachers, too eager to steal a march on their countrymen. There was an old Charlestown saying, "Up to me, up to me, but never above me." No son of Joe Kennedy's was going to clamber over Bernie's head.

Moreover, Bernie was committed to Charlestown's own candidate for Congress, John F. "Fish" Cotter, a popular figure who had served as secretary to Curley and before that to Congressman John P. Higgins. When Higgins resigned his congressional seat, Cotter had been appointed to fill out his unexpired term. During his years in Washington, he had dispensed countless favors to his fellow "Townies." The Kirks had received more than a few of them, and now Bernie Kirk was determined to return the favor.

Among the Townies who had committed themselves to Fish Cotter was a young Air Force veteran named Dave Powers. One night in January 1946 there was a knock at the door of the three-decker that Dave shared with his widowed sister and her eight children. When he opened it, there stood a gangly fellow who stuck out his hand and said, "My name's Jack Kennedy. I'm a candidate for Congress." Sitting at the kitchen table, Powers explained that he was working for one of Kennedy's opponents. But he liked his young visitor, and when Kennedy mentioned that he was speaking the next week to Gold Star Mothers at Charlestown's American Legion Hall, Powers agreed to go with him.

The next Tuesday, Dave stood at the back of the hall as Kennedy gave what seemed like "the world's worst speech"—halting, awkward, clumsily worded. But then the candidate looked out across the phalanx of women, all of whom had lost sons in the war, and said, "I think I know how you feel, because my mother is a Gold Star Mother too." (Jack's older brother, Joe, had been shot down over Germany.) In the back of the room, Powers could hear some women weeping and others turn to their neighbors and say, "He reminds me of my boy." When the speech was over, the young aristocrat was mobbed by dozens of working-class women, ardently promising him their support. Powers was convinced.

A few denounced him for deserting Cotter, but working with other veteran operatives, Dave mounted a crisply efficient campaign. On a routine day in Charlestown, Kennedy started at 7:00 a.m., shaking hands outside the Navy Yard, then rang doorbells at every three-decker along Bunker Hill Street. In the afternoon he dropped into grocery stores and barbershops, ending up back at the Navy Yard, where he shook the hands he'd missed that morning. In the evening there'd be a rally at the American Legion Hall or a get-together in somebody's parlor.

Meanwhile, Jack set out to acquire the more formal badges of Irish Catholic orthodoxy, starting with membership in the Knights of Columbus. Shrewdly, his aides directed him to the Bunker Hill Council, oldest in the state, much honored among Boston's Celts. Appropriately enough, induction in the Third Degree took place on St. Patrick's Day. The ceremony began with fifty "candidates" marching through Charlestown's streets to the Knights Hall, each with a "relic"—an oversized key, cross, or candle—to lug along the three-mile route. Jack was assigned a special burden—a live, frisky billy goat which the future President hauled on a leash past hundreds of amused spectators. A powerful symbol in Knights ritual, the goat was intended to teach humility: the candidate might think he was leading it, but as would eventually become clear, the goat was leading him. After the initiation, Jack adjourned with his fellow Knights to Sully's Cafe on Union Street for the traditional hoisting of the brew. It was a moment that would remain sacred to all those who stood that night at Sully's beer-stained bar.

But the climax of the Charlestown campaign was the annual Bunker Hill Day parade on June 17. The night before, Townies and their guests celebrated at a half dozen banquets and balls. Jack addressed no fewer than five, then went on with Powers to an after-hours joint called the Stork Club, where he stayed until 2:00 a.m.

Hours later, he was back in town for the traditional round of house calls before the afternoon parade. With the primary only hours away, each candidate sought to make a final splash. Seeking to exploit his image as a war hero, Kennedy marched that day under the glittering new banners of the Lieutenant Joseph P. Kennedy Post of the Veterans of Foreign Wars, named after Jack's late brother. Hatless, dressed in a dark gray flannel suit, he strode up Bunker Hill Street with more than a hundred supporters marching three abreast behind him. Every few steps, someone broke from the crowd to pump his hand or ask for an autograph.

The Kirks watched the parade from a friend's stoop on Monument Square. As Kennedy went by, Bernie stood stonily with arms folded; he was sticking with Cotter. But his wife, Gertrude, and his three daughters had long since succumbed to Jack's charms. Alice, then only nine, was desolate that she couldn't cast a vote for the dashing young candidate.

The next day, Kennedy lost Charlestown to Cotter by only 337 votes, and elsewhere in the Eleventh District he outpolled his nearest competitor by nearly two to one. That night at a victory party, eighty-three-year-old Honey Fitz clambered up on a table and croaked out his famous rendition of "Sweet Adeline."

Almost overnight Jack Kennedy had become an honorary Townie. Charlestown voted overwhelmingly for his return to Congress in 1948 and 1950, for his election to the Senate in 1952 and 1958, and to put him in the White House in 1960. And Kennedy returned the attention. He appointed Bob Morey, his Townie driver, to be U.S. Marshal for Massachusetts, and he brought Dave Powers into the White House as boon companion. Powers took pains to see that loyal Charlestown supporters received appropriate recognition. In April 1961, the President received some three hundred members of the Bunker Hill Council of the Knights of Columbus—*his* council. For nearly an hour, the proud Knights milled across the White House lawn, jawing with *their* President.

The substance of Kennedy's policies did nothing to alienate Charlestown. In foreign policy, he was perceived as a tough guy, a battle-hardened veteran, not unlike the thousands of Charlestown men who had fought in the two world wars and Korea (there is a legend that Charlestown sent more boys into World War II than any community of its size in the country). Charlestown's vets thrilled to Kennedy's rhetorical flourishes, applauded his firm resistance to international Communism, cheered the attempted invasion of Cuba and the brinksmanship of the Missile Crisis.

In domestic matters, Kennedy suited the Townies nearly as well. For although he came to be considered a liberal, he was deeply suspicious of the conventional pieties. One strain in him, to be sure, rang with lofty purpose, summoning the nation to live up to its highest aspirations ("No problem of human destiny is beyond human beings"). But another side was ironic, intensely aware of man's limitations ("Life is unfair," he liked to say). Something deep in Kennedy's Irish soul bespoke a tragic view of life; the Kirks and their neighbors responded to that.

On civil rights, Kennedy's stance was deliberate and intensely political. Convinced that he didn't have the votes in Congress to enact significant rights legislation—and afraid that the attempt would cost him Southern support for the remainder of his legislative program—he was determined to move in this area only by executive order. Yet even here he was laggard, delaying more than two years in signing an order to ban discrimination in federal housing programs, something which, during the campaign, he had airily declared "the President could do by a stroke of his pen." With this delay, Martin Luther King said, Kennedy had "undermined confidence in his intentions." Summing up the President's first year in office, King found it "essentially cautious and defensive"; Kennedy had the understanding and political skill, but "the moral passion is missing." Even when Kennedy finally introduced a civil rights bill in February 1963, black leaders bemoaned its lack of teeth.

It took the Birmingham crisis of late spring 1963—with Bull Connor's cops using nightsticks, dogs, and fire hoses on King's marchers—to create a sense of national urgency to which the President could respond. And respond he did in a nationally televised address that June, in which he said the country confronted "a moral issue . . . as old as the scriptures and as clear as the American Constitution." That night, the President announced that he would bring in a new, stronger civil rights bill, embodying "the proposition that race has no place in American life and law." To support the bill, a quarter million Americans marched on Washington on August 28. That evening, Kennedy received ten black leaders at the White House, greeting them with the very words King had used at the Lincoln Memorial just hours before—"I have a dream." At last, it seemed, the dreams of Martin Luther King and the political exigencies of John F. Kennedy were about to converge. Less than three months later, the President was dead.

When Lyndon Johnson capitalized on the nation's grief to push Kennedy's civil rights bill through Congress, Alice McGoff and her neighbors concurred. But before long they detected a not so subtle shift in the rhetoric of civil rights. No longer were politicians, professors, and editorial writers talking merely about giving Negroes an equal shot at life, liberty, and the pursuit of happiness. By the mid-sixties, they were proposing to take real things—money, jobs, housing, and schools—away from whites and give them to blacks.

This notion of preferential treatment for blacks originated with a young Irish-American, Assistant Secretary of Labor Daniel Patrick Moynihan. When Lyndon Johnson agreed to deliver the commencement address at Howard University on June 4, 1965, Moynihan drafted the text. "Freedom is not enough," the President said that day. "You do not take a person who, for years, has been hobbled by chains and liberate him, bring him up to the starting line of a race, and then say, 'You are free to compete with all the others,' and still justly believe that you have been completely fair. We seek not just freedom but opportunity. We seek not just legal equity, not just equality as a right and a theory, but equality as a fact and equality as a result."

The more Alice McGoff heard about this doctrine, the less she liked it. The government picked several races and called them minorities, but the Irish, they weren't a minority; the government was saying the Irish were well off, they'd never had a hard life. Sure, slavery had been a great injustice, but she didn't see why whites who weren't even alive during slave times should be penalized for it. How could you make slaves of the majority to free the minority? Was that justice?

Moreover, she knew full well which whites would pay the price for all of this. It wouldn't be those who worked in the big corporate and law offices downtown, the ones who dined in those Back Bay clubs and lived in the comfortable, all-white suburbs. No, as usual it would be the working-class whites who shared the inner city with blacks, competed with them for schools and jobs and housing, and jostled with them on the street corners.

Before long, the issue of compensatory rights had helped to drive a wedge between the Townies and the remaining Kennedy brothers. Nobody proved a more impassioned advocate of the new doctrine than Robert Kennedy. And Bobby was among the first to point his finger at Northern cities like Boston. "In the North," he told one reporter, "I think you have had *de facto* segregation which in some areas is as bad or even more extreme than in the South. Everybody in those communities, including my own state of Massachusetts, concentrated on what was happening in Birmingham, Alabama, or Jackson, Mississippi, and didn't look at what needed to be done in our own home, our own town, our own city."

For Alice McGoff, that was sheer political posturing, designed to curry favor with Martin Luther King and the "limousine liberals" at the expense of working-class whites. But Bobby was an increasingly remote figure in Massachusetts. To Alice, the Kennedy survivor who really mattered was Ted.

When Ted first ran for Jack's old Senate seat in 1962, there were those who regarded him as grossly unqualified for the job and resented the Kennedys' "arrogance" in forwarding his candidacy. But Alice and most other Townies had no such reservations. Indeed, so fierce was Charlestown's loyalty to the President that it gave his brother a whopping 86.8 percent of its vote, the highest of any neighborhood in the city. Two years later—with JFK's assassination fresh in most minds and Ted in the hospital after a near-fatal air crash—the Townies tendered him an incredible 94.8 percent.

But Alice's enthusiasm waned as Ted took up the cudgels for minority rights. In June 1965—just months after the Selma march and Martin Luther King's address on the Boston Common—Ted put himself squarely behind efforts in the Massachusetts legislature to withhold state funds from cities and towns with racially segregated schools. Receiving an honorary degree from Northeastern University, he told a throng at Boston Garden, "We in the Northeast say we have given opportunity to each wave of immigrants that has come to our shores, but if this is our tradition, why have we failed so far to offer similar opportunity to Negro citizens who have come from other states? It should be clear that a Negro child in Massachusetts has as much of a right to an integrated education as a Negro child in Mississippi or Alabama."

Jerry Doherty, a Townie ally of Ted's, warned that such positions would cost him heavily in Charlestown. And indeed they did, for Teddy had never been so much an object of Charlestown's affections as the beneficiary of its special relationship with Jack. And if Jack's advance to the White House had released the Boston Irish from their anxiety about being only half American, so it had made them secure enough to reject an Irishman as well. Ultimately, many blue-collar Irish unloaded on Ted the pent-up envy and resentment they'd never dared to direct at Jack.

By the spring of 1968, at age thirty-one, Alice McGoff was beginning to feel some of her father's sense of grievance at the Kennedy clan. She was still a committed Democrat; she couldn't imagine herself voting for a Republican. But she found herself wondering whether the Kennedys were genuine Democrats any longer, whether they really had the interests of the white working class at heart.

Hours after Martin Luther King's death, Ted Kennedy delivered an impassioned eulogy to the fallen prophet. "He was a noble man, eloquent, patient, and brave," the Senator told reporters. "He loved his fellow man, white and black. He died because he was willing to go throughout this country, as a leader and a symbol, in an effort to bring them together."

Watching the Senator on television, Alice felt a rush of anger at his smug, preachy tone. As usual, Ted seemed to care more about blacks than he did about his own people. The Kennedys had never had it tough in their lives— who were they to sit down there at Hyannis Port and tell her what to do for the minorities? As fires stained the night sky over Roxbury, Alice turned off the set and went to bed.

4

Diver

SCARLETT: You, Mammy, go dig those yams like I told you!
MAMMY: Diggin's fiel' han's business! Po'k an' me's
house niggers!
SCARLETT: If you can't work you can both get out.
PORK: Where'd we git out to, Miss Scarlett?
SCARLETT: You can get out to the Yankees for all I care!

A stab of yellow light in the aisle, then a hand lightly jogging his elbow brought the Mayor of Boston back from the fields of Tara. "Mr. Mayor, there's a message for you," said the usher, thrusting a slip of paper into his hand. In the flashlight's beam, Kevin White read: "Martin Luther King has been assassinated in Memphis."

For a moment, he sat there wondering what he should do. Then he thought: There's nothing I *can* do. The man is dead. So he slipped the note into his pocket and went back to *Gone With the Wind*.

A few moments later another figure loomed in the aisle beside him, the Gary Theater's manager whispering, "Mr. Mayor, I'm sorry to disturb you, sir, but the Police Commissioner is on the phone. He says he needs to speak with you." The Mayor told his secretary, Mary McCarthy, he'd be right back, but when he picked up the phone in the manager's office, Commissioner Edmund L. McNamara said, "Mayor, we got trouble," and went on to explain that gangs of black youths were out in Roxbury smashing store windows and overturning automobiles. With that, Kevin White abandoned Scarlett, Rhett, and Mammy in mid-saga and briskly walked the four blocks to police headquarters, where he stayed for several hours, helping coordinate efforts to control the violence, before joining his staff at City Hall.

In a corner of the Mayor's cavernous office, his chief aide, Barney Frank, was scribbling a statement: "The assassination of Martin Luther King is a tragedy which diminishes us all. This brutal and senseless act has deprived America of one of our foremost leaders at a critical time. I hope the people will recognize anew the necessity of working together for the principle for which Dr. King lived and died: the equality of all men."

From his outer office, the Mayor and Frank could hear the staccato bursts of a police radio tracking splatters of violence across Roxbury and the South End. Every few seconds a phone rang in the mayoral suite, bringing fresh alarms and cautions.

Just after 9:00 p.m., Police Superintendent Bill Bradley called to say that a bus carrying a dozen whites was trapped by blacks on Blue Hill Avenue. The crowd had done nothing violent yet. They were standing back, chanting and jeering at the terrified faces behind the glass, but at any moment they might rush the vehicle. "What should we do?" Bradley wanted to know. "Should we send our men in?"

The Mayor's first instinct was to summon the police. But Barney, mindful of similar incidents during a riot the year before, warned that an armed response might only set off worse violence. At his urging, the Mayor agreed to let black ministers and community workers try persuasion first. Within an hour, Dan Richardson, Chuck Turner, and the Reverend Virgil Wood had quieted the crowd and rescued the white passengers.

That set the pattern for the rest of the night. Wherever possible, the Mayor held the police back, letting black leaders calm their own people. Meanwhile, two black plainclothesmen cruised the community in an unmarked car, relaying intelligence to police headquarters. When they reported that the worst incidents were caused by white curiosity seekers blundering into black crowds, the police sealed off Roxbury and the South End, diverting white pedestrians and motorists. By 2:00 a.m., the racket from the police radio began to ebb. The Mayor and Barney slumped on the office couch, trying to make sense of what was happening out there.

Kevin White had been Mayor of Boston for barely ninety-five days. With scarcely time to fill out his cabinet and learn his secretaries' first names, he didn't know whether his untried machinery could handle a crisis of this dimension. The only previous test had been an arctic cold snap in mid-January when below-zero temperatures burst water pipes, ruptured gas mains, and left hundreds of families throughout the city shivering and hungry. White had stayed in his office all one night, and for the next ninety hours city officials manned a round-the-clock operation at City Hall, which took 1,500 emergency calls and found temporary housing for seventy-four families. Partly as a result of that crisis, the Mayor decreed that City Hall would henceforth remain open twenty-four hours a day, with two staffers on duty at all times to handle emergencies—reflecting the Mayor's broader effort to open up "new lines of communication" with an electorate widely believed to be alienated from government.

White's creative response to the winter crisis had piqued Colin Diver's interest in him. Here was an energetic young mayor who was eager to confront challenges, not run away from them. White seemed to be cut in the John Lindsay mold: bold, imaginative, innovative, and decisive, he talked about refocusing national attention on the cities, bringing new resources to bear on pressing human needs. He had good ideas and the ability to attract first-rate people. After the cold snap, Colin watched the Mayor with new curiosity, eager to see what he would do next.

In fact, nothing in Kevin White's experience had remotely prepared him for the racial explosion he faced in April. True, he had won election the previous November over Louise Day Hicks in a contest heavily shadow-ed by racial confrontation. A member of Boston's School Committee, Mrs. Hicks was regarded as the leading spokesperson for the "white backlash" then believed to be sweeping Boston and other Northern cities. Her bland refrain, "You know where I stand," was generally interpreted—in light of her fierce opposition to school desegregation—as a not so veiled declaration of bigotry. National commentators and news magazines had quickly identified the Hicks-White race as a critical test of the racial climate in America's cities, and Kevin White's victory, though narrow, was seen as a triumph for racial enlightenment.

Since then, the Mayor had done his best to live up to that image, naming several blacks to important posts, pledging more low-income housing for the heavily black South End, announcing plans to hire twenty-five black police cadets. When the Kerner Report was issued on March 1, White promptly de-clared war on white racism, calling for a "profound and massive change" in public attitudes.

But during his first three months in office the Mayor had been preoccupied less with black alienation than with white disaffection. For Kevin White was even then pointing toward the 1970 governor's race, and he remembered the 1966 race, in which the Mayor of Boston, John Collins, bidding for the U.S. Senate, lost twenty-one of the twenty-two wards in his own city. With that statistic in mind, White had drawn quite a different conclusion than most people from his victory over Mrs. Hicks the previous November. To him, the margin of only 12,429 out of 192,673 votes seemed less a triumph for racial enlightenment than an ominous sign of continued estrangement in the city's white working-class neighborhoods, where Collins had been most soundly re-jected and from which Mrs. Hicks drew her greatest support. It was those white neighborhoods which held the key to his political future and it was in them that his greatest energies had been expended. So—despite his bold pro-nouncements—White had given little thought to the plight of Boston's blacks, had spent little time in the black community, and knew few blacks well. He was ill prepared to deal with a major racial confrontation—which, at 3:00 a.m. on April 5, is what Boston appeared to be facing.

The Mayor felt utterly powerless, but he didn't think he should leave the office. At 6:00 a.m. he stumbled to the same couch on which he had spent the subzero night of January 11, pulled a blanket over his head, and, to the wail of police sirens, fell into a troubled sleep.

He woke at nine to eerie silence. The sirens which had sounded in the night were stilled; someone had shut off the police radio; the phones had stopped ringing. Where the hell was everybody?

Then, shortly after nine, the first call of the morning came—from the black Councilman, Tom Atkins. "Kevin," said an agitated Atkins, who had been up most of the night patrolling Roxbury's streets, "something terrible is about to happen."

Atkins had just received a call from a black disk jockey named James Byrd, known to his fans as "The Early Byrd." In addition to his duties on WILD, Boston's soul-music station, Byrd was the New England representative for rhythm-and-blues star James Brown, who was scheduled to hold a concert that very night at the Boston Garden. But Byrd told Atkins that the Garden, concerned about more violence, was canceling the concert. It didn't take long for Atkins to realize what would happen, and now he sketched it in graphic terms for the Mayor.

"It's too late to cancel it; the word won't get around in time. There'll be thousands of black teenagers down at the Garden this evening, and when they find those gates are locked they're going to be pretty pissed off. King's death and Brown's cop-out will get all mixed up together and we'll have an even bigger riot than last night's—only this time it'll be in the heart of downtown." They should not only reinstate the concert, Atkins said, they should get a television station to carry it live, then appeal for kids to stay home and watch it on TV.

Neither the Mayor nor Barney Frank had ever heard of James Brown— Barney thought he was a football player, the Mayor kept referring to him as "James Washington"—but they immediately agreed that Boston needed him that night. So began a frantic seven hours of negotiation.

The urbane David Ives, president of WGBH, Boston's public television station, agreed to televise the concert, but when Atkins called Byrd to tell him, the disk jockey exploded. "You can't do that," he said. "James is in New York to tape a show. They're giving him a pile of money, but on the condition he doesn't do any other television on the East Coast until after it airs. You put this thing on TV here and you'll violate James's contract. He isn't going to like that."

When Atkins persisted, Byrd suggested he call Greg Moses, Brown's man-ager. Moses was dubious: "Look, even if we can work out the contract thing, we got another problem. It's going to kill our gate. We're going to take a bath on this thing. Who's going to take care of James?"

Atkins called White and said, "We gotta tell these people we'll guarantee the gate." At first, the Mayor flatly refused; ultimately, under Atkins' pleading, he agreed. "But for Christ's sake," he said, "don't tell anybody. If word ever gets out we underwrote a goddamn rock star with city money, we'll both be dead politically."

Atkins called Moses back and assured him the city would guarantee the difference between what Brown would have made from a full house and what he actually took in that night. Moses gave a tentative, very uneasy assent, for he had been unable to clear it with Brown, already on his way to Boston in his private Lear jet. Atkins promised to meet the singer at the airport and explain the whole thing.

In the Mayor's limousine, led by a wedge of police motorcycles, Atkins rushed to the airport, picked up Brown, then sped back through the Callahan Tunnel while hurriedly outlining the situation to the outraged star.

"No way," Brown shouted. "They'll sue me in New York."

"James, James," pleaded Atkins. "We'll work this out! But right now you have an opportunity to help save this city."

"I'll have to think about it," Brown grumbled.

When they screeched up to the Garden, Brown was met by Eddie Powers, the Garden's manager, who reported that people had been coming in all day getting refunds.

"This concert has been killed!" Brown roared.

At that moment the Mayor pulled up and he, Brown, and Atkins huddled in the manager's office. By then, Brown had figured out what the whole thing was going to cost him and demanded a city guarantee of $60,000.

"Sixty thousand!" the Mayor exclaimed. Martin Luther King had just been killed and here were two black guys putting the squeeze on him for $60,000. One of them, he'd been told, was the highest-paid black performer in America who made $2 million a year, had a Victorian mansion, a Rolls-Royce, two Cadillacs, two radio stations, a record company, a production staff of forty-two. Now he was worrying about the gate from one measly concert!

But White was running out of options. "Okay, Mr. Brown," he said. "You've got your commitment. Now get up on that stage!"

Barely 2,000 young people, most of them black, were scattered around the 14,000-seat arena when Tom Atkins advanced to center stage.

"I'm not going to sing, but I do want to say this," he began. "James Brown has donated his money and his time to help people. He donated one of his biggest-selling records to the young people of our country. And tonight he's making a twenty-five-hundred-dollar contribution to the Martin Luther King Trust Fund. For those of you who are not with us here tonight, but are watching, I think it would be sort of great if you were to make out a check to the Martin Luther King Trust Fund and send it to City Hall care of Mayor Kevin White. Anyway, this country owes James Brown a great debt and we're lucky to have him here tonight with us. Give a great round of applause to James Brown."

The audience thundered its approval.

Then Atkins went on. "I'd like to bring now to the microphone the man who is making the program tonight possible, the man whose foresight and leadership has given the city of Boston and the whole metropolitan area a new lease on life. He's a man who's young, he's a man who cares, and he's going to make this a great city. The Honorable Mayor . . ."

Dapper in a dark blue suit, button-down shirt, and rep tie, Kevin White ducked into the spotlight. The crowd's response was—at best—subdued. It was the first time since King's assassination that the Mayor had confronted a large group of blacks. Sensing the ghetto's new rage at whites, Atkins and other black advisers had urged him to stay off the streets. Gazing now into the vast arena, squinting against the klieg lights, White feared that someone up there in the balconies might try to avenge the prophet's death.

Sensing the Mayor's anxiety and the crowd's hostility, Brown took the microphone. "Just let me say," he assured his constituency, "I had the pleasure of meetin' him and I said, 'Honorable Mayor,' and he said, 'Look man, just call me Kevin.' And look, this is a swingin' cat. Okay, yeh, give him a big round of applause, ladies and gentlemen. He's a swingin' cat."

With the crowd more receptive now, the Mayor said, "All of us are here tonight to listen to a great talent, James Brown. But we're also here to pay tribute to one of the greatest Americans, Dr. Martin Luther King. Twenty-four hours ago, Dr. King died for all of us, black and white, that we may live together in harmony. Now I'm here tonight to ask you to make Dr. King's dream a reality in Boston. This is our city and its future is in our hands. So all I ask you tonight is this: Let us look at each other, here in the Garden and back at home, and pledge that no matter what any other community might do, we in Boston will honor Dr. King in peace. Thank you."

As White finished, Brown cried, "The man is together!" Then he launched into the distinctive routine which had earned him the sobriquet "Mr. Dynamite." Flanked by two moaning saxophones, lit by pulsing strobes, he batted the microphone between his palms, bringing it close, pushing it away, gyrating, twisting, and sliding. His skin slick with sweat, he stripped the jacket from his three-piece suit, tossed it into the wings, then began a frenetic rendition of "Has Everybody Got the Feeling?"

At that, his young fans in the front rows could no longer contain their enthusiasm. Jumping on the stage, they grabbed at their idol's hands and hair. Police pushed them back, while Brown pleaded, "Let me finish the show! We're all black. Let's respect ourselves. Are we together or are we ain't?"

"We are," the crowd chorused back. And they were. Scattered violence erupted in Roxbury that night, but the downtown riot never materialized. As expected, thousands of young blacks stayed home to watch the concert.

But three days later, the city's delicate deal with Brown came close to collapse. On Monday morning, Greg Moses called Atkins to say the city was backing off. Atkins quickly dialed the Corporation Counsel, Herb Gleason.

"We never really gave the guarantee," Gleason said. "We were only discussing it."

"Herbie," Atkins said. "It was a firm agreement."

"Well, I don't know where we're going to get the money."

"Write a damn check on the city treasury."

"We can't do that."

"Well, I'm not going to let you back off," Atkins said, warning that if he hadn't heard from Gleason by noon, he was going to introduce a resolution in the City Council laying out the whole story and calling on the Mayor to fulfill his commitment.

At 11:50, Gleason called to say, "Brown will get his money."

But the Mayor didn't have the money. Everyone agreed it couldn't come out of the city treasury. Tom Atkins' televised appeal for a "Martin Luther King Trust Fund" had elicited barely $5,000, most of it from liberal white suburbanites. A few large private donors were tapped, with little success. So the Mayor turned to the one source which could come up with such money on short notice—the Vault.

In the late 1950s, shabby and decrepit Boston had drifted toward a financial crisis, a forerunner of the credit squeeze which would plague many municipalities two decades later. When Boston tried to raise desperately needed capital with a bond issue, Moody's Investor Service rated its bonds lower than those of any other large American city. The Athens of America, once the financial capital of the colonies, the home of generations of parsimonious Yankees, was now ranked below Cincinnati or Denver. To the Brahmin bankers, this was simply unacceptable.

Convinced that Boston was headed for municipal bankruptcy, the sachems of State Street resolved to control that process. If the city had to go into receivership, then the banks and major corporations were determined to have a mechanism in place to administer the wreckage. This effort was spearheaded by Charles A. Coolidge, senior partner in Ropes & Gray; Lloyd Brace, president of the First National Bank of Boston; Carl Gilbert, president of the Gillette Company; and Ralph Lowell, board chairman of the Boston Safe Deposit and Trust Company. Widely known as "Mr. Boston," for his astonishing range of civic enterprises, Lowell became chairman of the new group, which met in his company's boardroom. Lloyd Brace brought his bank's senior vice-president, Ephron Catlin, along as treasurer.

The consortium convened in utmost secrecy, but a few scraps of information inexplicably reached the press. One newspaper dubbed the new group "the Vault," and the name stuck.

By 1959, State Senate President Johnny Powers seemed all but certain to become Boston's new mayor. Distrusting Powers, whom they saw as the prototype of the big-spending Irish pol, the bankers considered several ways of forcing the city into bankruptcy and giving them control of municipal finances. Nevertheless, regarding Powers' election as a foregone conclusion, they reluctantly supported him. Only at the last moment did several Vault principals quietly open channels to Powers' opponent, Register of Probate John Collins. When Collins scored an astonishing upset, he shrewdly forged an alliance with

Charlie Coolidge and his colleagues. Every other Thursday at 4:00 p.m., Collins met with the Vault in the boardroom of the Boston Safe Deposit and Trust Company. Against all precedent, the Irish mayor and the Yankee bankers collaborated intimately on the "New Boston," then rising on the twin cornerstones of "fiscal responsibility" and a "revived downtown." Time and again, the Vault produced substantial sums for the Mayor's cherished projects, while raising money for him to hire experts at salaries well above budgeted levels.

When Collins decided not to run for reelection in 1967, he mobilized his financial backers behind a handpicked successor, Redevelopment Director Ed Logue. If Kevin White instinctively distrusted the Yankee establishment, he particularly resented its determined support for his opponent. Once in office, he pointedly kept his distance from the business community, only reluctantly attending a couple of Vault meetings. Yet now, as he sought the money for James Brown, his thoughts naturally turned to the Vault. Why shouldn't he tap their ample resources? Indeed, with all the money represented around that table, why stop at $60,000? The "long, hot summer" was nearly upon them. Even in the best of years, funds would be needed to put young blacks to work and expand inner-city recreation.

One day in mid-April, White made his pitch to the Vault. Around the mahogany table that afternoon was the core of the original membership—Lowell, Coolidge, Brace, Gilbert, Catlin. And there were some new members too, for the Vault had gradually expanded to embrace most of Boston's principal business and financial leaders, among them Frank Farwell of the Liberty Mutual Insurance Company, Eli Goldston of Eastern Gas and Fuel Associates, Richard Chapman of the New England Merchants Bank, Richard Gummere of Filene's Department Store, and Edward Mitton of Jordan Marsh. Had a Marxist revolutionary sought to wipe out the city's ruling class in one stroke, he could scarcely have done better than plant a bomb in the boardroom of the Boston Safe Deposit and Trust Company that day.

Seated at the head of the long, polished table, the Mayor delivered his appeal. He explained "the James Brown problem," then went on to talk of the "tinderbox" in Roxbury, the need for emergency palliatives to "cool things off" until longer-range projects could be brought to bear.

"How much, Mr. Mayor?" asked the blunt Eli Goldston.

"Well," White ventured nervously. "It's hard to put a dollar figure on it. But I should think, well, it cost me a million to run for mayor, so maybe in the neighborhood of a million dollars."

After a short pause, Ralph Lowell spoke up: "Mr. Mayor, in all the years we dealt with your predecessor, we never came up with anything remotely like that. I'm afraid the figure you mention is out of our league."

Oh, come off it, the Mayor thought, looking around the room at all those pinstripes. But what he said was, "Well, gentlemen, the city is at stake here, so whatever you think you can do." Then he got up and walked back to City Hall.

When he entered his office, barely half an hour later, his secretary said, "You have a call from Charles Coolidge."

The Mayor picked up the telephone and Coolidge snapped, "Mayor, you have a hundred thousand dollars on account. Have one of your people talk to Eph Catlin."

Catlin later explained what had happened in the boardroom during the Mayor's walk. "Well, we had some pretty fierce arguments about that James Brown thing—some of our fellows just didn't go for that at all. But the Mayor had persuaded us that if we didn't come up with the money, the blacks were going to burn the city down. So we thought we better do something."

Over the next year, the money in what came to be known as the Mayor's Special Fund was doled out to a long list of projects, controlled by Barney Frank. Off the top, of course, came $15,000 for James Brown (reduced from the original $60,000, largely because the city put pressure on the Garden to waive its share of the receipts). Some of the money went to the city's new Human Relations Task Force, set up after the assassination to help "cool" things in the black community (the task force and its successor, the Office of Human Rights, were principally financed from the regular city budget, but the Special Fund secretly paid a small cadre of black informants and operatives who, had they been on the official payroll, might have been accused of "selling out" to the establishment). Most of the money went to more prosaic projects in the black community: the Roxbury Beautification Program and a similar "cleanup" drive, both designed to keep black youngsters busy during the summer; equipment for a teenage football team; a contribution to the Roxbury YMCA; tickets for two hundred black kids to see the "Ice Capades" at the Garden.

The Orchard Park housing project, where Rachel Twymon and her six children lived, received a disproportionate share of the money, perhaps because it had been the site of some of the worst violence following King's assassination. Some $1,500 went to finance a summer festival there called "The Orchard Park Thing," a week-long bash of rock concerts, games, and food, hugely enjoyed by the Twymon kids. Another $600 helped equip an Orchard Park Security Patrol, made up of men in the project fed up with crime and vandalism. And $100 went to the nearby Robert Gould Shaw House, the settlement house which Mrs. Twymon, her brothers and sisters, and now her children attended.

Such expenditures were merely stopgaps—firebreaks to hold back the holocaust. More grandiose plans were being contemplated.

The Sunday after King's assassination, Sheldon Appel, a Boston paper box manufacturer, was at breakfast in suburban Newton when he noticed an article on page one of the *Herald* headlined "City's Negroes Cool Their Own." It told how Bill Wimberly, director of the Roxbury YMCA, and his sidekick, Marvin Butler, had rescued a white man badly beaten in Roxbury that week, and how they had otherwise sought to control violence in the black community following King's death. The *Herald* had selected Wimberly and Butler to represent the hundreds of black community leaders, ministers, and social workers who had been out in the street trying to cool things during the riots. The reporter closed his piece: "Bill Wimberly sat in his office with the green curtains drawn back and the April sun shining in on him, thinking about the summer. 'We need a gym here real badly. It will cost $250,000. . . . We can't raise it in the black community. We need help.'"

Shelly Appel had been overwhelmed by King's assassination, and was feeling, as he later put it, "the guilt of centuries." Putting down the paper, he exclaimed to his wife, "Somebody ought to help these guys. Here their leader has been gunned down and they spend all their energies trying to save white people. My God, I've got to do something! This is something I can do."

During the next few days, Appel called friends and acquaintances asking them to help raise money for the gym. Someone suggested he try Ralph Hoagland, president of Consumer Value Stores, a Massachusetts chain of cut-rate drugstores.

Hoagland was something of a phenomenon in Boston business circles—a Princeton and Harvard Business School graduate who, while still in his twenties, had built CVS into a multimillion-dollar enterprise. But he approached his social responsibilities with equal intensity. In 1961, while still at the business school, he asked one of his professors how he could help Negroes. "Why don't you teach them what you learned last year?" the professor suggested. So that fall, Hoagland began teaching business at a Roxbury social service agency, to a mixed group of clothes pressers, junk men, and house painters. He was convinced that if he could pass along what he knew to these black men, they could make it in the business world. But it rarely worked, usually because his students lacked the necessary capital. Once he founded CVS, he dropped the course, but he retained a burning conviction that such men could make it if only they could put expertise and capital together. Staggered by King's death, he was more than receptive when he got a call from Shelly Appel.

Nine people gathered in the Hoaglands' living room on Saturday, April 13. Quickly, they abandoned the gym idea. As Ralph Hoagland put it, "Blacks don't need more basketball courts. They do very well as it is bouncing the ball off a stoop. We have to shoot for something bigger than that." But they couldn't agree on what that should be. One by one, the guests began drifting away, leaving Appel and Hoagland staring at each other over the coffee cups. "Well," Shelly Appel said, "I guess it's up to us." They agreed to meet again at Appel's home on April 22.

In the meantime, Hoagland spoke with his black friends, among them Bryant Rollins, a young writer and social activist, who told him, "You want to help us, then give us the money and let us decide what we're going to do with it. The time is over for white people to be telling blacks what to do. We're going to control our own destiny now." In part, Rollins reflected the stance of the Black United Front, a new umbrella organization embracing nearly all of Boston's major black groups—from the Urban League to the Black Panthers—formed that January following a visit by Stokely Carmichael. After King's assassination, the Front demanded a large dose of self-determination—or, in the lingo of the times, "community control"—for Boston's black neighborhoods. On April 8, five thousand blacks gathered in a Roxbury sports stadium. With whites excluded, they approved twenty-one demands, among them:

"As of Monday, April 8, all white-owned and white-controlled businesses will be closed until further notice, while the transfer of the ownership of these businesses to the black community is being negotiated through the United Front.

"Every school in the black community shall have all-black staff, principals, teachers, and custodians.

"All schools within the black community are to be renamed after black heroes. Names will be selected through the United Front.

"The black community must have control of all public, private, and municipal agencies that affect the lives of the people in this community.

"The Mayor's office is to mobilize the Urban Coalition, the National Business Alliance, and the white community at large to immediately make $100,000,000 available to the black community."

The United Front's demands drew an angry response from Kevin White, who could hardly be expected to welcome steps which would weaken his political control over the city. "I understand and feel the anguish which spawned it," he said. "I will not by one word or one act add to the delusion that it is rational, workable, or dignified either for black or white. Racism is obscene by whomever proposed, black or white, and social reform rarely benefits from expropriation." The Mayor coupled his flat rejection of the Front's demands with praise for simultaneous proposals by the Boston branch of the National Association for the Advancement of Colored People, which had broken with the Front. White called the NAACP's proposals—which included stricter housing code enforcement and the hiring of more black policemen—"a worthy basis for serious implementation."

Ralph Hoagland did not share the Mayor's reservations. Indeed, he was excited by the boldness of the United Front's vision (ultimately, the Front saw the black community separating politically from Boston and forming a new city). When he, Appel, and half a dozen others met on April 22, Hoagland persuaded the group to accept an extraordinary proposition: that they set out to raise the $100 million included in the demands and give it to the Front "no strings attached." To screen out those not truly dedicated, they would ask for a minimum of $1,000 per person and one day a week to be devoted to a "skills bank" which would help blacks develop expertise in business and finance. Moreover, they agreed that the real problem was not in Roxbury but in Newton and other suburbs like it where "white racism" prevailed. While striving to help the black community, they must also educate the white community on their "moral responsibility" to erase racial inequality. They resolved to begin with a series of recruiting breakfasts held in their homes at seven o'clock on weekday mornings. The hour was Appel's idea. "People are always telling you they're tied up for lunch or dinner," he explained. "But nobody can tell you they're busy at seven a.m. The only reason for refusing a seven a.m. invitation is that they're too lazy or not committed enough. We don't want those people anyway."

The founding members of what came to be known as FUND—Fund for United Negro Development—could scarcely be accused of either laziness or lack of commitment. Ralph Hoagland, in particular, largely abandoned his drugstore chain for months on end as he worked sixteen hours a day raising money for FUND and serving as the principal go-between with the black community.

Hoagland, Appel, and the others brought the same almost religious zeal to their recruiting for FUND—one FUND officer told another, "Now I think I know what it must have been like in the early days of Christianity"—and at first it paid off. Over the next months, they held hundreds of seven o'clock breakfasts throughout Boston's ring of white suburbs and brought in an impressive roster of members at $1,000 apiece. At the start, the recruits came principally from among their friends in the liberal Jewish communities of Newton and Brookline. But gradually during the weeks following King's assassination it became fashionable to ante up for the black community. Senator Edward Kennedy was an early donor. So were Mrs. Henry Cabot Lodge, wife of the Ambassador to the Federal Republic of Germany, and the Ambassador's son, George. FUND's membership list was a tightly held secret, but most of those who joined the organization were substantial citizens of the Yankee suburbs: among them, Robert Saltonstall of Ralph Lowell's trust company; Philip Weld, Jr., publisher of the Beverly *Times;* Standish Bradford of the law firm of Hale & Dorr, and Francis Hatch, a state representative from the North Shore. One wealthy suburbanite even gave FUND his Porsche.

There were failures too. Hoagland took a long walk up the Ipswich beach with novelist John Updike, but came away empty-handed. And Joan Diver went to a FUND meeting at the home of friends on Beacon Hill, but gave nothing, partly because the Divers didn't have that kind of money, partly because they harbored doubts about FUND's approach.

The early money raising went so well that on May 23, FUND presented the United Front with its first installment—a check for $75,000. But that was a long way from $100 million. Soon FUND's leaders realized that if they were going to reach that goal they needed to get it in larger chunks. One day Hoagland and Harvard theologian Harvey Cox lunched with Robert Slater, president of the John Hancock Insurance Company and chairman of Boston's branch of the Urban Coalition, a year-old organization which sought to enlist big business in the war on urban poverty. In a private dining room at the Somerset Club, they asked Slater to funnel some of his vast resources into FUND.

"No, I won't," he said, "and I'll tell you why. The people you're dealing with are Mafia and Communists."

Indeed, much of Boston's establishment—black as well as white—regarded the United Front's leaders as either crooks who would take the money and run to Brazil or revolutionaries who would buy guns and bombs. Among those who harbored such suspicions was Kevin White. When FUND's leaders went to see him at City Hall, he castigated them for "picking the wrong black cats" and warned, "If they go out and buy machine guns, I'm holding you people personally responsible for the bloodbath that ensues."

Six months later one of the Front's leaders—an ex-con named Guido St. Laurent, who headed the New England Grass Roots Organization (NEGRO)—was in fact gunned down with two of his aides in what police called a "gangland-style murder." But most United Front members were well-intentioned if clumsy social activists. The $1 million which FUND presented to the Front between 1968 and 1972 went principally into loans for small black enterprises, most of which eventually went out of business.

Quixotic and ill conceived as it was, the FUND–United Front alliance outraged City Hall and State Street principally because it skirted the traditional channels of private philanthropy and good works; because it involved—both as donors and as recipients—volatile new forces in the community who wouldn't play by the old rules; and because it threatened established institutional relationships. If substantial money could flow from progressive Jewish businessmen and their guilt-ridden Yankee allies to a bunch of militant, aggressive blacks determined to control their own community, it could at least temporarily discomfit the old money represented in the Vault, established interests among the black middle class, and, of course, the Mayor, whose political ambitions depended on mobilization of existing power bases.

Not surprisingly, in the weeks following FUND's affiliation with the Front, these traditional interests began to coalesce. Robert Slater besieged the Mayor's office, seeking "socially responsible channels" through which the Urban Coalition and the Hancock could deal with Boston's urban crisis. So impatient did Slater become that one mayoral aide dubbed him "the quivering mass of money." The Mayor was characteristically skeptical about this abrupt shift in the business community's stance. "All of a sudden," he said, "everybody wants to enlist in the battle to save the black man and the city."

White was particularly bemused by Bob Slater, a flamboyant wheeler-dealer, who took big chances with the Hancock's money and talked of running for governor. Early in 1968, Slater announced plans for a spectacular new company headquarters, sixty stories of reflecting glass towering over the Back Bay. There were some who believed that his passionate attention to minority needs was somehow related to the new building's precarious site on the rim of the black community; its five thousand windows would make tempting targets in any disturbance. Skeptics suggested that the company was taking out "riot insurance."

For the time being, though, Robert Slater's interests coincided with Kevin White's. On May 13, 1968, in a full-dress City Hall news conference, White proclaimed that Boston's banks and insurance companies would provide $50 million for low-income housing—through new construction, rehabilitation, and liberalized mortgages on existing homes. In addition, he announced formation of a Boston Urban Foundation to invest $6 million in minority business ventures, and a "skills bank" to assist such businesses.

Much of the program—notably the foundation and the skills bank—bore striking similarity to the FUND-Front program. The Front's response was predictable, labeling the Mayor's scheme "a sham, an insult to the black community, a hypocritical and superficial political move." Indeed, little came of it—except for some increased mortgage financing and a few ambitious, though ultimately abortive, projects sponsored by the Hancock. Years later, Kevin White conceded that the whole thing was a "floral piece." The ubiquitous Ephron Catlin, who cropped up again as one of its promoters, privately called it a "wind puppy," an old Yankee term for a dog who looks pregnant but is actually bloated by gas.

Not all of Kevin White's activities in this period were so flatulent. An intensely political man, White responded to political imperatives—and, after King's assassination, the black community claimed his attention. Wasting no time, he loosed a volley of statements and gestures that soon led working-class whites to label him "Mayor Black."

On April 9, the day King was buried in Atlanta, White issued a statement describing himself as "Dr. King's disciple." By then the mood in Roxbury had cooled sufficiently for the Mayor to walk the streets. Accompanied by Jeep Jones, he strolled up Blue Hill Avenue that afternoon, played basketball with a group of teenagers, dropped in on several "civil rights" organizations, and shook every hand in sight. Three days later, White swallowed his pride and met with fifteen representatives of the United Front, saying, "I have no desire to stifle the dialogue that is so necessary to make progress in this critical area." And on April 20, he spent all day at a conference on black employment, sponsored jointly by his office and Roxbury churches. Closing the conference that Saturday afternoon, he concluded that "the overriding need in the ghetto is not employment per se, but rather the development of black entrepreneurship."

Three hours later, Kevin White kept a long-standing commitment to address the eighty-first annual banquet of the *Harvard Law Review,* which was held in the central hall of the Harvard Club, a vast, four-story chamber with a floor of Tennessee marble, walls of Flemish oak, and six arched windows rising to a beamed ceiling hung with Italian chandeliers. Assembled in this baronial splendor were the current editors and their predecessors from years gone by—members of Congress, federal and state judges, professors from the leading law schools, distinguished practitioners from Wall Street, State Street, and Broad Street, all turned out in white starched shirts, black ties, and dinner jackets. After an ample dinner, the speeches began.

Erwin Griswold, former dean of the Law School and now the U.S. Solicitor General, spoke of "differing perspectives in Cambridge and Washington."

Nicholas Katzenbach, the former Attorney General and now Under Secretary of State, spoke of respect for the law.

Kevin White spoke of the agony of the American city. "The holocaust that has ripped through our cities over the last two years, indeed during the past three weeks," he said, "gives us ample testimony to the magnitude of the problem. I bring tonight the conviction that if we are somehow to escape destruction, we must accept without reservation the proposition that the plight of the black man is the greatest single crisis in America today—the axis around which every other problem revolves."

The Kerner Report, he said, had outlined the alternatives open to American cities. They could stick with present policies, relying on economic growth to improve the condition of blacks. They could choose "enrichment," increasing spending for social programs, but leaving the Negro isolated in the ghetto. Or they could opt for integration, reversing the nation's drift toward two societies, black and white, separate and unequal.

White declared for integration. "The time has come for me after one hundred days in office, and for this nation after one hundred years, to put, as Lincoln did, the preservation of the Union above all else, the creation of a single society of white and black above all else. This is our commitment in Boston. I need your assistance. I hope there are those here among you, among the very best young lawyers America has produced, who will choose to join us in this commitment."

As the Mayor's words died away, there was a split second of silence, then the rustle of hundreds of napkins against dinner jackets as the phalanx of lawyers rose to give him an ovation.

At his table in the rear, Colin Diver stood transfixed, staring at the youthful Kevin White behind the rostrum. On the ride back to Cambridge, he and David Mann shared their enthusiasm for the Mayor's speech. Somehow White had captured just the sense of urgency, of moral commitment, of sacrifice that had been gestating in them all through that long winter. Back at the Divers' apartment on Flagg Street, Joan Diver and Betsy Mann were waiting. Over coffee, their husbands told them about the Mayor's speech. For more than an hour, the two couples talked of cities, blacks, integration, and community control.

It was well past 1:00 a.m. when Colin turned abruptly to David Mann and said, "I dare you to come down with me next week and take the Mayor up on his offer."

"What offer?" Mann countered. "That wasn't an offer."

"Sure it was," Colin replied. "He said he hoped some of the bright young lawyers in the room would help him out. There were only twenty-four guys in the room who're graduating this year. We're two of them. He must have meant us."

"Oh, who knows if he even has any jobs."

"Let's find out."

Joan and Betsy reinforced Colin's enthusiasm. Neither woman wanted her husband to sign on with a corporate law firm. The more Joan thought of Colin's idea, the more she liked it. "It's the right thing to do," she said. "We've been saying all along we don't care that much about money. What's important is doing something for people, helping the city survive."

On Monday, Colin called Barney Frank to set up an appointment. Barney seemed taken aback, but said, "Sure, come on down." On Thursday, he met with the two law students for an hour but could promise nothing concrete; he was simply unprepared for volunteers. When the Mayor heard that two *Law Review* editors had actually responded to his speech, he was flabbergasted. It had never occurred to him that anybody would take him literally.

Put off by Barney's vagueness, Dave Mann backed out, deciding to stick with his Cincinnati job. But Colin wasn't easily discouraged. He called Sam Merrick, one of the mayoral aides who Frank said might need an assistant. Merrick did and offered him the job. It paid only $8,000—a $6,000 cut from what he could have earned in Washington. But by then Colin's mind was made up. He called the partner who had hired him for Wilmer, Cutler & Pickering and told him he'd changed his mind. The partner made it plain that he regarded the young man at the other end of the line as a naïve fool.

Colin didn't care. In July he went to work as an assistant to the Mayor. For the first time in months he felt that life held some purpose. He was confronting society's critical issue—nothing less than the American dilemma itself.

5

Twymon

About the last of August came in a dutch man of warre that sold us twenty Negars," John Rolfe, a Virginia colonist, recorded laconically in 1619. The first blacks to enter an English settlement in the New World, their arrival marked the start of American slavery.

The "Negars" were landed at Old Point Comfort, a sandy spit which divides the James River from the broad sweep of the Chesapeake Bay. Later the point was incorporated into Hampton, the village to which the English settlers repaired after they abandoned Jamestown in 1610. Over the next two centuries, Hampton became an unusual antebellum community, combining small-town intimacy with the refinement of Tidewater planter society. Living side by side for 250 years, master and slave reached a rough accommodation. Laws against teaching slaves to read and write were widely ignored. Many whites permitted their slaves to hire themselves out to factories or artisans, returning a fixed payment to their masters.

But the Civil War put Hampton in immediate jeopardy. By then on Old Point Comfort reared Fortress Monroe, a powerful Union bastion manned by 6,000 Northern troops. In May 1861, command of the fort was assumed by Major General Benjamin Butler, later governor of Massachusetts and a great favorite of Charlestown's Irish. Butler confronted a difficult situation. Only weeks after his arrival—and eighteen months before the Emancipation Proclamation—three slaves belonging to Colonel Charles Mallory of the Virginia militia escaped to the fort, claiming that their master wanted them to work on Confederate fortifications in North Carolina. Needing laborers of his own, Butler granted the Negroes asylum. When Colonel Mallory protested, invoking the Fugitive Slave Act, which required that slaves be returned to their rightful owners, Butler said he was seizing the slaves as "contraband of war." Butler's dictum raced through Hampton. Within days he was besieged by hundreds more "contraband" seeking refuge at what they called "Fort Freedom." Slaveholders, realizing that they could no longer maintain their property in the shadow of the Union fortification, fled North with their valued chattel.

Among the departing slaves were the Jenkinses—George and Amy, both in their mid-seventies; their son, Frederick, and his wife, Charlotte; and their grandchildren, James, Amanda, and Frederick Jr.—who in early 1861 set sail with their masters for Nova Scotia. Although 850 miles to the north, the island was a logical refuge for Virginians. Trading ships had long shuttled between Nova Scotian and Tidewater ports. Moreover, though Canada had for many years been a haven for runaway slaves, it served Southern whites too as a shelter from the approaching apocalypse. Slavery had been abolished in Canada, but slaveholders could import their chattel as "servants." In the months just before the Civil War, hundreds of Southern whites and their Negroes arrived in Canada.

Landing on the Bay of Fundy, the Jenkinses and their masters soon settled thirteen miles to the south in the village of West Nictaux, which was populated by New Englanders who had arrived there soon after the British expelled the original French settlers. By 1861, West Nictaux was a tiny farming community, its hills dotted with orchards which produced apples for export to Boston, New York, even London.

The Jenkinses were the only black family in town. Elsewhere in the Annapolis Valley were remnants of earlier waves of black immigration—"loyalist" blacks who had gone over to the British cause during the Revolution and were later settled in Nova Scotia; the slaves of American Tories, brought by their masters to the island; and Negroes who had served in British units during the War of 1812—but these Negroes had clung together in tight little settlements.

While remaining in the service of their "masters," the Jenkinses didn't feel free to join one of these black enclaves. Even after the master-servant relationship dissolved, they stayed on in West Nictaux, doing odd jobs for white farmers and orchardmen: butchering pigs, threshing buckwheat, sawing wood, splitting birches for the hoops on apple barrels. At first they lived on the Nictaux road next door to the two-room schoolhouse, where the Jenkins children were the only blacks. In class, they were regarded as quaint curiosities, the white kids chanting, "Thick lips, flat nose / On the head, the wool grows." The family attended the Nictaux United Baptist Church, where they were assigned a special pew on the side aisle.

Soon after George Jenkins died at ninety-one, his family moved from the schoolhouse site to the Middle Road, a desolate track where the village's poorest residents lived in tar-paper shacks. But they retained a sense of their own uniqueness, their special relationship with white folks. They never mixed with the blacks of North Street in Middleton, a settlement barely four miles away. North Street was called "the bog," partly because it was built on swampy ground, partly because it was the home of indigent 1812 refugees known for their drinking and other "low behavior." Charlotte Jenkins would warn her kids, "Stay away from those niggers in the bog!" It was a strange life. Embraced by neither whites nor blacks, they occupied a sort of racial no-man's-land in which conventional allegiances were suspended.

By 1885, Frederick Jenkins, Jr.—then twenty-five—was growing restless. He had become a lumberman, cutting white ash, black birch, and rock maples, then riding the logs down the river to a sawmill in the valley. But there wasn't much money in that, and other opportunities were scant. Black Nova Scotians had begun migrating to New England, where jobs were more plentiful, and when Frederick heard of a job with a Massachusetts lumber company, he packed his meager belongings and took the overnight ferry to Boston. When the job fell through, he worked successively at a tannery, a coal yard, and an asphalt company, while moonlighting as a janitor and rag merchant. Eventually, he settled in Lower Roxbury, where he married Rachel Baker, a recent migrant from Virginia. In 1905, their only child—Helen—was born.

The Jenkinses lived in Lower Roxbury for more than thirty years, nineteen of them on Flagg Street. Predominantly Irish and Italian, their block had only a smattering of blacks, and the races lived side by side with little tension. On warm summer nights, the neighbors gathered on someone's front stoop to drink beer and play cards. Maintaining his family's tradition of association with whites, Frederick Jenkins exchanged visits with two Scottish families from Nova Scotia and often played the fiddle at Irish wakes.

Helen was raised on sausage and sweet pastries which her mother sent her to buy at the Italian markets on Northampton Street. Only one childhood incident marred her sense of well-being. In 1923 her cousin Moses Baker was temporarily stationed as a seaman at the Charlestown Navy Yard. One night, walking the Charlestown waterfront on his way back to base, Moses was assaulted by several men and beaten so badly he spent weeks in the hospital and eventually had a kidney removed. Helen, then eighteen, was horrified and resolved to stay away from Charlestown.

After graduating from the High School of Practical Arts in 1925, she went to work for the Marshalls, a Yankee family who lived in a big house in Jamaica Plain. She never regarded herself as a maid, more as a companion and helper. In the summers, Helen accompanied the family to their house in New Hampshire, where she had her own room all through the hot weather. They were good to her.

One Sunday in 1930, when Helen was twenty-five, she was walking down Camden Street, coming home from the Zion Methodist Church, when someone hailed her from across the street. It was Jim the laundryman, but Helen noticed he had another man with him, a nice-looking fellow. So she said, "You come over here to talk with me and leave your friend over there?"

"Well, he's single, so I didn't bring him over," Jim said. It wasn't considered proper for single men and women to meet in such circumstances. But later that afternoon, Jim came by the house and introduced Helen to his friend Quinnie Walker, who had found his way to Boston by a very different route from the one the Jenkinses had taken.

.   .   .

If Hampton's slaves enjoyed certain dispensations, seventy miles upriver at Richmond many blacks were at least nominally free. Many Virginians, taking the rhetoric of independence with utmost seriousness, had recognized the irony of fighting for freedom while denying it to others. "The glorious and ever memorable Revolution can be justified on no other principles but what do plead with still greater force for the emancipation of our slaves," said a petition from Hanover County in 1785. Although Thomas Jefferson retained 150 slaves, many of his neighbors invoked his ringing phrases to justify the liberation of thousands of their own chattel between 1785 and 1800.

But soon this fervor cooled. After a number of free Negroes joined Gabriel Prosser's and Nat Turner's rebellions, they were denounced as "degraded, profligate, vicious, turbulent, and discontented" persons whose "locomotive habits fit them for a dangerous agency in schemes wild and visionary." Although they continued to work as tobacco processors, coal miners, iron forgers, and draymen, the legislature imposed stern new restrictions on their religious and educational activities, and vigilante bands made sure that they knew the penalty for violating such regulations.

Free blacks had to remain alert for another breed of freebooter—the kidnapper. For, with the invention of the cotton gin in 1793, "cotton fever" had seized the Deep South, sharply raising the price of slaves needed to pick the crop. By the 1830s, Virginia's depleted soil was no longer suitable for large-scale cotton production and slaves themselves became the state's most valuable crop. Pressed by creditors, many old families turned their plantations into giant breeding farms, until the state resembled "one grand menagerie where men are reared for the market like oxen for the shambles." Between 1830 and 1840, no fewer than 117,000 slaves were sold into other states. Virginia Negroes were in particular demand along the frontiers of Georgia and Mississippi, where every rustic seemed to hanker after a Virginia-bred black as his coachman, a Virginia slave as his lady's maid. Bands of kidnappers roamed the state, seizing free Negroes and selling them into slavery in the Deep South. Richmond's 2,000 free Negroes—feared, despised, and now particularly vulnerable—were prime targets for such raiders.

Late in November 1833, an eight-year-old girl named Fanny—the daughter of a free black man and a Cherokee Indian woman—was playing on the dusty roadway in front of her Richmond home when she heard the strains of a popular tune drifting down the street. Looking up, she saw a pair of horses drawing a flatbed wagon in which a band of white musicians were scraping on fiddles and tooting on horns. As the wagon drew abreast of her house, it stopped. The driver looked down and asked if she wanted a ride. Fanny hesitated. Her mother had warned her about going off with strange whites, but the tune was so enchanting that Fanny couldn't resist. She hopped up beside the driver and the wagon clattered off down the street.

One can only imagine what Fanny must have felt when she realized some hours later that the musicians were kidnappers, part of a gang which had been snatching Negro children off Richmond's streets. But the loss of a freedom then enjoyed by barely 180,000 blacks among 2.5 million in the slave states must have brought with it a special sense of anguish. That day could only have bequeathed a grievance against white people which would linger in Fanny's family for generations to come.

Fanny and the other captives were formed into a "coffle," a long train of slaves fastened together for the march south. The women and girls were tied to one another by ropes wound like halters around their necks, while the men and boys wore iron collars linked by a thick chain, their wrists cuffed behind their backs. The white drivers rode on horseback alongside, carrying whips which they cracked in the air whenever the coffle lagged. The slaves walked twenty-five miles a day, pausing in the morning and evening for meals of corn mush and boiled herring. At the day's end, still wearing their shackles, they lay down by the roadside to sleep.

After two weeks, Fanny's coffle reached Augusta, a center of the slave trade for the Savannah River basin. Augusta held its major auction on the first day of every month, when the slaves were led through the crowded streets to the city market, a gleaming white structure topped by a gold cupola. Its ground floor, which opened to the street through rows of Doric columns, was jammed with butcher stalls and fruit stands. In the rear, farmers sold cows, horses, and pigs. Out front stood a large wooden slave block to which, on auction days, the bell in the clock tower summoned a throng of prosperous planters, small farmers, overseers, commission agents, hackmen, gamblers, and blacklegs.

In the crowd that day in early 1834 was Job Gresham, a middle-aged planter from nearby Burke County who had come to the city to stock up on provisions. His wife had long wanted a lady's maid, and when he spotted little Fanny on the block, he resolved to take her home as a surprise.

Job Gresham was a native Virginian too, but by age twenty-four he'd found his way to Burke County, where he married into a pioneer family. The colonists who had settled that portion of eastern Georgia in the 1740s were drawn by its astonishingly rich soil, ideally suited to the Southern plantation system. "I don't know exactly what the Good Lord was thinking when he made Burke County," one early planter said, "but I believe he was thinking about cotton."

But while King Cotton thrived in Burke's intense heat, white men working the fields suffered "wasting and tormenting Fluxes, most excruciating Cholicks." To elude these fevers, Burke's planters worked out a pleasing accommodation to the climate. Turning the cultivation of their cotton lands over to resident overseers, they arranged to spend much of the year just across the line in Richmond County. There, on a high plateau covered with oak and pine, they founded a resort colony called Brothersville, replete with gleaming bungalows, lush lawns, and picnic grounds. Job Gresham had a house in Brothersville, where he stayed from June through October, returning to his plantation on Briar Creek in November and remaining through the spring planting. As the housemaid, Fanny accompanied the family wherever it went: first cleaning, washing dishes, and polishing silver, later cooking and waiting on table.

Several years after she came to the Greshams', she accepted the attentions of a field slave named Jack Bennefield, five years her elder. One spring they were married in the traditional slave wedding ceremony: jumping over a broom. Since Fanny was a house slave and Jack a field slave, they held different social positions on the plantation. Normally, Jack would have lived with the other field hands in an Indian-style lean-to. But since he was married to Fanny, the master gave them permission to share one of the little huts behind the Big House.

When Job Gresham died in 1846, his slaves were divided between his two sons—John Jones, then practicing law in Macon, where he twice served as mayor of the city, and Edmund Byne, who remained at home to run the family estate. John received thirteen blacks. Edmund took twenty-two—among them, Fanny and Jack Bennefield.

By 1860, Edmund owned ninety-nine slaves, ranking him tenth in the county. He and his wife, Sarah, treated their slaves with some consideration. But like his father, Edmund spent much of his time in the pine-scented cool of Brothersville, leaving personal supervision of the plantation to his overseer, Henry Ward. Ward was a hard man who drove the slaves relentlessly, and his wife was even harder. Once, when a cook burned the biscuits, Mrs. Ward made her strip to the waist and—as Fanny watched in horror—beat her with a willow branch until the blood ran down her back.

As war drew near, Edmund played a growing role in the county's affairs. One of three delegates from Burke to Georgia's Secession Convention, he sat down in his hotel room at Milledgeville on January 9, 1861, and wrote his wife: "This day will be long remembered by Georgia. We have passed the ordinance of secession by a vote of 208 to 89. The ordinance will be signed on Monday at 12 o'clock and now, while I am writing, the cannon is firing, the bells are ringing and every other demonstration of joy you can conceive of is going on." Once the fighting began, the Greshams did their part. At age fifty-two, Edmund was too old for active duty, but both his sons saw service.

After the Confederacy's capitulation in April 1865, Augusta's ex-slaves petitioned the government for some means of marking their emancipation. Authorities scheduled a massive parade on July 4, the date most closely identified with American freedom. Before dawn that day thousands of former slaves from surrounding counties—Fanny and Jack Bennefield among them— set out on foot for Augusta. Whites retreated behind shuttered windows, leaving the streets to the Negroes, who lined the parade route ten deep. At noon a detachment of the Thirty-third United States Colored Troops proudly stepped off, leading a procession of 4,000 wildly exultant Negroes. Later, some 10,000 blacks assembled before the city market—where thirty-one years before Fanny had been auctioned on the slave block—to hear the Reverend James Lynch deliver his "liberation sermon."

In those first months after the war, thousands of freed slaves descended on Waynesboro and Augusta to agitate for change. To Fanny and Jack Bennefield, emancipation meant sweet revenge on their overseer, Henry Ward, and especially on his terrible wife. When Union soldiers heard about Mrs. Ward, they made her "dance the jig" all the way to Waynesboro, more than twelve miles. On the outskirts of town she collapsed in the dusty road.

With the Wards gone, Edmund and Sarah Gresham spent more time at the "Home Place," bringing their more benevolent style to the fields. The Freedmen's Bureau, charged with protecting the rights of freed slaves, established a "contract" system with minimum wages, stipulated rations and sick time—able-bodied males like Jack received $8.00 a month, a woman hand like Fanny $4.00. But the relationship between employers and laborers hadn't changed greatly from prewar days. The "hands" still lived in the slave quarters, drew rations from the smokehouse, worked in gangs under white "managers." The Greshams provided virtually everything Fanny and Jack needed for their daily lives, subtracting the value of those goods and services from their wages: $3.00 for a pair of shoes, 75 cents for two plugs of tobacco, 25 cents for a dose of castor oil. At month's end most hands had little, if anything, coming to them.

So long as the freedman accepted his new lot, his life was bearable, but if he objected, arguing that this wasn't the emancipation they'd been promised, retribution could be swift and sure. In 1866, flogging "as in slave days" was common in Burke (Jack Bennefield's back, his grandson recalls, looked like a "washboard" from all the beatings he'd taken). By March 1868 the Ku Klux Klan was active in the county. In a single month that spring, three freedmen were shot to death by whites.

For the Greshams, Reconstruction was a trying period. It took time to accommodate themselves to the new realities. When John Jones Gresham married one of the county's belles, his uncle wrote from Macon: "I am sorry that circumstances are such that I cannot give him a Negro, but I must do the next best thing left, that is give him a mule."

Of all the Greshams, young Job—a grandson of the original Job Gresham—was the most capable. Mustered out of the Georgia Volunteers at Appomattox, he walked the four hundred miles back to Burke County, where he took over a plantation which had belonged to a distant cousin named William Byne. It was a pleasant spread, with nine hundred acres of cotton land, an orchard, a smokehouse, and an iron foundry—a big place that needed more than Byne's hands to farm it. After Edmund Gresham died in 1872, his widow sent over four men to help her son—among them, Jack Bennefield.

Jack and Fanny Bennefield had one child, Cornelia, who married Frederick Walker, one of Edmund Gresham's slaves. By 1880, Fred had joined Jack on Job Gresham's place. Each tilled a "plow"—about twenty-five acres of cotton land, a few more for corn and vegetables—for which they paid Job a bale of cotton. They relied heavily on their wives and children to hoe and weed the fields, then pick the cotton in the fall, harvesting about ten bales a year. With prices averaging $50 a bale, they earned about $500 a year. But they didn't keep much of it. Off the top came the bale each owed Job. Moreover, Job provided them with seed, implements, and food, to be paid for, with substantial interest, after the harvest. Once those debts were paid, the Bennefields and Walkers had just enough to squeak by on until it was planting time again. In 1881, Jack Bennefield had a $50 mule, $25 worth of farm tools, and $10 in household furniture—a net worth of $85.

Later they got their credit from merchants in nearby Keysville, who had a wider range of goods than Job could provide but who squeezed every cent of interest they could out of the farmers. If a tenant failed to pay his debts, the landlord or merchant would seize his crop, his meager belongings, even his dog or cat. The desperate farmer often tried to hide a few vegetables to feed his family. Once Sol Walker—Fred's brother—was beaten severely by his landlord for attempting to conceal some corn inside his mattress.

Job's Negroes sought solace from the hardships of this world at the Antioch Baptist Church. The Bennefields and Walkers were all members of Antioch, and Sol Walker was long one of its deacons. The Reverend Seaborn Jones, its pastor for fifty years, was a preacher of great passion and greater volume, whose Sunday-morning sermons, it was said, could be heard half a mile away. And everybody up and down the old "Gresham Highway" could hear Jake Mitchell, the church drummer, as he marched by banging the drum to proclaim the death of an Antioch member.

One morning in 1892, Jake banged his drum for old Jack Bennefield, dead at seventy-two. (Fanny lived nearly half a century longer, dying in 1933 at the age of 108, when she was buried in the Gresham Cemetery a few feet from her first master, Job Gresham.) By the time of Jack's death, Cornelia and Frederick Walker had nine children of their own with whom they lived in a two-room, tin-roofed shack made of logs with gaping chinks through which the wind whistled.

Fanny and Jack Bennefield had never learned to read or write—Georgia law before the Civil War prescribed a stiff fine for anyone caught educating a slave—and Cornelia and Frederick had had only a year or two of grade school. The Walker children didn't do much better. They went to the all-black Spring Hill School, where they received the rudiments of learning, but most of them left well before the eighth grade to join their parents in the fields.

Soon, however, those fields were ravaged by the boll weevil. As late as 1918, Burke County had produced a record 70,877 bales of cotton; by 1921, production had plummeted to 14,386 bales. White planters, who had once bet a dozen bales on a poker hand, were lucky to harvest that many from their blasted land. And black tenant farmers, with no resources to fall back on, were devastated. In 1922, the Waynesboro Women's Club, chaired by Mrs. Orrin Gresham, Job's niece, launched a campaign to assist needy children suffering from the winter cold. Appealing for sweaters, coats, and shoes, she said, "This is not only to supply a need but to let these people realize we mean to see them through."

But Burke's Negroes had little faith in their former masters. In 1922 alone, 5,000 of the county's 24,775 blacks departed, joining a massive flood of Negroes streaming North. Many who boarded the Dixie Flyer or the Southland in Augusta disembarked in Baltimore, Philadelphia, and New York, but others stayed aboard until their train reached Boston. Though wages were lower there than in the mid-Atlantic cities, there was something about Boston that drew Southern Negroes. It was from Boston that the abolitionists had issued their calls for a holy war against slavery. It was there that many blacks fled in the underground railway, relying on Bostonians to forward them to Canada. It was to Boston that David Walker, a North Carolina Negro, fled in 1825, and there that he issued his fiery pamphlet *Walker's Appeal* ("Brethren, arise, arise! Strike for your lives and liberties!"), which was widely distributed in Georgia.

The image of Boston as a sanctuary was encouraged by black writers who, over the years, described it as "a city of refuge, a place of light, life, and liberty," the one place in America "where the black man is given equal justice," and even, euphorically, "the Paradise of the Negro."

In 1923, Fanny Walker—Frederick and Cornelia's third-oldest daughter— grew weary of wresting cotton from the wasted fields. Arriving in Boston, she sent word back that jobs were plentiful, wages nearly triple what they had been in Burke. That sounded good to her younger brother Thomas Quinnie Walker.

Quinnie had already done some roving. At the age of seventeen, he had gone to work for the Southern Bell Telephone Company, laying long lines through the Georgia swamps. Three years later, just as the boll weevil hit Burke County, he returned to try his hand at tenant farming. One day, he went to the store seeking some corn and a hoe, but the shopkeepers refused to advance him the supplies, claiming that he owed them forty dollars. That did it. Quinnie gave his mule to his sister Sarah, packed his belongings in a worn cardboard suitcase, and boarded the Dixie Flyer. Years later he would tell his daughter—the future Rachel Twymon—that when the train pulled into Boston's South Station that morning in 1925, he felt "as if my life were starting all over again."

After a year in which they saw each other every Sunday, Quinnie and Helen Jenkins were married. And so a circle was completed. The wedding united two Virginia families who had begun barely seventy miles apart. Once they had been remarkably similar: slaves for hire in the urbane seaport, free blacks in the sophisticated capital. But the tortuous route each family had traveled to Boston opened a chasm between them. One, transported to Nova Scotia, had found themselves the only blacks in a white village, proud of association with their neighbors yet never quite accepted by them. The other, sold into slavery, had lived for ninety years in rural Georgia surrounded by others of their race, fearing and resenting their white overlords. The marriage of an old Bostonian and an illiterate sharecropper proved an uneasy one, reflecting deep fissures in Boston's black community.

"Slavery was repugnant to the Puritans and was regarded by them with abhorrence," wrote William Sumner, a Massachusetts soldier-historian, in 1858. On the eve of the Civil War that was a convenient version of history, lending the North a moral superiority in the coming struggle. But it was bad history, at odds with the ample record of Massachusetts' dominant role in the slave trade. Boston was never quite so distinctive as it liked to pretend. Through the eighteenth century, Boston's sailing men provided Negroes to the West Indies and the Southern colonies. Slaves, bought in Africa for five pounds sterling, brought from thirty to ninety pounds in the West Indies, a differential which laid the foundation for many New England fortunes.

In comparison with the Southern colonies, there were never many slaves in Massachusetts, partly because the harsh climate and stony soil did not permit a plantation agriculture requiring numerous field hands. Yet, by the eve of the Revolution, 5,249 Negroes, most of them slaves, were counted in the colony.

Still, Massachusetts' brand of slavery *was* distinctive, probably more benign than in any other colony. Following the Hebraic tradition passed down through the Old Testament, the Puritans regarded slaves as persons divinely committed to their stewardship. Usually referred to as "servants" rather than slaves, they were often treated as members of the family in which they lived. A visitor in 1704 complained that New England masters were "too indulgent . . . to their slaves; suffering too great familiarity from them, permitting you to sit at table and eat with them (as they say to save time), and into the dish goes the black hoof as freely as the white hand." Since salvation required a knowledge of the Bible, many masters even taught their slaves to read and write. The legal status of slaves in New England was somewhere between that of Southern plantation slaves and that of indentured servants. They could acquire, hold, and transfer property; they were entitled to a trial by jury. Most important, they could sue whites and could carry their suits on appeal to the highest courts in the colony.

By the mid-eighteenth century, slaves were taking advantage of that right, bringing civil suits for their freedom, arguing that slavery was "contrary to ye laws of Nature." Such entreaties eventually reached the Puritan conscience. Like Virginians, many Massachusetts citizens perceived the contradictions between their own struggle against Britain and their enslavement of others. Abigail Adams, in a letter to her husband, John, wrote: "It always appeared a most iniquitous scheme to me to fight ourselves for what we are daily robbing and plundering from those who have as good a right to freedom as we have."

Once the colonies won their independence, the Massachusetts Constitutional Convention adopted a Declaration of Rights, holding that "all men are born free and equal." But slavery persisted. Not until 1783 did the state's chief justice declare it unconstitutional.

Although conscience played a role in all this, more practical considerations were also involved. As John Adams noted: "The common people would not suffer the labour, by which alone they could obtain a subsistence, to be done by slaves. If the gentlemen had been permitted to hold slaves the common people would have put the Negroes to death, and their masters too, perhaps."

Unlike Southern slaves, who were overwhelmingly cultivators of cotton, rice, and tobacco, those in Massachusetts had been employed in a wide variety of crafts: as printers, blacksmiths, tailors, ship's carpenters, coopers, masons, rope makers, or sailors. But with the end of slavery in the state, white artisans largely reclaimed those jobs, and by the early nineteenth century Negroes were heavily concentrated in service positions.

At first, most blacks lived along the wharves of the North End, a quarter known as "New Guinea"; later they edged into the West End and onto adjacent Beacon Hill. Since many Negroes were servants to the wealthy whites who lived on the hill's south side, they settled in the crowded alleys on the reverse slope, which came to be known as "Nigger Hill."

It was there—in the African Meeting House, Boston's first black church— that William Lloyd Garrison and eleven other white men founded the New England Anti-Slavery Society and proclaimed two goals: the eradication of Southern bondage and of Northern discrimination. Although the former struggle took precedence, Garrison and other Boston abolitionists worked to ameliorate the lot of Boston's blacks side by side with such Negro leaders as Frederick Douglass and Lewis Hayden.

One of their principal objectives was the integration of Boston's public schools. The city's school system had been segregated since 1798. In 1849, a black parent, Benjamin Roberts, brought suit against the city in the name of his daughter Sarah, seeking reintegration of the schools. Arguing Roberts' case before the Supreme Judicial Court, Charles Sumner said: "[A] school, exclusively devoted to one class, must differ essentially, in its spirit and character, from the public school known to the law, where all classes meet together in equality. It is a mockery to call it an equivalent." But Chief Justice Lemuel Shaw disagreed, ruling that the segregated schools did not deny Negroes equal protection of the law.

Justice Shaw's ruling—the "separate-but-equal doctrine"—was to have a profound effect on the nation's history. The Roberts case was the chief precedent cited by the Supreme Court when it enshrined that doctrine in *Plessy* v. *Ferguson* (1896) and, thus, the genesis of the legal principle which was to govern the country's race relations until 1954.

Not in Boston, however. Spurned by the courts, black parents, supported by abolitionists of both races, carried their fight into the political arena. In 1855, the Massachusetts legislature passed a bill prohibiting segregated schools. It was the first of several notable victories achieved by the same coalition in the decades before the Civil War—among them, lifting the ban on interracial marriages, adding Negroes to the jury rolls, and abandoning segregated seating on the state's railroad cars.

By the eve of the Civil War, Massachusetts Negroes had achieved a fair measure of political and civil rights. Although their economic position was precarious and they were excluded from most social circles, they were probably more secure than their counterparts elsewhere in the nation. This progress prompted the New York *Herald* to lament: "Now the blood of the Winthrops, the Otises, the Lymans, the Endicotts, and the Eliots, is in a fair way to be amalgamated with the Sambos, the Catos, and the Pompeys. The North is to be Africanized. Amalgamation has commenced. New England heads the column. God save the Commonwealth of Massachusetts!"

The war itself quickened the sympathies of Boston's whites for their black fellow citizens. On May 28, 1863, thousands of Bostonians gathered to watch Colonel Robert Gould Shaw, a young Yankee aristocrat, lead his Fifty-fourth Massachusetts Volunteer Infantry—the first Northern black regiment in the Civil War—through the city's streets to Battery Wharf, where they embarked for South Carolina. Scarcely two months later, Shaw and several hundred of his Negro soldiers died together in an assault on Fort Wagner. Their common martyrship helped cast a glow of brotherhood over the city's race relations. When a monument to them was dedicated at the crest of Beacon Hill, the philosopher William James declaimed: "There on foot go the dark outcasts. . . . There on horseback among them, in his very habit as he lived, sits the blue-eyed child of fortune, upon whose happy youth every divinity has smiled. Onward they moved together, a single resolution kindled in their eyes, and animating their otherwise so different frames. . . ."

Indeed, for a time, it appeared that Boston's whites and blacks might march together toward the common goals of a just and equal society. Within months of the surrender at Appomattox, Massachusetts broadened the legal immunities of its black citizens. After Negroes complained about racial discrimination at Boston's Globe Theater and the Brigham Restaurant, the legislators banned such discrimination in licensed inns, public meetings, and "places of amusement," a prohibition which was eventually extended to all public accommodations.

Gradually, blacks played a more prominent role in public life. In 1867, two were elected to the Massachusetts legislature, where they maintained at least one representative until the end of the century. With their concentration in the West End, Boston's Negroes elected at least one City Councilman in every election between 1876 and 1895.

But as Boston's blacks tasted the fruits of this "golden era," their community was already being transformed by successive waves of freed slaves from the South. The first to arrive were some of General Butler's "contraband" from Hampton. Massachusetts officers had supervised these Negroes in the refugee camps which sprang up around Fort Monroe. When the Freedmen's Bureau sought to relocate them after the war, it looked first to New England because there was "no region . . . more desirable as a home for the Negro." Back came stacks of applications for "colored girl servants" and, over the next few years, nearly two thousand ex-slaves were sent North as domestics for white families in the Boston area. For the next three decades, Tidewater Virginia remained the principal source of black migrants to Boston. Most of the ex-slaves who settled in Boston in the first years after the war were urban, literate, semiskilled, light-skinned Negroes or mulattoes—products of the relatively benevolent slave system of the Upper South.

But even such comparative sophistication didn't assure these migrants a warm welcome in the black community. For Boston's Negroes—sheltered by extensive legal protection, succored by a few principled abolitionists, favored by a certain latitude in the city's public life—were intensely proud of their "special relationship" with whites. They did not take kindly to the influx of recently freed slaves who reminded them of the indelible stamp of servitude which lay on the brow of all black men in America.

This pride in their heritage of freedom was, for some Boston blacks, a goad to action. Accustomed to dealing with whites on a plane of rough equality, such Northern Negroes were determined to extend Boston's racial climate to the nation at large. The chief spokesman for this group of "Boston Radicals" was William Monroe Trotter. Born with an unusually light complexion, raised in white Hyde Park, Trotter had graduated *magna cum laude* from Harvard and inherited a modest fortune of $20,000. He inherited as well the racial militancy his father had developed while fighting for equal pay in one of the two black regiments Massachusetts sent into the Civil War.

Trotter's principal target was Booker T. Washington, the Sire of Tuskegee. In almost every respect, Washington was Trotter's antithesis: born a dark-skinned Southern slave, he derided "high-flown" intellectualism and emphasized practical "industrial education" for blacks. To Trotter, Washington was the quintessence of the Southern Negro whose spirit had been crushed by slavery. For Bookerites, Trotter was a dangerous overreacher, "a brave, roaring, make-believe lion."

This conflict came to a head on July 30, 1902, at the African Methodist Episcopal Zion Church on Boston's Columbus Avenue. Some two thousand spectators had gathered that night to hear Washington lecture on "the dignity and beauty of labor," but before he could begin, one of Trotter's supporters scattered cayenne pepper on the stage. Fistfights broke out in the audience and Trotter himself clambered onto a chair to read a list of nine challenges. After Trotter was arrested, a Bookerite journal cried, "What is the matter with these Boston Negroes?" But "the Boston riot" became a landmark in American race relations less because it deepened the rift between Trotter and Washington than because it persuaded W. E. B. Du Bois, another highly educated Massachusetts Negro, to break with Washington and found the more militant National Association for the Advancement of Colored People, with its first branch in Boston.

The newly aggressive mood did not persist among Boston's black elite. Trotter had never represented the privileged community into which he was born. The further the abolitionist past receded into history, the less militant Boston's blacks grew. By the second decade of the twentieth century, their leadership had fallen into the hands of some thirty black families known as the "Black Brahmins." There was J. H. Lewis, a merchant-tailor who kept a stable of racehorses; Gilbert Harris, New England's largest wigmaker; and the poet William Stanley Braithwaite. "Like the white Brahmins," writes one historian, "they spent Friday afternoons at the Symphony, vacationed at Newport or on the Cape, and lived in Beacon Hill apartments or in large, brick homes in the

South End, 'filled with books, potted palms, dull colored plants near the window and antique furniture.' Children learned their social graces at Mr. Papanti's dancing school." They generally belonged to white churches, rather than the Baptist and AME churches founded by blacks. Many summered at Oak Bluffs on Martha's Vineyard. So proud were they of their roots in the city which Oliver Wendell Holmes had called "the hub of the solar system" that they organized a Society of the Descendants of Early New England Negroes, which had twenty-four members in 1903. Though the true "Black Brahmins" were a tiny fraternity, their influence greatly exceeded their numbers. Aspiring to their status, thousands of Boston-born Negroes took on the Brahmins' complacency, their aloofness from social problems, their reluctance to participate in any movement that might set them apart from the white mainstream.

By the turn of the century, whites as well as blacks were retreating from the race question. In the South, the end of Reconstruction was followed by the imposition of rigid segregation, underscored by Klan raids and lynchings. In Boston, the changes were slower and subtler, but even there the passing of the abolitionist leadership and weariness with the "old issue" took their toll. Once Boston's cultural institutions and public accommodations had been open to all. Now segregation became the order of the day: the nursing school of the Massachusetts General Hospital denied a black woman's application; the black editor Frederick Douglass was forcibly ejected from a first-class railroad car and compelled to take a seat in the "Jim Crow car."

As blacks were deserted by their old Yankee allies, they found little sympathy among the Irish, who had long resented the abolitionists' alliance with the Negro. Blacks and Irish competed for jobs, with the Irish gradually displacing Negroes in many traditional occupations. Some intermarriage took place—particularly between Irish maids and black servants—but the children of such unions found themselves spurned by both groups. For a time after the turn of the century, Mayor James Michael Curley hinted at an alliance of Irish and black workers against the Yankee "codfish aristocracy," but even Curley proved a fickle ally. When Trotter spearheaded a protest against the showing of D. W. Griffith's *Birth of a Nation,* Curley overrode objections to the film's racial message and authorized its run. "Where is the valiant Jim Curley of old," Trotter asked bitterly, "the friend of the people, lovable Jim Curley, whom we coloured people supported for the mayoralty against the advice of our white friends? If this were an attack on the Irish race he would find a way pretty quick to stop it." The alliance died aborning.

White Bostonians—Irish and Yankees alike—were responding, in part, to the Southern ex-slaves who had flooded North in the decades since the Civil War, expanding Boston's black community from barely 2,280 in 1860 to nearly 14,000 in 1910. These late arrivals were likely to be dark-skinned field hands from rural Georgia or Alabama. Even W. E. B. Du Bois conceded in 1901: "As a whole, it is true that the average of culture and wealth and social efficiency is far lower among immigrants than natives." It was one thing for white Bostonians to attend the Symphony with the Lewises or visit the Authors

Club with William Stanley Braithwaite, quite another to brush shoulders with a former Georgia sharecropper. Whites recoiled and gradually that recoil hardened into permanent withdrawal.

To Boston-born blacks, the lesson was clear: the newcomers—soon dubbed "Homies," from "down home"—were dragging them under, destroying their "special relationship" with whites. In 1912, a white social worker was strolling through a black neighborhood with Butler Wilson, a prominent "Black Brahmin" and leader of the NAACP. Arguing about the establishment of a settlement house for black youth, they passed a group of young Negroes playing craps. "What's to become of them?" the social worker asked. "Let them rot!" snapped Wilson.

As the Homies swarmed into black neighborhoods, Boston's blacks began to disperse, hoping to put some distance between themselves and the interlopers. Even before the turn of the century, older Negro families began moving out of their traditional quarter on the back side of Beacon Hill, establishing themselves in the South End, Dorchester, or the more remote suburbs.

Soon the South End became the principal landing place of the Southern migrants, for jobs were readily available there in the Boston & Albany Railroad yards and the hotels of Copley Square. Many railroad porters and waiters settled in a narrow strip between the tracks and Columbus Avenue, within easy walking distance of Back Bay Station. One boardinghouse in the neighborhood catered exclusively to Southern-born waiters; Ebenezer Baptist Church, established to serve Southern fundamentalists, soon became known as "the Jay Bird Tabernacle" because of the loud shouts of "Glory to God!" which punctuated its services; and the Southern Diner on Columbus Avenue appealed to Homie tastes with hush puppies and sweet potato pie.

After World War I, another ingredient was added to the stewpot of black Boston: West Indians, particularly from Barbados and Jamaica. Highly motivated and hardworking, they came to Boston intending to make some quick money and then to go home. Many stayed on, but they continued to regard themselves as "His Majesty's Subjects," and formed their own set of institutions: St. Cyprian's Episcopal Church, the Eureka Cooperative Bank, the Crispus Attucks Drum and Bugle Corps. West Indians were known in Boston as "Black Jews" and "monkey chasers," but most often as "Turks." By the 1920s, Boston's black community formed a triangle, with Brahmins, Homies, and Turks all protecting their prerogatives and regarding each other with ill-disguised suspicion.

This chronic fragmentation enfeebled the community, but there were other sources of weakness. The vaunted "special relationship" between the races—though short-lived and much exaggerated—seduced Negroes from the development of strong black institutions which might have created a substantial middle class (for years, Boston's largest black business was Chisolm's Funeral Home). Then there was the community's size: throughout the nineteenth century blacks never exceeded 2 percent of the city, and even by 1970 they had reached only 16.3 percent, compared with Washington's 71 percent or Detroit's 43 percent. Boston blacks lacked the critical mass necessary for effective political or social action. This became particularly important in 1949, when the City Charter was amended to replace ward-based elections with an at-large system. With the black community unable to muster enough votes citywide, only one Negro—Tom Atkins—was elected to the City Council over the next quarter century. Finally, the community had no historic center to provide a sense of continuity and cohesion. Boston Negroes have always lived in segregated space, but that space has shifted steadily from north to south. There has never been a place where Boston's blacks could say with certainty, "This is what we are, this is where we make our stand."

By the mid-twentieth century, black Boston had three separate centers: Intown, Crosstown, and the Hill.

The Hill was the latest refuge of the Brahmins and their imitators. It had been a Jewish neighborhood until the 1930s, when upwardly mobile Negroes seeking better housing leapfrogged over a resistant Irish community and settled on the slopes leading to the green of Franklin Park. By the forties, they were firmly established in the big Victorian houses on the tree-shaded side streets off Humboldt Avenue. It was there in the summer of 1940 that Malcolm Little—later Malcolm X—moved in with his sister Ella; he found it a "snooty black neighborhood" whose residents "prided themselves on being incomparably more 'cultivated,' 'dignified,' and better off than their black brethren down in the ghetto."

Crosstown, back in the South End, was "the Great Black Way," "Black Broadway," or, to its denizens, simply "the Avenue." Its red-hot center was the intersection of Massachusetts and Columbus avenues, where jazz and blues blared from the open doorways of the Hi-Hat, the Wig-Wam, Kelly's, Wally's Paradise, and the Big M. And there were seedier establishments, gin mills like Hardy's or the 411 Lounge, where the three biggest pimps in town hung out with their stables. The high rollers parked their long cars at the curb, searching the sidewalk for the litany of Crosstown Pleasures—dope, booze, the numbers, the horses, and high-yellow women.

Intown was where the Walkers—and the Jenkinses before them—lived, a largely working-class neighborhood embracing Lower Roxbury and the outer South End. The narrow side streets—Kendall, Hammond, Davenport, Ball, Flagg—were predominantly black, though still with a liberal admixture of Irish, Italians, and Jews. On the major thoroughfares were the offices of the black doctors and lawyers, the undertakers, barbershops, and hairdressers, and the best restaurants—Slade's Barbecue, where chickens roasted tantalizingly in the front window, and Estelle's, where a customer could munch ribs and ogle the black celebrities.

Shortly after Helen Jenkins and Quinnie Walker were married in 1931, they moved into a little row house on Davenport Street in the heart of Lower Roxbury—a shabby house on a shabby street. Quinnie worked steadily—first at the P. H. Graham Wastepaper Company, hauling cardboard boxes from the downtown department stores; then, during the Depression, on several WPA construction projects. But there was never enough money to go around, particularly after the Walkers started having children, eight in all, beginning with Rachel in 1934.

They were poor, at times desperately poor, but somehow they managed. From his sharecropping days, Quinnie knew how to draw food from the earth. In their backyard he planted a vegetable garden where he grew collard greens, wax beans, cucumbers, and tomatoes. When the produce was ripe, he wrapped it first in waxed paper, then in brown paper, twisting it in a special way to keep out the air; then, after the first frost hit, he stored the packages in barrels sunk deep in the frozen earth, so the family had greens all winter long. In those first years, the marriage seemed to work, but gradually the gulf between the Bostonian and the Georgia Homie grew wider.

Between 1940 and 1960, Boston's black population mushroomed from 23,675 to 63,165, nearly tripling in twenty years what it had taken three centuries to build. Most of the newcomers were Cotton Belt Southerners, some arriving during the war to work in military facilities or industry, others surging North in the postwar boom. For many Boston blacks this latest wave of Southern immigration was devastating, the final liquidation of their special relationship. In the narrow alleys of Intown, a remnant of old Bostonians struggled to retain some shred of that distinctiveness. Sometimes they were driven to extreme measures. One woman who grew up in Lower Roxbury recalls how outraged her mother was when an Alabama family moved next door and began hanging its laundry on the front porch. Her mother went over and explained, "That's not the way we do things here. We put our laundry in the backyard." When the Alabama woman told her to mind her own business, the Bostonian instructed her children to spatter the laundry with mud. They had to do it three times before the newcomer got the message and moved her wash to the rear.

This battle of region and class was fought out *within* the Walker household. Helen felt that she'd married beneath her. Quinnie, who had quit school in the fifth grade, could neither read nor write. He was not without talents. A natural mechanic, he could fix your lawn mower or water pump, and people said he could hear a car go by two blocks away and tell what was wrong with it. But such skills carried little weight with Bostonians like his wife, who regarded him as a Georgia farm boy.

Quinnie thought Helen was "uppity." He sensed that she felt superior to him because her folks had been "house niggers" while his had been "field niggers," and he couldn't stand her "house nigger" ways. He didn't understand why she had to set the table every day with forks, knives, and spoons—down where he came from, people weren't afraid to pick up good food in their hands. He ridiculed her because she didn't know how to clean a fish or pluck a chicken, simple jobs for any eight-year-old Burke County girl.

Much of the conflict focused on the Fourth Methodist Church, just down Shawmut Avenue. Although its pastors and membership were black, it was part of the overwhelmingly white Methodist Episcopal Church and thus gained some of the traditional prestige Boston blacks attached to such churches. A devout member, Helen served on several of the church's committees, while sending her children to its Sunday school. Quinnie, though nominally a Baptist, had little use for religion. For a few years he reluctantly joined Helen at Fourth Methodist, yet soon he stopped going and did whatever he could to prevent her from attending "that fancy, white folks church."

As the atmosphere at home deteriorated, Quinnie spent most of his time playing whist at the Independent Social Club or lounging on orange crates with the other neighborhood men outside Dolly Bolt's Tropical Variety Store. Injured in an accident on a WPA project, he received some insurance money and promptly spent it on a secondhand Cadillac, in which he loved to tool up and down the avenue. A spiffy dresser, he wore dazzling white shoes which he polished every day. Quinnie also savored his whiskey: old Grand-dad gulped straight from a big juice jar. And he relished his women. The family knew he was running around, often spotting him with some new girlfriend coming out of a Crosstown bar.

A "massive dude"—his six-foot frame carried 250 pounds—Quinnie could be a tyrant at home. When he thought it was time for guests to leave, he would go downstairs and pull all the fuses out of the box. He refused to buy Helen clothes, so she couldn't go out. When he went to work in the morning, he often turned the furnace off and locked the basement door, leaving Helen and the children to shiver in a frigid house.

Not surprisingly, the Walker kids were caught between their mother's Brahmin reserve and their father's street savvy. On most issues Rachel took her mother's side, but the ferocity with which she defended it owed not a little to her father's style. Once when she saw one of Quinnie's women loading up her father's Cadillac outside Fulsom's Market, she grabbed the groceries and flung them all over the parking lot. And one particularly cold day, Rachel unscrewed the hasp on the basement door and—while her terrified mother begged her not to—went down and turned on the furnace. This set off a terrible row, during which Quinnie warned his rebellious daughter not to mess with the furnace again, and Rachel said she'd mess with it anytime she liked and the only way Quinnie could stop her was to carry the damn thing around on his back.

During World War II, Quinnie got a job at the Charlestown Navy Yard. Remembering what had happened to their cousin Moses Baker, the family was apprehensive, but every day Quinnie and two black co-workers rode the El to City Square and walked along the wharves to the Yard. Townie heads would turn, but nobody ever bothered them.

After the war, he went to work for the Begsford Construction Company, where he made good money. But Helen and the children didn't see much of it. When the kids wanted a dime for ice cream or candy, he'd say, "I can't afford to make the Jew rich" (most Roxbury stores were Jewish owned). Eventually, Helen went to work as a stitcher at the Goddess Bra factory to help pay the bills, but even that wasn't enough. In 1960, she got a court order requiring him to pay her fifty dollars a week, which he did only sporadically. In October 1962, Helen left him and moved in with her second daughter, Alva.

After all those years of wrangling, Quinnie—then fifty-eight—was at a loss without his wife. He moved across the street to a smaller house, where he was desperately lonely. When he asked some of his children if he could move in with them, they put him off. On February 5, 1963, he was standing on the platform of the Northampton Street El station during the evening rush hour. As a train roared in, Quinnie stuck his head directly in its path and suffered a fractured skull. He underwent delicate brain surgery, but died the next day. Although police called it an accident, some of Quinnie's children—Rachel among them—believed it was suicide.

Long before her father's death, Rachel had been having troubles of her own. In her third year at Brandeis Vocational High School, she'd grown bored with the dreary courses in sewing, typing, and office practice, so she hadn't put up much resistance when her father insisted that she quit school to help support the family. She took a job at Mack's Variety Store, where the owners trusted her so completely that they often went South and left the store in her teenage hands.

At nineteen Rachel left home for good, taking a room with a family friend and keeping time with Eddie Jones, a burly trucker who drove giant rigs on interstate runs to California and Arizona. In quick succession, she bore two of his children—Richard in 1954 and George in 1955. For a time, Eddie helped support his sons, but he never lived with Rachel and gradually they drifted apart.

Soon she met another man, a charming Alabamian with a Nike missile unit in suburban Squantum, and in July 1957, Rachel and Sergeant Haywood Twymon were married. When Haywood overstayed his leave, he was bumped to corporal, an ominous start to a marriage that soon went awry. For Rachel had largely recapitulated her mother's mismatch. Like Helen, she was proud of her roots in Boston, of her associations with whites. She cherished childhood memories of Lower Roxbury's ethnic hodgepodge—of Catholic holidays when Italian neighbors would invite her in for homemade wine and butter cake. She was nostalgic for that golden era of racial harmony when "people were people, whether they were black or white or whatever." Soon after her marriage, she sought out a six-room apartment on Dewey Street, two-thirds of the way from Intown toward the Hill, in a neighborhood still largely white.

Haywood, on the other hand, was not unlike Quinnie, a product of the Cotton Belt who felt ill at ease with the gentility of old Bostonians. At first, he was regarded as a prime catch—an Army sergeant with a technical skill and prospects for promotion. Jovial and friendly, he was good company—except when drinking. But as the years went by, he drank with increasing ferocity; as soon as he got his paycheck, off he would go on a binge, hitting all the bars along Massachusetts and Columbus avenues. One Christmas, he was found wandering the streets in his underwear.

In the meantime, he was saddling himself with family responsibilities. Four children came quickly: Frederick in 1958, Wayne in 1959, Cassandra in 1960, and young Rachel in 1961.

With little money coming in from Haywood, Rachel went back to work, joining her mother for a time at Goddess Bra, later working as a packer at Schrafft's candy factory in Charlestown, then as a maid for white families in the suburbs. With a child coming nearly every year—and often laid up with mysterious illnesses—Rachel couldn't take a steady job with a family. Instead, she did "day work," shuttling back and forth by bus and subway to the comfortable Yankee-Jewish suburb of Newton. This meant rising before dawn to reach the state employment office by 9:00 a.m., when the jobs were parceled out. The families Rachel worked for lived in big Victorian houses along Walnut Street. The brisk young housewives gave her the work they didn't want to do themselves—scrubbing bathtubs, cleaning toilets, scraping the grease out of ovens. Unlike her mother, who never regarded herself as a maid, Rachel knew just what she was and resented it bitterly.

In June 1960, three months after Cassandra was born, Haywood stunned the family by announcing that he was leaving the Army after eight years. Rachel, Helen, and other relatives urged him to reconsider; his military allotments had kept the children fed even when he drank up the rest of his pay. But Haywood wanted out.

Cousin Moses Baker chose that moment for one of his periodic visits to Boston. Retired from the Navy on a disability pension after the Charlestown beating, "Cuz" was a highly respected member of New Haven's black community, for years president of its NAACP chapter, a former butler to Yale professors. Some of the family found him pompous and self-important, but he was Rachel's favorite cousin, personifying the respectability she so badly craved. On his visits to Boston he invariably stayed with her because only she would put up with his demands—that his plate and cup be warmed before each meal, and his coffee served just so. For days before his arrival, Rachel scrubbed the house and prepared his favorite dishes. Haywood bitterly resented "the Great Cuz," grumbling, "He ain't nothing but a man, is he?" Cuz, in turn, openly disdained Haywood. The continuing debate over Haywood's decision to quit the Army made this visit from Cuz an especially tense one.

Haywood behaved well all week, but others could see he was building up a head of steam. The morning after Cuz had left, Haywood told Rachel that some friends were coming by to play cards and he needed ten dollars to buy whiskey and beer. Rachel, who could get very deaf when she didn't want to hear someone, simply ignored him. Pulling on his pants, Haywood warned, "When I get dressed you better have that ten dollars." Rachel didn't respond. Exasperated, Haywood grabbed his wife and dragged her down the hallway, bellowing new threats at her while she shouted her defiance. But Rachel wrenched free, grabbed a pot of boiling water off the stove, and as Haywood bolted down the stairs, emptied it on his head. Howling in pain, he lurched back upstairs, pulling the soaked undershirt over his head. With it came great swatches of skin from his chest, shoulders, and face.

Treated at the hospital for third-degree burns, Haywood came home, but Rachel wouldn't have him. "I'm sick," he appealed. "I don't care," she said. "I don't want you dying here. Get out and stay out."

After a month Rachel relented, but the relationship continued to deteriorate. In March 1961, Haywood walked out. Dependent on his $68 a week from Colonial Coal, out of work herself, with five young children to support, Rachel sought public assistance for the first time. The Welfare Department awarded her an "emergency grant" of $20. At the social worker's suggestion, she then swore out a non-support complaint against Haywood and the court ordered him to give her his full salary every week, which he did until mid-May, when he was laid off.

After a hospital stay in June, Rachel moved to her parents' house on Ball Street, taking her children with her. In July, she again went to the welfare office, "sobbing and somewhat hysterical," saying that her youngest child, Cassandra, was ill. She had no money except for the few dollars her parents could spare and feared that if she returned to Dewey Street Haywood would beat her. The social worker authorized "general relief" payments of $38.80 per week. Ten days later, a warrant was issued for Haywood's arrest for non-support. That August, Rachel obtained an uncontested separation from her husband, who was ordered to pay $40 a week in support of his family. Meanwhile, Rachel qualified for permanent Aid to Families with Dependent Children, with payments beginning at $257 a month. In September, she and the children moved back to Dewey Street, changing the lock to keep Haywood out.

For a time, Haywood met his obligations, but in July 1962 he was laid off again. Late in August he blew most of his $64-a-week unemployment check on a drinking binge. With no money to feed her children, Rachel swore out another complaint against him and this time the court sentenced Haywood to six months at the Deer Island Correctional Facility. The year before, Eddie Jones—father of Rachel's first two children—had spent several months at Deer Island for failing to support them and several children by another woman. Rachel insisted she never wanted to send either man to jail. All she wanted them to do was support the children they'd given her.

But this is just what Haywood couldn't—or wouldn't—do. On his release from prison in February 1963, he told Rachel he'd learned his lesson and wanted to come home. She refused, saying she didn't want him in the house until he proved he had stopped drinking and could support the family. Getting a job at the Tillotson Rubber Company, he resumed support payments. Late at night he would show up at Rachel's door, often with a bottle in his hand. To avoid trouble, she often let him in, then watched him fall asleep on the couch. But soon the support payments stopped again. In November 1963, Haywood was sent back to Deer Island, this time for a year.

By then, Rachel was utterly dependent on her welfare checks. For in late 1962, doctors at Boston City Hospital had finally diagnosed her frequent illnesses as manifestations of systemic lupus erythematosus, a disease which alters the body's immune system, giving rise to a legion of odd, seemingly unrelated symptoms: severe arthritic pains in the joints; inflammation of the lungs; red, patchy lesions of the skin; malfunctions of the heart, kidney, liver, or central nervous system. Characteristically, her lupus would go into remission for several months or even a year, only to be followed by a relapse. She was in and out of the hospital dozens of times over the next decade. For four days in 1964, she was completely blind, only to mysteriously regain her sight. Several years later, she required a total hysterectomy. Still later, she had to have all her teeth removed. At times she was profoundly depressed, preoccupied with fears of death or of life as a permanent invalid.

She was hospitalized so often that she was unable to provide a home for her family, and late in 1962, her children were placed in black foster homes. Richard and George, then eight and seven, went to stay with a Miss Bernice Cook on Braddock Park in the South End; Frederick and Wayne, four and three, went to the Sneeds in Malden; Cassandra, two, and Rachel, not yet a year old, went to the Freemans, also in Malden. They remained in these homes off and on for nearly three years until in late 1964 they returned for good, joining their mother at her new apartment on Fenelon Street.

Even when the worst of her hospital bouts were behind her, Rachel often found it difficult to care for her children. Occasionally, she suffered slight paralysis in her arms and legs; once she had a seizure while feeding two-year-old Cassandra and dropped her onto the floor. At such times, her mother or her sister Alva would look after the children, but most members of the family were reluctant to help out. One female relative told the Welfare Department she would take Cassandra and young Rachel if she got twenty dollars a week for each girl—four times the statutory figure. The social worker admonished her, saying that she should be willing to accept the responsibility "without demanding a profit."

Even Helen Walker didn't want to be saddled with her grandchildren for very long. As Helen was leaving Quinnie, Rachel implored her to move in with her so the children wouldn't have to go into foster homes. When her mother flatly refused, Rachel was deeply wounded.

Rachel never even considered asking for help from the aunts on her father's side—loud, coarse women from Burke County, stereotypical Homies. Sarah was a hopeless drunk; Fanny eventually went mad and was committed to Boston State Hospital for the Insane. The only one of Quinnie's relatives whom Rachel saw regularly was cousin Magnolia Williams, a late arrival from Burke County who settled in Boston in 1951. Although she was considerably older than Rachel, the two women managed a cordial, if ambivalent, relationship.

One day in April 1964, Magnolia paid a call on Rachel. That spring, many Massachusetts whites were heading South to protest racial segregation, often getting arrested to dramatize their cause. Over coffee and doughnuts in Rachel's kitchen that day, the two women discussed the movement's latest *cause célèbre*—the arrest of Mrs. Malcolm Peabody, mother of Massachusetts' governor, Endicott "Chub" Peabody. Known for her proper Bostonian zeal for good works, the white-haired Mrs. Peabody had gone to St. Augustine, Florida, late in March to demonstrate against segregated hotels and restaurants. When Mrs. John Burgess, wife of the first Negro suffragan bishop of the Episcopal Diocese of Massachusetts, was arrested in the lounge of the Ponce de Leon Motor Lodge, Mrs. Peabody and several other demonstrators courted arrest too. After two days and a night in jail, she proclaimed, "I will go to jail again if necessary to fight for civil rights." Martin Luther King sent a telegram lauding her as "an inspiration to generations yet unborn." When she and Mrs. Burgess returned to Boston, demonstrators met them at the airport carrying a banner which read: "Godspeed to the Gallant Ladies."

Rachel thought that Mrs. Peabody was a wonderful woman, a modern exemplar of the abolitionist tradition. Magnolia wasn't so certain. "Oh, yeah," she said, "that's fine, going down to Florida to integrate some motel. But what's that lady and her son, the governor, doing about things up here?"

"We don't have that kind of discrimination up here, Mag," said Rachel.

"You think you don't?"

"No," said Rachel, "or at least we never used to."

"You had it all along, honey, but you hid it under half a bushel."

"Mag, I'm telling you, we never used to have any of that sort of thing up here, and if we have it now, it's only because all you Southerners came up here and brought it with you."

"That's a damn lie," said Magnolia, slamming her coffee cup down on the table. "They don't want you up here any more than they wanted us down there. One of these days, you'll see how you been foolin' yourself."

Magnolia stormed out and the two women didn't speak again for weeks.

6

McGoff

Toward the close of the eighteenth century, the North of Ireland writhed in sectarian combat. Protestants and Catholics raided each other's settlements, burning, pillaging, and slaughtering. The Protestant banner was raised by the Peep o' Day Boys, so known because they appeared outside their victims' cabins just as dawn lit up the glens, while the Catholic Defenders matched their foes lash for lash, bludgeon for bludgeon. County Armagh was particularly vulnerable to these "outrages," as Protestants sought systematically to rid the county of Catholics. In 1791–92 alone, some 7,000 Armagh Catholics were forced to flee south into counties Louth and Monaghan.

Among those who took flight were a small clan of Kirks, for whom the religious warfare must have been particularly unsettling. For the Kirks had once been Protestants: Scottish Presbyterians from the lowland county of Dumfriesshire, who had emigrated to Northern Ireland around 1630. Sometime during the intervening century and a half, at least one Kirk had converted to Catholicism, apparently to marry a Catholic girl. By 1794, these Catholic Kirks had settled in a narrow corridor between Inniskeen in County Monaghan and Maghereah (also known as Kirk's Cross) in County Louth.

One of these was a Maghereah butcher named James Kirk, known to friend and foe alike as "Butchy." A beefy man with a blood-red face, Butchy wasn't popular with his fellow Catholics, who suspected him of illicit ties to the Protestant yeomanry. His enemies accused him of being an informer, furnishing the despised English with intelligence on the Defenders.

One day in 1796, Butchy fell into an argument with a worker named Pat Culleton, who flung a lead weight at his head, killing him outright. Kirk was to be buried in his family plot at Inniskeen, but when the funeral procession reached the river Fane, a party of Catholics seized the coffin and dumped it in the river. Recovered and buried at Inniskeen, it was dug up in the middle of the night.

The Kirk affair produced a series of celebrated trials. Pat Culleton was found guilty of manslaughter, twenty-nine others of disrupting Kirk's funeral. But the defendants were widely regarded as patriots, while generations of Kirks were labeled collaborators. For years, any Kirk walking a village path had to suffer the gibes of children shouting "Butchy! Butchy!"

About 1800, a farm laborer named Owen Kirk decamped from Inniskeen in search of more amiable surroundings. Tramping the hills east of Ardee in County Louth, he came on a humpbacked ridge of peculiar charm. On one side the land fell away through fields of barley and oats to the river Dee; on the other, a copse of Scottish fir inclined toward the river Glyde. Along the ridge's spine ran a dusty road straddled by the tiny village of Roodstown: two dozen thatched huts, a smithy, tailor's shop, and cooper's works. Towering over everything were the ruins of a sixteenth-century castle, its roof sheared off by wind and storm, but its square towers and mullioned windows still keeping a sentry's watch over the sleeping valleys.

The castle had been built by the Taaffes, Welsh warlords who had ruled Roodstown through the Middle Ages. By the eighteenth century it had fallen into the hands of Thomas Dawson, a loyalist rewarded by the Crown with the title of Lord Cremorne. From his seat in County Monaghan, he ruled his Louth estates through agents and overseers.

When Owen Kirk reached Roodstown in 1801, he rented a quarter acre of Dawson's land adjacent to the old Taaffe castle. His plot held a one-room thatched hut, a rutted "half road," and a small garden, barely large enough for a few rows of potatoes and parsnips, for which he paid an annual rent of five shillings. Before long he married Cath Creaton, and together they had five children. To support his family, Owen worked part-time as a laborer for other farmers, earning six pence a day.

Life was hard for Owen and Cath, but not without its pleasures. In summer, Roodstown was a green and fragrant place, overlooking two of Ireland's loveliest valleys. The Glyde and Dee teemed with salmon and eel. Grouse and woodcock fluttered in the copse. The Kirks attended the races at Haggardstown and the famed steeplechase at Mullacurry. Ardee and Dunleer held regular fairs at which jugglers, acrobats, and minstrels performed. On such occasions, Louthians downed prodigious quantities of Castlebellingham ale, renowned as Ireland's best malt liquor.

The opening years of the nineteenth century were relatively prosperous ones in Ireland, but then a severe recession revived the country's semi-permanent agrarian insurgency. Waged for decades by Whiteboys, Rightboys, Oakboys, and Hearts of Steel, now it was carried on by a new breed of rebels calling themselves Ribbonmen. Spawned by the sectarian warfare of the 1790s, the Ribbon Society came to focus on the economic grievances of small farmers and landless laborers. As famine and depression deepened during 1815–16, the Ribbonmen looked toward armed rebellion and started collecting weapons.

In April 1816, three Louth Ribbonmen appeared at Wildgoose Lodge, five miles northeast of Roodstown, demanding guns from its owner, a prosperous farmer named Edward Lynch. A donnybrook broke out and Lynch informed the authorities. When the three Ribbonmen were executed at Ardee, the Ribbon Society swore revenge. On October 30, some seventy-five Ribbonmen surrounded Wildgoose Lodge with smoldering turf torches and set it ablaze, killing Lynch and seven others. The night's events sowed terror among the Louth gentry, who responded with unusual vindictiveness. Eighteen persons were executed for the crime, their bodies publicly displayed at crossroads throughout the county for up to two years.

If Wildgoose Lodge and its aftermath set gentry and tenants at each other's throats, it also brought terrible pressures to bear on Catholics in surrounding villages like Roodstown. The Ribbon Society demanded unqualified allegiance to its insurgency, while landlords and magistrates threatened bloody reprisals against those who offered succor to the rebels. If the Kirks threw in their lot with the Ribbonmen, they were "degenerate felons" marked for execution; if they turned their backs on their own kind, they were "villainous traitors" risking Edward Lynch's fate. For a family long sensitive to the epithet "Butchy," it must have been an excruciating dilemma.

Unrest built in Louth as crop prices continued to fall. Then, during the 1840s, the potato crop—prime source of food for most Irish peasants—failed for five consecutive years. Turning potato fields throughout Ireland black with rot, the blight proved a national disaster of unspeakable proportions. Especially acute in the desolate West, the famine took a terrible toll even in fertile Louth. By October 1846, bands of starving men roamed the Louth countryside, forcing themselves on local relief schemes.

Many landlords took advantage of the Great Famine by evicting tenants who had fallen into arrears on their rent. Since eviction was the worst calamity that could befall an Irish farmer, the landlords' new strategy prompted a resurgence of Ribbonism. The society would issue one warning to those who pursued "this reckless policy," then if the landlord persisted, a Ribbon tribunal would sentence him to death.

In December 1851, James Eastwood, an English landlord with an estate in Castletown, decided to evict two of his tenants on the Sunday after Christmas. When Ribbon remonstrances proved fruitless, an officer of the society named Barney Quin came to the county seat of Dundalk to recruit assassins among Ribbonmen of the area. After meetings at Rafferty's Public House, Burns's Tavern, and Lawless's Public House, Quin selected Thomas Belton, twenty-four, Patrick McCooey, thirty-four, and an itinerant laborer, the forty-nine-year-old James Kirk.

A cousin of Roodstown's Owen Kirk, James had been born in Inniskeen just six years after Butchy Kirk's death. Bearing the very name of the informer, he must have grown up with special maledictions heaped upon him; according to legend, he had sworn to redeem the family honor. Casting his lot with the Ribbon Society, he did not shrink from the ultimate act of rebellion. On Christmas Eve, as light snow fell over Castletown, Kirk and his two accomplices intercepted Eastwood as he strolled his estates, clubbing him with heavy stones and leaving him for dead at the edge of a quarry. But the landlord survived. Five days after the attack, Kirk and McCooey were arrested on the information of a paid informer—publican Michael Lawless—who testified that he had overheard Quin and three men plotting the assassination in his tavern on the night of December 22. Largely on Lawless's testimony, Kirk and McCooey were sentenced to death.

On July 31, 1852, the most celebrated execution in county history took place in the square before the Dundalk courthouse. A double row of constabulary ringed the square, backed by a squadron of lancers. At ten minutes to twelve, the condemned men, arms pinioned with leather straps and white caps on their heads, were led to the scaffold. McCooey exhibited "much weakness," chanting over and over, "Holy Mary, Mother of God, pray for me." In contrast, James Kirk displayed his "usual firmness." At high noon, the hangmen wound strips of black crepe over the prisoners' eyes. Around their necks went ropes of silk, woven for the occasion by prisoners in the Cork jail. At a signal from the prison's governor, the two men were "launched into eternity." For an hour their bodies hung from the gallows, "an object lesson to those who watched."

But the Kirks drew a different lesson from the one the British magistrates had intended. In the family's collective memory, the exploits of James Kirk the Ribbonman soon exorcised the shame of James Kirk the Traitor—though they still might hear the chorus of "Butchy" in marketplace and tavern, somehow they succeeded in erasing all recollection of the informer. As generations went by, these themes of loyalty and betrayal were to run like bold threads through the family's history, weaving a tapestry in which heroes and villains, patriots and turncoats, were pitted relentlessly against each other, with the Kirks—and their descendants, the McGoffs—invariably enlisted in freedom's legion.

Before the Great Famine was over in 1851, death, eviction, and emigration to America had eroded the population of rural Ireland. In 1841, Roodstown had 208 residents; a decade later, only 172 remained. The Kirks hung on. Although Owen and Cath were dead by now, the cottage next to the old Taaffe castle was occupied by their oldest son, Bryan, his wife, Bridget, and their five children.

The Kirks were less dependent on the land than most of their neighbors, for Bryan was a tailor, an itinerant craftsman who made clothes for the villagers and outlying farmers. Through the first half of the nineteenth century, ready-made clothes were largely unknown in rural Ireland. At fairs and markets, one might find a few secondhand suits, known as "Lord-ha'-mercys" because they came off the backs of dead men, but most farmers still supplied hand-woven cloth to the village tailor, who made up a suit to measure. Sometimes Bryan Kirk worked at home; more often he traveled to his customer's home, carrying needles, thread, and scissors in a leather pouch.

The Kirks continued to live in spartan simplicity. The old thatched cottage Owen had built in 1802 was now divided down the middle by a flimsy partition. To the left was a kitchen with a stone hearth; to the right, a bedroom where the Kirks spent the night on straw pallets spread out on the clay floor. On either side was a small window which did little to relieve the dark, damp, and cold which pervaded the cottage in all seasons.

Other than Kirk the tailor, Hardy the blacksmith, and Rorke the cooper, Roodstown offered its twenty-five families little in the way of commerce or diversion. For those they went three miles east to Ardee or two miles west to Stabannon. By the 1850s, Ardee was a town of 2,500, with a tanyard, an oat mill, and eighteen alehouses. But it was to Stabannon that the villagers went on Sundays to hear Father Corrigan chant the Latin Mass in the whitewashed chapel; there they went to quaff ale at Geraghty's, or dance to the fiddling of old Jamie Farrell. And it was there that the Kirks' second son, Patrick, attended John Mackin's "hedge school," so known because it had long been illegal for any Catholic youth to get an education and priests and schoolmasters gave instruction hidden behind a hedge. By 1851, Mackin's school was legal enough, but it retained a clandestine air, conducted as it was in a former stable on a side lane behind a high thorn hedge.

As Patrick grew to manhood, he could see nothing to hold him in Roodstown. He had no wish to follow his father into the tailoring trade, even less to scratch out a living farming Lord Cremorne's land.

Nothing had happened since the Great Famine to improve the lot of the Irish peasant. Affronted by mounting Catholic belligerence, many landlords deserted Ireland for much of the year, taking their pleasure in England. The Third Lord Cremorne, a lord-in-waiting to Queen Victoria, shuttled between his London town house and his Monaghan manor, with little thought for his Louth estates.

Many Louthians had their eyes on events across the Atlantic, where the Union armies were crushing the Confederacy. In February 1865, the Dundalk *Democrat*—a principal voice of Louth's Catholics—detected "a curious affinity between the state of things in Virginia and the state of things in Ireland. In Virginia, planters have too much power—an unjust and cruel power over their laborers. In Ireland the landlords have too much power—a power of life and death to their tenants. It is a usurped power, precisely like that which buys and sells the Negroes."

When Lee surrendered at Appomattox, the same editor could scarcely contain his delight. A prolonged civil war "would have prostrated Kingdoms and Empires in its march," he wrote, "but based on Democratic liberty the American Republic has wrestled with it and conquered. The fact proves that a government of the people is more powerful than that of aristocrats and kings."

Evidently Pat Kirk was equally impressed by the American example, for just three weeks after Appomattox he crossed the Irish Sea to Liverpool, where—with 758 others—he boarded the S.S. *Bosphorus*. After six weeks in steerage he arrived in Boston on June 5, 1865.

Pat's first stop was an unlikely one for an Irishman fresh off the boat: suburban Somerville, then almost exclusively Yankee. Friends from County

Louth had found him a job in a Somerville brick works. They may also have introduced him to Mary Quinn, a recent emigrant from the Louth town of Drogheda, for on July 19, Pat and Mary were married at St. John's Church. A few months later they moved to South Boston's Lower End, then teeming with newly arrived Irish, and began building a family: a son, Bernard, born in May 1866; a daughter, Mary, in July 1869.

The Kirks sank shallow roots, moving every year or so from one grim tenement to another: 220 Second Street, 92 Athens Street, 110 Bolton Street. These flats were scarcely larger than the thatched hut Pat had left behind and, in most respects, were even less pleasant and healthful. Landlords had divided warehouses and town houses into ten or twelve apartments, stacking the new-comers in attics, basements, and closets. Most houses had only one sink and a single privy serving up to a hundred people. Lacking direct access to the street, tenants dumped their garbage into the courtyards, where it lay for months in stinking heaps.

In the winter of 1871, a tuberculosis epidemic raced through the squalid warrens of the Lower End, felling men, women, and children by the hundreds. The Kirks' two-year-old daughter, Mary, took ill in February and died in May. By then her mother had contracted the disease as well, putting up a longer fight but finally succumbing on July 26. A stunned Pat Kirk buried his wife and daughter side by side in Holy Cross Cemetery. For a few months longer he struggled to keep things together, working as a day laborer, but jobs were scarce, there was nobody to look after his four-year-old son, Bernard, and the cramped flat on Bolton Street was filled with painful memories of his two Marys. Late that fall, Pat packed his few belongings and took his remaining child back to Ireland, where they moved into the Roodstown cottage with his father, Bryan the tailor. For the next fifteen years, Pat worked other men's land as a hired hand, earning ten pence a day. He never remarried, relying on his mother and in-laws to help raise Bernard.

By 1890, the Irish countryside was once more in turmoil. Falling agriculture prices and fresh evictions made tenant farming more precarious than ever. To Bernard Kirk, then twenty-three, Boston beckoned much as it had to his father a quarter century before. Pat Kirk had never forgotten the hardships endured, the terrible losses suffered, in that flinty Yankee town, but Bernard ultimately overcame Pat's misgivings and, late in April, father and son set sail aboard the S.S. *Pavonia*. Pat's premonitions proved all too sound; only four months after his return to Boston, he died of a heart attack and was buried in Holy Cross Cemetery, next to his wife and daughter.

The Irish colonized Boston by county: emigrants from Galway settled in Roxbury, those from Cork in South Boston, those from Kerry in Bay Village. Counties Louth and Meath were drawn first to the North End, replicating there the social landscape of northeastern Ireland. In 1891, Bernard Kirk lodged in a rooming house at 239 Friend Street, a narrow lane hard by the docks, where he worked as a day laborer. Among other Louthians in that house were Peter and Bridget Sharkey from Ardee and their twenty-four-year-old daughter,

Catherine. Confronting each other daily in those close quarters, Catherine and Barney fell in love and were married on February 5, 1893. Six months later, the Kirks left the North End, crossing the narrow strip of gray water to Charlestown, where they settled at 72 Chapman Street in the southern lee of Breed's Hill. Like other North Enders who made that same move toward the turn of the century, the Kirks were known as "Dearos," after their occasional bouts of nostalgia for "the Dear Old North End." But, like other newcomers, they soon transferred their allegiance to Charlestown, which had huddled on that rocky coast for two and a half centuries.

On March 29, 1630, the brig *Arbella* set sail from Southampton, England, with a company of Puritans bound for Massachusetts. Aboard ship, the company's leader, John Winthrop, delivered a sermon expressing the extraordinary intensity of their community-to-be:

"We must be knit together in this work as one man. We must uphold a familiar commerce together in all meekness, gentleness, patience, and liberality. We must delight in each other, make others' condition our own . . . We must consider that we shall be like a city upon a hill. The eyes of all people are upon us."

On June 12, the *Arbella* landed at Salem, where an advance party of the Massachusetts Bay Company had established a commercial outpost. But Salem did not please the newcomers, and soon they resumed their search for their "city upon a hill," selecting the narrow Charlestown peninsula between the Charles and Mystic rivers, where a small party from Salem had settled two years before.

The new party of one thousand made Charlestown a substantial community and the capital of the infant colony. But it was not to be Winthrop's "city upon a hill." The peninsula was too cramped and lacked adequate drinking water. The bloody flux flashed through the travelers. Then came word that the French were preparing to attack. Through the autumn, small groups left Charlestown, establishing settlements at Watertown, Roxbury, Medford, and, directly across the Charles River, on the Shawmut peninsula, soon to be renamed Boston. Winthrop himself left for Boston in October. His dream of a single consecrated city was dead. But his notion of a Bible Commonwealth lived on in the separate towns which now dotted the tidewater flats. Although Charlestown was temporarily depleted, it soon began growing again and by midcentury had taken its place as one of the principal towns of the colony.

In some respects, New England towns were modeled on the English townships from which their settlers came, the ideal village they had left behind. But unlike those ancestral communities with their sturdy walls and mossy marketplaces, Charlestown and its neighbors were artificial creations, literally hewn from the wilderness and constantly in jeopardy—if not from wild animals or Indians, then from the vagaries and passions which can so easily rend such delicate human constructs. This perpetual state of crisis accounts, in part, for the intensity of their communal life, their almost desperate insistence on mutual obligations. Perhaps the greatest fear of all was of violating the "covenant," the sacred compact which the settlers had made with God and with each other. The covenant was the stone on which the community was built, the basis of its determination to become "a fellowship of visible saints." A townsperson who broke its stern commandments endangered not only himself but all his colleagues, and risked bringing down God's wrath on the entire community.

Thus the intense pressure for conformity to a shared set of beliefs, customs, and institutions. By the very act of joining the congregation, the Puritan accepted not only one God and one religion but one polity, one law, one allegiance. The town could not tolerate diversity; it could not live with aberration. So most towns took steps to guarantee homogeneity. Sudbury barred "such whose dispositions do not suit us, whose society will be hurtful to us." Dedham banned "the contrarye minded." In 1634, Charlestown's town meeting voted that "none be permitted to sit down and dwell in the town without the consent of the town first obtained." Even after a person was received into the town, he could be expelled by a process known as "warning out."

Such rigid enforcement of uniformity was possible in communities engaged only in subsistence agriculture and fishing. But by the mid-seventeenth century, Charlestown, like Boston, was breaking out of such isolation, becoming a trading center for the region. Rampant individualism and the increasing specialization of a mercantile economy had largely eroded Winthrop's dream of a community in which private concerns would forever be subordinated to public needs.

Still, Charlestown could never quite forget the purity of that vision. The less it resembled Winthrop's model, the more seductive became the memory of that archetypal New England town, harmonious, consensual, cemented by a single faith and a devotion to the common cause. For more than three centuries to come, that notion burned like a beacon, summoning the people of Charlestown to an increasingly unrealistic ideal of community.

Through most of the eighteenth century, Charlestown shunned insubstantial myth for the solid clink of shillings in the coffer. Then, in the 1770s, it found itself transformed once again into a potent symbol, an example which would help bring down an empire.

Charlestown's conspicuous role in the Revolution stemmed less from the revolutionary fervor of its populace than from its critical location. British-occupied Boston was like a pollywog, its tail connected to the mainland at Roxbury, its head pointing across the bay at Charlestown. It was to Charlestown that Paul Revere rowed on April 18, 1775, there to take horse and carry word of the British attack to Lexington; and twenty hours later, it was back through Charlestown that the battered British column retreated to Boston. By June, Roxbury and Charlestown were the fronts on which General Thomas Gage's 5,000 redcoats were bound to confront the 15,000 armed colonists who had massed around Boston.

Early in June came word that the British planned to break out of that vise by driving at Roxbury, then assaulting Charlestown. Resolving to fortify Bunker Hill, the Committee for Public Safety assigned the task to three regiments commanded by Colonel William Prescott. By error, Prescott built his redoubt on the lower, more vulnerable Breed's Hill. So when the battle was joined on June 17, General William Howe's light infantry, grenadiers, and Royal Marines could turn the colonists' flanks and attack the hill's defenders from three sides. Although Prescott's farmers and minutemen fought valiantly, the British ultimately stormed the hill, sending the Americans streaming back along the peninsula.

At first, the battle was widely regarded as a British victory, but both sides came to recognize how dearly the "victors" had paid for the hill—226 killed and 828 wounded compared to 138 killed and 276 wounded for the defenders. Moreover, "Bunker Hill" demonstrated how wrong the British had been in assuming the Americans wouldn't stand and fight. "Damn the rebels," wrote one lieutenant, "that they did not flinch."

Charlestown, too, paid a heavy price—the virtual razing of the town. When the Royal Navy in the harbor and British artillery on Copp's Hill laid down incendiary fire, the meetinghouse with its slim steeple, the two ministers' houses, the principal inn, and dozens of trim, clapboard houses crumbled in the inferno. "Beneath prodigious unextinguished fires," wrote a contemporary poet, "ill-fated Charlestown welters and expires."

But not quite. Armed now with a new myth to accompany Winthrop's old vision of community, Charlestown soon adopted as its motto: "Liberty, a Trust to Be Transmitted to Posterity."

Far from expiring, Charlestown grew faster than ever: in 1810, with nearly 5,000 residents, it was Massachusetts' third-largest town. Once more it benefited from its strategic location. Enfolded by two navigable rivers and Boston Bay, with the Lowell Railroad and the Newburyport Turnpike funneling goods in from north and west, Charlestown became a "vestibule" through which New England's produce was shunted into Boston's spacious mansion. The Charles River Bridge poured goods and vehicles into the capital. In 1800, the infant United States Navy had opened a shipyard in the bustling Charlestown harbor, which produced virtually all the Navy's rope on its giant ropewalk and where many a fighting vessel was shaped from New England oak and yellow pine. Clustering around the shipyard were wharves and warehouses, tanneries and brickyards, banks and insurance companies.

The Navy Yard and ancillary industries drew laborers from rural Massachusetts as well as Irish immigrants who, by the 1820s, were trickling into Boston. Before long, Charlestown housed a thousand Catholics—most of them Irish—who found it difficult to attend Mass miles away at the Boston Cathedral. Bishop Benedict Fenwick resolved to build Charlestown a separate church. When the cornerstone was laid in October 1828, overwhelmingly Protestant Charlestown witnessed the novel spectacle of a Catholic procession winding through its narrow streets led by a bishop in full regalia. For a town once indistinguishable from its church, the opening of St. Mary's Church, and later of a Catholic cemetery on Bunker Hill, must indeed have been disturbing. Soon religious tensions erupted into violence. After townsmen insulted a group of Irishmen coming home from a dance at Roger McGowan's restaurant, fighting broke out in which one Protestant was killed. The next night a gang of Protestants destroyed McGowan's house.

Another symbol of Catholic encroachment in Charlestown was the Ursuline Convent, established in 1826. From the start, the convent's presence had inflamed the Puritan imagination with wild images of torture and immoral practices. As stories spread, placards went up in town exhorting the people of Charlestown: "To arms!! Ye brave and free, the Avenging Sword Unshield!" On August 12, 1834, a mob of the "brave and free"—mostly bricklayers, apprentices, and sailors—laid siege to the convent and, after nuns and students had fled, burned it to the ground.

The Ursuline Convent affair grew only in part out of Catholic-Protestant contention. Most of the convent's forty-four students weren't Catholics at all, but Unitarians, daughters of Boston's aristocracy. To working-class Congregationalists, it seemed as if upper-class Unitarians and "foreign" Catholics had joined hands to undermine what they still regarded as their civil religion. Instinctively, the indigenous mob lashed out at this "unholy alliance."

Soon the Irish emerged as the principal threat to Charlestown's homogeneity. The great wave of Irish immigration began with the potato famine of the 1840s, during which millions of impoverished peasants were driven from the land. Between 1846 and 1856, some 130,000 Irish disembarked at the port of Boston. By the end of the Civil War, more than a third of Charlestown's residents were first- and second-generation Irish. Most of the newcomers settled along Warren Avenue, soon called "Dublin Row," where the town's old residents were horrified to find "any quantity of filth, rubbish, misery, and degradation."

By midcentury, the Protestants of the Native American Party were ready to launch an open assault on the alien influx. In 1845, the *Bunker Hill Aurora* warned that foreigners were landing at the rate of "13,400 a month!!! 466 a day!!! 19 an hour!!!" Three years later, the same paper declared: "Our country is literally being overrun with the miserable, vicious, and unclean paupers of the old country." Within days, the city fathers voted to expel illegal paupers—an echo of colonial Charlestown's "warning out" of undesirables.

But the influx continued, helping to trigger the greatest assault yet on Charlestown's autonomy—the movement for annexation to Boston. As Boston's Irish swelled toward a majority, a union with predominantly Protestant Charlestown appealed to many Bostonians as a means of containing "the foreign element." In Charlestown, the Protestant establishment sought a comforting alliance with State Street's bankers. In both cities, the Irish welcomed the merger as a way to pool their growing strength. Not surprisingly, the most virulent opposition came from Charlestown's Congregationalist artisans, who once more detected an unholy alliance among the Irish, the upper classes, and "outsiders" of all kinds. Opponents invoked nostalgia for ancient New Eng-

land towns, "the best nurseries of freedom, independence, and personal indi-
viduality." But it was too late. Irredeemably riven now by conflicting interests
and mutual fears, Charlestown was swallowed up by Boston in 1874.

Almost before the sealing wax was dry on the annexation papers, Charlestown was blaming its woes on the misconceived union. The Charlestown *Enterprise* called the town "ignored, neglected, and despised ever since she threw
herself into Boston's arms." Later, the Businessman's Association of Charlestown said, "Since Annexation we have gone backwards. We certainly have
gained nothing. When there is a big snow storm the teams and men of the
street department assigned to this district are at once hustled over to the city
proper and we can't get a cross-walk cleared."

Once a stately "vestibule" to the city, Charlestown was now a drab, utilitarian corridor through which goods and suburban commuters poured in and
out of Boston. The traffic had intensified in 1858 with the horse-drawn street
railway, which, for the first time, enabled laborers to work in Boston and live
in Charlestown. By the time electric cars started on the Charlestown run in
1892, many of the passengers were from outlying suburbs who often filled the
inbound cars, leaving no seats for Charlestown residents.

Then, in 1901, came the Elevated Railway, which not only quadrupled the
traffic passing through Charlestown but put much of the town in shadow. From
the West End, the El screeched across the bridge to Charlestown's City
Square, then up Main Street toward the suburbs. For long-range commuters,
it was a blessing, providing convenient service to downtown Boston. For
Charlestown, it was a curse, a hissing monster which brought noise, dirt, and
darkness to much of the town. Like the black dust which sifted through the
tracks onto the streets below, blight gradually blanketed the route. Within ten
years of the El's completion, a municipal commission called for its disman-
tling, but suburban commuters and downtown business interests had more
political clout than increasingly working-class Charlestown. The El became
an emblem of the exploitation which every Townie felt at the hands of the
outside world.

By the turn of the twentieth century, Charlestown's "native" population had
begun to depart in greater numbers. As the Irish moved from their enclaves
along the docks, creeping slowly up the slopes of Breed's and Bunker hills,
the Protestants either left altogether, retreated up the peninsula toward Somerville, or withdrew to the Yankee precinct at the top of Breed's Hill, which—
in the words of one historian—"like a shrinking dowager, kept lifting its skirts
to avoid the mud below."

With the natives entrenched on the heights and the Irish on the slopes, the
peripheral shorelands, expanded by landfills, were gobbled up by industry,
commerce, and institutions unwanted elsewhere. On the Mystic River side,
two sugar factories and a Schrafft's candy plant belched black smoke. On the
Charles River shore, freight cars banged all night in the Boston & Maine
railyards. Elsewhere, the great gray hulks of the State Prison, the Sailor's

Haven, and the Navy Yard walled off the water views which had once re-freshed the townsmen's eyes and spirits. The peninsula, largely surrounded by water, was only one square mile, yet soon it housed 40,000 people. All but the middle class on the hilltops were wedged into cramped three-deckers which fought for what little polluted air or dusky light filtered through the El or past the smokestacks.

But if Charlestown had become an industrial slum, at least it was an Irish slum. By the turn of the century it was Boston's most Irish neighborhood. Just as the Puritans had once sought to build an exclusive fellowship of saints on that peninsula, so now the inheritors of that myth sought refuge in an ethnic haven sealed off from the hostile world. When the most aggressive or luckiest among them joined the flight to the suburbs, those who remained were deeply ambivalent. Much as they might envy a relative or friend his tract house on a half acre in Everett or Malden, and his chance to raise his children in a world of broader opportunities, they dismissed the suburban life as a betrayal of the Irish-American heritage, treason to "the Town."

The Kirks' first years in Charlestown were difficult ones. In January 1894, Catherine bore her first child, christened Patrick Joseph Kirk after his late grandfather. But it was as if a curse attached to that name, for eight months later young Patrick died of the croup. Bernard Kirk must have been terribly poor, for he paid his son's $33.80 burial costs in installments of $2.00 and $5.00, spread over seven years. Eventually he found a job driving a horse-drawn trolley for the Boston Elevated. A stocky man with a handlebar mustache, Bernard cut an impressive figure in his blue uniform with its shiny brass buttons. Now that he was earning steady wages, the Kirks moved to Ruther-ford Avenue, where they remained for nearly three decades. Gradually he and Catherine built a family: three daughters and two sons, one of whom was named Bernard Jr., quickly dubbed Bernie by his father.

Coming of age in the 1930s, Bernie Kirk juggled multiple identities. From his father he inherited a dogged allegiance to the Irish rebel tradition, passed down from Whiteboys and Ribbonmen to Sinn Fein and the Irish Republican Army. Yet his father had been an American citizen since 1894 and Bernie proudly regarded himself as a second-generation Irish-American. His parents' sojourn in the North End gave him a Dearo's lineage, but his birth in Charles-town made him a full-fledged Townie. As a resident of Rutherford Avenue he was a "valley dweller," but his first loyalty was to the Arrows, a teenage gang which hung out in Thompson Square. Later, he graduated to a successor or-ganization called the Indians.

Embodying Townie allegiance to tribe and turf, the Indians extended a boyhood association well into mid-life. Founded in 1926 by alumni of the Arrows, Wildcats, Bearcats, and other valley gangs, it established a clubhouse in the old Owls Hall on Warren Street, holding regular dinners and card nights there. Each spring it gave a dance at Roughan's Hall, every fall a "Pow-Wow" at a Reading farm, featuring baseball, nail-driving, balloon-blowing, and a turkey dinner washed down with foaming kegs of beer. All through the twenties and thirties, Bernie Kirk was a leading Indian, serving on the Hall and Pow-Wow committees.

His father wanted to get him a job at the Boston Elevated—a position much prized among Boston's Irish—but Bernie preferred to strike off on his own. He found a job mixing ink for the George Morrill Ink Company in the South End, where he remained for twenty-five years. It was good, steady work, but the pay was meager: $17.50 a week until Franklin Roosevelt came along to push through a minimum wage bill.

In many respects Bernie was a conventional Townie, but he made a most unconventional marriage. Gertrude Wolfberg had been born to Eugene Wolfberg, a German-Jewish shoe clerk, and Mary Connors Talbot, an Irish factory worker. After a second daughter, Winifred, followed in 1912, the marriage broke up, and in 1914, Mary married William Frawley, a Medford laborer. Barely three months later she died of tuberculosis. Feeling little responsibility for his two stepdaughters, Frawley placed them with his late wife's cousins in Charlestown. The girls' "Jewish name" was an embarrassment in xenophobic Charlestown, so much so that Winifred began spelling it with two *f*'s "to show it was German," while Gertrude used her mother's first married name, Talbot. Yet none of that bothered Bernie Kirk, who'd grown up around the corner from Gertrude.

Children came quickly: two boys and four girls, the last of whom was Alice. As the family grew, it moved from rented quarters to a three-story brick house at 31 Monument Avenue. From their parlor window, the Kirks could see the Charlestown prison looming by the river. Sometimes on dark mornings, rising early for his job at the ink factory, Bernie Kirk swore he could see the bare bulb over the kitchen table dim for a few seconds. Prison officials insisted that executions didn't drain Charlestown's power supply, but old Townies maintained they could tell whenever the switch was pulled on a cop killer or rapist or even Nicola Sacco and Bartolomeo Vanzetti, who went to the electric chair there.

Short on cash, the Kirks occupied the first floor of their new house and the front of the second, renting the rear of the second and all of the third to a succession of sailors, salesclerks, and ancient pensioners. Gertrude Kirk further supplemented the family's income by stitching clothes for the Works Progress Administration, waiting tables at the Adams House restaurant, and selling china at Raymond's before she finally found steady work just over the hill at the Navy Yard Officers Club. Starting in 1958 on the lunchtime cafeteria line, she added the much-sought-after cloakroom job on Friday and Saturday nights. Warm and gregarious, Gertrude easily took home $70 in tips on Friday, $100 on Saturday. At week's end, the Kirk children gathered at the kitchen table to help count their mother's satchel of dimes and quarters. This extra income permitted the Kirks a few special pleasures. They bought a 1934 Ford, a green two-door sedan with old-fashioned running boards, in which they took

Sunday jaunts into the suburbs. In the summers they rented a cottage, first at Point Shirley, later on New Hampshire's Beaver Lake.

But there wasn't anything frivolous about Bernie Kirk. Whatever devilment he may have displayed as an Arrow or Indian had been leached from him by middle age and family responsibilities. Most nights he was content to eat his supper, then retire to his easy chair, where he read the Boston *Post* and listened to the radio for hours on end without uttering a dozen words. Only one evening a week did he venture out of the house. Every Friday night at seven sharp he put on his tweed cap and went down the street to Sully's Cafe, where he sat at the bar nursing a beer and talking with friends until eleven. Sometimes when he got home those nights his children caught flashes of puckish humor before his implacable reserve slammed down again.

More lively and fun-loving, Gertrude enjoyed playing beano or whist at St. Mary's. She and her sister Winnie had season tickets at Fenway Park, and when the Red Sox played the Cardinals in the 1946 World Series they were at every home game. Gertrude's three heroes were Franklin Roosevelt, James Michael Curley, and Ted Williams. Her children grew up in obeisance to that trinity. They were Americans at last.

Alice Kirk—later Alice McGoff—was a spirited tomboy, matching her male playmates stride for stride. For several years, she and her girlfriends hung out with a gang called the Crusaders down at the old colonial training field. On hot summer afternoons they cooled off by jumping from piers and bridges into the murky waters of the Charles River or the oil-slicked Little Mystic channel. In the evenings they caught a flick at the Thompson Square Theater, where two kids got a candy bar if they shared a single seat. Downtown Boston—with its movie palaces, shooting galleries, and malt shops—was barely a mile away, a short walk across the low bridge. But except to bowl at Sixteen Lanes in the North End or shop at Filene's Basement, Alice rarely went into "the city," as she called it. The Town was sufficient to her needs.

Indeed, her favorite day of the year was June 17, the anniversary of the Battle of Bunker Hill, the day on which Charlestown celebrated its own unique traditions. Throughout most of the nineteenth century, it had been a genteel ceremony, devoted to florid oratory and refined self-congratulation among Boston's Yankee elite. But as the Irish advanced ever further up the slopes of Breed's and Bunker hills, they had gradually appropriated not only the soaring battle monument on the heights but the civic spectacle dedicated in its name. By the time Alice was born, Bunker Hill Day had become a great Irish-American jamboree, a ritualized expression of the Town's solidarity, an exuberant statement of Charlestown's independence from the rest of the world.

The night before the big day, the Kirks would join thousands of other Townies at the American Legion and Knights of Columbus halls for prolonged bouts of drink, food, and patriotic rhetoric. Early the next morning, Bernie Kirk would throw open the bay window on the second floor and fix a giant flag to the standard there. Meanwhile, Gertrude cooked up a great batch of hot dogs, which she kept in a pot on the back of the stove, next to a dish of baked beans. The kitchen table was covered with platters of cold cuts, potato salad, and pickles. Beer and soft drinks rattled in ice. All day long, friends and neighbors stopped in to help the family celebrate.

Late in the morning, Alice and the other young Kirks would climb the hill to see the doll carriage procession and collect their free ice cream, lollipops, and miniature American flags. By 2:00 p.m., they were back on their stoop to watch the parade: 5,000 marchers, dozens of floats, military units, state and local politicians, high school bands, drill teams, color guards, Boy Scouts, bagpipers, the Irish American Association, the Knights of Columbus, the Charlestown High School cheerleaders, the Charlestown Militia Company. Along Bunker Hill Street they came, down Main Street, where the crowds stood six and eight deep on the sidewalks, up the steep slope of Monument Avenue, then around Monument Square, where American flags hung from the second-story balconies, past St. Mary's rectory, where a clutch of priests and nuns stood on the stoop, then down Winthrop Street to the emerald swatch of the training field.

From her front steps, Alice waved and shouted to friends in the line of march. Sometimes she was delegated to rush into the street and hand a bouquet of flowers to Frankie Marr, a cousin who led the Fire Department Band. Frankie would brandish the flowers over his head and bow low to the Kirks in front of their house. Alice would flush with pride. For Bunker Hill Day was her personal holiday, a day which few other Americans could share, a day on which she first understood what it meant to be a Townie.

7

Diver

"This day about four o'clock afternoon we set sail in the *Craw-ford Bridge,* bound for Boston, New England," wrote Dr. John McKechnie at Greenock, Scotland, on July 26, 1755. Forty-eight days later he and sixteen other passengers disembarked on Boston's Long Wharf.

The good doctor, in his diary, neglects to tell us why he quit his physician's post at a Paisley linen mill to confront life in the Massachusetts Bay Colony. But it seems likely that he was recruited by Silvester Gardiner, a Boston physician who had studied medicine in Edinburgh and was then encouraging emigration to the Province of Maine. For only months after he arrived in Boston, McKechnie pushed on to Maine, where he took a position with Captain John North, commander of Fort Frederick and a surveyor for Gardiner's company, the powerful Kennebec Proprietors.

In the mid-eighteenth century, Maine was largely untamed wilderness, a frontier territory hazardous to the unwary traveler but rich in opportunity for the audacious speculator. Nowhere were peril and promise held in more tantalizing equilibrium than along the mighty Kennebec, which swept 150 miles from the depths of Moosehead Lake to the rocks of Casco Bay. The Indians called it the Snake because its seething waters suggested the movement of a giant serpent beneath the surface. Kennebec winters were cruel and bleak; the Norridgewock Indians and their allies, the French, were determined to expel English settlers. But the river teemed with fish and fur; its banks bore miles of spruce, hemlock, and white pine; the sandy loam produced goodly crops of corn, rye, and flax.

The Kennebec Proprietors numbered some of colonial Massachusetts' ablest men. John Hancock was one of the company's principals, John Adams its attorney. Among the proprietors were James Bowdoin, a delegate to the Continental Congress, and James Pitts, who took part in the Boston Tea Party.

The company also included some notable Tories, among them Benjamin Hallowell, Boston's Commissioner of Customs, and Silvester Gardiner.

This diversity was the company's hallmark and ultimately the source of its downfall. John Adams once wrote in his journal: "Going to Mr. Pitts' to meet the Kennebeck Company—Bowdoin, Gardiner, Hallowell and Pitts. There I shall learn Philosophy and Politicks in Perfection from H.—high flying, high church, high state from G.—sedate, cool Moderation from B.—and warm, honest, frank Whiggism from P."

He was least drawn to Gardiner, who had "a thin Grasshopper voice . . . an affected Squeak, a meager visage, and an awkward, unnatural complaisance." Yet, for all that, it was Gardiner who made the company a powerful enterprise which disposed of vast resources, worked its will in the General Court, intrigued with royal governors, and struck marriages of convenience with military and civil authorities.

John North was a striking example of such reciprocity. Though a military man, North doubled as a company surveyor, helping to lay out many new settlements along the lower river. It would have made sense, then, for Gardiner to dispatch John McKechnie to serve an apprenticeship with North at Fort Frederick, initially as teacher to the North children. In 1757, the captain's command was enlarged to encompass neighboring Fort St. George's, and John McKechnie was appointed his lieutenant. Three years later, McKechnie asked for the hand of North's eighteen-year-old daughter, Mary. The captain wasn't pleased, in part because the suitor was a decade older than his intended bride, but ultimately he gave his consent and on New Year's Day 1760 performed the ceremony himself.

Family tensions persisted nonetheless, and soon the McKechnies left the fort, settling first at Townsend, later at Bowdoinham. The sixties were a decade of rapid development along the Kennebec, and John McKechnie played no small role in that growth, both as a surveyor for the proprietors and as a warden of their property.

In 1771, McKechnie took his family further up the river, settling in Winslow, a town founded that very year by six Massachusetts men. He and his family took up residence in the "Fort House," a gabled building within Fort Halifax. The fort was no longer a military installation. With four hundred surrounding acres it had been sold a year before to Silvester Gardiner. McKechnie had apparently been dispatched to Winslow by Gardiner himself, for soon he was functioning as the company's agent there, selling real estate, making grants to encourage fresh immigration, supervising the company's tax payments, above all surveying and planning new settlements.

Shrewdly he took advantage of his travels to search out the choicest lots in town. In the winter of 1774, he chose one at the intersection of the Kennebec and Messalonskee Stream. There, beside his log cabin, he built a dam and mills for grinding grain and sawing lumber, enterprises which soon made him a prosperous man. By 1775, only two of the sixty taxpayers in town had more land than McKechnie, only one a larger personal estate. Quickly he assumed a leading role in town affairs. As early as 1772 he was moderator of the town meeting. Two years later he was elected one of Winslow's three selectmen.

Like most Maine communities, Winslow was slow to apprehend the crisis brewing between the British Crown and its American subjects, but once the first shots were exchanged at Lexington, the Kennebec Valley was drawn into the hostilities. General Washington saw the Kennebec as a critical thoroughfare to British Quebec. Fearing that troops there might intervene in battles to the south, he decided to strike first. To command the expedition, he chose Colonel Benedict Arnold. On September 19, 1775, Arnold and 1,100 volunteers set sail from Newburyport. Three days later they landed at Gardiner, Maine, where they transferred to flat-bottomed "batteaux" for the journey up the Kennebec. The voyage was an arduous one. At every waterfall they had to empty the boats and carry them, with all their equipment, to clear water. Cold, wet, and exhausted, ravaged by fever, the troops limped into Fort Halifax on September 27.

Arnold had his own surgeon, but the ills besetting his forces were more than one physician could attend and during the expedition's brief stay in the Winslow area, John McKechnie lent a hand. His diary records some of his cases: "James Conner, with part of his toe cut off with an ax. Thos. Parks, Joshua Warren, Charles Bartlett, dysentery and fever. Joseph Carter, camp fever. Arnold, with a cut in his leg."

But these fleeting ministrations didn't establish McKechnie's revolutionary credentials. Like many colonists born in Scotland, he knew all too well the reach of English power, which left him little faith that the patriotic cause could prevail. Moreover, as an educated man of wealth and social standing, he had many dealings with prominent Tories, notably his sponsor, Silvester Gardiner. For years McKechnie had served as an intermediary between Gardiner and the town, and so long as it served their interest, the townsmen had been pleased to use McKechnie's influence with the proprietors; but now these connections no longer stood him in good stead. As patriotic fervor swept the Kennebec, bands of settlers roamed the countryside confronting known Tories and their suspected allies, demanding that they swear allegiance to the cause and, if they refused, tarring and feathering them or making them ride the rail. Gardiner was one of the mob's prime targets. In October 1774, some 150 armed men surrounded his house. Told he had already fled to Boston, they "rushed in, rifled the house, broke open his desk and perused his papers."

As Gardiner prudently remained behind British lines, agitation in the valley focused on his associates, among them John "Mahogany" Jones, who, like McKechnie, was a surveyor for the proprietors. Also known as "Black Jones," he was a particularly virulent Tory. In late 1774, the mob demanded that he sign a "solemn league and covenant" pledging to end all commerce with Britain. "Upon which," according to an eyewitness, "he stripped open his bosom and told them they might stab him to his heart, but nothing should induce him to sign that accursed instrument. They seized him with violence and threw him headlong into the river and then dragged him about till he was torn to pieces."

All this could scarcely have reassured John McKechnie, who had worked closely with Jones in laying out the territory.

By early 1777, Winslow was ready to proceed against suspected Tories in its midst. In July, acting on instructions from the General Court of Massachusetts, its Committee of Correspondence, Inspection, and Safety paid a call on John McKechnie at his cabin. The committee confronted the doctor with accusations they had received about his relationship with known Tories, and with remarks suggesting a lack of enthusiasm for the patriotic cause. McKechnie heard them out. Then, with characteristic hauteur, he told them, "Gentlemen, if at any time I have said anything you do not understand, I am sorry for it." With that, he ushered them out the door. No formal charges were ever preferred against him.

Several factors may have helped McKechnie slip the committee's net. First, while Gardiner belonged to the reviled Church of England, McKechnie shared his neighbors' Congregational faith. Second, he had made himself a valuable, if not indispensable, participant in Winslow's affairs. Whether as moderator or selectman, surveyor or agent, physician or miller, he had a thumb in every pot in town. A community of only sixty voters could ill afford to lose a man of his energy. Had he been a defiant loyalist of Gardiner's stripe, none of this would have saved him; but if he wasn't a zealous Whig, he was hardly a raging Tory either. The colonists would have called him a "trimmer," a shrewd opportunist, an entrepeneur alert to the main chance, a confirmed hedger of bets.

For two years, McKechnie remained under a cloud: for the first time since his arrival in Winslow he held no town office. Then he was rehabilitated—from 1779 to 1781 he served twice as moderator, three times as selectman. Those were good years for the McKechnies. The log cabin on the Messalonskee was so crowded—with thirteen children—that they built a new frame house, the first in town. The doctor read widely and studied astronomy until he died in April 1782.

He left a considerable estate—1,250 acres of land, a gristmill, a half interest in a sawmill, two horses, eighteen cattle, a library of forty-two books—the total valued at 1,074 pounds sterling. Even after it was divided among his widow and twelve surviving children, it left enough for everyone to live quite comfortably.

But John McKechnie left another, more durable, legacy. For generations to come, his descendants felt intimately connected to the stirring events of the American Revolution. If the doctor's own connection to those events was at best ambiguous, such quibbles were largely erased over time. As his leatherbound diary passed from father to son, often to be read aloud at family gatherings, what lingered were McKechnie's ministrations to Arnold's troops on the march to Quebec, his leadership of a New England village in the first brave years of the Republic. For more than two centuries—down to Joan Diver in contemporary Boston—the McKechnies would feel they were following in that noble tradition.

John McKechnie's third-oldest son, Joseph, strengthened his claim on that heritage by marrying Electa Bement, the daughter of a Revolutionary War major. In 1805, they pulled up stakes, settling thirty miles north in the little farming village of Athens. Purchasing eighteen acres on the brow of Chapman's Ridge, they and their nine children scratched out a modest living from corn, potatoes, and apples. For salt, sugar, candles, and rum, however, they depended on credit from local merchants, and soon McKechnie owed substantial sums to several storekeepers in nearby Norridgewock. By 1817 he was compelled to mortgage his farm for $250. Two years later, the firm of Selden & Fletcher sued him for $126.53 and, when McKechnie was unable to pay, the merchants took possession of his farm. The McKechnies hung on in Athens for another fifteen years, farming land which Electa had acquired from her brother; then in 1833, beset by still more debts, Joseph mortgaged his farm again and moved to Argyle Plantation on the Penobscot.

In a trip of barely fifty-five miles, they had gone from a bucolic farming community to the cutting edge of the Maine frontier. Few settlers had yet found their way to the banks of the Penobscot and those who had were a freewheeling breed disinclined to till the soil for a living. They had recourse instead to that oldest of frontier occupations, lumbering, which by its own logic bred a disrespect for the domestic virtues of more settled communities. Timothy Dwight, who visited Maine in those years, dismissed its lumbermen as a tribe of wastrels given to "prodigality, thoughtlessness of future wants, profaneness, irreligion, immoderate drinking and other ruinous habits."

Taking hyperbole into account, such was the setting in which the McKechnies now found themselves. Argyle Plantation was a heavily forested tract on the Penobscot fifteen miles north of Bangor. In 1834, Joseph McKechnie purchased a lot on the Bennoch Road, Argyle's sole "highway." To either side, the land fell away to swale and bog, covered with spruce, cedar, and white birch. It was there that Joseph and his five sons launched their lumbering operation. Each November when the swamps were frozen, they loaded a sled, hitched up a team of oxen, and set off into the wilderness. Establishing their camp in a likely stand of timber, they spent months felling trees, then hauled them to the edge of a stream. When the ice melted in April, the logs were launched into a network of streams until they reached the Penobscot, where they floated downriver to the sawmills clustered north of Bangor. From spring through fall, the McKechnie men worked the river, sorting the logs with huge pikes called "hookeroons." To a contemporary observer, watching loggers come home from a season on the Penobscot, they seemed "crisped to a blackness by the sun, baked with heat, bitten by black flies, haggard, gaunt, sore-footed." Not surprisingly, they sought relief in the grogshops of the river towns or in Bangor's notorious red-light district, the Devil's Half-Acre.

This life didn't suit everyone. One of those who wearied of the river was Joseph McKechnie's second son, Charles. A colleague once called him "too retiring for the logger's life, a born farmer if ever I saw one." In the Maine woods that wasn't a compliment. After barely a year on the Penobscot, Charles moved back to the farming belt of Central Maine, settling in the village of Ripley. There he married Elizabeth Hale, daughter of a prominent innkeeper and justice of the peace known as "Squire Hale," and bought a farm just down the road from the Squire's homestead.

If Charles McKechnie had been an indifferent logger, he wasn't much of a farmer either. By 1850 he had 113 acres, but only 25 of them cleared. His livestock holdings were typical for a farm his size: a team of oxen, a horse, two cows, and twelve sheep. But his crops of wheat, corn, oats, potatoes, hay, and butter were well below average.

Charles's five sons weren't much drawn to their father's placid life. Ripley's stubborn soil would have frustrated even the most avid agriculturists, but the young McKechnies had other reasons for shunning the farm. The aura of bracing peril and boundless opportunity which had attracted their grandfather to the territory had largely dissipated over the years. To many young people, Maine now seemed a somnolent backwater, while the nation's cities, pulsing with commerce and industry, offered a new challenge.

In 1854, Charles's second son, Hiram, struck off for Boston, where he found a job clerking in a clothing store. At his Salem Street boardinghouse he encountered another clothing clerk, named Myron Wilmot. One can imagine their conversation at the boarding table—their complaints about tyrannical bosses, their boasts about the kind of store they themselves would run. In 1856, they got their chance. Myron had raised some money and invited Hiram to come in with him—on one condition. The 1850s were an era of massive Irish emigration to Boston, the passenger lists filled with McNultys, McBrides, and McLaughlins, and Myron feared that his new partner would be mistaken for Irish. So he prevailed on him to spell his name in the Scottish manner. When the new enterprise opened that autumn at 332 Hanover Street, the sign above the door read "Wilmot and Makechnie, Gents' Furnishings." The stratagem didn't work—after three years the store declared bankruptcy— but the change of name stuck. Henceforth, every member of the family who found his way to Boston adopted the Scottish spelling.

In 1871, another brother arrived. George Makechnie took a salesman's position at Chipman Brothers, a well-known clothing store, but, like his brother before him, George dreamed of his own business. In 1883, he and Frank Ames launched Ames & Makechnie, Men's Furnishing Goods. This too was short-lived. By 1886, George was back as a salesman for Chipman Brothers, where he remained for a decade.

Soon after reaching Boston, George had married Sarah Ann Cram, the straitlaced descendant of a Revolutionary War officer. Settling in suburban Everett, they became stalwarts of the Baptist Church and the Republican Party while they raised three sons and two daughters. The oldest son, Charles, was a tennis star at Everett High, but intellectually undisciplined and apparently without ambition. He served for a time in Everett's Fire Department and managed the Standish Shoe Co. in downtown Boston. By then, his father was a salesman at a nearby clothing store, and twice a month father and son lunched at the communal tables of the Durgin Park Diningrooms, exchanging gossip of the trade over the clatter from greengroceries and meat stalls.

But all was not well between father and son. Charles had married a lively young woman named Mabel Downing, with whom he formed a dancing club for married couples. By secular standards it was innocent enough, but to devout Baptists like George and Sarah Makechnie it was outright blasphemy. Moreover, neither Charles nor his wife was a regular churchgoer. As the years went by, the older Makechnies grew increasingly concerned at their son's "immoral" behavior.

In January 1907, the young couple produced their only child, whom they named George, perhaps as a peace offering to his grandfather. That September, Charles Makechnie contracted typhoid fever, which the doctors blamed on "contaminated oysters." Six days later, at age thirty-one, he died. His parents put their own construction on his final hours. Shortly before his death, Charles had gazed up at a vaguely religious painting and muttered something unintelligible. Convinced that his mumbling constituted an act of contrition, George and Sarah proclaimed that their son had made his peace with God.

Unable to accept her in-laws' piety, Mabel became increasingly estranged from orthodox Christianity, eventually joining Charles Taze Russell's International Bible Students' Association. Russell had broken with his Presbyterian-Congregationalist faith to preach a millennialistic Christianity which eventually evolved into Jehovah's Witnesses. If the elder Makechnies had condemned their son's casual disregard for Christian dogma, they were horrified by Mabel's overt break. Soon young George Makechnie found himself a pawn in the spiritual tug-of-war between his mother and his grandparents. The elder Makechnies insisted that he attend the First Baptist Church, where he shifted uneasily through apocalyptic sermons. Meanwhile Mabel took him along to the Bible study association, where he wondered at the renegade faith of these fervent malcontents. Before long, his curiosity focused on the Irish and Italian Catholics then moving by the thousands into Everett's working-class neighborhoods. Ignoring his grandparents' admonitions, he sneaked into Mass at Immaculate Conception, where he was strangely stirred by the solemn Latin cadences.

Mabel Makechnie never remarried; somehow she supported herself and her son by stitching tennis balls and taking in lodgers. When George entered Boston University, he worked his way through as a custodian in a private mausoleum. After taking a master's degree in education, he served successively as assistant to the dean, registrar, and professor at the School of Education, ultimately becoming dean of the university's Sargent College of Allied Health Professions. Along the way, he married one of his students, Anne Schonland, a descendant of William Prescott, the colonial commander at Bunker Hill. In 1952, they moved to an eighteenth-century clapboard house a musket shot from the Lexington Battle Green, with their three children: Norman, Arthur, and Joan.

Although George Makechnie had long since left the Baptist Church, spiritual questions remained central to his life. In Lexington, he gravitated to the Hancock Congregational Church overlooking the Battle Green, but even that flexible doctrine seemed only a marginal improvement on Baptist dogma. When the black minister, Howard Thurman, became dean of Boston University's Marsh Chapel in 1953, George went to hear his colleague preach.

Almost from the beginning, he was intrigued by Thurman, who that very year had been named by *Life* magazine as one of America's twelve greatest preachers. His homilies were unlike anything George had heard before, utter departures from the rigid screeds of his youth. Thurman preached what he called "the love ethic," a mystic vision of an intimate relationship with God. His faith transcended all boundaries, it was "neither male nor female, Black nor White, Protestant nor Catholic." Soon George Makechnie resolved to attend Marsh Chapel and gradually his family followed suit. After the Sunday service, blacks and whites mingled informally at a coffee hour, where George and Howard Thurman—already professional colleagues—discovered that they were kindred spirits. The two couples began exchanging visits. Finding that each had been married the same day—June 12—they held an annual anniversary dinner. Before long, their families developed a profound rapport.

Thurman rarely preached on racial issues or urged his congregation to overt action. His lesson was more oblique—the unity of all mankind, indeed of the entire natural world. But those who listened closely detected a fierce commitment to equality.

George Makechnie was a willing listener. Just as he had broken with his Baptist heritage, so he had cut the moorings to his grandparents' hide-bound Republicanism. To him, the Makechnies' revolutionary heritage implied a commitment to New Deal–Fair Deal liberalism and racial equality. In 1945, when he became dean of Sargent College, he had quietly passed the word that Negro students would no longer live in the Cambridge ghetto, but would share college dormitories with whites. Southern alumnae and conservative faculty raised the roof, but the dean held firm.

George's second son, Arthur, felt the heavy weight of the past on his shoulders. Growing up a ten-minute walk from Lexington's Battle Green, Arthur had been steeped in his community's sacrifice for freedom. In 1965, seeking a subject for his master's thesis in history at the University of Wisconsin, he was browsing through Vernon Parrington's *Main Currents in American Thought* when he was struck by Parrington's description of Theodore Parker, the abolitionist minister from Lexington. Arthur knew that Parker was the grandson of the very Captain John Parker who had commanded the minutemen on the Battle Green. But not until that fall did he realize how Parker's abolitionist fervor grew from his sense of being rooted in Lexington's revolutionary tradition: "When a small boy my mother lifted me up, one Sunday, and held me while I read the first monumental lines I ever saw: SACRED TO LIBERTY AND THE RIGHTS OF MANKIND. Gentlemen, the Spirit of Liberty, the Love of Justice, was early fanned into flame in my boyish heart. That monument covers the bones of my own kinfolk; it was their blood which reddened the long green grass at Lexington. It is my own name which stands chiseled on that stone; the tall Captain who marshaled his fellow farmers and mechanics into stern array was my father's father."

Arthur had found his subject. All through the late sixties—through the agony of Newark and Detroit, the Kerner Report, and Martin Luther King's assassination—Arthur Makechnie labored on "The Anti-Slavery Viewpoint of Theodore Parker."

Not only was New England the wellspring of the Puritan "instinct for democracy," the birthing ground of the American Revolution, it was also for Parker the home of the "free idea." Parker regarded the Revolution as "a continuing undertaking, a New England crusade to implant the spirit of liberty throughout the continent." But the "free idea" wasn't merely an American doctrine; it was part of what Parker called "the higher law," rooted in the medieval notion of "natural law." When a man-made law like the Fugitive Slave Act came into conflict with "the higher law," Parker had no doubt what the moral man must do. "You cannot trust a people who will keep the law because it is law," he wrote, "nor need we distrust a people that will only keep a law when it is just."

Arthur's thesis breathed a sympathy for Parker's stands on human rights, though it frankly confronted his prejudices, notably his contempt for the Irish immigrant. Parker recommended that the Irish newcomers be quarantined for thirty-one years: "Certainly it would take all this time to clean a paddy on the outside. . . . To clean him inwardly would be like picking all the sands of the Sahara." Nor did Arthur disguise the central contradiction in Parker's world view: his zeal for the black man's abstract rights, his intense distaste for the Negro as a particular person. Despite these glaring paradoxes, or perhaps because of them, the abolitionists intrigued Arthur. When the time came for him to select a Ph.D. topic, he focused on yet another of them—Gerrit Smith, the wealthy New York farmer who helped arm John Brown for his raid on Harper's Ferry.

Surprisingly, for a man so obsessed, Arthur took no part in the civil rights movement of the sixties, attending to his studies while other Northern whites went South to participate in Freedom Rides and sit-ins. But he came to admire the demonstrators' courage, for Arthur had a tenacious will and a fierce determination on matters of principle.

This caused him great pain after his marriage to Heather Kellenbeck, a member of the Mormon Church, which at that time did not permit Negroes to enter the priesthood or participate in the sacraments. Nevertheless, so deeply did Arthur believe in the unity of the family that he determined to become a Mormon. In August 1971, he was baptized and for nearly three years he remained in the Church, even holding a series of minor offices. But he couldn't live with himself, particularly when he remembered that the abolitionists had called for people to "come out" of proslavery churches. In the summer of 1973, Arthur became so preoccupied with the matter that he couldn't study or sleep. Finally, that autumn, he told the bishop that he no longer considered himself a Mormon.

Few of the Makechnies could match Arthur's commitment. Through her high school years, his younger sister Joan was absorbed by cheerleading, glee club, field hockey, and student council. Even the Makechnies' switch from the suburban tranquility of Hancock Congregational to the more urgent ministry of Marsh Chapel didn't stir her to action. To Joan, Howard Thurman was "Uncle Howard," more a spiritual mentor and revered family friend than a prophet of social justice. But she wasn't immune to the mythology of her famous village. In school she studied the battles of Concord and Lexington in excruciating detail. Her parents took her to the Buckman Tavern, where the minutemen had convened; to the Battle Green, and the "rude bridge." Very early on she was conscious of being "special," of being rooted in this terribly important place, this spot where it all began.

Each April 19, Lexington commemorated "the shot heard round the world" with a day of solemn festivities. Every year since she was nine Joan had participated in those Patriots Day ceremonies, rededicating herself to the "self-evident truths" for which men had shed blood in that place. In the dim moments before dawn, the old town bell would sound the alarm. Soon church bells joined the clangor. But Joan had been up for hours, washing her hair, pulling on her Girl Scout uniform, then running to join her troop at the Monroe School. Promptly at 7:00 a.m., the Sunrise Parade stepped off along Massachusetts Avenue, led by the "Spirit of '76"—a hardware store clerk and an eighth-grader rapping on drums, an insurance man piping a wooden flute. Behind them came row upon row of Boy Scouts, Girl Scouts, and Brownies marching to the beat of high school bands.

Later in the morning, the modern company of Lexington minutemen massed before the statue of John Parker, dressed in leather jerkin and breeches, grasping his old musket and gazing sternly down the road toward Boston. At 1:00 p.m., two horsemen clattered up that road, impersonating Paul Revere and William Dawes, the colonists who had carried word of the British attack. Another horseman, playing Dr. Samuel Prescott, galloped off to Concord. Joan Makechnie liked that moment best of all, for her parents had told her she was related to Prescott—as well as to William Prescott, the colonial commander at Bunker Hill.

By then the town was filled with spectators, come to watch the afternoon parade with its military outfits from nearby bases, its "minutemen" in breeches and tricorns who streamed in from Acton, Chelmsford, and Tewksbury. Later that afternoon, as orators thundered from the bandstand, volunteers handed out souvenir "birth certificates." Joan invariably filled in her name so it read: "This is to certify that a certificate of birth was recorded for all Americans in the name of Liberty and Justice for all at the Birthplace of American Liberty, Lexington, Mass., on the 19th of April 1775. I, Joan Makechnie, American, do reaffirm my faith in the glorious tradition born that day."

By her senior year in high school, Joan had another reason for feeling special. When Massachusetts' own John Kennedy was elected President that autumn, she was elated. He was so handsome, so intelligent, so idealistic! He was one of their own, a spokesman for spare, principled New England and for an energetic new generation which was ready to take over from those drab, Eisenhower Republicans.

George Makechnie was also an enthusiastic Kennedy supporter, in part because he endorsed the Senator's brand of liberal politics, in part because he had known him slightly through the years. When Boston University awarded Kennedy an honorary degree in 1955, George had been chosen to escort the Senator to the stage; after he became President, Kennedy sent him an auto graphed picture, which hung on George's wall. Moreover, the college's receptionist was Rose Kennedy's sister-in-law, "Bunny" Fitzgerald, who kept the Makechnies well briefed on the Kennedys' doings. Through Bunny, George received two precious tickets to the inauguration. Anne Makechnie was ill, so George took Joan instead. With hotel rooms impossible to come by, George called a former student, who found them rooms in the dormitories at Howard University. So far as Joan could tell, she and her father were the only whites on campus. The girls in her dorm seemed bemused by her presence and a couple of them made sly references to "Mrs. White." Other than that, they treated her with elaborate courtesy.

For three days Joan and her father made the endless round of festivities. The night before the inauguration, they were dancing at the Shoreham when Kennedy stopped by to acknowledge the revelers' cheers and Joan caught a glimpse of her hero bathed in a spotlight. The next morning, through streets white with new-fallen snow, they found their way to the Capitol Plaza and stood in the sunlight as Robert Frost summoned "the glory of a new Augustan age," and the young President intoned those stirring phrases which would stay with Joan for years to come: "The torch has been passed to a new generation of Americans—born in this century, tempered by war, disciplined by a hard and bitter peace, proud of our ancient heritage."

Back in Lexington, she couldn't get the image of that bright winter morning out of her mind. But something else lingered too: those days at Howard when she'd been the only white girl in a black dormitory. "Now I realize what it must be like to be a minority," she told her father. "Now I see how a Negro must feel."

The next fall, Joan went on to Wheaton College, where she soon displayed the public spirit that John Kennedy was urging on her generation. Vice-president of her class, editor of the yearbook, she majored in political science and dreamed of government service. But what pleased her father most was Joan's defense of her roommate's franchise. Candy Yaghjian was a white girl from South Carolina, which had no provision for absentee ballots. When Joan organized a campaign to send Candy home on election day, George Makechnie sent his daughter a poem by the abolitionist James Russell Lowell:

When a deed is done for Freedom, through the broad earth's aching breast
Runs a thrill of joy prophetic, trembling on from east to west
And the slave where'er he cowers, feels the soul within him climb
To the awful verge of manhood, as the enemy sublime
Of a century burst full-blossomed on the thorny stem of Time.

Joan basked in her father's approval, but by then there was another man in her life. Neighbors and classmates, she and Colin had known each other all through high school, but only after Joan went to Wheaton and Colin to Amherst had they become romantically attached. The relationship bloomed in the summer after their freshman year and by the following fall Joan was spending every other weekend at Amherst.

Most people who knew the Divers assumed they were Yankees, associating the name with Dick Diver in Scott Fitzgerald's *Tender Is the Night*. In fact, it was a corruption of Dwyer, Dyer, and Dever, for the Divers were originally Irish Protestants. Colin's grandfather, Ben Diver, was born at Killybegs in County Donegal, but as a young man he emigrated to London, where he enthusiastically adopted the English way of life. In succeeding years, Ben consistently took the English side in the bloody rebellions tormenting his native land.

He found a job at Ward's, a tobacconist's shop in the Burlington Arcade, which catered to wealthy Londoners who could afford to have their tobacco mixed to order. The orders invariably arrived on stationery with the family crest, which Ben brought home for his son, Ben Jr., to paste in a scrapbook. Ben's wife, Sarah, was cook to General Sir Redvers Henry Buller, who, after violating military etiquette, had been forced to surrender his command and retire permanently to his country home, Downes, in Devonshire. Sarah shuttled between Downes and Sir Redvers' town house in London's Russell Square, often taking her young son with her. The general and his wife were entertainers in the grand style, and Ben Jr. grew up in a "real upstairs-downstairs world." Ben was fascinated by the electrical box on the wall which flashed the floor on which service was required. Every afternoon at four his mother would trundle upstairs with tea and scones, while Ben tagged happily at her heels.

When he was fourteen, Ben was apprenticed to the antiques department at Liberty's in Regent Street, where he was set to work polishing the suits of armor with Rangoon Oil and powdered pumice. When war broke out in August 1914, he signed on with Queen Victoria's Rifles and fought for two years on the Western Front until he was temporarily paralyzed by an exploding shell. Back home, he had difficulty finding work and emigrated to Canada, where he became a society photographer. Still he couldn't stay put. In 1924, he emigrated again, this time to Massachusetts, where he took a room in the South

End, Boston's shabby rooming-house district. Around the corner lived Ethleen Heuser, a young woman of German-Swedish ancestry who was a law student at Northeastern University. Eight years later—when Ben was forty-two and Ethleen thirty-two—they were married, and Ben got a job in the photo labs at MIT, where he worked for the rest of his life. The Divers found a tiny Cape Cod cottage in Lexington, where their only child, Colin, was born in 1943.

A precocious boy, Colin sailed through Lexington's public schools at the top of his class. But by his third year in high school he had begun to slack off a bit, regarding his academic superiority as a social liability. At that point his parents sent him for a year to Deerfield, a private school in western Massachusetts that would guarantee he was well prepared for an Ivy League college. But they were after something else too: a touch of social panache. To Ben Diver, schools like Deerfield and Choate were the closest America came to the English public school, an experience he had been denied by his family's modest circumstances but which he was determined that Colin should have.

The neighborhood in which the Divers lived throughout Colin's youth was still largely rural, and Ben Diver put in countless hours creating an English country garden in their backyard. And in the basement, where their neighbors installed pine-paneled recreation rooms, Ben built an odd medieval chamber, adorned with gargoyles and murals of feudal knights in armor.

For many who lived in them, suburbs like Lexington were refuges from urban calamity, havens from the dirt, noise, crime, and disorder which seemed to lurk around every city corner. They were sanctuaries as well from the dark-skinned races, those unsettling newcomers who had begun to take over the rotting cores of American metropolises. The young veterans of Anzio and Guadalcanal, fleeing to the countryside, were exchanging the ethnic hodge-podge of their parents' world for a more homogeneous environment in which the white middle class could taste the pleasures hitherto reserved for the Yankee elite.

Lexington had long been overwhelmingly white. Civil rights activists liked to recall that one of John Parker's ragged band of minutemen on that fateful day in 1775 was Prince Estabrook, a slave belonging to Benjamin Estabrook. After the Revolution, Prince was rewarded with his freedom, becoming a progenitor of the town's small free black community, which persisted well into the twentieth century. Yet by 1960, there were only thirteen black families among Lexington's 32,000 inhabitants.

That very year—to help send Joan through college—Anne Makechnie joined a real estate firm in adjacent Bedford. Before long she discovered why blacks found it nearly impossible to rent or buy a house in most of Boston's suburbs. Real estate agents feared a community boycott if they dared show a house to a black family. The agents were particularly concerned about the tests being conducted by "fair housing" groups. First, a black would try to buy a suburban house. When he was rejected, a white would immediately seek to buy the same house. If the white succeeded, that was prima facie evidence of discrimination, and the agent might lose his license. Anne's employer gave her strict instructions that if she saw a black enter the office she should make a dash for the back door. "If they can't find you," he said, "they can't test you."

She never had to make that dash because no blacks showed up in Bedford, but the firm's policy made her uncomfortable and she was receptive when Leonard Colwell, a Lexington real estate man, asked her to join his new agency. Colwell agreed with Anne that they should sell or rent to anyone who had the money. A year later, Colwell was the only one of Lexington's twenty-five real estate agents to sign a "good neighbor pledge," sponsored by a newly formed Lexington Fair Housing Committee ("I will accept families and individuals into my neighborhood without discrimination because of religion, color, or national origin"). Colwell signed the pledge with some trepidation; his livelihood depended on listings and he feared retaliation.

But the reprisals never developed. The Colwell agency sold or rented a couple of houses every year to blacks, often referred by the Fair Housing Committee. One of the sales, negotiated by Anne Makechnie herself, was to Howard Thurman's daughter and her white husband. By 1963, there were thirty-six black families in Lexington.

Late that summer, another black family came to town looking for a house. James Parker, a forty-one-year-old foreign service officer, had served in Liberia, Nigeria, and Spain before taking a year's leave for work at Boston University's African Studies Program. Now he and his wife, Odessa, were focusing their housing search on the western suburbs so that their three children could attend one of the area's outstanding schools. But the hunt wasn't going well. They would follow up ads only to be told that a property was already rented or that the landlord didn't take children.

When they answered an ad for a cottage at 11 Saddle Club Road, the owner, Mark Moore, Jr., agreed to show it to them on the evening of August 27, but Moore was clearly taken aback when he saw them. He was so unenthusiastic that Parker finally asked, "Do you have any objection to renting your house to Negroes?"

"Oh, no, no," Moore said.

"Well, we'd be interested."

"I should tell you, there are some people from MIT who have first refusal."

"Okay, but if they don't take it, we'd like it."

Moore said he'd let them know. But the Parkers had gone through all this before. Disheartened, they boarded a plane for Washington.

That night, a friend reported the incident to Barbara Petschek of the Fair Housing Committee, now a subcommittee of the Lexington Civil Rights Committee. Barbara and her husband had been active in the fair housing movement, and the Moore situation struck them as a perfect test case. Barbara began calling other subcommittee members, but none of them was home. Only then did they remember what was happening that evening. Thousands of civil rights activists were descending on the nation's capital for the next day's March on Washington, scheduled to culminate with a mammoth civil rights rally in front of the Lincoln Memorial. Just as Barbara Petschek began her calls, the Lexington contingent was assembling at St. Brigid's Church, so her husband sped to the church, where he found dozens of committee members milling around the parking lot. Explaining the Moore case, he asked permission to launch a test immediately, but with their minds already focused on the next day's events, the travelers could work up little enthusiasm for Harry's plan. "Don't do anything yet," said Charles Weiser, one of the committee's leaders. "Wait until I get back."

But the Petscheks were impatient. Scanning a list of committee members for a lawyer, Barbara found the name of Julian Soshnick, an assistant state attorney general. When she called him, Soshnick not only agreed that a test should take place immediately, he insisted that he be part of it. At 4:45 p.m. the next day—as the vast throng at the Lincoln Memorial was listening to Mahalia Jackson sing "I Been 'Buked and I Been Scorned"—a vice-president of Boston University called Mark Moore on Parker's behalf and was told the house had been rented to the people from MIT. Fifteen minutes later, Barbara Petschek called Moore, identifying herself as a Mrs. Julian Gardner, and asked if the house was still available. Moore said it was and agreed to show it to her at 7:30.

At the appointed hour, "Mrs. Gardner" and her husband—Julian Soshnick—arrived at 11 Saddle Club Road. After viewing the cottage, they asked when they could move in. "September 1," Moore said. Whipping out his credentials, Soshnick questioned Moore about his refusal to rent to the Parkers. Moore said he had "nothing against them," but he had $400,000 invested in a prospective subdivision on the property and if he rented to a Negro he might lose it.

The next day, Soshnick filed a complaint with the Massachusetts Commission Against Discrimination, a state body empowered to resolve the situation through conciliation or to bring suit in court. Meanwhile, the Boston Chapter of the Congress of Racial Equality (CORE) announced that it would stage a demonstration Saturday on the Battle Green to protest housing discrimination in Lexington.

When Lexington's delegation to the March on Washington returned late Thursday, still talking of Martin Lurther King's "I Have a Dream" speech, they were astonished to discover what had happened in their absence. On Friday, the executive committee of the Lexington Civil Rights Committee angrily confronted the Petscheks and Soshnick, accusing them of "rabble-rousing." Mark Moore, they said, was one of the town's most prominent citizens, a pillar of the Baptist Church; this wasn't the way to deal with a man like that. Moreover, Saturday was the start of the Labor Day weekend, the town would be filled with tourists come to view the historic sites, and the demonstration could only damage the town's reputation. The committee urged CORE to cancel the demonstration.

CORE refused. At 11:00 a.m. on Saturday, some thirty demonstrators—most of them from Boston CORE and the NAACP, but a few, like the Petscheks, from the Lexington Civil Rights Committee—set up a picket line on the Battle Green. For two hours they paraded around the green carrying signs that read: "Birthplace of American Liberty???" and "Freedom: Let It Begin Here." The demonstrators didn't fail to note that Jim Parker bore the most renowned name in Lexington history. As they passed the statue of Captain John Parker, one protester brandished a sign which read, "If John Parker could live here, why can't Jim Parker?"

On the sidewalk across the street, townspeople gaped in astonishment at the first political demonstration they had ever witnessed on that hallowed ground. Among the onlookers was Colin Diver, then about to enter his junior year at Amherst. He found the demonstration strange. He had followed the high drama unfolding in the South, where civil rights activists were confronting local authorities armed with whips, cattle prods, and fire hoses. Now here in his own New England village, on the gentle green where he had played as a boy, these demonstrators were suggesting that Massachusetts wasn't so different from Georgia or Alabama. Somehow the march seemed out of place. A demonstrator handed Colin a leaflet headlined: "There *is* discrimination in the North! It exists in Lexington too!" He stuffed it in his pocket and went downtown.

Among leaders of Lexington's Civil Rights Committee, the reaction was more intense. In statements to the press, they angrily denounced CORE for exploiting their historic battlefield to score cheap points. Dr. Warren Guild, the committee chairman, said that his group had placed eighteen Negro families in Lexington. "Our work has been quiet, dignified, unsensational, and, most important, effective. I sincerely hope our future usefulness in combating discrimination will not be impaired by unfavorable public reaction to today's picketing." Father Thomas E. MacLeod, Jr.—who seven months later was to be arrested during a sit-in at a North Carolina restaurant—said, "I am in complete sympathy with sit-ins in the South where they demonstrate against the laws which are both immoral and unconstitutional, but I deplore the action of CORE in this instance."

CORE was undeterred. "We go wherever there is discrimination," a spokesman said. The following Wednesday, they were back on the green for two more hours of picketing.

Meanwhile, in Washington, Jim Parker was equally adamant. He told the State Department that he would abandon his year in Boston unless the government found him appropriate housing. He flatly refused to live in Roxbury, where, he said, the schools were segregated and second-class. The Department was sympathetic. It was preparing a stiff letter of protest from Secretary of State Dean Rusk to Massachusetts' governor, Endicott Peabody, when word came that Mark Moore had capitulated. On September 7, just in time for the start of school, the Parkers moved into their pine-shaded cottage.

To Joan Makechnie and Colin Diver, now back at college, the bitter squabble in their hometown was only a passing distraction. The great national struggle over racial segregation was centered in places like Selma and Little Rock. Even the first murmurings of discontent in Boston's black community didn't convince Colin and Joan that the race issue had much relevance in their own backyard.

8
Twymon

In my school, I see dirty boards and I see papers on the floor," wrote a fourth-grader at the Christopher Gibson School in the spring of 1965. "I see an old broken window with a sign on it saying, Do not unlock this window are browken. And I see cracks in the walls and I see old books with ink poured all over them and I see old painting hanging on the walls. I see old alfurbet letter hanging on one nail on the wall. I see a dirty fire exit I see a old closet with supplys for the class. I see pigons flying all over the school. I see old freght trains throgh the fence of the school yard. I see pictures of contryies hanging on the wall and I see desks with wrighting all over the top of the desks and insited of the desk."

The Gibson was a crumbling, seventy-two-year-old brick schoolhouse on Ronald Street in the North Dorchester section of Boston. It was only three blocks from Fenelon Street, where the Twymons lived, so five of Mrs. Twymon's six children went to the Gibson that year: Richard and George in the fifth grade, Frederick in the first grade, Wayne and Cassandra in kindergarten.

They brought home stories which alarmed Rachel Twymon: tales of children being beaten with the "rattan," a thin bamboo whip still used then in the Boston schools to discipline recalcitrant children; of overcrowding so severe that classes met in the damp basement, which stank of urine and coal dust, or in corners of the auditorium, where glee club rehearsals drowned out most of what their teachers were saying; of shattered windows, broken desks, three-legged chairs; of chronic shortages of pencils, chalk, and erasers; of outdated textbooks, often with covers ripped off, pages missing or obliterated by ink stains; of racial slurs directed by indifferent white teachers at the black pupils who made up 60 percent of the school; and even reports of one teacher whose classroom was segregated, whites seated in front and blacks in the rear.

But when twenty black parents and a few concerned teachers called a meeting at St. Mark's Church that April to discuss conditions at the Gibson, Rachel

Twymon wasn't sure she would go. It had been barely a year since she and Magnolia Williams had heatedly debated racial discrimination in Boston, and Rachel was still loath to admit that "Southern" practices and attitudes had invaded her city. She did not see life in racial terms; temperamentally, she wasn't much of a protester; and the growing activity by the Boston branch of the NAACP made her nervous. Yet the tales her children brought home from school profoundly disturbed her. So she went along to St. Mark's that night, and gradually, almost against her will, Rachel was drawn into the mounting protest. In May, she joined a small delegation which called on Dorothea Callahan, the Gibson's principal. Miss Callahan smiled a great deal and shook hands with each of them. She conceded that the school was in disrepair and said she was trying to get funds from the school department for some badly needed improvements. But when the delegation mentioned the racial slurs, Miss Callahan grew aloof, saying that she didn't believe "any of that." Rachel left the school that afternoon feeling that changes would be slow in coming.

Then, on June 10, she learned that one of the white teachers who had been present at St. Mark's—indeed, the teacher most sympathetic with the parents' concerns—had been abruptly fired by Miss Callahan. His name was Jonathan Kozol, and he stood out among the other teachers at the Gibson, most of them middle-aged Irish women, veterans of some years in the system, strict disciplinarians who seemed resentful at spending their days teaching ill-prepared black children. Kozol was different. Only twenty-eight, a *summa cum laude* graduate of Harvard College, a Rhodes Scholar and published novelist, he was in his first year of teaching, brimming with enthusiasm for the job and concern for his students. At St. Mark's, he had spoken passionately about how black children were being "short-changed" by the Boston school system, and Rachel Twymon had liked him immediately.

Kozol had taught a fourth-grade class just down the hallway from Richard and George's fifth-grade classroom. Indeed, they still remember the commotion that afternoon when the school learned what had happened. The popular young teacher, they were told, had been fired for reading to his class a poem not included in the official "course of study." The poem was unlike most of the reading assigned at the Gibson—stories about characters like Miss Molly, Fluffy Tail, and Miss Valentine of Maple Grove School. It was a poem about the lives of black people in a big city like Boston and some of the black children in Kozol's class liked it so much they took it home and memorized it. Once Kozol's firing became known, mimeographed copies of the poem became prized items at the school, and even Richard and George could recite portions of Langston Hughes's "Ballad of the Landlord."

> *Landlord, landlord*
> *My roof has sprung a leak.*
> *Don't you 'member I told you about it*
> *Way last week?*

Landlord, landlord
These steps is broken down.
When you come up yourself
It's a wonder you don't fall down.

Ten bucks you say I owe you?
Ten bucks you say is due?
Well, that's ten bucks more'n I'll pay you
Till you fix this house up new.

What? You gonna get eviction orders?
You gonna cut off my heat?
You gonna take my furniture and
Throw it in the street?

Um-huh! You talking high and mighty
Talk on—til you get through.
You ain't gonna be able to say a word
If I land my fist on you.

Police! Police!
Come and get this man!
He's trying to ruin the government
and overturn the land!

Copper's whistle
Patrol bell!
Arrest

Precinct station
Iron cell
Headlines in press:

MAN THREATENS LANDLORD
TENANT HELD NO BAIL
JUDGE GIVES NEGRO 90 DAYS IN COUNTY JAIL.

Later, a school official told Kozol that Negro poetry was unsuitable for schoolchildren if it described suffering; the only poems acceptable for classroom use were those which "accentuate the positive," "describe nature," or "tell of something hopeful."

The Gibson parents had run out of hope—and patience. After workers from the Congress of Racial Equality knocked on doors in the neighborhood, telling parents what had happened, two hundred of them, including Rachel Twymon, showed up for an angry rally at St. Mark's. The next Monday, a dozen parents staged a three-hour sit-in at the school to protest Kozol's firing and conditions in the building. Their children all stayed home that day while the parents took their places at the battered wooden desks in Kozol's classroom. Police officers warned that they were violating the law, but the mothers and fathers stolidly refused to budge.

On the sidewalk outside, twenty more parents paraded with picket signs reading: "Harvard Summa Too Good for Negro Children," "Good Teaching Banned in Boston," and "Why Are Our Children Taught in a Boiler Room?" Meanwhile, a delegation met with Miss Callahan to present a list of twelve demands, including reinstatement of Kozol; elimination of the rattan; up-to-date, integrated school books; elimination of basement and auditorium classrooms; and more respectful treatment of children and parents.

The demonstration ended after school officials agreed to meet with parents. On Wednesday afternoon, Deputy School Superintendent Marguerite Sullivan met with fifteen mothers in a first-floor classroom and left two hours later, saying "a great deal of progress" had been made. The mothers didn't agree. They refused to leave the building, threatening to spend the night if their grievances were not attended to. This time, both sides seemed prepared for a long siege. Police ringed the building with orders to let no food or other supplies in. A hundred and fifty parents, children, and community leaders soon gathered outside waving placards and banners—among them Rachel Twymon, with Richard and George in tow. All through the long afternoon and into the evening they marched in a big circle on the sidewalk, singing "Let My People Go" and "We Shall Overcome." Then, just before 9:00 p.m., Thomas Eisenstadt, a School Committee member, arrived to meet with the demonstrators. After Eisenstadt pledged a "full, personal investigation" of the Kozol case, the sit-in ended. Weeks later, Eisenstadt issued his promised report, finding that school officials had been "fully justified" in dismissing Kozol. But school was out for the summer, the children were splashing in overflowing hydrants along Washington Street, and the parents had other things to worry about.

By then, the Twymons had moved from Fenelon Street to the Orchard Park housing project in Roxbury. Once the neighborhood had been an Irish enclave, fiercely resistant to black intrusion; and even when the project was built in 1942, whites were assigned to buildings east of Albany Street, blacks to the west in a section soon nicknamed "the Jet." The move was a step down the social scale for the Twymons—from the lower-middle-class single- or two-family housing of North Dorchester to the shabby brick blockhouses of the project, occupied by working-class families, many of them on welfare. But, on welfare herself now, Rachel needed Orchard Park's heavily subsidized rents.

The move, nearly two miles back into the heart of Roxbury, had a similar effect on her children's schooling. Starting in the fall of 1965, they went to the Dearborn School, right down the street from the project and attended by many project kids. While the Gibson had been nearly half white, the Dearborn was more than 98 percent black. It was even more shabby, decrepit, and overcrowded than the Gibson. The Dearborn was typical of the schools in Boston's predominantly black neighborhoods, and the more Rachel saw of them, the more she despaired of her children's ever getting a decent education there. They were hardly schools at all, she thought, more like warehouses where the kids were stored for a few years, sorted, labeled, and packed for shipment to the menial, low-paying jobs at which they would be doomed to labor the rest of their lives.

Rachel was ill disposed to raise her children in all-black surroundings. It wasn't merely because she believed they could get better instruction in integrated schools. She was still her mother's daughter, inheriting Helen Walker's pride in her Boston upbringing and in her association with whites. The Dearborn and schools like it were filled with the children of recent Southern migrants, the progeny of folks like her rough-hewn father and her former husband. Rachel wanted something better for her children. In part, she looked back to the genteel mixed community of her youth; in part, forward to a world in which racial discrimination would be systematically eradicated.

Her own impulses were reinforced by her younger brother Arnold. Since her separation from Haywood and her illness, Arnold had become Rachel's counselor and protector, a sort of surrogate father to her children. Several times a week, he would stop off at her apartment in the project, bringing groceries and advice. And increasingly his advice focused on schools, for Arnold believed body and soul in education. His own start hadn't been auspicious: a dismal decade at the Asa Gray and the Sherwin, two of Boston's worst ghetto schools. With deplorable reading and math scores, he had to repeat two grades. A succession of teachers, regarding him as unsuited to scholastic life, nudged him toward trade school.

But Arnold had two models pulling him in a different direction. One was John Shelbourne, a football All-American at Dartmouth, now a social worker at the Robert Gould Shaw House and director of its Breezy Meadows Camp: a shining exemplar of what a black man could achieve. Another of Shelbourne's protégés was Carl McCall, a product of Boston's elite Hill section who had played basketball at Roxbury Memorial High, won a scholarship to Dartmouth, then studied theology at Andover-Newton Seminary and the University of Edinburgh. Five years older than Arnold, Carl had served as head counselor at Breezy Meadows while Arnold was a "work boy" in the camp kitchens. Not surprisingly, Carl was both a model and an object of consuming envy.

At Boston Trade—where Arnold studied cabinetmaking—he was repeatedly discouraged from seeking a higher education. "Do yourself a favor," his shop teacher told him, "go out and make some bread and butter." But Arnold had higher aspirations. For six years, while working at Carroll's Cut-Rate, he attended remedial classes three nights a week, gaining the basic skills he should have picked up in the public schools. Ultimately, he went on to Boston State, the first member of the Walker clan to attend college.

As he rose in the world, Arnold was attracted to Audrey McCall, Carl's demure, sophisticated sister. From New York, where he'd entered politics, Carl expressed little enthusiasm for the relationship, but when the pair were married in April 1966, Carl reluctantly preformed the ceremony. At first his marriage seemed to double Arnold's self-confidence. Joining Kevin White's Youth Activities Commission, he earned a master's degree at the Simmons School of Social Work and was soon attending gatherings of Boston's black elite. But he was never altogether comfortable in that new world. Every summer Audrey and Arnold visited Carl and his wife at their cottage in Oak Bluffs, the fashionable black enclave on Martha's Vineyard. Simultaneously attracted by its style and nettled by its pretensions, Arnold threw up a protective shell. At the annual Labor Day tennis tournament, a friend found him "testy and belligerent," bristling at slights from blacks and whites alike. "Aren't you Bill Cosby?" a Yankee in J. Press sports clothes asked him on the Vineyard ferry one day. "No, sir," snapped Arnold, "we niggers just look alike."

Arnold grew restless at his painfully slow advance through Boston's social work bureaucracy. His academic credentials and family connections notwithstanding, he couldn't seem to break the logjam ahead of him. Increasingly, he seethed at the black "muckamucks" who hadn't helped him up the ladder more quickly.

The harder he pushed, the more mixed his feelings about the doors on which he was knocking. The more he felt rejected by the Black Brahmins, the more "street" he became. When Audrey pressed him to join her at the prestigious St. Mark's Congregational Church, he committed himself further to Louis X's mosque. Black Congregationalists were merely aping their white counterparts, while the Muslims were in touch with the black experience. Soon he informally changed his name to Hasan Sharif.

These resentments put a heavy strain on Hasan's marriage. He identified Carl McCall—by then New York City's Deputy Administrator of Human Resources—with all the middle-class blacks who'd turned their backs on him. Who the hell did Carl think he was? For that matter, who did Audrey think she was? Gradually Hasan and Audrey went their separate ways.

None of this did anything to diminish Hasan's passionate advocacy of education—and integration—for other family members. He arranged for his two daughters to join a voluntary program—Project Metco—under which small numbers of inner-city blacks were bused into Boston's white suburbs. Meanwhile, he urged Rachel to get her children out of Boston's all-black schools, away from those "Irish biddies" who didn't give a damn about educating a bunch of niggers. But sometimes Hasan wondered what all his devotion to learning had availed him. Was it really the key to life's achievements?

It was a question which, by the mid-sixties, had come to preoccupy many of America's leading social scientists. No other nation had ever invested so much of its resources—and its hopes—in the public schools. For more than a century, Americans had believed with John Dewey that "the office of the school environment [is] to balance the various elements in the social environment, and to see to it that each individual gets an opportunity to escape from the limitations of the social group in which he was born." Or, with Horace Mann, that "education, then, beyond all other devices of human origin, is the great equalizer of the conditions of men—the balance wheel of the social machinery."

Through the nineteenth and early twentieth centuries the myth remained largely intact. Each wave of European immigrants was said to have found in American classrooms the skills and assurance with which to launch its assault on the new continent. And nowhere were the schools more highly regarded than in Boston. Even after that confidence had begun to wane, Harvard's Daniel Patrick Moynihan noted that "no system that produced Leonard Bernstein and Teddy White could be all bad." Indeed, journalist Theodore White had been educated—four decades before—at the very Gibson School which now drew Jonathan Kozol's scorn. White credited the Gibson's sixth-grade teacher, Miss Fuller, with instilling his love of history. "She was probably the first Protestant I ever met; she taught history vigorously; and she was special, the first person who made me think I might make something of myself." It was an old story—but a powerful one—which reinforced the legend every time it was told.

Not until black demands for integration found an ally in the burgeoning social sciences did a systematic critique of educational performance begin to develop. As NAACP lawyers framed the attack on school segregation in the fifties, they turned for support to a young social psychologist at New York's City College. Kenneth Clark and his wife, Mamie, had been playing some interesting games with dolls. Their four baby dolls were identical in every way, except that two were brown and two were white. After showing them to Negro children aged three to seven, the Clarks said, "Give me the doll that looks bad," "Give me the doll you like best." The majority of Negro children tested—many of them in Boston and neighboring Worcester—showed "an unmistakable preference for the white doll and a rejection of the brown doll." The Clarks were surprised by this evidence of "self-rejection," the "truncating effect" it had on the children's personalities, and the cruelty of internalized "racism." With some trepidation—for the fruits of social science research were just beginning to find their way into the courtroom—the lawyers put Clark on the stand. The gamble paid off. In 1954, when the U.S. Supreme Court ruled in *Brown* v. *Board of Education,* it cited Clark's findings, among others, to support its most sweeping conclusion: "To separate [Negro children] from others of similar age and qualifications solely because of their race generates a feeling of inferiority as to their status in the community that may affect their hearts and minds in a way unlikely ever to be undone."

Over the following decade, this proposition congealed into an article of faith, which went somewhat as follows: If racial segregation impaired the self-image of Negro students, it must also impair their performance. Thus black schools were inferior to white, or integrated, schools, not simply in physical facilities, curricula, teacher training, and the like, but inherently, precisely *because* they were black. If Negroes were educated in integrated settings, they would achieve more academically and improve their prospects for a rewarding life.

As the social sciences became increasingly central to the formulation of public policy, this doctrine reinforced the political and legal drive for school desegregation. So powerful was the presumption that when Congress in 1964 ordered a survey on "the lack of availability of equal educational opportunity for individuals by reason of race, color, religion or national origin," James Coleman, the study's director, could tell an interviewer even before the field work was done: ". . . the study will show the difference in the quality of schools that the average Negro child and the average white child are exposed to. You know yourself that the difference is going to be striking."

So Coleman and most of the academic establishment were startled and dismayed eight months later by just how *little* difference his survey detected. When the results were in from this, the second-largest social science research project in history, they produced conclusions sharply at variance with the reigning doctrine. Popular impressions to the contrary, Coleman's investigators found little difference between physical facilities and curricula at black and white schools. Moreover, the differences they did recognize had little effect on black and white performance. Even racial integration had relatively little impact on student achievement, as measured by standardized tests. The significant variables lay, not in the schools at all, but in the homes from which the children came and the cultural and *class* influences surrounding those homes.

If the Coleman Report—as it came to be known—was a thunderclap in the cloistered world of social science research, its implications for public policy were even more earthshaking. *Science* magazine called it "a spear pointed at the heart of the cherished American belief that equality of educational opportunity will increase the equality of educational achievements." But its implications went even deeper than that. For if the family, not the school, made the difference; if the poor, the black, and the disenfranchised were less susceptible to educational influence than hitherto believed; if differences between Americans were rooted in the bedrock of class—then social progress would be far more difficult to achieve than most people of goodwill had assumed.

At Harvard, where the worlds of academic research and social policy so often converged, the report became a *cause célèbre* during that fall of 1966. Daniel Patrick Moynihan, professor of education and urban politics, and Thomas Pettigrew, professor of social psychology, convened a faculty seminar on the study. Meeting every week at the Faculty Club, it quickly developed into an intellectual "happening" of astonishing glamour, a cockpit in which the urgent issues of race, poverty, and the cities were thrashed out for hours on end, over brandy and cigars supplied on a grant from the Carnegie Foundation. As word spread, people began approaching Moynihan and Pettigrew in the Yard, asking if they could participate. Professor Abraham Chayes of the Law School—and the Kennedy State Department—was one of the eighty participants. So was Theodore Sizer, dean of the School of Education; Henry Dyer, vice-president of the Educational Testing Service; and political scientist Seymour Martin Lipset. Charles Silberman of *Fortune* magazine and Jason Epstein of Random House shuttled back and forth from New York.

The Harvard seminar produced no consensus. Instead, it spawned a whole range of recommendations across the ideological spectrum.

A committed Southern liberal, Tom Pettigrew found nothing in the Coleman Report to shake his faith in integration. He correctly pointed out that Coleman had devoted surprisingly little attention to desegregation; he had simply showed that mixing of social classes was more likely to improve student performance than mixing of the races. But since race and class were so often connected in America, desegregation struck Pettigrew as imperative.

But a young colleague of Pettigrew's who also participated in the Harvard seminar drew quite different conclusions. David J. Armor, associate professor of sociology, studied Project Metco, the voluntary busing program in which Arnold Walker had enrolled his two daughters. Using data from that and five other busing programs, Armor found no evidence that integration had improved academic achievement. In a slashing assault on the whole liberal agenda, Armor concluded that "busing is *not* an effective policy instrument for raising the achievement of blacks or for increasing interracial harmony."

A third participant in the seminar, Christopher Jencks, associate professor of education, pushed Coleman's position to its logical extreme. If the roots of inequality lay in family and class, then egalitarians ought to meet the issue head on rather than proceed by "ingenious manipulation of marginal institutions like the schools." That meant establishing "political control over the economic institutions that shape our society . . . what other countries usually call socialism."

Pat Moynihan and a colleague, Professor Frederick Mosteller, took a more cautious tack. Coleman had demonstrated that increasing the "inputs" (money, buildings, teachers, even racial integration) would have little effect on the "outputs" (educational achievement and equal opportunity). Continuing efforts should be made to "close the gap in educational achievement between the disadvantaged minorities and the white group," so long as nobody expected dramatic advances.

All through the late sixties and early seventies, the ideological wars raged on at Harvard, regiments of Left and Right marching and countermarching across the scarred battlefields, with no resolution in sight.

To Rachel Twymon such abstractions had little meaning. She'd never expected integration—in and of itself—to guarantee her children a better education. She regarded it principally as a means of ensuring that blacks got their equal share of resources which, at least in Boston, tended to go disproportionately to white schools. But she had another, more practical, consideration. For the foreseeable future, she knew, Boston would be a "white world," in which the Irish would keep their hands on the levers of power. If her children were going to make their living there, they would have to know how to get along with such people.

It was too late for Richard and George, by then entering junior high school at the Dearborn. All their friends were there and they didn't want to leave. Richard took the traditional route through the black inner-city schools. George, too, stayed on at the Dearborn several more years, but toward the end of that time he came under the influence of one of its few extraordinary teachers, Harriet Schwartz, who pulled strings to get him into Roslindale High, a better-than-average school in a largely white neighborhood.

Meanwhile, Rachel sought an escape route for her younger children. One day she encountered a nun doing social work in the projects who told her about St. Patrick's, a parochial school just around the corner. Like other Catholic schools in the changing neighborhoods of the inner city, St. Patrick's had been cut off from its former Irish and Italian constituency, and now found itself stranded in the midst of the black community. Since most blacks were Baptists or Methodists, there were powerful pressures within the Archdiocese to abandon such schools, but liberal Catholics, concerned about the Church's social responsibility, persuaded the hierarchy to open them to blacks. By the late sixties, at least four parochial schools were heavily black and Puerto Rican— and less than half Catholic.

For Wayne and young Rachel Twymon, who entered in 1969, and Frederick and Cassandra, who joined them in 1970, St. Patrick's represented a startling change. They were required to recite the catechism every day, attend Mass every Friday, wear neat black-and-white uniforms, and once a year walk around with "those funny ashes" on their foreheads. Cassandra hated the uniforms and the Sisters' strict discipline. The boys yearned for the days when they could cut school with impunity. But the classroom drills and the huge homework assignments paid off. In four years at St. Patrick's, the Twymon children learned more than they had in all their years of public school.

Parochial school cost Rachel several hundred dollars a year, for tuition, uniforms, and books—a heavy burden for a woman on welfare—but she considered it worth the price. And, in 1973, when Frederick, Wayne, and Cassandra graduated, Rachel was determined to keep them out of the overwhelmingly black high schools in Roxbury and Dorchester. She seized on the "open enrollment" program which permitted pupils to go to any public school in the city where there were vacancies, so long as they provided their own transportation. After surveying the options, she picked the Joseph H. Barnes Junior High School in East Boston. It was an unusual choice. A tightly knit Italian community, East Boston didn't welcome outsiders of any kind. Only a handful of blacks lived there, most of them in the housing projects; and few blacks were willing to make the long ride from Roxbury with such an uncertain welcome at the end of the line.

But for the Twymons it proved a successful experiment. The only uneasy moments each day came at the Maverick Square subway station, on the bus they took from there, or the walk from the bus stop up the hill to the school.

Outside the vegetable and fruit markets, the old Italians with their shopping baskets would stop and stare at them. In the little candy stores where the children paused to buy chocolates or soda, the clerks served them with a scowl and, once their backs were turned, rattled off something in Italian. Cassandra, who took Italian at school that year, occasionally made out a phrase like "dirty little monkeys."

But once they reached the school, they had no trouble. In an enrollment of 350 there were barely 30 blacks and Puerto Ricans—never enough to threaten the white majority, just enough to make them objects of genuine curiosity. At first the Italian boys asked Frederick a lot of questions—"What's that thing you got stuck in your head?" they would inquire about his hair pick, or "Why do you wear sneakers every day, why don't you wear shoes?"—but soon his toothy grin and bold irreverence made him a popular figure in class. Frederick and Wayne both played varsity basketball. Cassandra made two close friends among the Italian girls—Rosemarie Lamonica and Maria Carli. Rosemarie had a younger sister, Lucy, with long, curly hair, and Cassandra loved to comb it, running her fingers through its silky strands.

But her real girlfriend was Maria Carli. They sat together in class, passing notes back and forth, and during recess they chatted excitedly about boys and clothes and parties. One evening, Maria invited Cassandra to dinner. Mrs. Carli welcomed her in the parlor, saying, "The bathroom's upstairs, dear, if you want to clean up. I won't show you up because my feet are killing me, but you just go on up and make yourself at home." Cassandra liked that because it was just what her mother would have said. Later, they sat down around the kitchen table to huge platters of spaghetti, hamburgers, and corn on the cob, followed by ice cream and cake. Then they all watched television for a couple of hours. When it was time to leave, Mrs. Carli gave her an imitation-alligator purse as a present from the family, which made Cassandra so happy she felt like crying. Maria insisted on walking her to the subway—"just to make sure you get home all right"—but when they passed a sidewalk flower stand, Cassandra bought a bouquet of gardenias, which she took back to Mrs. Carli to thank her for "my best evening of the whole year." Cassandra never forgot that night in East Boston. For her, it was a symbol of the way black and white people could get along if only they forgot about what color they were and just enjoyed each other.

Only once during the year did East Boston's simmering resentment against blacks break into a boil. It happened in October 1973, following several racial incidents in Roxbury. On Monday, October 1, René Wagler, a twenty-four-year-old white woman who lived in a racially mixed feminist collective in Roxbury, was walking along Blue Hill Avenue when she encountered three young blacks who told her, "Honky, get out of this part of town." She shrugged it off. But Tuesday night, as she carried a can of gasoline to her stalled car on the avenue, she was set upon by the same trio and three others. They dragged her down a narrow alley to a rubble-strewn lot, forced her to pour two gallons of gasoline over herself, and then touched a match to her soaked clothes. Burning like a torch, René managed to stagger four hundred yards to a liquor store; she was rushed to a hospital, but died five hours later. Her body was so charred, doctors said, that except for the bottom of her feet "you couldn't tell whether she was white or black."

On Thursday, Louis Barba, a retired contractor of Italian extraction, was fishing in Pleasure Bay Pond behind the Columbia Point housing project when a group of black youths stoned him and then stabbed him to death with his own fish knife.

On Friday, in apparent retaliation for the two killings, whites at East Boston High School badly beat a young black. The following Monday was Columbus Day and the schools were closed. But on Tuesday, another gang of whites chased six black students from the high school down Saratoga Street toward the Barnes, which was then just letting out.

When Frederick and Wayne came banging out the door that afternoon, they found the street in front of the school filled with more than a hundred whites, milling back and forth, seeking targets of opportunity. "There's some niggers! Get the niggers!" shouted the crowd. A dozen whites ran toward them, brandishing baseball bats and sticks. Wayne and Frederick quickly retreated to the school, helping to barricade the front door. Rocks and bottles beat a savage tattoo on the brick façade. Cassandra, hunched by a window, watched the angry faces surging in the street below. Eventually, the police arrived and dispersed the crowd.

For the rest of the week, small knots of white youths gathered across the street from the Barnes each afternoon, loudly threatening to "kill the niggers." Police escorted the blacks to and from the subway until things quieted down.

It was the first racial violence the Twymon children had ever been exposed to. Frederick, then fifteen, and Wayne, fourteen, seemed to take it in stride. Cassandra, thirteen, felt it more deeply. Though most of her memories of East Boston were warm ones, in years to come she would occasionally dream of a dark street, lined with fruit markets, down which white boys with baseball bats relentlessly advanced, shouting "monkey, monkey."

Alone among the Twymon children, Richard remained locked in Boston's "ghetto" schools. Graduating from the Dearborn in 1968, he entered English High, then rapidly becoming the principal black inner-city high school. English was America's oldest non-exclusive public high school. From its massive brick pile on Avenue Louis Pasteur, it had produced a distinguished roster of alumni, among them J. P. Morgan and General Matthew B. Ridgway. By the late nineteenth century, English was the principal stepping-stone from which Irish, Italian, and Jewish immigrants made their leap into the middle class. When the class of 1916 held a reunion three decades later, its 459 living members included 24 physicians, 22 lawyers, 7 college professors, 20 politicians, 50 owners of their own businesses, and no fewer than 5 millionaires.

By the early 1960s, the schools' Irish and Italians began giving way to blacks. Since Roxbury had no boys' high school of its own, English—located on the northwestern edge of the black community—became the logical alternative. As more blacks chose to go there, whites preferred to remain at their own district high schools. Soon the School Committee put its imprimatur on the shift, creating a set of predominantly black junior highs which fed blacks to English. By 1965, the school was 25 percent black; by 1971, 50 percent. The freshman class that year was 80 percent black.

Asked to perform for blacks the same assimilating role it had played for others, English by then was ill equipped for the task. In 1967, following a study which condemned its curriculum, physical plant, and library, the New England Association of College and Secondary Schools placed English on a two-year probation. Moreover, as its student body grew progressively black, that change wasn't reflected in the school's staff and administration. Its headmaster was white, as were seventy-four of its seventy-seven teachers, and all of its guidance counselors. By the time Richard Twymon entered in September 1968, the black community would no longer tolerate such imbalance. Martin Luther King's assassination four months before had bred a new air of militancy in Roxbury. Prompted in part by New York's battle over control of the Ocean Hill–Brownsville schools, Boston blacks demanded their own version of "community control." As classes began that fall, black parents at the embattled Gibson, supported by five white teachers, withdrew their children and opened a "liberation school," refusing to return unless a black principal was appointed and black parents were given a major voice in operating the school.

Two weeks later, the new spirit reached English. On September 17, two black students were suspended for wearing dashikis to school. "When a considerable number of students dress differently it constitutes a divisive influence," explained Headmaster Joseph Malone, an Irish veteran of forty-five years in the system. But four days later, some two hundred blacks—many of them dressed in vividly colored robes and beads—massed in front of the school. A bomb threat forced evacuation of the building. Malone abruptly caved in, lifting his ban on "African garb," recognizing the Black Students' Union, and announcing a new "black history" course.

For Richard Twymon, that week's events were puzzling. Raised to cherish his association with whites, he found the new black militants a bit silly. Everybody was "runnin' their mouths but not sayin' much." He certainly wasn't going to wear one of them jive "dasheekees." And when other black freshmen held a ceremony to burn their neckties, he didn't know what to do. His mother didn't want to hear anything about his burning a perfectly good three-dollar necktie, so Richard discreetly left it in his locker that day.

By his sophomore year, he began to absorb the new style. Richard's guide was Hugh Jenkins, one of the school's three black teachers and faculty adviser to the Black Students' Union. Jenkins had taught at English for eight years, seething at the insensitivity of his white colleagues, one of whom once told him, "If it weren't for us, you'd still be in Africa." He taught the new black history course, seeking less to create black heroes than to "set the record straight about the American experience." He didn't want to lionize Crispus Attucks; he wanted to show his students how Woodrow Wilson, the great peacemaker, had helped establish racial segregation in the District of Columbia.

But Richard learned more from Hugh Jenkins outside class than in. Born and raised in North Carolina, Jenkins had lived half his life under rigid segregation, and he had no patience with the accommodationist spirit of Boston Negroes. "Don't let the white man walk all over you," he told Richard. "Don't be docile. If you have a disagreement with him, let him know. Speak right up. That's what you got a mouth for."

One day in the school cafeteria, a white boy cut into line in front of Richard. In the old days, he would have shrugged it off. But now he said, "Hey, man, I waited my turn, you wait yours." When the white kid said, "Shut up, nigger," Richard hit him over the head with his tray, knocking him to the floor.

The next year, Richard was asked to sit in on meetings of the ten-man committee which ran the Black Students' Union, now renamed the Afro-American Society. Although not a committee member, he was the "eleventh man," the "scribe" who took notes on its agenda: such as the complaint from one boy that his teacher sang "Bye, Bye, Blackbird" as a public invitation for him to quit school. After the committee lodged a formal protest, the teacher was reprimanded.

That winter the grievance procedure broke down. When two black students were disciplined for allegedly stealing clothes and money from an employee's locker, some three hundred blacks seized the school auditorium, demanding the pair's reinstatement. The next morning, members of the Afro-American Society—Richard Twymon among them—roamed the corridors gathering blacks for a still larger meeting which broadened the protest, calling for more black teachers, new "black studies," and an end to actions by school officials which were "detrimental to the pride and spirit of black students." By early Friday, officials determined that English was in "such a chaotic state" it should be closed down. Over the weekend, the headmaster warned that to reopen the school would be to "endanger the lives of the faculty, administrators, and student body."

As English remained closed, the protest spread to other city schools. For a week in early February, between a quarter and a third of the city's 5,000 black high school students stayed out of class. By then, several white administrators at English favored drastic reforms to make the school more responsive to its new clientele. Jim Corascadden, chairman of the Faculty Senate, said, "English is no longer functioning as an educational institution and won't function until the entire system is reorganized." But the Boston School Committee rejected such advice, branding it "appeasement." The committee voted to send police into the troubled schools, to suspend the "troublemakers" and prosecute the "ringleaders." Joseph Lee, one of the committee's five members, likened the school protests to recent kidnappings by French-speaking separatists in Canada. "You can't give in to kidnappers or protesters," he said, "or they'll take over." The committee drew powerful support from Mrs. Louise Day Hicks, by then a candidate for mayor, and for nearly a decade the symbol of white resistance to black demands in Boston.

9

The Chairwoman

The graduates sang "The Star-Spangled Banner." The glee club sang "The Battle Hymn of the Republic." Francis E. Harrington, principal of Roxbury's Patrick T. Campbell Junior High School, advanced toward the microphone, when suddenly a figure rose in the audience.

"A foul enemy of ours has been brought into this place!" shouted the Reverend Virgil Wood, Boston representative of the Southern Christian Leadership Conference, who only a year before had escorted Martin Luther King to that school. Now the audience sat in stunned silence as Wood made his way to the stage, brushed Harrington aside, and asked:

"If this were a synagogue, would you have invited Adolf Hitler?"

"No!" roared the audience.

"Is Mrs. Hicks interested in our children?"

"No!"

All the while, Louise Day Hicks—the scheduled graduation speaker at Campbell that June day in 1966—sat primly in a powder-blue dress and matching hat, her white-gloved hands folded in her lap, a faint smile on her face. Nor did her expression change when the audience and many of the 146 graduates (143 blacks, 2 whites, and 1 Chinese) began rhythmically chanting, "Get out! Get out! Get out!"

From the wings charged a phalanx of plainclothesmen, assigned to the exercises after black parents had threatened demonstrations against Mrs. Hicks. Two policemen stationed themselves on either side of her. Three others grabbed Wood, hustling him off the stage and out of the auditorium. Several hundred shouting young blacks ran after them. In a corridor outside, the youths surrounded the police, wrestled the minister from their grasp, and triumphantly escorted him back to the stage. Wood, whose blue suit coat had been torn off in the scuffle, stood at the microphone in his shirt sleeves. "I see Mrs. Hicks is still here," he said. "Do you still have a message for her?"

"Go home, Mrs. Hicks!" thundered the crowd, joined now by all but a few of the graduates.

Turning to Mrs. Hicks, Wood said, "You are a trespasser here. You don't belong here. Go home. I ask you to leave." Her hands still folded in her lap, Mrs. Hicks stared blandly back at the minister. Only when students began clambering onto the stage, where they were repelled by police, did Mrs. Hicks allow a captain to lead her to safety.

Later, across the city, Mrs. Hicks told newsmen, "The children were beautifully dressed and behaved. All they wanted was their diplomas. They started crying when that man exploded on the stage like a bomb." Asked whether her insistence on attending the graduation despite threatened demonstrations hadn't been a provocation, Mrs. Hicks said she had spoken at other largely black graduations. "Why, at one school," she said, "a Negro mother came up and threw her arms around me and told me how grateful she was for our work to improve education."

As so often with Louise Day Hicks, a listener could take his choice. Was she the woman whom Virgil Wood likened to Adolf Hitler, whom James Farmer of CORE called "the Bull Connor of Boston," whom columnist Joseph Alsop described as "Joseph McCarthy dressed up as Polyanna," whom others dubbed "the gentle demagogue," "the sly bigot," and "the Iron Maiden"? Or was she, as her disciples contended, Boston's earth mother, a bighearted Lady Bountiful, a dedicated laborer for better schools, a humble woman who had never lost touch with her Irish heritage, her working-class neighborhood, or the "little people" who supported her so fervently?

These same contradictions were to be found in the neighborhood with which she was so closely identified, her beloved South Boston. For a brief period in the 1850s, the peninsula which juts into Boston Harbor seemed destined to become the new home of the city's Yankee upper class, but by the 1860s, South Boston began filling up with Irish immigrants, people with social distinctions of their own. The Irish middle class settled in the City Point section at the peninsula's tip, where the grandest of the Yankee estates had been erected along the beaches, while the working-class immigrants gathered further north in a cramped quarter called Little Galway or the Lower End.

Straight off the boat, John and Julia Day settled in the Lower End, where they eked out a meager existence. But their eldest son, William J. Day, was a young man of formidable energy and prodigious charm. After working his way through Boston College and Boston University Law School, he established a law office in Barristers' Hall, right behind the Suffolk County Courthouse, and soon built a thriving practice, representing among others the Boston Musicians Protective Association, the Motion Picture Operators' Association, and First National Stores. One of his principal clients was the Mount Washington Cooperative Bank, of which he became counsel, a director, and, ultimately, a major stockholder. His own money went into shrewd real estate investments. In 1910, he married Anna L. McCarron, a fashion model from Charlestown, and after living several years on the slopes of Bunker Hill, they returned to South Boston, purchasing a three-story, eighteen-room house on Columbia Road, facing the sea. It had taken Billy Day barely thirty years to go from the squalor of the Lower End to the splendor of the Point.

In 1915, Governor David I. Walsh—the Commonwealth's first Irish governor—named Day a special justice of the South Boston District Court (a part-time job which permitted him to continue his other lucrative activities). He soon built a reputation for leniency, particularly when the defendant was a friend or neighbor. One or two days a week, he sat in the juvenile division, where his compassion was particularly evident. "There's no such thing as a bad boy, just bad luck," he would say, finding any excuse not to send a neighborhood youth off to reform school.

As a banker he was equally indulgent. Banking then was almost exclusively a Yankee preserve. South Boston's other bank was the South Boston Savings Bank, headed by the very Yankee Chandler Bigelow. So it was to Mount Washington—known as "the Irish bank" or simply "Judge Day's bank"—that the working-class families of the Lower End went for their mortgages, loans, and advice. Unlike the Yankees, the Judge rarely foreclosed a mortgage. If a family fell on hard times, he would suspend payments on the principal so long as the interest charges were met.

Soon the combination of banking, real estate, and law made the Judge one of South Boston's wealthiest men. He collected diamonds the way other men collect stamps. Once a week, he and a half dozen of South Boston's leading business and professional men gathered at Gallivan's Funeral Home to play cards in a group that became known as the Morgue Club. A pious Catholic, a daily communicant at St. Brigid's Church, and onetime State Deputy of the Knights of Columbus, he was a powerful orator who frequently addressed religious and community groups on the menace of Communism, the evils of divorce, the folly of prohibition, and the rising tide of immorality which was "raising its foul head and challenging the power of God over the hearts of men, perfuming the human emotions with the odor of the pig sty."

An imposing figure with florid face and curly white hair, Judge Day seemed ideally suited for politics, yet he never showed the slightest interest in running for office. Some of his political friendships were eccentric ones for a South Boston Democrat—notably with the Republican governor, and later President, Calvin Coolidge (it is said that Coolidge wanted to give him a job in Washington, but that Day refused because he didn't want to leave South Boston). "I think the Judge regarded party politics as beneath him," recalls John Flaherty, his onetime clerk. "He would walk down the street and people would tip their hat to him, as they would to a priest. He was 'the Judge,' a respected figure, and that's all he ever wanted to be."

To his daughter, the Judge was "the greatest fellow who ever walked this earth," "my first and only hero," and "the greatest influence in my life." Her mother had died in 1932, when Louise was sixteen. From then on, Louise was the only woman in a family of four men—her father and three brothers, William Jr., Paul, and John—and she quickly assumed many duties of wife, mother, cook, and housekeeper. Even after she married John "Jay" Hicks, a former ice-skating champion from Albany, New York, she did not leave her father. When Hicks got out of the Navy in 1945, he moved into the Judge's house. In 1946, they named their second son William, after the Judge. Louise was surrounded by men and boys, but the Judge remained her first love.

And she was his. He boasted to lawyers in his courtroom when she won a race in the annual swimming competition off City Point. He preened when, as a student at Nazareth parochial school, she won a statewide essay competition sponsored by the Ancient Order of Hibernians on "America's Debt to Ireland." When she was twenty-four, he made her a clerk in his law office, where she became expert in searching real estate titles. As a hearing examiner for the Office of Price Administration during World War II, he took her along on his travels. She was with him at the Paddock Club at Suffolk Downs on May 27, 1950, when he suffered a heart attack. She was at his side three days later when he died. And on his deathbed, she says, her father told her, "Take care of my people," the little people of South Boston who had come to depend on him for mercy in court, easy terms at the bank. No doubt these people genuinely revered the Judge. Shortly after his death, with wide community support, the roadway along the beaches of South Boston was renamed William J. Day Boulevard.

Mrs. Hicks has often called her father's death the "turning point" in her life. His final admonition, she has said, convinced her to become a lawyer so she could "carry on his work," though she has probably exaggerated this for political purposes. In fact, she had entered Boston College Law School in February 1949—fully fifteen months before the Judge's death—remaining there off and on until February 1951, when she dropped out.

Another event which the family doesn't talk about may have been just as important in nudging her toward a public career. On August 18, 1941, her oldest brother, William Jr., died mysteriously at age twenty-nine. There is strong evidence that he committed suicide. His father's heir apparent, Bill studied law at Boston College, but quit before receiving a degree. He had been a handsome and popular playboy who courted a show girl named "Bubbles" and drank heavily. Friends suspect his untimely death may have stimulated Louise's ambition, just as the wartime death of young Joe Kennedy prompted his younger brother John to enter politics. Ultimately, another Day brother, John, did become a lawyer and took over the Judge's practice. The third son, Paul, followed his father into the Mount Washington Bank. But neither boy had the Judge's ambition or flair for public life. A longtime friend of Mrs. Hicks says, "Louise loved being Judge Day's daughter. Growing up in South Boston, she'd been a princess. She might have preferred that one of her brothers carry on that family tradition, but when it became clear that neither of them was going to do it, she decided the torch had been passed to her."

Her father's death does seem to have given Mrs. Hicks a new sense of purpose. Until then she had proceeded somewhat aimlessly: a year at Simmons College studying home economics; three years at Wheelock College, where she got a teacher's certificate; two years teaching first grade in suburban Brookline, while she studied for an education degree at Boston University; then nearly ten years as a clerk in her father's law office; finally, her first attempt at law school. But soon after her father's death, she returned to Boston University to complete her education degree. Then, in the fall of 1952, she plunged into Boston University Law School.

For a thirty-six-year-old mother of two that would be somewhat unusual even today. In the early 1950s, when few women of any age studied law, it was rare indeed. But for a South Boston woman, steeped in the Irish mystique of home and family, it was extraordinary. It meant handing over much of the housework and the care of her children to a family retainer, Mrs. Augusta Manson, who had helped raise Louise and her brothers. John Hicks, never very successful in his "engineering" career, also picked up some of the burden at home. Even then, Louise's schedule was relentless: up at 4:00 a.m. to study for several hours before attending morning classes, afternoons in her brother's law office, home in time to have dinner with the family and put her children to bed.

There were only 9 women among the 232 students who started out in the class of 1955. Their male classmates tended to regard them as freaks—ambitious blue stockings tolerated in the classroom but largely ignored outside. So the women huddled together, seeking reassurance from one another. Within a few weeks, Louise had scaled a friendship with two classmates—Elaine Reeder, a Jewish girl from Newburyport, Massachusetts, and Isabel Gates, a black from Durham, North Carolina. They met in the ladies' lounge and soon were sitting together in classes, studying together, eating together.

Before long, the trio became the nucleus of an informal study group whose members helped one another prepare for examinations. Most of the others were either women or blacks. There was Elaine Sartorelli, an Italian girl from Chelsea, and Eleftheria Themistocles, a Greek girl from Newton. Two black men—Reuben Dawkins and Jim Purdy—were regular members, and the five other blacks in the class all attended from time to time. "It was a coming together of the scorned minorities," one member recalled years later. "The women knew what the blacks were going through, the blacks knew what the women were going through. The few white males who studied with us were those who could accept us as people, without being blinded by our color or our gender." The mid-fifties were years in which most Northern whites never exchanged more than a sentence or two with a Negro; for at least three years, Louise Day Hicks had far more contact with blacks than all but a handful of her contemporaries.

The study group usually met at Elaine Reeder's apartment on Peterborough Street. Elaine was known as "Perri," after Perry Mason, a nickname gained in childhood because of her passion for defending the underdog. She had been an early civil rights activist, setting out to become a lawyer because she was "enamored of the Constitution of the United States." She once told Jim Purdy that she wanted to become a judge so she could "right wrongs quickly."

Isabel Gates, too, spent much of her time in Roxbury, often attending the Twelfth Baptist Church, where she knew Dr. Hester, Mike Haynes, and, of course, Martin Luther King, then a student at the university's Divinity School. There were so few blacks at the university then that they all hung out together. Isabel was a frequent visitor at King's apartment on Columbus Avenue in the South End, and it was King who introduced her to her husband, Donald Webster. In later years, Isabel and Donald Webster were to become prominent leaders of the civil rights movement in Atlanta, but in those law school years, Isabel, Perri, and Louise rarely discussed such lofty matters. They talked about classes, about boyfriends, about clothes. Louise, ten years older than the others, often took them to the shrine of her patron saint, St. Anthony, where the three girls, Jewish, black, and Irish, knelt side by side in prayer. Or she brought them home to the house on Columbia Road, where they would sit around the kitchen table playing Scrabble. On St. Patrick's Day, South Boston's special holiday, they would don green hats and join the family's friends and neighbors for a party which lasted long into the night.

Louise had something of a head start on the others in the study group. Not only had she been to law school before, but she had a decade of experience in her father's office. "We shared the law," Louise says. "I learned more about the law from my father than from any book I ever read." She was particularly well versed in property law. Following her father's lead, she had invested heavily in real estate, purchasing several substantial apartment houses in the Back Bay. "My father collected diamonds," she told friends. "I collect buildings."

"Louise was a very pragmatic lady," says Perri Reeder. "She understood corned beef and cabbage; from *pâté de foie gras* she could have cared less. She had enormous respect for property and money. For her, the law was a means of making your way in the world; she didn't give a damn about constitutional law." During their second year at law school, the Supreme Court handed down its decision in *Brown* v. *Board of Education*. Perri and Isabel were stirred by the landmark school desegregation ruling, but they can't remember Louise reacting to it. "It probably rolled right off her back," says Perri. "That wasn't where her act was."

When she passed the bar examination in March 1956, Louise wrote Perri she felt "born again." She promptly went into partnership with her younger brother John. Operating out of their father's old office in Barristers' Hall, the new firm of Hicks & Day didn't make much of a splash in Boston legal circles. It was a crimped, hidebound practice, like hundreds of others across the city, dealing primarily in real estate transfers, trusts, and wills—the musty, fly-blown instrumentalities of the law. But soon Louise broadened her activities. She examined titles for the Suffolk County Land Court. She served as an unpaid counsel for indigent defendants in Boston's Juvenile Court, carrying on her father's concern for errant youths. And she started building a base of community support as a founding member of the Catholic Lawyers' Guild, treasurer of the Massachusetts Association of Women Lawyers (where she worked closely with Ethleen Diver), and regional chairman of the 1961 Cancer

Crusade. Then, in the spring of 1961, she announced her candidacy for the Boston School Committee.

Both of her brothers were against it. "If you've got to run for something," said Paul, "why don't you pick a job that pays?" "Why do you need it?" John argued. "What will it get you?" That was undoubtedly the position their father would have taken. "The Judge would never have approved Louise going into politics," said his ex-clerk, John Flaherty. "It wasn't dignified." But for a politically ambitious woman, a seat on the School Committee was the obvious office to seek. Here was the one body in the city to which women had traditionally been elected, presumably because children and their schooling were considered to be the mother's province.

Boston's School Committee had an honorable pedigree, running back as far as America's notion of the common school. In 1784, a town meeting declared that Boston's schools should serve "the Benefit of the Poor and the Rich; that the Children of all, partaking of equal Advantages and being placed upon an equal Footing, no Distinction might be made among them in the Schools on account of the different Circumstances of their Parents, but that the Capacity & natural Genius of each might be cultivated & improved for the future benefit of the whole Community." This high ideal was implemented five years later when Massachusetts passed the nation's first comprehensive school law, requiring every town to support an elementary school. A few months later, Boston established a twenty-one-member School Committee.

The committee changed shape over the years, responding to political exigencies. As long as Boston remained a relatively homogeneous Yankee town, the schools operated much as they had in colonial times, under relaxed local control, and the School Committee reflected local interests, ballooning to 116 ward representatives. Its members were doctors, merchants, and ministers—men of like backgrounds and rearing who, as Oliver Wendell Holmes put it, "carry the Common in our heads as the unit of space, the State House as the standard of architecture, and measure off men in Edward Everetts as the yardstick."

But by the mid-nineteenth century, following the flood tide of Irish immigration, such men became obsessed with the threat to the social order posed by "the ravenous dregs of anarchy and crime, the tainted swarms of pauperism and vice Europe shakes on our shores from her diseased robes." Education was quickly enlisted in the struggle for social discipline. "Unless [the children of immigrants] are made inmates of our schools," School Committeeman George Emerson warned in 1846, "they will become inmates of our prisons." The common school, once a reflection of natural community, became a means of wrenching community out of diversity, of assimilating foreign elements to American civic and moral standards. "The whole character of the instruction given," said the Boston School Report of 1853, "must be such, and only such, as will tend to make the pupils thereof American citizens, and ardent supporters of American institutions." These were the concerns which motivated Horace Mann, the first secretary of the Massachusetts Board of Education and often called the father of the American public school. If they were to compel immigrants to become "morally acclimated to our institutions," Mann argued, the schools themselves had to be centralized and professionalized. In 1851, after a long battle, the committee finally named a superintendent to run the system.

Meanwhile, the Irish themselves—the very newcomers who threatened to rend the social fabric—were gaining seats on the ward-based committee. Long before the interlopers were much of a factor in mayoral elections, the School Committee was the arena in which they and the Yankees did battle. By early in this century, they gained an iron hold on the School Committee which they maintained into the 1970s, doing unto the Yankees, the Italians, and the blacks as they had once been done to. Between 1905 and 1976, there were 48 Irish Catholic members, 8 Yankees, 5 Jews, and 2 Italians; after 1942, all but four members were Irish. And the committee took care of its own. Since 1920, all school superintendents have been Catholic and all but one have been Irish. During most of this period, the system's administrators and teachers have been overwhelmingly Irish. In the mid-1960s, one investigator counted 68 Sullivans, 61 Murphys, 40 McCarthys, 30 O'Briens, 25 Walshes, 22 Dohertys, 21 McLaughlins, 21 Lynches, 18 Kelleys, and 14 Kellys in the system.

It is perhaps noteworthy that the comparable body in New York is the Board of Education while Boston's remains the School Committee, for the committee seems less interested in education than in employment. Once Boston's schools had justly claimed to be among the country's best. But in the thirties—as Puritan rigor was abetted by Irish civil service rigidity—the system began to atrophy. ("We do not need to teach the current economic theories, nor the ever-changing concepts in government, nor the science of tomorrow," Superintendent Patrick Campbell said in 1935. "Let us remember that man must always learn from the experience of the past.") The proud boasts of another time ("Our common schools are a system of unsurpassable grandeur and efficacy," Horace Mann had said) became ritualistic obeisance to "our wonderful system" and "our dedicated teachers." By 1944, the Boston Finance Commission, a state watchdog agency, concluded: " 'Politics' has dealt a paralyzing blow to progress in Boston schools. 'Politics' is given as the cause of relatively incompetent persons holding responsible positions, of decisions being made that are contrary to [educators'] best judgment. . . . The result is deadly to honest thinking, professional initiative, courageous leadership, and progress in all portions of the school system."

A quarter century later, in 1970, the situation was, if anything, worse. Only 14 percent of School Committee votes concerned educational policy and curriculum, while 74 percent dealt with hiring, firing, promotion, and assignment of individual school employees. Appropriately grateful to the member who put them or kept them in office, such employees could be counted on to work on the member's future campaigns; indeed, elections were often decided by how many jobs a member controlled (the average member appointed 30–

40 custodians, aides, or night school teachers during his term on the committee; the chairman up to 200).

Although members were unpaid, they raised thousands of dollars each year through $25-a-plate "testimonial dinners" to which administrators, teachers, and businessmen seeking contracts with the system were "invited." ("Dear Friend," read a typical invitation, "Friends of Boston School Committeeman John J. Kerrigan are planning to honor him with a reception and cocktail party at the New England Aquarium on Thursday evening, October 19, 1972, from 5:30 to 7:30 p.m. The purpose of this party is twofold. The first is to honor John, an outstanding dedicated public official, who is an unpaid member of the Boston School Committee. The second is to honor John on the occasion of his fourteenth Wedding Anniversary. . . . Enclosed for your convenience you will find both a reservation card and a postage-paid envelope: Gentlemen: please reserve ___ tables at $250 each. Please reserve ___ tables at $500 each.") Failure to attend such dinners often resulted in the employee's demotion or dismissal or the loss of a contract. The funds raised went straight into the member's pocket for purely personal use or toward the escalating cost of incessant campaigns. For ever since Maurice Tobin had graduated from the School Committee to mayor, governor, and Secretary of Labor in Harry Truman's Cabinet, members had seen the committee as the ideal launching pad to higher office.

But in 1961 Louise Hicks gave no sign of such aspirations. She ran as a reformer, pledged to "take politics out of the School Committee." Indeed, the Judge's daughter seemed then the very prototype of the "lace curtain" Irish who had long collaborated on school reform with Yankee "Goo-Goos." She won endorsements from the Boston Teachers' Alliance and the League for Better Schools. She appealed particularly to women with her campaign slogan: "The only mother on the ballot" (not bothering to mention that her two sons went to parochial school). But her chief political asset was her late father. From the start, she always used her full name, Louise Day Hicks. People would call her campaign headquarters to ask, "Is she really the Judge's daughter?" The little people the Judge had helped and the big people with whom he had hobnobbed rallied round his little girl. Her campaign organization was rudimentary, built on her family. Her brother John reluctantly served as campaign manager. Her husband ran a sound truck. A neighbor, Marie Whelan, helped organize women's groups which met in kitchens and parlors across the city. Louise called on two friends from the law school study group—Perri Reeder, who canvassed the Jewish community, and Reuben Dawkins, who worked the black neighborhoods (Louise herself met with black parents at Freedom House, the black community's principal settlement house, and pledged her support for their objectives). Reform was in the air that fall and four new members were swept onto the five-member committee, among them Louise, who finished third in the balloting.

During her first year on the committee she was quiet and uncontroversial. At the start of her second year, in January 1963, her colleagues elected her chairwoman and for the first five months her direction of the committee was so unimpeachable that Citizens for Boston Public Schools, the principal reform lobby, contemplated endorsing her for reelection that fall. Then, on May 22, the Citizens released a report charging that thirteen of the city's schools were over 90 percent black; that eleven of these were at least fifty years old and the newest twenty-six years old; and that all were chronically shortchanged on funding (the average cost allocated to pupils in all-white elementary schools was $350 per year, while in predominantly black schools it ranged as low as $228.98). Paul Parks, the group's black vice-president, who had met Mrs. Hicks during her first campaign, invited her to a meeting at Freedom House that night at which he outlined the report's finding. Afterwards, Parks drove Louise home to South Boston. In the car, she assured him that she "understood and sympathized" with the black parents' grievances and would do what she could to alleviate them.

Three weeks later, on June 11, the NAACP went before the School Committee to call for correction of these conditions. By coincidence, they had chosen a critical moment in the national civil rights struggle. That very morning, in Tuscaloosa, Alabama, Governor George Wallace stood on the steps of the University of Alabama, symbolically blocking implementation of a court order for admission of two black students. But then, with 600 federal marshals and federalized National Guard units standing by to enforce the order, the Governor backed down, ending weeks of tense confrontation with the White House and Justice Department.

President Kennedy made it the occasion for his most important proclamation on civil rights. At eight that evening, over national television, he announced that he would introduce legislation to speed school desegregation and guarantee blacks access to all public facilities. Often criticized for being too cool and intellectual on such matters, it was an impassioned President who spoke to the nation that night on "a moral issue . . . as old as the scriptures and as clear as the American Constitution." It was not a sectional issue, he said, but "a problem which faces us all—in every city of the North as well as the South. . . . The heart of the question is whether all Americans are to be afforded equal rights and equal opportunities, whether we are going to treat our fellow Americans as we want to be treated. If an American, because his skin is dark, cannot eat lunch in a restaurant open to the public, if he cannot send his children to the best public school available, if he cannot vote for the public officials who represent him, if, in short, he cannot enjoy the full and free life all of us want, then who among us would be content to have the color of his skin changed and stand in his place? Who among us would then be content with the counsels of patience and delay?"

At that very moment in Boston, a crowd of 300, unable to gain entrance to School Committee headquarters, stood in the rain singing "We Shall Overcome." Inside the committee's grim third-floor meeting room a biracial delegation of 125 massed behind Mrs. Ruth Batson, chairman of the NAACP's education committee, as she demanded action. "I know that the word 'demand' is a word that is disliked by many public officials," she said, "but I am afraid that it is too late for pleading, begging, requesting, or even reasoning. We are here because the clamor from the community is too anxious to be ignored, the dissatisfaction and complaints too genuine, and the injustices present in our school system hurt our pride, rob us of our dignity, and produce results which are injurious not only to our future but to that of our city, our commonwealth, and our nation.

"We then make this charge. There is segregation in fact in our Boston public school system. To be sure, the 1954 Supreme Court decision dealt with deliberate segregation, but there can be no misinterpretation of the language used in that decision which stated that 'the separation of children solely on the basis of race generates a feeling of inferiority that may affect their hearts and minds in a way unlikely ever to be undone.' The NAACP's position on Northern school segregation is clear. We must work to reduce and eliminate school segregation wherever it exists. We do not accept residential segregation as an excuse for countenancing this situation. We feel that it is the responsibility of school officials to take an affirmative stand on the side of the best possible education for all children. This 'best possible education' is not possible where segregation exists. Inadequate educational standards, unequal facilities, and discriminatory educational practices exist wherever there is school segregation."

When Mrs. Batson had finished, Mrs. Hicks thanked her politely. For the moment, the chairwoman made no comment of her own. Instead, she turned the floor over to School Superintendent Frederick J. Gillis, who indignantly denied the NAACP's charges. "At no time during my service has any child been deprived of the right of attending any Boston public school because of his or her race, religion, or national background," said the sixty-four-year-old superintendent. "The Boston public school districts are determined by school population in relation to building capacities, distances between homes and schools, and unusual traffic patterns. They aren't bound by ethnic or religious factors."

The issue was joined. The next day—even as civil rights leader Medgar Evers was assassinated in Mississippi—angry, frustrated blacks announced plans for a symbolic one-day boycott of Boston's junior and senior high schools. The NAACP balked at first, but militants in the Massachusetts Freedom Movement insisted such tactics were necessary to wake the city's blacks from their lethargy. Ultimately, the NAACP agreed to support the walkout if the issues couldn't be resolved through negotiation.

On Saturday, June 15, the School Committee and four black representatives sought to break the impasse in a seven-hour session. The blacks presented fourteen specific demands, among them new training, counseling, and guidance programs; reduction in class size; new biracial textbooks; and fairer methods of intelligence testing. The committee finally accepted or agreed to study twelve of the demands. It tabled No. 10—"The elimination of discrimination in hiring and assignment of teachers"—which it could hardly be expected to accept since it had never admitted that such discrimination existed. And it flatly rejected No. 1—"An immediate public acknowledgment of the existence of *de facto* segregation in the Boston Public School system"—the single demand which the blacks regarded as essential to an agreement.

In part, the dispute was a semantic one. There was no disagreement on the facts: thirteen of the city's schools were at least 90 percent black. To many, that was *de facto* segregation—a term which had come into use to distinguish the Northern brand of racial separation from the legally mandated dual school systems of the South. But not to the School Committee. It conceded that "because of concentration of Negroes in certain sections of the city, we have Negroes predominantly in some of our schools," but it wouldn't admit that this was *de facto* segregation. The NAACP's position was characteristically moderate: it didn't accuse either the committee or its predecessors of deliberately segregating the system, asking only that it accept a generalized responsibility for the situation. The committee refused. "It's like a picture on the wall," one committee member explained. "Once you admit it's tipped, you have to put it straight. We're not admitting anything." Superintendent Gillis, about to retire after eight years in office, was particularly intractable on this point, fearing that any such admission would be a repudiation of his administration. Of the five School Committee members, only Arthur Gartland, a liberal Back Bay insurance executive, was willing to accept demand No. 1. When the deadlocked parties gave up shortly after midnight, Mrs. Hicks emerged grim-faced and obdurate. "All views have been expressed during the past seven hours," she told newsmen. "There is nothing more to say."

But Mrs. Hicks was less adamant than she sounded. The next day she met secretly with three blacks—Paul Parks of the NAACP and Otto and Muriel Snowden of Freedom House. The meetings produced a statement designed to head off the boycott. "This will do it," the Snowdens assured her. In light of Mrs. Hicks's later reputation as a confirmed bigot, it was a remarkably conciliatory position.

> *Because of social conditions beyond our control, sections of our city have become predominantly Negro areas. These ghettos have caused large numbers of Negro children to be in fact separated from other racial and ethnic groups. Ghetto living presents problems to the Negro family and to the Negro child which necessitate a total community effort to overcome and eradicate.*
>
> *Ghetto living, in itself, makes unique problems for the Negro youngster. We recognize this as a fact and we dedicate ourselves to the sympathetic, cooperative solution of these problems.*
>
> *In this city, so proud of its "Cradle of Liberty" spirit and the home city of the President of the United States, it is only fitting and proper that we*

*take the lead in recognizing the social revolution taking place across this
nation for Negro equality. The dignity of all mankind demands that all of
us work together with understanding and it is to this end that we dedicate
our sincere effort.*

Louise herself described this as "a strong, honest statement of policy and
intent designed to show the Negro people I fully understand their position,
their grievances, and their problems." Although it did not include the magic
words "*de facto* segregation," it went a long way toward meeting the black
community's demands in this area, and might have provided the basis for a
compromise.

But late Sunday evening, Mrs. Hicks angrily withdrew the statement. The
reason for her abrupt reversal remains in dispute to this day. According to Mrs.
Hicks, a reporter called her that night with a statement released in her name
by black leaders. Mrs. Hicks says it resembled the one she had drafted that
afternoon, but had been subtly altered—opening, "We regret," and omitting
the phrase "beyond our control"—to suggest greater committee responsibility
for segregated schools. Black leaders deny they tampered with her statement.
They suggest that she withdrew it when she failed to find majority support on
the committee, leaving her uncomfortably isolated as a racial moderate.

In any case, at a news conference the next day, she utterly disowned any
version of the statement. "Let me assure you," she told reporters, "the School
Committee members regret nothing, except that children are being encouraged
to remain out of school. If some black leaders would rather 'play with words,'
then I am indeed disillusioned."

On Monday night, Governor Endicott Peabody made an eleventh-hour effort to avert the boycott. He managed to extract relatively conciliatory statements from three members of the committee—Joe Lee, Thomas Eisenstadt,
and Gartland—and presented them to black representatives at a midnight
meeting in his Beacon Hill apartment. None of the statements mentioned "*de
facto* segregation," though Arthur Gartland assured the blacks that the statements constituted "a moral commitment that cannot be repudiated." But the
blacks stood firm, perhaps influenced by Chairwoman Hicks's sudden intransigence ("I repeat what I have said time and again," her new statement read.
"We do not have segregation in the Boston schools").

So the boycott began as scheduled on Tuesday morning—8,260 of Boston's junior and senior high school students remaining at home or attending
"freedom schools." No longer even faintly conciliatory, Mrs. Hicks lashed out.
"Our schools and our public officials preach obedience to the law, yet here we
have our Negro children being encouraged to flaunt the law." At a teachers'
meeting, she exclaimed with tears in her eyes, "God help them, they know not
what they do!"

By late June, the two sides had reached an impasse over two small Latin
words. To some, the dispute seemed ridiculous. Boston's Cardinal Cushing

urged the School Committee to "at least acknowledge the problem." The Boston *Herald* warned that "recognition of the existence of *de facto* segregation . . . is the necessary forerunner of appropriate correction action."

The strongest pressure came from Washington, where Boston's conflict was proving acutely embarrassing to John Kennedy. For just as the NAACP's June 11 challenge had brought Boston's racial antagonism into the open, so the President's June 11 address was a watershed in his administration's stance on racial issues, the start of a concerted drive to get a civil rights bill through Congress. Not surprisingly, Southern Democrats seized on the troubles in Kennedy's native city to brand him a hypocrite. Starting in midsummer, Mrs. Hicks began getting telephone calls from Presidential Appointments Secretary Kenneth O'Donnell, from Attorney General Robert Kennedy, and, ultimately, from the President himself. All delivered the same message: the President would greatly appreciate it if Mrs. Hicks could reach some sort of compromise with the NAACP. Louise, by then a staunch Kennedy supporter, was flattered by the attention; but, even after one presidential aide dangled a judgeship before her, she declined to bend.

Indeed, the more others pushed, the more the committee, led by its chairwoman, dug in its heels. On August 15, when NAACP members raised the issue again, Mrs. Hicks snapped, "The committee has decided not to discuss the question of *de facto* segregation. Kindly proceed to educational matters." The NAACP delegation walked out.

As Mrs. Hicks campaigned for reelection that fall, she was the target of demonstrations and denunciations by blacks who accused her of "the most vicious type of racism." Louise denied such charges, labeling them "a distortion of the truth," "an absolute lie," and "a complete falsehood." She even suggested that race wasn't a relevant category in American life, that it was only the liberals who were insisting on it. "I never think of people as Negro or white," she once said. "Boycotts and other actions have drawn a color line in our schools that never existed before." And when civil rights activists sought the hiring of more Negro policemen, she said, "God forbid the day we have to think of our policemen by color as we do of our schoolchildren." It was a convenient way to avoid dealing with the problem.

When George Wallace made overtures to her, she rebuffed him. "He's a segregationist," she told a reporter. "I don't want to be connected with him. As far as I'm concerned, he doesn't exist." Later, in a particularly revealing interview, she conceded, "A large part of my vote probably does come from bigoted people. But, after all, I can hardly go around telling them, 'Don't vote for me if you're bigoted.' The important thing is that I know I'm not bigoted. To me that word means all the dreadful Southern, segregationist, Jim Crow business that's always shocked and revolted me." Repeatedly she challenged her opponents "to find any statement or any action of mine tainted with racism." She said this so often and so vehemently, she may well have believed it.

Among others who believed it were the members of her old law school study group. Perri Reeder, Isabel Gates, James Purdy, and Reuben Dawkins had never seen the slightest trace of racial antagonism in Louise. "I spent too much time with her day in and day out to regard her as a racist," says Isabel. Perri couldn't believe it either, but confronting Louise one day, she warned her that she was beginning to "sound like a racist." To which Louise, with a wounded look, replied, "After all we've been through together, you should know better than that." When Isabel asked Perri that fall of 1963, "What in the world has happened to Louise?" they decided that their old friend was being "politically expedient."

Indeed, in retrospect, Louise seems to have acted less like a bigot than a politician on the make. She hadn't gone looking for the fight. In 1961, she'd campaigned in the black community and done reasonably well there (30.5 percent in one black district). During her first year and a half in office, she had shown some understanding of black aspirations. And her initial reaction to the NAACP's challenge was relatively sympathetic. Her retreat to a more conventional position apparently stemmed from personal pique at black leaders who, she felt, weren't sufficiently grateful to her; political caution, which drove her to seek shelter in the committee's majority; instinctive support for Superintendent Gillis, who doled out the committee's patronage; and deference to the view of her friends and neighbors in South Boston (her "non-political" stance and lack of organizational muscle made her particularly vulnerable to constituent pressure). Then, as chairwoman, she discovered that, while her intransigence brought denunciations from blacks and liberals, it gained still greater support in white working-class neighborhoods. She had found her issue or, more accurately, it had found her. If she had any doubts about its potency, they evaporated that November when she not only topped the School Committee ticket but recorded a staggering 74 percent of all votes cast, a record for a Boston municipal election and 20,000 votes more than John Collins received in his reelection as mayor. "My, my," she exclaimed.

Only rarely in years to come would she permit her old feelings about blacks to surface. One occasion was a 1969 "encounter group" run by a Boston radio station, during which Louise, several other white officials, and four blacks were locked in a tiny studio for twenty-two hours. Toward the end, worn down by fatigue and enforced intimacy, Louise and a young black woman exchanged tearful vows of mutual admiration. But most of the time she kept such impulses bottled up. Some friends believe the chronic hives which often blotched her arms and legs were the external signs of an inner war between emotions she long suppressed and political stands she felt required to take.

To most blacks it mattered little whether her position was motivated by bigotry or opportunism. In either case they held her largely responsible for what followed. Ruth Batson once cornered her in a classroom and, shaking a finger at her, shouted, "You had an opportunity to change history. Instead, history is going to record you as the woman who impeded history. A whole generation of children has been lost because of Louise Hicks." When Martin Luther King spoke on the Boston Common, the crowd sang, "Will you follow

Louise Day Hicks or Martin Luther King?" Which, as many people saw it, was the choice Boston—and America—had to make.

During the mid-sixties, she built a following much as School Committee members before her had done—through the extensive application of patronage. She became a particularly ardent supporter of the system's 500 custodians, consistently seeking pay raises and other emoluments for them. And she looked after her own family. Her brother Paul became manager of the Adult Education Center in Charlestown, earning $25 for each of fifty evening sessions. Her son Bill served as her administrative assistant at $178 a week, supplementing that with a $13-a-night job at the Adult Education Center in Dorchester.

In April 1965, the segregation battle resumed when the Advisory Committee on Racial Imbalance and Education, appointed by the State Education Commissioner, issued the most detailed analysis yet of racial division in the Boston schools (the phrase "racial imbalance" was used throughout to avoid the term "*de facto* segregation"). The committee found that half of the city's black students—some 10,400—attended twenty-eight schools which were at least 80 percent black. Sixteen schools in the heart of the black community were over 96 percent black. "Racial imbalance," the committee concluded, "represents a serious conflict with the American creed of equal opportunity. It does serious educational damage to Negro children, impairing their confidence, distorting their self-image and lowering their motivation. It does moral damage by encouraging prejudice within children regardless of their color. . . . Separation from others breeds ignorance of others, and ignorance breeds fear and prejudice." It recommended legislation to compel school systems to eliminate such imbalance. Boston's situation, the committee said, could be corrected by revisions in the open enrollment program, the closing of some existing schools, location of new schools so as to promote integration, and, perhaps, "the exchange of students between other school buildings"—a very carefully couched suggestion for limited busing to achieve racial balance.

Within hours of the lengthy report's release, the School Committee voted to reject it out of hand. Mrs. Hicks's reaction was particularly harsh, branding it "the pompous proclamations of the uninformed" and its busing proposal "undemocratic, un-American, absurdly expensive and diametrically opposed to the wishes of the parents of this city." Of the committee itself—which included Cardinal Cushing and four college presidents—she said, "We have in our midst today a small band of racial agitators, non-native to Boston, and a few college radicals who have joined in the conspiracy to tell the people of Boston how to run their schools, their city and their lives."

The constituency for change was larger than that. In June, Governor John Volpe introduced a bill empowering the State Board of Education to withhold state funds from any local school system that had not adopted an acceptable plan for eliminating imbalance. Although Boston's representatives howled with rage, the suburban and rural majority found the bill unobjectionable. (Its principal backers were Father Robert Drinan, a Newton resident, then dean of the Boston College Law School; Beryl Cohen, a Brookline legislator; and the Yankee lieutenant governor, Elliot Richardson.) For by defining imbalance as more than 50 percent black, the state committee had taken the onus off all but Massachusetts' three largest cities—Boston, Springfield, and Cambridge. There were simply no other communities with enough blacks to qualify. The committee conveniently ignored the question of whether 100 percent white schools in Brookline, Newton, Wellesley, and other suburbs within a short bus ride of the Roxbury ghetto were also imbalanced.

This, of course, was the formula for any successful civil rights legislation. The national Civil Rights Acts of 1957, 1960, 1964, and 1965 had all been imposed by Northern and Western majorities on Southern communities. Veteran lobbyists had long since deduced the applicable maxim: the probability of support for such legislation is inversely related to the proximity of its potential application.

Nor, for that matter, did the Massachusetts bill address the more complex question of whether quality education might not be possible in a predominantly black school. The moral fervor of the time—a few months after the outrages of Selma, a few weeks after Martin Luther King's impassioned address on the Boston Common—did not leave time for such quibbles. Few paused to wonder whether the moral imperatives of the Southern civil rights struggle could be applied mechanically to a Northern city where segregation had developed differently. When the legislature passed the Racial Imbalance Act on August 16, 1965, Massachusetts became the first state in the Union—and to date the only one—to outlaw *de facto* segregation in its public schools.

But the bill's passage only intensified the School Committee's determination to resist. Mrs. Hicks and William O'Connor, acting through a friendly legislator, introduced a bill to repeal the act. Meanwhile, Mrs. Hicks, serving her second term as committee chairwoman, left no doubt that she would rather lose all state funds than accept busing or other forms of balancing: "My father never yielded to pressure in his years on the bench and I never will." Once more her intransigence paid handsome political dividends. At the November elections, she again finished first. Though her percentage of the votes slipped to 64 percent, she finished 22,000 votes ahead of her nearest rival, and 40,000 ahead of Arthur Gartland, the lone dissenter on racial balance issues, who lost his place on the committee.

Talking to reporters after the election, Mrs. Hicks said she wanted to relax and "let peace settle in"; to which her colleague and political rival Tom Eisenstadt remarked, "She wants peace the way I want a heart attack." Indeed, there was to be no peace. Even before the election, Mrs. Hicks had obtained a gun permit, telling reporters she had acted after a man called her in the middle of the night to say, "I'm going to kill you. You're a pigeon and I'm going to get you." Following another threat, two policemen were assigned to her day and night as bodyguards. Later, she acquired—apparently from sympathizers on the police canine squad—a fierce German shepherd guard dog named Prinz. But some critics questioned whether Mrs. Hicks really wanted to avoid confrontations. They cited her appearance at the Campbell School graduation in 1966, despite advance warnings of demonstrations at the overwhelmingly black school, and a later incident in which she and an aide crept to the edge of a Black Power rally in Franklin Park until they were chased away by black youths. The critics suggested that she sought out such incidents to gain sympathy—and publicity—for herself.

To some who dealt with her during that period, Louise appeared remarkably clumsy and inept. Mayor John Collins called her "ineffective, confused, maudlin, a big gooey mass of uncooked dough." But the novelist Edwin O'Connor may have been more prescient in his portrait of Margaret Lucille Elderberry, a character in his novel *All in the Family* clearly patterned after Louise. Another O'Connor character, loosely modeled on Jack Kennedy, says of Margaret: "She's clumsy, but she's not stupid. You remember that the biggest compliment people used to pay a politician around here was to say that he was 'cute.' Well, that's what she is, she can shoot around corners. Pure poison . . . I think that given the right circumstances, Margaret Lucille might just come full-blown out of the woodwork."

All through the mid-sixties, Louise helped create the "right circumstances." Partly at her instigation, the School Committee used every means at its disposal to resist implementation of the Racial Imbalance Act. It tried ridicule, submitting "A Plan to End the Monopoly of Un-light Colored Pupils in Many Boston Schools," which included a proposal to "notify at least 11,958 Chinese and Negro pupils not to come back to Boston schools." It tried diversion, suggesting extension of compensatory education programs for black students in their own schools, which Mrs. Hicks called the "golden key" to the problem. And it tried delay, resubmitting a plan the State Board had already rejected.

Some School Committee members made little secret of their attitude toward the Negro pupils in their charge. "We have no inferior education in our schools," Bill O'Connor said in 1964. "What we have is an inferior type of student." The most outspoken member was old Joe Lee, an amiable Yankee eccentric, former naval architect, newspaper reporter, and unsuccessful candidate for mayor and governor, who liked to puff on a homemade hookah constructed out of a ten-cent test tube, a briar bowl, some surgical tubing, and a few rubber bands. "Now, the Negro people are the most likable people in the world," he once said. "And yet what have we done? By forcing this pace of imagined need for jet-set education, every student is almost a nervous wreck and all the qualities that I mentioned of pleasantness, obligingness, and so forth are kind of knocked out of them in their race to understanding the latest wrinkle in mathematics. . . ."

The State Board ultimately withheld $52 million in state funds from Boston. Meanwhile, the number of "imbalanced" schools in the city rose from 45 in 1965 to 62 in 1971. By the later year, 62 percent of the city's black students attended schools that were at least 70 percent black and 84 percent of white students attended schools that were at least 80 percent white.

The School Committee continued to insist that such racial separation was due entirely to residential segregation, combined with the tradition of "the neighborhood school." In fact, Boston had long since abandoned the neighborhood as an organizing principle for attendance at the middle and high school levels. Students shuttled around the city, following elaborate "feeder patterns." Even at the elementary level, where children generally attended schools close to home, they frequently had a choice of two or more schools and often didn't attend the nearest. As the School Committee fought the Racial Imbalance Act, it manipulated this Byzantine system in such a way as to keep blacks and whites separate. The few new schools or annexes built during this period were clearly located so as to be either heavily white or heavily black. Graduates of predominantly white lower schools were given preference at white high schools; students from heavily black schools were guaranteed seats at heavily black high schools. Even the "open enrollment" program, under which students could transfer to schools with vacant seats, aggravated segregation by permitting whites to escape predominantly black schools.

And yet the School Committee could hardly be blamed for the concentration of Boston blacks in an inner-city ghetto where they had little access to decent homes, good jobs, or wholesome recreation, much less adequate schools. Louise proved particularly irritating to the Massachusetts establishment because she had a way of spicing her predictable opinions with some facts most suburban liberals did not care to address. "If the Negro lacks mobility in finding housing, the School Committee cannot be held responsible," she said. "This is a problem for the entire community." And "Boston schools are a scapegoat for those who have failed to solve the housing, economic, and social problems of the black citizen." And still more pointedly: "If the suburbs are honestly interested in solving the problems of the Negro, why don't they build subsidized housing for them?"

Meanwhile, Louise herself had moved into a larger arena. In the great tradition of School Committee politics, her landslide victory in 1963 had aroused a taste for higher office. The following year, she tested the political waters with an unsuccessful but promising campaign for State Treasurer. In 1965, she toyed with a run for the City Council. She chose the School Committee again, she told reporters, after receiving a visitor to her home, a mother of four small children, who broke into tears when told Louise was not going to run again. "It would be a disservice if I didn't listen to that mother. I belong on the School Committee until the problems are solved." But that resolution proved short-lived. When she headed the ticket again that November, she detected "a hue and cry in the city that I run for mayor."

Eighteen months later, in May 1967, she stood in the Oval Room of the Sheraton Plaza, dressed in a peacock-blue outfit speckled with sequins, and proclaimed: "My chapeau is in the ring." Slicing into a gargantuan 475-pound cake in the shape of the new City Hall, she declared, "City Hall belongs to all of us. Let's eat it up." Then the band struck up her campaign song, "Every Little Breeze Seems to Whisper Louise," an adaptation of the 1929 ditty made famous by Maurice Chevalier: "The city's every need can be met by Louise / Her record and pace proves she should be in the race."

Indeed, her record in blocking school desegregation remained her principal qualification. "I have guarded your children well," she said. "I will continue to defend the neighborhood school as long as I have a breath left in my body." By then, of course, the phrase "neighborhood school" had accumulated layers of other meanings—it was not just a school to which one's children could walk, a school which enshrined one's own values and attitudes, but a white school safe from black inundation. It had become a potent political slogan, loaded with subliminal connotations.

That fall, Louise stumbled across an even more effective slogan. It came from her brother John, once again her campaign manager, who introduced her at rallies by proclaiming: "You know where Louise stands on every issue in this campaign. You know." Soon Louise borrowed the phrase, a perfect slogan because it allowed every voter to read into it his own fears. "You know where I stand," she said, and they knew.

The more famous Louise became, the less explicit she needed to be. She was a mistress of indirection. Her mayoral campaign was stunningly simple: few billboards, fewer television spots, almost no press relations, just the candidate herself strolling the streets, wearing a big button which read: "I am Louise Day Hicks," shaking hands, saying, "Hi, how are ya," with maybe an aide trailing behind handing out emery sticks ("Stick with Hicks, she's always stuck with you"). She was instantly recognizable, of course, with that dumpling of a face set on a bulky Helen Hokinson body, draped in royal-blue, kelly-green, or shocking-pink dresses, a strand of pearls draped around her neck, a corsage blooming on her lapel. It was always a surprise when, from that huge physical presence, issued that tiny, little girl's voice, often on the verge of tears, as she bemoaned the fate of "the little children."

To some listeners, "You know where I stand" was merely a bigot's code, a way of communicating racial hostility which the conventions of Massachusetts politics would not let her express openly. Whatever Louise's private feelings on race, that was certainly an aspect of her political stance. Her campaign speeches were loaded with sly allusions to the black threat: "I am alarmed that I, as a woman, can no longer walk the streets in safety. . . . I am alarmed to see lifelong Bostonians moving out of Boston in disgust. . . . I am alarmed to see rioters causing damage to property, injuring our policemen and firemen, and escaping any form of punishment. . . . I can reduce welfare costs by putting able-bodied welfare recipients to work. . . . Under my administration the parks, streets, and subways of Boston will no longer be a jungle of lawlessness." Only rarely did she lapse into explicit assaults on "a justice which means special privileges for the black man and the criminal" and on "black militants who tyrannize our schools, creating chaos and disruption, who sabotage, undermine, and frustrate every effort of our educators to create a learning atmosphere." When Martin Luther King said her election as mayor would be a "tragedy," she shot back: "Dr. Martin Luther King is the real trag-edy of our times."

But she stood athwart other ramparts too. For Louise had tapped a much broader sense of grievance, rooted less in race than in class: the feeling of many working-class whites that they had been abandoned by the very institutions—City Hall, the Democratic Party, the Catholic Church, the popular press—that until recently had been their patrons and allies. After eight years of Mayor John Collins, white neighborhoods were seething at the priority given to downtown development. Airport expansion, highway construction, and urban renewal had encroached on blue-collar communities across the city. Democrats in the age of Robert and Ted Kennedy no longer found the plight of the white workingman as compelling as it had been in the New Deal and Fair Deal eras. The Church and the press rallied to the new, fashionable causes. Friends, relatives, and neighbors had escaped to the suburbs and, pre-occupied with their own zoning and tax problems, no longer gave a damn about the old neighborhood. If the rioting in Watts, Newark, Detroit, and Rox-bury had persuaded government, business, and white liberals to give fresh attention to black needs, that was only the latest in a succession of snubs to neighborhoods like South Boston, Charlestown, and East Boston.

Louise had never really belonged to this dispossessed class of city dweller. Her father was part of South Boston's Irish aristocracy and her own shrewd real estate investments had kept her family's living standards well above most of her neighbors'. In addition to the eighteen-room house she and John Hicks shared with her brother Paul, they had a summer house at Weymouth on the South Shore, often called "the Irish Riviera." The Days had helped found the Boston Harbor Yacht Club, whose clubhouse on the Point was the bastion of South Boston's Irish elite. Louise's brothers had both served as the club's com-modore, her husband as fleet captain and trustee, and the Hickses kept two boats at the club—a sloop called *Scotty* and a powerboat dubbed *Lojobi*, from the first letters of "Louise," "John," and "Bill."

Yet although Louise was never one of the "little people," she was closely attuned to their fears and anxieties. Some critics called her a "conservative," even a "reactionary," but if she had any ideology at all it was an amorphous kind of urban populism. Proud of her identification with the Democratic Party, she resisted entreaties from George Wallace to be his running mate on a third-party ticket in 1968 and appeals from Richard Nixon for her support of the Republican slate. When the Greater Boston Labor Council declined to support her reelection to the School Committee because of her stand on desegregation, she seemed genuinely surprised. "I'm shocked not to be endorsed by labor," she said. "Why, even as a child I was taught never to cross a picket line just as other children were taught never to cross the street." Later, when she served in Congress, she drew far higher ratings from Americans for Democratic Action (62 percent) than from the conservative Americans for Constitutional Action (28 percent). A staunch patriot ("There's only one flag good and true and that is the American flag, Old Great Glory") and a vigorous supporter of the Vietnam War, she also supported much Great Society social legislation, particularly health care and old-age assistance. Her invective focused on "the special interests," "the rich people in the suburbs," "the establishment," "the outside power structure," "the forces who attempt to invade us." Just as telling as "You know where I stand," was her other slogan, "Boston for the Bostonians," and by "Bostonians" she meant "the workingman and woman, the rent payer, the home owner, the law-abiding, tax-paying, decent-living, hard-working, forgotten American."

Her critics in the press—usually suburban, upper middle class, and well educated—often revealed their class bias. To the *Globe,* she was anathema. Ridiculed on its news pages, scorned on its editorial pages, she was once depicted by a cartoonist as a bloody Bitch of Buchenwald bestriding the city. But nothing quite matched the lofty condescension of *Newsweek*'s 1967 cover story: "They looked like characters out of Moon Mullins, and she was their homegrown Mamie-made-good. Sloshing beer at the long tables in the unadorned room of the South Boston Social and Athletic Club sat a comic-strip gallery of tipplers and brawlers and their tinseled overdressed dolls. . . . After Mrs. Hicks had finished reading off her familiar recitation of civic wrongs the other night . . . the men queued up to give Louise their best, unscrewing cigar butts from their chins to buss her noisily on the cheek, or pumping her arm as if it were a jack handle under a trailer truck."

Sensing an opportunity to exploit class resentment against the New York media moguls, she promptly took out full-page ads in Boston newspapers addressed to *Newsweek*'s editors: "I am not disturbed that you undertook to insult me. As a candidate for mayor of Boston, I have come to consider myself an open target for publications in New York and elsewhere which, for some strange reason, assume the right to try to tell Bostonians for whom to vote and how to run their city. But I deeply resent your insults to Boston and its residents. . . . I am proud of my heritage. No article of yours can lessen that pride. On Tuesday, November 7, the people of Boston will give you their reply."

The response was an impressive outpouring of votes which fell just 12,249 short (out of 192,673 cast) of electing her mayor. The postmortems suggested that she had lost to Kevin White because she had run an amateurish campaign, compounded by a last-minute blunder in which she pledged to raise policemen's and firemen's salaries by one-third, without sufficiently explaining where she could get the funds. But Louise had more fundamental problems. She consistently did well in multi-candidate races where her opposition was splintered, but in head-to-head contests she could never muster a citywide majority. Many of Boston's white voters—less a conventional voting bloc than a movement of true believers—wanted Louise to speak for them in the councils of government. But those who had assiduously sought respectability often found her an unsettling reminder of less refined days and couldn't envision her as the city's chief executive. Thus, while she won a three-way race for Congress in 1970, and powerful pluralities swept her into the City Council in 1969, 1973, and 1975, she lost her second bid for mayor in 1971 and her congressional campaign the following year.

Her most bitter disappointments were personal. After her husband died of cancer in 1968, she invested her remaining emotional capital in her two sons, proudly boasting that Bill would be a doctor, John an astrophysicist. But that was not to be. Soon Bill was arrested for a fracas at a South Shore country club, during which he allegedly took a golf cart for a drunken ride along the fairway, assaulted a club employee, then rode the cart onto a public street (the assault charge was later dropped). Her younger son, John, found himself in much graver trouble, convicted of kidnapping a security guard, riding around the city for several hours, during which he threatened the guard with a pistol, fired several shots at billboards and buildings, and finally blasted a hole through the car door a few inches from the guard's elbow. A few years later, John was arrested again after allegedly storming out of a Weymouth restaurant threatening to "get a machine gun and clean out the place," hopping in his Cadillac, and leading police on a wild chase down the expressway, during which he bounced off several cars, sideswiped others, and forced still others off the road, until he finally abandoned the car and fled into the woods. Arraigned on twenty-four charges, including assault with intent to murder, he became a fugitive from justice. For a woman who had devoted her public life to a defense of home and family—not to mention law and order—John's escapades were embarrassing as well as painful. "It hurts a mother to see this sort of thing happen to her family," Louise told a reporter. "Maybe if I'd spent more time with them. I'm sure it wasn't easy being the children of Louise Day Hicks."

Ironically, as racial animosities sharpened in Boston, the woman who had come to symbolize them began losing control of her movement. Other, less inhibited politicians came along to ride the wave. There was Albert "Dapper" O'Neil, a pistol-packing former chauffeur for Governor Peabody, who first attracted notice in Boston by bellowing accusations of infidelity through a bullhorn outside the window of a newspaper editor who had offended him, then won a seat on the City Council, which he used as a platform for ardent declarations of faith in Governor George Wallace of Alabama and defamations of black leaders such as the Reverend Ralph Abernathy ("a perverted degenerate") and Bayard Rustin ("a homosexual fag"). There was Elvira "Pixie" Palladino, a tough-talking, street-savvy daughter of an Italian shoemaker from East Boston, accused of punching Ted Kennedy in the stomach at a rally and cursing a Catholic monsignor, who even after her election to the School Committee was heard muttering about "jungle bunnies" and "pickaninnies." And there was John "Bigga" Kerrigan, a former orderly at the New England Medical Center, who parlayed a friendship with one of his patients, Mayor John Collins, into election to the School Committee and the City Council, where he prided himself on unrestrained invective ("I may be a prick, but at least I'm a consistent prick"), particularly directed at blacks ("savages") and the liberal media ("motherfucking maggots"), and once, in the Federal Courthouse, found the perfect foil in Lem Tucker, a black correspondent for ABC News, whom Kerrigan described as "one generation away from swinging in the trees," a remark he illustrated by assuming a simian crouch, curving his hands upward, and scratching his armpits.

For all the discord she had sponsored, Louise could not and would not compete with this sort of thing. She was still the Judge's daughter who, more than anything else, wanted to be worthy of the pride and affection her father had lavished on her. Even in her toughest political battles, her most unyielding confrontations, she was always South Boston's version of a "lady"—demure and genteel as the nuns at Nazareth had taught her to be ("I don't drink, I don't smoke, I don't tell lies"); her schoolgirl's voice raised in pitch, but never in volume, her language a bit stilted, laced with her father's studied legalisms, "as to," "so as," "therefore." Vulgarity, obscenity, name-calling, boorishness—these she had associated in childhood with the rabble of the Lower End. She was from the Point, and although she had stayed on in the old house while other Point families moved to the suburbs, she shared their craving for respectability. Politics required that she cater to the anxieties of the Irish who had been left behind in South Boston, Charlestown, Dorchester, and Jamaica Plain, but she could never quite bring herself to play the strident demagogue. As the mood of racial confrontation deepened, Louise looked on with distaste and some measure of private misgiving, while the movement she had nurtured and exploited over the years, but which she could no longer control, swept the city closer and closer to the brink.

10
McGoff

As the bells in St. Mary's steeple tolled three, Alice Kirk and her schoolmates chanted a perfunctory "Hail Mary," then filed onto the crooked pitch of Winthrop Street. Nuns, severe in their coal-black habits, marshaled them into two lines, one facing up the slope toward the Bunker Hill Monument, the other downhill toward the shabby jumble of Main Street. Promptly at 3:15, the Sisters led their charges in opposite directions. When the "up-street line" reached the rectory at the top of the hill and the "down-street line" passed the church at the bottom, they broke for home. But they never forgot the catechism of class they learned in those daily processions.

For the nuns were steeped in Charlestown's social geography. Once, Breed's and Bunker hills had been a preserve of the Puritan ascendancy, while the Celtic newcomers huddled by the docks on either side. Now that the Yankees had decamped for the countryside, the heights were held by the lace-curtain Irish, with the lower slopes and valleys occupied by their less fortunate countrymen. Even the least experienced nun realized that donations from the hills were heavier than those from the valleys.

Alice and the five other Kirks who attended St. Mary's School were assigned to the "down-street line" because they lived nearer the bottom than the top of Breed's Hill. But soon they worked out a private accommodation with the Sisters that permitted them to cut through a firemen's alley from Winthrop Street to their back door on Soley Street. Strictly speaking, they were neither "up-street" nor "down-street" kids, but a third, ill-defined category, swimming in social ambiguity.

The Kirks' Monument Avenue address was enough to lend them a certain cachet. A graceful thoroughfare which ran straight up the hill toward the granite obelisk from which it took its name, the avenue had once been a Yankee bastion. In the years before World War I, a few Irish moved into the spacious brick town houses—among them Dr. Dan Hurley, the first Irishman to captain

Harvard's football team—but it was decades before they claimed the avenue as their own. During World War II, many of its stately dwellings were converted to rooming houses for sailors and war workers from the Navy Yard. In others, Irish spinsters and their bachelor brothers passed their declining years in a clutter of Victorian geegaws and dusty house plants, but it was still Charlestown's most prestigious thoroughfare.

The Kirks, with their six children, were naturally drawn to the few neighbors who had kids about the same age: among them the Galvins, who lived near the top of the hill at No. 49, and the McLaughlins, who lived near the bottom, at No. 25. The Kirks, at No. 31, were bracketed by Charlestown's most renowned family and what would soon be its most notorious clan.

Billy Galvin and Bernie Kirk had grown up together on Charlestown's streets and docks, later disporting themselves in the Indian Club, of which Billy was the longtime president. But the boozy camaraderie of a dozen "Pow-Wows" could hardly disguise their temperamental differences. If Bernie was an industrious plodder, Billy was a gregarious showman. For a time he worked as a candy packer, a jewelry salesman, and a real estate broker, but soon he gravitated to more flamboyant enterprises, which, during Prohibition, apparently involved liquor. At a political rally some years afterwards a rival leveled an accusing finger at him and shouted, "Are you going to vote for that guy? He ran the biggest booze joint in town."

"That's okay," Billy blithely responded, "you were my best customer."

After an unsuccessful run for office in 1935, Galvin made it into the Boston City Council in 1937, remaining four years, the last two as Council President. When Mayor Maurice Tobin was out of town, Billy served as acting mayor, the first time a Townie had occupied that exalted position. But in November 1941, he lost his Council seat to a younger challenger, the defeat attributed in part to his support for a controversial Charlestown housing project, in part to his support for Mayor Tobin in a district loyal to James Michael Curley. Six months later, Tobin rewarded his Charlestown lieutenant by making him city Superintendent of Markets, a political plum he held for twenty-six years.

On occasion, Billy could still flash his old street style. In June 1942 he came before the Boston School Committee to oppose a plan, devised by Chairman Clement Norton, which would postpone student holidays from summer to winter in order to save fuel. Galvin called Norton "Boston's No. 1 political faker." Norton called Galvin "Boston's No. 1 political gangster." As the epithets escalated, Galvin heaved a seven-inch plaster ashtray, which narrowly missed Norton and shattered against a wall. The Superintendent of Markets and the committee chairman had to be physically restrained.

But such exhibitions notwithstanding, Billy Galvin assumed the mantle of Charlestown's elder statesman, becoming known to one and all as "Mother Gal," ostensibly because of the favors he'd done for his constituents (though a few malcontents suggested that the name derived from the old days when he could be counted on to supply a bottle or two). Settling on Monument Avenue in 1935, he and his wife, a striking woman of Swedish descent, had seven daughters, one more beautiful than the next. Living just nine doors apart, the seven Galvin sisters and the four Kirk girls spent a lot of time together, sleeping over at one another's houses, trading clothes, doing each other's hair. Alice Kirk and Mary Galvin were particular friends, as were Donalda Kirk and Ellen Galvin.

But once "Mother Gal" became President of the City Council, a subtle change seemed to creep over the Galvins. Bernie Kirk remained loyal to his fellow Indian, but Bernie's wife and children thought their neighbors were putting on airs. Gertrude Kirk, in particular, resented Galvin's refusal to help reduce the assessment on their house, a favor he'd done for other families up and down the block. The Kirk and Galvin girls drifted apart. The Galvins sent their daughters to the best Catholic schools, gave them elocution and ballet lessons, and dressed them elegantly (Alice Kirk never forgot their little black velvet jackets with white ermine trim). They were getting a little "hoity-toity." Years later, when Kathryn Galvin married the up-and-coming Boston politician Kevin White, Alice wasn't surprised.

If the Galvins were quintessential "top-of-the-hillers," the Kirks' other neighbors, the McLaughlins, were characteristic valley dwellers. Johnny McLaughlin, a wizened railway clerk, and his wife, Annie, a gargantuan earth mother, produced eleven children—six girls and five boys. The McLaughlin kids were a little older than the Kirks, so the girls all served at one time or other as their neighbors' babysitters, and when troubles developed at the McLaughlins' house, several of their younger children came to live with the Kirks for a while. Georgie McLaughlin wanted to enlist in the Navy, but couldn't make the weight, so night after night he put down prodigious quantities of Bernie Kirk's mashed potatoes until the Navy capitulated.

The troubles began with the oldest son, Eddie, known to one and all as "Punchy." A longshoreman and a pretty good club fighter, Punchy began using his fists outside the ring. His public brawls with South Boston's Tommy Sullivan were legendary: once he went after Sullivan in a bar with a five-inch railroad spike. Soon he was working as an "enforcer" on the docks, collecting money for professional loan sharks. Inexplicably he was a shoplifter as well, arrested for stealing a pink negligee from a Roslindale department store. In the early fifties, Punchy went off to Montreal, where he served an apprenticeship with the mob. Returning to Charlestown, he muscled in on gambling and loan-sharking operations, gradually enlisting his younger brothers Bernie and Georgie.

Bernie became a renowned enforcer, specializing in "the vigorous treatment." If a guy didn't pay back a loan with full interest, Bernie beat him with a lead window sash weight wrapped in newspaper, often breaking an arm or a leg.

But the best known of the brothers was Georgie McLaughlin. Given a bad-conduct discharge from the Navy, where he was tagged a "psychopathic personality with marked aggressive traits," Georgie worked for a time as a longshoreman. But he kept bad company.

In August 1960, Georgie went to a party in a Salisbury Beach cottage with members of a gang which owed its allegiance to James "Buddy" McLean, a longshoreman from neighboring Somerville who "looked like an altar boy but fought like the devil." Georgie got drunk and insulted the wife of one of McLean's men, calling her a "whore," then spitting a mouthful of beer in her face. An hour later, McLaughlin's body was dumped on the lawn of a New-buryport hospital. The "going-over" left him virtually unrecognizable, with all but two teeth knocked out, his scalp split open from his forehead to the base of his skull, the tip of one ear bitten off.

Georgie refused to tell the police who'd beaten him, growling, "I'll take care of it my own way." Two days later, Punchy and Bernie went to Buddy McLean with an ultimatum: give us the guys who beat up our kid brother or we'll get you. McLean declined. The feud was on. Two months later, five sticks of dynamite were found in Buddy's car parked outside his Somerville home. The next day—Halloween—Bernie McLaughlin did some drinking at Charlestown's Morning Glory Cafe. Shortly after noon, he came into the mid-day shade beneath the El in City Square. Linda Lee, a nightclub singer he knew, sashayed by and Bernie said, "Hi, beautiful, how you doing?" For a few more minutes he stood in front of Richards' Liquor Store, boasting to a friend that he'd "squash" Buddy McLean.

"That's not the way I heard it, Bernie," said a man in tortoiseshell glasses who'd been lurking behind a stanchion of the Mystic River Bridge. Then he pumped five .38 caliber slugs into Bernie, jumped in a car, and sped away. Later, police arrested Buddy McLean and Alex Petricone for the killing, but the grand jury failed to indict. There'd been fifty-seven people in City Square when Bernie was killed, but not a one cared to testify.

Bernie wasn't widely mourned in Charlestown. It is said that as he lay dying on the pavement, a longshoreman who had suffered "the vigorous treat-ment" at his hands walked over, looked down at him, and said, "Whatever bastard did that should get a medal." But if nobody else cared, Bernie's broth-ers—and their associates—did. The newspapers described it as a war between Charlestown and Somerville gangs, but the men all had much the same back-ground, most of them having worked at one time on the Charlestown docks. Rarely holding a steady job, they lived by their wits—loan-sharking, robbing bookies, or pulling minor stickups. Most of them had done prison time together.

Now they were killing each other off at a record rate. One ex-con was beheaded and dumped in a car trunk. Another body was found dismembered in three suitcases in a parking lot. Harold Hannon, Georgie McLaughlin's best friend, was discovered floating in Boston Harbor, strangled to death with piano wire. In five years, forty-three men associated with the two gangs lost their lives.

In May 1964, Georgie McLaughlin was placed on the FBI's Most Wanted list for shooting a bank teller in Roxbury. After an eleven-month manhunt, he went on trial for murder.

That left only Punchy McLaughlin at large. But Punchy led a dangerous life. In November 1964, as he sat outside a Brookline hotel, a shotgun ripped half his jaw away. Eight months later, his right hand was shot off when his car was ambushed in Westwood. Barely a month after he was released from the hospital with an artificial hand, he began attending Georgie's trial. The police warned him he was a sitting duck, but he just shrugged. One morning in September 1965, as he was about to board a bus to the courthouse, a man in tortoiseshell glasses stepped out of the bushes and blew Punchy away with a shotgun blast. Georgie—who was soon convicted and is still in prison—was sitting at the defense table when a court officer told him what had happened. The baby of the family broke into tears. "One-two-three," he said. "The ball game's over."

If mutual decimation of the McLaughlins and the McLeans marked the end of Charlestown's "gangster era," a host of gangs endured in the Town. These were less criminal bands than expressions of territorial allegiance. Every street and alley, every park and pier had its own ragged troop which hung on the corner, played football, baseball, and street hockey, and defended its turf against all comers. The Wildcats hung at the corner of Frothingham and Lincoln streets, the Bearcats at Walker and Russell streets, the Falcons outside the Edwards School, the Cobras on Elm Street, the Jokers in Hayes Square, the Highlanders on High Street, the Crusaders at the Training Field. Each had its distinctive football jersey (on which members wore their street addresses), its own legends and traditions.

The Highlanders, for example, took their identity from the Bunker Hill Monument, which towered over their hangout at the top of Monument Avenue. On weekends and summer afternoons, they gathered there to wait for out-of-town tourists visiting the revolutionary battleground. When one approached, an eager boy would step forward and launch his spiel, learned by rote from other Highlanders:

"The Monument is 221 feet high, has 294 winding stairs and no elevators. They say the quickest way up is to walk, the quickest way down is to fall. The Monument is fifteen feet square. Its cornerstone was laid in 1825 by Daniel Webster. The statue you see in the foreground is that of Colonel William Prescott standing in the same position as when he gave that brave and famous command, 'Don't fire till you see the whites of their eyes.' The British made three attempts to gain the hill . . ." And so forth. An engaging raconteur could parlay this patter into a fifty-cent tip.

The Bobcats, a gang which hung out near the high school, were credited with a game called "halfball." Unique to Charlestown, it was played with a broom handle and a rubber ball sliced in half so that it wobbled like a dying quail. The batter stood in the street about fifteen yards from the school's granite façade. A ball which reached the sidewalk was a single, a blow off the first story a double, a hit off the second story a triple, and anyone who could swat the erratic missile off the third story was given a home run. Soon the game became Charlestown's "national sport." Every August, the town's best players competed in the All-Charlestown Championships, which drew hundreds of raucous, beer-swilling spectators.

But Charlestown's most characteristic pastime had long been the reckless sport of "looping." The young "looper" played by a rigid set of rules. First, he stole a car in downtown Boston. Then he roared into Charlestown, accelerating as he reached City Square, where the District 15 police station stood in a welter of bars, nightclubs, and pool halls. Often he had to take a turn around the square before the first policeman dashed for his patrol car or motorcycle. Then the chase was on: down Chelsea Street to Hayes Square, up the long slope of Bunker Hill Street to St. Francis de Sales' Church at the crest, then down again, picking up speed, often to 70 or 80 miles per hour, until a screeching left into Sullivan Square took him onto Main Street, where, dodging the stanchions of the El, he roared into City Square again, completing the "loop." All that remained was to ditch the car before the police caught up.

Looping was an initiation rite, proof that a Townie had come of age. But it was something else as well: a challenge flung at authority, a middle finger raised to the powers that be. Before long, looping became a kind of civic spectacle, pitting the Town's young heroes against the forces of law and order. Plans for a loop circulated well in advance. At the appointed hour, hundreds of men, women, and children gathered along Bunker Hill Street, awaiting the gladiators. When the stolen car came in sight, racing up the long hill, a cheer would rise from the spectators, followed by jeers for the pursuing policemen.

The first recorded "loop" was performed in 1925 by a sixteen-year-old daredevil named Jimmy "Speed King" Murphy, but most renowned of all was "Shiner" Sheehan, the teenage son of a federal alcohol agent, whose exploits so electrified the Town that he drew round him a group of young acolytes. Membership in their "Speeders Club" was limited to those who could produce newspaper clippings showing they had bested the police.

For some the sport proved fatal. In November 1932, two eighteen-year-olds were killed when their car, careering down Bunker Hill Street, smashed into a steel stanchion. Innocent bystanders also suffered. A twenty-two-year-old woman was killed when a car hit her as she waited for a trolley. A young attorney died while trying to cross the street.

By the early thirties, Boston's press began taunting the police for failure to capture the "young hoodlums." Stung, the police devised new "anti-looping" measures. Motorcycle cops were instructed to conceal themselves by St. Francis de Sales' Church and cut the loopers off as they crested the hill. But the drivers quickly caught on, heaving bricks or firing pistols at the cops. Then plainclothesmen were ordered to mingle with the crowds, sidle to the curb, and "shoot to kill" as the loopers passed; undeceived by the policemen's disguises, the crowds proved so hostile that this plan too had to be abandoned.

Finally, the police devised the "Magic Carpet," a forty-foot leather strip studded with 1,400 spikes. When police got word of a loop, they spread the carpet across the roadway. On several occasions it worked, but on June 5, 1934, as Patrolman James Malloy, dressed in plain clothes, unrolled the carpet across Bunker Hill Street, the car swerved directly toward him and dragged his lifeless body 125 feet. Two young Townies were charged with Malloy's murder. One confessed he had been seeking revenge on the cop for the death of two loopers in 1932.

By 1937, Charlestown's civic leaders were fed up with the practice, which had blighted the Town's reputation. A committee demanded that the Police Commissioner end looping "at all costs." Late that year, authorities announced that any captured looper would be publicly flogged on a platform in City Square. The plan was never implemented, but increased police surveillance led to the arrest of seventy-seven loopers in 1937 alone. The next March, Mayor Maurice Tobin ordered Bunker Hill Street dug up at three locations to create "bottlenecks" slightly wider than an automobile wheel base and filled with low concrete pyramids. If these traps weren't negotiated at low speeds the pyramids would rupture the car's undercarriage.

But all through the forties, as the Kirks grew up on Monument Avenue, an occasional looper still blazed his defiant path across the Town. As late as March 1949, police fired four shots while they pursued a twenty-two-year-old along Main Street. As the car screeched into City Square it overturned three times, pinning the looper beneath the wreckage. The Kirks and their neighbors watched as the police cut the miscreant out with a blowtorch and dragged him off to jail.

The Kirk boys were raised to shun such confrontations with the law. "Remember who you are," their mother warned. "You're the Kirks from Monument Avenue!" Each hung out with a street gang—Jim with the Jokers, Bobby with an unnamed outfit on Monument Square—but their activities were relatively innocuous: playing football, baseball, and halfball in the summer, coasting the icy hills in the winter, playing pinball at Vic's Place, occasionally jousting with rivals from an adjacent corner.

After hanging out with the Crusaders for several years, Alice Kirk transferred her allegiance to the Eagles, a gang which occupied a stretch of Bunker Hill Street dubbed "Stony Beach" because Townies took the sun there in canvas chairs as if it were an ocean beach. It was there, in the fall of 1953, that Alice met Danny McGoff.

Like the Kirks, the McGoffs were third-generation Irish-Americans, but their route to Charlestown had been more circuitous: a long stint as New Hampshire farmers followed by a stay in South Boston. Not until early 1941 did Mike McGoff, a supermarket accountant, bring his wife and six children to Charlestown to take a much-sought-after place in the brand-new Bunker Hill housing project.

The notion that government ought to play some role in providing decent housing for its citizens was not much older than the Charlestown project itself. It took the Depression—with its mass foreclosures, blighted housing industry, and runaway unemployment—to make most Americans see what Franklin Roosevelt called "one-third of a nation ill-housed, ill-clad, ill-nourished." In 1934, a limited housing program began under the Public Works Administration, but not until the Housing Act of 1937 did Congress accept the idea that the federal government should aid local authorities in providing housing for the poor at rents they could afford.

The program awakened large expectations. When Mayor James Michael Curley dedicated one of Boston's first public housing colonies, he boldly asserted, "With this project we will forever have solved the problem of housing in Boston." From the start, such projects were political prizes, strenuously sought by Boston's needy neighborhoods. The city's first—among the first in the nation—went to South Boston, whose congressman, John McCormack, was Democratic floor leader in the House of Representatives. Later came projects in the South End, Roxbury, and Charlestown.

Charlestown's twenty-four-acre site encompassed most of the "Point" section along the Mystic River, where Irish immigrants had first settled in the 1850s. The neighborhood had changed little, its narrow streets still lined with soot-stained clapboard dwellings, most of them without hot water, bathtubs, or central heating. Charlestown's civic leaders were dismayed by the Point's "odious condition," but to many of its elderly residents it was the only home they'd known. Long after the deadline for evacuation had passed, dozens of families held out in their houses, vowing to resist if deputy sheriffs tried to remove them.

Families evicted from the area received preference on new apartments in the project, so long as they met income criteria; 36 percent ultimately resettled there. But thousands of other Bostonians clamored for one of the 1,149 apartments ballyhooed in the Boston press as "modern, efficient, inexpensive and neighborly . . . a colony where sunshine and happiness are available." The forty-five three-story brick buildings, set around square courtyards, were almost painfully plain, with all embellishments—elevators, vestibules, even doorbells—omitted. But they boasted modern conveniences new to many tenants. When the first families moved in around Thanksgiving 1940, they were delighted by the white enamel sinks, gas stoves, refrigerators, and washable pastel walls. "I never thought I'd be able to afford anything as lovely as this," said Mrs. John Shackleford, the wife of a parking attendant. Rents were heavily subsidized: three-room apartments went for fourteen dollars a month, utilities included.

In April 1941, the McGoffs of South Boston learned that their application for the Bunker Hill project had been accepted (perhaps with a little help from Mrs. McGoff's brother, a policeman who knew James Michael Curley and John McCormack). They moved into a nineteen-dollar-a-month six-room apartment the following month, just in time to attend the project's gala dedication, which coincided with the annual Bunker Hill Day parade.

Six years old when his family moved into the project, Danny McGoff grew up in its alleys and courtyards, went to St. Catherine's parochial school, then on to Cathedral High in the South End. When his father died in 1952, Danny quit school, taking a job at the Schrafft's candy factory to help support the family. After work each day he joined the Eagles on Stony Beach across from the project. One afternoon, at Scalli's Coffee Shop, he met Alice Kirk. Soon the two teenagers were seeing each other regularly.

Without Mike McGoff's salary, his widow couldn't meet the project's modest rent, so in 1953 she and her six children moved in with her family in South Boston. The next summer Danny went into the Army, but when his mother died a few weeks later, he received a "compassionate discharge" to care for the younger children. With only a year of high school, he found it difficult to get much of a job. For a time he did street work in Charlestown. Later he worked at a Star Market in Chestnut Hill. In the wintertime he sold Christmas trees. Then he and his friend "Dizzo" opened a fish market in Charlestown's Hayes Square.

In September 1957—after dating steadily for four years—Danny and Alice were married by Father Fogarty at St. Mary's. It was a small, unpretentious ceremony; they didn't have the money for a splashy reception or a honeymoon. That autumn they moved into a five-room cold-water flat on Polk Street near the housing project and promptly started having babies. Over the next five years the children came with relentless predictability: Danny Jr. in March 1958, Billy in February 1959, Lisa in February 1960, Kevin in March 1961, Tommy in April 1962, and twins—Bobby and Robin—in October 1963.

While Alice was giving birth, Danny struggled to feed his growing brood. Not long after they were married, his fish market went broke. For a time, he took pickup jobs as a day laborer, and finally began tending bar at several of the taverns which clustered along lower Bunker Hill Street hard by the Navy Yard.

For years, Charlestown was said to have more bars than any other square mile in the world. When Charlestown's three commercial piers operated at full throttle during the forties, they employed about a thousand longshoremen. Another 3,500 laborers and skilled technicians worked at the adjacent Navy Yard. And when the Navy's great gray cruisers and destroyers stood into the Yard for repairs, their crews were set loose on the Town, sea pay rattling in their pockets. All three groups were prodigious drinkers. In the three short blocks of Chelsea Street between the Navy Yard and City Square, ten bars lit up the night with neon signs. There was the Morning Glory Cafe, popularly known as "the Glories," a favorite Navy hangout. Next door was Donovan's Tavern, a longshoreman's haunt. Then came Jack's Lighthouse, Ma Glassen's, Doherty's Tavern, Charlie's Delicatessen and Cafe, Tom Casey's, Glynn's Tavern, O'Neill's Cafe, and the Eight Bells. Nearby were Dot's Diner (a notorious battleground where a Panamanian sailor was once heaved through the plate-glass window), Rip McAvoy's, Speed and Scotty's, the D & H (whose initials stood for Driscoll and Hurley but were generally said to mean Drunk and Happy), the Big Spud (later called the Big Potato), the Pilsener Gardens (known simply as "the German's"), and a famed after-hours spot called the Stork Club. Most renowned of all was the Blue Mirror, known universally as "the Blue Zoo" because of the nature of its patrons. Fights at the zoo went on until the first blood speckled the sawdust. "No blood, no cops," the proprietor liked to say. But that was a hard rule to enforce. For many longshoremen still carried their general cargo hook, a lethal foot of curved steel used to lift bales of cotton or bags of cement. When a longshoreman went into a tavern he would twist his hook through the belt loops of his pants and generally it stayed there all night. Occasionally, if sufficiently drunk or backed into a corner, a man would use it as a weapon. One night, during a brawl at the D & H, a docker drove his hook through his opponent's lip and out the middle of his chin. The injured man staggered to the bar and knocked back a shot of whiskey, which dribbled out through the hole in his chin.

The Point and the Oldtimers, where Danny McGoff tended bar, rarely attracted that kind of clientele. A quarter mile away in Hayes Square, they catered to laborers from the Navy Yard during the day and neighborhood guys at night. The Point had been a speakeasy during Prohibition. Later it became a classic Charlestown tavern, with a long bar down one side, a jukebox, a cigarette machine, and a bookie permanently hunched over a whiskey in a back booth. Its tavern license required it to sell no food, serve no women, and close at 11:00 p.m.

The Oldtimers had a cafe license, allowing it to provide food, serve women, and stay open until 1:00 a.m. But its manager, "Bungeye" Donahue, ran it more like a tavern. So named because of his twisted left eye, Bungeye could be induced to serve a stale baloney sandwich to Navy Yard guys at noon, but otherwise he didn't want to hear about food. And he abhorred the very notion of women in his bar. On the rare occasion when some unsuspecting dame wandered into the place and ordered a beer, he would ostentatiously spit in a glass, draw a draft, and slide it across the bar. Few women ordered a second drink.

Danny started at the Point in 1959, but soon was working the Oldtimers as well, shuttling back and forth as the demand required. He generally worked from 8:00 a.m. to 5:00 p.m., when the night man came on. But the busiest time of day by far was the Navy Yard's "lunch hour," barely twenty minutes for the "Yardies" to down a sandwich and knock back three drinks. Charlestown's standard order was "a ball and a beer"—a shot of Old Thompson's rye washed down by a draft of Croft ale. At 11:15 each weekday morning Danny placed thirty shot glasses on the bar, filled them with rye, then drew thirty drafts, lining them up like a reserve battalion next to the shots. Promptly at 11:30, the door swung open and the Yardies demolished Danny's handiwork. Occasionally a Townie varied the order, asking for a "musty," half ale and half beer, or sending for a pitcher of beer, which was known as "rushing the growler." But bartending at the Point and the Oldtimers required no great imagination. The most exotic drinks Danny had to serve were a Tom Collins or a vodka-and-orange in the summertime.

What the job did require was firmness and understanding. Although barely five feet ten inches tall and thin as a barber pole, Danny was expected to keep the peace, which meant shutting off drinkers who'd had too much, ejecting troublemakers, and making certain that nothing too egregiously illegal went

on. Only once did he get in trouble himself. A new bookie was working one
of the bars, someone unknown either to the management or to the cops. Since
he hadn't struck a deal with the authorities, he got himself pinched and Danny
was picked up with him. But Danny didn't even know the guy. Tony Scalli, an
old friend from the coffee shop who'd become Charlestown's state representative, quickly got him out.

Through high school and the Army, Danny himself had drunk very little,
but serving drinks day after day to his friends and neighbors, he developed a
taste for the stuff. After work he often stopped by the Horseshoe Tavern, another neighborhood spot, which had once been Jack Kennedy's favorite bar in
Charlestown. The place had lapsed into decrepitude, becoming known as the
"Wax Museum" because the figures at the bar never seemed to move. Danny
could often be found among them, quietly sipping Old Thompson's.

With his friends, Danny was lively and gregarious. Fanatical hockey fans,
he and his pals had season tickets to the Bruins and attended virtually every
home game. Occasionally they saw the Celtics and the Red Sox as well. Late
at night, coming back from a game, Danny would unloose his gorgeous tenor
voice, breaking into a chorus of "Danny Boy" or "I'll Take You Home Again,
Kathleen." On nights like that, life seemed worth living.

The early sixties were hard years for Alice, who already had four young
children to raise. The Polk Street flat was cramped, badly maintained, desperately cold in winter. The heat never seemed to percolate through the ancient
radiators. She and the children often had to wrap themselves in blankets to
keep warm.

One night in November 1961, Alice went into the tub room to put some
clothes in her old wringer washing machine. When she turned on the light,
there was a rat the size of a small cat sitting on the machine. Alice screamed,
grabbed three-year-old Danny and one-year-old Lisa, and dashed into the
street. Telephoning her mother, she cried, "Ma, I just saw this huge, awful rat!
I've got to get out of that place!"

Months before, she'd tried to get into the Bunker Hill project, but apartments there were scarce, the application process heavily bureaucratic, and
she'd been told to wait her turn. Now her aunt Mary called the new state
representative, Jerry Doherty, who intervened with the Housing Authority. In
January 1962, the McGoffs moved to a six-room apartment at 74 Decatur
Street. The project was no longer so desirable as when Danny's parents had
moved there twenty-one years before. Trees, shrubs, and grass had long since
given way to acres of bleak macadam; benches and playground equipment had
been destroyed; hallways and basements were scarred by years of vandalism.
But the prewar construction was still structurally sound, the apartments relatively spacious. It was a vast improvement over the rat-infested cold-water flat
on Polk Street.

As the family went on growing, Danny started looking around for something that paid better than bartending, and in 1967 he took a job with the city
Parks Department. Three minutes' walk from the McGoffs' new apartment

was the William J. Barry Playground, popularly known as the "Oilies," after the thick sludge from the oil barges which washed up on its makeshift beach. The small park was largely devoted to a regulation-size baseball diamond, used every night during warm weather by Charlestown's two softball leagues. As the Oilies' new custodian, Danny was charged with watering and cutting the outfield grass, rolling the dirt infield, chalking the foul lines, replacing bulbs in the light stanchions, picking up trash and bottles. In winter he flooded the infield to make an informal ice-skating rink. He still had time at night to fill in occasionally at the Point Tavern, now renamed the Shamrock Pub.

Meanwhile, Alice went back to work: first at the Schrafft's candy factory; later at the Golden Egg, a diner on Mystic Avenue; then at a doughnut shop called Handy Andy's. In 1965, her mother suffered a serious heart attack which required open-heart surgery and kept her away from her job at the Officers Club. Alice took over, working three nights a week in the kitchen, Friday and Saturday nights in the cloakroom.

With this extra income, the family was more comfortable. But something was nagging relentlessly at Danny, and it seemed to grow worse the older he got. It seemed to be connected with his uncle Dan, who had died at age thirty-five. As a young man, Danny often said, "I'll never live past thirty-five." Now, as he closed in on that symbolic birthday, he fell into periods of morbid gloom. Always slim, he grew painfully thin, almost emaciated. At night he often retired to his bedroom for hours on end to watch television, eat quahogs, and sip Old Thompson's.

On Sunday, June 11, 1972, the Oilies was the site of a day-long festival sponsored by the Charlestown Militia Company, a quasi-military outfit which commemorated the Town's revolutionary past by donning colonial garb and drilling with flintlock muskets. Far into the evening, hundreds of Townies trampled the baseball field, guzzling beer, munching hot dogs, and leaving the diamond ankle deep in debris. The Parks Department had promised to send a special cleanup crew that Monday morning, but it never arrived. Danny, who'd been drinking the night before, complained to his supervisor, who told him to clean up the park himself. Seething with anger, he went down to the Oilies, accompanied by two of his sons—Billy, thirteen, and Tommy, ten—and another Parks employee. It was blisteringly hot. Toward noon, Danny went over to a cement water fountain for a drink. As he leaned over, he staggered and toppled to the ground. Tommy saw him lying there, shaking uncontrollably. Someone called an ambulance, which sped him to Massachusetts General Hospital, where he remained in intensive care for eleven days. At 8:00 a.m. on June 23, he died. The death certificate listed the immediate cause of death as "right lumbar pneumonia." Danny was thirty-seven years old.

Hundreds of friends and neighbors showed up for the wake at Sawyer's Funeral Home and the Mass at St. Catherine's. None of the McGoff children attended. The oldest was then fourteen. Alice didn't want them to remember their father lying in a box.

Alice missed Danny dreadfully. Despite his faults, she had loved him deeply; he would live in her memory as a good man, a conscientious husband and father who'd done his best to provide for his family. Now, at the age of thirty-five, Alice found herself a widow with seven young children to support. Somehow she'd have to get by on Danny's pension and whatever she could take home in salary and tips from the Navy Yard. Moreover, by 1972, the Bunker Hill project was scarcely the place she would have chosen to raise seven impressionable youngsters. In the decade since they'd moved in, the project had become even shabbier, and socially less stable.

Once, years before, the project had teemed with social activities: a Men's Club, a Women's Club, Boy Scouts, Brownies, movies, softball and football teams, a sewing club, a boys' airplane group, victory gardens, boxing and hopscotch tournaments, dances and block parties. In woodworking classes, the men made white picket fences, which they proudly installed around their neat front yards. Public housing in that era was regarded as a temporary haven for ambitious working-class families who might stay five years or so before moving on to the suburbs. Rigorous screening sought to exclude all but the most stable applicants, while strict enforcement ensured that disruptive tenants were promptly evicted.

Then, in the 1960s, several currents eroded that discipline. Extensive re-development of Boston's inner-city neighborhoods displaced thousands of poor tenants, who were dumped in public housing because there was no other place to put them. For the first time, these projects were designated as per-manent homes for the poor and dispossessed. Meanwhile, 1960s reform move-ments undercut the autocratic power of project managers to screen out or evict "undesirables." As the courts imposed stringent limits on their authority, many managers and their staffs simply gave up. Through the late sixties, supervision and maintenance in projects across the city fell off sharply.

This decline was exacerbated in Charlestown because, more than anywhere else in Boston, "the project" was seen as distinct from the community. The mass expulsion of families from the site had given it a bad name at the start, while the tenants imported from South Boston, Dorchester, Roxbury, and the West End were never regarded as true Townies. Increasingly, the middle-class residents of Breed's and Bunker hills viewed the project as an alien appendage which they would gladly lop off if they could. Those who lived there were dismissed as "riffraff," "project mugs," and—most explicitly—"project rats." Indeed, the project's population had changed markedly. In 1943, 15.5 percent of its families were without a father, 16.1 percent on some form of public assistance. By 1973, 68 percent were without a father and roughly 80 percent on welfare, while 66.3 percent had incomes under the $4,000 "poverty line."

If the project was now a dismal wasteland of crumbling brick and cracked macadam, its most grievous wounds were self-inflicted, for it had spawned a tribe of alienated youths who, turning early to drugs and alcohol, vented their frustrations on government property. When night fell, they pried open mail-boxes, burned laundry on the lines, smashed light fixtures, shattered windows, broke down doors, harassed and intimidated elderly tenants, and stole cars, stripping them of all valuables, then dousing them with gasoline and setting them afire. Tenants, afraid of their own children, dubbed half the project "the Combat Zone," half "the Jungle."

Alice McGoff struggled to insulate her seven children from the violence which raged about them. But much depended on where—and with whom— each kid hung out. Billy McGoff, who displayed formidable athletic prowess, spent most of his time with a gang of budding athletes in Hayes Square dunking basketballs through a rusty hoop. Kevin was a wisecracking maverick who refused to cast his lot with any group. Danny hung at the high school with a gang renowned for its fighting ability and, eventually, for some of its members' criminal exploits. But Tommy ran with the toughest bunch of all, a gang which had started at the steps of the Bunker Hill Monument, gradually working its way down the hill to a variety store at the corner of Monument and Bunker Hill streets.

"Bunker Hill Mini Mart" said the Coca-Cola sign out front—"Cold Cuts Center. Groceries. Sandwiches. Coffee. Film"—but it was widely known as "the Green Store" to distinguish it from the Union National Market on the opposite corner, which was called "the Red Store." Not surprisingly, Tommy and his colleagues became known as "the Green Store Gang," an outfit soon to grow legendary as it helped usher in a new stage in the Town's ongoing war with constituted authority. Nobody seemed to know quite when or how it began, but suddenly in the early seventies bank robbery became Charlestown's crime of choice. According to the FBI, nearly one-third of all bank jobs committed in the Boston metropolitan area during that decade were the work of young Townies.

For such youths, it seemed, these stickups were what looping had been to their fathers—splashy, public acts, certain to get prominent display in the newspapers, sure to earn their perpetrators instant acceptance from their peers. Like looping, they were an open challenge to the police, who watched banks with special care. Moreover, banks were potent symbols of economic and social power, appropriate targets for those intent on defying authority. The difficulty was that most Townies weren't very good at robbing banks. Boston police and FBI agents enjoyed regaling each other with tales of the robbers' ineptitude. There were the three youths who ran from their car, guns drawn, only to find the bank closed that day. On another occasion, two young men were spotted munching candy bars outside a bank; when the wrappers were retrieved after the robbery, they yielded fingerprints that sent the kids to jail. Then there was the time police responded to a robbery and found a stolen car parked outside the bank. While towing it away, they heard a voice from the trunk; inside, they found a Townie youth, a revolver, and a pillowcase full of money.

Soon the police learned to recognize the trademarks of a Charlestown bank job. The holdup men were young, sometimes no more than fifteen or sixteen; they invariably wore basketball sneakers, a windbreaker, and a knitted ski mask, and they loved to vault the tellers' counters. As soon as the police spotted those trademarks, they would seal off the bridges leading into Charlestown and, on more than one occasion, picked up the robbers heading home. By 1975, some forty Charlestown youths were in prison for bank robbery—ten or so from the Green Store Gang alone.

At times it seemed as if these young men from the project were acting out a free-floating rage which pervaded the Town. For Charlestown harbored a fierce sense of grievance which clung to the hills and valleys just as the coastal fog wrapped its rotting wharves at dawn. By the turn of the century, the Town had become a convenient site in which to dump prisons, asylums, poorhouses, and other institutions not tolerated in more affluent communities. Soon Boston inflicted the greatest indignity of all, laying the great steel stanchions of the El down Main Street, blanketing much of the Town with noise, dirt, and shadow. Later still, the Massachusetts Port Authority bulldozed dozens of homes to make way for ramps onto the Mystic River Bridge and others onto Interstate I–93, ramps which were often closed during rush hours so Townies wouldn't compete for space on the crowded highways with commuters from Wenham and Winchester. By the 1960s, the Town was shackled in rails, girders, ramps, stanchions, bridges, and highways, most of them designed to serve outsiders.

To many Townies, the drab and alien Bunker Hill project was sufficient proof of official malevolence toward Charlestown. But then, in the mid-sixties, came urban renewal, another federally subsidized program ostensibly designed to "restore Charlestown to its former glory." Even the proudest Townies conceded that their community could use some dressing up. Its population, once 40,000, had slipped to barely 18,000. Many of those who remained were old and poor; the Town's median income was $2,700, among the lowest in Boston. Except for the Bunker Hill project, virtually no new housing or public accommodations had been built in the Town since 1890.

But when the Boston Redevelopment Authority first proposed Charlestown's renewal, the plan met with profound skepticism. The only model most Townies had was the disastrous West End project of the fifties, in which one of Boston's functioning, if deteriorated, Italian neighborhoods was literally erased to make way for a phalanx of luxury apartment buildings. Ed Logue, the expert Mayor Collins imported to head the BRA, had taken no part in the West End fiasco; indeed, he rejected such wholesale clearance, favoring rehabilitation of existing housing wherever possible. But once he took a hard look at Charlestown, Logue realized that some demolition was inevitable. "What has happened to this historic neighborhood was a shock to me," he told one Charlestown audience. "Not the Monument, not the Square, but just a few blocks away on the slopes of this hill are slums as bad as any I have ever seen." The first plan, devised before Logue took office, called for demolishing as much as 60 percent of the Town's housing. Logue reduced that to 11.

But Charlestown feared something more than mere demolition. While thousands of upwardly mobile Townies had moved on to the suburbs after World War II, those who stayed behind grounded their sense of self-worth in an affirmation of Charlestown's traditional working-class culture. Now renewal seemed to call into question that stable, homogeneous world of church, home, tavern, and corner gang. For Ed Logue and his planners, architects, and social workers, there was something un-American about people who didn't move, strive, compete, improve. But that was precisely what many Townies wouldn't—couldn't—do. Logue's sophisticated arguments only fed the anger which seethed on Bunker Hill. Led by a group of determined opponents who called themselves the Self-Help Organization–Charlestown (SHOC), a thousand aroused Townies flooded a public hearing in January 1963 and shouted down the plan.

Logue spent the next two years assembling a coalition of his own: the Longshoremen's Union, the Teamsters, the Knights of Columbus, and, most importantly, the Catholic Church. The three monsignori who headed Charlestown's triad of parishes were concerned that a further exodus of Charlestown's stable households would destroy the Church's financial base there ("Salvation is free," one of them explained, "but religion costs money"). The prelates spoke out from their pulpits. Logue repeatedly explained what renewal would bring to the Town: new schools, playgrounds, a shopping center, a community college, low-interest loans for rehabilitation of existing housing, and—perhaps most important—demolition of the despised El. SHOC fought back, its sound trucks crisscrossing the Town, blaring its slogan, "Save Our Homes."

Finally, on a blustery afternoon in March 1965, some 2,800 Townies filled the armory atop Bunker Hill for a final hearing. Feelings ran so high that fifty Boston policemen, armed with Mace and truncheons, ringed the walls to maintain order, but even so the proceedings frequently threatened to get out of hand. As Monsignor Gerald Shea compared Charlestown to Dodge City in the TV serial *Gunsmoke,* a man leaped from the audience and landed a glancing blow on the priest's shoulder. Later, an ex-longshoreman shouted at Ed Logue, "This place is called Hell's Kitchen because the city made it that way. But it's my home, I fought for it, and that's all I want. So you can stick your money up your ass!" After three hours, one of the monsignori abruptly announced, "All those in favor of a renewal plan for Charlestown, please stand!" Something like half the crowd lurched to its feet. "All against!" About half stood again. When the chairman declared the resolution passed, a wild wail of protest rose from the hall. Part of the crowd surged forward and would have knocked Ed Logue off a table from which he'd been counting heads if six policemen hadn't pushed them back. Several weeks later, 350 SHOC activists—only half in jest—signed a petition to the state legislature seeking to "dissolve the ties between the City of Boston and the District of Charlestown and to authorize the citizens of Charlestown to form a government completely independent of the City."

Charlestown, which had long cherished its insularity, now veered toward outright xenophobia, reminiscent of the fierce Puritan distaste for alien intrusions. Nowhere was this more evident than in the enmity between Irish-American Townies and the Italian-Americans who had taken their place across the bridge in the "Dear Old North End." For years it was unsafe for a North

Ender to venture into the Town, and vice versa. Once detected, an intruder's best hope was to make for the bridge and try to outrun his pursuers to home ground. Some encounters on the bridge involved hundreds of antagonists and dragged on for hours at a time—you could go home for lunch and return to find the battle still underway. Fists, bottles, two-by-fours, and slingshots might be brought to bear, but the classic attack involved wrestling your opponent to the railing and heaving him into the polluted waters of the Charles River basin.

The struggle was less ethnic than territorial. Ultimately, as Irish and Italians began to intermarry, a few such couples settled in Charlestown. The Champas, Saccos, and Castranovas were "our Italians" or "white Italians" to distinguish them from "the goddamned Italians" across the bridge.

So long as they posed no threat, Charlestown could assimilate a limited number of aliens. For years, Jerry Yee Woo operated a hand laundry on Bunker Hill Street near the housing project; Charlestown's only Chinaman, Woo gradually evolved into a kind of Townie mascot. And at one time the Town had harbored a small but vigorous black community, whose founders had been slaves—Bacchus, Cato, and Jupiter—brought by the early colonists. After slavery was abolished, their descendants stayed on, settling near the Town wharves. As late as 1930, some two hundred Negroes remained, living in relative peace and security. Then, in October 1931, a longshoreman's strike threatened to paralyze the port. The shipping companies responded by trucking hundreds of black strikebreakers in from the South End. Charlestown's dockers responded with fury, showering the interlopers with bricks, stones, and two-by-fours. In the hostile racial climate that followed, most of Charlestown's own blacks fled across the river.

Not until the mid-sixties did they return in any number, this time as a result of deliberate government policy. When Boston began building low-income housing in the 1930s, all blacks were automatically assigned to a single project: Lenox Street in the South End. Only after civil rights organizations challenged such segregation in 1963 did the Housing Authority seek to integrate the all-white projects of Charlestown and South Boston. Beginning in 1964, the authority filled vacancies in the Bunker Hill project with black applicants, and soon there were nearly a dozen families there. White response was surprisingly mild. A rash of graffiti daubed on walls and doorsteps and a few rocks heaved through windows testified to some neighbors' disapproval, but on balance the blacks were grudgingly accepted. It was a time when "white backlash" still meant Bull Connor and Strom Thurmond, while most Northerners paid at least lip service to integration.

When Nettie Young and her two children moved into the apartment directly above the McGoffs, Alice was apprehensive, but she did what she could to make them feel at home. Later, the young McGoffs played with the seven children of David and Joyce Williams on nearby Corey Street. One day, when Danny came home for lunch from the Point Tavern, he found young Kenny Williams sitting at the table with his own brood. "Alice," he quipped, "you better keep that kid out of the sun."

But relations weren't always so smooth. For a time, young Danny McGoff ran with a black kid named Constantine Solman. One day the two boys came to blows, Constantine getting the worst of it. Mrs. Marion Solman, a huge, leather-lunged woman, charged down to McCarthy's Grocery, where she grabbed Alice by the neck before bystanders could intervene.

One night, another black woman from the project showed up at the Point Tavern seeking a drink. Told the tavern didn't serve women, she went berserk, swinging a bicycle chain in a lethal arc around her head. Ultimately she barricaded herself in her apartment while a crowd of angry whites gathered outside. When the police failed to respond promptly, a black troubleshooter called the Black Panthers, who, waiting until the crowd dispersed at midnight, transported the woman to safety in an unmarked van.

By then, mounting racial tensions in Boston and the nation at large had found their echo in Charlestown. In part, this new discord reflected dislocations which had shrunk the Townies' economic prospects. For three centuries, Charlestown had drawn its living from the sea, but by the early seventies the port no longer supplied an abundance of jobs. For in 1971 the new Moran Terminal brought "containerization" to Charlestown, its mammoth cranes hoisting metal containers from the ships' holds directly onto truck beds, unloading in four hours what it had taken a hundred longshoremen forty hours to handle with the old block-and-tackle gear. Meanwhile, the Port of New York negotiated a new contract with its 35,000 longshoremen, for the first time assuring them a guaranteed annual income. With the shipping companies committed to pay New York's dockers $250 a week whether they worked or not, it served their interest to divert ships there from Boston, which had no such guaranteed wage. As a result, Charlestown's Local 799, which had six hundred longshoremen in 1941, could count barely a hundred in 1973.

Then, that April, the Defense Department announced that the Charlestown Navy Yard would close the following year after 174 years of service. A Pentagon spokesman insisted that this was part of an economy drive throughout the military establishment, but others noted that Massachusetts—the only state not in Richard Nixon's victory column the previous November—was slated to lose not only the Navy Yard but two air bases, a military hospital, and sundry other installations. Whatever the motive, the Yard's closing was a grievous blow to Charlestown. To those like Alice McGoff, whose family had worked there for fifteen years, it would mean a direct loss of livelihood. Only a small percentage of the 5,100 civilian jobs at the Yard had been held by Townies, but the closing would take a heavy toll of the bars, restaurants, variety stores, and newsstands that served Yard employees and sailors temporarily stationed there.

Meanwhile, the Town watched yet another of its traditional employment sources dry up. Since the turn of the century, when the Irish seized control of Boston's City Hall, they had cornered a disproportionate share of municipal jobs, notably in the Police, Fire, and Public Works departments; nearly every Charlestown family had someone serving in at least one of those bailiwicks.

But through the sixties and early seventies a series of legal challenges shook such ethnic monopolies. In 1971, U.S. District Judge Charles Wyzanski ruled in the first of those suits, holding that entrance exams for Boston's Police Department gave whites a "discriminatory advantage," and ordered the department to correct such practices and hire fifty-three minority applicants who had failed the last exam. Over the next few years, other federal judges issued similar orders to Boston's Fire and Public Works departments. Soon all three services launched "affirmative action" programs designed to give preference to qualified black and Hispanic applicants. The numbers involved were comparatively small, but Charlestown's Irish fervently believed that jobs which had once been theirs by birthright would now go to dark-skinned interlopers across the city.

Such were the grievances alive in the Town on October 2, 1973, when three young blacks accosted René Wagler in Roxbury, doused her with gasoline, and set her afire. Later that week, after the white woman's death, white youths in the Bunker Hill project wreaked revenge on the black families living there and in the adjacent Charles Newtown development.

On October 5 a bottle was thrown through the window of an apartment occupied by Thomas and Correen Dubose at 27 Old Ironside Way.

On Sunday, October 7, a gang of white youths broke the rear window of a car belonging to Ronald Resca, who lived at 30 Old Ironside Way. Resca, a white man married to a black woman, ran out of his apartment to confront the vandals, who knocked him to the ground and beat him severely.

That same evening, a fire broke out in Marion Solman's apartment at 66 Medford Street. The Fire Department discovered that a Molotov cocktail—a bottle filled with gasoline and stuffed with a rag—had been thrown through an open third-floor window.

The next morning, Ronald Resca called the Fire Department to report that his car, whose windows had been broken the day before, was now on fire.

Over the next few days, several more firebombs crashed through the windows of other black families in Charlestown. All that winter and spring, as Boston edged closer to racial confrontation, a sour rage was accumulating in Charlestown.

Then on June 16 the Town celebrated Bunker Hill Day with the traditional round of banquets, balls, and house parties, culminating in the grand parade. As the last marchers slogged down Breed's Hill in a fine rain, gangs of youths roved the Town, swigging beer or wine from brown paper sacks, singing football songs, and accosting passersby. A grocery store owner was knocked unconscious by a beer bottle. A couple from Malden was robbed at knifepoint.

Tommy McGoff and his pals in the Green Store Gang clustered around an oil drum packed with ice and beer near the steps to the Monument grounds. At 3:40 p.m., they noticed two young men—one black and one white—strolling across the square. What the hell was a black guy doing in the Town on Bunker Hill Day? they wondered. Most Charlestown blacks had long since fled, and no dark-skinned outsider who knew the score would dare walk those streets, especially on the most sacred day in Charlestown's calendar. It had to be a provocation, a challenge flung in the Town's face.

In fact, Emil Ward, a black man who worked in Kevin White's Office of Human Rights, and his friend George Arthur were on their way to a Bunker Hill Day party at 20 Monument Square. The three young women who rented the handsome brick house—Pamela Fairbanks, a colleague of Ward's at City Hall; Elizabeth de Rham, a nurse; and Sarah Creighton, an artist—had already had some trouble with the young Townies. The women were newcomers to Charlestown, part of a small wave of "young professionals" attracted to the Town by the charm of its narrow old streets and its proximity to downtown. But such newcomers often encountered hostility from neighbors who regarded their cosmopolitan style as a threat to the traditional Charlestown way of life, and these suspicions were made worse by failures in communication. On several occasions that spring, the three women had asked the gang drinking on the Monument steps to quiet down, and when police moved the youths along, they held the women responsible (though, in fact, someone else had called the cops). One night a rock came crashing through the women's living-room window. A few nights later another window was broken and their cars, parked outside, were vandalized.

Now, as Emil Ward reached the steps, someone shouted, "Get out of here, nigger! We're going to kill you!" A full can of beer hit him on the back of the head, opening a jagged wound. Then two of the youths jumped on his back, pulling him down, beating him around the face and head. When George Arthur came to his friend's assistance, other young Townies, Tommy McGoff among them, converged on the pair. Somebody knocked Arthur to the ground, where someone else kicked him in the ribs. Only then did several policemen scatter the attackers. An ambulance rushed the injured pair to a nearby hospital, where six stitches were taken in Emil Ward's head.

Afterwards, several of the women from 20 Monument Square ran into the street, shouting at the Townies, "Those were our friends! Don't you dare do that again!" But the Green Store Gang wasn't through for the day. Two hours later, as the women and their guests were reviewing the afternoon's events, twenty youths appeared in the street outside. Using the oil drum as a battering ram, they broke down two sets of doors and beat up three male guests who tried to stop them. When the police arrived, they advised the women to leave the house for the rest of the day. That night when Pam Fairbanks and Elizabeth de Rham returned home, they found that someone had broken into the house once again, stealing a television set and some video equipment. As Elizabeth entered her bedroom, she found a dead and bloody bird in the middle of the floor, apparently a message from the gang. It reminded her of "the omen in a Greek tragedy."

Two nights later the group attacked again, breaking three windows, which the women replaced with Plexiglas. On June 22, the youths were back, chanting, "Get out of Charlestown!" Unable to break the Plexiglas with beer cans or rocks, they cracked it with hockey sticks.

On June 29, a neighbor told the women that down at the Blue Mirror Cafe he had overheard someone say he was going to firebomb the house to "teach people not to rent to nigger lovers." On June 30, the three young women left Charlestown for good.

That night, down on Bunker Hill Street, the Green Store Gang celebrated its defense of the Town's integrity. Once more, Charlestown had repelled an alien invader.

11
Diver

On steamy summer evenings in 1968, Colin played third base for the Mayor's office softball team, who, bristling with pride in their bold new administration, called themselves Kevin's Krusaders. Once a week, the Krusaders assembled to play teams fielded by the Police Department, the *Globe*, the distinguished Yankee law firm of Hale and Dorr, or the Association for Protecting the Constitutional Rights of the Spanish-Speaking. Dressed in white T-shirts, with "Boston Parks and Recreation" stitched across them in blue, their wives and children cheering on the sidelines, a case of beer cooling in a trash can filled with ice, they played a combative, knuckles-in-the-dirt brand of ball.

One August afternoon, Colin and Budget Director Dave Davis left City Hall early to pick up the Krusaders' bats, balls, and other gear, which Davis stowed at home. In the Budget Director's car, they drove past the Public Gardens, where white swan boats cruised the blue lagoon; along Newbury Street with its sidewalk cafes and expensive boutiques; through the Back Bay to spacious Copley Square, where the granite façade of the Boston Public Library confronted the Romanesque splendors of Trinity Church. Turning there, and crossing the railroad tracks, they entered a shabbier, scruffier part of the city which Colin had never visited before—the South End.

Not to be confused with remote South Boston, the South End was downtown's backyard, a largely neglected swath of the inner city, extending from Chinatown on the north to Roxbury's black heartland on the south, from the Back Bay on the west to the rushing traffic of the John F. Fitzgerald Expressway on the east. Colin had heard about the South End for years—idle boasts from high school classmates about their visits to sleazy bars or bordellos there or, later, from his friends at law school, tales of the great blues belted out at the quarter's black nightclubs. But, attracted by neither jazz nor sin, and largely unaware of its other assets, Colin had never set foot there before that afternoon.

As Davis' car crept through the crowded streets, dodging pushcart peddlers, skid-row bums, stickball players, and children scampering in the overflowing hydrants, Colin was intrigued by the animation around him. What he noticed first was the varied colors of the children—black, white, brown, even a scattering of yellow. He had seen enough of Boston's neighborhoods by then to know how rare this was. Most of the city was divided into ethnic enclaves, jealously guarded turfs where intruders of other nationalities, much less different races, were not welcome. Yet here, five months after Martin Luther King's assassination, blacks and whites were throwing baseballs, not rocks, at each other. It was exactly the kind of racial harmony which Colin was trying to foster in his work for the Mayor.

Next he was struck by the bow-front brick houses lining those narrow streets. Ever since his first summer working for the Cambridge Historical Commission, Colin had been charmed by Victorian architecture, and he quickly noted that behind the grime and disrepair and misconceived alterations, many of these buildings were fine examples of mid nineteenth-century domestic architecture. And when Dave Davis pulled up in front of his four-story town house on West Brookline Street and ushered him inside, Colin was struck by how comfortable, even elegant, the renovated building was. On their way to the ball field, he questioned Dave about the South End—about its history, its recent redevelopment, its surprising variety and racial integration.

Boston was still foreign terrain to Colin. During his first year at the Mayor's office, he and Joan lived in suburban Watertown. That was hardly unusual. Most of Kevin White's aides lived in the suburbs, a situation which was causing the Mayor increasing embarrassment. Hostile City Councilmen lost no opportunity to remind the voters that the Mayor's Whiz Kids had sought out sanctuaries comfortably remote from Boston's problems.

The second year, Colin and Joan moved just across the city line to Brighton, but that leafy, quasi-suburban neighborhood still seemed too detached from the pressing issues with which Colin grappled at work. Having committed himself to the war on urban poverty and injustice, he felt he should be living closer to the front line.

Moreover, both Colin and Joan yearned for the racial, ethnic, and class mix to be found only in the inner city. Weary of the long bus ride to and from City Hall, Colin wanted to be near enough to walk or cycle to work; they wanted to take more advantage of the city's theaters, concert halls, and restaurants. Finally, there was the prospect of restoring their own Victorian town house.

In the winter of 1969–70, they started looking in earnest—consulting real estate agents, scouring the *Globe*'s classified ads, or simply touring the city in their blue Dodge, surveying prospective neighborhoods. They looked at Federal town houses on the steep slopes of Beacon Hill and French Academic brownstones along the boulevards of the Back Bay, but soon concluded that such elegant surroundings were beyond their means.

Some Greek Revival houses around Charlestown's Monument Square were well within their price range. Indeed, Charlestown had many of the attributes they were seeking. But, overwhelmingly white and working class, it lacked the critical element of diversity. Moreover, its special sense of grievance, nursed over the centuries, had left Charlestown an insular community unlikely to welcome outsiders of any kind, much less Harvard-educated lawyers. The few Townies they encountered on their visits—longshoremen trudging home from the docks or teenagers lounging outside the taverns on Bunker Hill Street—glared at them suspiciously. Colin and Joan didn't want to be *that* far out on the urban frontier.

As they eliminated neighborhood after neighborhood, Colin's thoughts kept returning to the South End. He tried to communicate his enthusiasm to Joan, and on several occasions drove her through the area, pointing out graceful squares, copper fountains, leafy parks, a particularly fine doorway or roof line. But Joan was skeptical. So much of what she glimpsed from the car's windows was drab, deteriorated, or destroyed. Burnt-out shells violated the Victorian landscape. The alleys were heaped with trash. Drunks and derelicts lounged on street corners. The pedestrians seemed mostly black and Puerto Rican. Joan wanted to live in the city, she wanted diversity and integration, but how could she raise her children in a place like this? This was going too far. So, for a time, Colin stopped talking about the South End.

Then one day in February 1970, Joan fell into conversation with a friend. Linda MacGregor and her husband, Jim, had lived in the South End since 1965 and were enthusiastic advocates of its brand of city living. Joan began firing questions at her: What was it like? Was it safe? What did she do with her children all day? Linda bubbled with reassurance. Her two girls hopscotched and jumped rope on the sidewalk, rode their bicycles to the Charles River, flew kites in the park, made friends with Italian butchers, Irish bartenders, proprietors of Spanish *bodegas*. Most important, Linda told Joan about the John Winthrop Nursery School on Marlborough Street in the Back Bay, where many of the newer South End families sent their children. Linda raved about the Winthrop, its attention to the individual child, its concern with fostering independence, resourcefulness, and initiative; it sounded perfect, just the sort of school the Divers had been looking for. That evening, Joan excitedly told Colin what she'd learned, and with her doubts assuaged, she agreed to look for a house in the South End.

At first it seemed hopeless. Much of what the Divers saw fell into one of three categories: already rehabilitated town houses in the heart of the zone favored by the "young professionals" and thus priced at $50,000 or more; buildings which still needed lots of work, selling at $18,000 to $25,000 but well outside the rehabilitated zone and on the fringes of the black ghetto; or burnt-out shells and virtual wrecks which could be had for $5,000 to $10,000.

The first category was too expensive, the second too risky, the third too much work.

Those buildings which were habitable, cheap, and appropriately located were invariably rooming houses. Long Boston's lodging-house district, the South End still had about 235 licensed lodging houses accommodating 14,000 tenants, many of them elderly single people who had occupied the same house, sometimes the same room, for years. (Most were white; the rural Southern blacks who had flooded the district generally arrived in large families, settling in crowded apartments.) The lodging houses ranged from shabby but neat premises kept by gruff, demanding Irish landladies to sordid, crumbling warrens neglected by absentee landlords. One after another, they were snapped up by eager "young professionals," who evicted the tenants and converted the buildings to single-family dwellings.

Every weekend that winter, the Divers looked at rooming houses. When tenants reluctantly opened their doors to these visitors from a foreign realm, they revealed terrible scenes of squalor, desperation, and loneliness. Most rooms were dark and gloomy, drapes pulled tight against cold, light, and the outside world. A dank, musty smell—mixed of cooking oil, sweat, and garbage—hung in the air. Often a piece of cardboard was tacked over a broken windowpane. Chunks of ceiling plaster littered the floor. Gas burners roared perpetually to ward off the chill as the roomers huddled in ragged sweaters and overcoats. Some tenants, particularly the older men, were exquisitely polite as they showed the potential buyers around their cramped quarters. Others, knowing they might be on the street within weeks, regarded the Divers with sullen resentment.

But roomers were cowed, beaten people, not accustomed to challenging their fate. Only once did the Divers encounter open hostility. In one house with several tiny apartments, a young white couple glared ferociously at them. Then the husband hissed through clenched teeth, "I just want you to know that if you buy this house, we're staying. You aren't pushing us out!" It was particularly unsettling because the couple looked uncannily like the Divers—only a bit more bedraggled and desperate.

After weeks of this sort of thing, Colin and Joan decided not to buy a rooming house. They couldn't reconcile themselves to the prospect of evicting tenants, particularly old, helpless people, and they told the brokers they wanted a house from which only the previous owner would be displaced. The Divers realized that their stand contained an element of self-delusion. If they were to buy an empty house, they wouldn't inquire too closely as to how many tenants had been removed to make way for the sale. And even if they displaced nobody themselves, they knew they were part of a movement which was forcing hundreds, perhaps thousands, of people out of the South End.

If they hadn't fully recognized that before, it was brought home to them with some force on May 2, 1970, when they took the Fourth Annual South End House Tour. Sponsored by the South End Historical Society, the tour sought to attract families like the Divers into the neighborhood by displaying impressive examples of earlier restoration. One of the showplaces was the Brookline Street town house of Mr. and Mrs. Jerry Pinkney. Colin and Joan lingered there for half an hour, admiring the handsome marble fireplaces, the parquet floors, and the twelve-foot ceilings decorated with elaborate plaster-work. But when they emerged onto the high stoop, they found fifty demon-strators parading on the sidewalk below with signs reading: "Pioneers Out—Take Your Victoriana with You," and "The Historical Society Is a Lackey of the Real Estate Agents." From the bed of a pickup truck parked in the street, a man with a bullhorn harangued the crowd: "History isn't old houses. History is people!"

But who were the South End's people? For more than a century, wave after wave of immigration had broken over the district, each inundation washing away at least part of the previous one. The South End had been called "a nursery of democracy," because, in succession, Yankees, Irish, Italians, Greeks, Syrians, Lebanese, Chinese, Russian and German Jews, blacks, and Hispanics had learned there the ways of urban America. If middle-class professionals were now "discovering" the area, it had been discovered and rediscovered many times before, each group of settlers making it over in its own image.

Indeed, the South End had literally been "made" to accommodate its first inhabitants. When John Winthrop arrived from Charlestown in 1630, he found the hilly Shawmut peninsula almost completely surrounded by water and con-nected to the mainland by a narrow isthmus, or "neck." Not until the early nineteenth century, with the town rapidly running out of building lots, did Boston construct sea walls so that a network of streets could be laid out on the neck, the future South End. And only in the 1850s did the city fathers seri-ously attempt to develop the district. Fearing that central Boston would soon be an Irish ghetto, officials determined to build a fashionable new residential community in the South End which might serve as a magnet to the departing middle class.

It was an era of enthusiasm for nature; cities were regarded as sinks of squalor and corruption. To counter the lure of the countryside, the South End's planners studded their new district with grassy residential squares, parks, fountains, statues, and tree-lined avenues. Its architecture was distinctive too—red brick or brownstone town houses with mansard roofs, bulging bow fronts, and high stoops, the kitchens and dining rooms tucked under the stoops at street level, while the formal parlors opened from the top of the steep flight of stairs. Ranged in long rows down the avenues or in ovals around the parks, their russet façades gave the district a pleasing, restful symmetry.

In size and opulence, the dwellings varied according to the income of their occupants. The South End attracted few of Boston's genuine aristocrats; the old shipping and mercantile families preferred Beacon Hill or the emerging suburbs. But it drew much of the new wealth, the prosperous merchants in shoes, leather, liquor, and grain who built spacious houses ringing Blackstone,

Franklin and Chester squares, high-shouldered mansions, often with more than twenty-five rooms and costing up to $30,000.

As the district was extended west on new land claimed from the bay, its scale declined. Around Concord and Rutland squares, or in the adjacent cobblestoned streets, lesser merchants bought mass-produced houses. And in the alleys behind the squares, clerks and salesmen rented small row houses. Indeed, the city's original vision of the South End as an elite gold coast faded quickly. As early as 1855, confronted with lagging sales, Mayor Jerome Smith proposed that the South End be opened to "mechanics of limited means."

Meanwhile, the city began developing still another area of fine homes—the Back Bay. There it abandoned the tradition of intimate squares, modeled on London and Bath, for the more dramatic vistas and grand boulevards of Haussmann's Paris. Closer to the traditional upper-class enclave of Beacon Hill, the Back Bay immediately caught the fancy of many wealthy families who had resisted the initial enthusiasm for the South End. By 1870, the Back Bay became *the* place to buy—and the South End, after barely fifteen years in the limelight, was suddenly out of favor.

Socially conscious Bostonians were particularly prey to fears that they had bought in the wrong place. Once convinced of their mistake they did not linger long. John P. Marquand's George Apley recounts how his father came out on the front steps one day and glimpsed an unspeakable sight next door. "'Thunderation,' Father said, 'there is a man in his shirt sleeves on those steps.' The next day he sold his house for what he had paid for it and we moved to Beacon Street. Your grandfather had sensed the approach of change; a man in his shirt sleeves had told him the days of the South End were numbered."

Apley acted just in time. It was 1873, the year of "the Great Panic." The repercussions were felt first along Columbus Avenue, lined with expensive hotels and grand town houses. Hard-pressed owners defaulted on their mortgages, and banks quickly dumped the properties. The sharp drop in values spread to the rest of the South End, which slipped into precipitous decline.

Gradually, its town houses were converted to multiple dwellings—the larger homes to apartment buildings and tenements, the smaller ones to lodging houses. The city had been so concerned with retaining the middle class it had glutted the market with expensive homes, while virtually ignoring the needs of the working class, which now poured into the void. At first, the lodging houses catered primarily to young people from New England and the Maritime Provinces who had a "film of glorious prospects before their eyes, to be clerks and salesmen, to enter business college and blossom out as bookkeepers at six dollars a week."

So long as such young people predominated, the lodging houses were repositories of hope and ambition. But before long those on the threshold of their productive lives were replaced by others who had long since left theirs behind. In 1895, a Boston journalist visited "Gunn's Lodging House. Friendly Lodging House for Sober Men. Prices 15, 20, 25, 35, 50 cts. No Drunken Men Admitted." Behind the twenty-cent door was a dark, narrow room. "It contained ten cot beds, five on each long side with an aisle between the fives," he wrote. "Of two or three beds still vacant, I chose the one nearest the window. It was woven wire on a wooden frame a few inches high, had a grimy mattress, two dirty sheets, a bloodstained pillow and a single comforter with a great rent in the centre."

By 1900, with 37,000 lodgers, the South End was the nation's largest rooming-house district—a drab, dismal quarter which one social worker called "the city wilderness." Its once peaceful squares were now hemmed in by sooty factories, noisy machine shops, dusty brickyards, grim warehouses, and the incessant rumble of trucks and steam engines. As with Charlestown to the north, the South End had become a "vestibule" of the inner city. Through its narrow funnel passed five heavily traveled arteries, two railroads, and the Boston Elevated Street Railway, whose line from Scollay Square to the South End was completed in 1901.

The South End's deterioration was greatly hastened by the erection of the El along Washington Street. Just as in Charlestown, it blighted everything in its path with soot, noise, and darkness. Nor was it there to serve the immediate population. The El didn't even stop within the South End, only at its two extremities—Dover and Northampton streets. It had been built to provide the burgeoning suburban middle class with speedy service to and from their offices, and if, by so doing, it had to pass through Charlestown and the South End, then the businessman from Dedham or Wakefield could simply avert his glance and spare himself the bleak vistas which flashed past the windows.

The two El stations became centers of a garish night life. Three theaters offering vaudeville, popular plays, and operettas "turned night into day" on Dover Street. Around them spread a rash of saloons, all-night restaurants, dime museums, penny arcades, pawnshops, and pool rooms. "When the work of the day is over," wrote one social worker, "crowds of pleasure seekers fill the sidewalks; hotels and theaters become brilliant with lights; the hurdy-gurdy jingles merrily; and the street is changed for a time into a sort of fair, where evil offers itself in many attractive guises." Indeed, the innocent pleasures of the boulevard gradually attracted prostitutes, drug traffickers, confidence men, pickpockets, fences, and petty criminals of all varieties. And just as New York's alcoholics congregated under the city's elevated tracks along the famed Bowery, so portions of Washington Street, in the latticed gloom of the El, became Boston's skid row.

Yet, for many, the South End remained a residential quarter. As the Yankees departed, their place was taken first by the Irish, who clustered around the Cathedral of the Holy Cross on Washington Street, which in 1875 became the seat of the new Boston Archdiocese. For the next fifty years the Irish ruled the roost in the South End, a tough, contentious breed like John L. Sullivan, the heavyweight champion of the world, who trained at O'Donnell's gym on East Concord Street; "Pea Jacket" Maguire, the iron-fisted boss of Ward Seventeen; and James Michael Curley, born in a cold-water walk-up on Northampton Street.

It was the arrival of the Jews which pushed the Irish into Roxbury and Dorchester. In 1898, the family of Mary Antin, the future writer, settled on Dover Street, where she found a market teeming with the sounds and smells of Eastern Europe, surrounded by open sewers, filth-strewn alleys, houses of prostitution, raucous saloons. "Nothing less than a fire or flood would cleanse this street," she remarked. And yet, for Mary Antin, the South End was a door opening on the wonders of America. Long after she left it, she wrote: "I must never forget that I came away from Dover Street with my hands full of riches. I must not fail to testify that in America a child of the slums owns the land and all that is good in it." Antin's experience was largely replicated by many of those who followed her to the South End. Well into the twentieth century, the district was a classic port of entry that gave immigrants their first lesson in the American experience.

Easing those rites of passage was an extraordinary array of philanthropies. Edward Everett Hale once said the South End was "the most 'charitied' region in Christendom." From his South Congregational Church, Hale pursued the social gospel, culminating in the establishment of a settlement house in his name. Later, South End House was founded by Robert A. Woods, a staunch moralist who believed in "purifying" such neighborhoods by segregating the tramps, alcoholics, and paupers from the "deserving poor," a process he called "factoring out the residuum." Then there were the Lincoln House Association, Harriet Tubman House, Morgan Memorial, the Scots Charitable Society, the Boston Female Asylum, St. Joseph's Home for Sick and Destitute Servant Girls, and a dozen others. Many of these organizations were staffed by graduates of Boston's universities—earnest young men and women who hoped thereby to alleviate the glaring inequalities and injustices of industrial society. By the turn of the century, the South End had become Boston's traditional laboratory for such experiments in altruism.

So long as the "deserving poor" predominated, *noblesse oblige* thrived in the South End. But as stable working-class families continued to move out (the area's population declined from 57,218 in 1950 to 22,775 in 1970) to be replaced by ever more roomers and drifters, and as Anglo-Saxons or Middle European immigrants gave way to Slavs, Mediterraneans, Chinese, and ultimately to blacks and Puerto Ricans (who made up 47 percent of its population by 1970), traditional philanthropy seemed futile. Robert Woods was horrified by the Southern Negroes, whom he found "loud and coarse," "revealing more of the animal qualities than of the spiritual."

When Scollay Square and the West End were demolished in the late fifties and early sixties, many of their denizens migrated to skid row, which, by 1963, provided refuge to 7,000 homeless men, eleven poolrooms, twenty-four liquor stores, and forty-one saloons. More than ever, the South End became the principal haunt of the city's "night people," notably the "white hunters," suburban men who prowled the avenues of "Momma-land" in their late-model cars, looking for black prostitutes. A prominent Republican politician, running for lieutenant governor, had to drop out of the race after police picked him up not far from the 411 Lounge on Columbus Avenue with a black prostitute in his car. Increasingly, respectable people declined to cross the New Haven Railroad tracks into the South End. On warm spring evenings, the poet Robert Lowell felt a frisson of terror when he threw open his Back Bay windows to "hear the South End / the razor's edge / of Boston's negro culture." For most white Bostonians, the South End had simply ceased to exist.

But to some who stumbled on it accidentally, the district was a revelation; one visitor called it "the most beautiful slum in the world." The very suddenness of its decline had been its architectural salvation. A few buildings had gone through bizarre transformations: the magnificent Deacon House, once the South End's finest mansion, had become an art school, a dance hall, a hardware store; Edward Everett Hale's church became a Catholic cathedral, the Columbia Theater, then a burlesque house before it was demolished in 1957. But most private owners did not have the resources for extensive renovation. As town houses became rooming houses, sinks were merely moved into parlors. Architecturally, most of the South End remained frozen in a mid-nineteenth-century tableau.

From time to time, a few middle-class families made a stab at rehabilitating sections of the South End, but nothing came of it, probably because the neighborhood was too remote from the downtown business, shopping, and entertainment districts. Then, in 1965, the New Haven Railroad yards, just across the tracks in the Back Bay, were transformed into the Prudential Center—a fifty-two-story office tower, the 1,000-room Sheraton-Boston Hotel, a huge shopping mall, and three twenty-four-story apartment buildings. In effect, downtown had been extended a mile to the south and, suddenly, the South End was infinitely more attractive as an in-town residential district.

The first wave in the middle-class resettlement of the South End consisted of gays. An old real estate maxim advised, "Follow the fairies"; for, not welcome in many conventional neighborhoods, gays often gravitated to "fringe" communities where houses could be picked up for a song and later sold for a symphony. As they scrubbed and redecorated the old bow-fronts, word of the astonishing results spread to straight members of the artistic community—painters, sculptors, and, particularly, architects—who became the second wave of immigrants to "the new South End."

Then came others, more conventional young people, some of them drawn by the bargain prices on Victorian bow-fronts, some by the neighborhood's convenience to downtown, still others by the racial and social integration, the opportunity to participate in "a great urban adventure." It was the start of a phenomenon later labeled "gentrification," a British term for the resettlement of working-class neighborhoods by more affluent young families. The American model was Georgetown, Washington's charming enclave of Federal brick town houses, where private rehabilitation had begun as early as the 1930s. But soon the movement spread to Philadelphia's Society Hill, Baltimore's Bolton Hill, Park Slope in Brooklyn, the Upper West Side of Manhattan, and San Francisco's Mission District. And by 1963, several hundred middle-class families had established themselves in the South End, particularly on Union Park and other streets nearest downtown.

At first it wasn't easy. Mortgages were difficult, if not impossible, to obtain. Applications came back stamped "unstable neighborhood." The banks began to relent only after the city assigned the South End a high priority for urban renewal. In their 1960 development program, John Collins and Ed Logue lumped the South End with Charlestown as "gray" areas in need of immediate attention. But Logue sensed the neighborhood's exquisite ambiguity, describing it as "too promising to ignore, too near the edge of disaster for remedial action to be delayed." The South End was trembling on the edge of something. The question was: what?

Planning for renewal in the South End and Charlestown began almost simultaneously, but the fierce resistance which Logue met in Charlestown, culminating in the tumultuous hearings of January 1963, made him tread more carefully in the South End. The initial plan, calling for a grassy "common way" running the full length of the community, encountered some difficulty, so he quickly scrapped it. Logue realized that, unlike Charlestown, which was dominated by Irish Catholics, the South End had no single group with which one could bargain. The 606-acre renewal area was the country's largest, and probably its most diverse, so negotiations were opened with sixteen distinct interest groups. Even those with the least political clout—rooming-house tenants, skid-row alcoholics, black Southern migrants, and the "night people"— were loosely represented in the process by United South End Settlements. After two years of negotiations, the final plan was overwhelmingly endorsed at a South End hearing in August 1965 and later that year by the City Council.

It was a heavily political plan, with something for everyone. Demolition would be concentrated on the heavily trafficked, badly deteriorated avenues, displacing 3,550, or 19 percent, of the South End's households. Nearly 3,000 structures, most of them along the tree-shaded, still shabbily genteel side streets, would be rehabilitated. New construction would provide up to 2,500 federally subsidized low- and moderate-income rental units; 800 low-income public housing units; four schools and seven playgrounds. Forty-six of the community's 116 liquor licenses would be removed, which, it was hoped, would sharply reduce skid row and discourage the "night people." The sleaziest of the rooming houses were slated for demolition, but efforts would be made to refurbish the better ones.

There remained one acute, unresolved tension. Although the plan committed the redevelopment authority to provide "an economically, socially and racially integrated community" and to ensure "the availability of standard housing at rentals that all displaced low-income residents wishing to remain in the South End could afford," there were those who doubted that such objectives could be achieved. Already by 1970, the South End had changed markedly. In the decade since 1960, its median income had risen from $4,542 to $6,122; its proportion of professionals and technicians had increased 10 percent, while its laborers and service people had declined 15 percent. To some, this was a sign that renewal was working, that the shabby old slum was regaining some of its past grandeur, that—as the Boston *Herald* put it—the South End was "blossoming out as the 'in' place for affluent upper-middle-class, well-educated people to live." To others, it was a warning that the middle-class young professionals were inexorably squeezing out the poor, the old, and the black, and that the very racial, social, and ethnic mix which had attracted some of the newcomers was now being threatened by their presence. It was a tension that would sharpen in years to come.

The Divers almost gave up. In the month after they told their real estate agents they didn't want to buy a rooming house, not a single suitable house came on the market. They were about ready to forget the South End and look elsewhere when, in mid-May, one of the agents called to say she had "a really good deal." A Greek couple had bought a house on West Newton Street, had done some rehabilitation, but were in over their heads and wanted to get out. They were asking $36,000, but were so eager to sell that the agent was certain they would take less.

Late one afternoon, the Divers went down to look at 118 West Newton Street. When she saw it, Joan was dismayed. It was a total disaster, she thought, beyond all hope. The old spruce floors were rotting, the window sashes were splintered, the plaster ornaments had fallen from much of the parlor ceiling. The bottom two floors were livable, but the top two looked as if they had barely survived a hurricane—wooden lath showing through the walls, wire and cables trailing along the halls, two bathrooms with exposed plumbing and uncovered plasterboard.

But Colin's practiced eyes saw past the disarray to the essential features of the fine brick town house which had been built in 1865 (and first occupied by William S. Hills, a prosperous flour broker). The identical houses lining the block between Columbus Avenue and Tremont Street were fairly typical of that vintage, with their bow-fronts, mansard roofs, and high stoops. What particularly intrigued Colin was the interior detail—the Italianate marble fireplaces, the ornate plasterwork on the high ceilings, the cornice moldings, and the medallions in the center of each parlor from which chandeliers had once been suspended. And there were other attractions too: a large backyard in which the boys could play until they were old enough to go out on the street; a separate apartment on the bottom floor, with its own entrance under the stoop, which would bring in some badly needed income; and the prospect of a reasonable price. The house would take a lot of work, but that was precisely what Colin wanted, a tough job he could get his fingers into. Yes, he decided, this one would do.

Colin's enthusiasm soon won Joan over, and a few days later they made a bid of $27,000. To their surprise, it was accepted almost immediately. Though most banks were still disinclined to give mortgages in the South End, Suffolk Franklin Savings Bank was beginning to finance the young professionals moving into the neighborhood. The Divers got a twenty-year mortgage at 7 percent, requiring an $8,000 down payment—all they could scrape together. (Getting the house insured was more difficult. Insurance companies wanted nothing at all to do with the South End; they wouldn't write any theft insurance at all, and fire insurance was available only through a state-sponsored risk-pooling program.)

Their parents were flabbergasted when they learned where Colin and Joan were settling. Ben Diver, who had lived in the South End forty-five years before, associated the area with derelicts and shiftless Southern blacks; he didn't want any son—or grandson—of his living there. George Makechnie wasn't pleased either, and he had more recent evidence to support his position. Three years earlier, George had shattered his left arm in an auto accident. Unable to drive back and forth to Lexington, the Makechnies had sold their house there and moved into a Prudential Center apartment. Several days a week, George's route took him along West Newton Street. On almost every walk, he was solicited by prostitutes and once he saw a police car screech down the street, with policemen firing at an escaping felon. It was a dangerous street and he couldn't understand why Colin and Joan wanted to live there. As soon as George could drive again, the Makechnies moved back to Lexington, buying a new house there in June 1970, just as their daughter and son-in-law were moving in the opposite direction.

On Saturday, August 1, with some friends lending a hand, the Divers moved into their new house. It was a sweltering, humid evening and by the time they were installed they were aching, parched, slippery with perspiration. Out in the clamorous night, bottles shattered on the sidewalks, screams mixed with raucous laughter, while fire engines and police cars wailed up and down the avenues. As Colin and Joan thrashed on the damp sheets, unable to sleep, they asked themselves, what have we done?

But when Sunday dawned gold and green, the sun slanting off the rich brick façade across the street, their enthusiasm came surging back and they started putting their new house in order. For a few weeks, Joan worked at Colin's side, but soon she found that her two sons kept her so busy she couldn't be of any real help. So Colin, not unhappily, shouldered the whole job. Every evening when he got back from City Hall, he grabbed a quick supper, then changed into khaki pants and a T-shirt and set to work with his saws and planes and scrapers. He started on the fourth-floor bathroom—attaching the sink and toilet, laying down the tile, painting and wallpapering. Late one night after he had grouted the last tile, he summoned his wife and, for a few glorious moments, they sat cross-legged on the floor, happily admiring their first finished room.

Colin lavished hours on the backyard, once nothing but hardscrabble covered with weeds. He carted in gravel and soil, raising a mound, which he covered with a rock garden. From South End demolition sites, he gathered paving stones and old bricks with which to build a patio and terraced garden. And one day, walking by a water-main excavation, he noticed huge slabs of fir and spruce which had been driven into the ground to buttress the sides of the trench. Colin asked if he could have the wood when the job was done and the foreman said sure, it would save them from hauling it away. Colin took a truckful, enough to build a large deck.

The work he liked best was restoring the ornamental plaster on the parlor ceilings. It was an elaborate Victorian conceit—lacy filigree, scrolls, plumes, rosettes, wreaths, and leafery—but previous owners had covered it all with so much paint that the detail was blurred or obscured. Colin rigged up a plat-form—a broad plank supported by two ladders—where he would sit beneath the twelve-foot ceiling, squirting water from a Windex bottle, soaking the paint until it came loose, then flicking it off with tiny wooden molding tools. In many places, the decoration had already fallen away in chunks, so Colin made latex molds and cast new pieces to complete the pattern. Restoring the ceiling's original glory was meticulous, demanding, painfully slow work—a foot an hour, and each parlor had sixty-five feet of ornament. So for two years, Colin spent almost every Saturday afternoon up on the platform, wetting and scraping, scraping and wetting, while the Metropolitan Opera poured from a radio on the floor. His arms ached, his fingers cramped, water soaked his hair and got in his eyes, but it was his favorite time of the week.

The most demanding job of all was the octagonal window—sometimes called "the captain's bridge" because it looked like a ship's pilothouse—which jutted out from the mansard roof. Its wooden siding had rotted away, so one weekend Colin tied a rope around his waist, secured it to a radiator, and climbed out the window. Bracing himself like a mountain climber against the roof, he ripped off the old boards and hammered on new ones, then repainted them. Forty feet below, passersby shook their heads in astonishment at the strange new people in 118.

This bemused view of the Divers' urban homesteading was shared by many of their friends—notably Bill Cowin, Colin's colleague in the Mayor's office. A native of Brookline, Cowin had bought a house in nearby Newton and re-sisted all hints from the Mayor and Barney Frank that he should move into the city. Professionally, he could devote himself to the city's revival, but he would never subject his family to the rigors of city life and he needled Colin relent-lessly about his dedication to "the urban experience." One summer weekend in 1970, returning from Cape Cod, the Divers and the Cowins drove up West Newton Street to find a noisy crowd gathered around an automobile which had crashed into a house directly across from the Divers'. One of their neighbors, they were told, had drunk too much, staggered into his car, and fishtailed down the street, smashing into one of the brick bow-fronts. Standing on the sidewalk, watching the crowd, Colin sighed, "Well, I see things are normal around here. Home, sweet home!" At which Bill laughed, clapped his friend on the shoulder, and said, "Old buddy, you are absolutely crazy!"

Soon the Divers concluded that if they were crazy, it was "a special kind of craziness," which many of those around them shared, an outlook which united them with their neighbors in a way they had never experienced before. Their block was still a diverse one, roughly half black, with a heavy sprinkling of white lodging houses, but every year more young professionals had moved onto the street—engineers, lawyers, teachers, and artists. These early "pioneers," as they sometimes called themselves, were drawn together in part by shared values and concerns, in part by the very disapproval of their parents, the incomprehension of their friends, the gibes of their professional colleagues. Many had read Jane Jacobs' paean to urban living, *The Death and Life of Great American Cities*. Now they were fleeing suburban "sterility" and "ennui," discovering for themselves the perils, stimulations, tumults, and delights of city life, and this produced a vital sense of community. When George and Susan Thomas moved onto the block in 1963, they were welcomed in the adjacent alley by Jack and Arlyn Hastings, carrying a bottle of champagne and singing a song which celebrated the rigors of neighborhood life. That was the way it was, a constant shuttling between houses, to borrow an onion, a bike, or a plumber's wrench. The pioneers helped each other, sympathized with each other's misfortunes, laughed over the absurdities of South End life.

But it was a constricted community, defined as much by race and class as by geography. Though most of the newcomers had wanted to live in a racially and economically mixed neighborhood, once they were there they had little contact with people very different from themselves. A few middle-class black families eventually moved onto the block and were accepted into the community. But, with a few notable exceptions, the young professionals rarely mixed with the poor—black or white.

One exception was Eldred "Max" Hiscock. Raised in a Maine farming community, Max told of marrying a woman "for whom one man wasn't enough," and going with her to Boston, where she promptly ran off with a railroad conductor, leaving him to fend for himself in a city where he felt a stranger. Like many similar men, Max drifted into a South End lodging house, where he lived for nearly thirty years in a basement room, sleeping on a canvas cot, surrounded by piles of newspapers. A woman upstairs cooked his meals and cleaned his room. Then a doctor purchased the house and evicted the roomers. For a while, Max lived in another lodging house, but without his old friend to care for him, his room descended into such squalor that he was evicted again. He took to living on the streets, sleeping in doorways, cadging handouts, which he used to buy cafeteria meals and to support a serious drinking habit.

But Max had a kind of dignity. He disguised his drinking well; it never made him aggressive, only discursive. Even when the police took him away to "dry out," he came back and reported that he'd been to see his dying mother in Maine. He wasn't an alcoholic, Max insisted, just a man who'd fallen on hard times. Soon he became a kind of mascot on the block, ambling through the gutters or sitting out on one of the stoops, talking of the old days when there'd been seventeen rooming houses on that block alone. He adored children and they loved him. Often he could be seen in the street, trying to jump rope or play hopscotch, his arms extended like a Maine scarecrow, his black overcoat flopping behind him as he ran.

One day he fell into conversation with Josh Young, a trust officer at the State Street Bank, who lived on West Newton Street. When Max mentioned that he was sixty-two years old, Josh asked whether he was receiving social security. No, Max said, he'd never applied because he didn't have a copy of his birth certificate. Josh wrote off to Maine, obtained the certificate, and helped Max fill out the necessary forms; after a time, back came a check for $350.

Max was delighted, but bewildered. It was more money than he'd ever seen before and he didn't know what to do with it. Afraid to keep so much money on his person, he asked Josh to hold it for him, so the young banker deposited the check and subsequent payments of seventy dollars a month in a joint account at his bank. Every afternoon at four o'clock, when Josh came home, Max would show up on the Youngs' stoop to pick up three dollars. Gradually, he came to regard the stoop as his home, and Josh and his wife, Holly, often found him curled up on the stairs with a bottle cradled in his arms. They grew intensely protective of him; once, during the annual South End House Tour, police tried to remove Max from the stoop but they were driven off by an enraged Holly. Max returned the loyalty, presenting the Youngs with little gifts he picked up on his wanderings.

Then one afternoon in August 1970—a few days after the Divers moved onto the block—Josh came home to find Max lying on the stoop, dead. Holly laid a sheet over her old friend. Later that afternoon, as Colin returned from work, he saw the shrouded body stretched out at the top of his neighbors' stairs. He stopped and gaped. Here was something you would expect on the streets of Calcutta—an unsettling introduction to West Newton Street.

Once Josh had asked Max what should be done with the money in their account if anything happened to him, and Max replied, "Do something for the children." At the time of his death, the block's residents were already converting a vacant lot near the Divers' house into a vest-pocket park and playground, so the Youngs contributed the remaining $280 of Max's money to the project, which the neighbors named Max Hiscock Park. With its shade trees, sandbox, and jungle gym, the park was a protected spot to which the young professionals could bring their children, the legatees of the new South End; but for those who remembered Max, it was also a reminder of the old South End, which they were reluctantly—but relentlessly—displacing.

12

Twymon

Hello, Dolly!
Well, hello, Dolly!
It's so nice to have you back where you belong,
You're lookin' swell, Dolly,
We can tell, Dolly,
You're still glowin',
You're still crowin',
You're still goin' strong!

While the chorus massed against the tintypes of Olde New York, Dolly Gallagher Levi, in flaming plumage and red satin dress, sashayed down the bulb-lit runway, growling and rasping:

Wa, wa, wow, fellas,
Look at the old girl now, fellas,
Dolly'll never go away again!

The curtain fell across the Shubert Theater stage and Rachel Twymon lurched to her feet, clapping, cheering, calling for more. Her mother shouted "Bravo!"; her friend Ola Smith called "Encore! Encore!"; her two oldest sons, Richard and George, stomped and whistled. It had been a glorious evening. The theater was always a treat for Rachel, her favorite night out. Even better was a big, brassy musical, fresh from a long run on Broadway. And best of all was a black production such as this, headlined by two stars like Cab Calloway and Pearl Bailey.

After five tumultuous curtain calls, the house lights went up and the audience filed out. Rachel—still resonating to Pearl Bailey's portrait of a middle-aged black woman who triumphs over life's vicissitudes—was humming her

175

favorite song from the show, "With the rest of them / With the best of them /I can hold my head up high."

In front of the Shubert that icy night in January 1970 waited a line of taxis. Rachel headed for the first cab in the rank, opened the door, and said, "We'd like to go to the Orchard Park housing project."

"Un-unh," growled the white cabbie. "I ain't going to Roxbury tonight."

Rachel stiffened. One of those, she thought. Well, it was partly her fault; she shouldn't have mentioned the project—that always scared them. Walking to the second cab, she smiled and in a carefully modulated voice said, "Hampden and Prescott streets, please."

"Sorry, lady," said the driver. "Try somebody else."

The third cab turned her down. So did the fourth. And the fifth consented only after she changed her tactics, asking to be taken to Dudley Square. But that left them four blocks from Orchard Park, a long walk for Rachel along icy, snowdrifted sidewalks. By the time they reached home, chilled and tired, her sense of well-being had worn off. How could you hold your head up high when you couldn't even get a cab to take you home? "That's it," she told her children. "We're getting out of this goddamn project!"

The Twymons had lived in Orchard Park for nearly five years. Rachel had never wanted to live in public housing—she felt it was demeaning—but she hadn't had much choice. Utterly dependent on her welfare check, she couldn't afford a private apartment large enough for her family of seven. Yet as the years went by she had gradually become accustomed to project living. Her four-bedroom apartment was unusually spacious. She had furnished it with items provided by welfare or loaned by friends. Sunlight streamed through her windows, nourishing a forest of plants: pachysandra, wandering Jews, begonias, African violets, dieffenbachia. And she'd made some good friends in the project.

But the advantages of Orchard Park were increasingly overshadowed by the drawbacks. There were no elevators, and, with her arthritic legs, Rachel had difficulty climbing to her third-floor apartment. The buildings were thirty years old and showing their age: roofs leaked, plumbing failed, paint peeled. Then there was the location—deep in the heart of one of Roxbury's worst neighborhoods, far from the theaters, movies, and concert halls that Rachel patronized whenever she could afford them. And, of course, like other Roxbury projects, Orchard Park had a reputation for crime which kept cabdrivers, repairmen, and delivery boys away.

The project wasn't as dangerous as many whites imagined, but it was increasingly perilous. Some of the crime was merely annoying. Once, after the boys returned from a church-sponsored summer camp, Rachel had washed their dirty socks and underwear and hung them in the project courtyard to dry; by evening, somebody had stolen them all. Other crime was more serious. Once, when Rachel was confined to bed with a fresh outbreak of lupus, Richard and George took the family laundry to a nearby laundromat. On the way, they were set on by drug addicts who took all their money, then beat them because they didn't have more.

Rachel appealed to the Welfare Department, complaining that she had to send her sons on such dangerous missions because her own washing machine was broken, and the department bought her a new one. But her total dependence on welfare troubled her. She often complained to her social workers that she wasn't receiving everything she was entitled to. When her sons' socks and underwear were stolen, she asked for an emergency grant to buy new ones. Her social worker told her that "eighty-nine cents is excessive for a pair of children's socks and the price could be reduced with more careful shopping." Rachel exploded, accusing the social worker of discriminating against her. Later, she objected strenuously when the department failed to reimburse her for taxi trips to and from the hospital.

The "extreme hostility" which several of the welfare workers detected in Rachel—and about which they often complained in their reports—apparently reflected her shame and frustration. One social worker, who became friendly with Rachel, concluded that she was "anxious to become financially independent as she is very unhappy on welfare rolls." Her doctors had warned her repeatedly that her chronic disease would not permit her to take a regular job.

For a brief period in the late sixties, Rachel had seemed on her way to self-sufficiency. By 1966, her lupus was sufficiently in remission for her to take a part-time job as a saleswoman at Lindy's, a clothing store in the Dudley Station area. But as racial hostility built in Roxbury, the store's owner, Hyman Levy, wanted out. He'd grown fond of Rachel and asked her if she'd like to buy the store. Rachel only laughed. "Man!" she said. "You must be crazy." Of eighty-nine members of the Dudley Station Merchants' Association that year, only three were black. But Levy gave her a packet of materials from the Small Business Administration's equal opportunity program, designed to promote "minority" businesses. After weeks of hesitation, Rachel concluded that this was the chance she'd been waiting for. She applied for an SBA loan and, in August 1967, to the astonishment of her friends and family, she received a commitment for $18,000.

The agency clearly had some doubts that Rachel could make it. The loan was on a year's "trial basis," during which she was to take a course in retail store management at Boston University and would have two counselors from the Service Corps of Retired Executives (SCORE) to guide her. Although she could hire salesgirls and a bookkeeper, she couldn't pay herself a salary until the store began turning a profit, which the SBA said might be as long as three years. Until then, Rachel would have to rely on continued welfare payments, which, by 1967, had reached more than $400 a month. At first, the Welfare Department was not encouraging. If she could get an $18,000 loan from the government, it asked, why did she need welfare? Only after the SBA officials explained the loan's provisions did the department agree to maintain Rachel's Aid to Families with Dependent Children until the store turned a profit.

Rachel's Specialty Shop opened on November 17, 1967, at 2255 Washington Street in the heart of Roxbury's principal shopping district. For a time it seemed to do well. As one of the area's first black proprietors, Rachel was interviewed by newspapers and television—valuable publicity for a young venture. Her SCORE advisers—Leon Margoles and Abe Siegel—reported that she showed "business acumen" and "great dedication." Her welfare worker, dropping by the store one day, found her "much more composed and confident." She came through the riots following Martin Luther King's assassination with only a smashed display window. Then that summer Rachel went back into the hospital for ten weeks and the business began to languish.

Her advisers noted a strange phenomenon. White merchants in the area seemed to welcome Rachel (many of them had known her for years as Mrs. Jenkins' granddaughter or Mrs. Walker's daughter, the cute little girl with the hair ribbon who had run errands for the family). Some of them did everything they could to help, telling her where she could buy goods at the best discount or sending her their own customers. But for some reason, blacks were less supportive. They seemed to resent Rachel's new status. In November 1968, Siegel and Margoles warned: "A great part of the success or failure of such a venture depends on the community's response. One of the surprising elements in Mrs. Twymon's case is that she has not received as much community support as expected." The coming Christmas season, they said, would "make or break this venture."

It broke it. By mid-March, proceeds were so meager that Rachel and her advisers reluctantly decided to close the store. Its fixtures and stock were sold at auction for $4,000, which went back to the SBA. In April, a welfare worker visiting Mrs. Twymon found her "disappointed by the failure," with "no plans for the immediate future."

But three months later, when the worker called again, Rachel was "deeply involved with church activities, which help satisfy her tremendous energy." She had always found solace at her church, Union United Methodist Church in the South End. When her lupus acted up, money ran low, or her children gave her trouble, Rachel would be fortified by a few hours on the hard wooden pews at Union, listening to an uplifting sermon, chanting the responses, and singing a few selections from the *American Service Hymnal,* such as her favorite, "Pass Me Not."

> *Pass me not, O gentle savior,*
> *Hear my humble cry; while on*
> *Others Thou art calling, do*
> *Not pass me by.*
>
> *Savior, Savior, hear my*
> *Humble cry; while on others Thou*
> *Art calling, do not pass me by.*

Now Rachel focused even more of her energy on Union. Every week before services she taught Sunday school for an hour. She often volunteered at the day-care center in the church basement, and in the summers she helped out at the Vacation Bible School, taking children on field trips to the Science Museum, the Coca-Cola and Wonder Bread plants. She served on a multitude of commissions and committees. She became a board member and later chairman of the Cooper Community Center, the church-sponsored settlement house in the South End. In 1966, when Duke Ellington came to perform a concert of "sacred jazz" at Union, Rachel was assistant chairperson for the event.

It wasn't easy for her to get from Orchard Park to Union, more than a mile away. On Sundays, devout church members who lived nearby would drive her down and back; on weekdays, one of the other women who helped at the day-care center often took her there, but she usually had to find her way home alone. With her increasingly painful legs, that could be difficult or, if she took a cab, prohibitively expensive.

The January night in 1970 when she nearly froze coming home from *Hello, Dolly!* was the final straw; it convinced her to apply for an apartment in the new housing project, to be called Methunion Manor, which her church was constructing along Columbus Avenue in the South End. The project, she thought, would be the solution to all her problems: it would get her out of Orchard Park; off the third floor and into a building with an elevator; closer to the theaters, movies, and restaurants she loved; and right next door to her church, where she was already spending so much of her time. The more she thought about it, Methunion Manor seemed a godsend.

To the Reverend Gilbert Caldwell, pastor of Union Methodist, the housing project seemed like the answer to a multitude of problems confronting his famous old church. It would, he hoped, begin to resolve a tension between the church's duty to its members and its responsibility to the broader black community, between its century-old vision of itself and the social reality in which it was embedded.

Union United Methodist Church had its origins in a small group of Negroes who, beginning in the 1790s, attended Boston's predominantly white Bromfield Street Methodist Church. No sect had pursued Negro members more vigorously than the Methodists, and none had reaped a larger harvest. Blacks were attracted by Methodism's evangelical fervor, by its challenge to social conventions, most of all by its explicit opposition to slavery, passed down from its founder, John Wesley, who branded the slave trade "the execrable sum of all villainies." After baptizing the first Negro Methodist in 1758, Wesley asked in his diary, "Shall not our Lord, in due time, have these Heathens also for his inheritance?"

In the revolutionary era, Christianity's egalitarian implications were reinforced by the rhetoric of natural rights. Methodists responded with increasingly uncompromising stands against slavery. Finally, in 1796, the annual conference required members to emancipate their slaves or face expulsion. But this was an advanced position which the Methodists could not hold under fire. As the cotton gin made slavery more profitable, Southern Methodists realized they would be at a competitive disadvantage in the South if they maintained their adamant stance against "the peculiar institution." Faced with a choice between "purity and popularity," antislavery Methodists gradually worked out a temporary accommodation with their slaveholding brethren. As one delegate put it, "Slavery is a great evil, but beyond our control; yet not necessarily a sin. We must then quietly submit to a necessity which we cannot control or remedy." By 1840, Methodist ministers in the South were admonished, "Your only business is to promote the moral and religious improvement of the slaves . . . without in the least degree . . . interfering with their civil condition."

But the sectional conflict could no longer be papered over. Northern Methodists became ever more zealous in the abolitionist cause, and in 1844 Methodists separated into Northern and Southern churches—a division which William Seward, later Lincoln's Secretary of State, called a "sinister prophecy."

Even before the schism, Methodists North and South had segregated their congregations, compelling their black members to sit separately in the "African corner," or "Nigger Heaven." For some Northern blacks, such practices proved intolerable. In 1797, when black members of Philadelphia's St. George's Methodist Church were required to surrender their seats and stand "around the wall," they left the church and founded their own African Methodist Episcopal Church. A similar dispute in New York led to formation of the African Methodist Episcopal Zion Church.

But, especially where Negroes were few in number or where, as in Boston, they valued their relations with whites, most chose to remain within the predominantly white Methodist Church. Indeed, as Southern blacks migrated to Boston, frequently forming their own fundamentalist churches, membership in an established, predominantly white church became a badge of status. For a time, blacks and whites worshipped together in the little Methodist church on Bromfield Street. But the "colored" membership grew steadily and, in 1818, "it was thought desirable that they should have public exercises among themselves both for their own enjoyment and for the benefit of that portion of the city in which they resided." The whites had become uncomfortable with the "vigorous" forms of worship practiced by their colored brethren; the blacks wanted more freedom to worship as they pleased. The division of the congregation into "colored" and "white" meetings was a typical Bostonian solution, permitting continued formal association between the two groups without the need for much personal contact.

Over the next century the "colored" members moved frequently, each successive building paid for by the Bromfield Street Methodist Church, which continued to look after its former members—often referred to in church minutes as "our brethren in black." By 1928, when the congregation began construction of a new building in Lower Roxbury, it was on its own financially. The basement was complete a year later when the stock crash and subsequent Depression made further fund raising impossible. Construction ceased, and for the next two decades the congregation—by then known as Fourth Methodist—held its services and other activities in the spartan basement on Shaw-mut Avenue. Only in the relative prosperity of World War II could the church begin raising money again. Its membership was small and poor, so the new building fund had to be raised bit by bit. Adults contributed a penny a day; children chipped in a nickel a month; the church choir sang at white Methodist churches around Boston, the proceeds going to the building fund; and, ulti-mately, the New England Conference of the Methodist Church—impressed with the sacrifices Fourth Methodist was making on its own—appealed to its member churches to "come to the help of our loyal Negro friends with sub-stantial and generous gifts."

In 1948, just as construction was about to resume, an extraordinary oppor-tunity presented itself. With white Protestants leaving the city in ever-greater numbers, Union Congregational Church, once one of the South End's most distinguished congregations, put its building at the corner of Columbus Ave-nue and West Newton Street up for sale. Built in 1870 at the height of the South End's prosperity, Union was a Victorian Gothic cathedral of Roxbury pudding stone, with a 420-foot steeple towering over the neighborhood; a giant sanctuary, lit by eight stained-glass windows, which seated 1,500; a down-stairs banquet hall; a kitchen; six classrooms, a conference room and offices. All this was available for $65,000, far less than it would cost to complete the structure on Shawmut Avenue. The deal was irresistible. The New England Conference purchased Union and deeded it—debt free—to "our Negro friends." The long hegira of Bromfield Street's "colored members" was over.

But the new building proved less of a blessing than an albatross. As time passed, the cost of maintaining the huge structure increased geometrically while the congregation grew only modestly. On the average Sunday, barely 250 of the faithful filled the front pews of the vast, echoing sanctuary, and the dimes that dropped on the collection plate fell increasingly short of the church's needs.

This reflected a more essential problem. In moving from Lower Roxbury to the South End, the church had turned its back on the heart of the black community. The South End of those days was both less black and less respect-able than Roxbury. Thousands of white roomers filled the lodging houses around the church, and the Southern blacks who poured into the district fol-lowing World War II were more likely to attend Baptist churches or the fun-damentalist storefronts which cropped up along the avenues. West Indians generally preferred their own Episcopal churches. Some of Roxbury's older Methodist families didn't care to visit the South End, which they associated with vagabonds, alcoholics, and criminals. So as other black churches devel-oped new constituencies, Union Methodist continued to draw principally the old loyalists who had stuck by it through the lean days on Shawmut Avenue. Many of them had prospered, moving further out into Dorchester, Mattapan, or the suburbs, and the church remained their last tie with the ghetto. On Sundays, their large late-model cars filled the adjacent streets, a striking con-trast to overflowing trash cans, empty wine bottles, and ragged children. Every year, Union Methodist's members were further out of touch with the blacks who lived in the shadow of its impressive steeple. Even the church's seating pattern reflected the deep divisions within the black community. The Black Brahmins tended to sit up front, directly before the pulpit; a large group of West Indian Turks occupied the pews on the right, while a much smaller group of Southern Homies huddled on the left.

The Reverend Egbert C. McLeod, Union Methodist's pastor from 1948 to 1964, did little to bridge the gulf between his church and the broader black community. Indeed, he may have deepened it. McLeod was an aloof, patrician figure who, one parishioner later recalled, "acted as if the Lord picked his nose for him." Union Methodist began to turn a different face toward the community in 1964, when McLeod was replaced by his young assistant, Gil Caldwell. Gil's father was an old-style Southern preacher from Greensboro, North Carolina, eloquent on the rewards of eternal life, passive on racial justice in this world. But Gil had entered Boston University's School of Theology in 1955, just a year after Martin Luther King left. When King launched the Montgomery bus boycott, Caldwell invited him back to address a student audience and soon took him as a personal model.

In the summer of 1964, Gil went to Mississippi to aid the Student Nonviolent Coordinating Committee's voter registration drive. After two white volunteers and a black colleague were found in a shallow grave in Neshoba County, he wrote the Boston *Globe:* "I hope that Bostonians realize that they are not free until the Negro in Mississippi is free." The next spring, he answered King's call to Selma, where he was among the last people to see Jim Reeb alive. By then, Caldwell was vice-chairman of the Boston branch of King's Southern Christian Leadership Conference. In that capacity, he proudly served as master of ceremonies when King spoke on the Boston Common in April 1965. And like King himself, Caldwell gradually shifted his attention northward. After visiting the scene of the Watts riots, he addressed another warning to *Globe* readers. Watts, he reported, suffered from "unemployment, landlords, merchants with no sense of responsibility to their customers, a dramatic lack of municipal services, and arching over all this is a massive feeling of anger, frustration and despair. This is not much different from the Boston that I know. The main difference is that as of yet there has been no uprising, no revolution, no united attempt to 'take what's coming to me.' May we in Boston begin to act before it is too late."

As Union's new minister, Caldwell wasn't immune to the church's high-bourgeoisie style—in 1966, he and his wife launched Boston's first black debutante cotillion, called the Snowflake Ball because it took place in early winter. But beneath his middle-class attitudes, Gil Caldwell was an increasingly angry man. If he admired Martin Luther King, he also respected Malcolm X for "daring to describe what it was to be black in America." And he was disturbed by the assimilationist style of his own church. "The black church in the black community has an initial responsibility to its community," he wrote. "Unfortunately, the black church, like other institutions, has spent too much time, consciously and unconsciously, 'trying to be white' and thus has become irrelevant." In particular, he worried about his church's responsibility to its immediate South End community. By 1964, barely 15 percent of Union's membership lived within ten blocks of the church, and they came largely from the old black middle class, descendants of the conductors, porters, and other railroad workers who had settled along the tracks in the 1870s. Moreover, under Egbert McLeod, most of the church's programs were inward-looking—spiritual and social activities for its own members—rather than efforts to serve the surrounding community.

Determined to change all that, Caldwell began by moving his own family into the South End. Although Union Methodist had a comfortable parsonage in Roxbury, he bought a house on Greenwich Park, just two blocks from the church, and began walking the streets, chatting with neighborhood blacks who had never met a Union Methodist minister before. In the evenings, he sought out community groups, assuring them that the church cared about their problems. The church's basement meeting room, hitherto reserved for membership functions, was thrown open to the community.

It was about this time that Caldwell first heard of the city's search for non-profit organizations to sponsor low- and moderate-income housing in the South End. The neighborhood's renewal plan called for demolishing hundreds of crumbling tenements and apartment buildings, displacing some 3,550 households, most of them poor, many of them black. In return, the plan provided for construction of 2,500 new rental units in federally subsidized projects which, it was assumed, would ultimately house most of the families forced from their homes.

The new buildings were to be built under a program called 221 (d) 3, the centerpiece of John Kennedy's housing policy. Named after the relevant section of the Housing Act of 1961, it was designed to remedy defects in earlier efforts to house the poor and near-poor. Kennedy and his advisers had sought to steer a middle course between the bureaucratic insensitivity of public housing and the avarice of private development. Instead of the government building and administering housing for the needy, private groups were induced through government subsidies to provide such housing. Section 221 (d) 3 reduced interest rates on mortgages for such projects to 3 percent, which, in turn, permitted the sponsor to charge rents 20 percent below those in comparable non-subsidized apartments. This housing was intended for moderate-income families, not poor enough to qualify for public housing, yet unable to secure decent accommodations in the private market. In his housing message that spring of 1961, Kennedy declared, "In 1949 the Congress, with great vision, announced our national housing policy of 'a decent home and a suitable living environment for every American family.' We have progressed since that time; but we must still redeem this pledge to the 14 million American families who currently live in substandard or deteriorating homes."

Four years later, the pledge remained unfulfilled—indeed, racial and social unrest was provoking talk of an "urban crisis." In a March 1965 address on urban policy, Lyndon Johnson declared, "The modern city can be the most ruthless enemy of the good life, or it can be its servant. The choice is up to this generation of Americans. For this is truly the time of decision for the American city." Johnson unveiled an array of new housing programs, among them the rent supplement, which he called "the most crucial new instrument in our effort to improve the American city." Rent supplements took the subsidy concept one step further—for the first time directly paying a portion of the needy family's rent. As amended by Congress, they became an additional subsidy, piggybacked on 221 (d) 3, permitting low-income families who would otherwise have been relegated to public housing to live in subsidized projects. Such families paid only 25 percent of their incomes; the government paid the rest.

By 1965, 221 (d) 3 housing was heir to the loftiest idealism of the New Frontier and the Great Society: these were not to be mere real estate deals, but havens for society's disadvantaged. At first, the program was limited to non-profit groups—churches, fraternal organizations, and community groups. Later, limited-dividend commercial operations became eligible. But in Boston's South End, as elsewhere, the program retained a bias toward churches, which were assumed to possess the requisite altruism. The Boston Redevelopment Authority, trying hard to live down its high-handed treatment of the West End, had particular reasons to prefer non-profit sponsors rooted in the community. Moreover, since most of those to be rehoused in the South End were blacks or Puerto Ricans, it was hoped that black churches would have special credibility with prospective tenants.

Gil Caldwell wasn't sure that Union Methodist had much credibility, but he hoped to gain some from sponsoring comfortable, attractive, low-priced housing. Urban renewal too often meant "Negro removal," and the South End was already beginning to fill up with young white professionals, but the project would at least assure that a substantial number of blacks remained in the neighborhood. If some of them should express their gratitude by joining the church, all the better.

Gil Caldwell had an even larger vision: "We envisioned ourselves as not only putting up housing, but having an ongoing responsibility to the persons who lived there, whether they were members of our church or not. Here was a real opportunity to bring some of Union's middle-class blacks together with inner-city residents. People who had been able to move out of the South End and Roxbury could relate to their brothers and sisters who were still caught there. We envisioned a sense of reciprocity—residents and non-residents talking together about how you make that a human environment."

In March 1965—even before the South End renewal plan was approved by the City Council—two BRA representatives met with Caldwell in the pastor's study to outline procedures for a 221 (d) 3 project. Soon, the church formed the Columbus Avenue Housing Corporation to sponsor such a project. By May, a site had been selected, stretching four blocks down Columbus Avenue and occupied by several shabby apartment buildings, the five-story Braddock

Hotel, the notorious 411 Lounge, and other bars frequented by black prostitutes and the white hunters who pursued them. In place of all this squalor would rise four new buildings to be called Methunion Manor.

In December 1965, the church chose Henry Boles, a respected black architect, to design the project, and Boles came up with an ingenious idea: instead of flat slabs, he proposed a series of duplexes stacked one on another to form the six-story buildings. The two-story units would be staggered to create a grid, breaking up the concrete façades and echoing the surrounding blocks of nineteenth-century town houses. Caldwell and his housing committee were delighted; buildings like these would make a handsome contribution to the new South End, they thought—a lasting symbol of the church's concern for its neighbors.

But the design quickly ran into trouble. The BRA liked it, but the Federal Housing Administration—which would have to insure the mortgage—regarded it as "unrealistic" and overly expensive. Months dragged by in administrative wrangling. A Boston construction company which had bid on the stacked duplexes pulled out, to be replaced by Bonwit Construction Company of New York, which scrapped Boles's design and ordered him to come up with more conventional slabs. In the spring of 1968, Boles presented his new design to government officials and church representatives. The BRA didn't care for the cold, austere result, preferring a "more esthetic approach." Even Herman Boxer, Bonwit's president, conceded, "I'd have liked a better-looking building, rather than a plain box, but I didn't think it could be done with the money involved." Indeed, nobody was particularly happy with the redesigned project.

Less than a month later, Martin Luther King was shot in Memphis. In the black anger which followed his death, one target was the city's failure to complete housing for the poor displaced by the South End renewal program. Methunion Manor was still on the drawing boards more than three years after it had been conceived, and other projects lagged even further behind schedule. Kevin White and his BRA director, Hale Champion, had promised to speed up the program, and following King's death, they put increasing pressure on Boston's banks and insurance companies, seeking pledges of additional low-income housing. But black leaders were increasingly impatient. Reggie Eaves, a South End activist, warned, "Let's start stacking brick on brick, not word on word."

On April 26, 1968, forty demonstrators blocked entrances to a South End parking lot. The activists—members of a group called Community Assembly for a United South End (CAUSE)—handed out notices reading: "Dear Car Parker: South End people want to live in decent homes at reasonable rents. No housing has been built. People have been moved, of course. Housing should be built on this land." Sporadic clashes broke out during the day between the demonstrators and police. Five people were arrested.

But, as City Hall sought to cool the confrontation, CAUSE was temporarily permitted to occupy the lot. The demonstrators pitched tents and erected crude shacks; as the occupying force swelled past two hundred, support grew.

Martin Luther King, Sr., father of the murdered leader, took time from a memorial service in the city to visit the lot and pay tribute to its occupiers, who, he said, were acting in "my son's spirit." The Youth Alliance, which had helped restore peace after King's death three weeks earlier, now provided security. Churches sent barbecued chicken, potato salad, and fruit salad. At times, the occupation took on a carnival air. As night fell, a saxophone wailed as dancers snaked through the lot, now known as "Tent City."

When the demonstrators voluntarily struck their tents on April 30, they had won at least a symbolic victory. The next day, Hale Champion issued a sweeping edict halting further demolition of homes in the South End and promising that a major low-income housing program would be launched within ninety days. The Mayor, trying to pacify the city's black community, yet determined to show that he wasn't caving in to pressure, denied that Tent City had forced any changes; it had merely "called attention again to some of the urgent problems we have been working on for four months." But, whether power politics or guerrilla theater, Tent City publicly committed the city to a new sense of urgency on low-income housing.

Even the new political imperatives couldn't entirely break the Methunion logjam, for a new party had entered the dispute: the young white professionals, represented by the South End Project Area Committee (SEPAC), the committee elected by area residents to pass on the renewal program. Many of the newcomers were artists or architects; others had been drawn by the South End's aesthetics. When SEPAC representatives first saw the revised designs for Methunion Manor, they exploded. "The ugliest housing I've ever seen," said one architect. Objecting to the high density, minimal setbacks, lack of landscaping or adequate play space for children, the committee lobbied for revisions in the project design. City officials argued that it was too late, that a mortgage commitment had already been given on the basis of the current design; moreover, they warned, if the project was delayed again, or—God forbid—canceled, that could jeopardize the whole South End renewal program, from which the newcomers stood to benefit the most. Josh Young, the West Newton Street banker who had become one of SEPAC's leaders, told his colleagues, "We may not like the way it looks. But there are thousands of people in our neighborhood who desperately need decent, reasonably priced housing." Young's arguments prevailed. In autumn 1969, SEPAC reluctantly endorsed Methunion.

But the dispute left some of the newcomers with a sense of grievance against Union Methodist Church. On several occasions they had sought to discuss the project design with the Reverend William Bobby McClain, who, in mid-1968, succeeded Gil Caldwell as Union's minister. An Alabamian, educated at Boston University's School of Theology, McClain had worked for a time in Boston's poverty program. Gil Caldwell was an angry man, but McClain practically seethed with rage at white society. "God help me," he once told Rachel Twymon, "I hate white people so much!" Certainly he had no interest in debating architecture with them. When a delegation of whites called on him to talk about Methunion, he flatly refused to discuss the matter. "Those buildings will last a hundred years," he snapped. Later he charged that several South End whites had been so determined to block the project that they had offered to buy the church.

Bobby McClain was an electrifying preacher who mesmerized his congregation with the power of his language. To the quiet dignity of Union's sanctuary, he brought the evangelical techniques of Southern revivalism, and his message had a new, cutting edge. Black Methodists, he said, were "like Jonah in the belly of a white whale. We are still like Ezekiel in a valley of dry bones. We, like the man in the Good Samaritan story, are still 'fallen among thieves'—thieves of Jericho who have stolen our names, our heritage, our rights, our religion and robbed us of our culture and our self-concept." If Gil Caldwell's style had reflected the mid-sixties ascendancy of Martin Luther King, McClain's mirrored post-King disenchantment and militance.

During Caldwell's ministry, fifteen or twenty whites regularly attended Union Methodist, but McClain's denunciations made them deeply uneasy. Ultimately, Mary Holman, a prominent black parishioner, advised McClain to "go a little easy." McClain dismissed her words of caution. "If they can't take what I'm dishing out," he said, "they shouldn't come here anymore." In the following months, most whites stopped attending Union's services.

Before blacks and whites could worship comfortably together, McClain believed, the former slaveholders had to expiate their sins. In mid-1969, he devoted his formidable energy to the crusade for "reparations" from white churches, a notion introduced that spring by James Forman of the Student Nonviolent Coordinating Committee when he interrupted services at New York's Riverside Church to demand $500 million—"fifteen dollars per nigger"—as reparations for past injuries suffered by blacks. As chairman of New England Black Methodists for Church Renewal, Bobby McClain led a fight for $1,500,000 in reparations for his area. When the New England Conference allocated only $235,000, and failed to pay all of that, McClain leveled a polemic at his church, warning the white New England Methodist that blacks were now "coming to him as assertive missionaries rather than as docile menials who once accommodated his paternalizing charitable benevolence by saying 'please' for the crumbs under his table."

As her new pastor confronted the church's white leadership, Rachel Twymon looked on in astonishment. Still a devout integrationist, she would never permit herself to voice such open anger at white people. Yet she nursed her own quiet grievance at many white Methodists. As a board member of the Cooper Community Center, she resented the remote stance many white suburban church members adopted toward the needs of inner-city Methodists. They might send money, food, or secondhand clothing, much like the handouts they gave their maids or gardeners, but they rarely came anywhere near the center. It was clear to Rachel that suburban whites didn't mind blacks belonging to their church—indeed might even welcome them as a badge of virtue—so long as they didn't get too close. Gradually Rachel found her way into Black Methodists for Church Renewal, eventually becoming secretary of the New England branch, hoping the organization would become "a thorn in the side of our white brothers and sisters, so they won't forget we're here."

His dramatic struggle for "reparations" diverted Bobby McClain's attention from the technicalities of Methunion Manor. For many reasons negotiations dragged on. Not until April 7, 1970, did the FHA give its final mortgage commitment of $4,231,949. In only fifteen months, rising construction costs had added $1,275,100 to the project's bill. Five weeks later, on May 17, 1970, ground was broken at last. Rachel and her mother, Helen, were among the church members who gathered in the abundant sunshine across the street from the church as McClain led them in a litany written for the occasion:

MCCLAIN: Because we realize that "the earth is the Lord's and the fulness thereof; the world and they that dwell therein";
CONGREGATION: We break this ground.
MCCLAIN: To aid in removing blight of tenement, urban decay, needless want of shelter, and to provide comfortable surroundings and housing for those in search of a home;
CONGREGATION: We break this ground.
MCCLAIN: To create community and a sense of pride in living, in being a people sharing in the abundance of God's earth;
CONGREGATION: We break this ground.
MCCLAIN: To participate with God and community in providing shelter for families, widows, children and people of all backgrounds, races, classes and creeds.
MCCLAIN AND CONGREGATION: We break this ground this day as our hallowed task.

Then McClain and Mayor Kevin White took turns digging spadefuls of earth from the construction site. Methunion Manor was finally underway.

At the last moment, in yet another dispute over project design, Bonwit Construction Company was replaced by Starrett Brothers & Eken of New York. A large construction company, Starrett had built many of America's best-known buildings—the Empire State, Pittsburgh's Gateway Center—and such housing developments as New York's Stuyvesant Town and Peter Cooper Village. There could be no doubt about its qualifications. Yet rising construction costs soon squeezed the company's profit margin. In such situations, many contractors reacted by omitting work required in the specifications, replacing designated materials with less expensive substitutes, scrimping on craftsmanship and finishing. Even the most competent companies, aware that such projects were designed for the poor, cut corners in a way they wouldn't have dared had they been building private homes for the wealthy. Moreover, churches and other non-profit groups which sponsored so many 221 (d) 3 projects lacked the experience to ride herd on such buildings; this often resulted in shoddy, inferior, or defective work.

Witness the battle of the bricks. In July 1970, with two Methunion Manor buildings more than half complete, the Kelsey-Ferguson Brick Company reported that because of a wildcat strike at its plant, it was running short of Concord Blend brick. In August, Henry Boles authorized use of Quaker Town brick, which was more orange in tone, "provided that black bricks were added to effect the transition." But the black bricks were never added. In September, when the scaffolding was removed, passersby could easily detect a marked change in brick color. On September 28, Elliott Rothman, a South End architect, wrote Mayor White, "You would fight against such action in Back Bay, Beacon Hill or West Roxbury. The South End also requires enforcement of reasonable construction procedures." The BRA fired off a letter to the Reverend McClain, noting, "The great variance of brick colors detracts immensely from the aesthetics of the buildings. Much adverse comment is being received from various residents of the South End . . . You are requested to take immediate action for the removal of all brick facing varying from that as approved." But the two buildings were largely complete. The church decided the Quaker Town brick should be dyed to the color of Concord Blend. When officials contended that the dye would fade in sunlight, the contractors were compelled to set up a special escrow account to pay for further repairs.

After the brick fiasco, the BRA inspectors grew more vigilant and soon discovered other glaring deficiencies. Concrete foundations were "in poor shape and present a bad aesthetic appearance with poor patchwork, nonmatching mortar colors, very rough surfaces from worn-out or gouged forms." Stairs and landings had a reverse pitch, so they were "puddling badly and will create hazardous conditions during cold weather." Roofs leaked and created "stains and dampness on ceilings." Light poles in the parking lot were "very wobbly and globes are not set securely." Doors warped and sprang from their tracks. But by then it was too late for anything but minor repairs. The church had already opened a rental office and flooded the neighborhood with brochures announcing: "Convenience, Comfort and Safety in a New Community. 150 families will enjoy many fine facilities in the all new South End community developed by Union United Methodist Church. Methunion Manor is not only a new apartment complex, it is a new community. Convenient for Methunion residents will be many services offered in the 9,600 square feet of commercial space. All prospective tenants and their references are carefully reviewed."

By autumn 1970, Rachel Twymon was at work in the church's rental office, answering the telephone and helping applicants fill out their forms. Using her access to survey the available apartments, she settled on a four-bedroom unit at Columbus Avenue and Yarmouth Street. Relatively spacious, it had plenty of light for her plants. More important, its first-floor location would spare her from using either the stairs or the elevator. With its ordinary interest-rate sub-sidy, the apartment rented for $222 a month, but Rachel qualified for the rent-supplement program, under which she would pay only one-quarter of her monthly income, or about $75 (utilities included), while the Department of Housing and Urban Development picked up the rest. It seemed like a bargain.

Rachel was full of "great hopes" in June 1971 as she and her children left Orchard Park and began their new life at Methunion Manor. And for a time it seemed, indeed, like a new life. The buildings' brick fronts glowed in the summer sunshine. Fresh linoleum and bright paint gleamed in the hallways. The kitchens and bathrooms shone with new enamel. Everybody was excited about the crisp, modern feel of the place. Neighbors chatted eagerly in the hallways, exchanging tales of the "pigpens" they had left behind.

Rachel was happiest of all about Methunion's location. At last she was out of that dreary public housing, away from that deteriorating, crime-ridden neighborhood. Here she felt near the center of things. She agreed entirely with another tenant, A. L. Wesley, Jr., who wrote in the tenant bulletin:

> *I like the idea of knowing that I can walk down to the Common, or over to the Fenway and even to the banks of the Charles, all within the limits of an hour or less. I can look out my window and see the beauty of the Prudential Center, a colossus of steel, brick and concrete against the blue background of a sun-lit sky . . . I like to hear the ringing of the time from the belfry of the Christian Science Church. The chimes seem to make mu-sic, especially on a Sunday morning; chimes that rhyme filling the air with beautiful sounds. Langston Hughes epitomized it all in his poem "The City," in which he says:*

> > *In the morning the city*
> > *spreads its wings*
> > *making a song*
> > *in stone that sings*

> > *In the evening the city*
> > *goes to bed*
> > *hanging the lights*
> > *above its head.*

But Rachel's euphoria was short-lived. In midsummer, the toilets in both her bathrooms began backing up, flooding the apartment with water and caus-ing extensive damage to rugs and furniture. A plumber would get them work-ing only to have them back up again. It happened a dozen times that summer before engineers discovered that a four-inch sewer pipe had been installed where eight-inch pipe had been specified.

As winter arrived, Methunion's tenants confronted another problem. Their heat was controlled by a thermostat outside each building, which triggered a gas-fired boiler when the temperature on the street dropped below 57 degrees. There was no way to adjust heat to the actual temperatures in apartments. The thermometer often reached 85 inside Rachel's apartment, more than that on higher floors. The tenants could gain relief only by opening their windows. Some days the heat was so oppressive the Twymons streamed onto the sidewalk, panting for air. When her mother came to visit, she told Rachel, "They're trying to cook you niggers and you ain't got the message yet."

All kinds of little things went wrong: cracks opened in the plaster ceilings; when a heavy truck rattled by on Columbus Avenue, white dust sifted down, covering Rachel's plants; the basements flooded whenever it rained; bathroom grouting cracked; shower heads wobbled.

Some of Methunion's deterioration was due to tenant negligence. Once there had been brave talk of a "multi-racial, multi-class project," but no such balance was ever achieved. Of the 147 families who moved in that spring and summer of 1971, 130 were black, 7 Spanish-speaking, 4 Oriental, only 6 white. More important, the project never attracted middle-class tenants—there was a teacher, a nurse, and several salesmen, but many families were on some form of public assistance. Preference had gone to those displaced by urban renewal, most of them low-income. Thirty-eight families received rent supplements from HUD, twenty-two from the Boston Housing Authority. And the commitment to tenant screening had gone largely unfulfilled: most of those who met the income limits were automatically accepted.

Efforts had been made to secure tenant cooperation. The Codman Company, a management firm hired by the church to administer Methunion, put up large, brightly colored posters which called cheerily for the tenants' help: "Here at Methunion Manor we have an opportunity. The opportunity starts with a beautiful new building. We set the example we want our children to follow by taking care of our apartment. That's why we cooperate in keeping the halls and elevators clean and free of bicycles, baby carriages and children's toys. . . . That's why we realize that it's up to us to prevent an insect and rodent problem. If we take our garbage and trash to the trash chute in the hall every day this problem will not happen."

But such cooperation wasn't always forthcoming. In March 1972, Roland Peters, Methunion's manager, issued eviction notices to two tenants, both welfare recipients receiving rent supplements. Mrs. M.'s estranged husband had stabbed her nephew in her apartment the previous December. Since her separation, Mrs. M. had received numerous male visitors, with whom she could be found drinking and playing cards at all hours. "It would appear that Mrs. M. exercises little control over the behavior of her children. They write profane statements on the hall walls, in lobbies and commit other acts of vandalism." Peters described the other tenant, Mrs. K., as a "psychopath" because of "her speech impediment, her dermatology condition and her obnoxiousness, all of which subject her to ridicule from people who come in contact with her; her affinity for minding everyone else's business—which is further cause for rejection by other tenants; her antagonism to anyone, including a landlord, who suggests conformity to rules and regulations; her refusal to sign a lease; her refusal to pay rent."

In a letter to the Welfare Department reporting his action, an exasperated Peters said the cases illustrated "the problems we are encountering in attempting to make low and moderate income housing work. . . . Many tenants have asked where we get these families. Recently you asked me if we screen applicants. We try, but how is it possible for us to determine in any screening process how these human beings will behave in our units?" Some months later, another manager warned more bluntly that Methunion was becoming a "dumping ground for troubled families."

But many tenants held management largely responsible for conditions in the project. In June 1972, a group met with the board of the Columbus Avenue Housing Corporation to complain that the corporation and its management company had failed to maintain the buildings or enforce minimum standards among residents. The board promised to investigate, but barely two months later several dozen tenants signed a petition renewing their charges. "Leases have not been enforced," it alleged. "Tenants sit on the front steps, littering the steps and entrance. . . . Halls are not kept washed and waxed. Tenants too often play stereos at night, too loud. Children play out of windows. Light bulbs have been removed from the back of the building. . . . These are the same things that were brought before the Board at the mass meeting when the majority of tenants met at the church. It seems nobody cares." When the petition achieved nothing, twelve of the signers formed the Methunion Concerns Committee to work for an alleviation of tenant grievances.

Among the founders was Rachel Twymon. By now Rachel was deeply disappointed in Methunion. Gil Caldwell's dream had soured. Not only had the project failed to bring Union Methodist closer to the community, it had deepened the gulf between Union's members, mostly suburban and middle-class, and Methunion's tenants, mostly working-class or welfare clients. When the tenants complained, the Housing Corporation was deeply aggrieved. They had tried to do the right thing, they had devoted endless time and energy to Methunion, they had provided badly needed housing, and now the very people they had done all this for were raising all sorts of ridiculous objections. The complainers were "ungrateful" malcontents.

Only a handful of Methunion's tenants belonged to the church. As one tenant with a foot in both camps, Rachel found the mutual antagonism intolerable. At church she heard people complain about the "riffraff" at the project; in tenant meetings she heard people complain about the "uppity boogies" in the church. This conflict echoed the old tension within her own family, a conflict she had never fully resolved. She wasn't altogether certain on which side she belonged.

But by late 1972, the conflict between tenants and church was submerged in a larger issue. Methunion Manor was out of money. To insiders, this came as no surprise. Like many 221 (d) 3 projects across the country, Methunion had been in financial trouble long before it accepted its first tenant, for its rents had been determined less on economic than on political grounds. Under heavy pressure from South End community groups, the Mayor and the BRA desperately needed housing which would be perceived as replacements for the demolished units. In setting rents for these projects, HUD had shown little concern for the project's financial viability. And Gil Caldwell had his own agenda: the church's search for credibility with inner-city blacks. Eager to build, Union had allowed itself to underestimate Methunion's operating costs to ensure that the FHA would approve its mortgage application. And, of course, the FHA—which shared HUD's emphasis on housing production—could be counted on not to scrutinize the figures too closely. For there was a tacit understanding among all parties that the first priority was to get the buildings up and occupied; then, if expenses outran revenues, an appeal could be made to the nation's conscience, and the federal government would presumably ride to the rescue, as it had so often in the sixties.

Indeed, this might well have happened had the deficits been as modest as originally expected. What nobody could have anticipated was the inflation of the early seventies. Most devastating of all was the extraordinary surge in the cost of utilities. Natural-gas prices skyrocketed—a particular problem for Methunion due to its wasteful gas-fired heating plant. Electric rates went up as well. Boston's water and sewer rates increased 67 percent in April 1972 alone. Inflation affected virtually every operating cost: insurance, taxes, salaries, rubbish collection, and maintenance.

In 1972, its first full year of occupancy, Methunion's operating expenses ($182,024) were more than double those projected in its budget ($90,526). These deficits were further aggravated when some expected revenues failed to materialize. For more than three years, as Bobby McClain sought to develop a black-owned shopping center on the ground floor of one building, he turned away other potential commercial tenants; 9,260 square feet of space remained vacant and the project lost $30,000 a year in budgeted income. No wonder that a HUD internal memorandum finally conceded that Methunion's original budget was "too low." An official of the Codman Company put it more bluntly when he wrote in 1973 that "the amount of dollars allocated for operations [was] absolutely ridiculous even three years ago . . . the project was doomed to failure at the drawing board." Yet despite its financial crisis, the board made remarkably little effort to get HUD to raise its "political rents." The deficits deepened. By May 1972, barely a year after the first tenants moved in, Methunion could no longer meet its mortgage payments. It staggered along for several months on extensions from the mortgage holder, the Government National Mortgage Association, but in December 1972—owing $97,000 in debt service and $60,000 in back taxes—the project went into default. In May 1973, HUD honored its pledge to buy the bad loan.

By then, with Richard Nixon triumphantly launching his second term, benevolence had gone out of fashion in Washington. While Methunion's tenants were preoccupied with leaking roofs and backed-up toilets, HUD was deciding to "dispose of all acquired multi-family properties at the earliest possible date at the highest price obtainable in the current market." Even Rachel Twymon, with her close ties to Union Methodist Church, did not yet realize that this could mean foreclosure and sale of the property to the highest bidder. If that happened it would eliminate government subsidies, sharply raise rents, and force all but Methunion's most affluent tenants onto the street.

13

Diver

Some called it a "chicken coop," a "Mayan cistern," or "Disneyland East," but to Colin it was a symbol of the bold, imaginative Boston they were trying to build. It was different all right—a striking departure from the traditional school of municipal architecture and particularly from the old City Hall, that Second Empire pile of columns, pilasters, and arcades in which Colin had labored all that sweltering summer and through the fall. The old Hall, Boston's seat of government for 103 years, was redolent of the inflated rhetoric, ethnic warfare, and outright corruption that had been the stock ingredients of Boston politics during much of that era. In *The Last Hurrah*, his fictional account of the city's political combat in the age of James Michael Curley, Edwin O'Connor wrote of the old Hall: ". . . this inefficient tangled warren [was] the perfect symbol of municipal administration. . . . In its old, high-ceilinged chambers, the elected and appointed officials of government slumbered, mused or conducted the affairs of the city; in this they were guided by the opportunities afforded them and, to a somewhat lesser degree, by the strictures of conscience."

The new City Hall had risen from the rubble of Boston's sleaziest quarter—Scollay Square—with its cheap saloons, penny arcades, shooting galleries, pool halls, and "girlie shows." For generations the matrons of the Watch and Ward Society had inveighed against this "sinkhole of depravity," but not until the city planners added their weight did the Square finally give way to the gleaming new Government Center.

As conceived by its architect, I. M. Pei, the Center focused on a broad, fan-shaped plaza, flanked by the John Fitzgerald Kennedy Federal Building, two state towers, three private office buildings, a new police station, and a parking garage. But its highlight was the new City Hall which loomed like an inverted Aztec pyramid at the plaza's southeast corner. Built around a huge interior court—"a great agora, a place that proclaims the majesty of government by the people"—the Hall was divided into three levels reflecting the separate functions of city government. At its base was the public square, symbolized by the red brick floors which carried the pedestrian plaza inside. There, around the central court, were brick walkways lined by counters and offices where the public could purchase licenses, pay assessments, and make inquiries. On the top level, behind a massive, stepped cornice, the architects placed the agencies which dealt least with the public, the faceless bureaucracy. In between lay the "ceremonial" functions—the monumental City Council chambers and the elegant Mayor's office. As the base was rooted in the red brick of old Boston, so the upper reaches soared in shafts of gray precast concrete and exposed, roughly textured cement walls. Although the design was received with some skepticism in Boston, it was applauded by international critics. Ada Louise Huxtable of the New York *Times* pronounced it "a structure of dignity, humanism and power [which] will outlast the last hurrah."

The Hall aroused such expectations of immortality that in December 1967 outgoing Mayor John Collins moved into the still incomplete structure for his few remaining days so that he could be the first mayor to occupy it—and promptly contracted pneumonia from the chill winds that blew through his ill-heated office. Kevin White prudently remained in the cluttered jumble of the old Hall for another year. Only in February 1969, when the new Hall had been in use for a month, did the Mayor schedule a week-long inauguration of the edifice, which he plainly hoped to appropriate as a symbol of his new administration.

On the eve of the inaugural ceremony, the heaviest snowstorm in years swept through New England, forcing a twenty-four-hour postponement. The next day, February 10, huge drifts concealed the plaza as five hundred guests took their seats in the great central court, decorated for the occasion with Oriental rugs and tubs of greenery. From the first landing, Senator Edward M. Kennedy addressed the assemblage, deliberately evoking memories of his brother's time in a speech touched with urgency. "Urban life in the United States has come to a critical point of decision," he said, "caught between the narrowing walls of change and decay on one hand and, on the other, priorities created for another age. . . . If the city of Boston becomes a city filled with crime, if it becomes a city lived in only by the very rich and the very poor, if over the next fifty years it gradually becomes an all-black city rather than an integrated city, then our problems will overcome us."

Kevin White struck a more hopeful note. "It is not just an architectural event which we celebrate this morning," he said. "For, if you believe, as I do, that architecture both portrays and shapes men's lives, then you will agree that this building's major significance will be its effect on the people who use it. . . . Today, though our cities are beset with incredible problems, this building exhorts all of us to do better than we thought we could in dealing with them—to be hospitable to change, to try new ideas, to bring people closer to government."

Gazing up at the Mayor, who stood there in his tailored suit and blue-and-gold tie, his head thrown back, his blue eyes crackling in that beaming Irish pol's face, Colin was proud to be working for the man. The speech itself came as no surprise—Colin had contributed some ideas for it—but he found himself swept along by the lofty phrases. For Colin believed—as the Mayor had put it to Robert Coles the previous summer—that there was "no more time for politics as usual, not in 1968, not in our cities." He believed that, with strength and compassion, government could do something about the cities' problems. And he believed that Kevin White had the qualities necessary to lead the most successful assault ever launched by an American city on racial discrimination, poverty, and decay. As the Mayor concluded his remarks, Colin joined in the applause, and thought to himself, God, I'm glad to be here at this moment, doing what I'm doing, instead of showing some corporation how to save money on its taxes.

But then Colin checked his enthusiasm. He thought back to that other speech of the Mayor's, the one which had brought him to City Hall in the first place. He and Joan had laughed about that many times. A few days after he started work, he'd encountered the Mayor in a corridor of the old City Hall.

"Hey, Colin," White had said. "Is it true that you're here because you took my speech at the *Law Review* banquet as a personal invitation?"

"Well," Colin stuttered, "yes, I suppose I did."

The Mayor chuckled. "I don't think I really intended it that way. But it brought you here, and we're damn lucky to have you."

The place they had found for him was anomalous, not quite fitting any table of organization. His title was assistant to the Mayor; in fact he was assistant to an assistant—specifically to Sam Merrick, the Mayor's Special Counsel. At fifty-four the oldest of White's aides, Merrick was a Main Line Philadelphia lawyer who had spent most of his life in government labor relations, first with the National Labor Relations Board and then as the Labor Department's man on Capitol Hill. In September 1967, he had left for a year of "decompression" studying urban policy at Harvard, and late that fall he remarked casually that "it would be fun to work for the city of Boston" (in much the same tone as "it would be fun to go slide in the snow"), but when Barney Frank heard of his remark he called Sam's bluff. Soon Merrick was handling a package of special responsibilities for the Mayor: making sure the city was getting all the federal funds it was entitled to, dealing with the Labor Department and the Office of Economic Opportunity, and overseeing collective bargaining with city employees.

Colin was assigned a desk in the corner of Merrick's cramped office and set to work accumulating a library on federal funding so that he could advise city agencies on available resources. But there wasn't much to do. Merrick was an independent operator, keeping his own counsel, requiring little staff assistance.

Gradually, Colin began working for others in the Mayor's office. His study of federal funding led him into a general brief on the city's fiscal problems. Except for Budget Director Dave Davis, he became the mayoral staffer most familiar with state aid, federal aid, new forms of taxation, any source of funds the city might tap to narrow its budget deficit. He devised plans for getting revenues out of the staggering array of tax-exempt institutions—universities, hospitals, churches—which owned nearly a fifth of the city's real estate. He examined increased fees for municipal services. As a lawyer, he was a natural resource for legal work in the office. Although the Mayor had a separate Law Department, Colin was soon overseeing preparation of the Mayor's annual legislative package.

Despite his increasing responsibilities, for the first year or so he had little direct contact with the Mayor. He wasn't in the inner circle, which included Barney Frank; Sam Merrick; Bill Cowin; Hale Champion, Ed Logue's replacement as director of Redevelopment; and Corporation Counsel Herb Gleason. Colin was at the next level together with other young assistants like Jeff Steingarten, Rick Borton, and Paul Oosterhuis. When the Mayor's staff moved into the new City Hall in December, Colin and Steingarten shared a small suite just down the marble corridor from the Mayor's office where they were available to receive assignments from the Mayor himself or from Barney Frank, who was not only Kevin White's chief of staff and principal policy adviser, but his alter ego and, in many technical areas, *de facto* mayor. Frank had achieved his preeminence at age twenty-seven through a combination of intelligence, energy, and a caustic wit which, though it alienated some, lashed others on to prodigies of accomplishment. In a City Hall still populated principally by amiable Irishmen, Barney was an anachronism: a Jew from Bayonne, New Jersey, who delivered his stinging wisecracks in a thick "Joisy" accent, through billows of smoke from a cigar which looked like one of Hoboken's belching smokestacks. With his massive belly draped in perpetually rumpled suits, Barney did not *look* impressive, but few people could skip so nimbly through the corridors of Massachusetts politics.

Barney was a doctrinaire liberal, whose message to those around him was "Dammit, we can change things!" As he proselytized for change, his most important convert was the Mayor himself; for, despite appearances, Kevin White, when he took office in January 1968, was a remarkably non-ideological man. The general impression to the contrary was almost entirely a function of his having drawn Louise Day Hicks as his opponent in the runoff, for her stolid resistance to change and her racial innuendoes could only make him seem, by contrast, a trailblazer of the Great Society.

Once White took office, several factors encouraged him to follow through on his rhetoric about the urban crisis. Because he saw himself running for governor, not for reelection as mayor, his audience was different from his constituency; he was governing the city, but his actions were tailored to impress not just Boston's working-class Irish or Italians but the liberal suburbanites of Brookline and Newton, whose votes would be critical in the gubernatorial race. Moreover, White quickly realized that urban issues were "sexy," providing an opportunity for the coat-over-the-shoulder crisis management which John Lindsay had demonstrated in New York. The city's pressing problems—dramatic, tangible, out on the streets for everyone to see—genuinely intrigued the problem solver in White. And Barney Frank, constantly moving toward the boldest, most progressive position, pushed the Mayor still further along the path of social change. Finally, Martin Luther King's assassination forced White to give the race issue top priority.

The Mayor responded to the assassination with a blitzkrieg of attention to the black community: Lindsayesque walks up Blue Hill Avenue, with stops along the way to bounce a basketball; efforts to refurbish Franklin Park, the major green space in Boston's ghetto; creation of the Mayor's Office of Human Rights, headed by a black director; and the promotion of Herbert Craigwell, Jr., a black detective, over hundreds of white officers, to the rank of Deputy Superintendent of Police.

With remarkable speed, he forged his way into that small circle of mayors—Lindsay of New York, Carl Stokes of Cleveland, and Joseph Alioto of San Francisco—regarded as the spokesmen for America's embattled cities. In July 1968, appearing on a panel with Alioto and Stokes, he challenged suburban whites to come out from behind their "stockades" to help demolish "the towering torture chamber" of the Negro ghetto. A month later, testifying before the Democratic Party Platform Committee, he warned that urban America was being financially "starved" by federal and state government. And in April 1969, he joined five other mayors in a visit to Richard Nixon and Spiro Agnew at the White House. Agnew's description of the encounter—"We didn't have a nice exchange, but we had a frank one"—sharpened White's image as a tough fighter for the cities, a man who would do battle with vested interests wherever they were.

But it was White's evolving position on race that defined his administration and, by the end of his first year in office, put him at odds with many of his more parochial constituents. In his first State of the City address in January 1968, he said, "I cannot avoid a reference to perhaps the most disturbing of the city's problems—its continuing ethnic divisions which seem to resist every effort at resolution. The highest aspirations of this administration will be to reconcile this city's people. The finest contribution that we could conceivably make to this city is the creation of an atmosphere in which every man might recognize the human dignity and worth of every other man."

It was a bold attempt to address Boston's racial tensions, but it didn't work. As the Mayor moved into his second year, he found that such words were well received in the affluent suburbs, but utterly rejected in the city's white working-class neighborhoods. The pattern was almost reflexive. When Herbert Craigwell was promoted to Deputy Superintendent of Police, liberals in Wellesley and Weston welcomed the appointment as an act of courage, but white inner-city neighborhoods rang with racial epithets. The Mayor's men reported that whenever they appeared at a community meeting in those neighborhoods, somebody invariably rose to denounce "that S.O.B. who's giving everything away to the blacks." Nearly every morning, hate mail showed up on Colin's desk addressed simply: "Mayor Black, City Hall."

Eventually this assault so disconcerted the Mayor that he ordered his staff to find out exactly where city dollars were being spent. Colin helped compare actual expenditures on parks, schools, playgrounds, streetlighting, garbage collection, and other city services in the black community with expenditures in white neighborhoods. Boston's black community was small in comparison with most major Northern cities—16.3 percent in 1970—but the staff found no evidence that the Mayor was disproportionately concentrating funds in black neighborhoods, even on a per capita basis.

Such data made no dent in the conviction of white neighborhoods that they were being "screwed." For what had changed was not so much the flow of cash or city services as City Hall's attitude toward the black community, what Kevin White called "the psychological side" of government. In an interview ten months after he took office, the Mayor said that the black unrest of the mid-sixties—in particular the massive Detroit riot of August 1967—had helped focus attention on the psychological needs of the black community. "Detroit," he said, "was a city with massive federal aid, low unemployment rate, black participation, and a progressive mayor, and yet its riot was the biggest holocaust, bigger than Newark or Watts. We wound up seeing that there was a psychological side which had been missed. Lindsay in New York was the first to see this. He then set out to provide it. We have tried to do the same thing here. I think we have given the blacks confidence." It was this effort to make blacks feel they were full-fledged citizens of Boston that had made the white neighborhoods perceive themselves as victims; if the blacks were getting new attention, the whites concluded, it had to be coming from somewhere, it had to be coming out of their share.

Such resentments were inevitable, Kevin White and his aides came to realize, because the unmet psychological needs of the city's neighborhoods—white and black—were so enormous. The neighborhood problem was rooted in the profound cynicism with which many Bostonians had come to regard their municipal government. A decade earlier, the extraordinary upset of State Senate President Johnny Powers by the relatively unknown John Collins in the 1959 mayoralty race had prompted a Boston University political scientist to warn of the frightening "alienation" of many Boston voters. In a book that made "the alienated voter" a catchphrase in Boston politics, Murray T. Levin argued that Powers had been defeated because many voters perceived him as the quintessential insider, "a leader of a powerful and corrupt group of politicians, businessmen and unsavory elements who govern the city for personal enrichment rather than for the general welfare." Collins, in turn, was regarded as a spokesman for "the little man" against the politicians. "Angry, resentful, hopeless and politically powerless," Levin wrote, such voters were "crying out, sometimes blindly, sometimes articulately, for candidates who make sense and for political life that has meaning."

But in the long run, the 1959 election only heightened the neighborhoods' alienation, for when Collins entered office, Boston was facing a fiscal crisis— a declining tax base, spiraling property taxes, a low credit rating, and a business community that had utterly lost confidence in City Hall. A shrewd, able man, determined to "prove that all Irish politicians aren't crooked or stupid, or both," Collins gave the city prudent fiscal management combined with an ambitious urban renewal program designed to rebuild the city's tax base. But as part of his campaign to regain the confidence of the business community, he struck an implicit deal with them, through the Vault, to give priority to the redevelopment of the city's aging, decrepit downtown. Under Collins, the New Haven Railroad yards in the Back Bay were transformed into the Prudential Center, a vast, forbidding office and apartment complex erected around the fifty-two-story headquarters of the Prudential Insurance Company. Across town, the predominantly Italian West End, which had been demolished under Collins' predecessor, John B. Hynes, was replaced with the sterile luxury apartments of Charles River Park. Scollay Square gave way to Government Center. Meanwhile, Collins reduced property taxes five of his eight years in office. As a result, while downtown gorged on plump new developments, the working-class neighborhoods were systematically starved. Few new schools, playgrounds, parks, or community centers were built during the Collins years. City services in the neighborhoods deteriorated. Boston's voters got their revenge when Collins ran for the U.S. Senate in 1966 and lost twenty-one of the city's twenty-two wards, leaving him so weakened politically that he dared not run for mayor again. But this didn't mollify the neighborhoods. When Kevin White succeeded Collins in 1968, he inherited a refurbished downtown and a pack of aggrieved communities, utterly disbelieving of all politicians.

Determined to escape his predecessor's fate, White began looking for ways to reassure the neighborhoods even before he was elected. His very first campaign position paper argued that the "fundamental problem" of Boston's city government was "communications between government and the people." To meet the problem, he promised to create a new Neighborhood Service Department, with offices in all city neighborhoods, to "assure each citizen of a voice in his community's affairs." Then he gave a promise shrewdly calculated to appeal to alienated voters: "The target area of the next administration must be the neighborhoods of this city." Soon this evolved into a sort of campaign slogan, with White replacing Collins' old theme of "The New Boston"—which had come to mean "The New Downtown"—with the more modest and appealing "City of Neighborhoods."

White had little notion of how a Neighborhood Service Department would function, so after his victory in November he appointed a study group, headed by Harvard political scientist Samuel Huntington, to transform the idea into a workable program. The group examined other efforts at urban decentralization, particularly John Lindsay's Little City Halls and Urban Action Task Forces. The New York program focused almost exclusively on poorer—usually black—neighborhoods, and in that respect was a model for the "Neighborhood City Halls" recommended that winter by the Kerner Commission. Huntington's study group quickly concluded that in Boston such a limitation would be disastrous, that the program would work there only if it encompassed the white working-class neighborhoods as well. It also argued that, to alleviate neighborhood alienation, the operation had to be more than a citizen complaint and referral service; it had to have a role in framing city policies.

The Mayor accepted the recommendations and in March 1968 established the Office of Public Service to oversee fifteen "neighborhood centers" throughout Boston. Soon, like their forerunners in New York, the centers became known as Little City Halls. The first three were located in white areas—Italian East Boston, Irish Field's Corner, heterogeneous Allston-Brighton. By the end of 1968, ten Little City Halls had opened, most of them in brightly painted fifty-foot trailers. The Mayor inaugurated each one with a full-dress ceremony, accompanied by high school bands and prancing drum majorettes.

Those rickety trailers may have been more potent symbols of Kevin White's governance than the massive City Hall. For if the astonishing structure downtown represented White's spirit of innovation, the Little City Halls proclaimed his willingness to listen to the people of the neighborhoods, to grant them a measure of self-determination.

Not every neighborhood welcomed the halls. Charlestown—still recoiling from its urban renewal battles—was so suspicious of municipal programs that at first it refused to accept a trailer, which it regarded as "the Mayor's fifth column." Not until a year later, after watching other halls function, did a Charlestown delegation petition the Mayor for one of their own. But such suspicions never entirely disappeared, for the Little City Halls were asked to perform multiple, often conflicting, functions. They were expected to improve the delivery of city services to the neighborhoods by funneling residents' complaints about potholes or broken streetlights to the appropriate departments, or simply by leading confused, frustrated people through the municipal bureaucracy. They were also meant as catalysts for community action, mobilizing neighborhoods to tackle their own problems. But their most important function was to be the Mayor's "eyes and ears," monitoring the community's fear and resentment, identifying problems while they were still manageable, alerting him to potential crises. White liked to tell his Little City Hall managers, "It's not your job to come in and tell me your neighborhood is on fire. If you do, I'm going to throw you in the fire. You've got to tell me when the neighborhood is *going* to catch fire."

Little City Halls could be effective tools in the political game, particularly when a shrewd manager identified a potent issue which the Mayor could exploit for his own purposes. The first such conjunction of circumstances came in East Boston, where street-wise Fred Salvucci became Little City Hall manager in July 1968. Despite his MIT education, Salvucci had never strayed far from his ethnic roots, still living in a Brighton three-decker with his parents downstairs. Speaking Italian as well as he did English, Salvucci was ideally equipped to understand the clannish Italians of East Boston. It didn't take him long to identify Logan International Airport as the overwhelming issue in the community, one that threatened to erupt into a full-blown crisis.

For years, Logan had abraded nerves in "Eastie." Huge jets swooping in for landings made sleep difficult and daily life distressing. Planes knocked down television antennas, stripped trees of their leaves, and so weakened a church steeple that it had to be razed. Service vehicles rattled through the streets. Then, as air traffic grew in the late sixties, the airport sought to expand its runways. By the time Salvucci arrived, the neighborhood's patience was exhausted. Suspicion of all public "improvements" was so intense that many residents believed their new ice-skating rink was actually a hangar in disguise. Like Charlestown with its El and highways, East Boston felt abused by outsiders. "Why don't you tear down all of East Boston and turn it over to the airport?" one resident asked at a community meeting. "Then you could have real long runways, all the way to Dover and the other suburbs—save commuting time for the travelers."

Late in 1968, the Mayor assigned Colin to ride herd on the airport, and on the Massachusetts Port Authority, the autonomous body which ran Logan and the Port of Boston. For years, complaints had proliferated against the sprawling Authority and its strong-willed director, Edward F. King. Colin compiled a "laundry list" of charges against the Authority and prepared a hard-hitting press release, winning a rare accolade from the Mayor, who stopped him in the hall one day and said, "Hey, I didn't know you had that kind of political instinct."

But the bulk of the grievances came from East Boston, channeled to City Hall by Fred Salvucci. Superficially at least, Colin and Salvucci were about as different as two men could be, and, at the beginning, the advocate and the analyst eyed each other warily. The first few times Salvucci came to lay an Eastie complaint on Colin's desk he found the young lawyer remote, even aloof, while Colin was taken aback by Salvucci's urgency. There are a dozen neighborhoods out there, he thought, and I'm damned if I'll be stampeded into devoting all my attention to one of them just because it has a passionate spokesman. Moreover, East Boston was hardly the kind of neighborhood for which Colin had intended to go to war. Salvucci and his people would have to wait their turn.

But, resourceful as he was ardent, Fred Salvucci invited Colin to tour East Boston one day. They met in Fred's trailer and spent the morning trudging through the neighborhood around the airport. Stopping his ears against the screech of the jets, Colin marveled at the tenacity of the families who lived beneath those flight paths. Later, Fred regaled him with airport "horror stories" over lunch at Tony's, an East Boston bistro known for cutting a customer's tie off if he failed to finish his meal. Beneath hundreds of ties which hung from the rafters like multicolored spaghetti, Fred and Colin felt their way toward an understanding. Before long, they were close allies in the battle against the Port Authority. The more Colin learned about the airport's encroachment on East Boston, the angrier he got. This was no struggle against a faceless bureaucracy; it was a personal duel with its director, and Ed King was an easy man to hate. One day, as Colin examined blueprints at the Authority, the director himself walked in and fixed him with a glare "as cold as ice." Colin returned to City Hall more determined than ever to teach the arrogant S.O.B. a lesson.

He got his chance early in 1969 when the Authority moved under "eminent domain" to take over a stretch of road at the end of runway 15–33. While lengthening the runway to 10,000 feet, the Authority had already demolished several Victorian houses on Neptune Road. Now it wanted to take 720 feet of uninhabited road with its grassy median strip and thirty-six elm trees on either side. The afflicted residents on the remaining two blocks were fighting to preserve the stub of roadway and the trees as a buffer against the airport and as a play area for their children. At Salvucci's urging, Colin was assigned to bring a suit to enjoin the Authority from taking the road and trees. In the State Supreme Judicial Court it was argued for the city by Corporation Counsel Herb Gleason. Colin, who had prepared all the papers, sat by him at the counsel table, increasingly confident that they would prevail. He was astonished when the court ruled in the Authority's favor.

The very night after the ruling—before the city could bring further legal action—Port Authority bulldozers rumbled onto Neptune Road and under cover of darkness knocked down the elms. The next morning, angry residents gathered to shout in impotent fury at the workmen. Colin seethed quietly and wondered at the speed with which Ed King had moved. Jesus, he thought, nothing in government happens that quickly; he must have had those damned bulldozers waiting for days with their motors idling!

The movement to limit airport expansion was closely linked with opposition to new highway construction. If the business community traditionally favored planes and cars, workers generally supported buses and trains—not only because they could afford such conveyances, but because their neighborhoods were invariably the ones ripped up to make way for new runways, highways, and interchanges. By the late sixties in Boston, a broad coalition of neighborhood groups had been forged to fight a number of new highway projects. It was a remarkably diverse coalition—dashiki-clad members of the Black United Front, longshoremen from Charlestown, housewives from Jamaica Plain, Cambridge professors, and South End welfare mothers.

One day in early 1969, Colin paid a call on John Lynch, who had recently taken over as Little City Hall manager in Jamaica Plain. A predominantly Irish neighborhood just southwest of downtown, Jamaica Plain had been the first of Boston's communities to make an open stand against the Southwest Expressway, which was scheduled to cut a swath through dozens of its residential blocks. With Lynch that day, Colin attended a meeting in a church basement to plan a petition drive against the highway. Colin was already anti-highway, but the fervor of those working-class mothers and small merchants determined to protect their homes aroused new sympathy in him. In the months that followed, he added his voice to those of Frank, Salvucci, and Lynch, urging the Mayor to support the resistance movement publicly.

Finally, in December 1969, Kevin White put his signature to Frank's bold letter calling on Governor Frank Sargent to proclaim "an immediate halt to any land-taking, demolition or construction now taking place or contemplated for new highways." Citing "the anguished objections of neighborhood residents," the Mayor said highway construction caused "the loss of housing, additional air pollution, disruption of long-established neighborhoods, the disappearance of open space and the growth of feeling among our citizens that government is an unfeeling, unthinking monolith unconcerned with their needs and unresponsive to their wishes." The moratorium proposal was an extreme one, designed in part to seize the highway issue from the Governor, against whom White planned to run the following year. In an editorial, the *Globe* termed it "about as practical as a petition to the Weather Bureau for a moratorium on snow in New England." But Colin thought it a useful bargaining position, one that identified the Mayor with the enlightened interests of the city's neighborhoods.

Once he had taken the neighborhoods' side on both the airport and highways, it was natural for the Mayor to support them on a whole range of other issues, and frequently Colin was assigned to such questions. When tenants in Allston-Brighton clamored for rent control, Colin examined legislation in other cities, prepared the Mayor's rent control ordinance, and lobbied for it in the City Council. Later, he again rode to the defense of Allston-Brighton, helping to block the proposed purchase of a large apartment complex by Boston College, which would have converted the apartments to dormitories. In the Fenway, the South End, and Dorchester, he helped other neighborhoods fend off tax-exempt institutions seeking to expand their plants at the expense of precious open space.

These neighborhood grievances were blessings in disguise for Kevin White; they were pains he could minister to. For they stemmed from encroachments by external forces and, as Saul Alinsky had long since demonstrated, nothing unites a neighborhood like a well-defined external enemy. It was easy for the Mayor to take stands against such outsiders. Even when he lost, the neighborhoods gave him full credit for trying. But the Mayor's situation became more difficult when the force seeking change in white neighborhoods was the city itself. Yet this was inevitable. To fulfill his pledges to the black community, White had to encroach on the jealously guarded prerogatives of places like Dorchester, Jamaica Plain, and Charlestown.

A notable example was the "infill" housing program initiated by the Mayor in March 1968. "Infill" was designed to provide 1,000 units of low-income housing—particularly for chronically ill-housed large families—without having to go through time-consuming land acquisition. It would have erected prefabricated housing on city-owned vacant lots throughout Boston, rents to be subsidized under federal programs, so that most tenants would pay about 23 percent of their incomes. This imaginative program was calculated to provide decent housing for the poor—quickly, cheaply, and without the social problems that invariably resulted when large numbers of the disadvantaged were herded together in high-rise projects. But the program met fierce resistance in the white neighborhoods, much of it rooted in fears that "infill" tenants would be primarily black. One after another, Charlestown, Jamaica Plain, West Roxbury, and Dorchester declined to accept "infill." The only units ever built were in the black neighborhoods—Roxbury and the South End—and most of those were never occupied.

Time and again during those first years, the Mayor encountered determined opposition from communities afraid that his ambitious projects were merely subterfuges designed to introduce unwanted blacks. Sometimes the fear of blacks cost the communities improvements they would otherwise have welcomed. When the Mayor insisted that a proposed new municipal swimming pool in Dorchester must be open to all races, the residents refused to accept it, claiming that it would become an "inkwell."

The most persistent opposition to the Mayor's programs generally came from Irish neighborhoods. Colin found himself at a disadvantage in dealing with such communities because he knew so little of Boston's Irish. His only close contact with them had come in the summer of 1964, after his junior year at Amherst, when he got a job at a meat-packing plant in a grubby industrial zone on the edge of South Boston. Filling in for men on vacation, he worked at many jobs: at the strapping machine, chopping hamburger, lifting sides of beef off the hooks and sliding them across the bench to the butchers, or wheeling the steaks from the cutting room to the packing room. The hours were long—7:00 a.m. to 6:00 p.m.—because everyone worked overtime. It was dirty, dreary, monotonous labor which required few skills and therefore attracted the least trained workers, often immigrants just off the boat.

There were Irish from Charlestown and Southie, Italians from the North End, Lebanese, Syrians, but only a handful of blacks and a few Hispanics. Colin had little in common with most of them, other than bitter resentment of the working conditions and of the foreman who made everybody's life miserable. At lunchtime, many of the laborers—even middle-aged men with a brood of children to feed—went upstairs to the locker room and gambled their wages away at poker. What money they kept went into cars—big, expensive sedans which struck Colin, who drove his family's little Nash Rambler, as an irresponsible squandering of their resources. But he felt a certain sympathy for these men, many of whom were clearly stuck in their jobs for life, with nothing else to look forward to until they retired or dropped dead of a premature heart attack.

With only one of his fellow workers did Colin develop anything like a friendship—a young Irishman named Jim Ryan who came from the industrial city of Chelsea. Colin and Jim usually ate lunch together sprawled outside in the sunny yard, exchanging tales from their very different lives. Jim was an accomplished raconteur and, before long, Colin felt he understood a little of what it was like to grow up in an Irish working-class family in a dirty industrial town. But every evening Colin would climb in his Rambler and head for Lexington. He never visited Jim at home and, once the summer was over, they never met again.

After that, the only glimpse Colin got of Irish life was on an occasional visit to South Boston's St. Patrick's Day celebration. There he would gape at the flamboyant figures who marched in the parade or massed along the sidewalks—boisterous men and women, decked out in bottle green, waving shillelaghs, bawling ballads, their faces flushed from frequent pit stops at dozens of saloons along the route. But when the last marchers disappeared over the hill and roving bands of Southie kids began scuffling on the beer-spattered streets, Colin and his friends made a quick getaway.

Such forays helped form Colin's picture of the Irish as coarse, unruly, hot-tempered, sometimes violent, but vital, humorous, lively, with intense loyalty to their Church, generous attachment to friends and neighbors, a passionate allegiance to their tight little community. And it was precisely this devotion to tribe and turf that proved so resistant to Kevin White's entreaties for racial justice. Yet that was an old tension in American life—between the notion of community invoked by John Winthrop when he set out to form a "city upon a hill" and the idea of equality enshrined in the Declaration of Independence.

Tocqueville recognized that Americans had not one but two political systems: "the one fulfilling the ordinary duties and responding to the daily and infinite calls of a community; the other circumscribed within certain limits and exercising an exceptional authority over the general interests of the country." For seventy years this delicate balance prevailed, reassuring Americans that the demands of nationalism were compatible with the intimacies of community. In the mid-nineteenth century, the revolutionary settlement broke down, the centralizing impulse dashing on the hard rock of particularism. The battle was joined in the Lincoln-Douglas debates, in which Lincoln argued that the essence of democratic government was "the equality of all men" derived from natural law, while Douglas insisted it was the "principle of popular sovereignty," the right of American communities to decide fundamental issues, like slavery, for themselves. Ultimately force of arms held the nation together, but the tug-of-war between community and equality was by no means resolved. In one way or another, it has persisted to this day.

In the flowering of 1960s idealism, Americans persuaded themselves that community and equality were not only compatible but mutually reinforcing principles. In 1964, with the nation still mourning Jack Kennedy's death and determined to fulfill his interrupted promise, the Johnson administration secured passage of the Civil Rights Act and the Economic Opportunity Act. The Civil Rights Act empowered the federal government to cut off federal funds to districts guilty of racial discrimination, an unprecedented role for the executive branch in the struggle for racial equality. The Economic Opportunity Act, with its guarantee of "maximum feasible participation" in community action programs, granted poor people an opportunity to control their own neighborhoods. Impelled by the same benevolent impulses, enacted by the same congressional coalition, they were twin expressions of the nation's conscience at mid-decade.

But soon the inherent tensions between community and equality reasserted themselves. Civil rights legislation sought to override local law or custom— often equated with bigotry—in the name of a national commitment to human rights, while the poverty program encouraged "community control" as an antidote to bureaucratic centralization. Moreover, it wasn't long before disadvantaged whites saw that they could invoke, in a spirited defense of their own interests, the very doctrines designed to aid blacks.

Ironically, nobody had done more to empower the disenfranchised neighborhoods than Kevin White. From the start, his campaign appeals to a "city of neighborhoods," his Little City Halls, his stands on the airport, highways, and other community issues had encouraged Boston's neighborhoods to demand self-determination. Nobody could doubt that he was equally serious about his demands for racial equality. But the two impulses no longer pulled in tandem. As Kevin White completed his second year in office and prepared to run for governor, the two great ideals of equality and community were drifting dangerously apart in Boston, with many of the Mayor's boldest ventures foundering in the gulf between them.

The Mayor loved popcorn. He gobbled it almost as voraciously as he did politics. Popcorn and politics, his staff suspected, could keep Kevin White going for months on end.

One summer evening in 1970—during his gubernatorial campaign—the Mayor summoned several senior aides to his Beacon Hill town house to discuss the fate of his embattled "infill" housing program. When Colin arrived, the Mayor was in the kitchen making popcorn and mixing drinks. Colin volunteered to help, and for a few minutes the city's chief executive and his young aide were alone together. Suddenly the Mayor said, "Colin, I've been thinking about what I'd like you to do when I'm governor."

"Oh?" asked Colin. The Mayor was still in a three-way race for the Democratic nomination. If he won that, he faced a tough battle against the Republican incumbent, Frank Sargent. The issue seemed a bit premature. But the Mayor rushed on. "I've decided I want you as my legal counsel. How does that strike you?"

"Well, Kevin, of course I'm flattered. But I just haven't thought about it."

"That's okay. Just remember, I want you with me."

Then, with the Mayor carrying the popcorn and Colin the tray of drinks, they climbed to the second floor, where the others were already gathered in the rear parlor: Barney Frank; Deputy Mayor Ed Sullivan; the new redevelopment director, John Warner; and several others. It was a muggy night and the officials had their coats off and their shirt sleeves rolled up as they began laying out options for rescuing the housing program, then stymied by neighborhood opposition. It was a gritty, technical discussion, filled with costs per unit, HUD subsidies, and FHA financing. After ten minutes, the Mayor had lost interest. Soon he was on the telephone with State Treasurer Bob Crane, his close friend and political adviser, and Jimmy Hosker, his campaign manager. As the conference droned on across the room, the Mayor sprawled in his favorite arm-chair talking politics and gobbling popcorn.

My God, thought Colin, we've lost him. He hasn't the faintest interest in infill housing. He isn't interested in governing Boston anymore. All he can think about is that damn governor's race!

In two years at City Hall, Colin had learned a lot about politics and even more about Kevin White. By now he realized that White had sought the may-oralty principally as a stepping-stone to the State House. Yet his own interest was in the Mayor as mayor, not the Mayor as candidate, or even the Mayor as governor. He was still fascinated by the task of governing the city, and when the demands of the state campaign made it increasingly difficult for any of them to do that, he grew impatient.

As the race progressed, not only were the Mayor's energies diverted from the city, but so were those of his staff. By September, when White won the Democratic nomination, his senior aides were spending 80 percent of their time on the campaign. Then, in mid-October, the Mayor was hospitalized with a perforated ulcer. He emerged on October 24 clearly lagging behind Acting Governor Sargent, who had proved a formidable opponent. The Mayor's ad-visers, desperately searching for issues with which to capture public attention, came up with off-track betting as a way to alleviate the fiscal crisis confronting many Massachusetts towns and cities. Overnight, Colin and three other may-oral assistants cobbled up a position paper.

Last-minute gimmicks notwithstanding, White lost to Frank Sargent that November. To a man whose entire political career had been targeted at the State House, it was a grievous blow. Even more devastating was the loss of his own city by a whopping 17,000 votes. Worse yet, the incumbent Irish Catholic mayor of a heavily Irish Catholic working-class city had lost on his own ground to an Episcopalian Yankee acting governor from the horsey suburb of Dover. Indeed, the Mayor had done worst in the heavily Irish neighborhoods of South Boston, Roslindale, and West Roxbury. His own people had publicly humiliated him. He wouldn't forget that.

Indeed, for the next few months Kevin White could think of little else. The day after the election, he told aides, "I'm through. I'm not going to run again." Then he left for a Puerto Rican vacation. Even when he returned, he didn't—in his own words—"give a shit about governing Boston." He was preoccupied with his own survival. In January, he hired Tully Plesser, a New York pollster, to test the political waters for him. The next month, Plesser came up with encouraging news. The Mayor wasn't dead politically, but he would have to remake his image. His constituents regarded him as too liberal, too pro-black, too faddist and flighty. Most important, in a city that prided itself on its tough-ness, he was regarded as weak and indecisive. Plesser urged the Mayor to "toughen up."

Armed with this judgment, the Mayor sought reelection. But he took Plesser's advice to heart. For the rest of the year, "toughness" was Kevin White's watchword. His advertising relied on slogans emphasizing his fighting spirit: "When the landlords raised rents, the Mayor raised hell," and "Logan Airport had plans to tear up East Boston, the Mayor tore up the plans." Some of the shift was pure flackery, deft manipulation of the Mayor's image. But some of it was real. For White himself sensed that it was time to edge to the right. In part, this reflected a change in his audience. For three years, as a mayor running hard for governor, he had devised his political messages with one eye cocked toward the liberal suburban vote. Now, compelled to seek reelection in the city, he beamed his messages at ethnic, working-class Boston. This realignment was underscored by the departure of some of the aides who had given White's first term such a liberal tone—Special Counsel Bill Cowin, who left in May 1969 to head the State Public Utilities Commission; BRA Director Hale Champion, who in July 1969 became vice-president of the University of Minnesota; and most important, majordomo Barney Frank, who resigned after the November election, ostensibly to return to Harvard. The effect of these and other liberal defections was reinforced by a new aggressiveness among the traditionalists on the Mayor's staff—old-liners like Ed Sullivan, Larry Quealy, and Barbara Cameron, who had bristled at the "trendy" tone of the first three years. Soon after White's loss to Sargent, this "conservative caucus" began compiling a briefing book that emphasized many of Tully Plesser's points.

So a new Kevin White began to emerge during 1971. He downplayed his Office of Human Rights, Model Cities, and other programs designed to aid the black community, while talking tough on crime and drugs, beefing up the police, and promising to hold the line on taxes. Symbolic of his new stance was White's campaign for the removal of Doris Bunte from the Boston Housing Authority. Three years earlier his appointment of Mrs. Bunte—a black tenant in the Orchard Park housing project—had been seen as a commitment to give public housing tenants a powerful voice on the Authority, and with two others of similar views, she formed a tenant-oriented majority on the board. But soon that trio and the Mayor found themselves at odds over patronage. Determined to regain control, White charged the outspoken Mrs. Bunte with five acts of misconduct. After a thirteen-day "trial" before the Mayor and City Council, she was found "guilty" of three charges and removed from the board, only to be reinstated by a court. The Mayor said Mrs. Bunte had been dismissed because "she did not bring about reform," but others saw the episode as a clear signal that henceforth the Mayor would adopt a more skeptical attitude toward the black and the poor. To Colin Diver, the Bunte affair was "a colossal mistake—embarrassing, humiliating, and stupid." Partly a personal vendetta, partly a power play, partly a political message, it was the Mayor at his worst.

By the summer of 1971, Colin was growing uneasy in the Mayor's employ. It wasn't for lack of responsibility. With the departure of Frank, Cowin, and Merrick, Colin's role had expanded rapidly; he took over some of the substantive policy making from Frank, most of the speechwriting from Cowin, some of the federal liaison from Merrick. Advancing into the inner circle of advisers, he spent nearly as much time in the Mayor's spacious office as he did in his own cubicle down the hall. Indeed, so shorthanded were they in City Hall that year that he became a jack-of-all-trades, with a hand in almost everything that passed through the Mayor's office. Bob Weinberg, the Mayor's new majordomo, would shout down the corridors, "My God, let's do something. Get Colin!"

But the closer he got to the center of power, the less it appealed to him. Three years before, he had enlisted in Kevin White's crusade against racial injustice, poverty, and urban decay, and they had accomplished some fine things during those years. But now the Mayor was so preoccupied with his political ambitions that he had little energy left for the substantive issues. Increasingly, White seemed to regard blacks and other disadvantaged groups as political liabilities. Colin found the Mayor's new priorities dismaying and frustrating.

There were other frustrations as well, which could hardly be blamed on Kevin White. For three years now, Colin had spent most of his time contending with demands from the resurgent neighborhoods. In one sense, he knew, that was as it should be; government ought to respond to the legitimate complaints of an aroused electorate. The trouble was that Boston's white neighborhoods seemed primarily concerned with *stopping* things. Colin, who had joined the White administration to act on behalf of the disadvantaged, was becoming, instead, an expert in blocking action. And even when he or the Mayor took positive action, Colin was no longer confident that it would produce the intended results. He knew now that even the best-intentioned programs sometimes produced dubious social consequences.

A prime example that summer of 1971 was the "B-BURG" program, an effort by a consortium of twenty-two Boston savings banks (the Boston Banks' Urban Renewal Group) to provide mortgages for the city's low-income black families. B-BURG had been founded in 1963 to answer Ed Logue's appeal for rehabilitation loans, and during the next six years the program had puttered along, committing only $2 million. Then, after Martin Luther King's assassination, Boston's business community was galvanized by fear of retaliatory violence and by anxiety over the alliance struck by the militants of the Black United Front and FUND's suburban liberals. When Kevin White appealed to banks and insurance companies to come up with a counter-program, the savings banks hastily agreed to revitalize B-BURG, pledging $20 million in new mortgage money, most of it for low-income blacks. Indeed, when the commercial banks and insurance companies largely defaulted on commitments they had given at the same time, B-BURG became the only segment of White's program to bear fruit, its member banks providing $29 million in mortgages to more than 2,000 families over the next three years. Here, it seemed, was an example of effective government–private sector activism on behalf of the black and the poor—precisely the sort of program for which Colin had been pressing all along.

But by early 1971, the unintended consequences of B-BURG began to crop up—and they didn't look positive at all. Unbeknownst to most Bostonians, the consortium had granted mortgages to blacks only within a narrow zone stretching from the South End through Roxbury into Dorchester and Mattapan, for nearly a century the route of black—and, earlier, Jewish—migration, a path that generally skirted the Irish Catholic neighborhoods on either flank. The Irish neighborhoods had resisted Jewish encroachment and were likely to repel blacks even more adamantly. By taking the line of least resistance, B-BURG had done nothing to help blacks break out of the ghetto. It had merely enlarged and reinforced the ghetto.

That was only one of the unintended consequences. The combination of heavy black demand for the newly available mortgages and the sharply constricted B-BURG district created a classic breeding ground for blockbusting. As the first blacks bought houses there, unscrupulous real estate people warned Jewish families that they had better sell quickly before their property lost its value. Speculators snapped up the homes at panic prices, then resold them at huge profits to incoming blacks. Real estate agents made big commissions on the rapid turnover. Once begun, the process fed on itself. In a few years, the Jewish population of Mattapan plummeted from about 90,000 to barely 1,500—an abrupt shift that was accompanied by fierce social conflict. Through much of 1970 and 1971, Boston's newspapers were filled with stories of murders, rapes, and muggings, many of them committed by young blacks on elderly Mattapan Jews. The Jewish Defense League patrolled the area, armed with rifles and baseball bats. One Defense League pamphlet warned: "We will not run from Mattapan. We are determined to fight to the finish these elements and enemies of our people. If need be, we will fight in hand-to-hand combat that our Jewish blood shall be avenged."

In May 1971, a Senate subcommittee announced that it was coming to Boston in September to hold hearings on the B-BURG program. Assigned to develop the city's position, Colin discovered that the B-BURG zone had been no secret to city, state, and federal officials. Fortunately, several city officials had protested to the banks, drawing a curt reply that the banks weren't interested in the city's suggestions but were simply advising it "what we are and are not willing to do." This starchy attitude allowed Colin to disassociate the city from the worst aspects of the B-BURG fiasco; the statement he drafted, and which the Mayor submitted to the subcommittee, insisted that the city had always preferred a program which would allow blacks to purchase housing anywhere in the metropolitan area.

Although the White administration managed to escape B-BURG's worst fallout, the episode had a profound effect on Colin. He may have taken its lesson particularly to heart because it echoed the theme of a book he was reading that summer—*Urban Dynamics*, an unlikely volume to find favor in Kevin White's City Hall. Its author, Jay Forrester, was a professor of management at MIT, where he had formed an alliance with White's old adversary, former Mayor John Collins, and Forrester's thesis reflected Collins' suspicion of liberals who thought they could solve the urban crisis through social activism and welfare programs. Using computer language, Forrester argued that most of man's intuitive responses developed from "first-order, negative feedback loops." For example, when a man warmed his hands by a stove, the only important variable was his distance from the burner. If his hands were too far from the burner, they wouldn't get warm enough; if they were too close, they'd get burned. Cause and effect were closely related. Such intuitive responses—which governed the way we perform most daily tasks—were accurate and reliable.

But, Forrester warned, the modern city didn't function like a simple, first-order loop. Instead, it had a multiplicity of intersecting feedback loops, each with many complex variables. Thus, such systems were "counter-intuitive." If one looked for a cause near in time and space to the symptom, one usually found something plausible, yet it was generally not the true cause, but merely another symptom. Conditioned by our training in simple systems, we applied intuition to complex systems and were led astray. "Very often," Forrester concluded, "one finds that the policies that have been adopted for correcting a difficulty are actually intensifying it rather than producing a solution."

When applied to urban systems, Forrester's analysis suggested that "humanitarian impulses coupled with short-term political pressures lead to programs whose benefits, if any, evaporate quickly, leaving behind a system that is unimproved or in worse condition. Job-training programs, low-cost housing programs, and even financial aid, when used alone without improvements in the economic climate of a city, can fall into this category." Forrester's prime example was subsidized housing. Intuitively, projects such as Methunion Manor might seem a mandatory response to the needs of the poor and the near-poor for standard housing at rents they could afford. In fact, Forrester argued, such housing generally made things worse for everyone, including those it sheltered. First, the availability of subsidized housing—along with other welfare services—attracted the needy to the city, building a constituency for even more such housing and further straining city services. Then, the housing took valuable land, reducing the land available for non-subsidized housing and business enterprises which produced both jobs and tax revenue. The result: the growth of a dependent welfare class, the exodus of productive businesses and tax-paying employees, and a fiscal crisis for the city.

By 1971, *Urban Dynamics* had become the bible of the "conservative caucus," which was urging the Mayor to retrench his social programs and concentrate on improving delivery of more traditional services, such as police and fire protection, sanitation, street paving, lighting, and recreation. Colin wasn't ideologically predisposed to the Forrester thesis, but his experience with B-BURG and other misfired programs prepared him for the notion of unintended consequences. All that summer, he brooded over the book, wondering whether government was making things better or worse in Boston. And yet he clung to the values which had brought him to City Hall in the first place. What had changed were not his beliefs but his expectations. After three years in the Mayor's office, he no longer believed that government could establish racial justice or eradicate poverty; those problems, it now seemed to him, were too complex, the resources too limited, the instruments too imprecise, the competing interests too intractable. Money could probably be spent more effectively on improving conventional services. But that didn't mean government should retreat to mere housekeeping; even with diminished expectations, one should do what one could to reduce social injustice. To that degree, Colin was still an activist—and inevitably that brought him into conflict with the increasingly cautious Mayor.

Rockland Towers was an eleven-story public housing project for the elderly which the Boston Housing Authority planned to build in West Roxbury. When announced in 1970, the proposal stirred vigorous protests from neighborhood groups, for it was the first low-income project ever designated for that last bastion of the city's Irish middle class. With its single- and two-family homes set well apart on tree-lined streets, West Roxbury looked more like suburbia than like an urban neighborhood. With the exception of Beacon Hill, it was Boston's wealthiest community, and it was certainly one of the whitest; only a handful of blacks had managed to find homes there. Not incidentally, it was Kevin White's birthplace.

But West Roxbury hadn't showed much loyalty to its native son. In his 1970 race for governor, it gave him his lowest percentage anywhere in the city—a meager 31.6 percent. To win reelection as mayor he had to do better than that; so, although he had initially endorsed the West Roxbury project, as soon as opposition developed he began to back away.

Some of the opposition was directed against high-rise apartments of any kind—residents had blocked two other apartment projects which they feared would destroy the suburban feel of their community. "These people wouldn't approve a ten-story palace for the Pope," argued one City Hall lobbyist. But Rockland Towers was no ordinary apartment project. It was "public housing"—a code phrase for the black and poor. Much of the opposition was grounded in West Roxbury's determination to remain as affluent, and as white, as possible.

Early in the summer of 1971, Larry Quealy, the mayoral aide who kept in close touch with Irish neighborhood groups, brought a West Roxbury delegation in to see Kevin White. Colin, who had been arguing forcefully in support of Rockland Towers, was asked to sit in, as were Bob Weinberg and the Mayor's housing adviser, Andy Olins. After the delegation had made their pitch and been ushered out, the Mayor asked his four aides to stay behind for a discussion of the issues. Larry Quealy, who himself lived in West Roxbury, led off by scornfully dismissing the project. "It's bad for these people, it's bad for the neighborhood, it's bad for you," he told the Mayor. "That's three strikes against it. In baseball and politics, that means it's out." As Quealy spoke, the Mayor leaned back in his leather desk chair, eyes half closed, nodding his head in apparent agreement.

Colin could see the Mayor's mind closing down. If he gave in on this one, it would be just another in a series of capitulations to aroused neighborhoods which opposed his programs. How often was he going to let them exercise their veto? Shouldn't the Mayor stand up for citywide interests, not to mention those for whom nobody else would speak? As Quealy finished, Colin broke in: "I can see which way this thing is going. I'm sure this serves no useful purpose other than to vent my spleen, but I'm going to say it anyway." He could feel his face burning, the way it did on those rare occasions when he lost control. In three years with the Mayor, he had never exploded like this. Indeed, he struck his colleagues as the quintessential man of reason, so much so that some of them, behind his back, called him "the iceman." Sometimes Colin himself worried that all the passion had gone out of his commitment to the city, that he had bogged down in a mechanical cost-benefit analysis. Well, he might be making a fool of himself now, but he didn't care. He plunged on.

"I don't think the reasons those West Roxbury people gave are the least bit convincing," he said. "Does anyone really think they're concerned about height and density? Do you believe that, Larry? I can only conclude that their real reason for opposing the project is a cynical combination of fear and bigotry. And let me say this, Kevin, the city will be displaying the same kind of fear and bigotry if it caves in to them." Then he got up and stalked from the room. As he closed the door, he could see the Mayor gaping after him.

Soon afterwards, Colin resigned. He hadn't lost faith in government, merely in the relentlessly political administration of Kevin White. And he had an intriguing job offer. Bill Cowin—who had left the Mayor's office two years before to take a post with the state—liked Colin and admired his "astonishing intelligence." When Bill was given a new job—Secretary of Consumer Affairs—he asked Colin to be his assistant secretary.

Colin's resignation prompted no recriminations. The Mayor threw him a going-away party and presented him with a Raleigh bicycle. That fall Colin ran two South End precincts for the Mayor, helping him win reelection over Louise Day Hicks.

Early in October 1971, Colin rode his bicycle to the State Office Building to begin his new job. As Secretary of Consumer Affairs, Bill Cowin concentrated on improving the work of the state's regulatory agencies. As his principal assistant, Colin helped implement the state's new no-fault insurance law and set up a cable television commission. It was interesting work, but just as Colin got the feel of it, he changed jobs again. Bill Cowin was the rising star of the Sargent administration. In September 1972, Sargent asked him to leave Consumer Affairs and take over as Secretary of Administration and Finance— the principal fiscal, budgetary, and administrative officer in state government. So important was the A & F Secretary that he was sometimes called Deputy Governor, and as Under Secretary, Colin became, in effect, the Deputy Governor's deputy.

Colin had less contact with the Governor than he had had with the Mayor. His job was to manage the huge A & F department while Bill concentrated on liaison with other state agencies and on advising the Governor, as a member of Sargent's "kitchen cabinet." Yet as Bill's trusted deputy, Colin was sometimes included in those sessions, which gave him an opportunity to observe the Governor at close hand.

In some respects, Frank Sargent and Kevin White struck Colin as remarkably similar men. To be sure, Sargent was a classic New England Yankee. A great-grandson of the legendary Brahmin banker Henry Lee, he had used a Cape Cod sporting goods store called the Goose Hummock as a stepping-stone to a fifteen-year career as a professional "fish and game man" (director of the state's Marine Fisheries and Natural Resources departments). But if many Yankees were parched and parsimonious, Frank Sargent was an ebullient, natural politician. His personal magnetism reached across party, ethnic, and class lines. To many of Boston's Irish, he was an honorary Irishman.

Though he was a lifelong Republican, Sargent's stance on most issues wasn't very different from Kevin White's. After Martin Luther King's assassination, as lieutenant governor, he pledged to "make the changes that King dreamed of—the change of heart, the change of mind." In 1970, as acting governor, he ordered the State House flag flown at half-staff in memory of the students killed at Kent State. He was frequently criticized by other Republicans for straying from the party line and for appointing too many Democrats. If anything, Sargent was more liberal than White: no Republican could be elected statewide in Massachusetts without appealing to Democrats and independents.

Colin discerned one major difference between them: White carefully calculated most of his moves, but Sargent governed from the gut. Compared to White, he wasn't a particularly strong leader: his staff pulled and hauled him in different directions. Yet when he had to make a decision, he invariably came down on the humane side. Indeed, the essence of Sargent's liberalism was a human response to human needs. He and his progressive appointees improved conditions for the retarded in state schools, expanded the Public Welfare Department's human services, closed many of the worst youth detention facilities, and carried out a sweeping reform of the archaic prison system.

Colin generally supported these initiatives, but increasingly he was less concerned with the substance of Sargent's programs than with how to execute them. That was his job at A & F—making sure that state policies were carried out effectively with the least possible waste, duplication, or corruption. Somewhat to his surprise, Colin found that he took enormous pleasure in such tasks as revising the state's personnel procedures, centralizing computer functions, even setting up a state motor pool. In part this inclination might be temperamental: a man who loved restoring his house, remaking ornamental plaster, and laying bathroom tile was likely to enjoy the nuts and bolts of government. But there was more to it than that. Traditional liberals, he decided, had exaggerated the importance of ideas. Four years earlier, Colin himself had thought that all City Hall needed was bright, innovative, creative ideas. Now he felt that the most important job in government was *implementing* ideas. Of course, if issues abstracted from management made no sense, then neither did management abstracted from issues. But there were plenty of people around just bursting with ideas, and not that many who could make them work.

There was at least one idea, though, on which Colin's commitment had never wavered—the notion of racial equality. It had been Martin Luther King's death more than anything else that brought him into government, and it was King's dream more than anything else that kept him there. At times the new aggressiveness of black spokesmen irritated him. Once Elma Lewis, a black cultural leader, met with Colin and Bob Weinberg to demand city money for one of her projects. When they hesitated, Mrs. Lewis launched into what Colin called her "three-hundred-years-of-slavery speech," a polemic in which she blamed whichever white she happened to be with for every indignity that had oppressed her people since the African slave trade. But such incidents hardly interrupted the strong flow of Colin's feelings about racial injustice, feelings which intensified in 1974 as the long battle over Boston's school segregation finally came to a head.

For nearly eight years, the State Board of Education and the Boston School Committee had engaged in a fruitless tug-of-war over implementation of the state's Racial Imbalance Act. Year after year, the board pressed for action to reduce the number of Boston's "unbalanced" schools (those more than 50 percent black) while the School Committee flatly refused, delayed, evaded, and, when pressed to the wall, adopted token measures. Meanwhile, the number of unbalanced schools rose steadily from forty-six in 1965 to sixty-seven in 1971.

Colin had little direct experience with the schools issue—in three years at City Hall, school questions had rarely crossed his desk, since the Mayor had virtually no control over the school system. Only once in the Mayor's office did Colin get a close look at the schools. When White appointed a Home Rule Commission to study the city's governmental structure, Colin served as one of its staffers and drew the schools as part of his assignment. For weeks he prowled the tangled warren of School Department headquarters, interviewing the Superintendent, his staff, and committee members. The experience filled him with despair. He found the department a hive of entrenched timeservers more concerned with buttressing their official positions than with educating children. The School Committee itself, utterly preoccupied with politics and patronage, had dug itself in for a long war of attrition on racial imbalance. Colin concluded that the best solution was to abolish the committee altogether and make the Superintendent directly responsible to the Mayor. As a fallback, he proposed an enlarged committee, elected by district so it would better reflect the city's ethnic and racial composition. The Home Rule Commission adopted his recommendations, but—as with so many of his assignments for Kevin White—nothing came of it. So long as the schools remained outside his ambit, White wanted nothing to do with them. Moreover, he had ill-disguised contempt for the School Committee. Whenever Colin urged him to do something about the schools, the Mayor responded, "If I'm publicly identified with those idiots, I'm going to be held responsible for what they do."

Only when the city faced a loss of state aid did the Mayor intervene in the desegregation dispute. Such was the case in 1971 when the State Board of Education and the School Committee reached an impasse over enrollment at the new Lee elementary school, built largely with state funds on the condition that it open "balanced." To facilitate that result, the school was placed near the border between black and white Dorchester. But, due in large part to B-BURG, that border had shifted, leaving the neighborhood around the school largely black. To balance the Lee, the School Committee would have had to take the unpopular step of transferring white children from adjacent elementary districts, and not surprisingly, the committee balked. The state threatened to withhold funds, which could mean an increase in the city's tax rate in an election year. The Mayor used what influence he had, and the committee eventually voted 3–2 to balance the school—53 percent white and 47 percent black.

But the settlement was short-lived. Outraged white parents launched a campaign against it, and at an emotionally charged public hearing, School Committeeman John Craven dramatically switched his vote, permitting white parents to keep their children in their neighborhood schools. Craven explained his reversal by charging that he had been "completely misled" by the School Department staff. "The truth is that it is impossible to racially balance the new Lee School without forced busing," he said, "and I've always been opposed to busing." (In fact, no busing would have been necessary, since the longest trip required under the plan was four-fifths of a mile.) Craven, who had been hissed when he entered the auditorium, was cheered and embraced on his way out. Ever since Louise Day Hicks had led the way in 1963, most School Committee members had fed the fires of resistance to school desegregation, but there could be little doubt that they were fairly representing the mood of their constituents. If democracy meant responding to the will of the majority, Mrs. Hicks was probably justified in describing the second Lee School hearing as "an exercise in participatory democracy."

But constitutional democracy also protects a minority from the unrestrained exercise of majority power, and sooner or later, Boston's struggle of majority will vs. minority rights was bound to find its way into court. Late in September 1971, concluding that the School Committee had "taken official action to increase and encourage racial isolation," the State Board of Education ordered an immediate freeze on $200 million worth of new construction in Boston and withdrawal of $14 million in state aid. In October, the School Committee brought suit in Superior Court, challenging the board's actions, and the board countersued, asking the court to enforce the Racial Imbalance Act in Boston.

At almost the same moment, black parents in Dorchester, dismayed by the Lee School fiasco, began contemplating a federal suit and approached Stephen Rosenfeld, then director of Boston's branch of the Lawyers' Committee for Civil Rights. Through the sixties, Northern attorneys in the Lawyers' Committee had defended indigent blacks in Mississippi and Alabama, and when they returned home they founded Northern branches to carry on the struggle there, using the *pro bono* services of private firms. When the Dorchester group approached Rosenfeld, he took the case to Foley, Hoag & Eliot, which assigned the case to two young associates—Roger Abrams and John Leubsdorf (a former *Law Review* colleague of Colin Diver's). Neither Abrams nor Leubsdorf had any experience trying school desegregation cases, so they were delighted to learn that two former Justice Department officials, then across the river at Harvard, were planning to file just such a suit.

J. Harold Flannery and Robert Pressman were veterans of the Southern civil rights struggle. Flannery had served for twelve years in the Justice Department's Civil Rights Division, trying dozens of Mississippi desegregation suits; he left the Department in 1970 to become deputy director of Harvard's Center for Law and Education. In 1971, "Nick" Flannery told Nathaniel Jones, counsel of the NAACP's Special Contribution Fund, that Boston was a "sitting duck" for a school suit, and several months later the NAACP agreed to finance a Boston suit.

Late in 1971, Leubsdorf and Abrams, representing the Dorchester clients, met with Flannery, Pressman, and Jones, representing the NAACP, and decided to merge their two suits. The fifty-three plaintiffs, representing a "class" of black children and their parents, were chosen from lists supplied by both groups. As lead plaintiff the lawyers selected a twenty-four-year-old mother of three school-age children named Tallulah Morgan, and the case became *Morgan* v. *Hennigan* (James Hennigan was then the School Committee chairman). Filed in March 1972, it began its passage through the Federal District Court as the State Board's battle with the School Committee worked its way through the state courts.

Eighteen months later, in October 1973, the Massachusetts Supreme Judicial Court ordered the School Committee to put a state-drawn desegregation plan into effect the following September. "The committee must understand that the time for testing the meaning of the statute has long since passed," the state court said, "and the time for prompt action to implement it is at hand." The first-stage plan would have reduced the number of unbalanced schools from sixty-one to thirty-one, by busing some 17,000 students. Though it directly affected only about three-fifths of the city, the plan exchanged students between Mrs. Hicks's beloved South Boston and the black heartland of Roxbury, a notion not calculated to assuage the fears of either community.

Although the School Committee's lawyer advised that "all legal avenues have been exhausted" in the state case, the plan's opponents were determined to try one more gambit. If they could repeal the Racial Imbalance Act, they believed they could nullify any court decree under its provisions. (Lawyers were by no means sure of that, but the opponents pressed ahead.) On April 3, 1974, opposition spokesmen paraded before an all-day hearing in the State House auditorium while, outside on the Boston Common, 25,000 others staged a massive demonstration demanding repeal.

From his office window high on Beacon Hill, Colin could see the huge throng swarming across the great lawn which swept from the State House steps down to the Park Street Station. Like a medieval army, they wore bright insignia of their sacred turf: green armbands for South Boston, brown for Charlestown, purple for Hyde Park, red for Dorchester. Colin made out the banners and placards jostling in the spring air—"No Forced Busing," "Down with Unjust Laws," and "Suburban Meddlers Go Home." He could hear the rhythmic chants borne upward on the wind—"Never! Never!" and "Hell no, we won't go." And he watched with mounting distaste as one group of youthful demonstrators clambered atop the Saint-Gaudens monument to the Brahmin Lieutenant Robert Gould Shaw and his black regiment, the youngsters' sneakers scraping the bronze visages of the soldiers who had marched to death together in 1863.

Three weeks later, the state legislature repealed the Racial Imbalance Act. Abruptly the focus shifted to the Governor. Should he veto the repeal or not? Frank Sargent was running for reelection that November, very likely facing Michael Dukakis, a liberal Democrat with strong support in Boston's suburbs. Sargent's conservative advisers warned him that his backing in traditional Republican circles was already draining away, that he could ill afford to alienate the Boston Irish. Since Dukakis would presumably preempt the liberal vote— though even he had backed away from busing by proposing "community control" of schools—Sargent should move to the right and identify himself with the anti-busing forces. He should sign the repeal.

The Governor's liberal advisers, on the other hand, contended that school desegregation was an overriding moral issue which could not be blinked. Moreover, for the Governor, who had supported the Racial Imbalance Act from the start, to back away from it now on the eve of its long-delayed implementation would be widely perceived as an act of self-serving cowardice. Finally, whatever they did about the state law, the federal court was on the verge of a decision. If, as was widely expected, the court ordered Boston desegregated anyway, all that repeal would accomplish would be to give aid and comfort to those determined to resist *any* court order. The Governor had no choice, the liberals said; he had to veto.

Both Bill Cowin and Colin strongly favored a veto. "Christ, Bill," Colin said at lunch one day. "The Governor's got to stand firm. This is no time to be copping out. It's the law. It's right. Let's get on with it." At several kitchen cabinet meetings during the next few days Bill urged that position on Frank Sargent.

On the evening of May 10—barely twenty-four hours before the deadline for action—the Governor went on statewide television to announce: "We have not come down a nine-year road only to turn our backs on those who deserve their place in the sun, their right to a quality education. I will not repeal the racial imbalance law. This afternoon, in the office from which I now speak, I have vetoed the legislation that would repeal that law." But then he shocked many of his supporters by revealing that he would soon seek to replace the old law with a new one which employed voluntary rather than mandatory methods. Instead of two-way busing for both races, he proposed a one-way "freedom of choice" plan for black children, plus an emphasis on "magnet schools" designed to attract integrated enrollments.

Louise Day Hicks welcomed the Governor's plan as "a vindication of all those who have opposed forcible busing." Doris Bunte angrily denounced it as "a backdown on the commitment to desegregate Boston schools."

Colin, too, was bitterly disappointed. The Governor had lost his nerve. Experience in the South showed that "freedom of choice" simply didn't work. But perhaps they had all expected too much of a politician in an election year. Now, Colin thought, it was all up to the federal court.

14

The Judge

$\mathbf{N}$o one can understand the feeling that comes to a Southern Negro on entering a federal court," wrote Martin Luther King, "unless he sees with his own eyes and feels with his own soul the tragic sabotage of justice in the city and state courts of the South. The Negro goes into those courts knowing that the cards are stacked against him. But the Southern Negro goes into the federal court with the feeling that he has an honest chance of justice before the law."

King's colleague, the Reverend Ralph David Abernathy, put the same sentiment more theatrically. When Judge David Holcombe Thomas lifted the legal barriers to King's march in Selma on March 15, 1965, Abernathy declared, "God spoke from the federal court."

From the late fifties well into the sixties, the federal judiciary was, if not quite the voice of God, then the voice of the United States Constitution in the former Confederate States. When all other avenues were closed, when sheriffs, cattle prods, hound dogs, and fire hoses stood between the black man and the rights he sought, the United States district courts were his last, best hope. Not all Southern district judges lived up to their responsibilities. Some were consistently hostile to civil rights suits. But they were generally overruled by the judges of the Fourth and Fifth Circuit Courts of Appeals, who, further from the political grass roots, were freer to challenge public resistance. Most members of the Southern federal bench ultimately put loyalty to the Constitution above loyalty to regional attitudes.

Yet a federal judge's order was not, at the start, sufficient to ensure compliance with the law. For years, Southern politicians routinely defied such orders, convinced that they could do so with impunity, and that even if they faced legal sanctions, those would only enhance their political fortunes. Only after Dwight Eisenhower and John Kennedy sent federal troops to enforce desegregation rulings in Arkansas, Mississippi, and Alabama did the lesson begin to sink in. Governor Earl Long of Louisiana is said to have warned Leander Perez, the die-hard segregationist of Plaquemines Parish: "Look, Leander, don't you understand? The feds have the atom bomb."

But it was one thing to threaten force against the South, long regarded as the country's most benighted region, and quite another to marshal it against the North, home of the nation's leading banks and corporations, its most powerful media, and the very liberals who most passionately supported the civil rights movement. For more than a decade, the federal government's legal guns were locked into place, facing south. Only in the late sixties and early seventies did they begin to swivel and train their barrels on the hitherto exempt cities of the North.

In the United States District Court for the District of Massachusetts, cases are allocated among the judges by a complex lottery system whose purpose is to distribute the work load evenly and to preclude even a whisper of suspicion that a case had been intentionally assigned to a particular judge. At the start of each court term, a set of envelopes is prepared for each of the legal categories heard by the court: admiralty, bankruptcy, civil rights, habeas corpus, libel, patent, and so forth. In the spring 1972 term, each of these sets comprised fourteen small brown envelopes—two for each of the seven judges then sitting. In each envelope, a deputy clerk placed the typewritten name of one of the judges. The fourteen envelopes were then shuffled, secured by a thick rubber band, and placed with the other stacks in a blue card drawer on the clerk's desk. At 10:30 on the morning of March 15, 1972, when the complaint in *Morgan* v. *Hennigan* was filed, the clerk reached for the "civil rights" stack, took the first envelope off the top, ripped it open, and retrieved from it the tiny slip of white paper. On it was typed the name "Garrity."

Once, back in County Sligo, the name had been McGarrity. Patrick and Bridget McGarrity's three sons were high-spirited miners in Sligo's rock quarries who became embroiled in the Young Ireland rising of 1848. When the English routed the ill-prepared rebels, the three brothers fled to the New World, where they made their way under the Americanized name of Garrity.

Thomas Garrity settled initially in Charlestown, where he was among the first Irishmen to find a foothold on the inhospitable slope of Breed's Hill. But, uncomfortable there, he worked his way north into New Hampshire, laying track on the Boston & Maine Railroad. In late 1850, he reached the little village of Milford, where he decided to follow his ancestral craft of stonecutting in the local granite quarry. Other Irishmen were attracted to Milford by the Souhegan Cotton Mill, and gradually an Irish quarter grew up around the mill. There Thomas and his wife, Ellen Fallon, raised eight children.

Though it had only 1,500 inhabitants, Milford at midcentury was a remarkable place, a hotbed of temperance and abolitionist agitation. The village's most fervent abolitionists were a family of musicians called the Singing Hutchinsons, whose Sunday prayer meetings drew people from miles around to hear their songs and a rousing call to action by William Lloyd Garrison or Wendell

Phillips up from Boston. Although most Irish at that time were hostile to the antislavery movement, resenting the Yankees' preferential treatment of Negroes, there is some evidence that the Garritys became abolitionists.

Charles Garrity—one of Thomas's eight children—was a cooper, but he hankered to buy a farm. One day, according to family legend, he went to a probate court auction and won a prime parcel, only to be refused title because a county custom prohibited the sale of probate court land to "Indians, Negroes and Papists." (New Hampshire had a long history of anti-Catholic feeling, rooted in its fear of French Quebec.) It was that experience, so the story goes, which persuaded Charles Garrity to pull up stakes in 1883 and move his family to Worcester, Massachusetts.

Charles's wife, Margaret, had come to Milford as an infant and evidently absorbed its social conscience. Passionately devoted to politics, an avid supporter of William Jennings Bryan, and an early suffragette, she named one son Clarence, after Clarence Darrow, another Wendell, after Wendell Phillips. Why Phillips? Perhaps because the Garritys remembered him from his appearance at the Hutchinsons' camp meetings. Perhaps because they admired his antislavery stance. Perhaps because Margaret appreciated his support for women's rights. And perhaps because, in the years after the Civil War, Phillips openly identified with the plight of the Irish immigrant, particularly with the reformers in the Irish-American Land League. In December 1879—six years before Wendell Arthur Garrity was christened—the patrician Phillips told a mass meeting in Boston, "I said in the great rebellion, 'Give the Negro a vote and forty acres of land.' Give every Irish a vote and forty acres of land to stand on."

Whatever the reason for the Garritys' admiration of Phillips, it reflected a partial truce in the cultural war which had long pitted the Irish immigrant against the Yankee reform tradition. By the 1880s, many Irish-Americans had begun to emerge from the big-city shanty towns, becoming regular wage earners, respected craftsmen, even middle-class burghers. Having gained some stake in the larger society, they came to identify with broader national concerns. This was particularly true of those who settled in semi-rural towns like Milford or in medium-sized industrial communities like Albany or Worcester. They were beginning to feel American.

Certainly Charles Garrity made his way in the Yankee world of Worcester. A skilled cooper and minor inventor, he turned from barrels to houses. During the last decades of the nineteenth century, Worcester's population exploded and Charles built many of the grim three-deckers which still scar its gritty hills. For his own growing family, he built a large house on Vernon Hill, the city's Irish stronghold. Charles made houses and money, but Margaret made the deepest impression on her children. It was she who persuaded two of her sons to enter the practice of law—Charles, who ultimately became a member of the state legislature, and Wendell Arthur Garrity.

Wendell—more often known as W. Arthur, or simply as Arthur—went to Holy Cross, just across town, and then on to Harvard Law School, among the first of the Worcester Irish to attend that august institution. Graduating in 1909, he came home and went into partnership with a lawyer named John Sheehan. Among the most prominent Irish lawyers in town, Sheehan and Garrity prided themselves on the breadth of their clientele. Garrity used to boast that, unlike most Irish lawyers, he didn't get his clientele through the priests. The firm supervised the division of assets between two branches of the once virulently anti-Catholic Masons, and represented the Methodist Church. Arthur kept up with his old college mates at the Holy Cross Club and still hoisted a few with the Irish lads down at the Knights of Columbus, but he had begun to transcend the fierce ethnic loyalties which preoccupied so many of his contemporaries. Asked once to list his favorite authors, he included John P. Marquand, recorder of Boston's Yankee aristocracy.

In 1919, he married Mary Kennedy, whose father was a coachman to Jonas Clark, a prominent Yankee merchant. Reared in the Clark household, and intensely grateful for their many kindnesses, Mary to her death wouldn't let anyone speak ill of the Yankees.

From childhood, their son, Wendell Arthur Garrity, Jr., was marked as an achiever: a vigorous athlete whose promising sports career was cut short when he broke the same leg three times in bruising football and hockey matches, a diligent student who skipped three half-grades in grammar school.

Like so many middle-class Irish families of that era, the Garritys worshipped education. The Belmont Street School which they attended was the very model of the American neighborhood school. It was a five-minute walk from the Garritys' new house, and from houses roundabout came other Irish children, Germans, and particularly Swedes—for the family had completed its ethnic emancipation by moving to predominantly Swedish Green Hill.

From across Belmont Street, site of Worcester's small black community, came several dozen Negro children, who made up 10 percent of the school's enrollment. As a child, young Arthur accepted this black presence with little curiosity. Years later, his brother Jim remembered the Negro boys removing straight razors from their pockets and stowing them in their shoes before they joined the Irish and Swedes in barefoot football games at Green Hill Park, but the sight filled him more with wonder than with fear. For Worcester's black community was too small—and too passive—to intimidate anyone. The Garritys retained a special sympathy for blacks. Their mother sometimes drew a parallel between the Irish and black experience by expanding the old slogan to go: "No Irish, *No Negroes,* Need Apply." And in the 1940s and 1950s, long before civil rights became a fashionable cause, W. Arthur Garrity, Sr., was one of a tiny handful of Worcester Irish in the NAACP.

After twelve years of public education, all the Garrity boys went across town to the College of the Holy Cross—that much was preordained. It was their father's alma mater and it exercised a powerful hold on the imagination of Worcester's Irish. Moreover, the Garritys were devout Catholics, saying the rosary together for forty-eight straight days during Lent, keeping an altar to the Virgin Mary during May. Their mother harbored a secret wish that one of her sons would grow up to be a priest, but if that was not to be, she was determined that her boys should at least have "an intellectual basis for their faith."

Holy Cross in those years was a stern place with compulsory daily Mass, a strict dress code, and an intellectual life which was just as rigorous. The Jesuit curriculum included great quantities of Latin, Greek, ethics, philosophy, and theology, but the reigning intellectual influence was that of St. Thomas Aquinas. Thomism is a relentlessly logical discipline, its chief analytical tool the syllogism, an argument in which two premises lead to an inevitable conclusion (as in "All crimes against nature are wrong / This is a crime against nature / This is wrong"). Building from major premise to minor premise to thundering conclusion, St. Thomas constructed a self-contained moral system grounded in the immutable nature of the universe. Its principles could be discerned by man in the natural law, which, in turn, was "the rational creature's participation in [God's] eternal law."

This doctrine had obvious appeal to the Catholic Church operating within a secular state, for it held that natural rights sprang not from man-made law but from the divine will of God. Since the state had not made these rights, it could not take them away. As a limitation on secular authority, natural law buttressed the Church's moral authority. But the theory could likewise serve rebels against a tyrannical regime, helping to kindle the English and American revolutions, later fortifying the abolitionists. Against the Fugitive Slave Act, William Lloyd Garrison would argue: "When rulers have inverted their functions and enacted wickedness into a law which treads down the inalienable rights of man to such a degree as this, then I know no ruler but God, no law but natural justice." To that extent, Arthur Garrity's training in Thomistic philosophy may have reinforced the abolitionist inclinations which had persisted in his family for three generations.

For the moment, Garrity had little time for such lofty considerations. At Harvard Law School in the fall of 1941, he plunged into the dreary particulars of evidence, property, and torts. After graduation, he clerked for Federal District Judge Francis J. W. Ford, who became almost a second father to the young lawyer. Later he served as an assistant U.S. Attorney, then entered private practice with several colleagues.

In 1952, Garrity married Barbara Anne Mullins, an elementary school teacher, and moved with her to a garden apartment in suburban Wellesley. A delicate woman known as "Bambi" from the monogram—BAM—embroidered on her blouses, she had graduated in 1945 from Regis, a Catholic women's college with a certain social status. She kept up with some of her schoolmates in the Ace of Clubs, a group founded by Rose Fitzpatrick, later John Kennedy's mother. Excluded from Yankee sewing circles, Rose had established the Ace of Clubs as an alternative for well-bred Irish Catholic girls, and it grew into an exclusive society, whose activities culminated in a spring dance at Boston's Ritz-Carlton Hotel.

In their first married years, the Garritys' social life centered on Barbara's

Regis and Ace of Clubs friends and their husbands, most of them graduates of Boston College and Holy Cross. These were second- and third-generation Irish-Americans, who after the war had moved out of Boston's ethnic enclaves, finding homes in the suburbs and making their way in law, medicine, or business. In the elaborate hierarchy of the Boston Irish, they were the "two-toilet Irish," an emerging professional class no longer comfortable with the claustrophobic world of their fathers.

For such families, the annual rite of spring—St. Patrick's Day—posed a dilemma. They were too Irish to ignore it altogether, too assimilated to enjoy the raucous, boozy, sometimes violent celebration in South Boston. (Arthur Garrity's sister Peggy once attended the South Boston parade and came away horrified. "My gosh," she told a friend, "they're a very different kind of Irish than we have in Worcester.") Eve Carey, daughter of the chairman of American Airlines, was a friend of Bambi Garrity's from Regis. In the mid-fifties, she solved the St. Patrick's Day dilemma for her friends by founding a group called the Mystery Nighters. Every year, on the Saturday nearest the holiday, a hundred couples would be invited to "a night of intrigue and adventure." Once they were taken to Logan Airport, where they boarded an American Airlines plane, which then taxied into a hangar, where the real festivities began. Another year they went to a Charlestown funeral home for a cocktail party among the caskets, where a man dressed in a green top hat told Irish jokes. Several Townies wandered in off Bunker Hill Street to gape at the suburban visitors. A number of Mystery Nighters recall Bambi and Arthur Garrity as regulars at these annual revels.

The Mystery Nighters were a classic John Kennedy crowd, the kind of upwardly mobile young Irish who responded most enthusiastically to his wit and modish idealism. So it was hardly surprising that Arthur Garrity should join the Kennedy camp, working hard for Jack in the 1952 senatorial campaign, helping him swamp the incumbent, Henry Cabot Lodge.

Six years later, when Kennedy was up for reelection, Garrity got even more deeply involved. His law partner Dick Maguire had long been close to Kennedy—serving as treasurer for his first congressional campaign—and in 1958 Maguire persuaded Garrity to put in several hours a day at the Senator's headquarters. Kennedy already had his eye on the presidential nomination two years hence and he set seemingly irreconcilable goals for 1958: a landslide victory in Massachusetts, but plenty of time to campaign elsewhere for candidates who might return the favor in 1960. Between the September primary and the November election, he spent only seventeen days in Massachusetts, and Garrity's job was to make the best use of every available minute. Kenny O'Donnell called Garrity "a genius" at the scheduler's game: in what may have been a record for a single day, he got Kennedy through fifteen speaking engagements in fifteen different towns and yet to bed by 11:00 p.m. That split-second timing paid off when the Senator won reelection by 874,608 votes, the biggest majority ever achieved by a candidate for public office in Massachusetts, and a favorable omen for 1960.

Arthur Garrity had earned a place on the Kennedy team—not as one of the publicized stars like Ted Sorensen or Larry O'Brien, but as a solid regular who could be counted on to do his job—and in 1960 he drew a tough one: running the Milwaukee headquarters for the critical Wisconsin primary. The Kennedys hadn't wanted to enter Wisconsin, where their main rival, Hubert Humphrey, was almost as popular as in his adjacent Minnesota. But once they went in, they threw all their resources into the battle—the entire family, dozens of friends and supporters from back home. Garrity coordinated logistics for the far-flung operation. In seven weeks, he earned the Kennedys' renewed admiration for his meticulous attention to detail and his capacity for hard work. On April 6, Kennedy won two-thirds of Wisconsin's delegates. Later that spring, Garrity helped plan a national voter registration drive.

To this day, Garrity insists that he had no ulterior motives in these labors, but if he didn't, Dick Maguire surely did on his behalf. Maguire, who had become a political adviser in the White House, immediately proposed his law partner as the new United States Attorney for Massachusetts. It was a much-sought position; dozens of lawyers who had labored for the Kennedys felt they deserved it. Arthur Garrity was the leading candidate from the start, however, and on March 24, 1961, his name went to the Senate.

But the Administration seemed content to let the Republican incumbent, Elliot Richardson, remain in office a while longer. High on the U.S. Attorney's docket was the tax evasion trial of Boston industrialist Bernard Goldfine. Goldfine's lawyer was Edward Bennett Williams, a Holy Cross classmate and close friend of Garrity's. It might be better, the Kennedys thought, to let Richardson handle the Goldfine case.

The trouble was, Richardson had another investigation underway which promised to be more embarrassing. Since World War II, nearly a billion dollars in federal money had financed new expressways in Massachusetts, creating ample opportunity for graft. Just how ample became evident in proceedings Richardson launched against Thomas Worcester, an engineer who had obtained highway contracts through kickbacks to state officials. After Worcester was sentenced to eighteen months in prison for tax evasion, Judge Charles E. Wyzanski offered to suspend the sentence if he testified about the kickbacks. This Worcester did, conceding that he had paid $275,000 to state legislators, a congressman, even William F. Callahan, the influential Chairman of the Massachusetts Turnpike Commission, a power broker with ties to virtually every important Democrat—and many Republicans—in the state. It was a scandal with lush possibilities.

Charles Wyzanski was the most brilliant judge on Boston's Federal District Court. A protégé of Felix Frankfurter's at Harvard, a member of Franklin Roosevelt's "brain trust" at twenty-six, and frequently mentioned as a candidate for the Supreme Court, Wyzanski was also unpredictable, impetuous, and abrasive. "By temperament," he once said, "I believe with Heraclitus that strife is the source of all things. I have the joy of battle." On January 5, 1961, he lived up to his militant reputation with a peroration from the bench which found that "a network of corruption" permeated the state, and scolded law enforcement officials, politicians, the press, and the bar for tolerating "this venal system." It was a polemic which not even a President-elect could ignore. As he gained in national stature, John Kennedy had held himself aloof from the morass of Massachusetts politics, but with his inauguration barely two weeks off, he had to heed such a sweeping indictment of his own state's political morality. Four days after Wyzanski's tirade, Kennedy came home to address a joint session of the Massachusetts legislature. Invoking John Winthrop's memorable phrase, he declared, "Our governments, in every branch, at every level, national, state and local, must be as a 'city upon a hill,' constructed and inhabited by men aware of their grave trust and their grave responsibilities."

Thus pledged to clean house in Boston as well as in Washington, Jack Kennedy and his brother, the new Attorney General, wanted to avoid anything which might look like obstruction of Elliot Richardson's investigation. So, well into April, Richardson presented evidence to a federal grand jury. Then, on April 12, he sent a draft indictment of six persons to the Justice Department for comment. The next day, Garrity's appointment was rushed through the Senate Judiciary Committee, past an unsuspecting Senate, and sped to the White House for the President's signature. The following morning, the commission was put on a plane for Boston, where Joe Maloney, one of Garrity's law partners, retrieved it at Logan Airport. At four that afternoon, Arthur Garrity was sworn in as the new U.S. Attorney.

It was not an auspicious start. Elliot Richardson felt badly used by Bobby Kennedy and, although the Attorney General named him a special assistant to carry on the Goldfine prosecution, Richardson soon was charging "cover-up." The implication was that the Kennedys had shut down the highways investigation before it reached prominent Massachusetts Democrats.

Judge Wyzanski was even more outraged by the turn of events. An intellectual Russian Jew, Wyzanski had clearly enjoyed his collaboration with the elegant Yankee prosecutor in cleaning the Augean stables of Irish politics. He plainly regarded Arthur Garrity as a Kennedy stooge, placed in office to frustrate his own reforming zeal, and he wasn't afraid to say so. When one of Garrity's assistants brought an Army private into court charged with unauthorized duck hunting, Wyzanski wanted to know whether the U.S. Attorney thought justice was best advanced by prosecuting "matters of this sort" as opposed to the highway prosecutions on which Garrity had "failed to follow through."

As such sniping persisted, the Wyzanski-Garrity feud was the talk of the Federal Courthouse. To some, the dispute took on larger proportions: a clash between Yankee/Jewish rectitude and Irish/Kennedy pragmatism. Certainly Arthur Garrity was a Kennedy loyalist, but he was no stooge. For a time he did seem to be dragging his feet on the highway frauds. But, ultimately, he brought nearly twenty indictments, including five of the six recommended by Richardson, and about half of the defendants were convicted. Eventually, even the most skeptical Yankees conceded that the delay was due not to some Kennedy-inspired cover-up, but to Garrity's characteristically meticulous work habits.

Indeed, by the end of his five-year stint as U.S. Attorney, Arthur Garrity was so widely respected in Boston's legal establishment that he moved rapidly into the leadership of the very Yankee Boston Bar Association (as distinguished from the Irish-dominated Massachusetts Bar Association). In 1966, he served as the association's vice-president and would have become its president—only the third Irish Catholic ever to hold that post—had he not been made a federal judge.

Ever since the new seat on Boston's Federal District Court was created by Congress in May 1961, Jack Kennedy had been under heavy pressure from his father to appoint an old crony, Boston Municipal Court Judge Francis Xavier Morrissey. A ruddy-faced operator who knew his way around the seamy side of Boston politics, Morrissey had served as Joe Kennedy's agent in his son's camp. But when the American Bar Association found him "lacking in intellectual capacity," Kennedy temporized, and at his death the seat remained empty. Morrissey kept pressing for the job, supported by Ted Kennedy, and two years later Lyndon Johnson obliged, shrewdly mousetrapping his Massachusetts rivals. When the Boston *Globe* revealed that the judge had falsified his credentials, the legal establishment—led, not surprisingly, by Charlie Wyzanski—excoriated the appointment. The Kennedys, not Johnson, had to shoulder the blame and in October 1965 Ted threw in the towel.

Publicly humiliated, the Kennedys badly needed a candidate whose credentials couldn't be challenged, so Ted turned to another man who had served the family well. A judge, the old saying goes, is just a lawyer who knew a governor. Arthur Garrity had known a President, an Attorney General, and a senator—and he was amply qualified. His nomination encountered no significant opposition, and on July 6, 1966, Garrity was sworn in by the presiding judge of Boston's District Court—none other than Charles Wyzanski—who made some coolly polite remarks about his new colleague.

As a judge, Garrity proved the very antithesis of his old antagonist. Where Wyzanski was flamboyant, Garrity was the soul of propriety; where Wyzanski was bold, Garrity was cautious; where Wyzanski was self-aggrandizing, Garrity was self-effacing. His bald head bowed over the bench, squinting down through horn-rimmed glasses, he was unfailingly polite to lawyers ("Permit me, if you will," "If you'll pardon me for saying so") and careful to tell criminal defendants what he was doing ("Now, the law requires me to . . ."). If anything, he was conscientious to a fault—the smallest procedural matters had to be submitted in writing. Unlike other judges, who delegated heavily to young law clerks, Garrity read everything that crossed his desk, often working twelve hours a day, and such diligence meant that years might go by before he decided a complex case. Inmates at Boston's antiquated Charles Street Jail filed suit in January 1971 to have the prison closed or its conditions improved. Not until June 1972—after spending a night in jail to make his own assessment—did Garrity open the trial. His decision did not come down until a year later. In a Worcester police brutality case, Garrity took twenty-one months to rule. But his caution paid off: among New England's federal judges, he had one of the lowest rates of reversal by the First Circuit Court of Appeals.

In at least one area, however, passion overrode judicial reserve. On criminal matters, especially those involving moral transgressions, Garrity was the harshest sentencer in the district. In bank robbery cases, one lawyer recalls, "you could send your client Christmas cards in prison for years if Arthur was the judge." Drugs, in particular, aroused him. In thirty drug cases which came before him between 1971 and 1973, Garrity sent twenty-nine of the defendants to prison, for an average of 4.2 years. "It is essential to take these harsh steps to endeavor to bring the country out of this scourge," he said in sentencing one young man to three years in prison for a "relatively innocent" cocaine offense (thereby drawing a rare, if indirect, rebuke from the Court of Appeals). Pornography, too, horrified him. After ruling on some sexually explicit magazines, Garrity told an attorney for the defendant, "It is because of lawyers like you who take these cases that people are able to import this trash." Garrity often struck a high moral tone. Sentencing a convicted murderer, he explained, "There is an aura of evil about this case."

"Garrity is a puritan," said one criminal lawyer who has practiced before him. "Like all puritans, he has a great superego, great control. That's the side he shows most of the time—contained, dispassionate, methodical. But, take my word, underneath is a boiling cauldron of prejudices, biases, notions of how people ought to behave. Like all puritans, he has a pathological fear of losing control. Drugs and pornography represent loss of control, and that's why they have to be punished so severely."

Such reservations notwithstanding, by March 1972, when his name was drawn from the little brown envelope, Garrity struck many Bostonians as the ideal arbiter for the long-standing battle of majority rule vs. minority rights in the city's schools. For not only did he have a reputation for integrity, fairmindedness, scrupulous attention to detail, and hard work, but he was an Irishman—a Kennedy Irishman at that. The day Garrity got the case, his old adversary, Charlie Wyzanski, told a friend at lunch, "Boy, I'm glad I didn't get it. You need an Irish name, a Catholic, to do it." If anybody could sort out the decade-old muddle, it seemed to be Arthur Garrity.

Garrity wasn't so sure. He knew how tangled school desegregation law had become in the eighteen years since the Supreme Court, in *Brown* v. *Board of Education,* had held that separate school facilities for black and white children were "inherently unequal" and therefore violated the Fourteenth Amendment's equal protection clause. And he knew the complexities involved in applying the evolving doctrine to Northern cities like Boston.

Ironically, Boston was the only city to which the Court in *Brown* had given a clean bill of health. To gain maximum support for that landmark decision, Chief Justice Earl Warren had not wanted to point an accusing finger solely at the South; after all, *Brown* itself was a Kansas case and, as Warren wrote in a footnote: "In the North segregation in public education has persisted in some communities until recent years. It is apparent that such segregation has long been a nationwide problem, not merely one of sectional concern." To underline that point, Warren noted that the separate-but-equal doctrine itself had originated with *Roberts* v. *City of Boston* (1850). But, referring to the Massachusetts legislature's subsequent action in abolishing legally mandated school segregation, Warren added, "Segregation in Boston public schools was eliminated in 1855."

That remark would have surprised the black plaintiffs in *Morgan* v. *Hennigan* and the white liberals who had drafted the Racial Imbalance Act eight years earlier. To be sure, Warren had been writing still earlier, before the wave of black emigration from the South had intensified the imbalance in Boston's ghetto schools. But in any case, the Chief Justice felt bound by the Court's long-established position that the equal protection clause only prohibited discrimination by the state, not by private practices. Thus *Brown* applied only to separation imposed by racially explicit statutes, what became known as *de jure* segregation, not that which stemmed from social conditions, or *de facto* segregation. As the law stood in 1954, Boston's schools were plainly not segregated.

In 1955, in a decision that came to be known as *Brown II*, the Court ordered desegregation to proceed with "all deliberate speed," but left specific remedies in the hands of district judges who were closer to local conditions and thus better able, the Court said, to balance "public and private needs." But for the next decade little progress was made. For a time, indeed, Southern judges found in the *de facto–de jure* distinction a loophole through which to slip continued segregation. It was put most starkly by Judge John J. Parker of the Fourth Circuit Court of Appeals, a Virginian whose appointment to the Supreme Court in 1930 had been torpedoed by the NAACP when it turned up a speech of his filled with racial slights. In 1955, Parker wrote: "[The Supreme Court] has not decided that the states must mix persons of different races in the schools or must require them to attend schools or must deprive them of the right of choosing the schools they attend. What it has decided, and all that it has decided, is that a state may not deny to any person on account of race the right to attend any schools that it maintains . . . but if the schools which it maintains are open to children of all races, no violation of the Constitution is involved even though the children of different races voluntarily attend different schools, as they attend different churches."

This so-called Parker Doctrine was seized on by other Southern courts as a rationale for approving various evasive techniques, among them "freedom of choice," which permitted black and white children to attend any schools in their districts so long as there was room. In theory, at least, that was desegregation. In practice, it was not. Few black families would take the initiative to send their children to predominantly white schools where they might be in a vulnerable minority, particularly when parents feared that whites might retaliate against their jobs, their homes, or their persons.

For nearly fifteen years after *Brown,* "freedom of choice" and its variations—"open enrollment" and "local option"—frustrated school desegregation in districts throughout the South. Not until 1968, in *Green* v. *County School Board of New Kent County, Va.,* did the Supreme Court finally put the Parker Doctrine to rest. "Freedom of choice" in New Kent County, the Court declared, "operated simply to burden children and their parents with a responsibility which *Brown II* placed squarely on the school board." It was not enough to eliminate assignment by race, the Court said. Boards which had operated dual systems were "charged with the affirmative duty to take whatever steps might be necessary to convert to a unitary system in which racial discrimination would be eliminated root and branch." The object, the Court said, was not a mere cleansing of the statute books, but results in the schools.

Up to that point, virtually all school segregation cases had come from rural school districts where blacks and whites lived side by side as they had since antebellum days. In such districts, desegregation could usually be accomplished merely by assigning children—black and white—to the school nearest their homes. In *Swann* v. *Charlotte-Mecklenburg* (1971), the Supreme Court finally came to grips with the "flinty, intractable" problems of desegregating a major urban area—the most populous school district in North Carolina, with some 83,000 pupils. Since blacks and whites in Charlotte and surrounding Mecklenburg County generally lived in separate neighborhoods, assigning students to the nearest school would only ensure that most of them continued to go to school with children of their own race. In *Swann,* the Court held that, everything else being equal, students should be assigned to the school nearest their homes, but "all things are not equal in a system that has been deliberately constructed and maintained to enforce racial segregation." In such districts, the very residential pattern would presumably have been influenced by the location of segregated schools, black neighborhoods often clustering around black schools, white neighborhoods around white schools. Thus, to assign students by neighborhood would perpetuate the effects of the dual system. Since the Court in *Green* had required a "root and branch" extirpation of such systems, it ruled in *Swann* that district courts could order a variety of measures, including those which were "administratively awkward, inconvenient and even bizarre," to accomplish that end. Specifically included in the catalogue of approved means was the busing of children from one neighborhood to another.

But sweeping as such an edict was, *Swann* had much less national impact than might have been expected. For though the justices might pretend otherwise, legally mandated segregation—as the Court defined it up to that time—was almost exclusively a sectional problem, a Southern problem. Yet Southern spokesmen, notably Senator John Stennis of Mississippi, were pointing out that school segregation existed in the North too, achieved there merely by different means. Even Senator Abraham Ribicoff of Connecticut, a prominent Northern liberal, indicted his own region for "monumental hypocrisy." Such critics noted that because Southern blacks and whites had always lived adjacent to each other on plantations or tenant farms, the state had had to enforce segregation in order to limit social contact between the races. No such legislation had been needed in the North, where blacks and whites, since colonial days, had tended to live separately. There was some truth to that old bit of Negro folk wisdom: In the South, the white man doesn't care how close you get if you don't get too high; in the North, the white man doesn't care how high you get if you don't get too close. But the effect on school attendance was much the same in both places: whether by law or by neighborhood, whites and blacks went to school separately. Why, the South now began asking, should the courts treat the Northern form of segregation any differently than they did the Southern?

The same question came to preoccupy the NAACP and particularly its general counsel, Robert Lee Carter, who in the legal attack on "separate but equal" had been Thurgood Marshall's principal lieutenant. For years they had worked closely together, but gradually Carter had grown resentful of the older lawyer—a friction exacerbated by the disparity in their backgrounds. Marshall's parents were each half white, and young Thurgood had grown up in the conservative mulatto aristocracy of Baltimore, at that time very much a Southern city. That experience did not leave Marshall an Uncle Tom, but he was a cautious, deliberate man who took orderly steps toward a carefully conceived goal. Bob Carter, on the other hand, was a dark-skinned product of Newark's Central Avenue ghetto—one of the very few NAACP leaders of that vintage to have grown up in the North, which left him with an acute resentment of Northern white hypocrisy. More a hot-blooded advocate than a cool analyst, Carter had always been temperamentally disinclined to settle for half measures.

In the early 1960s, after leaving Marshall's Legal Defense Fund and moving over to the NAACP proper, Carter established his own legal office and launched a novel assault on Northern segregation. He set out to show that racial segregation in and of itself—regardless of its cause—was unconstitutional. Attacking at its heart the Court's time-honored interpretation of the Fourteenth Amendment, Carter tried to demonstrate that the equal protection clause not only required an end to state-enforced school segregation, but actually conferred a right to an integrated education. It was a characteristically bold departure, a brave raid on the very heart of the Northern defenses, and it failed. In three separate suits in three Northern cities—Gary, Cincinnati, and Kansas City—Carter's theory was rejected, not only by Courts of Appeal but later by the Supreme Court. Although the Court never wrote a full opinion on the matter, its affirmations of lower court opinions made clear that it was unwilling to take that broad a step away from its traditional view of the Fourteenth Amendment. By the mid-1960s, the failure of this venture had left the civil rights movement feeling mortally wounded. With the Court apparently accepting *de facto* segregation, the nation seemed doomed to a double standard which could only become increasingly embarrassing to advocates of desegregation. To many able attorneys, it looked as if the assault on Northern school segregation had reached a dead end.

But cooler, more analytic lawyers at the Legal Defense Fund—notably Jack Greenberg, who succeeded Marshall when he went on the Supreme Court in 1967—saw a different route to desegregation in the North. Greenberg and his colleagues harked back to a line of lower court cases which had shown that the Court's definition of "state action" might be broadened beyond explicit statutes to include a whole range of subtle techniques used by Northern school boards to reinforce and maintain school segregation. In Hillsboro, Ohio, in 1956, New Rochelle, New York, in 1961, and South Holland, Illinois, in 1968, federal courts had found that schools could be effectively segregated by gerrymandered districts, selective transfers, discriminatory feeder patterns, and the like. Where there was intent to segregate, "it makes no meaningful difference whether the segregation is maintained directly through formal separation, or indirectly," wrote Judge Irving Kaufman in the New Rochelle case. "Constitutional rights are determined by realities, not by labels or semantics. The Supreme Court has affirmed that courts must look through the guise in which school officials seek to clothe their unconstitutional conduct."

By 1972, when Arthur Garrity began hearing the Boston case, the Supreme Court had not yet ruled specifically on this emerging lower court reinterpretation of "state action" (although lawyers and judges were eagerly awaiting the Court's decision in a Denver case which it had accepted for review). Lacking a definitive Supreme Court precedent on which to rely, Garrity studied the Gary, Cincinnati, and Kansas City cases on the one hand and the Hillsboro, New Rochelle, and South Holland cases on the other. But the case which weighed most heavily on him was the only school desegregation suit tried by a federal court in Massachusetts since the *Brown* decision, a case decided by his colleague on the Boston bench George C. Sweeney, and reviewed by the same First Circuit Court of Appeals that would hear any possible appeal from Garrity's Boston decision.

The suit had been brought by the NAACP in 1964 against the Springfield, Massachusetts, Board of Education, arguing—at least in part—the Carter thesis. This time it prevailed in the District Court. Judge Sweeney found that the Board of Education had not deliberately segregated Springfield's schools; it had impartially assigned students to neighborhood schools which, purely because of residential patterns, became racially identifiable. Nonetheless, Sweeney ruled, such *de facto* segregation violated the Constitution. "It is neither just nor sensible," he wrote, "to proscribe segregation having its basis in affirmative state action while at the same time failing to provide a remedy for segregation which grows out of discrimination in housing, or other economic or social factors." And he closed his opinion with these explicit words: "There must be no segregated schools." But a year later, the Court of Appeals bluntly reversed Sweeney in declaring: "We can accept no such constitutional right."

Moreover, Chief Judge Bailey Aldrich suggested that Sweeney had gone much too far to accommodate the NAACP, warning: "It would be no better to consider the Negro's special interests exclusively than it would be to disregard them completely."

Arthur Garrity had no great affection for Bailey Aldrich, a prominent Yankee who occasionally betrayed a touch of arrogance toward Irish lawyers and judges. Now Garrity's normal anxiety to be affirmed on appeal was reinforced by his disinclination to let Aldrich or his colleagues slap him down as they had George Sweeney. Arthur Garrity, a cautious judge on most cases, was going to be doubly cautious on this one.

In May 1972, as Garrity heard preliminary motions in the Boston case, Nick Flannery thought he detected in the judge a strange confusion—"almost a purposeful obtuseness"—about whether the plaintiffs were bringing a *de facto* or a *de jure* case. Over and over he would ask them, Are you claiming that the School Committee or other public bodies deliberately caused the schools here to be racially identifiable, or are you saying that segregation in and of itself is unconstitutional? Finally, Flannery realized that Garrity was sending them a message. Listen, he seemed to be saying, if this is a *de jure* case, fine, let's move ahead; but if you're going to get me into the mire Sweeney got into in Springfield, I may not want any part of it. So that June, Flannery and his colleagues wrote the judge a memorandum in which they spelled out—"almost in block letters"—their answer: he was not being asked to revisit Springfield; he was not being asked to do anything that would get him out on a doctrinal limb; indeed, he would be presented with a straightforward, almost a classic, *de jure* case. After that, Arthur Garrity seemed more at ease.

As promised, the argument presented by the plaintiffs in the two-week trial the following spring relied heavily on the "state action" premises of the Hillsboro, New Rochelle, and South Holland cases. Racial imbalance in Boston's schools, they contended, was neither fortuitous nor innocent; it had been reinforced and maintained over the years by a whole host of techniques devised by the Boston School Committee: optional attendance zones, manipulated district lines, differential grade structures, open enrollment, feeder patterns, site selection policies, portable classrooms, and various pupil assignment practices. To make such a case required enormous time and effort. Unlike Southern plaintiffs, for whom it was often sufficient to cite a racially explicit statute, those in the North had to comb through School Committee minutes, district maps, and departmental regulations in search of documentary evidence of segregative practices and intent. Fortunately, the Boston School Committee had made things easier by keeping verbatim stenographic accounts of its meetings, providing a clear record of resistance to desegregation, as well as hints of its motivations. It was these transcripts which, more than anything else, had convinced Nick Flannery that Boston was a "sitting duck" for a school case.

The School Committee was represented by James St. Clair of the Boston firm of Hale and Dorr, who only nine months later would become President Nixon's chief Watergate lawyer. Known in Boston as "the Silver Fox" because of his handsome shock of gray hair, he had also been called "the best trial lawyer in the country." But he needed all his skill and resourcefulness to rebut the massive evidence assembled by Nick Flannery's team. At the trial, St. Clair argued that Boston's racial imbalance stemmed merely from a "neighborhood school" policy neutrally applied to a city whose residents tended to live in tight ethnic enclaves. In other words, it was a case of pure *de facto* segregation, no more unconstitutional than that of Gary, Cincinnati, Kansas City—or Springfield.

Three months after the trial ended, while Arthur Garrity was pondering these arguments, the Supreme Court clarified his problem when it handed down an eagerly awaited decision in the Denver case, *Keyes* v. *School District Number 1*. For the first time in its series of landmark school cases, however, the Court was not unanimous. Because of the fierce opposition to integration in the South, the justices had struggled through *Brown, Green,* and *Swann* to hold together their fragile façade of unanimity on desegregtion. But in *Keyes* that effort collapsed—in part because Nixon had appointed two new justices, Lewis Powell and William Rehnquist, who were ideological foes of aggressive desegregation, and in part because the Court had greatly expanded its concept of *de jure* segregation.

In *Keyes,* seven justices put the capstone on the evolving doctrine of Northern school desegregation. Denver's schools had never been officially segregated—their segregation probably grew out of relatively innocent housing patterns. But henceforth the origin of segregation—whether by law or by residence—would not matter. What would matter was the immediate cause. In cities like Denver, the issue would be whether local authorities had maintained, reinforced, or expanded residentially based separation by covert techniques, and then whether their actions were guided by "segregative intent." In answering the first question, the Court did not even demand that such techniques be found throughout the city. So long as their use could be proved in *one* neighborhood, and so long as that one neighborhood was not "a separate, identifiable and unrelated unit," the Court presumed that such techniques would infect other parts of the system. Likewise, if "segregative intent" was proved in one section, that created an inference that segregation elsewhere in the city was also intentional and shifted the burden of proof to the school authorities to refute that assumption. If they failed to do so, a court could order "root and branch" desegregation in the entire city.

By then, the line between *de facto* and *de jure* segregation had become so fine as to be almost indistinguishable to the layman's eye. Some held that whether the segregation was intentional or not, the very fact of separation harmed black children; if that were so, why not cut through the doctrinal underbrush and attack the problem directly? But others, some liberal constitutionalists included, thought it a distinction worth preserving: surely, a free society ought to defend the right of its citizens to make genuinely private choices, no matter how reprehensible. If government could abolish purely voluntary school segregation (if such a thing really existed), then what was to prevent it from requiring a private citizen to accept Irish, black, or Portuguese guests at his dinner table?

In July 1973, Garrity reopened the record so that the parties could argue *Keyes*'s relevance to Boston. But the plaintiffs didn't think they needed *Keyes*'s elaborate structure of inferences and presumptions—theirs was a more old-fashioned case, relying on sturdy, direct evidence of discrimination. At best, *Keyes* was a "moreover"; if their argument hadn't already prevailed, they thought, the new doctrine would surely buttress it.

Privately, Arthur Garrity agreed. Boston seemed to him an infinitely more compelling instance of intentional segregation than Denver had been. But the judge was determined to produce such a tightly reasoned decision that it would satisfy even Justice Powell, whose opinion in *Keyes* had outlined a rigorous standard of proof for such Northern school cases. So Garrity worked hours each day at the long table in his chambers, beneath the signed photographs of Jack and Robert Kennedy; then, after a quiet supper at home, he worked well into the night in his second-floor study. But the job went slowly, partly because he was burdened with several other major cases, partly because his diligence required that he personally examine each of the thousand-odd exhibits—depositions, minutes, charts, computer printouts. As the spring of 1974 came and still no decision was forthcoming, some of the plaintiffs' lawyers grew uneasy: if Garrity waited much longer, he would leave school and city authorities little time to prepare for any desegregation he might order that fall. The lawyers briefly considered the unusual step of asking the Court of Appeals for a writ of *mandamus* requiring the judge to issue his order forthwith.

The decision might have come down somewhat earlier had the state's Supreme Judicial Court not still been refining its order well into the spring. Garrity wanted to let the state court complete its record so he, in a sense, could ride its coattails. By fusing these two strands of litigation, he hoped that each would reinforce the other, thus winning wider community acceptance. Another factor in the delay may have been a concern about violent student protests if the decision came down while school was still in session. On June 6, an exasperated Kevin White called the delay "a crucifix, a crime to those who are apprehensive and uncertain."

On June 21—the last day of school and fifteen months since the end of the trial—Garrity finally released his opinion. Following the "blueprint" of *Keyes,* he found that the School Committee had used covert techniques to segregate the system, and had done so with "segregative intent." But in those findings he relied principally on the direct evidence supplied by the plaintiffs from committee transcripts and other documents, and only in one narrow area on the inferences permitted by *Keyes*. "The court concludes," he wrote, "that the defendants have knowingly carried out a systematic program of segregation affecting all of the city's students, teachers and school facilities and have intentionally brought about and maintained a dual school system. Therefore, the entire school system of Boston is unconstitutionally segregated."

In support of his decision, the judge had written a 152-page opinion, five or six times the length of similar rulings in other cities. Tom Atkins, the former Boston City Councilman, now a lawyer specializing in school cases for the national NAACP, called it "the most thoroughly documented, tightly reasoned opinion on school desegregation I have ever seen." In producing such a document, the judge had two principal objectives: first, to ensure against reversal on appeal, and second, to overwhelm Boston's persistent opposition to desegregation by the sheer weight of evidence and the power of his logic.

He achieved his first goal. Six months later, the Court of Appeals upheld Garrity, noting, "In the light of the ample factual record and the precedents of the Supreme Court, we do not see how the court could have reached any other conclusion." And six months after that, the Supreme Court itself let that ruling stand. But Garrity's impressive opinion did nothing to mitigate the opposition to desegregation in Boston's white neighborhoods. Indeed, the judge's critics argued that he had been naïve to imagine that many Bostonians would wade through his complex legal analysis. Moreover, his decision dealt only with the first segment of the case—the "liability" portion, in which he determined whether or not there had been a violation of the plaintiffs' constitutional rights. Now came the more difficult part—the "remedy" phase, in which he had to decide what to do about it. That was no mean task. Some of the fifteen months which Garrity had spent crafting his immaculate "liability" finding, his critics contended, might better have been spent beginning the search for an appropriate remedy. Now, with barely three months left before the state plan was scheduled to go into effect, the judge felt he had no recourse but to adopt that plan as his first-stage remedy (what would become known as Phase I) while he began devising a permanent remedy (Phase II).

The chief architect of the state plan was a thirty-five-year-old Episcopalian minister named Charles Glenn. A veteran of the civil rights movement, Glenn had marched at Selma, been arrested in North Carolina, worked with a black church in Roxbury, and helped organize Boston's first school boycott. By 1971, he was director of the State Education Department's Bureau of Equal Educational Opportunity, which put him at the center of the department's efforts to implement the Racial Imbalance Act. Even as a bureaucrat, he displayed a passionate zeal on racial issues. In his dealings with the Boston School Committee, Charlie Glenn was more than strong, he was implacable. When the Supreme Judicial Court ordered the State Education Department to prepare a plan for Boston in 1973, the job fell to Glenn. Jack Finger, a desegregation expert from the University of Rhode Island, supplied the basic concept, but Glenn did most of the work. As he describes it, the task was largely mechanical. "We simply took a large map and started moving across the city in a big arc from northwest to southeast, dividing it into districts so that each school would include the right proportions of black and white kids. When we got to the end of the arc, we were left with South Boston and Roxbury. We didn't have any choice but to mix those two neighborhoods."

Others aren't so sure. Knowledgeable educators believe there were several alternatives to cross-busing between South Boston, the stronghold of opposition to desegregation, and Roxbury, the community generally regarded as the heart of Boston's black ghetto. One would have been to integrate South Boston instead with blacks from adjacent North Dorchester, a community with a historical relationship to South Boston. Many people from South Boston had moved to Dorchester, the two neighborhoods were represented by the same state senator, and thus the area was less alien—and less frightening—to Southie. Or South Boston and Roxbury students might have been bused to several neutral sites where they could have been diluted with students from other inner-city neighborhoods. In any case, the process didn't have to be quite so mechanical as Glenn describes it. And there are those who suspect that Glenn's approach was less mechanical than deliberate. One former colleague says, "Charlie's patience had long since been exhausted by dealing with those bigots on the School Committee. I think he said to himself, 'We've had enough of you racists in South Boston; you're going to Roxbury; let's see how you like that.'"

Danger signals flared. In early 1973, Professor Louis Jaffe of the Harvard Law School was designated by the State Board of Education to hold hearings on the plan. In his report, Jaffe warned, "[South Boston's] people are intensely hostile to blacks. . . . I conclude, therefore, that this part of the plan should be restudied." It is not clear what Jaffe was suggesting. To have omitted South Boston completely from the plan would have been to let its very racial hostility frustrate integration there, a principle repeatedly rejected by the Supreme Court. But Jaffe proposed no alternatives. In any case, the State Board—and later the Supreme Judicial Court—overrode his warning and ordered the plan, including the South Boston–Roxbury pairing, into effect.

For the time being, Arthur Garrity didn't want to confront such problems. On June 27, 1974—six days after he had adopted the state plan as the first-stage remedy for Boston—Garrity announced from the bench, "I saw the state plan for the first time late yesterday afternoon." To some critics, this was a damaging admission that he had adopted the plan without even reading it. But it was scarcely an inadvertent remark, for Garrity repeated it several times that day. In retrospect, his strategy seems clear. Because he had taken so long to rule on the constitutional violation, he had not yet produced a remedy himself. Some officials suggested he postpone all remedies a full year—until September 1975—to permit time for systematic planning, but the state court had already ordered a plan into effect that fall; it would be most unusual for a federal judge to override a state remedy if he had nothing with which to replace it. In midsummer, Garrity gave the School Committee a chance to suggest an alternative, but the committee refused to endorse any plan which required busing. Precedent required Garrity to implement the "best available plan," and for the time being the state plan was the best—indeed the only— plan available. By stressing his ignorance of its details, Garrity seemed to be saying, "If, as some predict, this plan provokes violence in the fall, don't blame me." It wouldn't be his plan; it would be Charlie Glenn's plan.

· · ·

The predictions came to pass—with a vengeance. When the school year opened on September 12, 1974, most of the eighty schools affected by the plan were relatively peaceful. But when buses carrying black students pulled up at South Boston High School that morning, groups of angry whites shouted, "Niggers, go home!" And six hours later, as buses from the high school rolled back down Day Boulevard—that memorial to Louise Day Hicks's father—crowds pelted them with eggs, beer bottles, soda cans, and rocks, shattering windows and injuring nine students. Television flashed the scene across the city and the continent that evening. Whatever the situation at other schools, then and in the future, that image of "busing in Boston" was indelibly stamped on the national memory, as irrevocable as the scene outside Central High School in Little Rock seventeen years before.

And that was only the beginning. On September 16, after a planned protest march was banned by the city, South Boston youths attacked blacks at a subway station, overturned benches, and ripped out pay phones. During the next weeks, the Tactical Patrol Force had to break up wild racial melees in the cafeterias of both South Boston and Hyde Park high schools.

October brought an escalation of the violence. On October 7, a Haitian-born maintenance man named André Yvon Jean-Louis drove into South Boston as usual to pick up his wife, who worked at a laundry there. As he stopped for a red light, a crowd of whites rocked his car back and forth, smashed the windows, hauled him out, and chased him down the street. "Get that nigger!" they screamed. In desperation, Jean-Louis tried to climb over a wrought-iron fence onto a porch, but his pursuers threw him to the ground, where he was kicked repeatedly and beaten with a hammer and a sawed-off hockey stick until rescued by a policeman. The next day, black students in Roxbury—who had generally kept the peace until then—responded with a wild rampage during which they stoned cars and attacked passing whites. A few days later, Governor Sargent called out the National Guard.

While the city reaped the whirlwind of Phase I, Judge Garrity was working toward a better plan for Phase II. The framing of such remedies is theoretically guided by the same legal principles which govern awards to plaintiffs defrauded, or otherwise damaged, in business dealings. The victim is to be compensated for his loss or, in legal terms, to be "made whole." Practically speaking, in constitutional questions like school desegregation, things are not so simple, for by the time the court can bring a remedy to bear, the plaintiffs themselves, and even the contemporaneous "class" they represent, have either left school or are so far along that they have suffered damage beyond judicial repair. Thus, remedies in such cases must extend far beyond traditional notions of compensation to devise schemes which guarantee the rights of future generations of black students. Judges may maintain the legal fiction that they are merely trying a lawsuit between two parties, but their remedies affect the rights of parties who, strictly speaking, are not even represented before the court. A judge in such a case is no longer primarily concerned with adjudicating past wrongs; he is seeking to alter the future behavior of large sections of the population. Though he may still see himself as a neutral arbiter, he is, in fact, making social policy.

Though a trial judge has broad discretion in framing a remedy, he is by no means unrestrained. Particularly in the heavily litigated field of school desegregation, he is bound by a whole body of precedent. Indeed, barely a month after Garrity's ruling on the constitutional violation, the Supreme Court effectively cut off one possible avenue of remedy. In *Milliken* v. *Bradley,* it overruled a district court which had required cross-busing between Detroit and its surrounding suburbs. Since the lower court had found *de jure* segregation only within the city and not in the suburbs, the Supreme Court held that a metropolitan-wide order "would impose on the outlying districts, not shown to have committed any constitutional violation, a wholly impermissible remedy." *Milliken* marked an important turning point in the Court's approach to school segregation. Albeit by the narrowest margin (5–4) in any major school case yet, the Court halted the advance of school desegregation at the city line. Although many students of the matter believed a clear pattern of "state action" could be detected in the suburbs—notably in government housing loans and highway construction policies which operated to keep them predominantly white—the increasingly conservative Court majority declined to push its broadened doctrine of *de jure* segregation that far.

In a scathing dissent, Thurgood Marshall accused his colleagues of relying less on "neutral principles of law" than on a "perceived public mood." If so, it would hardly have been the first time the Court had ruled with an eye on public opinion. Prudent justices had long recognized that the Court itself had no battalions, that it drew its special power from the reverence in which most Americans held it, a veneration which could quickly evaporate if the Court collided too often with the critical interests and deeply held convictions of most Americans. The suburbs contained not only the nation's economic and social elite, but the broad reach of its white middle class, precisely the constituency which the Court would least wish to alienate. But a majority does not need the Court to protect its rights; a minority relies on the law for protection precisely because it does not have the numbers to prevail in the political realm. Marshall and other critics warned that by exempting suburban whites from school desegregation, the Court itself had discriminated against the powerless (white as well as black), had ensured that urban remedies would increasingly pit poor whites against poor blacks, and had permitted whites who could afford it to escape integration by fleeing to the refuge beyond the city line. Henceforth, the suburbs would be to the inner city what for so long the North had been to the South.

But even had the Court ruled the other way in *Milliken,* the NAACP and other black plaintiffs would probably not have sought a metropolitan solution in Boston. In the months following Garrity's liability ruling, the plaintiffs' attorneys began meeting with a broad cross section of Boston's black community, seeking a consensus on the optimum remedy. Virtually no blacks favored a metropolitan solution, largely because they believed it would dilute their meager influence in the sea of white suburbia. Indeed, there were some who opposed *any* remedy aimed principally at mixing blacks and whites, and sought instead some form of black "community control" of their own schools. However, most Boston blacks, recognizing that they were still a small minority (22 percent) in their own city, and knowing the tenacious grip of the Irish on the city's school system, had little faith in community control. They concluded—in some cases reluctantly—that the only way their children could ever gain their fair share of competent teachers, up-to-date books, and adequate facilities would be to attend the same schools as white children.

But before the plaintiffs could propose a remedy, the defendants had to be given a chance to frame their own plan. Arthur Garrity had scant expectation that a School Committee which had obstructed the Racial Imbalance Act at every turn would now submit an acceptable proposal for "root and branch" desegregation. Nevertheless, on October 31, he gave the committee six weeks to do so. In fact, for most of that time a majority of the committee was probably moving toward submission of a plan. Then, five days before the judge's deadline, a seventeen-year-old white boy was stabbed by a black student at South Boston High School. Within minutes, thousands of angry whites ringed the school, trapping hundreds of blacks inside, crying for revenge. Louise Day Hicks hurried to the school and, shouting through a bullhorn, urged the crowd to let the black children go back to Roxbury. "Do it for me," she pleaded. "I'm asking you because I've been with you all the way. Please help me." "No," they chorused back. "Niggers eat shit!" And a burly man yelled, "Shut up, Louise." For the first time in her decade-long leadership of the movement, she had lost control of "my people." Ashen-faced, she retreated.

After the stabbing at Southie, the School Committee was unwilling to risk the repudiation Louise had suffered. On December 16, it voted 3–2 to defy the judge and refuse to submit a desegregation plan drawn by the School Department staff. Garrity held the three-man majority in contempt of court and for a time considered sending them to jail. But fearing that would only make martyrs of them, he let them purge themselves of contempt by submitting a palpably unacceptable "voluntary" plan.

Long before that, Garrity had been preparing to devise his own plan. Even if he received a School Committee proposal, he would need to evaluate it in comparison with the plaintiffs' plan and critiques from other quarters. At the very least, he would need an "expert" in such matters to assist him, perhaps even a "master"—a legal surrogate to conduct hearings and recommend a remedy.

His first two choices as "expert"—a Harvard sociologist, Thomas Pettigrew, and the dean of Harvard's School of Education, Paul Ylvisaker—both turned him down. So the judge turned to Robert Dentler, the dean of Boston University's School of Education and a specialist in drawing desegregation plans. In mid-December, Dentler proposed a more complex structure than the judge had contemplated, involving a team of experts and masters. By then, Garrity had adopted another close adviser—Martin Walsh, the New England regional director of the Justice Department's Community Relations Service, who became the judge's "eyes and ears" in the city. Once Dentler recommended the team approach, Walsh began a search for the players.

In February, the judge selected four masters: former Massachusetts Attorney General Edward J. McCormack; Jacob J. Spiegel, a retired justice of the state's Supreme Judicial Court; Francis Keppel, a former United States Commissioner of Education; and Charles V. Willie, a black professor of education at the Harvard School of Education. Rounding out the team were the two experts: Dentler and Marvin Scott, a black associate dean at BU. These six men were installed in their headquarters—the chambers of Garrity's old and ailing mentor, Francis Ford, just down the hall—and by mid-February began their search for an acceptable way of desegregating Boston's schools.

But if the judge was assembling his own apparatus, that went largely unremarked. To Bostonians already rankling at his orders, or those apprehensive of dicta yet to come, the responsibility for their afflictions lay with Garrity alone—no longer a mere judge interpreting the law, but the personification of all the injustices heaped on them over the years by unfeeling or uncaring authority.

Morgan v. *Hennigan* came to be perceived as *Garrity* v. *Hennigan,* even *Garrity* v. *Boston.* Across the city that fall of 1974, slogans appeared on walls, bridges, and roadways: "Bus Garrity," "Fuck Garrity," "Kill Garrity." He was hung and burned in effigy. Affixed to a gazebo in the Boston Common one morning was a carefully lettered sign:

> *THE CITY IS OCCUPIED*
> *A BOYCOTT EXISTS*
> *A TYRANT REIGNS*
> *LAW IS BY DECREE*

And anti-busing activists in South Boston wrote a song about their tormentor, sung to the tune of Frank Sinatra's "My Way":

> *This man doesn't have the common sense of a third-grade level.*
> *I think he's in disguise, he really has to be the devil.*
> *But God is on our side just as it was in the beginning.*
> *This judge has almost reached his final inning.*

Thousands of letters poured into his chambers, some reasoned arguments against busing, but most of them fierce attacks on his character and lineage ("nigger lover," "Nazi," "child murderer"). Telephone callers besieged him at his office and home (where he stubbornly refused to get an unlisted number because, he said, he didn't want to disrupt his teenage daughters' social lives). One who called several times at home was Louise Day Hicks, who, angered because she couldn't get an appointment with the judge, took out her frustration by telephoning Mrs. Garrity and posing as a mother distraught at the fate of her children (Louise's two boys were long since out of school).

Many of the angriest letters and phone calls emphasized the judge's remoteness from Boston, his long residence in affluent Wellesley, where his family and friends were exempt from his court orders. One night in October 1974, a cavalcade of 350 cars, horns honking and headlights flashing, rolled out to 40 Radcliffe Road in Wellesley, where the Garritys' cream-colored colonial house stood on a green hillside. About two hundred demonstrators remained there for two hours. Though kept at a distance by the police, they paraded through the normally placid neighborhood waving American flags and brandishing placards. Throughout this period he received frequent death threats, and at least two attempts were made on the judge's life. A former mental patient in Dorchester was arrested one night with an M-16 rifle after telling his wife he was going to shoot Garrity. And a young Wellesley man, who had denounced the judge as a "dictator," was apprehended on the way to Garrity's house with a homemade bomb. After that, two deputy federal marshals were stationed outside the house day and night.

But physical danger worried Garrity less than the social ostracism to which he was subjected. Some old friends stopped calling; at cocktail parties he would often look up to see a pair of angry eyes glaring at him; and on the commuter train to and from Boston's South Station, men with whom he once had chatted now turned their backs on him. Garrity was a gregarious man and these slights hurt him deeply. Once he asked Kenny O'Donnell why he was no longer invited to parties held by a group of former Kennedy appointees. "The fellas," he wondered, "are they all mad at me now?" No, O'Donnell assured him, they were simply respecting the delicacy of his position as a federal judge immersed in controversy. A few days later when O'Donnell called to invite him to one of the parties, Garrity was delighted, but still apprehensive. "Are they all going to say the same thing, 'You were a nice Irish guy and then you moved to Wellesley and you changed'?" When his old friends welcomed him warmly, Garrity told them, "I haven't been so relieved in my life. You understand my position. I just have to carry out the law."

Throughout his travail, Garrity rarely missed the three dinners held every year by Boston's Clover Club, the city's best-known Irish society. Founded in 1883 by twelve Boston Irishmen, the club faithfully maintained its traditions: members wore clover medallions on green ribbons around their necks and smoked Irish clay pipes. But there was a self-conscious wistfulness in these Celtic trappings, as if the members were trying to reassert their Irishness in the face of relentless assimilation. For the two hundred Clovers—as the members called themselves—were the city's Irish establishment, drawn principally from the utilities, law, politics, and the press (Joe Kennedy once called them "a bunch of damn Republican Irishmen"). By 1970, with their political parodies and organized sing-alongs, they more closely resembled Washington's Gridiron Club than the tight little Irish drinking circle of a century before.

Yet Garrity's faithful attendance at Clover Club dinners was frequently invoked by friends as evidence that he had not ceased to identify with Boston's Irish. In a city whose public life is still largely dominated by men of Irish ancestry, such rituals are important acts of obeisance to a cultural tradition which has become largely a cultural myth. And nothing so demonstrated the continuing power of that myth as the persistent debate over just how Irish Arthur Garrity was.

His friends also cited his love of song and dance, always important indices of "Irishness" in Boston. His sister remembered how Arthur loved to sing around the piano at home. A friend recalled that Garrity was the first man in their crowd to learn the twist. Others enjoyed his sense of humor, but it was plainly not the jocularity of the caricature Irishman, rather a droll wit delivered so deadpan that only his quivering nostrils gave him away. Once, as he expressed annoyance at plaintiffs who were late in filing, his law clerk said, "We'll have to noodge them along." The judge asked, "You mean nudge?" No, said the Jewish clerk, "noodge." Weeks later, on another matter, the clerk said, "I think you ought to fudge that point." Garrity deadpanned: "You mean foodge, don't you?"

More boisterous men found him a bit prissy. His law clerks had never heard him tell a dirty joke. His strongest epithets were "criminy" and "good heavens." Once, while conferring with a more blunt-spoken assistant at the U.S. Attorney's office, Garrity said, "That, as you would say, is the goddamnest thing I've ever seen." The assistant asked, "Which of us has to go to confession tomorrow, Arthur?"

Bemused by his austere, almost ascetic devotion to the task at hand, some of his critics regarded Garrity as a "hoper"—Boston slang for "a man who goes to bed Irish and hopes to wake up Yankee." But Garrity's style was not so much Yankee as middle-class, the assimilationist manner of countless third- and fourth-generation Irish who have made it into mainstream America. And Boston's busing struggle was less a battle between Irish and Yankee—or even between Irish and Yankeefied Irish—than a family feud between the Irish who had made it and the Irish who hadn't. Indeed, the struggle in Arthur Garrity's courtroom that year often resembled an Irish morality play, fought out between various conceptions of what it meant to be Irish in contemporary Boston. On the bench, of course, was Garrity himself, the Clover Club Establishment Irishman. Representing the plaintiffs was Nick Flannery, whose service in Washington, New York, Detroit, and Mississippi qualified him as the Cosmopolitan Irishman. Speaking for the State Board of Education was Sandra Lynch, the Emancipated Irishwoman. On the other side of the aisle, Kevin Maloney, faithfully representing Kevin White's ambivalence toward desegregation, was the Political Irishman. And doing battle for the School Committee—after Hale and Dorr backed out in late 1974—was the indomitable J. J. Sullivan, playing the role of True Irishman.

James J. Sullivan's career began as if he were going to challenge John Kennedy for the title of Super Irishman. A bricklayer's son, Sullivan grew up in the tough Mission Hill district of Roxbury, but graduated from Boston Latin, Harvard College, and Harvard Law School, and worked for Henry Cabot Lodge in both the Senate and the United Nations before returning to Boston, where he served as an Assistant U.S. Attorney, then Real Property

Commissioner and City Corporation Counsel under John Collins. Once Kevin White took office, Sullivan found himself in political eclipse. Gradually, he shucked his patina of sophistication, resuming his earlier identity as a Roxbury Irishman, a belligerent battler for traditional values against the impractical notions of social experimenters. Sullivan had warned when he took over the School Committee case that he intended to try it as an "adversary proceeding," and he kept his promise. But his adversary was not so much the plaintiffs as the judge himself, whom Sullivan privately ridiculed as a "pansy." His taunts enraged Garrity, who, in his chambers, seethed at "that little stinker."

The Garrity-Sullivan skirmishes revealed the political nub of the case. Sullivan was charging Garrity with being a traitor to his own kind, an apostate who had forgotten that an Irishman's ultimate loyalty was to his family, his clan, his turf, his blood. Garrity was accusing Sullivan's clients of being false to a still higher value, to the requirement of their faith that they love and respect all God's children. Arthur Garrity was harder on his fellow Irish Catholics than any Yankee judge would likely have been in such circumstances. To him, racial hatred and prejudice were moral transgressions as great as drug peddling and pornography. From the bench he lashed out at "the frenetic, hate-mongering fringe in South Boston." He would not countenance that kind of conduct, and if people thought he was harsh, so be it. The dictates of their Church required a certain standard of behavior and he was going to hold them to it. Dick Maguire, who knew Arthur Garrity as well as anyone, said, "Whenever I hear that line from 'The Battle Hymn of the Republic': 'As he died to make men holy, let us die to make men free,' I think of Arthur."

On March 13, 1975, the Boston Bar Association gathered to honor the man who had once been in line to be its president. Outside the association's Beacon Street headquarters that evening, anti-busing demonstrators chanted, "Don't honor him! Impeach him!" Inside, a hundred judges and lawyers applauded as Garrity received the Public Service Award for his "steadfast devotion to the law." Then Garrity walked to the microphone. "There's much more to the rule of law," he said, "than constitutions and statutes themselves and their faithful construction by the courts and enforcement by officials of government. The rule of law encompasses the entire process whereby social order is achieved and preserved." But such order depended in turn, he said, upon "another body of rules which exist independently of constitutions and statutes and have been described by Professor Lon Fuller as 'the fundamental rules that make law possible.' These are the traditional principles of liberty, justice and decency commonly called the natural law."

Then he quoted from Walter Lippmann's *The Public Philosophy*. "Is there a body of positive principles and precepts which a good citizen cannot deny or ignore? . . . Indeed, there is such a thing as the public philosophy of civility. It does not have to be discovered or invented. It is known. But it does have to be revived and renewed."

As one might have expected from his Thomistic training at Holy Cross, Garrity felt some affinity with the early-American judicial tradition—exemplified by John Marshall—in which judges do not "make" law, but "find" it in a body of immutable truths. The judge declared what those truths were; he was the oracle, the secular priest, who received and interpreted the law. This was a tradition later rejected by Oliver Wendell Holmes and other positivists, who argued that judges were law*makers,* deriving their decisions not from some body of revealed truth but from the gritty sum of man's experience. But to Arthur Garrity the law was indeed something beyond mere experience. Right was right. Wrong was wrong. Racial justice was commanded not only by the United States Constitution but by divine law and natural law.

Apparently in reference to the angry shouts from outside, Garrity declared that night: "In reaching decisions which arouse the passions of the community in such matters as abortion and school busing, the Constitution forces the court in some degree to rely on natural law."

Even so, it remained unclear just how natural law might guide a judge in such a complex task as desegregating Boston's schools. For natural law could be argued on both sides of the case. Indeed, Ray Flynn, a state representative from South Boston, tried that one day, rising in Arthur Garrity's courtroom to remind the judge that they had both gone to Catholic colleges and learned there a doctrine which held that parents had natural rights above and beyond those of the state, chief among them the right to control their own children. In reply, Garrity found himself arguing constitutional law against Flynn's version of natural law.

No, natural law was fine for Bar Association disquisitions, but in devising a Phase II remedy, Garrity preferred to rely on a street-wise pragmatic Irishman. Although the judge had adopted Dentler's recommendation for a "team" approach, Eddie McCormack was clearly first among equals, the team's unofficial captain. It was a shrewd choice. A native of South Boston, McCormack was regarded as a loyal son of Southie, but he was also a lifetime member of the NAACP, and when he was State Attorney General, his strong civil rights stance had won the respect of Boston blacks. Moreover, he was a nephew of the former Speaker of the United States House of Representatives, John McCormack, a bellwether of the Democratic Party. The McCormacks, to be sure, had jousted with the Kennedys for control of the state party—Eddie had run against Ted Kennedy in a bitter primary contest for Jack's vacated seat in 1962. But even that was a point in his favor, because Arthur Garrity knew he could count on the Kennedy faction; he chose McCormack in part because he represented "the other camp" of the Boston Irish. Finally, McCormack was a tough, resourceful politician, adept in the art of consensus building.

He and Garrity never reached a firm agreement on what the job entailed, in part because there is no precision in legal circles about a master's duties. He is often viewed as a purely legal officer, a surrogate for the judge, who holds hearings on a complex subject and then recommends a course of action. But while Ed McCormack was an able lawyer, that was clearly not his principal qualification for the job. He was chosen because he had the savvy to broker a politically acceptable settlement consonant with the constitutional requirements. Yet that kind of activity was a legal no-man's-land. Garrity never told McCormack just how far he could go; McCormack never said just what he would do.

But broker he did—boldly and aggressively. He and his colleagues went through the motions of formal hearings, taking testimony on various plans which had been submitted to the court. But the real work was done in private meetings with leaders from all parts of the city in which McCormack asked, "How far would you be prepared to go?" In weeks of shuttle diplomacy, he negotiated a Phase II plan with broad support.

Unlike the Phase I plan, which affected only 40 percent of Boston's schools, the Masters' Plan covered the entire city (although East Boston, which the masters seemed to regard as a separate community under the *Keyes* doctrine, was largely exempted from its provisions). The city was divided into nine community school districts like slices of a pie, each wedge including black neighborhoods toward the pie's center and white communities toward the edge. Integration was achieved by busing whites toward the center of each slice and blacks toward the periphery. Each student had the right to attend a school within his own district if he chose to; however, he could also opt for one of thirty-two citywide "magnet schools" offering specialized programs. Magnet school enrollments would be held close to the racial ratio prevailing in the system at large—51 percent white, 36 percent black, 13 percent "other minority." But district schools would be allowed to reflect the racial composition of their own district. Thus, the percentages of white students would fluctuate widely—from 95 percent in East Boston and 80 percent in West Roxbury to 25 percent in Dorchester's Burke district and 30 percent in Madison Park. Another significant change would have eliminated the busing between South Boston and Roxbury, desegregating South Boston principally with blacks from nearby Dorchester. The plan had been designed to minimize busing throughout the city, and although its scope was greatly increased over Phase I, the number of students to be bused was actually reduced from 17,000 to 14,900. Parents were given some control over their children's schools through elected district councils. Finally, the city's universities and major business institutions were to offer assistance to individual schools.

To some, the plan seemed a skillful balancing of the constitutional requirement for racial integration with the craving of many parents for neighborhood autonomy. Moreover, Eddie McCormack had woven a powerful mystique around the plan. It seemed to promise both justice and order, an attractive combination to the afflicted city. That expectation mobilized a broad middle ground behind the plan, including the *Globe* and *Herald,* Mayor White and Governor Michael Dukakis (who had defeated Frank Sargent the fall before).

But not everybody liked it. Pixie Palladino labeled it "a rotten plan because it still requires mandatory busing." And to the NAACP the plan "looked like Munich, as if the governing constraint had been accommodation and tranquillity, not justice." Objecting particularly to the omission of East Boston and the wide fluctuation in racial ratios, the NAACP threatened to take the case to the

Court of Appeals. The State Board of Education submitted a detailed critique which argued that the masters had grossly miscalculated the ratios in several areas. Finally, new data obtained from the School Department showed that there were substantially fewer students in the system than hitherto believed, which altered many of the masters' calculations. By mid-April, it was clear to Ed McCormack that Garrity was under heavy pressure to revise the plan substantially, by busing more students and imposing greater uniformity on the city. Moreover, he heard that the judge was considering putting Roxbury and South Boston back in the same district. "You can't do it, Arthur," he told Garrity. "It'll blow the plan."

From his experience in the state courts, McCormack's colleague Jacob Spiegel thought he knew what was worrying Garrity. Although the Supreme Court in *Swann* had rejected integration by inflexible ratios, it also disapproved of schools whose racial composition was substantially different from the system-wide percentage. Garrity, Spiegel assumed, was afraid of being reversed on appeal if he adopted the Masters' Plan, but Spiegel believed that appellate judges would sanction considerable variation, particularly within a city like Boston, which was so Balkanized by ethnic neighborhoods. "Arthur," he argued, "do me a favor. Don't change a comma. Let it go to the Court of Appeals. I'll represent our side up there and I'll guarantee you, they won't overturn it."

The judge offered no assurances, but the masters retained some hope for their plan. Ed McCormack realized that the judge was not simply a Jesuit-trained jurist concerned with constitutional rights and remedies; he was also a practical man, intensely concerned with what worked. After all, he had long been associated with the Kennedys, the most pragmatic of public figures, and from them Garrity had learned to practice the art of the possible. "There is no such thing as perfection," he once declared. "It is a great mistake to think that there is." Garrity loved to get his hands around hard, stubborn, intractable details. Once he told Bob Dentler that what he had enjoyed most about running Jack Kennedy's Wisconsin campaign was the chance to administer a complex logistical operation. He seems to have fulfilled that part of himself in the school case. As the School Committee continued to defy him, he was drawn into administering the system himself—establishing school hours, hiring and firing personnel, ordering roofs repaired and hallways painted. One day he instructed South Boston High to purchase twelve MacGregor basketballs and six Acme Tornado whistles. Nor did he neglect to instruct a school that was being converted from elementary to middle grades to raise the height of its urinals.

Garrity most clearly revealed his practical side on the day he dedicated a plaque to his mentor, Francis Ford, who had died late in 1975. Garrity noted that Ford had been shaped in part by his experience in municipal politics. "It gave him, or perhaps strengthened in him," Garrity said, "a streak of skepticism, even suspicion, lest he embrace a judicial doctrine without an understanding of its practical consequences. In pondering a legal problem, he subscribed to the prayer of the poet Yeats:

> *God guard me from those thoughts men think*
> *In the mind alone.*
> *He that sings a lasting song*
> *Thinks in a marrow bone."*

Ed McCormack prayed that Arthur Garrity's marrow bone would prevail.

Finally, on May 10, 1975, Garrity handed down his decision. He retained much of the Masters' Plan, but changed significant portions: enforcing a more uniform racial ratio on the entire city (except East Boston); abolishing a district, the Burke, because it was too black; again placing South Boston and Roxbury in the same district; and sharply increasing the number of students to be bused, from 14,900 to 25,000. It was a characteristically cautious, by-the-book ruling. "Arthur threw the ball right across the center of the plate," a friend says. "He doesn't like to work the edges."

Ed McCormack was so angry he couldn't bring himself to read the newspapers the next morning. He felt betrayed. After encouraging them to build consensus for a plan, the judge had kicked the props from underneath it. If the plan had needed refinement, why couldn't Garrity have handed it back to them for "fine-tuning" instead of simply overriding them? Now people could say, "I supported the Masters' Plan, but I can't support the judge's." Garrity claimed to have retained 90 percent of the original plan, but McCormack was sure that the revisions, modest though they might be, had destroyed the plan's mystique and therefore its efficacy. He could not guarantee that his plan would have brought peace to the city, but he was certain that the judge's remedy would ensure more violence.

Arthur Garrity, too, was pained by the hard choices he had to make. Particularly difficult was the decision to increase busing. "Toward lessening widespread misunderstanding on the point, it may be stated that the court does not favor busing," he wrote. "If there were a way to accomplish desegregation in Boston without transporting students to schools beyond walking distance, the court and all parties would much prefer that alternative." But, as he saw it, there was no alternative. And there was no way to retain certain aspects of the Masters' Plan without violating the plaintiffs' constitutional rights. The jurist in Arthur Garrity had prevailed over the pragmatist; John Marshall over Oliver Wendell Holmes; Thomas Aquinas over Jack Kennedy; the mind over the marrow bone.

15

McGoff

Alice had heard that sound before. A rhythmic slap, like the wings of a giant bird trapped in a closet. But what was it? The mad flapping echoed somewhere near the base of her skull, and try as she might, her sluggish brain couldn't decipher it.

Abruptly she came awake. Outside her window, eerie blue lights played on the brick façade of the housing project. A siren wailed over the hill. And there was that sound again. Chock, chock, chock.

A garbage truck? An airplane? A helicopter?

That was it. But what was a goddamn helicopter doing in Charlestown at six o'clock in the morning?

Groping to the window, Alice could see a cluster of kids in the street, pointing up the hill toward the Monument. A police car blocked the roadway, its blue light pulsing. The sound was louder here, but still she couldn't see anything. Stumbling into the parlor, Alice pulled back the curtains. Peering into the steel-gray sky, she saw not one but three helicopters circling the towering white shaft of the Bunker Hill Monument, hovering over the town.

It was Monday, September 8, 1975, the opening day of school, the start of Arthur Garrity's Phase II plan for Boston, the first day of busing in Charlestown, a day Alice had been anticipating with apprehension bordering on hysteria. The day before, she had awakened with a neck so stiff that by midafternoon her son Danny had to take her to Massachusetts General Hospital, where an emergency room doctor could find no physical source for her ailment.

"Are you suffering from any particular nervous stress or strain?" he had asked.

"Not that I know of," she replied.

"Oh, no," Danny chimed in. "She's only got seven kids and busing begins tomorrow."

Ah, said the doctor, she was the fourth mother he'd had in there that week-end; like the others, Alice was probably suffering an anxiety attack. He gave her some muscle relaxants and encased her neck in a huge foam-rubber Thomas Collar, which eased the discomfort somewhat but made it impossible to sleep. Eventually, she'd taken it off, but the neck was throbbing and aching worse than ever.

Gazing out the parlor window now at the helicopters, she thought: It's like we're the Nazis and they're the Americans, and they're going to shoot us. It's crazy!

She put the collar back on, twisted painfully into her bathrobe, and made herself a cup of coffee. By now the noise from the copters had wakened her children and they came clattering out of their bedrooms.

"What the hell's going on?"

"Choppers, dummy! Whirlybirds!"

"It's the Vietcong!"

"It's the fuckin' Marines!"

Alice tried to get the kids some breakfast, but everybody was too excited to eat. Pulling on their clothes, they piled out the door onto Walford Way, cut through the alleys of the project onto Bunker Hill Street, then up the steep hill toward Monument Square. Even before they reached the corner, they could hear the sound of trucks maneuvering on the narrow streets around the Monument, the thud of feet on the pavement, the sharp commands ringing in the autumn air. But they weren't prepared for what they saw when they reached the square. Hundreds of police lined the sidewalks around the Monument: Boston police in regulation blue uniforms, with yellow rain gear tucked under their arms; Metropolitan District Commission police in light blue shirts and helmets; state police in breeches, boots, and broad-brimmed trooper hats; deputy U.S. marshals in gray business suits; and—most distinctive of all—the city's Tactical Patrol Force in jumpsuits, leather jackets, riot helmets, and Plexiglas visors, pounding wooden batons into leather-gloved hands.

Danny hadn't realized there were that many cops in all of Boston. And these guys meant business—they looked as if they were ready for combat in Vietnam.

Then Billy grabbed his arm and pointed toward the roof of Charlestown High School across the square. Danny could make out two policemen behind the rooftop balustrade, one with binoculars methodically scanning the street below, the other hefting a rifle with a prominent sniper scope.

Snipers on the rooftops! Helicopters! Riot police in combat gear! Hell, this wasn't school desegregation—they were being invaded!

By then a blazing orange sun was inching over the crest of Breed's Hill. For a moment, the McGoffs and their friends stood transfixed by the martial array drawn up before them, half admiring the military precision with which the police had seized the high ground, half seething at the edict they were there to enforce.

"Hell," said Danny, quickly recovering his characteristic bravado. "They can drop the damn atom bomb on the Monument if they want to. They'll never get this town to cave in."

Like most Townies, the McGoffs were resisting Garrity's order as best they could. Alice had sworn she would never put her children on a bus to Roxbury, and even before her three youngest were assigned there, she'd enrolled them in Catholic schools in Malden and Everett, nearby working-class suburbs—Tommy at Immaculate Conception, the twins at St. Anthony's.

Under Garrity's plan—which designated certain age groups in each "geocode" to be bused and others to remain in their neighborhood schools—Billy, Lisa, and Kevin were assigned to Charlestown High. Anti-busing leaders had called for a boycott of all Charlestown schools that first week to express the community's determined opposition to the judge's order, and many of the McGoffs' classmates—under pressure from their parents—had already pledged not to go to school that morning. Alice had left the decision up to her kids. "I hope you won't go," she said. "It'll show the judge we mean business. But I won't stop you. You're old enough to make up your own minds."

Billy and Lisa decided to go. A senior that year, Billy had already been elected co-captain of the football team; he would probably be co-captain in basketball as well, and he expected to be chosen senior class president as his brother Danny had been before him. Busing or not, it was going to be a good year and he was eager to get started.

Lisa felt even more strongly about it. As she told her mother that morning, "If we don't go, we're letting Garrity and all those police keep us out of our own school. I don't care if they bring the whole Army in here, I'm going to school."

A few minutes before eight, Lisa looked at her watch. "Well," she said, "I guess it's time."

Alice sat at the kitchen table, rubbing her aching neck with both hands. "Oh God," she moaned. "I'm frightened for you kids. Please, stay out of trouble. If any fighting starts, just come home. And, Billy, for crying out loud, look out for your sister!"

Then the two of them set off along Bunker Hill Street. At Monument Street, where the Red Store and the Green Store manned the corner like old friends, they paused for a moment to gather their courage—buying some candy at the Red Store, exchanging greetings with the regulars around the counter—before starting up the hill. As they reached Monument Square, their path was barred by three policemen demanding identification. When they produced cards stating their names, grades, and school assignments, the cops waved them through.

Before them lay the grassy flanks of the Monument grounds, enclosed by a high wrought-iron fence and now by another wall of Metropolitan District Commission police, standing guard at ten-foot intervals. As the McGoffs turned right and headed toward the high school, whose gray granite façade dominated the northwest corner of Monument Square, they noticed for the first time a huge throng of press people massed behind the fence. There were newspapermen scribbling in stenographer's pads, photographers festooned with cameras, television cameramen with Minicams strapped to their shoulders, sound men with long black booms which they poked between the rungs of the fence, hoping to capture some murmur of approaching confrontation. The principal object of their attention was a group of about seventy-five Townies, most of them women, who had gathered on the corner of Concord Street as it emptied into the square, hard by the high school. Brandishing homemade placards with messages like "No forced busing!" and "Never!" the women were straining against another line of police thrown up across the intersection.

As the McGoffs reached the corner, they were halted again by a police sergeant who asked once more for their identity cards, then waved them through a cordon of police toward the school's front door. Passing along the corridor of blue uniforms, Lisa was simultaneously excited and terrified. Never in her young life had she been the center of such a maelstrom of activity; never before had so many people seemed so passionately interested in what she was doing. Yet the very passion, the intensity, the sheer physical presence of so many armed men intimidated her, and she hurried toward the safety of the familiar school door, Billy close at her heels.

But as she stepped through the doorway into the gloomy marble lobby, the scene confronting her was anything but reassuring. Immediately in front of the door stood three large, rectangular metal detectors—like those she had seen at airports—through which her schoolmates were now filing one by one, closely scrutinized by teachers and school administrators. And suspended above the detectors was a cardboard sign, hand-lettered in bold, black characters:

NO UNAUTHORIZED PERSONNEL MAY CARRY ONTO SCHOOL PROPERTY, CARRY ON HIS PERSON, OR USE WITHIN SCHOOL PROPERTY ANY ITEM OR ARTICLE THAT MAY BE USED AS A WEAPON.

THE FOLLOWING ITEMS ARE TO BE CONSIDERED WEAPONS:

A. Firearms of any kind.
B. Any knives, razors, or other objects sharpened into blades.
C. Clubs, athletic equipment such as baseball bats, hockey
sticks, umbrellas, karate sticks (moonchucks), or rods of any kind.
D. Pipes, brass knuckles, and other metal objects
(screwdrivers, wrenches, hammers, other metal tools).
E. Chains, whips, ropes, or any object fashioned into such.
F. Combs with metal teeth, rat tails.
G. Scissors, metal nail files, hatpins.
H. Mace and other chemical sprays such as
spray paint and spray deodorants.
I. Bottles.
J. All other instruments or articles not listed above
which may inflict bodily harm upon another.

Lisa stared at the sign in disbelief. This wasn't the school she had left the June before—it wasn't her school at all anymore. It was an alien place, ruled by judges, bureaucrats, police, and criminals with knives, pipes, bottles, and clubs intent on doing her harm. With clenched teeth, she submitted to the metal detectors and a long, painstaking search of her handbag. Then, filled with anxiety, she climbed the marble steps toward her homeroom.

From the corner of Concord Street, Danny McGoff watched his sister and brother enter the school, almost wishing he was going with them. He'd had a hell of a good time up there and put together an impressive extracurricular record—president of the senior class, editor of the school paper, manager of the hockey team. He'd hoped to be the second member of his family—after his uncle Jim—to go to college, but he'd squandered so much of his energy on the hockey team and hanging out on the corner with his friends that his grades and board scores had been too low to get him in anywhere decent. The guidance counselors said he needed a year to "brush up" his English and math, so when the 502 Club—a group of teamsters up in Sullivan Square—offered him their annual scholarship, he grabbed it and selected Berwick Academy in Maine. For weeks now he'd been so busy getting his school gear together he hadn't had much time to think about busing, but as he stood on the corner surveying the massive display of city, state, and federal power drawn up around his old school, he could feel the anger rising in him. He'd always thought the job of the police was to catch crooks, not to ram unpopular laws down people's throats. Turning away in disgust, he jogged down the hill toward Bunker Hill Street, where a group of his pals had gathered outside the Green Store, restless and looking for action, hungry to vent their anger at the alien presence in their town. Many were already pulling on cans of Bud or bottles of Narragansett beer. And there were younger kids as well—among them his two youngest brothers, fourteen-year-old Kevin, who had stayed out of Charlestown High to see what was happening on the streets, and thirteen-year-old Tommy, whose classes at Immaculate Conception hadn't yet begun.

An impish-looking sophomore named Jimmy Walsh had an idea. Together with a friend, he ran down the street to his family's apartment in the Bunker Hill project, pulled an old pair of jeans and a sweatshirt from a closet, and stuffed them with wadded newspapers. Fashioning a head from a black plastic garbage bag, they hung a cardboard sign: "Nigger beware!" around its neck. Tying a rope around the effigy, they climbed to the project roof and flung it over the edge. "Look at the nigger!" Walsh shouted as the crowd below cheered.

On the first throw, the dummy caught in the limbs of a tree and dangled there for a few minutes. Soon the boys retrieved it and tossed it further out onto the street. The crowd in front of the Green Store broke and ran toward the dummy, kicking and stomping it in a frenzy of release. "Let's burn it!" someone shouted. A match was produced. The dummy, doused with gasoline, erupted in flame. Prancing around the fiery "corpse," the boys shouted, "Burn, nigger, burn!"

Several patrol cars came screeching up Bunker Hill Street, as Captain William MacDonald, Charlestown's police commander, hurried down the hill to take charge of the situation. At once he ordered the crowd to disperse, but by then the burning effigy and police sirens had drawn still more youths out of the housing project. Sensing a confrontation, they refused to move.

MacDonald seized a bullhorn and shouted, "This intersection must be cleared immediately. You have five minutes to comply with this order or the police will move you." But that brought only a chorus of jeers: "We ain't going nowhere!" "This is our town, you get out!" Abruptly, down the street in Hayes Square, appeared a squad of the dreaded Tactical Patrol Force, visors in place, ready to move. "Sit down!" a man shouted, and most of the teenagers obeyed, squatting in the street around the blackened object on the pavement. On a signal from MacDonald, the TPF began jogging up the street, and from around the corner came six motorcycles of the Mobile Operations Patrol, driving straight for the kids, scattering them right and left.

Until then, Danny McGoff had been merely a spectator. He kept telling himself: "I'm not going to get arrested today. I'm going to school in a week and I don't want to come down here to court. I'd better stay out of this." But now as the battle was joined, as friends all around him began pelting the police with beer bottles, rocks, and pieces of wood, Danny heaved a Narragansett bottle at the police cars in the intersection and watched it shatter against a fender. Aroused, he charged into the fray, heaving whatever came to hand.

All around him, others—even grown men—were losing control. Vinnie Donovan, a beefy neighbor of the McGoffs, charged Captain MacDonald and kicked him in the groin. As the captain doubled up in pain, two policemen seized Vinnie by the arm, but his friends grabbed him by the other arm and for a few seconds a bizarre tug-of-war ensued, each side hauling at him until the weight of the crowd prevailed and they pulled him back into their midst. By now, the TPF were angry too, flailing about them with their nightsticks, drawing blood. The motorcyclists roared onto the sidewalks, chasing some of the crowd into the project.

Danny, Tommy, and Kevin McGoff scrambled down Carney Court and into O'Reilly Way, a narrow road behind the first row of project buildings. There they were relatively safe, for they knew all the project's alleys and courtyards, all the doors and passageways which led ever deeper into its protective maze.

So the battle became a game which Danny and Tommy joined with gusto while Kevin maintained his usual role of detached observer. The kids would sneak down an alley, jump onto Bunker Hill Street, and heave a barrage of rocks and bottles at the police, but once the cops gave chase, they would dart back into the project and disappear into a building, only to reappear a few minutes later two blocks away. For most of the morning and into the afternoon, the McGoffs and their friends played cat and mouse with the police.

But eventually they tired of that. In midafternoon, about three hundred Townies, most of them teenagers, staged a march up Breed's Hill, chanting the high school football cheer, "Here we go, Charlestown, here we go!" Along the way, they overturned five small cars and set fire to a sixth. On the other side of the hill, demonstrators forced their way into the lobby of the Bunker

Hill Community College and assaulted a nineteen-year-old black student, knocking him to the ground and injuring his arm. Then, their anger spent, the crowd drifted back up the hill, heading home through the gathering dusk.

Still immobilized by her aching neck, Alice hadn't moved from her apartment, where she followed the day's events on radio and television. Several local stations had preempted their normal programming for coverage of the crisis. Prone in bed, her neck cradled by four pillows, she viewed with growing horror the massive array of forces around Monument Square, the frightening scene outside the high school, the battle of Bunker Hill Street, the march to the community college. As she watched the images flickering across the screen, and listened to the newsmen summing it all up in their Harvard accents, she thought: The scene they're showing is barely three hundred yards up the hill, but for all these guys know, it might as well be on the other side of the moon. They just don't understand. By the time her children straggled home, Alice was deeply agitated and she pleaded with them to stay in that evening, to keep off the streets. But soon most of the boys had rushed out again, unable to resist the skirmishes still sputtering along Bunker Hill Street. At about ten o'clock, somebody threw two firebombs into the Warren Prescott School, and when firemen arrived they were stoned by a hostile crowd. Another group set up a barricade of blazing trash barrels, which brought the TPF racing back to clear it. Until well past midnight, police cars streamed through the project.

As she lay in bed, watching headlights race across her bedroom ceiling, Alice could feel her neck growing stiffer by the minute. It seemed to her as though all the pain of that terrible day had collected in one knot and lodged at the base of her neck.

The pain had been a long time gathering. Alice had paid little attention to the early phases of Boston's desegregation struggle—preoccupied with raising her seven children, she told herself that the legal battle was unlikely to affect Charlestown for years to come. But by 1973, as both state and federal courts prepared to grapple with the central issue, it suddenly seemed less remote.

In the early seventies, Alice had four of her children at the Harvard-Kent, a new elementary school directly across the street from the Bunker Hill project. Like most of her neighbors, she was delighted to have the new school—the first in Charlestown in more than thirty years—but she was determined to keep a close eye on her children's education. Having paid her one dollar to join the Harvard-Kent Home and School Association—Boston's equivalent of the Parent-Teacher Association—she regularly attended its monthly meetings in the school's spacious auditorium. In March 1973, after the state's Supreme Judicial Court set an accelerated timetable for "racial balancing" of the city's schools, Charlestown's Home and School Association called a mass protest rally. Alice was among five hundred parents who gathered to listen to anti-busing leaders from around the city. The evening's most rousing address came from Mrs. Olive Costello, a Dorchester mother, who warned that indiscriminate mixing of blacks and whites would be a disaster. "The three R's will be turned to Riot, Rape, and Robbery," she said. "Wake up Charlestown, before it's too late!"

To Alice, the idea of sending her children to a school halfway across the city when they had a perfectly good school right across the street was utterly ridiculous. Moreover, what she knew of conditions in Roxbury strengthened her resolve not to put any of her children on a bus. Riot, Rape, and Robbery might be a little strong, but she knew it wasn't safe over there, and when the chairman asked for recruits to help form a Charlestown chapter of a new state-wide organization—Massachusetts Citizens Against Forced Busing—Alice raised her hand.

Charlestown's nascent anti-busing movement was led by a small circle of women: Gloria Conway, editor of the Charlestown *Patriot,* the town's weekly newspaper; Peg Pigott and Ann Doherty, both active in the Home and School Association; and Judy Brennan, a telephone operator. All were mothers from stable "lace curtain" families, public-spirited, moderate, even circumspect. They fitted well into Massachusetts Citizens, a cautious organization which concentrated on public education, lobbying in the state legislature, and orderly demonstrations to capture media attention.

Though Alice lived in the project among a different breed of Townie, she'd been born and raised on Monument Avenue among women much like these. Now she threw herself into Massachusetts Citizens—signing up new members, handing out leaflets, attending demonstrations. Often she took her older children along—Lisa in particular became a regular in the protests outside City Hall and the State House. On April 3, 1974, when five hundred Townies marched in the huge procession to Beacon Hill, Alice, Danny, Lisa, and Kevin walked arm in arm in the second row of the Charlestown contingent. And later that afternoon, as the sun set, they were among the 3,000 diehards who remained on the Common singing, to the tune of the World War I song, "Over there, over there, our kids aren't going over there."

When Arthur Garrity issued his long-awaited ruling two months later, making it clear that some kids would indeed be going over there, a new desperation crept into Boston's anti-busing movement. With the federal court order overriding state laws, lobbying was now useless. A new brand of protest was needed to show the judge that Boston's white neighborhoods would never bow to his dictates. That June, Louise Day Hicks and her advisers pulled together a coalition of anti-busing activists in a new organization. To express the group's militance, they called it ROAR (Restore Our Alienated Rights). The first demonstration under the new label was scheduled for September 9, 1974, the Monday before the limited first phase of busing was to begin.

With the federal court taking jurisdiction of the case, the September protest focused on Massachusetts' two U.S. senators—Ted Kennedy and Ed Brooke—who had recently voted against a narrowly defeated anti-busing rider to the federal aid to education bill. The rider wouldn't have bound a federal court, but ROAR wanted to voice its outrage at the senators' stand.

Neither man actually advocated busing. In April 1965, Ed Brooke—then the first black to serve as Massachusetts Attorney General—said, "I don't believe any parent, black or white, wants to have his children bused from a superior school to an inferior school. It's just not natural. The sane and sensible approach is the destruction of the ghetto." Ted Kennedy was equally skeptical. On *Meet the Press* in March 1964, he told a reporter, "If your question is asking me whether I oppose 'busing' students, I do." But as support for busing became a touchstone of commitment to racial equality, both senators gradually altered their positions, and when Arthur Garrity handed down his decision, Kennedy and Brooke rallied round the embattled judge.

Ted Kennedy was especially close to Garrity—closer than his brother Jack had ever been. The two men saw each other with some frequency over the years, and not surprisingly there were those in Boston who regarded Garrity as Ted Kennedy's front man. At anti-busing rallies, it was not uncommon to see signs linking the two, as in "Impeach Kennedy—and Impeach Kennedy's Puppet, Judge Garrity."

Late in August of 1974, ROAR's leaders asked both senators to meet with them in their Boston offices in the John F. Kennedy Federal Building before the September 9 rally. Brooke said he would not be in Boston that day, but he designated two assistants to meet the delegation and receive their demands: "That you restore our alienated rights. That you use your influence to obtain an immediate moratorium of the court-ordered busing plan decreed by Federal Judge W. Arthur Garrity, a Kennedy political appointee. That you, failing this, do each day what you force us to do—put your children on a bus and send them into a high crime area. That you support us now or we will not support you."

Ted Kennedy had never responded to ROAR's request for a meeting. But he was in the city that morning, having flown up from Hyannis Port at 9:00 a.m., ostensibly to visit four high schools which were to be desegregated that week. When the delegation appeared at his office, an aide invited them to sit down. For nearly an hour, the six mothers waited impatiently. Suddenly a man appeared in the doorway, calling, "Kennedy's here! He's on the bandstand."

Why the Senator had changed his plans and headed directly for the platform is not clear. Perhaps it was a column in the previous day's Boston *Globe*, written by Mike Barnicle, a young columnist who was a friend of the Senator's. Born in Fitchburg of Irish-American parentage, Barnicle saw himself as a spokesman for the city's misunderstood white working class. The column, entitled "Open Letter to Senator Kennedy," sought to express the feelings of those Irish-Americans who would march in that day's demonstrations. "Dear Senator Kennedy," it began.

> *Tomorrow, they'll be marching . . . people who have worked hard just to stay even, never mind get ahead. Many of their minds can still race back in time and history to the night that "one of their own," John Fitzgerald Kennedy, became the President of the United States of America.*

*That was an earlier, easier time for them, a time when it was easy to smile
and laugh. But there will be few smiles tomorrow and little laughter. . . .
Senator, you are the one man who can heal the divisions that have arisen
over the issue of busing. You have the one voice that can help keep this
city calm, leaving the clear ring of justice and common sense. . . . You
could recall your memories of your brother, Bob, being driven through
the streets of Gary, Indiana, with hands reaching out to touch him, hands
that came out of a gray factory dusk and touched him in a night of brotherhood, hands—black and white—that were alive with hope. You could
tell them, Senator, that law knows no neighborhood, that justice is not
confined to any one block, that fear must be put aside and the fact of law
adhered to. And, to you, Senator Kennedy, they would listen.*

Perhaps Kennedy was responding to a telephone call Barnicle made to
Hyannis Port that weekend, urging the Senator to go to the rally and confront
the crowd. Perhaps it was Kennedy's own sense of what was required of him.
As he said later, "I felt I had a responsibility to do it. I felt it was important
that they hear my views." Or, perhaps, it was merely his instinctive response
to a challenge. Although he had been invited to meet with the delegation upstairs, Kennedy apparently thought the group was daring him to address the
rally. "They had thrown out a challenge, implied that I didn't have the guts.
So I felt it was important not to back down from that, to go ahead and confront them."

For whatever reasons, after brief appearances at South Boston and Dorchester high schools, instead of visiting the other two schools on his itinerary
he told his driver to head for Government Center. There he halted the car at
the plaza's edge and walked to the temporary platform set up in front of City
Hall, where 8,000 people were listening to the speeches.

Mrs. Rita Graul, one of Mrs. Hicks's principal lieutenants, had just introduced two figures in chicken masks—"the white chicken, Senator Kennedy,"
and "the brown chicken, Senator Brooke." All of a sudden, there was Kennedy
himself—that distinctive mop of brown hair, his face tanned from the late-
summer weekend on the Cape. There was a brief but heated discussion over
whether to let the Senator speak. Ultimately, Kennedy advanced to the microphone, but when the crowd realized who he was they booed and jeered:

"Impeach him. Get rid of the bum!"

"You're a disgrace to the Irish!"

"Why don't you put your one-legged son on a bus!"

"Yeah, let your daughter get bused, so she can get raped!"

"Why don't you let them shoot you, like they shot your brother!"

Kennedy's face tightened and his fist grasped the microphone more closely,
but each time he tried to speak the clamor grew. Some in the crowd chanted,
"No, no, we won't go." Others sang "God Bless America." Then, slowly at
first, more quickly as the idea caught on, the crowd turned row by row to face
the Federal Building named for his brother, the late President. Kennedy

abruptly left the platform and started across the plaza toward his office, a few women pursuing him, shouting further insults. Then out of the crowd sailed a ripe tomato, smashing on the pavement, splattering his pin-striped suit. "Ahhh," sighed the crowd. Another tomato and several eggs rained down on him. Kennedy quickened his pace, head down. With the object of their resentment in full flight now, the pursuers closed in. Screaming with rage, one woman with a tiny American flag in her hair flailed at the Senator, striking him on the shoulder. He stumbled, then righted himself and hurried on. An elbow caught him in the ribs. A man aimed a kick at his shins.

At last Kennedy reached the Federal Building and darted through the swinging door, secured behind him by uniformed guards. Outside, his pursuers pounded their fists on the tinted glass, howling with frustration. Suddenly, one large pane gave way, the jagged shards shattering on the marble floor as the demonstrators stepped back and cheered, shaking their fists over their heads. Surrounded by a ring of security men, Kennedy told reporters, "People have strong emotions—and strong feelings—and they've certainly expressed them. They have—ah—a right to their position. Anyone in public life has to expect this." But pouring cream into a Styrofoam cup of coffee, his hand trembled.

And well it might. For something had happened that day on the slippery stones between the soaring white tower named for Jack Kennedy and the Aztec pyramid of City Hall which Ted himself had dedicated only seven years before. Something had happened there to puncture a notion deeply cherished by the Kennedys, by the city in which they had come to power, and by the nation which had embraced them with such warmth. Many Americans had allowed themselves to believe that John Kennedy's accession to the presidency had completed the assimilation of the Irish into mainstream America. His style, grace, and wit, his beautiful wife and handsome children persuaded many that centuries of Gaelic rage and frustration had been dissipated in "one bright, shining moment." It was widely believed that Kennedy's breakthrough to the pinnacle of national power had marked a watershed in Irish-American history, a continental divide on whose broad, grassy forward slope the new breed of assimilated Irishman would henceforth accept the standards and mores of the American consensus.

Bobby Kennedy, to be sure, was less assimilated than Jack, more the brooding, mercurial Irishman. Nevertheless, the belief persisted, especially following the Indiana primary, that Bob could rally both blacks and working-class whites—working-class Irish—to his vision of social justice. When that promise was dashed by his own assassination, such hopes were transferred to Ted. In October 1968, Sam Beer, a Harvard professor and friend of Ted's, wrote him of a conversation he had had that summer with a Croatian construction worker in Chicago who had told him, "We're fucking tired of feeding niggers." Beer warned Kennedy: "The racist appeal opens up to economic conservatives a superb method of bamboozling the working class. . . . One of your strengths is that you could reduce the flow of working men in the racist direction. Like RFK in Indiana, you could, I believe, hold both Negro voters and blue-collar Slavs. . . . We cannot simply let the racist Democrats go over to the GOP and trust to some new force, e.g. young people, to counterbalance the loss. We must hold the elements of the old coalition as well as win the new ones (by 'we,' of course, I mean 'you')."

Ted Kennedy never responded to Sam Beer's appeal. Perhaps it seemed fruitless during the late sixties and early seventies when millions of working-class Democrats deserted their party to put and keep Richard Nixon in the White House. But through those bleak years, Kennedy remained confident that when the time came he could bring the working-class whites back home where they belonged. Indeed, he felt free to take some of his bravest stands—against the Vietnam War, for government-financed abortions, against IRA violence in Northern Ireland—precisely because he was so confident that Irish Catholic voters in particular, no matter how they might differ with him on a given issue, would rally round him when the chips were down. After all, the Boston Irish were the Kennedy voters par excellence, the people who had sent Jack to Congress thirty years before, who had cherished his family through the best times and the worst. Now, in the heart of Ted's own city, in the plaza beneath his own office window, in the shade of a building dedicated to his brother, those people had not only deserted him, they had publicly humiliated him.

Nowhere was the resentment against Ted Kennedy more intense than in Charlestown. Some two hundred Townies had led the march to City Hall that September morning, chanting, "Here we go, Townies, here we go," and had joined in turning their backs on the Senator. (The McGoffs weren't among them. Barely a week before, Alice had begun a new job—as an operator for the New England Telephone Company—and she couldn't get away for a weekday demonstration.)

The turnabout in Charlestown's feelings toward Kennedy had come quickly. As late as June 1970, the Bunker Hill Day parade had been dedicated to Ted "for his continuing tireless and dedicated work in behalf of the residents of Charlestown [and] his self-sacrifice in carrying on in the great Kennedy tradition." That morning, a huge throng at the base of the Monument had thundered its approval as Kennedy, in the day's oration, asked, "Did not the men on this hill seek a life for their children free of repression, free of other men's prejudice, free to advance to the limit of their talents? Then how can we avoid the same search, how can we flee from problems of our society only to seek quiet—when prejudice and repression exist."

Yet by June 1974, his staff had warned that it would be unsafe for him to appear publicly on Bunker Hill Day. He did show up at Jerry Doherty's traditional "time" following the parade. Hunched down in a friend's car, he was driven through the crowded streets, face averted from passersby. Inside Doherty's house on Washington Street, he threw himself into the spirit of the occasion, slapping old friends on the back, plucking a beer from the pails of ice, a ham and cheese sandwich off the kitchen table. As the party roared late into the evening, friends suggested he join them for a nightcap or two down the street at Sully's Cafe. After all, Sully's was a traditional Kennedy gathering spot—Jack had often stopped there while campaigning in the Town; both Jack and Ted had adjourned to Sully's after their inductions into the Knights of Columbus Fourth Degree; and Ted's ceremonial sword still hung on the wall. It was a temptation on that boozy night so reminiscent of celebrations past to join the others down at the tavern, to belly up to the bar with the Townies and try to reestablish the easy camaraderie of years gone by. But Ted resisted. It was okay there at Jerry's house, but the streets and taverns of Charlestown were enemy territory now. Once when a friend asked him what he thought Sully was saving his sword for, Ted smiled ruefully and said, "Stick it in my gut, I guess."

Now the incident at City Hall Plaza only intensified Charlestown's bellicosity. Gloria Conway, the newspaper editor and newly elected secretary of Massachusetts Citizens Against Forced Busing, had been Charlestown's representative on the podium that day. She had no great love for Ted Kennedy, but she didn't believe in assaulting U.S. senators. Her misgivings were shared by the other women who had led Charlestown's anti-busing movement those past few years. Three days after the Kennedy incident—just as busing was getting underway in South Boston and Roxbury—Mrs. Conway called a meeting to assess the situation. Present in the basement of the Bunker Hill Post of the American Legion were many of her own supporters, but they were joined that day by others, Townie parents who had been mobilized by the dramatic events of the past few days and who suddenly realized it was only a matter of time before their children were going to be bused. Many of these newcomers were residents of the Bunker Hill project, the poorest, most vulnerable members of the community, those least able to evade the problem by sending their children to private or parochial schools. The project families were spoiling for a fight, and they got one soon enough.

From the start, Mrs. Conway and her supporters found themselves on the defensive. Some of the newcomers had already joined ROAR. Now, one after another, they rose to challenge the leadership of Massachusetts Citizens Against Forced Busing.

"What the hell have you done?" asked Tom Johnson, a burly ex-longshoreman. "A lot of talking and marching, none of which has made a bit of difference. The time has come for some action."

"What kind of action are you talking about, Mr. Johnson?" asked Gloria Conway, her voice edged with sarcasm.

"I'm talking about action in the streets."

"But our children are going to be out in the streets," Gloria said. "Would you sacrifice one of our children?"

For a moment the room was still, as all faces turned toward Tom Johnson. "Yes," he said, "if necessary."

The meeting at Legion Hall left the Charlestown movement irrevocably split. Uncomfortable with the aggressive new street tactics, disquieted by the intimations of violence, disinclined to associate too closely with the "project people," most of the Massachusetts Citizens crowd soon retired from the field. Henceforth, Peg Pigott worked the creaking machinery of the Home and School Association, while Gloria Conway published editorials in the *Patriot*, thundering against busing yet pleading for non-violence. But the movement's leadership had passed into new hands.

Virtually alone among her colleagues in Massachusetts Citizens, Alice McGoff did not back away from these new elements. She had always been something of an anomaly in the old crowd anyway, a widow from the projects surrounded by a clutch of club women from the slopes of Breed's and Bunker hills. The new recruits were her friends and neighbors, people she saw every day along Bunker Hill Street, at the Red Store and the Green Store, in the courtyards of the project itself. They didn't frighten or repel her. Like Gloria and Peg, she was temperamentally disinclined to violence; the assault on Ted Kennedy had dismayed her, and when she heard of Tom Johnson's remarks at Legion Hall they struck her as dangerous bravado. Yet she had come to doubt the efficacy of the Massachusetts Citizens' approach—the endless lobbying, the interminable parading around the State House and City Hall, pleading for a fair shake. Those were labor union tactics—the patient, plodding, hat-in-hand approach she'd seen Charlestown's workingmen take for years. What did it ever get them? A couple of extra dollars. Another day off. Scraps for the dogs!

No, Alice thought, if they were going to make Garrity back down, they would have to learn something from the civil rights activists and anti-war demonstrators of the sixties. They would have to take a leaf out of Martin Luther King's book—civil disobedience, non-violent resistance, sit-ins, boycotts, guerrilla theater. They had to go into the streets and stay there until they won. To Alice, ROAR seemed more likely to prevail in such a struggle than the staid Massachusetts Citizens.

On September 25, Alice attended a community meeting where three hundred angry Townies constituted themselves the Charlestown branch of ROAR, under the name Powder Keg. Pat Russell, an outspoken neighbor of Alice's from the project, was elected president, narrowly defeating Tom Johnson. Alice was elected to the fifteen-member executive board. On November 11, Powder Keg opened a one-room office next door to a laundromat in the Charles Newtown project. Several hundred people turned out for the ceremony, many of them wearing the blue windbreakers and white tam-o'-shanters topped by blue pompons which had become the uniform of Charlestown's anti-busing movement. Louise Day Hicks and "Dapper" O'Neil were there to cut a red ribbon stretched across the doorway and slice a big chocolate cake that had green frosting spelling out "Welcome Powder Keg." When a reporter asked Pat Russell why they had chosen that name, she looked him in the eye and said, "Because we have a very short fuse."

To those who knew Charlestown's history of violence, the name was profoundly unsettling. How long was the fuse, they wondered; how big would the explosion be? Several members of Charlestown's establishment—among them the pastors of St. Mary's and St. Francis de Sales' churches—asked for a meeting with Powder Keg's leadership, and at a testy confrontation on November 18, the group agreed to clarify these matters in a letter to the *Patriot*.

"We the people of Powder Keg [it read] are not violent people. Our name was selected to go along with this slogan, 'Stop the fuse; stop forced busing.' We only wanted something to catch people's attention. In no way do we condone violence. In fact, we have marshals on every march and motorcade and rally so that if any confrontations occur they can be quickly and efficiently stopped."

Not everyone was reassured. As Arthur Garrity framed his Phase II plan, he came to believe that the town where his immigrant grandfather had first settled would be "the hardest nut of all to crack," even tougher than South Boston. His apprehension about Charlestown stemmed in part from his own experience as U.S. Attorney, when he had prosecuted more than a few Townies, but principally from Marty Walsh, regional director of the Justice Department's Community Relations Service, which played an unusual role in Boston. The CRS usually functioned as a racial conciliator, "helping people resolve their differences through cooperation rather than as adversaries on the streets." But when Arthur Garrity realized how little he could rely on Kevin White or his police for disinterested intelligence, he designated the CRS as the official monitor of Boston's desegregation, his watchdog on the city's streets.

The effort was headed up by Walsh, a former Catholic priest. With little knowledge of Boston's political subculture, Walsh was regarded by the Mayor's office with ill-disguised contempt, but his five years in the priesthood, his single-minded devotion to desegregation, and his very distance from Boston's political infighting all commended him to Garrity, who increasingly came to rely on his advice. After observing the violence of that first fall, Walsh concluded that city, state, and federal officials had underestimated South Boston's capacity for resistance and had done little to contain it. He was determined to avoid that mistake.

In planning for Phase II, Walsh focused on Charlestown. He sought out veteran policemen, who told him stories from the annals of Charlestown crime: tales of the loopers, epic brawls at the Blue Mirror and Alibi Cafe, the feud between the McLaughlins and the McLeans, bodies floating in the harbor or dismembered on vacant lots. The cops passed on rumors that Townie gangs were planning to block Garrity's order with tactics of their own—that cars would be overturned on bridges to block the school buses, that firebombs would be tossed through bus windows, that machine guns would come out of closets. The former priest concluded that busing into Charlestown could prove "one holy hell."

So he set to work trying to smother the smoldering fuse. As point man, he selected a thirty-five-year-old Boston Edison meter reader named Moe Gillen.

At first glance, Gillen hardly seemed a likely spearhead for the United States Justice Department. A blunt-spoken Townie, fiercely proud of his community and scornful of the "pointy-heads" who wanted to change it, he was adamantly opposed to the Garrity order. Moreover, his wife, Hunna, was a founding member of Powder Keg. But Moe Gillen's very pride in the Town had led him to become active in the Kennedy Center, Charlestown's anti-poverty agency, where he rose to become chairman of its community affairs committee. Gradually he came under the influence of the center's two professionals, Director John Gardiner and Assistant Director Bob O'Brien, both of whom strongly recommended him to Marty Walsh.

At first Moe distrusted the man from the Justice Department, fearing that Walsh wanted to turn him into "a stooge for Garrity," but gradually the two Irishmen established a rapport. Walsh made one particularly telling point. At that very moment, Arthur Garrity—with his masters and experts—was devising a full-scale Phase II plan which would certainly include Charlestown. In Eddie McCormack, South Boston had a persuasive advocate within the planning process. But Charlestown had none. Jesus, Moe thought, Charlestown was going to get screwed once again! They'd better get their oar into this thing before it was too late.

In early 1975, Moe formed a group which he hoped could evolve a reasoned community position, and on February 21, the Charlestown Education Committee gathered for the first time in the boardroom of the Kennedy Center. Around the table sat many of Charlestown's recognized "leaders": State Representative Dennis Kearney; Little City Hall Manager Bobbie Delaney; John Gardiner and Bob O'Brien; Father Robert Boyle, pastor of St. Mary's, and Father Lawrence Buckley, a curate at St. Catherine's; Gloria Conway and Peg Pigott; and representatives of the Boys' Club, the Bunker Hill Health Center, the Bunker Hill Community College, and Charlestown's public schools.

Powder Keg was amply represented by Pat Russell and five other parents, but Moe Gillen wanted to deal with "known quantities," people he trusted. He and Alice McGoff had grown up playing together on Soley Street, and since Alice had recently been elected secretary of the Charlestown High School Home and School Association, he asked her to represent the association on the new committee. At the last moment, he added two Charlestown High School students who would be directly involved if the judge included the town in Phase II. His choices were Lisa McGoff and her friend Trudy. Alice, Lisa, and Trudy sat side by side at the big table, proud to be part of these deliberations.

But at the head of the table sat Marty Walsh as "ex officio" member. Though he was aggressively friendly, calling them all by their first names, Alice couldn't forget that he was a government agent, there to implement the judge's order, an edict to which she would never bow. Though they might join forces temporarily, Alice couldn't bring herself to trust him.

That afternoon, Walsh told the committee it was too late for them to testify before Garrity's masters, but they could still submit a written statement. John Gardiner, Bob O'Brien, and Gloria Conway were appointed to draft the statement, and four days later they returned with one which the committee promptly adopted. Charlestown's "Plea for Mercy" urged the judge to declare a "moratorium" on all compulsory busing in Boston. But its central argument was a plea for preservation of community as a value competitive with—yet ironically essential to—equality. An ethnically or racially homogeneous neighborhood respected another community's integrity more easily than a weak, threatened neighborhood did. Thus, strong neighborhoods were the solid building blocks of a healthily diverse city. The statement ended on a plaintive note: "We ask the Court to forestall a crisis for our children which, though not of the Court's making, is within the power of the Court to alleviate."

But it was too late for such accommodations. Garrity's masters were concluding their deliberations. And when they submitted their Phase II plan to Garrity on March 31, it did little to relieve Charlestown's anxiety.

On April 2, the committee met again to assess the plan's impact on their community. Whatever enthusiasm there might be elsewhere for Eddie McCormack's political settlement, it didn't extend to Charlestown. Bob O'Brien told the committee that Charlestown would bear a disproportionate share of the city's busing, and when he completed his analysis, parents around the table sat in stunned silence. Alice glared angrily up the table at Marty Walsh. Lisa and Trudy were in tears.

So as O'Brien sat down that evening to draft the community's response, it was edged with frustration and anger. Adopted by the Education Committee on April 7 and entitled "A Cry of Protest," it called the masters' treatment of Charlestown "inconsistent, inequitable and counter-productive." First, it argued that Community School District 8, into which Charlestown fell, failed to meet the masters' own criteria for a "natural" unit. The unusually diverse district included eight neighborhoods containing, among others, Irish, Italians, Chinese, blacks, and Hispanics. Moreover, while District 8 had only about 10 percent of the city's students, it accounted for almost one-third of its compulsory busing. "This inequity is compounded by the fact that of all the neighborhoods of Boston, the District 8 communities are among the least able to accommodate the burdens by virtue of their universally low status in terms of economic opportunity and resources."

The committee also objected to the masters' recommendations to transform Charlestown High from a district high school into a "magnet" school, offering retailing and electrical training for students from throughout the city.

The protest ended with a thinly veiled warning: "In the absence of constructive action by the Court, we can anticipate a recurrence in our community of the tragic disorders and street protests which characterized the attempted implementation of Phase I in other communities of Boston."

This time, with Marty Walsh underlining the committee's warning, Garrity heeded some of Charlestown's protests—in his revised plan, released on May

10, 1975, Charlestown High was retained as a district school. But the community still bore a heavy share of the Phase II busing. Garrity's final plan called for 1,209 blacks and Hispanics to be bused into Charlestown High, the Edwards Middle School, and the town's four elementary schools, while 848 Townies were to be bused into Roxbury and the South End.

But well before Garrity completed his deliberations, Alice McGoff had abandoned hope for justice from the federal bench. As 1975 wore on, she had become exasperated with the notion of a non-elected judge handing down edicts on where, how, and with whom her children should be educated. She found it particularly galling that Garrity didn't even live in the city on which he was passing judgment. How could a two-toilet Irishman from Wellesley understand what it was like to be a Charlestown widow trying to raise seven children in a five-room apartment in the Bunker Hill housing project? But that was what liberals were like, she had come to understand; it was easy to be a liberal about other people's problems. Maybe that was why all the problems were in the city and all the liberals in the suburbs.

Alice learned something more about liberals that winter when she and other Bostonians tried to compel the Governor's Commission on the Status of Women to address busing as a women's issue. The Governor's Commission, a forty-one-woman advisory body, had called a meeting with two principal purposes: for Governor Michael Dukakis to proclaim 1975 "International Women's Year" in Massachusetts, and for representatives from Governor's Commissions throughout New England to confer about issues to be raised at the International Women's Congress in Mexico City.

But any Massachusetts woman was welcome, and when ROAR heard about the meeting it dispatched its own delegation to City Hall. Alice McGoff had a special reason for wanting to be there. A week earlier she'd seen a photograph of Governor Dukakis walking one of his children to school in suburban Brookline—a provocation to many Boston parents who no longer enjoyed the privilege of walking their children to school.

At eleven that Saturday morning in January 1975, Alice and eighty other ROAR women paraded into the conference room on the eighth floor of City Hall, brandishing placards and small American flags. Alice wore her white tam-o'-shanter and a blue windbreaker with her name stitched in white birthday-cake script on her left shoulder, a big powder keg with a smoldering fuse embroidered on the breast. Taking a seat in the second row, she glanced up at the stage, where the women sat dressed in their Town and Country tweeds, Pierre Cardin silk scarves, and eighty-five-dollar alligator shoes. They seemed to be looking down at her with contempt, and that look caught Alice like a punch beneath the ribs, sucking all the air out of her. My God, she thought, have I really sunk that low? Am I really that disreputable? Then, with a rush of hot, red anger, she thought: No, I may live in the projects. I may be poor. But I'm still a Kirk. A Kirk from Monument Avenue. Nobody was going to look at her that way and get away with it.

For a few moments the commission members ignored the newcomers, proceeding through their agenda. But the ROAR women wouldn't be brushed off that easily. At a preordained signal, they launched into their anthem, a parody of the official state song:

> All hail Massachusetts
> That grand old Bay State
> Once the leader of our Nation
> Once the molder of our faith
> We've given you our everything
> But our children, that's too damn much
> And we tell the whole damn nation
> That the bus won't work for us!

This brought a sharp rap of the gavel from Chairwoman Ann Blackham, a Winchester real estate agent and former vice-president of the National Federation of Republican Women. "Ladies," Mrs. Blackham said sternly, "this is an open meeting. You are welcome to attend as long as you maintain decorum. But I am afraid we cannot permit this kind of disruption."

Elsewhere in the room, other confrontations broke out. One slim redhead in a cashmere jacket turned to Alice McGoff and demanded, "What are you doing here?"

"Exactly what you are, honey," she replied.

"But this is the Governor's Commission on the Status of Women."

"And I'm a woman," Alice shot back. "Or the last time I looked I was."

Pixie Palladino, her stocky torso draped in a "Stop Forced Busing" T-shirt, rose in the front row and began reading a prepared statement. The nurturing, raising, and educating of children was a mother's function, Pixie argued, and it was the duty of a commission on the status of women to defend mothers' rights against usurpation by the state. Yet, she said, the commission and the Governor had ignored the plight of Boston's mothers. "Why don't you represent us? We are poor people locked into an economically miserable situation. All we want is to be mothers to the children God gave us. We are not opposed to anyone's skin. We are opposed to forced busing of our children to schools other than in our neighborhood. You are supposed to defend women's rights. Why don't you defend ours?"

Ann Blackham banged her gavel harder now. "The commission has no mandate to get involved in busing. That has nothing to do with what we're discussing. Now, please, you are our guests here, and if you don't behave, I'll have to ask you to leave."

"No!" shouted Pixie, gesturing toward the commission, whose members came principally from such suburban towns as Wellesley, Belmont, Newton, and Lincoln. "You're *our* guests. This is *our* City Hall. No bunch of ladies from the suburbs is going to kick the women of Boston out of their own City Hall."

After conferring with her advisers, Mrs. Blackham concluded that the atmosphere was too tense to risk an appearance by the Governor. A few minutes later the meeting broke up in tumult and acrimony.

Alice was sorry it ended that way. She had nothing in principle against women's liberation, for she came from a long line of strong, independent women. Her mother had been a gutsy dame who had survived a series of crippling illnesses to raise a houseful of children and keep them on the straight and narrow. Her aunt Mary had held a responsible position in City Hall for years. Cousin Mamie had worked at the Registry of Deeds, been a friend of Mayor Curley's, a union organizer, and a suffragette. In fact, Alice had always thought of herself as a liberated woman. In one sense, there was nothing quite so liberating as a husband's death, the burden of supporting your family and raising a bunch of kids by yourself.

As a woman on her own, she could well understand why women like her cousin Mamie had fought for the vote, equal pay for equal work, the right to a good education. But this kooky new movement that had sprung up in recent years made no sense to her at all. It seemed to be led by a bunch of college girls and chichi women from the suburbs who stewed over such burning issues as whether a girl could join an all-male soccer team or whether ads for cosmetics and designer jeans were "demeaning" to women. Once she had seen a bunch of college-age demonstrators of both sexes all pile into a single bathroom to "integrate" the toilet. No wonder these women seemed oblivious to her needs.

Through the spring and summer of 1975, Alice grew progressively angrier at the power, wealth, and privilege arrayed against her. An unelected judge, an unresponsive senator, and uncaring suburban liberals had joined hands to wrest from her the one thing in the world over which she still exercised some control: her family. If they could move her children around the city like pawns on a black-and-white chessboard, then what could Alice call her own anymore? As month after month went by, bringing them ever closer to September, Alice raged at those who would do her this final injury.

When a jangling telephone woke her on the second day of school, her neck was still throbbing painfully.

"Alice, dearie," shouted Pat Russell, "get out of bed and get on down here. We need you."

"I don't know, Pat," she said. "My neck still hurts like hell."

"Well, we've got something that'll make it feel a lot better. Since the cops won't let us walk our own streets, we're going to pray. Even those bastards wouldn't dare break up a bunch of praying women." Back in World War II, Pat explained, Charlestown mothers used to hold prayer marches for the boys in service. Now someone had suggested they try a prayer march against busing. Pat had cleared the idea with Captain MacDonald.

Alice hauled herself out of bed, put on her Thomas Collar, and joined the women who were already gathering in Hayes Square. Word had spread quickly through the town, and by 10:30 about four hundred mothers—many wearing shorts and sandals on this steamy Indian summer day—began lining up in the middle of Bunker Hill Street. Some cradled infants in their arms, others pushed strollers or held young children by the hand. On the sidewalks, knots of teenagers and adult males—among them Danny McGoff—had gathered to watch. When some of the men tried to join the march, Pat Russell—wearing her "Mother Power" T-shirt—borrowed an electric bullhorn from the police. "No men or boys in this march today," she bellowed. "This is a woman's march. We don't want any of you guys in it."

"That means you," Alice warned Danny. "No matter what happens, stay on the sidewalk."

Pat gave the women their marching orders. "We are going to pray in silence," she told them. "We are going to pray for our children; we are going to pray for our families; we are going to pray for our town. If Martin Luther King could do it, so can the women of Charlestown." Then they set off up the street, led by a three-year-old girl carrying an American flag.

From the start, the women were in no mood for silent devotion. One group, performing for men lounging in front of the Horseshoe Tavern, struck up the football cheer, "Here we go, Charlestown, here we go." Others down the line broke into "The Battle Hymn of the Republic," "He's Got the Whole World in His Hands," and "We Are the Girls from Charlestown."

This wasn't quite what Pat Russell had in mind. Waving the march to a halt, she huddled with Powder Keg's leaders. Since silent prayer wouldn't work, it would have to be a vocal prayer march. Pat, Alice, and their friends began reciting the rosary, intoning their "Hail Marys" in the singsong murmur familiar to generations of Charlestown mothers:

Hail Mary, full of grace, the Lord is with thee.

Others picked up the chant, savoring the old rhythms.

Blessed art thou among women, and blessed is the fruit of thy womb, Jesus.

Slowly, all up and down the line, the prayer caught on.

Holy Mary, Mother of God, pray for us sinners.

Soon, all four hundred women had joined in, flinging the prayer in defiance against the shabby brick walls of the housing project.

Now and at the hour of our death, Amen.

At School Street, Pat Russell executed a sharp left turn and led her mothers toward the Warren Prescott School. This violated a new order by Judge Garrity prohibiting the gathering of three or more persons within a hundred yards of a Boston school (an order drafted for the judge by the Justice Department, despite private doubts there about its constitutionality). "Get some equipment across the street," an apprehensive police officer muttered into his walkie-talkie. As the women passed the school, a mother near Alice shouted up at the open windows, "Ain't none of our children in there. Just niggers!" But the marchers moved past the school with no further incident and turned left onto High Street, heading toward Monument Square, where, around the corner, Charlestown High School reared opposite the Bunker Hill Monument.

As soon as Captain MacDonald saw the women turn onto High Street, he left the line of march and headed up the hill to take charge of his men surrounding the high school. "I figure they're headed up this way," he told his sergeant. "Tell the men they're to maintain the integrity of the hundred yards around the school."

As they advanced on Monument Square, the women encountered a phalanx of police drawn up across High Street at the corner of Cordis Street, still a block and a half from the high school. A formidable force confronted them there. First a double line of a hundred MDC police, each holding his baton horizontally before him to form an unbroken wall. A few feet behind them stood another hundred Boston police. Next came two Black Marias, their doors open, ready to receive prisoners. And behind them, held in ominous reserve, were about sixty members of the Tactical Patrol Force. Up a side street roared half a dozen motorcycle police of the Mobile Operations Patrol, and at the foot of the Monument stood five mounted police in helmets and flak jackets. On the sidewalk nearby were six deputy U.S. marshals, part of the riot-trained Special Operations Group, which had recently returned from Guam, where it had policed Vietnamese refugee camps. Dozens of reporters, local and national, crowded the stoops on either side, ready to record the battle for posterity. Television crews maneuvered for position.

In the second row of marchers, Alice gaped in astonishment at the small army drawn up in their path. Ten feet short of the first policemen, the women stopped. Pat Russell stepped forward and told Superintendent Lawrence Carpenter of the MDC police that she had Captain MacDonald's permission to continue, but Carpenter told her that if she went past that point she and her followers would be arrested. Then he ordered them to disperse.

Indignantly, Pat refused. "We have permission to march and offer our prayers to God. That's what we're going to do."

"Beyond this point, you'll be within a hundred yards of the high school. We'll have to arrest you."

"What are you talking about?" Pat cried. "We just marched right by the Prescott School, so close we could reach out and touch it. Why don't you people get your stories straight?"

"I don't care what you just did," Carpenter said. "I'm telling you now, you can't go any further."

At this, most of the women sank to their knees and began praying again, the "Our Father" this time: "Our Father, who art in Heaven, hallowed be thy name . . ."

Meanwhile, the two police wagons and the detachment of motorcycle police circled behind the marchers and stationed themselves in the middle of High Street at the rear of the procession. The marchers were surrounded.

Negotiations began. Pat Russell spoke for the mothers. Representing the authorities were Police Commissioner Robert DiGrazia, Police Superintendent Joseph Jordan, Public Safety Coordinator Peter Meade, MDC Superintendent Carpenter, Captain MacDonald, and Marty Walsh. In the center of the discussions was an animated figure in a business suit who, the astonished Townies soon learned, was J. Stanley Pottinger, U.S. Assistant Attorney General in charge of the Civil Rights Division. Pottinger had been designated as the Senior Civilian Representative of the Attorney General for Boston's school desegregation—the personification of federal power in the crisis—a role he had previously played during the Indian uprising at Wounded Knee and the confrontation at Kent State. His presence on Breed's Hill that day symbolized the Justice Department's growing concern over the Boston situation, just as, a decade earlier, Burke Marshall and John Doar had signaled Washington's determination to enforce the law in Mississippi and Alabama.

For nearly an hour, as the mothers prayed and the police twirled their batons, the negotiators huddled in the street beneath the Bunker Hill Monument trying to resolve their impasse, but they were caught in a stalemate which offered neither side an attractive option.

The mothers, and their male supporters who were quickly gathering on the adjacent sidewalks, sensed that this might well prove to be the crucial confrontation with Judge Garrity and his enforcement mechanism. If they gave in now, they might never again be able to muster this much moral indignation against his orders, yet the manpower massed against them was so overwhelming that physical resistance seemed out of the question. Nor could the police afford to give in. Believing that their "low profile" policy in South Boston the year before had only encouraged violence, police officials—vigorously seconded by the Justice Department—were determined to show the people of Charlestown that a repetition of last year's disorders would not be tolerated. Yet a melee in which heavily armed police attacked defenseless women and children was unthinkable, if only because it would provide a *cause célèbre* which could fuel the anti-busing movement for months to come.

The negotiators met first together, then in separate caucuses on either side of the street. In the police caucus, fears of a major debacle were rising. "If we let them go through," Joe Jordan warned, "we're going to face this every day."

"But, Joe," said another official, "look at all those TV cameras. Can't you just see *The NBC Nightly News* tonight showing us beating on a bunch of women in shorts and sandals."

"This is starting to look like Porkchop Hill, with everybody digging in to make their stand," warned Stan Pottinger. "We've got to find some graceful way out for these people."

Ultimately, the police decided to offer the women a "face-saving" compromise. They would be permitted to walk single-file down the south sidewalk of High Street—the side furthest from the high school—to the Training Field, a shady park where eighteenth-century Townies had drilled their militia and where the anti-busing movement often rallied.

Pat Russell took the proposal back to her caucus, where Powder Keg's leadership promptly rejected it. "We're not a bunch of cattle who can be led down a chute," said Alice McGoff.

"We're going through," Pat told the police. But Commissioner DiGrazia insisted that the offer be communicated directly to the rank and file of mothers. For that, he turned to young Dennis Kearney, who, as state representative for the district, had faithfully supported the anti-busing movement, yet who, as a Harvard-educated pragmatist with high political ambitions, wanted to be viewed as a responsible moderate. He promptly agreed to make the appeal. Borrowing a bullhorn from the police, he stood at the head of the march and addressed the mothers: "Nobody's going to win anything by violence here. Our intent has been to show how strongly we feel about busing. We've done that. Now let's do it by walking quietly, single-file, along the sidewalk to the Training Field, where we'll have our rally. We've come this far with respect and dignity. Let's not spoil that."

The mothers wavered, unsure what to do. From the sidewalk, bystanders urged them not to give in. "That's a sellout." . . . "Go back to Harvard, Kearney!" . . . "Bust on through those goddamned police." Others, among them several priests from St. Mary's, implored the mothers to accept the compromise.

Danny McGoff was anxious about his mother. "Ma!" he yelled from the sidewalk. "Ma! You got a bum neck. For Christ's sake, get out of there." But Alice didn't budge.

Slowly, about one hundred mothers—the elderly, the sick, and those with infants and small children—rose to their feet and straggled up the sidewalk to the Training Field. Nearly three hundred remained.

Now Superintendent Jordan took the bullhorn. "Ladies," he warned, "you will not be permitted to march past this point. You have fifteen minutes to walk to the Training Field or you will be subject to arrest."

The remaining mothers seemed determined. Grimly, those still accompanied by children shunted them to husbands, relatives, or friends on the sidewalk.

Danny resumed his pleading. "Ma, for crying out loud, you're sick! Get out of there!" Alice's neck was killing her now; the excitement of the march had only intensified the pain, but having come this far, she was going to see it through. Removing the Thomas Collar, she flipped it across the street to Danny. "Here, take this," she said, "and shut up."

The minutes ticked by. A few mothers, mindful of the analogy which Pat Russell had drawn with Martin Luther King's marches, struck up "We Shall Overcome," but the song trailed off after a few seconds. Nobody seemed to know the words. Just then Pat Russell shouted, "Okay, girls, this is it. We're going through. Heads down. Hard and heavy. But keep your hands at your sides. If they touch a woman, they won't be able to hold this town—and they know it."

Alice struggled to her feet. From her position in the second row of marchers, she could look across the ten feet of pavement directly into the gray eyes of an MDC sergeant who glared grimly back at her. Pain stabbed down her neck and along her spine, but she squared her shoulders, trying to look as fearless as she could. She was so close she could hear Commissioner DiGrazia as he moved rapidly along the police lines, whispering urgently, "Don't push anybody. Just stand in line, shoulder to shoulder. But don't let them through. If they charge brutality, we'll have the film."

With that, the women moved forward in a tight platoon, many still chanting "Hail Marys" and "Our Fathers" under their breath. Some were already weeping. Others had their eyes closed, with purses, shopping bags, or pillows over their faces to ward off the expected blows.

Alice couldn't bend her neck, so she walked with her head erect, arms slightly raised in front of her.

The front line of police obeyed orders, legs braced to meet the column with an unmoving picket of batons, arms, and shoulders. But here and there the women threatened to break through. Struggling to repel them, some policemen pushed back too vigorously. Scuffles broke out.

Abruptly, the Tactical Patrol Force waded into the bobbing sea of women. Quickly, the mothers were herded into two groups, one shoved down the steep hill of Cordis Street, the other pushed back along High Street. Alice had advanced barely four yards when the force of the TPF charge sent her reeling down Cordis Street.

Here and there, the TPF—whose job was to intimidate—used more force than was necessary. Women screamed and stumbled. Some fell against cars or sprawled on the street. A few husbands and sons tried to help their women, but the TPF would brook no male interference. One youth was heaved against an automobile. Several men were arrested.

In five minutes the skirmish was over. For some, good humor returned quickly. Ann Considine, a husky mother of five, had wrested a baton from an MDC policeman. "Yoo-hoo!" she crowed triumphantly. "Anybody lose this?" No policeman would claim it. Finally Superintendent Carpenter stepped forward, while police and women shared a laugh.

On Cordis Street, Alice leaned against a tree, tired but exhilarated. She felt as if she'd just fought the American Revolution. They'd gone up against the toughest cops in the city and survived. For the first time in four days, her neck didn't hurt at all.

16

Twymon

Born nine months before John F. Kennedy was elected President, Cassandra Twymon had only the haziest notion of the Southern civil rights movement. Montgomery, Little Rock, Nashville, Greensboro, Birmingham, and Selma were simply names to her, as exotic as Kinshasa and Katmandu. And except for Martin Luther King, most of the blacks who had struggled and prevailed in those places—Rosa Parks, Medgar Evers, James Meredith, Fannie Lou Hamer, Hosea Williams—were equally indistinct, so obscured by time that she could never be sure whether the tales she heard about them were fact or fiction.

Once, when she was thirteen, a black teacher assigned her a book about the integration of the University of Georgia. The events which it described took place in January 1961, when Cassandra was not yet a year old. But passages had stayed with her, perhaps because the author, Calvin Trillin, wrote so vividly; perhaps because her mother recalled that the University of Georgia was barely a hundred miles from the family's early home in Waynesboro; probably because the principal figure was a young black girl with whom she could identify. Years later, Cassandra still remembered Trillin's evocation of that terrible night on which Georgia students forced Charlayne Hunter and her black classmate Hamilton Holmes out of the university:

"Just after ten a small crowd of students gathered on the lawn in front of Center Myers and unfurled a bed sheet bearing the legend, 'Nigger Go Home.' Then three or four of them peeled off from the group, ran toward the dormitory, and flung bricks and Coke bottles through the windows of Charlayne's room. . . . As more people came up the hill from the basketball game—a close loss to Georgia Tech—and a few outsiders showed up, the mob grew to about a thousand people, many of them throwing bricks, rocks and firecrackers. . . . Dean Williams suspended Charlayne and Hamilton, informing them that it was 'for your own safety and the safety of almost seven thousand other students.' . . . The area around Center Myers looked like a deserted battle-field, with bricks and broken glass on the lawn, small fires in the woods below the dormitory, and the bite of tear gas still in the air [as] Charlayne, who was crying by this time and clutching a statue of the Madonna, walked right out the front door into the state police car, watched only by a few straggling reporters."

That image lodged somewhere deep in Cassandra's memory—a lone black girl, frail and defenseless, weeping bitter tears of shame while clasping the Virgin Mary to her breast. It became her private symbol of the civil rights movement, just as for others it was·Montgomery mothers walking to work, water hoses and police dogs in Birmingham, or the confrontation at Selma's Pettus Bridge.

Yet Charlayne's experience seemed terribly remote, something that had happened very far away and long ago. So as the civil rights movement moved northward and people began talking about a possible battle over school integration in Boston, Cassandra couldn't imagine that such scenes would actually be repeated there. Her own experience in the Boston schools had been relatively uneventful. She'd always gone to school with whites, and only once—when whites in East Boston sought to retaliate for the killing of René Wagler—had she been the target of racial violence. Although occasionally she still had nightmares about that day, Cassandra wasn't inclined to worry about such things. By nature cheerful and optimistic—some might say boisterous, even belligerent—she had adopted her mother's faith in the benefits of integration. Like most of her friends, she was absorbed by rock music, television, clothes, and boys—increasingly boys—but when she paused to think about the schools she supposed things would turn out all right. Indeed, when Arthur Garrity adopted the state racial imbalance plan in 1974, Cassandra and her brother Wayne found themselves on the bus to Brighton High, one of the least troubled of Boston's high schools. Their younger sister, Rachel, was assigned to Brighton's equally peaceful William Howard Taft Middle School.

Brighton was the working-class district in northwest Boston where Colin and Joan Diver had lived briefly in 1969–70. Although predominantly white, it was neither as physically isolated nor as ethnically self-conscious as South Boston, Charlestown, and the North End. Irish predominated there, but they were substantially diluted by Italians, Greeks, Eastern Europeans, even some Hispanics and blacks. Moreover, for years, Brighton High had drawn part of its student body from the black, Hispanic, and Chinese sections of the South End and Lower Roxbury. As early as 1972, 15 percent of its enrollment was black, another 15 percent Chinese. Teachers and students were so accustomed to substantial non-white presence in the school that even when it rose to nearly 50 percent under the state plan, there was remarkably little racial tension.

The Twymons' year at Brighton was marred by only two incidents. In a corridor on the way to class, an Italian girl once brushed past Cassandra, then turned and said, "Watch out, nigger." A shoving match developed, but was quickly broken up by teachers. More serious was a prolonged impasse with one of Wayne's teachers. First, she refused to accept his transfer into her class; when the office insisted, she told him he'd have to order his own textbook directly from the publisher; and when Wayne complained, she closed the classroom door in his face. Soon the teacher discovered that she had Wayne's sister in another class and began making derogatory remarks about Cassandra. That was too much for Rachel, who got both children transferred to another teacher.

On balance, the Twymons enjoyed their year at Brighton, especially when they came home each night to watch television coverage of the violence at South Boston and Hyde Park. The kids who braved the fury of those places were street celebrities, seasoned veterans of the school wars. But the Twymons didn't crave that kind of celebrity. So Cassandra and young Rachel were dismayed when they opened their Phase II assignments on July 7, 1975, to discover that they would be bused into Charlestown that fall—Cassandra to Charlestown High and Rachel to the Edwards Middle School. (Wayne escaped Charlestown altogether by gaining admission to a special pre-college program on Beacon Hill.) Neither girl had ever set foot in Charlestown—by the time they were teenagers, the Town was already regarded as unreceptive to blacks. But their mother had been there—first on school outings to the Bunker Hill Monument and the USS *Constitution;* later when she worked for a time as a packer at Schrafft's Candy Co. And she vividly remembered the day when cousin Moses Baker had been beaten along the Charlestown docks. She wasn't very comfortable at the thought of her daughters going to school there.

But if they had to go, she would do what she could to protect them. A few days after the girls got their assignments, Rachel received an invitation to a meeting at City Hall, where parents of children assigned to Charlestown High were to elect a "Racial-Ethnic Parents' Council." Judge Garrity had directed that every high school form a council composed of five white parents, five black parents, and—if enough Hispanic or Chinese students were enrolled— five "other minority" parents. Such councils would be elected by separate racial caucuses at the start of each school year. The parent groups, Garrity said, should "help achieve peaceful desegregation [by] meeting regularly to talk frankly and deal with racial problems." Rachel had served on the council at Brighton High, where black and white parents had worked well together, help ing resolve a dispute over racial balance on the basketball team. Believing that this kind of cooperation had contributed to the relative calm at Brighton, Rachel hoped that similar councils might make things easier for her daughters at Charlestown.

But ROAR had condemned the councils, warning that parents who joined them would be "traitors" and urging its supporters throughout the city to boycott the elections. White parents in South Boston had boycotted the councils the year before and now Powder Keg was calling for a similar boycott in Charlestown.

On the evening of July 15, Arnold Walker drove his sister to the meeting. As they approached City Hall along New Congress Street, they could see a cluster of demonstrators in blue Powder Keg jackets, waving placards which read: "A vote for multiracial councils is a vote for forced busing" and "Don't be a stooge for Garrity!" The protesters jeered as Rachel, alighting from Arnold's car, hurried through a corridor of policemen toward the glass doors.

Riding the elevator to the eighth floor, she found five other black parents on folding chairs in one corner of a large conference room. Fifteen Charlestown parents huddled in another corner. The no-man's-land in between was occupied by Charlestown's headmaster, Frank Power, and a young history teacher named Vince Braudis, the parent council "coordinator." After Power had welcomed the parents and Braudis distributed guidelines for the election, each race convened in its own corner. The blacks swiftly completed their "election." With six parents present, they had just enough to fill the required slots—five representatives and an alternate. But one mother, clearly unnerved by the demonstrators outside and the hostile atmosphere across the room, refused to serve, so Mr. and Mrs. Rodney Brown, Mrs. Marie Eaves, and Mrs. Edythe Lewis filled four of the regular slots, while Rachel, pleading her church commitments and the year she'd already served on the Brighton council, took the alternate's spot.

Across the room, white parents were embroiled in a fierce debate with Power and Braudis. Occasionally, the blacks in their corner overheard snatches of the exchange. "I ain't going to sit in the same room with a bunch of niggers," one Charlestown mother declared. "You're sitting in the same room with them right now," Power replied. "Why can't you work together?"

Nevertheless the whites, led by a Powder Keg contingent, remained adamant. At 9:30, Power gave up and adjourned the meeting. The blacks hurried out to Mr. Brown's station wagon, while the whites emerged from the hall holding their fists aloft in a sign of victory, provoking cheers from their supporters.

The evening left Rachel deeply apprehensive. If adults couldn't even discuss their differences, how could they expect children to resolve theirs? And what was the alternative to discussion? Yet she didn't entirely abandon hope; Charlestown parents must fear for their children's safety as much as she did for hers. Eager for a look at the places her children would be going, she quickly accepted an invitation to an August 27 "open house" at Charlestown High.

At dusk, just as lamps began to light up the streets, their yellow school bus crawled up the slope of Breed's Hill. As it swung onto High Street, led by three police motorcycles, Rachel noticed other police lining both sides of the street. When the bus reached the square and turned left, she could see that the near slope of the Monument grounds was thick with men, women, and children, but only as the twenty-five parents disembarked in front of the high school could she hear the rhythmic chant thundering down at them from the hillside: "Niggers, go home! Niggers, go home!"

Forming a cordon between the bus and the crowd on the hill, the police hurried the minority parents inside the school, where Frank Power led them upstairs to the third-floor auditorium. The school had done its best to make them feel welcome. A coffee urn and platters of doughnuts were laid out near the entrance, and around the walls teachers waited behind desks, ready to answer questions about their courses. A few white parents were there too, but they kept to themselves; when Rachel looked toward them, their faces were so filled with cold resentment that she didn't dare approach them.

Scanning the room for a friendly face, Rachel saw only one. James Howard was a black music teacher who had taught her children ten years before at the Dearborn School. She was so relieved to come upon an old acquaintance there that she rushed to his desk, embraced him, and fell into an animated conversation. Howard was almost as glad to see her. One of three black teachers in the school and the only one there that night, he too felt unwelcome. But he was hardly in a position to offer Rachel the reassurance she so obviously sought.

When Frank Power rose to welcome the parents, he did his best to neutralize their hostile reception. Charlestown High, he told them, was going to carry out the law of the land; administrators, teachers, and aides would do their best to assure the safety and well-being of every child. Violence, intimidation, or racial slurs would not be tolerated. "Charlestown High School is dedicated to providing a quality education for every student," Power said. "As long as I am its headmaster that's what we're going to do. I have too much pride in this school to permit anything less. I hope you and your children will soon be as proud as I am to be members of the Charlestown High School community."

But as Rachel looked over the school later, she wondered whether she could ever be proud of a place as old, shabby, and dreary as this. Paint peeled from ceilings and walls; windows were broken; linoleum was scraped and worn. When she asked to see the cafeteria, she was told that Charlestown had none, the only high school in the city without a hot-lunch program. On the walls she noticed racial epithets only partially erased or painted over: "Welcome Niggers," "Niggers suck," "White Power," "KKK," "Bus is for Zulu," and one she would never forget, "Be illiterate. Fight forced busing."

When aides began rounding up the parents for their trip home, Rachel was more than ready to leave. But she wasn't prepared for the roar which went up from the crowd on the Monument grounds. If anything, the crowd had grown during the past two hours, and this time, as the parents boarded the bus, they were met by jeers and catcalls. "That's right," people were shouting. "Go home, niggers! Keep going all the way to Africa!" Rachel hunched down in her seat, away from the bus windows, which she feared might shatter at any moment. Outside, she could hear the police radio crackling with urgent communications, then the whine of the sirens as patrol cars joined the procession. All the way down the hill and across the bridge, she thought to herself: My God, what kind of hell am I sending my children into?

When she reached Methunion Manor, young Rachel and Cassandra were waiting for her report. As calmly as possible, she told them. She told Cassandra that Charlestown High was a "raggedy-ass school" which should have been torn down years ago. She told Rachel that, although she hadn't seen the Edwards, she understood it was somewhat newer and in better condition than the high school. Then she recounted exactly what she had seen at the Monument, sparing her daughters none of the details. "There's a lot of prejudiced people in Charlestown," she said. "They don't want me over there and they don't want you over there. I'm afraid this isn't going to be an easy year for either of you. You're going to be called a lot of ugly names. You're going to be spat at, maybe pushed around some. But it's not the first time this has happened and it won't be the last. It's something we have to go through—something *you* have to go through—if this city is ever going to get integrated."

But later, as she lay in bed, Rachel wept bitterly. Her strong faith in integration had been badly rattled that night, the old verities called into question. What good, she wondered, could possibly come from all this? What could her children learn at a school like that, except how to hate?

"Fellow citizens," Charlestown's mayor, George Washington Warren, told a large assemblage on Monument Square one morning in October 1847. "When all of us shall have passed away from the stage of life, when there shall not be one of the present generation living to inform the men of the Twentieth Century of the doings of these times, may the Institution this day planted yield its good fruit, and be ever fondly cherished by the people. . . . As long as this Monument shall commemorate the successful contests of our fathers for National Independence, may the High School standing up proudly by its side, serve, by its generous and ennobling influences, to perpetuate and guaranty the blessings of that Independence to our children's children unto the remotest generation."

The new school, a handsome three-story brick building overlooking Monument Square, was dedicated on Bunker Hill Day 1848 and opened to its eighty-eight pupils two days later. Originally its curriculum was heavily weighted toward the classics (Xenophon's *Anabasis,* Virgil's *Georgics,* Cicero, Greek and Latin composition) as well as rhetoric, natural philosophy, French, ancient history, astronomy, and trigonometry. It was a classical education, appropriate for those who studied on the hilltop called by some "the American Acropolis." But gradually the high school adapted its offerings to the needs of nineteenth-century commerce, and as the Town's Yankees fled ever faster from the inrushing Irish, the trend toward vocational education accelerated. By 1906, when planning began for a new Charlestown High, the old vision of a classical education on an American Acropolis had long since given way to the urgent necessity of training the "unlettered, uncouth, unruly immigrant class."

It is said that one of the first Irishmen to graduate from Charlestown High—Joseph J. Corbett of the class of 1881—was responsible for the school's being rebuilt in the same white granite used for the adjacent Bunker

Hill Monument. By then a judge of the Municipal Court and a member of Boston's Board of Schoolhouse Commissioners, Corbett lived directly across the square in a fine town house, and he used his position on the schoolhouse board to make certain that the new high school should lend a fitting dignity to its corner of the square. When completed in 1907, the granite facing—embellished with eight Ionic columns, a large clock and matching compass—did give the new school a certain authority. But it was hardly the "architectural gem seemingly from Mars' hill" acclaimed by the euphoric Charlestown *Enterprise*. Perhaps its best features were the stately staircases which ascended right and left from the narrow entrance lobby. But the rooms to which they led on the three upper stories were bare, unadorned boxes, with little grace or charm. Indeed, the school's interior design seems to have been dictated less by Corbett's pride in his surroundings than by the need for economy and a spare, utilitarian focus on the school's new function. The education offered at the school was clearly defined by the Boston *Globe:* "It stands for the training of ordinary boys and girls to do the ordinary work of life. . . . The ordinary human being, who used to be turned loose upon the work-a-day world at the age of fourteen, to hunt for a job, and perhaps, missing it, to join the ranks of the worthless, here may find occupations for his idle youth and training for his useful manhood." This emphasis was soon confirmed by the erection of an annex to house the school's electrical shops. The Charlestown electrician's course was part of a program in which several Boston high schools provided technical training—sheet-metal work at South Boston, cabinetmaking at Dorchester—open to students from all over the city. Those enrolled in such courses also received academic instruction, but this was clearly peripheral to their preparation for a lifetime of manual labor.

As the high school's academic offerings shrank, so did its reputation. As early as 1917, the Boston *Traveler* asked in an editorial, "What's the matter with this school?" It noted that Charlestown, with 39,601 residents, had only thirty-five high school graduates while Hyde Park High, serving barely half Charlestown's population, had eighty-three. "Not one of the Charlestown boys and girls graduated this year with 'honors' or 'high honors.' . . . Something is wrong somewhere. Where it is the *Traveler* does not claim to know. But whatever it is it should be corrected before another school year begins, or the school should be closed in the interest of educational efficiency."

Something was wrong indeed. Charlestown families with aspirations for their children were abandoning the school, sending them to the Boston Latin School, English, Trade, Technical, or one of the new Catholic high schools. But Boston Latin required extra intelligence, the other "in-town" schools took extra initiative, the Catholic schools cost extra money. By 1920, Charlestown High had become a school of last resort for those without such resources.

Yet for some Townies the high school on the hill had its own attractions, less educational than symbolic. Apprehensive of the alien city, they renounced the opportunity, advancement, and adventure Boston offered for the reassurance of community, solidarity, and camaraderie. Rejecting the American imperative to get ahead, they opted for the Charlestown ethic of getting by. Like the Monument itself, the granite school by its side became a rallying point for those who would reaffirm their choice with cries of "Boom Charlestown" and "Townie Pride." So what if Yankee institutions like the *Traveler* criticized its academic standards? Who cared if colleges like Harvard and Wellesley ignored Charlestown graduates? What if the lace-curtain Irish preferred Boston Latin or Malden Catholic? The high school was the real Charlestown—tribal, resilient, pugnacious, indomitable. The school cheer might evolve over the years from "Rah, rah, rah for dear old Charlestown" to "Here we go, Charlestown, here we go," but the message remained the same: the hell with the rest of the world, Charlestown was Number One.

Charlestown's girls had particular reason for turning necessity into a virtue. Most Townie families of limited means generally allocated tuition money to their sons, which meant that the boys went off to Catholic high schools while the girls went up the hill to Charlestown High. For years, the school was led by a group of bright, restless girls eager to assert their worth.

Most boys who went there were less academically inclined, but they found other fields in which to excel. One was the Charlestown Corps of Cadets, a quasi-military outfit which marched every year in the Bunker Hill Day parade.

Then there were sports, to which the Townies brought a demonic ferocity. Through much of the thirties and forties the school didn't fare very well in competition. Not only was its male enrollment the smallest of any Boston high school, but most of the Town's best athletes were siphoned off by the in-town schools or the Catholic powers. Then, in 1951, Frank Power, Jr., became Charlestown's football and baseball coach. Determined to reverse the school's athletic fortunes, he worked hard to recruit young Townies. From the mid-fifties through the early sixties, Charlestown produced exceptional teams in all sports, and Frank Power quickly became the Town's newest hero. He was invited to address banquets of the Knights of Columbus, the Holy Name Society, and virtually anyone who could rustle up some chicken à la king and a Boston cream pie. Down at Sully's, every longshoreman in the place wanted to buy him a beer. And when he marched in the Bunker Hill Day parade, he got more applause than the pastor of St. Mary's and the U.S. Marine Band put together.

In 1961, with his reputation at its peak, Power shocked the Town by accepting a similar teaching/coaching job at Hyde Park High, nearer his home in Southwest Boston. But his heart was still at Charlestown High, and seven years later he returned there as headmaster. Taking office at midyear, he bided his time. Then, on September 3, 1968, he welcomed his faculty back to school with a speech none of them would ever forget. Power had detected "a certain lack of pedagogic duties, an unnecessary social atmosphere, a country club familiarity." But teaching was "not just a job from eight to two, an interlude in our more important projects, but a privilege and a solemn duty." Teachers who "find the job a bore, who are clockwatchers, who do not like children, such people do not belong in education." To Frank Power it was "a calling as sacred as that of the ministry." In the summertime and on weekends he took students' records home with him and, while watching television, thumbed the cards until he knew by heart every student's name, where he lived, who his parents were, his strengths and weaknesses.

A large man with an athlete's physical presence and enormous charm, he knew the effect he had on others and used it shrewdly. "Among placid men," said one teacher, "Frank Power rippled." But by the late sixties, the problems confronting Charlestown High would have challenged the most forceful personality. First was its continuing slide into academic mediocrity. Scarcely 15 percent of its graduates went on to college, the lowest percentage of any city high school. A few more entered technical or nursing schools, but the vast majority ended their education at Charlestown High. Low expectations had become institutionalized: students who anticipated failure were reinforced by teachers who had come to expect nothing more.

The quality of education was constrained by sheer physical obsolescence. By 1968, the granite fortress on the hill was sixty years old, one of the oldest school buildings in the city. Designed for 450 students, it now held 600 (with 150 more in the Electrical Annex and the Charlestown Boys' Club). With no cafeteria, no library, no athletic fields, its facilities were clearly inadequate for a modern urban high school. In 1964, the New England Association of Schools and Colleges had warned that unless these deficiencies were promptly corrected the school would lose its accreditation. Even the students—who generally displayed a grudging working-class passivity—became infected by the activism of the era and began agitating for better conditions. On one occasion, 125 of them staged a walkout and rally on the Monument grounds, where they burned their bag lunches to protest the lack of a cafeteria. When Frank Power appeared they chanted, "We like Frank, but we want beans." Although Power mollified them with promises of a hot-lunch program, the only long-term solution was construction of a new Charlestown High.

But with the state pressing for enforcement of the racial imbalance law, that wouldn't be easy. Since the law defined racial imbalance as more than 50 percent non-white, Charlestown High itself was not an immediate target. Yet with only ten non-whites out of 721 students enrolled there in 1967, it was clearly the white counterpart of the nearly all-black ghetto schools. The State Board of Education approved funds for a new Charlestown High, on the basis of vague assurances from the Boston School Committee that the school would open 30 percent non-white; but as the board came to question the committee's good faith, the project bogged down in seemingly endless wrangles between the two bodies.

Frank Power quickly recognized that to get the new school he so badly wanted he would have to demonstrate Charlestown's willingness to accept minority students, and realizing that the Town wasn't ready to welcome large numbers of blacks, he concentrated on attracting Chinese and Hispanics. Beginning in the late sixties, he made regular trips to middle schools in those communities, preaching the virtues of Charlestown. By 1971, he had reaped tangible results: 89 non-whites, of whom 49 were Chinese, 25 Hispanic, and 15 black.

To some this strategy smacked of hypocrisy: "desegregation without blacks," one critic called it. Certainly it was a convenient delaying tactic. But those who knew the headmaster never questioned his ultimate intent. For Power had grown up intensely aware of the parallel liabilities suffered by blacks and Irish Catholics. In his desk he kept an editorial from the *Irish News* of Belfast, warning: "Prejudice in any form is a dreadful thing," and under the glass top, the lyrics of a song from *South Pacific:* "You've got to be taught to be afraid / Of people whose eyes are ugly made / And people whose skin is a different shade." Frank Power harbored a private passion for racial justice.

During his career in the Boston schools, he had found time to coach freshman basketball at Boston College, where he came to know a black student named David Nelson, who went on to a career in Boston politics. In 1970 when Louise Day Hicks announced for the congressional seat being vacated by Speaker of the House John McCormack, Nelson challenged her. Ultimately, another Irish candidate, John Moakley, made it a three-way race. Needing all the Irish support he could find, Nelson called on his old friend from BC days. After conferring with his family, Power took $1,000 they'd been saving for their summer vacation and donated it to the Nelson campaign. A few weeks later, the Powers threw a fund-raiser for Nelson in their Hyde Park home. And two nights a week for the rest of the summer, Frank and his wife, Eunice, campaigned door to door in white neighborhoods. Frank marched with Nelson in the Bunker Hill Day parade and on primary day he manned a polling place in the North End. Nelson finished a close third, but the episode may have cost Power the biggest prize he ever sought. By 1972, his reputation as an administrator had spread and he was widely regarded as the leading candidate to become Boston's School Superintendent. But several votes on the School Committee switched at the last moment and the job went instead to Director of Curriculum William Leary. Some believe Power lost the job because of his refusal to play traditional school politics, but Congresswoman Hicks may also have blackballed the man who had dared to campaign against her.

At Charlestown High, he had to tread more carefully, but even there Power occasionally revealed the depth of his feeling on racial questions. Through the fifties and sixties, the school had only one black teacher and a handful of black students. Good athletes won respect on the playing field, but others suffered abuse. Whites leaned over the railings of the school's big central stairwell and spat on minority students below. Racial epithets rang through the hallways. Some blacks and Hispanics withdrew at midterm. In June 1972—two months after he lost his bid for the superintendency—Power used his graduation speech to address changes in the school which worried him deeply. When he first came to Charlestown "the kids that frequented the Monument area knew precisely the historical significance of the battle and could relate it accurately to visitors." But now, he said, consider "a gray granite school dominated by the Bunker Hill Monument, that citadel dedicated to the proposition that 'All Men Are Created Equal,' except those at whom we whisper or shout 'nigger, spic, chink' and occasionally 'guinea.' Yes, all men are created equal, but are some of us created more equal?"

By then, the principal source of friction at the high school was the presence of several hundred students from the predominantly Italian North End, which had no high school of its own. For years many of its teenagers had gone to the in-town high schools, but as those schools became increasingly black, the North Enders sought sanctuary at Charlestown High. There they were regarded as interlopers and often derided as "guineas" and "wops." As long as they recognized that the high school was Townie turf, an uneasy peace prevailed, but in September 1973 the Italians fielded their own slate of senior class officers. At first, the Townies took them lightly—no North Ender had ever held such an office. But the Italian candidate for class president was a charmer named Mark Forziati, who ingratiated himself with the girls in the class and campaigned hard with the "shop mugs" in the electrical course who came from all over the city and felt no particular loyalty to the Town. When the votes were tallied, the unthinkable had happened. Not only had Forziati won, he had carried a North End girl in with him as class secretary.

The Townies were stunned, then angry. Fights broke out in the corridors, ostensibly over courting rights to Charlestown girls. One morning, after a boy was suspended for punching a North Ender, he went home, got a revolver, and came back gunning for his rival, until an assistant headmaster wrestled the weapon away from him. That evening, as several Townies hung out on their regular corner by the high school, a car screeched around the square and shots ricocheted off the granite façade. When the Townies retaliated, they were usually led by twenty-five male students who called themselves the HOBARS, an acronym for "Help Our Boys Against Radical Suckers." Initially, the HOBARS were little more than a joke, a secret society formed by athletes and big men on campus to bamboozle the rest of the school. By the early seventies, though, they had focused on the newly aggressive North Enders. Some teachers and administrators, holding the HOBARS responsible for the harassment of blacks and Hispanics as well, suggested that their name should really stand for "Hoodlums Opposed to Basic American Rights."

But whatever the HOBARS represented, it was less ideological than geographical, the defense of Townie turf against all comers. Like the Town itself, the school felt short-changed, exploited, assailed on all sides by outsiders seeking to erode its identity. The long-promised new building was still bogged down in disputes over racial balance, and in 1974, after Judge Garrity ordered Charlestown High transformed from a three-year to a four-year institution, it was more grotesquely overcrowded than ever. Its enrollment—spread over three buildings—had ballooned to 1,150, with 800 of them in the obsolete main building alone. But fire laws permitted only 636 students in the building at one time, so they were shuttled in and out all day, an elaborate game of musical chairs which made serious education all but impossible. Teachers and students feared things could only get worse the following fall when the judge's desegregation order embraced Charlestown.

The old school on the hill might not be much. Its building was crumbling, its academic record was dismal, most of its alumni were destined for dreary blue-collar jobs. But to many Townies, it stood for priorities they staunchly professed: community above achievement, solidarity over mobility. Precisely because Charlestown High embodied notions scorned by the outside world, the Townies valued it all the more. It was theirs and nobody was going to take it away from them.

Cassandra Twymon woke that morning in September 1975 torn between fear and anticipation. Part of her wanted to pull the blanket over her head and stay there for hours, snug and secure. Yet another part of her reached for the new day, craving the action, the color, even the danger it promised. If nothing else, she was going to be a celebrity that day, a TV star like the kids at Southie the year before. She didn't want to miss that. Hurriedly she pulled on the new outfit her mother had made for the occasion—dark blue pants and a matching smock, decorated with a light blue transportation motif: little men on bicycles, a horse and buggy, a railroad train and a switchman with a stop sign. She had new blue shoes and stockings. She knew she'd look good on TV.

At breakfast their mother fed her and young Rachel a little lecture about staying out of trouble. "Yes, *Mother*," Cassandra said with a weary nod. She was so accustomed to her mother's homilies that she hardly listened anymore. By the time the hand on the kitchen clock touched seven, she was almost relieved and rushed for the door (Rachel had another three-quarters of an hour before the bus returned to take her to the Edwards). With a jaunty wave, Cassandra ran across the avenue to the corner of Columbus Square.

The bus had been scheduled to arrive at 7:15, but already it was 7:30 and still no sign of it. Four other kids were standing on the corner by then—two black girls named Darlene Wynn and Diane White, and a brother and sister, Enrique and Janeth Rivas, who said they came from Bogotá, Colombia. Cassandra didn't know where Bogotá was, but it seemed a long way to come just to go to school in Charlestown.

It was chilly that morning, and the kids at the bus stop broke into an impromptu dance to keep warm. Finally, at 7:40, bus No. 354 came creaking up the avenue. It had already picked up thirty-two students in Lower Roxbury and most of its seats were taken when the group from Columbus Square boarded. Cassandra squeezed into a rear seat beside a skinny little girl who had clearly been crying, but most of the kids seemed anything but cowed by the morning's events—shouting, stomping their feet, pointing out the window at passersby as the bus wound through downtown Boston. Although Cassandra knew they were just trying to cover up their nervousness, she joined in. Somehow, it made her feel better too.

The clamor subsided as they turned onto the Gilmore Bridge. To their left, in a large vacant lot overgrown with weeds, five other buses stood waiting in a row. Quickly, police formed them into a convoy: a police car, two motorcycles, a bus, two more motorcycles, another bus, and so forth. The flashing blue lights of the patrol cars, the canary-yellow buses, the navy-blue uniforms of the policemen standing guard along the sidewalks wove a bright band of color through the desolation left by Charlestown's urban renewal. To Cassandra, peering out the bus window, the scene had a festive air, like one of those Armed Forces Day parades she had watched as a little girl down on Boylston Street.

As the convoy climbed Breed's Hill, the blue corridor thickened, patrolmen standing shoulder to shoulder on either side; and, turning onto the square, it moved through a vast blue sea—police on the sidewalk, in the streets, on the grassy slope beneath the Monument. Here and there behind the cordon, civilians jeered and hooted as the buses rolled by. When they pulled up to the high school, Cassandra's attention was diverted to the horde of reporters and cameramen straining against the wrought-iron fence. Someone flung open the doors and shouted, "Everybody out, and make it quick!" As she clambered down, Cassandra turned toward the clicking Leicas and whirring Minicams, posing for one exquisite moment like a movie star on her way to a Hollywood premiere. Then, wheeling on her platform heels, she did a syncopated little strut through the schoolhouse door.

But inside the crowded lobby her spirits faded. With so many minority students trying to get through the metal detectors at one time, the lines were long and slow. When her turn finally came, an aide searching her handbag confiscated the hair pick she used to tend her Afro. Protesting bitterly, she was ultimately allowed to keep it after she pointed out that its prongs were plastic, not metal. But the long wait and the dispute left her in a sour mood as she climbed the curving staircase to her homeroom on the third floor.

Room 38 was a bare brown box with fourteen scarred wooden desks lined up in three files before the blackboard. As Cassandra entered, she saw that the first file contained only two black girls at the first desk and a Puerto Rican girl directly behind them. Cassandra took the seat next to the Puerto Rican. In the middle file sat the two Colombian students and one black boy. As the white students came in, Cassandra noticed that all twelve of them squeezed into the third file of desks by the windows, as far as they could from the minority students. So much for integration, she thought.

Just then Frank Power came on the public address system, officially opening the new school year at Charlestown High. The headmaster congratulated them on the orderly manner in which the day had begun and assured them that measures were being taken to make school "a pleasant and rewarding experience for all of you." He cautioned: "We have only one hard-and-fast rule at this school: respect the rights of others. We are going to do that this year. We are going to respect other people's right to get an education here. We are going to respect their rights as human beings. Now, let's get to work. Remember, you're here to learn. That's the purpose of this school."

But not much learning got done that day. First, their homeroom teacher, a business instructor named John Rowley, had to take down all their names, distribute cards for them to fill out, and read them a seemingly endless list of rules and regulations. Cassandra noticed that as he sat on the edge of his desk, he turned slightly toward the white students by the window, so that she often had difficulty hearing him. From the corner of her eye, Cassandra could see the white kids whispering and giggling. Occasionally she caught a message hissed in her direction: "Anybody smell something peculiar in here?" or "Throw them a banana, Tarzan."

So it went the rest of the day, as she shuttled from history to biology to typing, music, office practices, and physical education. Some of her classes were half empty, since many whites were boycotting, while some blacks and Hispanics had stayed away in fear of trouble (of the 883 students Judge Garrity had assigned to Charlestown High, only 315 showed up that day—235 whites, 66 blacks, and 14 Chinese and Hispanics). In some of her classes, the teachers made them sit in alphabetical order, but none of the whites she sat next to so much as acknowledged her presence. The whispered gibes continued and, once, on the way into her office practices course, a white boy blocked her path, refusing to move until a teacher ordered him out of the way.

Nevertheless, the day ran its course without major incident. When the final bell rang at 1:32 p.m., the whites were held in the classrooms until the "minority" students could be loaded onto buses. Riding down the hill toward the bridge, Cassandra saw a pretty blond girl about her age standing on the sidewalk. The girl raised her hand as if to wave at the buses, and Cassandra was about to acknowledge the gesture when she saw that the girl wasn't waving at all. Only the middle digit on her hand was raised. She was giving them the finger.

At home that night, Cassandra told the story of her first day at school over and over, accompanied by comic pantomimes and caricatures of the whites she had encountered, and Rachel chimed in with similar tales from the Edwards Middle School. Their brothers—Richard, George, Wayne, and Freddie—alternated between hysterical laughter at the dramatic recitations and outrage at the indignities their sisters had suffered. Eventually, talk turned to revenge, each brother topping the others with some notion of how to pay "whitey" back. This brought a stern lecture from their mother. "I don't want to hear that kind of talk from you," she said. "I'm sending you to get an education. If you get into fights, you're going to get suspended. And if you're suspended, there's no way you're going to get an education. So if somebody wants to start something with you, don't you oblige them. If they hit you, don't you hit them back. All they've done is prove how inferior they are to you. Just turn your back and walk away."

"Aw, come on, Ma!" exclaimed Richard. "Even the old-time religion said, 'An eye for an eye, a tooth for a tooth.'"

"Shut up, Richard!" his mother snapped. "When I want a sermon from you, I'll ask for it."

The rest of the kids just rolled their eyes to the ceiling. There wasn't any point in arguing with their mother when she got in one of those lecturing moods.

In the weeks to come, Cassandra tried to heed her mother's admonitions, but day by day it became more difficult. Everywhere she turned at the high school, she encountered fresh evidence of the Townies' hostility. On the third day, she arrived in her homeroom to find a bizarre picture scrawled in Magic Marker on her desk: a fierce-looking African with rings in his nose and bones in his hair. Other blacks in the class were welcomed with similar drawings, some of them labeled "bushboogie," "spearthrower," or "monkey man." A few days later, when she opened her history textbook, she found "Niggers Eat Shit" scribbled on the title page.

Slogans and taunts she could shrug off, but it was harder to dismiss the physical incidents which broke out with increasing frequency. Whenever a teacher turned his back, erasers, bits of pencil, or scraps of chalk rained down on the black kids' heads. In the breaks between periods, as students walked the long, dark corridors to their next class, white boys would often jump a black kid, pinning him against a locker or knocking him to the floor. And when Cassandra and her friends went to the ladies' room, white girls sometimes elbowed them away from the sinks or ripped paper towels from their hands.

But efforts were underway in the black community to support the students being bused into Charlestown. One day in mid-September, a notice went up on the school bulletin board proclaiming: "Students! Things to do after school!" The Community Education Resource Center (CERC) offered swimming, gym, basketball, martial arts, African dance, a teen lounge, tutoring ("any subject you need help on"), counseling ("someone to rap with"), workshops ("Why are we in Charlestown?"). The program would run two afternoons a week at the Clarendon Street YWCA, a drafty Victorian edifice just a few blocks from Methunion Manor. Buses would pick students up at the high school every Tuesday and Thursday at 1:00 p.m. CERC sounded good to Cassandra, so she joined fifty-eight other students at its registration meeting on September 29. The center was staffed by two black social workers—Steve Moss and Nathan Spivey—street-wise veterans of South End youth programs who also served as "desegregation aides" at Charlestown High. In early October, as the students began spending two afternoons a week at the Y, Steve and Nathan played a major role in framing the black response to conditions at the high school. Between slam dunks and karate chops, they talked for hours with Cassandra and her friends, eventually suggesting that they organize a Black Students' Caucus at Charlestown High.

On October 6, Frank Power gave permission for nine black students to meet in a small classroom off the auditorium. Each of them had some tale of horror to report and for more than an hour they simply exchanged stories. Then someone sat down at a desk and wrote out a brief declaration: "We the black student body of this school are tired of the abuses they are subjected to, such as 1) We feel that we are not able to walk in the school halls without being abused, 2) Also by the name-calling that we are subject to while working in the classrooms. We feel that these are also the reason that black and white students are not able to get an education at Charlestown High." Four students—Clarence Jefferson, Charles Butler, Sandy Payne, and Cassandra—were elected to speak for the caucus. Then all nine walked across the hall to present their grievances to Frank Power.

The headmaster felt harassed that day. He'd spent the morning mollifying outraged white parents and was in no mood to deal with a bunch of angry blacks. But slumped against the counter of his outer office, he listened to the students tensed in a semicircle around him. Although the group had designated four people to represent them, the spokesman's role was preempted by Clarence Jefferson, a husky, aggressive junior who loved the limelight and frequently got it. But Clarence had been in almost constant trouble that fall—he had been suspended several times for fighting with white boys, while his performance in the classroom was anything but impressive. Instantly, Power decided he wasn't going to deal with Clarence, so as the youngster launched into his harangue—he was sick of getting beat up, the school better get its act together—the headmaster cut him short. "I'm not listening to any more of this," he snapped. Surveying the delegation, he lit on Cassandra, who seemed self-contained and reasonable. "I'll deal with this young lady," he said. "She can be your spokesperson." Adept at pacifying unhappy students, he temporized, hoping time would defuse their anger. "Look, angry speeches aren't going to get us anywhere. Sit down and draw up a list of your demands. Give me specifics. Then when it's all done, have Cassandra bring it in and I'll go over it with her."

It was an effective tactic. Predictably indignant, Clarence muttered maledictions at Power, but the others, satisfied that they were making progress, shut him up. And they all kidded Cassandra about her new boyfriend, the headmaster, a notion she loudly scorned, though secretly she was pleased to have been singled out.

The caucus set to work drafting its demands, a task which, as Frank Power had anticipated, proved more difficult than they had imagined. They got plenty of help. Steve and Nathan were still advising the caucus, aided by two of the school's other black aides, Mark Maddox and Dick Gittens. At their suggestion, the group broadened its constituency to include Chinese and Hispanic students, changing its name to the Minority Students' Council. That, in turn, brought them a valuable recruit—a shrewd, articulate freshman named Robert Chin, who quickly became the council's secretary. For several afternoons, the council met in the sixth-floor library at the Y, sorting through their grievances. Finally, Bob Chin produced a summary which satisfied nearly everyone.

"This year in Charlestown High School," he wrote, "almost half of the student population consists of minorities. These minorities, being second and third world people, lack the proper representation even though these people have legitimate demands. It should be understood that these demands are made so that minority students can acquire an education. Recently a Minority Council was formed to represent these people."

The statement went on to list twenty-three demands, among them:

"Mr. Power meet with this council regularly.

"This council be (a) notified of all incidents with minorities, (b) be allowed to confer with these students, (c) allowed to investigate the faculty members involved and (d) obtain legal assistance for the students.

"Teachers treat students as adults.

"More minority teachers be added to the faculty.

"Teachers do not segregate classes.

"All punishment to be equal; i.e. suspensions or releases be equally applied.

"Minority students to be given complete protection.

"All racial profanities be removed from school property.

"White students stop referring to minorities as niggers, chinks, etc."

They mimeographed the list, handed it to all minority students, and gave a copy to Frank Power. On Monday, October 13, Power sent word that he was ready to meet with Cassandra, but the council said no; unwilling to let the headmaster select his negotiating partner, they chose their own team—Bobby Chin, Clarence Jefferson, and Charles Butler—telling Power he must meet with them or nobody at all. Knowing he'd been outmaneuvered, the headmaster gave in. Unable to make his old personal magic work, he felt control slipping away. Under increasing pressure from both blacks and whites, he was still playing for time, hoping to cool tensions before his school exploded under him. That afternoon, he met with the minority representatives and, without committing himself to specifics, indicated that he would do what he could to implement most of the demands.

It was a fragile accommodation, destined to collapse under the first serious strain. The crash came only seven days later when several white boys began hassling a black sophomore named Eddie Malloy as he walked the third-floor corridor. Racial epithets were exchanged, Malloy was knocked to the floor, several passing blacks jumped in, and before long fifteen youths of both races were pummeling each other up and down the hallway. A sixteen-year-old girl was bitten on the hand. An administrative assistant to the headmaster was floored, sustaining a bloody nose. When teachers and aides failed to stop the fighting, twenty-five MDC police had to be called in to restore order. The police arrested four whites, charging them with assault and battery or disorderly conduct. But—under the school's policy of penalizing both parties to any fight—five blacks were suspended for three days.

On the buses home that afternoon, the minority students were in an uproar. The attack on Malloy was only the latest evidence that Frank Power, despite the assurances he had given them, was unwilling or unable to guarantee their safety. They were even more outraged at the suspension of blacks who, they felt, had only been acting in self-defense. Through the buses that afternoon raced a message from the Minority Council: boycott tomorrow. To make their point more emphatic, they should board the buses as usual, then refuse to get off when they reached the school.

When Steve Moss got wind of the plan, he had visions of a disaster the next morning. If the students refused to enter the high school, what would happen to them? Could they be forced off the buses and compelled to walk through hostile Charlestown to the nearest subway stop? Quickly consulting CERC officials, Moss alerted the Y to be ready to receive the students if he could get them there.

To Cassandra, the boycott was the best thing that had happened all fall. It would show Mr. Power and the teachers that they meant business, that they wouldn't stand for being assaulted, abused, and insulted. As she boarded the bus at Columbus Square that morning, she turned excitedly to Charles Butler and whispered, "Is it going down?"

"We're down," Charles said with a broad smile. "Everybody's in."

Indeed, when the buses rolled up in front of the high school, only ten of the ninety-six students got off, among them Janeth and Ricky Rivas, the Colombians, who had never felt part of the Minority Council.

Frank Power, who was suffering from high blood pressure and nervous exhaustion, had a doctor's appointment that morning. When his assistant, Bob Jarvis, realized what was happening, he boarded each of the buses, pleading with the students to get off. "I know you've got some grievances," he said, "but this isn't the way to get them dealt with. This is just what some of the white community wants you to do, so they can picture you as disruptive. You're playing right into their hands. Now come on inside and we'll work this thing out, I promise you." But on bus after bus the students refused to move. When his pleas failed, Jarvis tried threats. "I'll give you five minutes," he warned. "Anybody who doesn't get off will be suspended." Still nobody budged.

On instructions from black aides and the students themselves, the drivers drove to the Y and the eighty-six students were ushered into the auditorium, where Steve Moss and Nathan Spivey suggested they use the time to write down the specific grievances which had prompted them to boycott. In the pages of her spiral notebook, Cassandra wrote:

"Mr. Power told Clarence Jefferson to leave the meeting without asking questions.

"Why doesn't Mr. Power suspend the white kids?

"Dispose of the teachers that are prejudiced.

"Whites throwing things at the minorities.

"Stop all the racial slurs.

"The school needs to be cleaned up, painted or something."

When Rachel Twymon learned of the boycott from a radio bulletin, she and her brother Arnold hurried to the Y, where they found a dozen black ministers, politicians, and youth workers milling about in the hallway. Ultimately, the Minority Council came out to state its position. A senior named Beverly Merritt tried to read the list of grievances, but when she became too upset to continue, Cassandra took over. At 1:45, the buses returned to take most of the students home. Only four—Bobby Chin, Clarence Jefferson, Beverly Merritt, and Cassandra—went on to a news conference at Freedom House, where Bobby read a prepared statement:

"As long as we attend Charlestown High under present conditions our lives are in danger. Today we have stayed out to protest present conditions under which we must attend school. . . . We feel there is a small group of white students intimidating us as minorities. We also feel that the parents of the majority have a lot to do with what their children are doing. Teachers and aides in most cases are incapable of maintaining discipline. If the white parents and teachers aren't making a move to help solve the problem they are part of the problem. We hope that this protest will make it safer to attend Charlestown High School."

When Cassandra reached home she found her own family decidedly unenthusiastic about the day's events. Her mother praised her cool demeanor through the ordeal, but expressed deep misgivings about the boycott itself. Arnold was even more vehement. Determined to shepherd his nieces and nephews into college, Arnold wouldn't tolerate absences from school for whatever reason. "Okay, you've had your fun today," he told Cassandra. "But if you ever do this again, I'm going to put my foot in your behind." Cassandra—who'd expected to be a heroine at home—burst into tears.

Rachel understood what her daughter was going through. A half dozen times that fall, as a member of the Racial-Ethnic Parents' Council, she rode the bus up the hill to inspect Charlestown High and was dismayed at what she found: hostile demonstrators keeping vigil on the Monument grounds, police massed at the doorway, belligerent whites rampaging through the hallways. And she didn't hesitate to tell school officials how she felt.

One day in mid-October, Cassandra came home with a three-day suspension for skipping most of her history class. She told her mother she had lingered an extra half hour in her music class because she felt so close to James Howard, the black music teacher. The only black adult at the school with whom she enjoyed any rapport, Howard had enlisted her for the school Glee Club, her one extracurricular activity. Moreover, she disliked the history teacher, who she thought was prejudiced against blacks. When Rachel heard her daughter's explanation, she concluded that school authorities had grossly overreacted in suspending her. The next morning she rode the bus to Charlestown, stormed into Mr. Jarvis' office, and demanded that the suspension be revoked. Although Jarvis refused, he respected her fierce defense of her daughter's rights.

Soon Rachel recognized that there was little she could do at Charlestown High. The Parents' Council was a paper organization; its five black members met once a month at a "neutral site" downtown, but, with whites continuing to boycott the council, it had no real function. Recognizing this, Judge Garrity ordered new elections to fill vacancies in Charlestown and elsewhere. But once again the black turnout was small and the Powder Keg delegation sat stolidly across the room, determined in their boycott. Frank Power pleaded with the whites to relent; when they persisted, he publicly apologized to the blacks. Rachel felt sorry for him. The headmaster was no longer the bold, confident man she had first seen two months before. In a voice loud enough to carry across the room, she told him, "It's too bad some people are determined this thing should fail. It's too bad they insist on teaching their children to hate."

"Nobody here hates anybody!" one of the Charlestown women shot back. "Everything would be okay if you people just left us alone. And that means you too, Power, you traitor!"

A few days later—on October 23—Frank Power resigned from Charlestown High. The newspaper accounts said he was going on sick leave until the end of the year, when he would become an assistant to Bob Cousy, the former Celtics star, who was then commissioner of the American Soccer League. He was replaced at Charlestown by Bob Murphy, a veteran assistant headmaster at Boston English.

Rachel was sorry to see Power go. He struck her as a well-meaning man who had struggled to find some middle ground on a battlefield where no compromise was possible. His resignation did not bode well.

In late October, Rachel received an invitation from a group of black parents who were meeting at the Cooper Community Center to plan new action on Charlestown High. She was reluctant to attend, particularly when she learned that the parents' plan included a massive boycott intended to force the closing of Charlestown High and the return of the minority children to schools in their own communities. Soon she began receiving material from one of the meeting's sponsors, the African Liberation Support Committee, which argued that busing served the needs of "the U.S. Ruling Class, not Third World people." It had been forced on the people of Boston by "the Rockefeller and Ford Foundations, the Kennedys, the NAACP, etc." Poor people gained nothing from "the forcible busing of our children from a dilapidated working class school in the black community to one in the white community." Such measures did nothing but "pit poor and working people from both communities against one another. We can no longer fool ourselves thinking equality of oppressed nationalities will come under capitalist society."

There was much in the pamphlet with which Rachel agreed. Certainly busing did pit poor whites and poor blacks against each other, and over what? A broken-down old school, worse than many of those in Roxbury. The tract echoed many of the doubts about busing which had been growing in her all fall. Nevertheless, she concluded that the African Liberation people were wrong in demanding that Charlestown High be closed and black children returned to their community. That would be a reversal of everything she had fought for those last ten years.

Cassandra would have been delighted with such a solution. By mid-autumn she was pleading with her mother to use her position on the Parents' Council to arrange a transfer out of Charlestown. But with Garrity's experts keeping a tight watch on school assignments, such transfers were virtually impossible to obtain, and in any case, Rachel would have resisted her daughter's pleas. One night, as Cassandra renewed her complaints about the school, Rachel explained why she thought it was important to stick it out in Charlestown. The African Liberation Committee might pretend that Boston's black community was equivalent to an African republic, but this wasn't Ethiopia or Zambia. Boston was a white city—it always had been and, so far as she could tell, it always would be. So Boston blacks had to learn how to deal with whites, how to jolly them along, how to play their little games. She wasn't talking about toleration, about Brotherhood Week; she was talking about survival. She had worked in factories where black people had to be careful when they went to the bathroom because whites would smear filth all over the toilets or the faucets when they saw them coming. She had friends who worked in offices where white waitresses would tip coffeepots or jam jars over on tables served by blacks so they would get a reputation as sloppy. There were a lot of good white folks out there, but there were a whole lot of nasty ones too. You couldn't avoid them by retreating into your own neighborhood the way the African Liberation Committee wanted you to. If you were ever going to make it out there in the big city, you had to know what city life was all about, and for that Charlestown High was the best possible education.

It was an education all right. Ever since the October 20 melee, ten policemen—five plainclothes detectives and five uniformed police—had been stationed in the school every day. But the uniformed police played cards in the auditorium, on call only for emergencies, and the plainclothesmen were spread too thin to be effective. The dark hallways and stairwells, particularly on the upper floors, remained as dangerous as ever. As the jousting continued through the fall and winter, Cassandra and her friends learned how to survive at Charlestown High.

They learned that some whites were friendly enough one-to-one, but turned hostile in larger groups. Knowing how much pressure there was on such students to conform, they didn't trust them in delicate situations.

They learned never to walk the corridors or the stairways alone. After a student passed through the metal detectors he was supposed to go directly to his homeroom. But after several blacks were jumped, they found ways to linger in the lobby long enough to form small convoys.

They learned to resist provocation. It was hard to be cool when someone shouted "coon" or "bushboogie" at you, but Steve Moss and Nathan Spivey warned that whites wanted them to lose control, to strike back in ways that would discredit them—and desegregation. Moreover, they were vastly outnumbered: by November, daily attendance averaged 292 whites, 77 blacks, and 17 "other minorities." Charlestown High was enemy territory; it was foolhardy to fight on such terrain. Occasionally, one of the hotheads—Clarence Jefferson, Curt Shepherd, or Eddie Malloy—would defy the odds and lash back at their tormentors. But most blacks growled, "Get off my back, honky," and walked away.

The Minority Council hadn't abandoned efforts for redress of its grievances. But it had made little progress that fall, except for the appointment of Alan Cornwall, a black business teacher, as an additional administrative assistant sharing disciplinary duties with Bob Jarvis. Following Frank Power's resignation, the council took a new tack. Bobby Chin, Clarence Jefferson, Charles Butler, Sheila Keyes, Cassandra, and other council leaders began meeting twice a week in the basement of the Union Methodist Church under the auspices of Lois Dauway, the church's community worker, who believed that the group would accomplish more by operating in a larger arena. Their first step was to join forces with a similar caucus from South Boston High, an alliance they hoped would lead to formation of a citywide minority students' organization. Next they sought meetings with officials who could address their problems on the highest level.

One letter went to Arthur Garrity. "Dear Judge Garrity," they wrote. "We are writing this letter on behalf of the minority students of Charlestown and South Boston High Schools. We, as the black student body, feel that changes should be made now. . . . There are several blacks and whites that are afraid to attend these schools for the simple reason they know they will get picked on if they are black or white. There have been blacks that have been attacked by three or more whites. . . . Education is the most important thing to us because we can't live without it. There is a very weak education going on in Charlestown. When the whites boycott or walk out there isn't any kind of education going on. . . . We would like to hold a meeting with you as soon as possible."

The judge—in keeping with his firm policy of not meeting privately with parties in the case—politely but firmly declined their request.

The next letter went to School Superintendent Marion Fahey, who accepted on condition that the students submit their questions in advance. Back went a long list of queries: "What have you done about the troublemakers in the two schools? Why since September haven't more materials concerning minorities been added to the schools' curriculum? Is it possible to have more minority aides in the schools and fewer aides from the neighborhoods? What can the School Department do to make Charlestown High School more attractive and bearable?"

Ms. Fahey spent half an hour with them in the basement of Union Methodist. She was sympathetic, but provided no assurances on any of the students' complaints. Cassandra left the church that evening fuming with frustration.

The holiday season provided a brief respite, but when the students returned from their ten-day vacation they detected a marked increase in tension. Through January, white students staged a series of increasingly vehement demonstrations in and around the school.

Thursday, January 22, began peacefully enough. Piercing winds and drifting snow kept demonstrators off the Monument grounds as the buses crawled along the icy streets toward the school. Inside the steamy lobby, students clapped mittened hands together and stomped snowy boots. Upstairs in Room 38, Cassandra chatted happily with her seatmates—Josie Flores, Sheila

Keyes, and Julia White—largely oblivious by now to the resentful stares from across the room. Sheila, the high scorer on the girls' basketball team, had made 18 points the night before and the other girls crowded around her, offering their congratulations. "Kareem Abdul Keyes," Julia called her, and they all guffawed. It was good to know that a black could excel in something at Charlestown High.

History period went quietly. But walking toward her biology class, Cassandra heard a commotion on the floor below and, peering down the stairwell, saw nearly a hundred white students milling around the office. Uh-oh, she thought, here we go again. When she got to the biology room, it was nearly half empty; most of the whites had joined the demonstration. The teacher did his best to keep the remaining students occupied, but it was difficult to concentrate on binary fission in protozoa with all the noise coming from below.

At ten o'clock, Mr. Cornwall interrupted the class to say they had "a bit of a problem" downstairs. For their own safety, he said, all minority students would be concentrated in three classrooms on the upper floors. Cassandra, Sheila, and Josie ended up in Room 36 with Mrs. Mathews, the English teacher. For a few minutes, she read them a short story, something about Puritans in a New England village on the first Thanksgiving. Suddenly there was a clatter in the corridor, the door burst open, and a white boy stood there with a chair poised above his head. With an angry roar, he heaved it across the room at Mrs. Mathews, who dodged and slipped to the floor as the boy charged off down the hall.

When she regained her composure, Mrs. Mathews ordered someone to barricade the door with a desk. Then she told them what little she knew: The white students were staging a sit-in on the main staircases. A few of the white boys had gotten loose on the upper floors. They were being rounded up by teachers and police—there was nothing to worry about—but they would all have to stay put until the staircase could be cleared.

For the first time in her months at Charlestown High, Cassandra was frightened. The clamor from downstairs grew deafening. First the demonstrators sang a song, then they broke into a rhythmic chant. In the hallway outside, she heard more footsteps, a shout, then the sound of shattering glass. Mrs. Mathews tried to keep the students busy. She read them another short story. They played cards. They sang songs. Some of the younger kids drew pictures. But as the hours went by and nobody came to get them out, they grew increasingly agitated. Tempers flared. Nerves frazzled. Every noise in the hallway made them flinch.

Not until 12:45 did Bob Jarvis knock at the door to report that police had isolated the whites on the staircase, freeing the fire stairs on either side. Buses were drawn up in the adjacent alley, ready to receive the minority students. Detectives would lead them to safety. Cassandra sobbed with relief as she followed a burly cop down the narrow staircase.

Just then, the whites got wind of what was happening. "They're getting away!" they shouted. "They're going out the side!" Around the corner raced a dozen white boys, heaving stones at the buses as they rumbled down the alleys.

From her window, Cassandra gazed up the snowy slope toward the high school, hunched there in the shadow of the Monument. Only when the bus had crossed the bridge into the winding alleys of the North End did she stop trembling.

17

McGoff

From the start they knew they were special—"Big '76," the "Bi-centennial Class," the "Class of Destiny." For years they had played, fought, and daydreamed beside the granite obelisk. Every morning on their way to school they had walked by the bronze statue of Colonel Prescott, his arm outstretched, surveying the colonial lines. And every evening, descending the central staircase, they had passed beneath Trumbull's epic painting of Dr. Warren expiring in the arms of his lieutenant as waves of redcoats overran the valiant garrison. So drenched were they in revolutionary mythology they hardly needed to be reminded that they would be graduating two hundred years after the first shots in the struggle for independence.

Unwilling to let the anniversary pass unnoticed, Charlestown High launched "Project '76," a three-year program that would culminate in a week-long visit by the entire class to Boston, England. Although the British had agreed to welcome the visitors, the trip would be expensive, and starting in their sophomore year, the class set out to raise funds for the charter flight, hotels, and other expenses. They sold American flags, Bunker Hill flags, red-white-and-blue candles, and sweatshirts emblazoned "Charlestown Townies." And on June 17, 1975, the two hundredth anniversary of the Battle of Bunker Hill, they sponsored their own float in the Bunker Hill Day parade—a flatbed truck, decked out in bunting, bearing a large model airplane labeled "The Spirit of '76."

Nobody was more beguiled by the prospect of a week in England than Billy McGoff. He'd never been farther from home than Worcester, for a Holy Cross football game. Merry Olde England sounded like the perfect way to top off his high school years, and nobody worked harder to make the dream come true. He served on the Project '76 Committee, sold sweatshirts, ran car washes, and helped build the float. He talked so much about England that his friends said, "For an Irishman, McGoff, you sure talk like a bloody limey." Then, in September of their senior year, Frank Power passed the word: there would be no trip to England. No reason was given, but Billy and his classmates assumed that busing had killed it. Some said the blacks couldn't go because they hadn't worked to pay their way; but if they *didn't* go, Garrity would ban the trip as segregated. In fact, the decision had nothing to do with busing. The funds so painfully accumulated had simply disappeared—school officials discovered that the teacher responsible for holding the money had blown it all at the racetrack. One administrator scribbled a fitting epitaph for Project '76: "Their kingdom for a horse!"

To protect the teacher's reputation, the incident was never publicized, and the class of '76 went on believing that busing had cost them the trip for which they had worked so hard. Hurt and angry, Billy and his classmates began to emphasize another of their distinctions. No longer did they call themselves the "Bicentennial Class." That autumn of 1975, little green-and-white stickers began appearing on walls and lockers at the high school, bearing the initials "TLWC"—"The Last White Class."

Strictly speaking, the slogan wasn't accurate—there were three blacks in the class. But Garrity had given that year's seniors the option of graduating from their present schools, and the class had remained overwhelmingly white, whereas the freshmen, sophomores, and juniors were substantially integrated. This—plus their two years of aborted labor on Project '76—had lent the 204 white seniors a special sense of mission: they were the last graduates of the real Charlestown High and, by God, they were going down fighting.

Billy McGoff wanted badly to be class president. His brother Danny had been president the year before, and Billy was a leader in his own right: co-captain of the football team, co-captain of the basketball team, editor of the yearbook. But he had strong competition—a lively Townie girl named Michele Barrett, who had been class president for two consecutive years. When the votes were in, Michele had edged Billy once again, carrying with her an all-female slate. That was as it should be, said some Townie girls. The anti-busing movement was largely a woman's enterprise, led by militant mothers like Louise Day Hicks, Pixie Palladino, and Pat Russell. It was fitting that women should lead The Last White Class into battle.

Billy soon recovered from his disappointment. Now he could concentrate on sports, which had long been his principal interest. A husky kid (six feet one, 175 pounds), with speed and coordination to match, Billy was a four-letter man—in football, basketball, baseball, and track—earning his schoolmates' respect in the arena which mattered most to Townies.

As a former coach, Frank Power recognized the powerful hold sports had on Charlestown's imagination. Indeed, he remembered all too well an incident the previous March in which a hockey game had nearly set off a full-scale riot. Now he had visions of similar rioting instigated by Townie sportsmen against the black community, and to neutralize the school's athletes, he announced that any student who boycotted school was prohibited from practicing that day; anyone who missed a practice couldn't play in that week's game.

The year before, South Boston High had been so rattled by desegregation that it had failed to field a football team for the first time in nearly a century. At the same time, the endless boycotts and demonstrations had cost Charlestown the services of Howie Long, an outstanding prospect who simply wanted to play ball (he went on to star for the Oakland Raiders of the National Football League).

It was a matter of pride to The Last White Class that, no matter what happened in the fall of 1975, eleven kids would somehow take the field for every game wearing the red, white, and blue Townie jerseys; Billy and his two co-captains had sworn a solemn compact on that. When practice began in the last week of August, the holdovers from last year's squad would assemble every afternoon in the choking dust of the J. J. Ryan Playground for two hours of calisthenics and light contact drills. It was murderously hot in the line, where Billy alternated between center and left tackle, but he loved the sweat and stink of the trenches, the surge as the linemen got off the mark together, the thud of shoulder pads as the two lines collided.

The holdovers were all white, but when the first full practice was held on September 15, four blacks showed up. Nobody had expected that. Blacks had played football for Charlestown before, but the team had been all white for three consecutive years and in the new climate of hostility engendered by busing, nobody had imagined blacks would try to crack the Townie monopoly.

That first afternoon, the four blacks practiced separately at one end of the field, most white coaches and players barely acknowledging their presence. Mike Sheeran, beginning his ninth year as the Townie coach, was an opponent of busing, impatient with the complications it required him to deal with. Many of his players were more vociferous. "Only a Townie can make this team," said defensive back Mark Burns. "The rest of the school is falling apart. They've taken everything else away from us. This is the only freedom we have left."

When Charlestown played its first game against South Boston on September 20, only eighty-four spectators showed up at White Stadium in Roxbury's Franklin Park. Fourteen white cheerleaders—selected the previous spring to preempt the racial issue—tried to rouse the meager Charlestown rooting section with chants of "Here we go, Townies, here we go!" But South Boston drubbed the Townies, 36–6. At left tackle, Billy McGoff spent a long, frustrating afternoon butting heads with a bruiser from Southie. It must have been a frustrating afternoon for Mike Sheeran too. Disgusted with his team's performance, unable or unwilling to resolve its racial problems, he approached his principal assistant, John Green, and said, "You've always wanted a crack at this job, John. Well, it's yours. I quit."

Even John Green, a more relaxed and patient man, couldn't defuse the racial issue. Confronted with active or passive hostility from most of the white players, the four blacks dropped off the team within a week. And yet Frank

Power's strategy paid off. The Townies suffered through a dismal season—no wins, six losses, and a tie—but all that fall Billy and most of his teammates stayed in school, shunning walkouts and demonstrations.

Billy's aloofness irritated his sister Lisa as she found herself being drawn more deeply into the anti-busing struggle. Since her father's death, she had felt particularly close to her mother, and as Alice plunged into the movement, so did Lisa, accompanying her to Powder Keg meetings, ROAR rallies, and innumerable marches to City Hall and the State House.

Lisa had grown up with no intense feelings—one way or the other—about black people. In a town so overwhelmingly white and so insulated from the rest of the city, race wasn't much of an issue; through most of her childhood, the handful of blacks in the housing project were more curiosities than anything else. But the approaching storm of school desegregation had changed all that. As it swept across South Boston, Hyde Park, and Dorchester, its repercussions were received in Charlestown with profound alarm, and as the adults of Powder Keg girded for battle, they passed their anxieties on to their children.

Ten days before the first buses rolled into Charlestown, rumors had raced through the Bunker Hill project that "the blacks are coming," that they were going to ride up and down Bunker Hill Street shooting anything that moved. A few kids went down to the bridges to serve as lookouts, and for nearly a week many project families, including the McGoffs, slept with baseball bats by their beds. No carloads of blacks ever showed up, but Lisa never quite forgot that terrible week. Like most of her contemporaries, she believed that when the buses came, the black kids would step off armed to the teeth and ready to rumble. She believed that most black boys were out to molest and rape white girls, that black girls would attack white girls in the ladies' room, and that blacks of both sexes carried knives, razors, scissors, stickpins, and other weapons with which to assault whites.

But Lisa had been raised not to betray her fears and doubts; she prided herself on being a tough Townie chick who gave as good as she got. Moreover, she was a born leader, blessed with a strength of will that made others follow her. Though only a junior, she was accepted on equal terms by the circle of energetic girls who had taken control of that year's senior class. She felt particularly close to two of them: Trudy, an honor student, basketball and softball player, and leader of Project '76; and Doris, the class secretary, a cheerleader and three-sport athlete. Trudy, Doris, and Lisa all lived in the Bunker Hill project, and all three had parents active in Powder Keg. Soon they emerged as the acknowledged leaders of the school's anti-busing activity. Certain teachers labeled them "the unholy trinity."

But the girls rarely acted on their own. From the start, Powder Keg had called the shots at the high school. The year before—as Charlestown demonstrated its support of embattled Southie and geared up for its own ordeal—Pat Russell had relayed orders to the students through her daughter Patricia. Every morning at 9:40, between the second and third periods, Pat assumed her position on the slope beneath the Monument, while Patricia went to a window facing the Monument grounds. From her mother's hand signals she could tell whether students loyal to Powder Keg should walk out or stay in school that day. But the "Bunker Hill semaphore," as it became known, was too crude for the more difficult decisions which had to be reached the following fall, and the Town's anti-busing forces found more efficient means of getting the word into the high school.

In June 1974—exercising his traditional right to designate the head of the high school's Home and School Association—Frank Power had selected a maverick. Virginia Winters, a mother of eleven from the Bunker Hill project, didn't openly favor busing, but she supported peaceful implementation of the court order. That made her useful to the embattled headmaster, but earned her only enmity from most Charlestown parents. The association's other officers— among them, Alice McGoff as secretary—regarded her as a traitor to their cause. When the time came to elect new officers in June 1975, Alice was returned to office, along with the vice-president and treasurer, but the association defied Frank Power by refusing to reelect Ginny Winters. Instead, it chose Tom Johnson.

It was a crucial choice, for the association president had ready access to the high school and Tom Johnson took full advantage of that privilege. In his blue ROAR jacket, he became a familiar figure in the school lobby, where he served as the white students' adviser and advocate, and through him, Powder Keg maintained direct contact with student leaders like Lisa, Trudy, and Doris. Frequently, the students attended Powder Keg meetings to plan tactics for the school.

Through September, most of Charlestown's protests took place on the streets. In the mornings, the now familiar procession of mothers filed up the hill, "Our Fathers" and "Hail Marys" sounding in the still autumn air; and at night, the kids in the Bunker Hill project played cat and mouse with the police. For the moment, Charlestown High was a sideshow, its students content with an occasional boycott to demonstrate support for the featured players in these daily dramas.

All that changed abruptly in early October as the Minority Council began making its presence felt. The notion of a black pressure group presenting de- mands and forcing concessions was offensive to white parents and students alike. For years, they had watched black student organizations in action at Boston's inner-city schools. It seemed as if they always got their way, that all blacks had to do was grow bushy Afros, brandish their fists, and chant, "Burn, baby, burn," for white administrators to start caving in. Now this terrify- ing scenario seemed to be playing itself out right up the hill at Charles- town High.

And who was it making concessions to the blacks but the Town's old stal- wart, Frank Power! The Townies simply couldn't understand why Frank had deserted them. It had begun back in July when the School Department mailed out the fall's assignments. In the days that followed, Power had been besieged by Charlestown parents, imploring him to use his influence downtown to get their kids transferred back to Charlestown. Invariably, they invoked a special relationship with the headmaster: they had scored two touchdowns for him in the Eastie game back in 1957, their sister had gotten a B in his advanced geometry class. Frank would greet them warmly, embrace the mothers, wrap a big arm around the fathers. There was nothing he'd rather do than help, he'd say, but what could he do—it was a federal court order. "Come on, Frank," the parents would say. "You know us. You've pulled strings for us before." Again he would explain: the judge controlled the whole thing. As they left, he could see the wounded look in their eyes.

But that was nothing compared to their sense of betrayal when he began negotiating with the Minority Council. It was one thing for Power to accept the court order, quite another for him to deal with the interlopers themselves, giving away, piece by piece, the time-honored prerogatives of Charlestown High. And none of Power's dealings with the caucus stayed confidential very long. When he accepted most of their demands in principle, the Townies could not contain their anger. That afternoon, coming into a vacant classroom, he saw scribbled in big block letters on the blackboard: "Mr. Power is a backstabber. He sold us out." And a few days later, during a white student boycott, a girl he'd known for years spat in his face.

At first, he tried to shrug it all off; the haters might be in control now, he told himself, but eventually the moderates would rally around him as they always had, and Charlestown High would be Frank Power's school once again. But as Indian summer turned to raw New England autumn, he could feel the resentment congealing into hard rage. He received death threats, half-legible warnings scribbled on postcards, slurred voices on the phone telling his wife he was going to get "a bullet in the head." The daily confrontations took their toll: dizzy spells and other symptoms which his doctor told him reflected dangerously high blood pressure. Seeking solace, he turned to the priests at St. Mary's. In the murky light of dawn, after opening the school, he would walk across Monument Square to the rectory. Sitting at the big dining-room table under steel engravings of the saints, he would sip a mug of black coffee and tell the Irish priests about the forces pulling him apart. How, he asked, could he reconcile his deep love of Charlestown, and his personal relationship with hundreds of Townie families, with his commitment to racial justice? "It's tearing me in two, Father," he told Pastor Bob Boyle one morning in early October. "I don't know how much longer I can take it."

On October 14, some 175 white students walked out of school to protest Power's meeting with Minority Council representatives. That afternoon, a list of complaints—drawn up by members of The Last White Class—circulated in the school. "The blacks aired their grievances," it said, "now we would like to air ours." Among them:

"All the vulgarity by the blacks in the classroom and nothing done about it.

"Obscene gestures and acts against the white girls from black boys. Shoving of white girls in the corridors.

"Metal detectors do not work. The blacks get in with picks concealed in their hair.

"Black aides entering classrooms to talk to black kids.

"Persecuting the whites before the blacks."

The protest continued the next day as a hundred white students occupied the stairway between the second and third floors, refusing to move until granted an audience with the headmaster. When Power appeared, they complained vehemently about his "favoritism" toward blacks and demanded that he meet immediately with the white students in the school auditorium. Power expressed sympathy for their frustrations, but such a meeting, he said, was out of the question; Judge Garrity had expressly forbidden segregated school assemblies.

That brought a hail of abuse down on the headmaster's head.

"Who runs this school, you or Garrity?"

"How come you met with the blacks, then?"

"Power, you suck!"

Frank Power glared up the narrow stairwell. He wasn't going to take this from the kids. Yet every time he tried to speak, a new volley of catcalls drowned him out.

Lisa McGoff sat halfway up the stairs, wedged between Trudy and Doris. Looking down at the headmaster as he paced uneasily in the dim hallway, she felt sorry for the man. She'd always liked Frank Power—even though he didn't live in Charlestown, he acted like any of the Townies you met on Bunker Hill Street. But since busing began, something had happened to him: he was definitely favoring the blacks over the whites. So despite her lingering sympathy for the headmaster, Lisa joined in the jeers that were now cascading down the stairway.

Never before in his fifteen years at the school had Frank Power been treated this way. Teachers standing nearby were horrified by the effect it had on him. Once he realized he'd utterly lost control of the situation, his shoulders sagged, the color drained from his face, his hands began to tremble.

Eventually, to get the students back to class, he agreed to meet with a small delegation, and that afternoon Power sat down with twenty members of The Last White Class in the school library. When they accused him again of favoring the blacks, he insisted that he was being evenhanded. Wasn't he meeting with them, just as he had with the Minority Council? They had to understand, though, that the school couldn't run without certain rules. They should come in and talk things over with him and they'd work everything out as they always had. That was enough to mollify some of the seniors, among them Billy McGoff. But others wouldn't be placated. When they renewed their accusations, the headmaster grew testy. "Look," he said, "I've done the best I can. Maybe somebody else should take a crack at it."

Frank realized that he could no longer hold the school together with personal magnetism alone. Feeling deserted by the moderates who might have helped him isolate the extremists, he would have to fall back on coercion, the naked clout of the federal court, and that wasn't his style. He had no quarrel with Garrity, but he wasn't comfortable with judicial authority: it was too abstract, too rigid, too remote. It was one thing to sit up there in black robes passing decrees, quite another to sit here in your shirt sleeves pressing human flesh. Frank had been in Charlestown too long, he was too close to the Townies to be the cool, dispassionate agent of the federal court.

Moreover, he wasn't well. His doctor had warned him that he was suffering from serious hypertension. "One of these days you're going to run up those stairs and they're going to carry you down," he said. Frank's wife, Marie, had pleaded with him to quit. On October 17, the headmaster told Superintendent Marion Fahey he was ready to leave.

Once the decision was made, he wanted to turn his back on the old school forever, but he had to stick around another week to break in his successor, Bob Murphy. Finally, during the lunch hour on October 23, he asked to say a few words over the public address system.

"As you know by now," he said, "this is my last day at Charlestown High. I'm going on sick leave starting Monday. This has been a painful decision for me. I love this school. I love this town. I will always love them. But the federal court has ordered some far-reaching changes. However we may feel personally about those changes, we have no alternative but to obey the law of the land. My position this fall—with which some of you have disagreed—has been that Charlestown High would stay open whether there were five hundred students, fifty teachers, and five police . . . or five students, fifty teachers, and five hundred police. Goodbye and God bless you all."

Then he picked up his briefcase, tucked some manila folders under his arm, and walked out the side door.

The Townies were ready for their new headmaster, having moved beyond resentment of black demands to assertion of their own rights. Through mid-October, Lisa, Trudy, and Doris were among twenty white activists who met each evening at the Knights of Columbus Hall to frame a declaration. With Powder Keg's ample assistance, the "White Caucus" drew up a list of fifteen demands that bore a striking resemblance to a list submitted two weeks before by the whites of South Boston High. They fell into five broad categories: decorum, patriotism, education, security, and community rights.

In the interests of decorum, the Townies wanted "the obscene gestures, abusive language and racial slurs stopped immediately."

To promote patriotism, they demanded "to be allowed to pledge allegiance to the American flag in the morning, and to sing the National Anthem."

To improve education, they asked "accelerated education programs for those students who are above the average grade levels" and demanded that "quality education be returned to Charlestown High."

For improved security, they wanted more "modern and sophisticated metal detectors." They wanted any student found with an "Afro pick" or knife to be arrested. And they demanded that "when white students wish to leave the school because they feel their safety is in jeopardy they be allowed to do so, instead of being locked in like convicts."

To secure the rights of the Charlestown community, they demanded that "community representatives"—Powder Keg and its allies—be permitted "access to the school," be allowed to "act as spokesmen for the white student body," and be permitted to "negotiate white student grievances."

The demands were ready for submission to Bob Murphy on October 24, his first day as headmaster. At eight that morning, 125 white students occupied the main stairway, compelling the blacks to stay on their buses for half an hour. (Eventually, the blacks were sent home for the day while Murphy tried to end the sit-in.) The new headmaster offered to discuss the fifteen demands with a small delegation of white leaders, but the demonstrators booed, stomped their feet, and chanted anti-busing slogans until he finally consented to meet them all in the third-floor auditorium.

It was a daunting prospect for Murphy on his first day, and for support he summoned Charlie McGonagle, one of the school's five Townie teachers and among its most popular figures. McGonagle's engaging essays and light verse appeared regularly in the Charlestown *Patriot*. The fall before, his piece called "The Neighborhood Tavern" had become an instant favorite in the Town, where it could be found tacked up above beer-stained counters or taped to barbershop mirrors.

> "*I'm sorry sir [it went in part] but you can't come in here anymore.*"
> "*What do you mean CAN'T? I've been coming here for years. All I want is a beer.*"
> "*I'm sorry, sir, but you've been reassigned.*"
> "*Reassigned? . . . You're kidding!*"
> "*No, sir. But don't feel too badly about it. We have a bus to take you there and back again.*"
> "*Hey, I want to drink with my friends, not a bunch of people I don't know.*"
> "*I'm sorry, but I really can't do anything about the situation. The State Board of Social Drinking, with the support of the Federal Board of Imbibers, has succeeded in getting a court ruling saying all taverns must be ethnically balanced.*"
> "*. . . What have I been assigned?*"
> "*Well, let's see, sir . . . Ah, here we are. Oh yes, Lim Wong's Bar and Grille, in Chinatown.*"

His scorn for Garrity's order thus established, Charlie enjoyed the trust of the school's white activists. Knowing this, Bob Murphy asked him to go to the auditorium and try to keep the demonstrators in check while the headmaster and others considered the fifteen demands. As Charlie mounted the stage, there were a few catcalls from the Townies, but he bantered good-naturedly with the kids, assuring them that their demands were being studied.

Down in his office, Murphy huddled with District Superintendent John McGourty and representatives of the Faculty Senate, going over the white students' grievances. With the sit-in paralyzing the school, they were eager to make concessions which might mollify the demonstrators; but, after reviewing the demands one by one, they found few to which they could accede.

Security was already tight. Airport metal detectors were in place and hand detectors had been ordered. Obscene gestures and racial slurs were already prohibited. Students couldn't be permitted to walk out anytime they felt themselves in danger. A daily pledge of allegiance seemed excessive, but once a week might make sense. Murphy saw no justification for dealing with Powder Keg, but he agreed to meet with representatives of the Home and School Association or the Charlestown Education Committee anytime they wished. As for "quality education," as the day's events amply demonstrated, it was hard enough in the current climate to guarantee any education at all.

When Murphy and McGourty entered the auditorium, they were greeted with thunderous boos. Virtually every white in the school was there and now they surged to their feet, chanting rhythmically, "Here we go, Townies, here we go!" As the din crashed about her, Lisa felt tears welling in her eyes. God, she was proud to be a Townie! Townies stuck together. They weren't going to let a judge or a bunch of black kids take their school away from them!

Finally the clamor subsided and Murphy outlined the steps agreed on in the office. As for the remaining demands, he hoped further discussions could take place with student representatives, but he would not stand for this kind of disorder. Nobody was going to drive the blacks out, so they'd better get used to them. At that, more than a hundred of the students—Lisa among them—rose and filed out. In the doorway, one student turned and shouted, "Mr. Power wouldn't have treated us this way!"

Bob Murphy knew it would be futile to compete with Frank Power's legend. He wasn't even going to try. Although he'd been at Charlestown High before—as a science teacher and guidance counselor from 1964 to 1970—he realized that the Townies regarded him as an outsider. But that might prove more an advantage than a handicap, he thought; without encumbering friendships and loyalties, he could play a role foreclosed to Power: the stern, uncompromising disciplinarian.

The new headmaster set out to show the activist students and their adult supporters that he meant to enforce the court order at all cost. His hard line quickly surfaced as he dealt with an epidemic of bomb threats that fall. When the first ones occurred, all students had been promptly evacuated, left to mill about on the Monument grounds until the police could search the school. Since no bombs were found, Murphy soon concluded that such threats were mere harassment, designed to keep the school in constant turmoil; moreover, once black students left the school they were particularly vulnerable to attack. So he revised his strategy. At first warning, police were summoned, but no evacuation was ordered unless they actually found a bomb—which they never did.

The new policy led to an angry confrontation with Tom Johnson. One day in October, after yet another threat was received, Johnson rushed into the headmaster's office, demanding that the alarm bells be rung immediately. "You're playing with these children's lives!" he said. "Get them out of here now!"

Murphy refused, citing his new policy.

At that, Johnson put a finger against the headmaster's chest and growled, "If there *is* a bomb in here, and if one child gets hurt, you bastard, I'll be the first in line to punch you out, and there'll be twenty thousand people behind me waiting their turn."

Relations between the two men went from bad to worse. Johnson saw Murphy as a "carpetbagger," an itinerant bureaucrat ready to sacrifice Charlestown's interests to advance his career. Murphy regarded Johnson as a troublemaker, an unscrupulous roughneck fomenting unrest. Eventually, the headmaster banned him from the building. When Johnson insisted that his position in the Home and School Association guaranteed him access, Murphy shook his head. "We're on different teams, Tom," he said.

"You're damn right we are," Johnson shot back. "Is your NAACP card paid up yet?"

The battle lines were clearly drawn now. For the first time white activists found themselves pitted not only against the black students but against a school administrator determined to give them no quarter.

Skirmishing continued through early November. When whites again occupied the front stairs on November 21, the headmaster lost his patience. Turning to Captain MacDonald, he said, "We've lost control of this situation, Bill. I think it's time for the police." MacDonald addressed the students, warning them to go to class, leave the building, or face arrest. The demonstrators' only response was a chorus of "God Bless America." What happened next surprised even the headmaster. The front door burst open and in charged a platoon of the Tactical Patrol Force in their leather jackets, boots, and Plexiglas visors. Wading into the students, they heaved them down the staircase. Girls screamed. Boys who resisted got a billy club on the arm or shoulder. Sitting halfway up the stairs, Lisa McGoff was spared the initial charge, but soon cringing with fear, she permitted herself to be herded out the front door. The students huddled in small groups on the sidewalk, still dazed from the TPF assault and shaking with indignation. What right did the police have to violate their sanctuary? It was their school, wasn't it? Didn't they have a right to sit on their own steps?

In the week that followed, Murphy discovered just how tenacious Townies could be in defense of their children. He was besieged by Charlestown institutions—the Little City Hall, the Kennedy Center, the Education Committee, and Powder Keg—all demanding assurances that the TPF would never again be called into the high school. Murphy insisted that he had no responsibility for the TPF. Once he informed the police that he had lost control of the situation, it was up to them to respond as they saw fit. But that satisfied nobody.

The students responded with three consecutive days of boycott. Every morning, 150 of them marched up the hill to jeer as the blacks got off the buses, then adjourned to the Knights of Columbus Hall for angry rallies. Murphy retaliated by suspending all the boycotters, imposing a heavy five-day suspension on a student who had pushed him during the November 21 demonstration. The student—a prominent football player—was outraged because he would be prevented from playing the Thanksgiving Day game against Brighton and he warned Murphy that if he wasn't allowed to play, none of the team would show up for the game. Murphy and Coach Jack Green agreed: they weren't going to be blackmailed. If the kids didn't want to play, there wouldn't be a game.

Billy McGoff was stunned. The Thanksgiving Day game against Brighton was the traditional climax of the Townies' season, the last football game he would ever play for Charlestown High. Were they really going to give that up for the sake of another damn boycott? On the other hand, Townies were supposed to stick by their buddies. For twenty-four hours, Billy and his teammates debated what to do. Then back came the answer: they would play. On Thursday morning, all but four of the team turned out, losing to Brighton, 6–0.

Lisa was furious at her big brother. How could he torpedo the boycott? It was the same dispute which had been simmering between them all fall, but now she'd had enough and a few days after the Brighton game she exploded. "Hey, big shot," she said, "why can't you think about anybody but yourself? A few of us are trying to get this school back in shape. You're the big man on campus around here. If you walked out, a lot of kids would go with you. But, oh no, all you want to do is play your silly game."

Billy, as usual, was imperturbable. Smiling back at his younger sister, he said, "You got it. That's all I care about. My game."

By then the game was basketball and it consumed Billy as football had only a few days before. But he knew that this season was going to be different. The football team had stayed white all fall, but the basketball squad was clearly going to be integrated. He had watched some of the black kids bouncing a ball around the gym. They were showboats, but they had some good moves, and one of them could execute a passable slam dunk. There was no way to keep these guys off the team, and even if Billy had wanted to, he knew the coach would never permit it.

Larry Mathews, a Boston Irishman from St. Thomas Aquinas Parish, had taught business and coached basketball at Charlestown for a dozen years. A John Kennedy liberal, he hoped that blacks and whites could learn at least a grudging respect for each other on the basketball court. In years past, he had tried to recruit black ballplayers for his team, without notable success. Now Garrity had done it for him. Before the first practice that fall, Larry took his returning lettermen—all of them white—into the gym and delivered a stern lecture. This was going to be a difficult year, he warned; people on both sides of the busing issue would try to draw them into it. But racial politics had no place on the basketball court.

Of the forty players who tried out for the team, about half were white and half black. Ultimately, the starting five had three blacks (Howard Eaves, Joe Strickland, and Roy Bone) and only two whites (Billy McGoff and Wayne Perry). It was the first time in anyone's memory that a Townie team had a black majority. And when Mathews named Billy, Wayne, and Howard as three co-captains, the school was predictably incredulous. An anonymous note went up on the bulletin board: "Niggers sweat too much to play basketball." But the commotion subsided almost as quickly as it had begun. Soon the players were joshing with each other in time-honored locker-room style. On the way back from a scrimmage against Natick High, the blacks began asking where the bus was going to leave them off. "We're going to drop you *boys* right in front of South Boston High," said a white player in the exaggerated drawl of a Southern sheriff. Everybody chuckled. Just then, they passed Bromley Heath—a notorious black housing project—and Joe Strickland exclaimed in mock horror: "Don't leave me off here!" The laughter was louder this time. Then Roy Bone yelled at Billy McGoff, "Hey, Flash, you don't need to be afraid out here. We'll just tell 'em you're our token Irishman." The bus rocked with laughter.

Billy and Joe Strickland—the team's two starting guards—got along especially well. Billy admired Joe's ability as a ballplayer, but he warmed most of all to Joe's ebullience, his pure love of the game. Had circumstances been different, they might have become real friends. Strickland made overtures in that direction: on several occasions he invited Billy to parties at his Lower Roxbury home. Billy was flattered, but he had to say no; he knew how foolhardy it was for a Townie to set foot in the black community. That was the way to get yourself killed. Strickland seemed disappointed.

But if the Townie players had come to terms with their black teammates, the same couldn't be said for the Charlestown community. The high school had no gym, so the team practiced and played its home games at the Harvard-Kent, across from the Bunker Hill project. The black players rode to and from the gym with a police escort. As a further precaution against racial incidents, the School Department had prohibited spectators at all basketball games that season.

Performing without a rooting section was demoralizing for any team, but it proved excruciating for Jeremiah Burke, a predominantly black high school in North Dorchester, which dominated the league that season. Burke was eager to show off its winning style, so when Charlestown paid them a visit it found the stands filled with Burke fans cheering their team on to a 70–52 victory. There were no disorders and, after the game, the Burke coach readily agreed that Charlestown could admit spectators when his team paid a return call the following week.

A boisterous crowd packed the stands at the Harvard-Kent for the Burke rematch. When the visitors took a commanding lead in the first half, the crowd turned ugly, showering racial epithets and ripe fruit on the Burke bench. Some of the slurs were directed at Charlestown's black players. At halftime, Larry Mathews gave his team a pep talk, reminding them that this was their last home game of the season, their last chance to show the home fans what they could do. The Townies went out and played their best ball of the year. With Joe popping jumpers from outside and Billy driving in for lay-ups, they tied the game, 68–68, in regulation time, then outscored the league leaders in overtime to win, 76–71. It was a stunning upset.

But Townie fans had something else on their minds. Massed out front, they hooted and jeered when Burke's black players boarded their bus, then pelted the vehicle with rocks as it sped away. The police warned Larry that it would be unsafe for his own black players to leave by the front door, so the triumphant Townies slipped out the back, boarding their bus for a surreptitious getaway. Billy, Joe, and the others rode in glum silence through the dark streets, a humiliating retreat for a team which had just pulled off its biggest victory of the season.

But the aggravations which beset Larry Mathews were minor compared with the problems his wife faced on the girls' team. Maryann Mathews, an English teacher, knew nothing about basketball—she'd been drafted at the last moment to assist Irene Kelly, a nun who had long coached the girls' squad. Sister Irene promptly went into the hospital, leaving Maryann in charge. Larry helped her with strategy—diagramming plays on napkins at the dinner table—but he could do little to ease her racial troubles, which proved far more acute than his own.

The boys had a big stake in their season—they had trained for years to make the varsity, and some of them hoped to parlay their skills into college scholarships. But most of the girls cared little about the game itself; to them, basketball was partly recreation, partly a social occasion, and—for some—another arena in which to wage the anti-busing struggle.

The troubles began as soon as three black girls signed up for the first practice. Lisa's friends, Doris and Trudy, promptly announced they weren't playing with "niggers" and quit the team. Lisa and the others agreed to give it a try. But when the three blacks all proved they were good enough to make the team, further dissension developed. The Townies dramatized their resentment by refusing to pass the ball to the black girls in practice. Their passing drills locked into racial stalemate, with a cluster of white girls camped under one basket, a clump of blacks under another.

Gradually the hostility abated as most of the white girls reluctantly accepted their new teammates. But one day, after an orderly practice, some of the white players went out for a Coke and half an hour later Michele Barrett returned to the gym in tears. She'd been accosted by a group of white girls, including Lisa McGoff, who had denounced her as a "nigger lover." Later that day, Lisa told Maryann she was quitting the team because she couldn't play with blacks.

Eventually, Maryann's team jelled beyond her wildest hopes. One black girl proved a spectacular center; another developed into a high-scoring forward. Three whites, including Michele, rounded out the first string, which ran off twelve straight victories to become Boston's city champions. In the first round of the state tournament, they demolished Tyngsboro, 49–25, before losing to suburban Ipswich in the quarterfinals.

Sports were Charlestown's principal ritual, dramatizing the issues as little else could. But some of the tension at the high school that winter focused on another, purely symbolic question: how much, how often, and in what manner to express patriotic sentiment. In ordinary times, Charlestown's Irish-Americans were zealous nationalists, determined to prove they cared as much for their country as had the Yankee farmers who first shed their blood on Bunker Hill. Now, with the Bicentennial year only weeks away, patriotic feeling was at fever pitch in Charlestown—and throughout the city.

For Boston, of course, was the "cradle of liberty." No city in the nation boasted so many revolutionary events—the Boston Massacre, the Boston Tea Party, Paul Revere's ride, the battles of Concord, Lexington, and Bunker Hill—America's ABCs chalked on the blackboard of our collective memory. Any Boston mayor would have ordered up festivities to commemorate such occasions, but to Kevin White they were more than anniversaries— they were God-sent opportunities to draw the nation's attention to him and his city. He established a public agency—Boston 200—charged with organizing the most elaborate celebration of the nation's birthday to be held anywhere in the land.

But White was hardly the only Bostonian seeking to make capital of American history. Bostonians' stake in their tumultuous past had been reinforced by their turbulent present. Nor surprisingly, the violent anti-busing demonstrations, the sight of police on horseback clattering through the narrow streets, the placards, banners, and effigies, had stirred recollections of an earlier battle over men's rights. All sides in the Boston busing struggle discerned—or claimed to discern—striking parallels between their own conflict and the revolutionary spectacle of two hundred years before.

White proponents of school desegregation invoked the liberties for which Americans had fought at Concord, Lexington, and Bunker Hill. Some Boston blacks derided the Bicentennial as "a birthday party for a two-hundred-year-old white man," but others identified their present struggles with that of Crispus Attucks, the former slave who was one of five men killed in the Boston Massacre.

Opponents of busing saw themselves as victims of the same oppression which had beset eighteenth-century Bostonians and said they were fighting for the same right to control their own lives. State Representative Ray Flynn

warned: "The sacred principles on which this nation was founded are threatened by a new tyranny, a tyranny dressed in judicial robes."

But sorting out the lessons of the past wasn't always so simple for the
Townies. Charlestown had its own militia company, patterned after the original
Charlestown Militia which fought at Bunker Hill. The modern version had
been founded in 1967 by a longshoreman named Jim O'Neil, who hung out at
the Thompson Square Tavern, where his obsession with colonial military history had earned him the nickname "General Jim." Many of the militia's four-
score members were recruited from the tavern's regulars. Their wives made
their uniforms—cocked hats, ruffled shirts, and breeches—and they brandished replicas of colonial muskets. As the Bicentennial celebrations got
underway, the Charlestown Militia was in heavy demand for historical pageantry, starting with the 1975 reenactment of the Boston Massacre.

Powder Keg and its allies in ROAR had different plans for the occasion.
Minutes before the reenactment was to begin at the historic site on the Boston
waterfront, some 400 anti-busing demonstrators loomed in the street. Led by
two drummers beating a funeral dirge, eight black-clad pallbearers carried a
pine coffin marked "R.I.P. Liberty, Born 1770–Died 1974." Behind them
came rank upon rank of marchers, keening in the high-pitched wail long used
to mourn the Irish dead.

By then, it was time for the formal ceremonies. Some 150 men in colonial
dress—drawn from the Charlestown Militia and suburban minutemen companies—came marching up the street toward the Old State House. But when
Dennis Kearney, Charlestown's state representative, tried to read a proclamation marking the occasion, the anti-busers hooted him down. An ugly confrontation was shaping up between two groups of Irish-Americans—each trying to
use history for its own purposes. Then Jack Alves, president of the Charlestown Historical Society, stepped to the microphone in his flowing black cape
and cocked hat. "I see you there, Pat Russell," he said. "And I see you too,
Tom Johnson. We all know each other. We let you do your thing. Now let us
do ours."

The demonstrators grew still. The Massacre proceeded, with Medford's
64th Regiment of Foot portraying the squadron of seven British soldiers who
fired into the crowd of colonials, killing five of them. But as the shots echoed
off the glass-and-steel skyscrapers, all 400 demonstrators dropped to the pavement, lying there for a moment as still as Liberty in her coffin, as if to say:
We, too, are victims.

If the Townies differed on how to commemorate the Massacre, there was
nothing equivocal about June 17, 1975, the two hundredth anniversary of the
Battle of Bunker Hill. This was Charlestown's big day, its moment in the
Bicentennial spotlight, and the Town's factions temporarily shelved their differences to mount a splendid show. Militia companies from thirteen states took
part in a reenactment of the battle—hundreds of defenders in shirt sleeves and
red-stained bandages manning a redoubt beneath the Monument, cannon sal-
vos echoing across the harbor, and the relentless line of redcoats pressing up

the hill until they overran the gallant defenders. Thousands of onlookers packed the sidewalks to watch the spectacle. But the threat of Garrity's order hung like the clouds of cannon smoke over the hill, and Powder Keg lost no opportunity to draw parallels with 1775. One large banner draped from a Monument Square rooftop said it all; in bold black letters against a red background it proclaimed: "We're right back where we began 200 years ago."

To The Last White Class—already primed by Project '76—such parallels seemed self-evident. As one senior wrote in a history paper that fall: "The dictatorship our ancestors fought to defeat has been reestablished here. We are living in a new tyranny. Garrity is the same as King George. He is appointed for life. Nobody can say nothing to him. His decisions are like laws. They are as unjust as taxation without representation. Senator Edward Kennedy is like one of the Tories, a traitor to his own people. And the people of Charlestown have no choice but to revolt."

Such comparisons not only buttressed the students' case by linking it to the first American cause but gave them a powerful weapon, one they never hesitated to employ. At sit-ins and demonstrations, they invariably sang "The Star-Spangled Banner," "God Bless America," and other patriotic anthems. At school, they pressed for more patriotic observances and demanded flags in every classroom.

But their most insistent demand was for daily recitation of the Pledge of Allegiance. In earlier years, Charlestown High had said the pledge every morning, teachers and students alike rising and placing their hands over their hearts. During the sixties, some liberal teachers refused to say the pledge, prompting a burst of protests from patriotic Townies. So Frank Power simply bypassed the dissenters by intoning the pledge over the public address system, with students following in their classrooms. But when busing began that fall, beleaguered administrators rarely reached the office in time to say the pledge, and the practice fell into disuse.

It was a perfect issue for the white activists. Since the sixties, the pledge had assumed a powerful symbolism. Ironically, Powder Keg had devised a parody which was frequently recited at anti-busing demonstrations: "We will not pledge allegiance to the order of the United States District Court, nor the dictatorship for which it stands; one order, under Garrity, with liberty and justice for none." But that only intensified their devotion to the true pledge, which they now insisted be restored as a regular feature of the school day. Bob Murphy refused—he simply had too much else to do at the start of every day. A compromise was reached: individual teachers could say the pledge one day a week.

That only shifted the battle to the classroom. Most blacks simply didn't believe there was "liberty and justice for all" in America, much less at Charlestown High; they couldn't say those words with a straight face. So while whites would rise to say the pledge, blacks often remained seated. And as the words "one nation, indivisible" echoed in the classroom, the two groups stared at each other in mutual incomprehension.

By year's end, Powder Keg and the school's white activists, concluding that most of the demands they had pressed that fall were bearing no fruit, decided to concentrate on a single issue: education. The new campaign got underway on December 2, when Moe Gillen, chairman of the Charlestown Education Committee, charged that most of Boston's schoolchildren were being short-changed educationally. Teachers, he said, were tailoring their instruction to the lowest common denominator in their classroom, ignoring the needs of students who could move faster. "The majority of students—both black and white—are being held back until the minority catches up," Gillen declared. He didn't identify what "minority" he was talking about, but the implication was clear: the blacks bused into Charlestown were dragging down academic standards and hampering the education of white students.

There was a kernel of truth in this. Teachers at Charlestown High discovered that most of their black students scored lower than whites in basic skills such as reading, writing, and mathematics. About 70 percent of the black ninth-graders, for example, read at or below a sixth-grade level, and all of the slowest readers in the remedial reading classes were black. But the white scores were nothing to cheer about either. Eighty-five percent of all ninth-grade students—white *and* black—read below their grade level. Long before busing, the school's staff had recognized that Charlestown High drew the Town's least proficient students, and busing had only aggravated that situation. Over the summer, many parents who could afford it or had high aspirations for their children had enrolled them in parochial or private schools. The gap between white and black achievement, therefore, was never so wide as to hamper a white student who really wanted to learn.

Bob Murphy knew he had to confront the education issue. Three days after Moe Gillen spoke out, Murphy sent a letter home with each student. "Dear Parent," it began. "I am writing to you on a topic that is of great concern to both of us: a quality education for your child. I would like to report to you what we at the school are attempting to implement in this regard. In addition to standard programs that are designed to provide your child with adequate tools for either college entrance or gainful employment, we have made special efforts this year to reaffirm the basic skills and individualize instruction." The headmaster went on to describe several new features of the school's curriculum: a remedial reading teacher, a new "learning center" equipped with the latest audiovisual equipment, and advanced instruction. "We believe that we have a lot to offer for the total education of your child. Please take advantage of it."

But nothing could have deflected the campaign by then. Over the holiday season, the anti-busing movement had resolved to bring Charlestown's educational problems before a wider audience, including officials downtown. The adults framing the campaign recognized that the students had frequently failed to make their best case; to confront the policy makers would require the most articulate voice they could muster and that was Lisa McGoff. Though only a junior, Lisa had already proved herself to be the movement's most effective spokesperson at the high school. Some kids said she simply had a "big mouth," others called her a "show-off." But Lisa didn't see it that way. If they were ever going to accomplish anything, somebody had to speak up, and the other kids were afraid to say what they thought. She never hesitated to tell anybody what was on her mind, and if they wanted her to represent the school down-town, what the heck, she didn't mind.

The campaign got underway on January 7, when eighty-five white students walked out of school and marched across the low bridge to School Committee headquarters, where a delegation of fifteen was admitted for a meeting with Superintendent Fahey. As the students crowded the small lobby of the Super-intendent's office, Lisa stepped forward and delivered her carefully prepared remarks: "We're not trying to get out of school, Miss Fahey. We want to get an education and go to college. But the way things are going, we're never going to get a decent education. Ever since busing started, we've been doing work we completed one, two, even three years ago. What we need is acceler-ated classes so students can work as fast as they want without worrying about the blacks who can't keep up."

After other students added variations on the theme, Ms. Fahey thanked them politely but said she would need more information before she could respond. She promised to appoint a team to visit the school and recommend appropriate action.

Five days later, two officials appeared at the school and spent three hours talking with students, teachers, and administrators. Their report to Ms. Fahey remained confidential, but officials said it gave little credence to the student complaints.

When they received no further response from the Superintendent, the students moved on to the second stage of their campaign. On January 19, a small delegation appeared at a School Committee meeting. Lisa, as usual, led off: "My name's McGoff, Charlestown High. I want to tell the School Committee personally our complaints that I've already stated to Miss Fahey. One is our math program. In math, the standards have been lowered badly. In my opinion, they have fallen a grade since the minority students have come in. It's not the teachers' fault, because they try their best, but since the black kids have come in we have to wait until they catch up to our work. I have gone into classes and seen addition, subtraction, and multiplication tables on the blackboards."

Then it was Bob Murphy's turn. His students had "some legitimate con-cerns," the headmaster said, "but the teachers are more than willing and anx-ious to help remedy the situation that does exist. We've been addressing the situation." Then, with a little nod to Lisa, he added pointedly, "I am sure most of the students are aware of that."

Lisa wasn't going to accept that. Pushing her way to the microphone, she said, "We've had all kinds of meetings with Mr. Murphy, but it doesn't seem that anything gets done. When we talked to him at the beginning, he said, 'I can't do it because the judge won't let me.' It seemed nothing was done when we asked for it to be done. Now I can see that Mr. Murphy has been doing something. But still, what about the seniors this year who have to graduate and take their college boards? How can they take boards when they are doing geometry and algebra that we have done before? It's just that everything has been lowered. All you have to do is sit in your seat and you can pass."

When Lisa sat down, Trudy slapped her on the back. "Hey," she said. "You really handed it to old Murph!" Lisa glowed. She'd done better than she expected to.

Then another student, Bobby Stearns, stepped to the microphone, carrying a pile of tattered textbooks. "These are the books we are learning out of," he said. "It's really hard to learn out of something like this." Stearns displayed one particularly scruffy volume, *The Origin of Mankind*. Its cover was falling off, many of its pages were ripped. The committee examined it with distaste, then handed it to Bob Murphy, who said, "To the best of my knowledge this book has been phased out. This must be a random copy that was around on the bookshelf or something." When Stearns conceded that he had picked the book off a counter in the English room, Murphy said with a broad smile, "I think you can go to any school and find old books lying around." Lisa was furious. She'd stood up to Murphy and come away looking like a winner. Then Stearnsie had blown the whole thing.

The humiliation, the sense that their new campaign was foundering, the conviction that nobody took them seriously—all these feelings converged three days later. At 9:40 a.m., some one hundred white students assembled outside the school office. Moving en masse along the second- and third-floor corridors, they flung open classroom doors, calling on the whites inside to join them. Then they began a sit-in on the main staircase. When Captain Mac-Donald ordered them to move, they broke into a derisive chorus of "Old MacDonald Had a Farm." But when a detachment of Charlestown police arrived, the demonstrators retreated upstairs. By then, the black students had been consolidated in several classrooms on the upper floors. "Let's get the niggers!" someone shouted, and the whites surged toward the third floor.

On the landing at the top of the stairs, they encountered a half dozen teachers and aides, arms locked to form a human barrier. Among them was a black history teacher named Bill Thomas, who was something of a celebrity at Charlestown High. Once a star fullback at Boston College, he'd been the Dallas Cowboys' No. 1 draft pick in 1972, but his promising football career was cut short by disabling injuries. Quitting football in 1974, he returned to Boston to teach school. At six feet three and 210 pounds, Bill Thomas was an imposing obstacle on the landing that morning.

But the demonstrators on the stairway gave no sign of being intimidated. As they tried to force their way through the barrier, something happened. Later, investigators had difficulty sorting out conflicting versions. Lisa's friend Doris, who was leading the charge, claimed that Thomas hit her in the face. Thomas said Doris hit him in the chest. Several eyewitnesses thought Doris collided inadvertently with Thomas' elbow and, believing she had been hit, struck out at him. In any case, several white youths promptly rallied to Doris' aid, assaulting Thomas and flinging him down the stairway, where he was pulled to safety by police.

Word quickly spread through the school that a black teacher had attacked a white girl. Within minutes, some two hundred whites had gathered in front of the school office, demanding that Thomas be arrested, but this action quickly produced another martyr to the cause. Police waded into the demonstrators and, after a brief scuffle, emerged with Pat Russell's sixteen-year-old son, Kevin. As Kevin was led to a paddy wagon, bleeding from the nose, he complained that three officers had held him while a fourth beat him around the head.

That brought Pat Russell rushing to the school, where she began issuing orders. "Okay, kids," she said. "They made their mistake when they attacked my Kevin. Now, everybody, sit down and don't make a move! Nobody's going to get out of this goddamned building today." The two hundred students sat down, blanketing the main stairway, blocking passage in and out.

In the library, Bob Murphy conferred with Deputy Superintendent John Kelly, District Superintendent John McGourty, and Captain MacDonald. Murphy and MacDonald wanted to call in the TPF, but, worried about community reaction, John Kelly warned that police overreaction could only make matters worse. As they debated what to do, a car pulled up out front and Pixie Palladino rushed through the front door. Informed that some officials wanted to eject the students, the School Committeewoman flew into a rage. "You can't do that," she shouted. "These are my kids. They're just expressing their First Amendment rights. I don't want anyone to touch them."

In a system where the School Committee had the last word, Pixie had just delivered it. The students stayed where they were. Hour after hour, they camped on the stairway, running through their usual repertoire of patriotic songs and random chants of "Bushboogies, back to Africa!" and "Niggers suck!"

Lisa McGoff was aware that the black kids, locked into classrooms on the third and fourth floors, could hear the chanting, and in a way she felt sorry for them. They probably didn't want to be in Charlestown any more than the Townies wanted them there. But the battle was bigger than all of them—it was a fight over principle, over who controlled this school. Nobody was listening to them; the judge, the Superintendent, the newspapers and TV were all taking the black kids' side. The Townies had to do something to make people wake up, so Lisa joined in the songs and chants which echoed up the stairwell.

Shortly after noon, she noticed police taking up positions around the lobby. Suddenly, there was a cry from outside: "They're getting away!" Lisa and a few others raced around the corner, only to see the buses filled with black kids disappearing down the hill. The boys heaved rocks after them, but Lisa turned and walked away, feeling outmaneuvered once again.

The next day, fifty white students met at the Harvard-Kent School to consider their next move. They wanted revenge, but the old tactics didn't seem to be working; they needed something new. Finally somebody came up with an idea: if they couldn't block the stairway, surely they could sit in their own classrooms. If the police came, they should insist on being arrested.

As often happened, though, someone warned Bob Murphy of what they were up to. Over the weekend, the headmaster prepared carefully for the demonstration. On Monday morning, as the students arrived at school, each was handed a directive warning that "all students must attend their regularly scheduled classes or leave the building on request of the school administration." Students who failed to comply were "subject to police action." The warning was largely ignored. When the bell rang for the first period, most of the white students sat still, refusing to leave their homerooms. But Murphy was ready for that. Accompanied by John McGourty, Captain MacDonald, and several aides, he went from classroom to classroom, asking each student either to go to class or to leave the building.

At first the students were full of bravado, daring Murphy to bring on the police. But as the lengthy process dragged on, their resolve wore down and most of them agreed to leave the building. Only six insisted on arrest.

As one of the demonstration's organizers, Lisa was determined to go to jail. When Murphy and his team reached her homeroom, she stared stonily ahead of her, and when the headmaster began asking questions, she answered in monosyllables.

"Is this your homeroom, Lisa?" Murphy asked.

"Yes."

"Will you go to your first-period class?"

"No."

"Well then, will you leave the building with one of these aides?"

"No."

Captain MacDonald took over. "Lisa," he said, "you are trespassing in a public school. That is a crime for which you can be arrested. Do you still refuse to leave quietly?"

"Yes."

MacDonald nodded and left the room. Lisa's face burned. Her hands trembled. She'd done it—she was actually going to be arrested.

But when the door opened again, it wasn't the uniformed policemen she expected, but juvenile detective Nick Minichiello, an old family friend, who came over to her and said, "Lisa, honey, do you know what you're doing? If you go through with this, you're going to have a police record for the rest of your life. That's a serious matter. Your mother will never forgive me if I let you get a record. Now come on, you've made your point. Let me walk you out of here."

Nick's familiar voice brought her back to reality. For a moment, she hesitated; she'd sworn to hold out to the end. Moreover, her own resolve had persuaded friends to join the demonstration, perhaps to get arrested too. But Nick was right: this was a futile gesture which would follow her as long as she lived. As apprehension overcame chagrin, she allowed the detective to lead her from the school.

Outside, an icy drizzle fell over Breed's Hill. Lisa stood in the lee of the school, brooding over the collapse of their plan. She was furious at herself for caving in, still angrier at the authorities for refusing to let them make their case. By then, more than a hundred whites were milling about in the rain, muttering with rage and frustration. When the six arrested kids were brought out to a paddy wagon, the crowd cheered lustily; and when the wagon headed downtown, the demonstrators set off after it, a bedraggled column scuffling through the muck. At the District 1 station house in Government Center, however, police wouldn't let them assemble, citing the danger of heavy icicles falling from the Kennedy Federal Building across the street.

"Let's go see the Mayor," someone shouted. It was one thing they hadn't tried, so off they marched to City Hall, where Louise Day Hicks ushered them into the City Council chamber, served them hot chocolate, and soon returned with Kevin White.

It was a heady moment for Lisa as she rose to tell the Mayor of Boston what was happening at Charlestown High. Once more she ran through the familiar litany of demands and grievances, adding several new ones for the occasion: the School Department's "refusal to permit our peaceful demonstration this morning," "the unjustified arrest of six students," and "several acts of police brutality last week." She concluded: "Mr. Mayor, your wife is from Charlestown. She knows what it's like to be a Townie and have everything stacked against you. Ask her whether she would put up with what we've had to go through. Please, Mr. Mayor, help us!"

When she finished, the Mayor said, "Thank you, Miss McGoff. My wife understands—and I understand—how you feel. Believe me, I will do everything I can to help you. But you have to understand the limits of my authority. The School Department doesn't report to me. I have no responsibility whatsoever for busing, which has been ordered, as you know, by a federal district judge. Nor do I control the police in such matters. Only school officials can call police into their buildings. Certainly I will look into your charges of police brutality. If I find the police are guilty, I can assure you they will be disciplined. But I have no way of dealing with most of your grievances."

Rebuffed yet again, the white students had run out of options. Not until April 5 did they try again, this time with the notion of appealing to the ultimate authority—Judge W. Arthur Garrity himself.

Lisa, Kevin, and Tommy McGoff were among 120 whites who left Charlestown at nine that morning. Carrying American flags, Bicentennial banners, and anti-busing placards, they marched across the bridge to City Hall Plaza, where they joined 150 whites from South Boston High. After a brief meeting with Mrs. Hicks in the City Council chambers, they left for the Federal Courthouse, where they hoped to present their grievances to the judge.

At that moment, Ted Landsmark was hurrying across the plaza, late for a meeting at City Hall. The route which had taken him to that place was an unlikely one for a black man reared in a Harlem tenement. Born Theodore August Burrell, the son of a New York subway conductor, he showed early academic promise and, after graduating from Stuyvesant High in 1963, applied to Yale. The college turned him down, but it was sufficiently impressed to arrange a "transitional year" at St. Paul's, the New Hampshire prep school, where he learned to play hockey and read J. D. Salinger. Admitted to Yale in 1964—one of 16 blacks in a class of 1,090—he found the ratio unsettling and took two years off before earning his B.A., followed by a joint law and architecture degree from Yale Law School. By then, prestigious law firms throughout the country were looking for young blacks with his credentials. While at Yale, he had married the daughter of a white Massachusetts surgeon, so he accepted an offer from the distinguished Boston firm of Hill & Barlow.

But something was eating at Theodore Burrell. His adoption by the white establishment left him well connected but disinherited. Welcome in New Haven courtyards, Boston clubs, and New York boardrooms, he was no longer at home in the streets of black America. Seeking some part of his heritage with which to identify, he found it in his maternal grandfather, a West Indian Garveyite named Landsmark. As he left for Boston in 1973, he changed his name to Theodore Landsmark.

That was only the beginning of rapid disenchantment with his brave new world. A social chasm divided him from his prosperous white in-laws. His marriage ended in divorce. Hill & Barlow seemed too stiff, too white, too elitist. All this culminated in a visit to his ancestral homeland, the Caribbean island of St. Kitts, where he lunched with the black governor and met dozens of black doctors, lawyers, and bankers, plainly in control of their lives. Returning to Boston, he hailed a cab at Logan Airport. When the white driver asked where he was going, he gave an address on predominantly black Chester Square. The driver nodded, but when Landsmark turned to get his bags, the cab sped off.

In March 1974, he quit Hill & Barlow, becoming executive director of the Contractors' Association of Boston, a black trade association which sought a greater share of construction contracts for minority builders. At 10:00 a.m. on April 5, 1976, he was scheduled to chair a community liaison meeting at the Boston Redevelopment Authority. When he couldn't find a parking space and had to leave his car a quarter mile away, he knew he was going to be late, so he steamed along, heading for a side entrance to City Hall. Passing the New England Merchants Bank and entering the plaza, he saw a group of young whites rounding the corner of City Hall, moving toward the Federal Courthouse, brandishing banners and placards. Before he could reach the City Hall steps, someone yelled, "There's a nigger! Get him!"

The first student hit him from the rear, knocking his glasses off. He tried to right himself, but a second blow from the front brought him to the ground. Other students moved in, kicking him in the ribs, the shoulders, the head. He struggled to his feet, but someone grabbed him around the neck and pulled him down again. Once more he got up. Then he saw a student carrying an American flag on a long staff. Advancing across the plaza, the kid leveled the staff like a spear, as if to impale him. It struck him a glancing blow on the face.

Finally, Landsmark broke free, managing to reach the City Hall steps, where a policeman came to his aid. A moment later they were joined by Deputy Mayor Jeep Jones, who, along with Kevin White, had watched the attack from an upstairs window.

Lisa, Kevin, and Tommy McGoff had been among the stragglers rounding the corner of City Hall. Lisa had looked up in astonishment to see the black man in his three-piece suit walking toward them, and she had watched in horror as some of her Townie friends beat and kicked him. Instinctively fleeing the violence, she ran across the side plaza, hiding behind a wall which skirted the bank and adjacent travel agency. As she huddled there, face in hands, she felt like weeping—from pure shock, from fear, from dismay at the terrible thing happening in front of her. And she understood immediately that whatever was going on out there could only damage the cause she believed in.

She hoped the black man wasn't hurt seriously, but she didn't feel much sympathy for him; in fact, her first thought was: This has to be a trick, because no black guy in his right mind would walk smack into the middle of an anti-busing demonstration. He must have done it on purpose, bopping along like that, almost as if he were saying, Hey, come and get me, beat the shit out of me, so you'll look like a bunch of white racist pigs. If that was his plan, she thought, they'd fallen right into it.

Charlestown took much of the blame for the attack. When the police arrested four youths, two of them proved to be Townies: a fifteen-year-old juvenile whose name has never been released and Eddie Irvin, seventeen, vice-president of Charlestown High's junior class.

Lisa knew Eddie Irvin well. Although enrolled in the electrical course, he was active throughout the school. A funny guy who clowned around a lot, Eddie liked to boast of how tough he was, but she'd never detected a mean streak in him, never seen him commit a violent act before. That morning on City Hall Plaza he must have felt his bluff being called. Kicking a guy while he was down was no way to prove one's manhood, Lisa conceded, but Eddie was essentially a good guy who was going to get strung up for one stupid act. Moreover, he was a Townie, a kid from her class. So Lisa attended all the court proceedings in his trial for assault, and when he was convicted—and given a one-year suspended sentence—she felt bad for him.

Ted Landsmark hadn't anticipated what would happen to him on City Hall Plaza that morning, but once it happened, he was determined that Boston extract the full lesson. Not unwilling to become the city's black martyr—a twentieth-century Crispus Attucks—he appeared at press conferences and interviews with broad white bandages covering his broken nose and face lacerations (it had taken eight stitches to close his cuts). Relentlessly, he drove home his message: if a Yale-educated lawyer in a three-piece suit could be attacked on his way into City Hall, then what black was safe in Boston?

The incident's impact was magnified by a remarkable picture taken that morning by a *Herald American* photographer. It showed the white student advancing across the plaza, the Star-Spangled Banner billowing in a breeze, the flagstaff leveled at Landsmark's chest. The picture appeared on front pages across the country and went on to win that year's Pulitzer Prize for news photography. In America's Bicentennial year, its symbolism required no commentary.

18

Diver

The mail was splayed across the hallway floor. Returning from work on a muggy July afternoon, Joan Diver stooped to retrieve it, then sank onto the couch to sort through the stack. Ripping open a small envelope marked "Boston Public Schools," she read: "Official student notification: Bradford Diver is assigned for the school year 1974–75 to the Carter School, 496 Northampton Street."

There had to be some mistake; it made no sense. Brad was attending the Bancroft, an elementary school scarcely two blocks away on Appleton Street. Although, strictly speaking, the Divers weren't in the Bancroft district (the district line ran down the middle of West Newton Street), they and fifteen other families in that slice of the South End had routinely sent their children to the school under the city's "open enrollment" program. For the Bancroft was a most unusual school, an experiment in ungraded, unstructured education, wrenched from a skeptical school system by a group of determined South Enders. Now, after years of skirmishing, the department finally seemed reconciled to the aberration. Moreover, since the South End was the most diverse neighborhood in the city, the Bancroft was one of the few schools in the system already naturally integrated—whites, blacks, Hispanics, and Chinese attended in something very close to their citywide percentages—and the parents had been assured by their friends in the State Education Department that the Bancroft would therefore be exempt from Charlie Glenn's racial balance plan. Since June, when Arthur Garrity had accepted Glenn's plan as the basis of his Phase I order, they felt confident that the judge's decree would leave their children untouched.

Now Brad was to be shunted from the Bancroft to the Carter, of all places, a makeshift school assembled in 1971 from portable classrooms to alleviate overcrowding in the heart of Lower Roxbury's black community. It was eight long blocks away; to get there, seven-year-old Brad would have to walk down

Columbus Avenue, past the Methunion Manor housing project and a line of ramshackle tenements, then across the notorious intersection of Massachusetts Avenue, sometimes called "the drug capital of New England."

As she sat in the fading light of that summer afternoon, holding the notice in her hand, Joan smoldered; it seemed so silly, so pointless, so unfair. And as she told Colin about it when he got home from work an hour later, he slammed his briefcase down on the dining-room table.

Racial equality had remained one of Colin's passionate concerns. For a decade he had followed Boston's school wars with mounting sympathy for the embattled blacks. Only three months earlier, he had watched in distaste as thousands of white demonstrators swarmed across the Common demanding repeal of the Racial Imbalance Act, and after urging the Governor to stand fast, he had been dismayed when Frank Sargent opted for a discredited "freedom of choice" plan. But six weeks later his chagrin had turned to satisfaction as Arthur Garrity cut through the State House debate, finding a clear violation of constitutional rights, and adopting the racial balance plan as a first-stage remedy. He had read the judge's massive opinion, relishing—as only another lawyer could—the richness of its research, the logical ordering of its arguments, the craftsmanship with which Garrity had marshaled his judicial precedents. At last, Colin thought, the full weight of the federal courts had been thrown behind black demands for racial justice in Boston.

But precisely because he knew the history of the battle so well, Colin found Brad's assignment inexplicable. The racial imbalance law had been designed to reduce the heavy concentration of Boston blacks in crowded, inadequate ghetto schools by mixing them with white students huddled in their own overwhelmingly white schools. Colin and Joan had once lived in Brighton, one of the city's white neighborhoods. They had looked at houses in other such communities—Beacon Hill, the Back Bay, and Charlestown—where the schools were almost completely white. Instead, they had chosen to live in Boston's only integrated neighborhood and to send their children to a fully integrated school. Now they, and others who had made the same decision, were being penalized. Here was Charlie Glenn's plan, which affected fewer than half the city's schools, breaking up the Bancroft! What purpose, Colin asked himself, could possibly be served by tearing apart precisely the kind of school that Glenn and Garrity were supposed to be fostering?

Colin was still seething when he went to work the next morning. He had left the state administration that May to manage Bill Cowin's campaign for Attorney General. They had set up a small office on Boylston Street, from which they were waging a shoestring effort as the underdogs in a three-way race. When Colin told Bill what had happened, his friend couldn't resist a few gentle jabs. "Ah ha!" he exclaimed. "The brave urban liberal hoist by his own petard!"

"Get off my back, Bill," Colin growled.

"No, really, this is funny," Bill went on. "All these years you're the big liberal, the dedicated city guy, going to change the world. Then the first time they put the screws on you, you're just like anybody else."

Bill was enjoying himself, as he often did, at Colin's expense, a loose irreverence central to their friendship. But his teasing that morning had a cutting edge. Bill was no less supportive of Garrity's order than Colin was, but he would never have chosen to live in the city, certainly not in a crazy neighborhood like the South End, and he had always been somewhat skeptical about Colin's insistence on living out the implications of his urban liberalism.

Colin was stung. He knew that he and Joan had options which few other city dwellers enjoyed, and perhaps they were guilty at times of seeking to preserve their advantages at the expense of their ideals. But not this time. The Bancroft was the most thoroughly integrated school in Boston, probably more integrated than the Carter would ever be. In objecting to Brad's school assignment, the Divers weren't seeking to avoid integration; of that, Colin was certain.

It was a potent argument, one which the Bancroft parents skillfully mobilized in their struggle that summer to get the school assignments reversed. Only fifteen or so families out of about 150 in the school had been affected by the shift to the Carter, but they included some of the most active participants in the Bancroft experiment. The others rallied around them, barraging school officials and Garrity's clerks with petitions, letters, phone calls, and personal visits. Joan Diver—who had delivered a petition that spring asking that the Bancroft be preserved intact—weighed in again with calls to friends in city and state government. Eventually, the parents' hard work and good connections paid off. Late in August, a letter arrived from the School Department stating that any student who had attended the Bancroft the year before would be permitted to return in 1974–75.

The Divers, of course, were enormously relieved. Here was a victory, they thought, not only for common sense and justice, but for the vision of the South End community which they and the other young professionals had cherished. Indeed, the Bancroft was a cornerstone of the New South End; without it, or something very like it, the Divers might never have moved there, and unless it could be preserved they would find it difficult to remain.

By the late 1960s, many Boston parents regarded the public schools as a hostile environment, a rigid, authoritarian structure ruled by shriveled spinsters and timeserving bureaucrats. This perception had originated in the black community, an outgrowth of its long, wearying battle with the School Committee. By 1966, many black parents had abandoned hope of getting a decent education for their children in the public schools and had begun to search for alternatives. Some, like Rachel Twymon, turned to the Catholic schools. Others sent their children to the white suburbs under the Metco program. Still others formed "free schools," private academies run by black parents but funded by white foundations so that needy students could attend free of charge. The first of Boston's free schools was the New School for Children, which opened in Roxbury in the fall of 1966 with Jonathan Kozol—late of the Gibson School—as its guiding spirit. Quickly three other black free schools sprang up in Boston.

The blacks' distrust of the public schools soon converged with a similar brand of white suspicion. Even more than blacks, the young professionals who had staked out a beachhead in the South End in the mid-sixties expected a great deal from education. Most of them were products of suburban school systems or New England private schools who had gone on to college and then to graduate school. When they turned their backs on their parents' suburban world, their chief misgiving was usually the public schools. Few had school-age children when they began restoring their dilapidated rooming houses, but they realized that it was only a matter of time before they would need a decent school. The problem was particularly acute in the South End, where the public schools were notoriously bad.

One night in August 1967, two dozen young professionals gathered in a Union Park town house to consider founding a private school. As they haggled over curriculum, Susan Thomas whispered to Piers Lewis, "If we put a fraction of this energy into a public school, I bet we could make it into what we want." Lewis blurted out her proposal and others quickly agreed. Someone suggested that the nearby Charles E. Mackey School might be receptive since its implacably orthodox principal was being replaced by a more flexible man.

From that meeting grew a group called Friends of the Mackey, and when the new principal, Francis Xavier Murphy, arrived that September, Susan Thomas was there to offer him help. Soon a dozen South End volunteers went to work at the Mackey, helping to establish a library, serving as tutors and teacher's aides. Quietly they worked to transform the school, encouraging good teachers and supporting fresh ideas. But they had to tread carefully, for they lacked official standing, either as teachers or as parents.

Late that winter they began recruiting families with children already at the school to form a second group: the Mackey Parents' Association. The driving force among the parents was Albie Davis—wife of City Budget Director Dave Davis, who had introduced Colin to the South End—a strong-willed woman determined to provide something better for her children.

Their strategy evolved into something very like the "good cop–bad cop" technique of police interrogation. Friends of the Mackey remained sympathetic allies of the school, doing everything they could to assist Frank Murphy and his overworked staff, while the Mackey Parents' Association were more openly aggressive, demanding immediate measures to improve their children's education.

They knew what they didn't want, but what kind of school did they expect the Mackey to be? It was still the sixties, a heady time in America when everything seemed possible. A committee that met that year decided that its object was "not just to make the Mackey a better school but to make it a Model Urban School."

Among its goals:

"That teachers and all school personnel show respect for the dignity and potential of each child.

"Such respect means that the authoritarian atmosphere of the public school and its emphasis on strict discipline must be replaced by an emphasis on self-discipline and responsibility.

"Children must be encouraged to go beyond the present limited expectations to the extent of their interests and abilities.

"In other words, each child must be treated as an individual with his own strengths and weaknesses. Only when these conditions are present can true enjoyment of learning be fostered; and only then can children grow to be truly productive members of their community."

Many of the parents' ideas were drawn from the literature of "open education." A loose bundle of educational techniques whose roots went back to Rousseau and Tolstoy, it stood, in almost every particular, 180 degrees from traditional public education. A teacher in an "open classroom" was less an authority figure than a facilitator and experimenter; instead of desks lined up before a blackboard, the "open classroom" was divided into several areas in which children could work individually or in groups on whatever interested them; the standard graded classroom was replaced by broader groupings—grades 1–3, for example—in which younger children often learned as much from older students as they did from the teacher; instead of being assigned pages from a textbook, students were given a wide choice from a variety of materials; traditional decor gave way to a riot of colors and textures, with paintings, games, tools, and other objects displayed on walls and counters; rigid schedules, fixed periods, bells, and recesses were replaced by a continuous stream of activity in which students were encouraged to make their own decisions.

To most principals, "open education" was anathema, the worst sort of professional heresy. But not to Francis Xavier Murphy. A native of Charlestown who had gone on to Boston Latin and Harvard, Murphy didn't shrink from innovation. When Albie Davis asked him for four open classrooms in the Mackey, he consented so long as they found four teachers to teach them. In September 1969 the "open education" program began in two classrooms at the Mackey and two at the adjacent George C. Bancroft School, an annex previously used for bilingual classes. One hundred students were enrolled and the South End's experiment in model urban education was underway.

It wasn't an independent school yet, just the Mackey's "ungraded program"; but already it was something more than a school, a community enterprise capable of attracting extraordinary commitment. Suddenly, it had more volunteers than it could use. Five parents served with two teachers on the Managing Committee, which made most of the decisions on how the program was to be run. Parents led neighborhood walking tours, taking students on expeditions to the firehouse, the Flower Mart, the Cathedral, and Blackstone Park, ending with cocoa and cookies at someone's house. Other parents taught courses in weaving, pottery, bicycle repair, leatherwork, drama, poetry, and philosophy.

As its reputation spread, the program had more applicants than it could accommodate in four classrooms. Murphy added a fifth room and moved all five open classes into the Bancroft building, where henceforth it was known as the "Bancroft Program."

Their appetites whetted, the parents focused on a new problem: the plight of children soon to complete their Bancroft education only to be plunged into the city's junior high schools. Serving adolescents who were just beginning to rebel against authority, Boston's junior highs were tumultuous, sometimes violent places. Bancroft parents had ample reason for wishing to extend their program to the seventh and eighth grades.

They had Murphy's blessing, but there was no space for additional classrooms. When their gaze fell on the adjacent Rice Building, then occupied by a language center teaching English to immigrants, veteran school officials denied their request for room there—the department was hardly inclined to bend yet another rule for the South End's troublesome young professionals.

That didn't deter the parents. On the opening day of school in 1971, twenty mothers went to the Mackey, where Albie Davis told Murphy, "Frank, we've waited long enough. We're going to form our own junior high." Then they marched a block to the Rice Building and into a first-floor classroom, empty except for a white-haired woman named Madeleine Reilly, a former chairwoman of the Boston School Committee, now a teacher at the language center. Taking hammers and screwdrivers from their handbags, the mothers began unbolting desks from the floor. "You can't do that!" Mrs. Reilly shouted, but the women didn't stop until they had moved every desk and chair—symbols of the traditional curriculum they rejected—into the street.

Mrs. Reilly summoned William Mellen, director of the center, who called school officials, demanding that police be sent in to evict the mothers. But the officials—knowing how much political clout the Bancroft parents could muster—declined to intervene, and over the next few days, the mothers transformed the drab classroom. From their homes they brought a rug, floor lamps, and paintings. Later came puzzles, games, and toys. In late September, the Bancroft's new junior high opened in the "liberated classroom."

The raid on the Rice was the talk of the South End that fall, a dazzling piece of guerrilla theater that served, like a neon sign, to draw neighbors' attention to the gutsy little school in their midst. But Joan and Colin Diver had been aware of the Bancroft for some time.

Like so many of their class who had settled in the South End, the Divers had regarded the Boston public schools as the principal peril of their new environment. "What in the world are you going to do with the kids?" a college classmate had asked Joan shortly before the move, and the Divers took the question seriously. It was one thing to sacrifice themselves for what they believed in, quite another to sacrifice their children.

The short-term problem had been solved when they learned about the John

Winthrop Nursery School, a private school in the Back Bay where many of the new South Enders sent their children. It was the kind of innovative institution the Divers had feared would be unavailable in the city—a nursery, kindergarten, and day-care service which, for a time, met their needs perfectly. But at best it was a temporary expedient. In the long run, the Divers knew, they couldn't afford private schools. Moreover, they didn't really approve of them. Except for Colin's year at Deerfield, a concession to his class-conscious father, both were products of public education, and they shared Horace Mann's vision of the common school, in which all segments of American society were educated together. One reason urban schools were so bad, they believed, was that so many educated middle-class parents took their children out; they weren't going to make the situation any worse than it already was.

But even before they moved to West Newton Street in August 1970, the Divers had reason to believe that they wouldn't have to send Brad and Ned to private school. They had heard intriguing accounts of changes underway at the Mackey, reports quickly confirmed by sympathetic neighbors. Many children who had completed kindergarten at the John Winthrop had gone on to the Bancroft, with impressive results. In October 1972—a year before Brad would be ready for the first grade—Joan arranged to sit in on the school's primary classes.

Lois Varney's classroom was unlike anything Joan had ever seen before. The walls were covered with brilliant tapestries, Japanese cloth fish hung from clotheslines, and jugs of wildflowers brightened the bookshelves. The room pulsed with excitement. When the excitement threatened to become excessive, Lois shrewdly calmed her pupils with recorded music or round-robin songs. Joan was so pleased with what she saw that at once she enrolled Brad in Lois' class for the following year.

Joan knew Brad needed a sensitive teacher. A cautious child, he would dip his toes in the swirling waters of life before taking a plunge. Their first winter in the South End, he had spent his afternoons sitting at the window of his room, assessing the situation on the street below; only after months of observation did he venture out to make friends. When Colin bought him his first bike, Brad refused for weeks to get on it, waiting until he felt he was ready. Then one day when he was home sick and all the other kids on the block were at school, he went out and learned to ride. Once he had confidence in himself, he could handle almost anything, but Joan knew that if a teacher pushed him too hard, he would only get frustrated and turn off school.

Lois Varney handled him deftly, never applying pressure, letting him take his time and feel his way into things. Gradually, Brad came out of his shell. One day, Lois' students put on a little play for their parents. Brad played a duck, waddling around the room, quacking and squawking. Joan and Colin were delighted.

When Brad was reassigned to the Carter, the Divers dreaded losing Lois' gentle touch; when the assignment was reversed, Joan pledged to work still harder for the school. By late 1974, the parents were preoccupied with how the Bancroft would be treated in Arthur Garrity's Phase II plan. All that winter and spring, Joan worked with the other parents, writing letters, circulating petitions, and calling on officials to urge that the school be preserved intact.

Garrity's masters and experts admired the Bancroft for "its exceptional achievement of quality desegregated education." As dean of Boston University's School of Education, Bob Dentler had supplied the Bancroft with student teachers, knew many of its founders, and admired its brand of education. But the masters envisioned only two kinds of schools: district schools, to which all students would be rigidly assigned by geocode; and magnet schools, offering special programs, drawing applicants from throughout the city, and guaranteeing only a quarter of their seats to the district in which they were located. The Bancroft could make a good claim for either status. Open education was a special program which should attract students from other neighborhoods. But the program had been founded by South End parents, enlisted enormous community support, and gained much of its character from the neighborhood.

An early plan drawn by the School Department had granted the Bancroft magnet status, and Bob Dentler was inclined toward that solution, since it would maintain the principle of voluntary selection; any parents choosing the Bancroft would presumably want an open education for their children. But since a magnet would exclude some, perhaps many, of the students already in the program, Dentler decided to solicit the parents' opinions. Which designation did they prefer?

To the parents, it was an unpalatable choice; they could have either their cherished program or their beloved community, but not both. Many of them resented such alternatives. Why *couldn't* they have both? one outraged mother asked Dentler. The dean bridled. He'd done everything he could for the Bancroft, but he was growing impatient with its endless demands for special status. No one school could be exempted from "root-and-branch desegregation," which had to be enforced uniformly across the city. "Look," Dentler explained, "we're like a restaurant with two kinds of ice cream on the menu— strawberry and vanilla. A customer may want pistachio, but he can't have what isn't on the menu."

In mid-February, the parents gathered at the school to make their choice. Colin and Joan were deeply torn. If they opted for a district school, some families assigned to the Bancroft might not be in sympathy with its educational style. But what good would a magnet program do the Divers and other South Enders if their kids were assigned elsewhere? Reluctantly, they voted with the majority to become a district school.

The judge acted accordingly, but his May 10 plan abruptly eliminated the Bancroft's hard-won junior high classes. Once more the parents mobilized. Letters flooded into Garrity's chambers, this time accompanied by appealing photographs of the school's pupils. Finally, on June 5, the judge reversed himself. As a special concession to its unique program and thorough integration, the Bancroft was the only school in the system permitted to remain kindergarten-through-eighth grade. The parents celebrated, their children wrote thank-you notes to Garrity, and the Bancroft adjourned for the summer, convinced it had fared extremely well.

A month later, 90 of its 175 returning students received notices assigning them elsewhere, while 140 new students were designated for the school. The parents were stunned. Only weeks before, parent representatives had spoken with Bob Dentler, who had assured them that the Bancroft district would be drawn so that the maximum number of students would be retained. Now the court had substantially reshaped the district. Most of the white middle-class families in the "gentrified" sections of the South End remained, but the plan excluded the district's former black neighborhoods, Methunion Manor and other buildings north of Columbus Avenue, replacing them with several housing projects in adjacent Lower Roxbury. As a result, while most white students were happy with their assignments, most black families who had wanted the Bancroft's open education were to be supplanted by blacks who did not.

On August 5, the Bancroft's Managing Committee sent Garrity a heartfelt appeal: "We have spent much time pondering why a school voluntarily integrated for six years by children of mixed races from the same neighborhood who sought a particular type of instruction would be torn apart in the name of integration. . . . Please, Judge Garrity, do not destroy what we have all tried so hard to build!" The committee urged Garrity to transfer thirty students whose families had voiced objections to open education and to readmit forty former students. The judge declined.

The Divers got the assignments they wanted—Brad was among the white children remaining at the Bancroft, while Ned was to enter the primary class that fall. Nevertheless, Colin and Joan found Garrity's order dismaying, a double threat to the program they had been struggling to preserve. First, it would overwhelm the school with families hostile to its basic premises, undermining the consensus on open education which had been at the heart of the Bancroft's success. Moreover, since most of the dissenting families were black, the order threatened to erode the racial harmony that was equally central to the Bancroft experience.

Although the school's founders had been largely white and middle-class, racial integration was one of their first principles. When enrollment in the first few years threatened to become overwhelmingly white, the parents had fanned out across the South End, knocking on tenement and housing project doors, soliciting black and Puerto Rican children. And they had met with considerable success. Many blacks found the Bancroft an attractive alternative to the Irish Catholic orthodoxy of other public schools. By 1974, the school had 85 white students, 47 blacks, and 33 "other minorities" (principally Chinese and Puerto Rican).

Brad's class was evenly balanced and, once he overcame his initial shyness, he made friends with black and white classmates alike; after school, he often brought his friends home to play. Colin hung a swing in the backyard, which quickly became a favorite gathering spot for kids from the school and neighborhood; many afternoons, the Divers' house and yard were filled with

South End children—black, Hispanic, and white. Brad and Ned were particularly friendly with two black brothers, Hamilton and Gregory Williams. One day, Joan stood at her kitchen window and watched Gregory, who was somewhat older than the others, teaching Brad to pass a football. She watched Gregory wrap his long fingers around Brad's hand, showing him how to grasp the ball along its seams. And she saw the smile of delight on Brad's face as he lofted the ball into the bright autumn sunlight. What a beautiful scene! she thought. This is why we're in the city, this is what it's all about.

Occasionally, there were less pleasant scenes. One of the Bancroft's black students was Bobby Mallory, whose mother was a stripper at the Normandy Lounge in Boston's "Combat Zone." While she was at work, Bobby stayed with his godmother at 146 West Newton Street, and he was often a visitor at the Divers' house. He was an awkward, sensitive child who, having little of his own, was awed and puzzled by the relative plenty of the Diver household. Joan once found him drinking a bottle of salad oil from the refrigerator. Another time, she discovered him hunched in an easy chair before their stereo, Colin's earphones clamped to his head, frantically clicking all the dials on the amplifier. Then, one winter morning, Bobby found his mother strangled to death with her own panty hose. The murder—committed by a jealous lover she had brought home from the nightclub—became an instant *cause célèbre* at the Bancroft. As white families rallied around Bobby to ease him through his loss, the murder became an occasion to demonstrate the Bancroft's commitment to a multiracial community.

But long before the summer of 1975 there had been rumblings of racial discord at the school. Joyce King, the only black parent in Friends of the Mackey, had withdrawn early, sending her children to a black-controlled parochial school. Mrs. King—the wife of South End black activist Mel King—concluded that open education had little to offer black children. Intangibles like warmth, creativity, openness, and trust might be important for white middle-class children, she argued, but they were hardly priorities for working-class blacks. An emphasis on personal choice was fine for children with a lifetime of choices ahead of them, but not for the poor, who would need discipline and order to prevail over life's rigors. Joyce King's break with her former colleagues led to bitter recriminations on both sides, particularly after she took the floor at a 1970 meeting to tell the young professionals: "You folks keep talking about love. Well, I don't need white people to love my children. I can supply the love. What my children need is reading, writing, arithmetic, and the other tools they've got to have to compete with your children. So don't tell me any more about love."

The Kings' indictment of the Bancroft went far beyond matters of curriculum. The white middle-class settlers, they charged, were trying to make the South End—and the Bancroft—over in their own image; in effect, they had turned the Bancroft into a private school, serving their own needs and priorities. They might talk a lot about racial integration, about how much they wanted blacks and other minorities at the school, but they weren't about to give blacks any real power (the Kings dismissed the two black parents on the school's Managing Committee as "window dressing"). Moreover, the white middle-class parents could go off anytime they wanted and pay for a genuinely private education. Blacks and the poor didn't have that option; they *needed* the public schools, which shouldn't be turned into chic, elite institutions like the Bancroft.

Joan Diver knew that many blacks in the Bancroft community shared at least some of the Kings' reservations. She had sensed mute resentment from minority parents who clearly felt excluded from the inner circle which ran the school, and she could appreciate what they experienced, for even she felt shut out at times by the tight little group of founders. In the winter of 1974, she had tried to remedy the situation by setting up a meeting with black parents. When her first overture was rebuffed, she and Lois Varney concluded that it would be better if a black parent made the gesture, so they asked Dusenia Smith, a tenant at Methunion Manor, to invite black and white parents to her home. On the appointed day, Mrs. Smith was the only black to show up at her own party. For an awkward hour, Dusenia, Lois, Joan, Colin, and a few other white parents sat around with coffee cups on their knees, trying to make conversation.

The resentments ran in both directions. Joan had heard white parents complaining that teachers were giving too much attention to minority students, that their own kids were being short-changed because they could do things on their own, while black and Puerto Rican children needed constant guidance. These complaints irritated Joan, for they came from some of the very parents who had insisted that the school be integrated. How could you have integration—by race *and* class—without some discrepancies in educational background? One went with the other. Moreover, if they were serious about integration—and she was—the benefits of diversity ought to outweigh any temporary imbalance in the teachers' attention.

But if racial tension had long been simmering at the Bancroft, it was Arthur Garrity's order that summer of 1975 which brought it to a boil. For the first time, black and white parents were pitted directly against each other. Most of the white families had selected the Bancroft, supported open education, and were determined to preserve it. Most blacks that year had been assigned to the school against their will, had no vested interest in open education, and increasingly saw it as unsuited to their needs.

Even the judge's provision for a Racial-Ethnic Parents' Council exacerbated the situation. In years past, blacks and whites had served together on the school's Managing Committee with little open discord, but now Garrity required that blacks and whites meet in separate caucuses to elect members to the REPC. At first, Bancroft parents balked, arguing that such methods were appropriate only to schools being desegregated for the first time; at the Bancroft, with its long tradition of integration, caucuses could only be divisive. But the judge refused to exempt the school from his order and the parents complied. Joan Diver was one of five white parents elected to the council, and played an active role throughout the year on various administrative issues. Black parents elected a slate, but its members took little part in the council's functions, declining to take on assignments. It was as if the formation of white and black caucuses had institutionalized the school's racial impasse.

And there were those who foresaw yet another divisive consequence to Garrity's order. As gentrification swept across the South End, the new white families concentrated in a narrow strip between Columbus Avenue and Tremont Street. To the north, the area between Columbus and the railroad tracks—one of the earliest sites of Negro settlement—remained overwhelmingly black. Three of Methunion Manor's brick fortresses reared along the north edge of the avenue in grim contrast to the parks and town houses of the white enclave. The old Bancroft district had embraced both sections, blacks from Methunion Manor mixing at the school with children of white gentry. Now Garrity's aides had drawn the district's northern border down the middle of the avenue, reinforcing the significance of that boundary. In a letter that summer, the school's Managing Committee warned the judge: "The Bancroft school has been an integrating force, bringing children from both sides of Columbus Avenue together. Now that they are not allowed to attend the same school, they will not easily meet each other. This has the potential of causing future racial strife and making Columbus Avenue a barrier across which hostility may develop."

By late 1975, the Bancroft's predicament was rich with irony. Founded by parents determined to fulfill their civic obligations, the school had become an institution determined to preserve its own prerogatives. Dedicated to the proposition that children of all races and classes should be educated together, it was torn by racial and class struggles rooted in divergent concepts of what an urban education ought to be. Designed as the cornerstone of the New South End, it had become an object of contention splitting the community down the middle. Parents like the Divers were tugged first by self-interest, then by their vision of a model urban school, their motives so mixed they couldn't disentangle them.

There were times when Joan Diver wearied of the delicate balancing of private want and public weal that life in the South End demanded; at such moments, she was grateful for a career which required dispassionate judgments, with nothing personal at stake, about what was good for the community at large.

As long as she could remember, Joan had wanted to work for the poor and disadvantaged. She supposed it was something she had inherited from her father, who had nurtured it in her with a subtle blend of praise and prodding. Her first jobs, in the Radcliffe and Emerson College development offices, had done nothing to satisfy that need—raising money from "fat cat" alumnae for capital improvement wasn't her idea of humanitarian endeavor, particularly since neither college was greatly involved in the community. Joan wanted work that would have a direct impact on the lives of ordinary people.

In late 1969, nearly a year before the Divers moved to the South End, a friend suggested that she explore the foundation world, and she talked with Bert Waters, director of the Associated Foundation of Greater Boston, a recently formed league of the city's private philanthropies. No position was available, but Waters kept her name on file, and a year later he called to say that a job had opened up—part-time secretary at the Hyams Trust, Boston's second-largest foundation. In November 1970, Joan saw Bill Swift, a partner at the old Yankee law firm of Hutchins & Wheeler, who was Hyams' managing trustee. At the start it wouldn't be much of a challenge for a bright college graduate, Swift said apologetically—answering the phone, opening mail, and drawing up the agenda for board meetings, which were held every six weeks between September and June. But the board was thinking of expanding the job to include research on potential grantees.

The job seemed exactly right to Joan. With Ned barely a year old and Brad only three, she couldn't accept full-time work, but as the boys grew older, she'd be able to take on more, and she felt confident that she could handle anything the board assigned her. Moreover, she was intrigued by philanthropy on this scale—Hyams supported a broad range of community programs that confronted most of the social ills besetting Boston. She particularly liked the notion of tackling the same urban issues which Colin was addressing a few blocks away at City Hall. So, early in December 1970, Joan became the foundation's administrative assistant.

In the starchy world of Boston philanthropy, the Hyams Trust was something of an anomaly, rooted not in old Yankee money but in a relatively new Jewish fortune. The Hyamses were Polish Jews who had emigrated to Ireland in the seventeenth century and thence to Boston's South End. When Godfrey Hyams graduated from Harvard in 1881, the university gave him a position teaching mineralogy, but he was in great demand with mining interests and soon signed on with Henry Rogers' Amalgamated Copper. One of the era's most ruthless businessmen, Rogers built an empire in oil, steel, banking, and railroads, but his boldest stroke was his attempt to corner the world's copper market. Hyams was a loyal lieutenant in these wars and Rogers cut him in on the lucrative Virginian Railway. By 1910 Hyams was a multimillionaire, but perhaps because of his role in some of the period's least savory business practices, he had become virtually a recluse. For years, he maintained a small office in Room 301 of the Sears Building, with no name on the door. If visitors got past a protective secretary, they found a slight man in gold-rimmed spectacles, reticent in the extreme about his activities.

Hyams had one secret he kept hidden from even his closest confidants. He was married to a gentile, most unusual then for a Jew in his position, and he went to extraordinary lengths to conceal this aberration. He lived in a large house in Dorchester with his two unmarried sisters, Sarah and Isabel, and even they were unaware that their brother kept a wife—Mary Irene Wilson—in a rented apartment nearby.

Hyams' marriage reflected his yearning for identification with the Yankee community. His family had emigrated to Ireland so far back that he thought of himself as British, and like many Jews of similar extraction, he was eager to distinguish himself from the later waves of Russian Jews who flooded into Boston around the turn of the century.

But his sister Isabel had another life, which kept her in close touch with the less advantaged class of Boston immigrants. Among the first women to attend MIT, she conceived a passion for the new science of "public health." In 1895, she founded a settlement program in the South End to teach home economics and social hygiene to young girls, calling it the Louisa May Alcott Club, in part because the author of *Little Women* had lived for a time in the South End, where she followed a family tradition of "good works" for the poor.

But even as she taught young South Enders to cook and clean house, Isabel Hyams dreamed of a wider scope for her philanthropies, and not surprisingly, her thoughts turned to the fortune her brother was accumulating in copper and railroads. Over dinner in Dorchester she may have reminded Godfrey that the Boston Yankees they both admired generally left part of their wealth to assist less fortunate members of the community. What could better complete the Hyamses' transformation into Yankees than a family trust to benefit deserving Bostonians down through the centuries?

Godfrey liked the idea. He turned for advice to a Yankee lawyer, H. Le-Baron Sampson of Hutchins & Wheeler, who drew up a document conveying Hyams' substantial holdings in several corporations to a charitable trust. Sarah and Isabel were named as trustees, but so long as he lived, Godfrey managed the trust himself, contributing anonymously to Harvard, Massachusetts General Hospital, and other venerable institutions. On his death in 1927, the bulk of his remaining estate went into the trust, bringing it over $7 million—at that time the largest philanthropic gift ever made in Massachusetts.

The trustees soon concentrated their philanthropy on social welfare activities favored by Isabel—hospitals, clinics, settlement houses, neighborhood centers, camps, and other agencies assisting the poor and disadvantaged. Through two smaller trusts, they supported good works in East Boston and several unincorporated charities.

Like many Boston foundations, Hyams operated from the law firm which had drawn up the original trust—in this case, Hutchins & Wheeler. Between board meetings, decisions were made by Sampson, who, once Isabel and Sarah were dead, knew the benefactor's mind better than anyone. Sampson remained the foundation's managing trustee for forty-one years, relying heavily on the advice of a part-time consultant, an official of Boston's United Fund named John Moore. His only other staff were two aging women—Janet Graves, the part-time secretary, and Thetis Questrom, Godfrey Hyams' personal book-keeper, who stayed on with the trust for more than four decades. Only when Bill Swift succeeded Sampson in 1970 and Joan Diver replaced Janet Graves later that year were the solemn rhythms of the trust at last interrupted.

Joan began slowly, spending twenty hours a week in the little office tucked away in a corner of the law firm. At first, she worked from nine to one o'clock, leaving Ned with a babysitter, then hurrying back to the South End after work to pick Brad up at the John Winthrop Nursery School. When the Winthrop added a day-care service, she put in several full days a week at the office, staying home with her children on the others. Joan knew too many women who, in the name of "doing good" for society, neglected their own families, and she wasn't going to let that happen to her.

But gradually the trust absorbed more of her energies. She brought work home from the office, poring over reports as her two rambunctious boys tore around the house. She grew preoccupied with the "philanthropic dilemma": how to use the limited charitable dollars to the maximum benefit of society? Thumbing through the trust's files, she realized how perfunctory its research had been. John Moore was a well-meaning man, but he generally suggested that Hyams put its money into the stodgy, traditional charities favored by the United Fund. How much did the trustees really know about the way their money was being used? Joan asked Bill Swift if she could take a closer look at several first-time applicants: among them, the Bromley Heath Teen Cave and the Protestant Guild for the Blind. When Swift agreed, she visited each agency, observing their operations, talking with staff and clients. The board accepted her recommendations and, impressed with her initiative, expanded her duties. In January 1971—after only two months on the job—she was promoted to Assistant to the Secretary of the Trustees. At the same time, the board authorized her to hire an assistant of her own to take over the steno-graphic and custodial work, freeing her to concentrate on Hyams' grant-making procedures.

To Joan, the old Hyams Trust was symbolized by a set of panels which decorated the foundation's boardroom. Purchased by Godfrey Hyams on a trip to London, the panels were said to be copies of ones which had hung in the House of Lords. Depicting common people bowing and scraping before the King and nobility, they struck her as incredibly patronizing, the flip side of Yankee *noblesse oblige*. There was something wildly anachronistic too, she thought, about those aristocratic tableaus hanging above the trustees' heads as they deliberated on racial unrest, juvenile delinquency, teenage pregnancies, and heroin overdoses. The times had changed, the social needs of the city were different than they had been in Godfrey Hyams' day. They could no longer be addressed from the lofty reaches of traditional Boston philanthropy.

From the beginning, charity had been among the most prized of Yankee vir-tues. "We must be willing to abridge ourselves of our superfluities, for the supply of others' necessities," John Winthrop admonished his shipmates aboard the *Arbella*. And seventy years later, Cotton Mather could report with satisfaction, "For charity—I may indeed speak it without flattery—this town has not many equals on the face of the earth."

Yet, from the start, the Puritans were tortured by their own beneficence. For if, as they believed, worldly prosperity was a reward for virtue, how could they indulge the improvident? Even Cotton Mather warned Bostonians "not

[to] abuse your charity by misapplying it. The poor that *can't* work are objects for your liberality. But the poor that *can* work and *won't,* the best liberality is to make them. Find them work; set them to work; keep them to work." It was a distinction which seemed even more essential as Boston grew from a small village to a bustling seaport. It was one thing for a few hundred native-born vagrants to wander the town's dusty lanes, quite another for many thousand "destitute and desperate Papists" to swarm the tenement districts. To the Protestant gentlemen who administered the city's charitable organizations, the host of impoverished Catholics was more than a drain on their resources; it was a threat to their stable, homogeneous world. To stem these tides of disintegration, the charity reformers of the 1870s urged the city's philanthropists to alleviate "pauperism" (a pitiable state brought on by youth, age, physical or mental disability) but keep hands off mere "poverty" (a necessary condition of mankind).

This distinction was grounded in the persistent moralism of Protestant Massachusetts. For if poverty derived from a defect in character, a failure of the poor man to follow in Christ's way, then the remedy wasn't reform of social inequalities, but religious transformation. To the Reverend William Ellery Channing, the true Christian's duty was to "rescue the poor from the degrading influence of poverty, to give them generous sentiments and hopes, to exalt them from animals to men, into Christians, into children of God." When Boston's Congregational churches founded a charitable body, they called it the Boston Society for the Moral and Religious Instruction of the Poor.

Theirs was a Protestant God, so Catholic immigrants were denied the society's ministrations, unless they would convert. Others who did minister to the Irish often felt guilty about it. "Are we not building up Catholic faith on Protestant charity?" asked Abby Alcott, Louisa's mother. She preferred to assist Boston's Negroes. "This much neglected class of native Americans should be more regarded by our philanthropists," she wrote. "To me they are far more interesting than the God-invoking Irish who choke you with benedictions and crush you with curses."

Such philanthropists did not trouble themselves much about the efficacy of their methods. When the ladies of the Hollis Chapel founded a Flower Mission in 1869, they never doubted that blossoms would lighten the slum dwellers' burden. One matron reported: "As soon as the first flower was handed out, the news spread like wildfire, and the children would come in crowds from the garret and cellar for the prizes, while men, rough laborers, would stop and beg—more humbly than children—for 'just one flower, Miss.'"

By the late nineteenth century, though, another movement was underway which sought to make charity more effective. "Scientific philanthropy" was as intent as the earlier movement on distinguishing "honest need" from "mere pathos," but it did so by applying empirical techniques borrowed from the physical sciences. "Data" would be gathered and analyzed, "hypotheses" tested and revised, until a body of "sound, scientific principles" evolved. A new social science came into existence, at first called "philanthropology," later—more modestly—"social work."

Boston's principal outpost of the new science was Robert Woods's South End House, which occupied a brick town house on one of the district's parks. There Woods presided over a dozen university graduates, most of whom were middle-class Yankees raised with a sense of social obligation. Woods regarded South End House as "a sort of shaft sunk into the thickest part of society with a view of studying the various strata." The young workers would advance by "patient experimental action, leaving aside the sentiments of pity and mercy which have been outworn by the spread of democratic ideas." And they would no longer seek the cause of poverty in a poor man's character, but in his environment. "The real trouble," wrote Woods, "is that people here are from birth at the mercy of great social forces which move almost like the march of destiny."

By late in the century, the flood of Catholics arriving in Boston was matched by the tide of Congregationalists and Unitarians ebbing toward Dover and Ipswich. Henceforth, the displaced Yankees no longer felt much responsibility for the "scourings of Europe's streets," seeking instead to preserve those institutions they still regarded as their own: Harvard, Massachusetts General Hospital, the Museum of Fine Arts, and the Symphony Orchestra.

As Boston's early mercantile energies gave way to a cautious preoccupation with preserving established fortunes, charitable trusts became the philanthropists' favorite instruments. This preference grew more pronounced after a Massachusetts judge decreed that trustees need only behave as "men of prudence," allowing Boston trustees greater latitude in investments than their counterparts elsewhere. But the provisions of such trusts—like one which provided money for a boat to deliver Sunday papers to the Boston Lightship—remained frozen forever or, as *Fortune* put it, "beyond the reach of any power but the Communist International."

By the twentieth century, so much of Boston's philanthropic wealth had fallen under the "dead hand" of irrevocable trusts, it had become difficult to meet current charitable needs. Into that vacuum, in 1915, stepped the Boston Safe Deposit and Trust Company with the notion of pooling trusts into a "community foundation"—the Permanent Charity Fund—to guarantee benefactors sound management of their money while permitting flexible adaptation to changing conditions. Boston Safe wasn't being entirely altruistic. Already the city's preeminent trust company, it would gain from the new device an even larger share of that business.

Forty-five years later—in 1959—the Permanent Charity Fund's principal was abruptly doubled. Albert Stone, Jr., an eighty-two-year-old bachelor, had lived alone in a Back Bay town house, investing in "sound common stocks." Now his bequest of $19.4 million made the Fund the country's second-largest community foundation. It could hardly have come at a more appropriate moment, for, barely a year later, John F. Kennedy was elected President, bringing with him a new determination to solve America's human problems. Armed with vastly increased resources, and challenged by the national mood, the Fund went in search of a new director, settling on Harvard's dean of admissions, Wilbur J. Bender.

It was a shrewd choice, for Bill Bender was in perfect tune with those strenuous times, having done more than anyone to transform Harvard from "a finishing school for the St. Grottlesex crowd" to a more representative institution. At the Permanent Charity Fund from 1960 to 1969, Bender displayed the same commitment to a more open society. With astonishing speed, he made the Fund a major force for social change in Boston. His critical decision was to phase out operating subsidies—once 90 percent of its grants—in favor of vastly increased support for pilot programs, demonstration projects, and other innovations. Often, the Fund supplemented, reinforced, or even prefigured Washington's social experiments. In the early sixties, for example, it presented $344,000 to Action for Boston Community Development, which became the city's anti-poverty agency, and another $250,000 for its first centers in Charlestown and Roxbury.

Philanthropists, Bender believed, should do "more than react to what comes to us." They should be "catalysts," with a "questing, questioning, non-doctrinaire openness to [their] community." In his final report—issued only months before he died in March 1969—he captured the sense of urgency which was a hallmark of that era: "The young are impatient, the poor are impatient, the mood of violence exists, and we are in a race between the ability of a lumbering, perplexed, imperfect society to move fast enough—and catastrophe."

Behind Bender's Permanent Charity Fund stood larger forces with an interest in accommodating themselves to the sixties' multiple insurgencies: liberal Harvard; the Boston *Globe,* at last awakening from its years of lethargy; the progressive wing of the Catholic Archdiocese; Irish Democrats enlisted under John Kennedy's banner; the most enlightened elements of the city's financial community, represented by the Boston Safe Deposit and Trust Company; and their allies in the Yankee law firms, like Hutchins & Wheeler, which served as counsel to Boston Safe. Those worlds converged in the person of Ralph Lowell, chairman and president of Boston Safe, who had recruited Bender for the job. Sometimes known as "Mr. Boston," Lowell was a member of Harvard's Board of Overseers, an officer or director of forty-four other corporations and institutions, including the *Globe,* as well as the dominant figure in the Vault. Of his own philosophy, he once said, "Most of us are given a great deal, in one way or another, and I believe it is our duty and privilege to return that bounty to our fellow man in whatever way our talents direct us." Not himself a Kennedy liberal—he was more of a Bull Moose Republican— Lowell felt the gales of change rushing across the harbor and, like the yachtsman he was, knew enough to put the wind at his back.

If the Permanent Charity Fund was the principal channel for such endeavors (by 1969 its endowment had reached $68 million and its annual grants totaled $2.4 million), then the Hyams Trust and its associated trusts, with assets of $38.6 million and annual grants of $1.6 million, were a respectable second. The foundations were closely linked—Boston Safe served as a trustee for both and Hutchins & Wheeler was counsel to both, with partners sitting on each board. The only foundations in town with professional staffs, by 1970 they were situated only three floors apart in Boston Safe's new bronze tower, and the traffic between their offices was heavy, for though they differed on certain issues, they shared an underlying philosophy—a curious amalgam of Puritan conscience and Yankee *noblesse oblige;* nineteenth-century scientific philanthropy and twentieth-century social work; a focus on the inner city and a cautious commitment to social change.

Not everyone in Boston's philanthropic world shared this sense of urgency about the city's social needs. Greater Boston had some 900 foundations, most of them tiny trusts, administered by banks and law firms, or relatively small corporate operations, and few of these greatly realigned their priorities during the sixties. By far the largest philanthropy in the city was the Massachusetts Bay United Fund, whose annual campaign in the late sixties was raising more than $14 million. Launched in the depths of the Depression, it was Boston's equivalent of the Community Chests and United Appeals which had consolidated public giving in communities across the country, and for years, service to the United Fund was considered *de rigueur* for public-spirited Bostonians. But, relying ever more on corporate contributions and payroll deductions, the United Fund had become increasingly dominated by business executives whose notions of charity scarcely extended beyond Boys' Clubs, Girl Scouts, and the USO. Each September, the Fund raised a four-story gas beacon called the "Torch of Hope," which burned on Boston Common until the campaign ended in mid-November. But many Bostonians placed little hope in the United Fund.

Blacks were especially disillusioned. Of the $14 million the United Fund raised in 1968, some $10 million went to the suburbs. That left $4 million for the city, of which $1.3 million was spent in the black community. But more than two-thirds of that amount was channeled through white-controlled agencies, leaving only $500,000—or 4 percent of the total—to black organizations. So skewed were the allocations, blacks argued, that the YMCA in the affluent suburb of Newton received more than the Roxbury Y in the heart of black Boston.

Black dissatisfaction came to a head in 1969, mobilized by the New Urban League. In most cities, the Urban League was a tame outfit, dedicated to improving black access to jobs and housing, but in the mid-sixties, young blacks led by the South End's Mel King seized control of Boston's League. King's imposing stature (six feet five inches), shaved skull, and dashikis made him look much fiercer than he was, and many whites found him an unnerving figure. As the League's new executive director, he sought substantially more money from the United Fund. Instead, the League's allocation was reduced: from $66,500 in 1968 to $61,500 a year later.

In October 1969, the League challenged the Fund's allocations process.

Traditionally, 45 percent of the monies raised by the Fund were handed directly to the Red Cross, the Salvation Army, Combined Jewish Philanthropies, the USO, and several large Boston hospitals, which had insisted on that arrangement in exchange for abandoning their own fund drives. The remainder went to the Fund's allocating wing—United Community Services—which distributed it to 225 Greater Boston agencies. The New Urban League labeled that process "paternalistic colonialism," because it required blacks to "shuffle" for their dollars. Henceforth, it demanded, 20 percent of the United Fund's total must go directly off the top to a black-controlled agency, which would distribute it to black institutions. The United Fund flatly refused to consider this form of "community control."

On December 18, 1969, the United Fund held its annual Awards Luncheon at the Statler-Hilton Hotel. Nearly seven hundred guests were just finishing their coconut custard pie and coffee, and Charles Francis Adams, a lineal descendant of the Adams Presidents, board chairman of Raytheon, and leader of that year's campaign, was preparing to make the awards, when thirty black members of the New Urban League filed into the vast ballroom. Taking up positions around the walls, they stood with arms folded, staring coldly at the diners. James Bishop, the League's president, strode to the platform, where, flanked by two aides in black leather jackets, he denounced the United Fund as a "racist organization that collects funds from black people and friends of black people, but can't allocate them in a way that will help black people." As he spoke, his colleagues moved through the stunned audience gathering half-eaten French rolls and pieces of coconut pie, which they tossed into a large laundry bag marked "Our Unfair Share—Black Crumbs." Then Mel King—his shaved head glistening in the ballroom spotlights—held the bag high over his head and dumped the leftovers in front of an astonished Charles Francis Adams. "We've been getting crumbs," King said. "We're no longer going to accept crumbs."

When Adams had brushed the pie off his lap, he rose to say, "There's a great deal of truth in what our black friends say. But it's not as simple as that. Our friends tend to oversimplify. I hope negotiations with the Urban League will continue, but the real solution is to increase the total we raise, rather than taking from one deserving group to give to another."

But that was precisely what the New Urban League was demanding: a shift of money from whites who needed it to blacks who needed it even more. Over the next several years, contributions to the "inner city"—a euphemism for the black community—did rise to $2.1 million, and the Fund did establish a Committee on the Inner City to consider ways of giving blacks a greater voice in their own allocations. But when negotiations reached an impasse, the Black United Front established its own United Black Appeal, seeking an annual $4 million for black institutions and agencies. The drive was launched in the middle of the United Fund's fall campaign, a point which chairman Ben Scott emphasized when he said, "We have a message to the black and the white individual who cares about urban problems and the emergency needs of the black community: Give to the Black Appeal, because the United Fund is inadequate to the growing needs of our community."

This bold attempt by Boston blacks to augment—and control—the flow of private money into their own community was the talk of Boston's philanthropic world when Joan Diver arrived at the Hyams Trust, and she felt a certain sympathy with the challenge; surely, if one considered the pressing needs of Boston's black community, it had been short-changed over the years by the major Boston philanthropies, the United Fund in particular. Joan hoped that Hyams and other private foundations could fill that gap, but as she came to know the foundation world better, she recognized that Hyams couldn't simply hand money over to the black community. The sad saga of FUND had demonstrated the dangers inherent in doing that. In the wake of Martin Luther King's assassination, FUND's white liberals had set out to raise $100 million and give it, no strings attached, to the Black United Front; in fact, it had raised barely $1 million, most of which was quickly dissipated in bad loans to small black businesses. And, within weeks of its inauguration, the United Black Appeal indicated its own unreliability when it took a $20,000 grant from Polaroid, intended for Boston's blacks, and presented it to the civil rights activists in Cairo, Illinois, and South African "freedom fighters." No, if Hyams wanted to step up its assistance to the city's black community—as Joan surely did—it would have to identify specific black agencies doing valuable work there and then fund them.

But that wouldn't be easy, Joan realized; excepting East Boston, where much of its early work had been concentrated, Hyams had little personal contact with any Boston neighborhood, much less the black community. For decades, it had remained aloof from the city it was pledged to assist. Reflecting Godfrey Hyams' own reclusiveness, the foundation published no annual reports, prohibited newspaper publicity for its grants, and discouraged visits to its offices. Many potential applicants were utterly unaware of Hyams' existence, and those who did apply had little contact with the trust. Their proposals were turned over to John Moore, whose recommendations to the board were based largely on his own experience at the United Fund. Most board members had little independent knowledge either of the communities they assisted or the agencies they funded. And there was little follow-up to determine how well the money had been used.

This time-honored procedure had worked reasonably well so long as the city's social agencies remained limited in number and applicants to the trust were old friends. But, energized by the War on Poverty and the movement for community control, new agencies were popping up every month. Determined to make the foundation more responsive and accessible, Joan published an elaborate annual report, opened channels to the press, and began meeting regularly with agency representatives, seeking more information about their operations than could be gained from written proposals. These conferences frequently took place in the foundation boardroom beneath the House of Lords panels, and one afternoon during a meeting with two young black men she noticed that they couldn't stop staring at the panels, which clearly disconcerted them. After checking with Bill Swift, she replaced the panels with stark black-and-white photographs of communities the trust was assisting: two black kids in the South End, a construction worker with a cold cigar in his mouth, an Italian woman in a North End market, black teenagers buying rhythm-and-blues records, an Irishman with a beer belly fishing in the harbor.

Gradually the new decor was matched by a shift in the trust's priorities. It has always devoted the bulk of its assistance to the city's poor and disadvantaged. Now, without abandoning the white ethnic neighborhoods, it allocated more of its resources to blacks and minorities. Meanwhile, it slowly phased out its support for some of the most conventional institutions whose needs were being amply met by other Boston philanthropies. In 1971, for example, the board had voted a $10,000 grant to the 90th Anniversary Fund of the Boston Symphony Orchestra—perhaps the most popular of all Boston charities. Two years later, instead of supporting the adult orchestra, it gave $2,000 to the Greater Boston Youth Symphony Orchestra "to support inner-city youth participation," as well as $10,000 to the Museum of Afro-American History for restoration of the African Meeting House on Beacon Hill, and $2,500 to Radcliffe College to help publish the proceedings of a conference on "The Black Woman: Myth and Realities." By the mid-seventies, about a quarter of Hyams' grants were going to agencies serving black or minority populations, while another quarter served mixed populations.

Hyams' greatest expenditure had always gone to settlement houses and other neighborhood centers—a direct legacy of Robert Woods's pioneering work at South End House. Like Jane Addams in Chicago, Woods believed that the urban poor could best be helped by strengthening their neighborhood institutions, "securing the local identity and local loyalty out of which the feeling of social responsibility springs." Appropriately enough for a philanthropy so influenced by Woods's thinking, Hyams had long supported the United South End Settlements, a social agency which had grown out of South End House. It had also helped to fund settlements in East Boston, Dorchester, South Boston, and Roxbury, and in 1971, shortly after Joan went to work, it made a major new commitment—to the Lena Park Multi-Service Center, which served the burgeoning black populations of Dorchester and Mattapan. By the mid-seventies, it was giving Lena Park $45,000 a year.

Unlike the Permanent Charity Fund, Hyams had decided to continue its annual operating grants, which were the lifeblood of places like Lena Park and United South End Settlements. Joan and Hyams' trustees debated long and hard on this issue. They could see powerful arguments for abandoning these grants to concentrate on more innovative projects, but Joan felt—and the board ultimately agreed—that because so few other foundations provided unrestricted funds, Hyams had an obligation to go on doing so. Moreover, she reasoned, such grants might in themselves become a spur to innovation. Many of the settlement houses, now called multi-service centers, were trying to develop new techniques to meet the pressing social problems of their communities, but how could they experiment with new programs unless they knew where their annual operating expenses were coming from?

After John Moore died in 1972, the trustees promoted Joan to executive director and authorized her to hire an assistant director. This allowed her to concentrate still more of her time on evaluating applicants and assessing how Hyams' money was spent. By then, she had become the linchpin of Hyams' operations.

As she made a name for herself in Boston philanthropy, she was invited to join other undertakings. Responding to mounting criticism, the Massachusetts Bay United Fund had at last gone through a major overhaul, designed, in part, to make it more responsive to "inner-city needs." In early 1973, the United Fund and United Community Services were merged into a single organization—the United Way of Massachusetts—which assembled a new set of review committees. Joan was named to the Committee on Social Services for Families, Individuals, and Children, which evaluated all applicants and recommended allocations in that area. It was a field in which she had considerable experience and quickly she became one of the committee's most influential members. She played a major role, too, in the Associated Foundation of Greater Boston, the league of philanthropies which she had first approached for a job in 1969. Founded by Bill Bender to enhance the effectiveness—and social activism—of Boston's foundations, Associated examined the city's problems and tried to nudge its thirty-two members into a coordinated approach to a solution. As the league's largest members, the Permanent Charity Fund and Hyams often set the pace, and Joan eventually was named a vice-president.

The early seventies were heady days for the Divers. Colin was rising within the Mayor's office, assuming new responsibilities, rapidly becoming one of Kevin White's principal aides. Joan was moving just as quickly at Hyams, advancing from secretary to executive director in barely three years, becoming a leading figure in Boston philanthropy. For a time they both found their work enormously rewarding, precisely the kind of service they had hoped to perform for their community. And somehow the fact that they were grappling with the same issues made it even more satisfying. At times they joked with each other about their overlapping responsibilities for the city's condition: with Colin handling the public sector, and Joan the private, how could Boston go wrong?

But they had frustrations in common too: the sheer intractability of the problems they confronted, the relative paucity of their resources, certain unintended consequences of their actions, the difficulty they faced in assisting one group without seeming to injure another.

By 1974, the three Hyams trusts made grants totaling $1,917,530—a lot of money by most people's standards, but very little indeed if one was trying to help stem the torrent of urban ills which cascaded across Joan's desk every week: alcoholism, drug abuse, mental retardation, crippling diseases, congenital handicaps, truancy, vandalism, juvenile delinquency, gang warfare, rape, overcrowded prisons, overburdened courts, deteriorated housing, ill-managed projects, broken families, wife beating, child abuse, unemployment, untrained workers, discrimination, and racial violence. Everybody had a program designed to meet one of these problems, but there simply wasn't enough money to go around.

Once Joan had hoped that Hyams could meet the needs of disadvantaged homes and deteriorating neighborhoods across the city. But gradually she had scaled down those expectations. Philanthropy was not generally effective in two areas critical to a just society—public schools and jobs. In other fields, only the federal government had the requisite resources. At best, foundations like Hyams could supplement federal spending, fill in some of the gaps, point the way toward projects which deserved government funding, and take calculated risks on a few ideas which might bear fruit.

Joan was disheartened when some of the programs for which she had the highest hopes ultimately proved unworkable. And to her chagrin, more often than not, it was the black agencies and institutions which were unable to make a go of it—not because they were black, but because the individuals involved had little experience in running such programs. Among the casualties were the Roxbury Federation of Neighborhood Centers; the Ecumenical Center in Roxbury; Open Ear Associates, a program for black alcoholics; and the Black Heritage Camp. She learned to resist the emotional tug of such programs, to look coolly at their prospects for survival. It was all very well to help a worthy black effort get off the ground, but if it didn't last out the year, the money could probably have been used more productively elsewhere.

Joan was particularly eager to find some effective instrument for easing the racial tensions which stemmed from Arthur Garrity's desegregation order. Boston's philanthropists—although generally sympathetic to the judge's stand—had remained aloof from the problem. As the Associated Foundation described its members' original position in an internal memo late in 1974: "Desegregation was perceived as a responsibility of the school system, the police, and City Hall. Because it was regarded as a racial problem, it was viewed as a problem between the Irish and black residents of Boston and one that the commuting white suburban population could not affect. For these reasons, the philanthropic community felt it could not play a significant role . . ."

Eventually Associated itself helped break the logjam. In a memorandum to the league's members, Executive Director Janet Taylor warned: "The problem is not simply the responsibility of the public sector . . . It requires a redirection of many of the services already funded by Associated's members to focus on the school setting. A concerted effort, of which our members are a part, can have a real impact."

Not everyone was convinced by Miss Taylor's argument: twenty-five of Associated's members were quite content to leave the busing question to the public sector. But eventually seven of Boston's most socially committed philanthropies allocated $198,000 in 1974–75 and $242,500 the next year to fourteen separate programs designed to reduce racial tensions and violence during the desegregation process. Determined to avoid a partisan stand on so divisive an issue, Hyams trustees made no grant the first year. Later, at Joan's urging, they concluded that they couldn't turn their back on the crisis. Yet finding an appropriate grantee was difficult. Joan conducted prolonged talks with a coalition of black social agencies, but the negotiations fell through when the group failed to submit adequate data. Ultimately, Hyams provided $45,000 to three organizations—the Citywide Educational Coalition, School Volunteers for Boston, and Freedom House—which sought peaceful compliance with the court order and "quality education" in the city's schools. Meanwhile, the United Way—in the middle of its 1974 campaign—committed $200,000 to several "special projects" intended to "reduce tensions and help guarantee the safety of our children in all neighborhoods." They included an effort by the South Boston Committee of Community Agencies to get students back into school, a counseling service by the People's Task Force of Hyde Park, and "sensitivity training" by the Greater Boston YWCA.

The action by Associated's members had attracted little public notice, but the United Way's special grants prompted an outcry in Boston's white neighborhoods. ROAR and its ally, the Home and School Association, called for a boycott of the United Way. A ROAR representative toured comfortable suburban communities urging residents not to contribute to the fund drive, but instead to give directly to their favorite charities. Hundreds of pledge cards were returned defaced with anti-busing slogans. The United Way was compelled to extend its campaign by several weeks in a vain effort to meet its target.

This protest crested on April 13, 1975, when three hundred cars streamed from the city to the Wellesley home of William C. Mercer, president of the New England Telephone Company and chairman of the United Way campaign. More than a thousand demonstrators pressed against the green privet hedge around Mercer's colonial house, located not far from Arthur Garrity's. Barred from the driveway and lawns by a platoon of helmeted Wellesley police, the protesters chanted anti-busing slogans, sang patriotic songs, and waved miniature American flags. A ROAR speaker, Adam Kasprzak of Brighton, said the United Way had "clearly misused the money given to it by the people." And Kasprzak added a warning which struck at the heart of Boston's philanthropic tradition: "If those who control our city's charities think they can also control our lives, they are very much mistaken."

19
McGoff

Alice McGoff stood at the hedge, gazing up the sweep of lawn toward the handsome house on the hill. Thickets of ash and silver birch partially screened it from Falmouth Road, but she could make out the broad façade of red brick, punctuated by a graceful white doorway and two rows of windows with bright green shutters. It was a grand house, all right, just where you'd expect to find the president of the New England Telephone Company, her boss, the illustrious William Chauncy Mercer.

Suddenly there was a movement at one of the narrow windows flanking the door. The gauzy curtain was pulled aside and a tall, silver-haired man appeared for a moment behind the glass. My God, Alice thought, it's Mercer! In the eight months she'd worked for the telephone company, she'd met the president only once—when he came through the operators' room at Christmas, shaking hands and expressing appreciation for all the overtime they'd put in during the holidays. He'd smiled at her then, that toothy smile she'd come to expect from Yankees of a certain class, and Alice had nodded back respectfully. But now, as he peered through his window, Alice wondered, "What if he recognizes me, one of his own operators, demonstrating in front of his house?" Oh no, she thought, that's silly—the company had hundreds of operators, thousands of repairmen and clerks. Why would Mercer remember *her* face? If he noticed her there at all, she would look like just another overweight Irishwoman out from the city to trample his bushes and scuff his lawn.

Well, she thought, that's what I am. She had nothing personal against Mercer—he was probably a decent man—but he was the United Way chairman, and $200,000 of the money he had raised was going to support forced busing, much of that money collected from people like herself, the very ones who were bearing the brunt of such social engineering. Indeed, the telephone company had put pressure on its own employees to support the fund drive, but Alice had flatly refused to contribute and she had urged her co-workers to boycott as well, spreading the word through a letter to the Charlestown *Patriot*. "I will not give any of my hard-earned monies to an organization that is so dramatically opposed to my beliefs. I would like to suggest to my fellow Townies that they make their contributions directly to the organizations of their choice." She had sent her ten dollars to the Charlestown Girls' Club, whose funding had been cut off by the United Way after its parent organization was accused of "financial irregularities."

In years past, Alice—like many of her neighbors—had usually given the United Way a few dollars. But Charlestown had never thought very highly of philanthropy controlled from downtown by Yankee bankers and businessmen. It was too remote from the Town, too lofty and condescending, too dedicated to its own social agenda (John Boyle O'Reilly, the poet-priest who lived in Charlestown for many years, called it "Organized charity, scrimped and iced / In the name of a cautious, statistical Christ"). Besides, Charlestown had long prided itself on its self-sufficiency, and it resented charity as a badge of dependency. When the United Citizens' League, a Protestant reform organization, opened an unemployment relief station there during the Depression, a letter to the Charlestown *News* complained that "this intrusion of soup-eating benefactors" was needed in the Town "like we need smallpox." The writer, an old Townie, asserted: "The needs of the poor in Charlestown have always been looked after in first-class shape by our St. Vincent de Paul Society."

In short, Catholics would take care of their own, without meddling from Protestant do-gooders. For traditional Catholic philanthropy had never shared the Yankee predilection for social reform. To the St. Vincent de Paul Society and the Catholic Charitable Bureau, charity wasn't a lever for change, but a balm to make the Catholic worker more content with his meager lot on earth. "It is through alms-giving on the part of the wealthy and gratitude on the part of the poor that we are saved the dry rot of communism or a war of the classes," the Reverend William G. Byrne, a Boston priest, wrote in 1880. And three years later, Pope Leo XIII put his imprimatur on that doctrine when he declared: "Christian charity . . . unites the rich and poor by sweet bonds of holy affection."

For generations, Charlestown's Catholics had lived comfortably with such passivity. Whatever they might expect from City Hall, the State House, or the White House, the parishioners of St. Mary's, St. Catherine's, and St. Francis de Sales' looked to their churches not for reform but for solace. As one Townie put it: "When I saw Christ bleeding on his cross, I knew he was there suffering for my sins. That was good enough for me. I didn't expect him to climb down and start lobbying for a minimum wage, urban renewal, and peace in Vietnam." When the Church began reinterpreting its position in regard to social issues in the 1960s, that created a new source of conflict for many Townies.

Alice had been raised a devout Catholic, but the Kirks differed widely in their attitudes toward the Church. Resentful of ecclesiastical power, her father, Bernie, rarely attended Mass. Bernie Kirk respected priests so long as they stuck to theological issues, but he wasn't about to let the Church instruct him in his temporal duties. This ambivalence was evident at the dinner table, where, in one breath, he would inveigh against Cardinal Cushing, "that red-hatted old politician," and, in the next, would command his children to obey the good pastor of St. Mary's, Monsignor Frederic Allchin.

Alice's mother was more conventionally religious, perhaps to eradicate the Wolfberg in her. It hadn't been easy growing up half Jewish in a relentlessly Irish Catholic town, and Gertie Wolfberg soon recognized that the quickest route to acceptance was full immersion in the Church. By the time Alice was born, her mother had adopted all the rituals of Charlestown Catholicism. The Kirks always ate fish on Fridays, fasted on Ash Wednesday, and occasionally even joined the Cardinal in his nightly recitation of the rosary, kneeling side by side on the hard parlor floor as Cushing intoned the familiar phrases over the radio. On hot summer nights, Alice could hear that harsh voice droning from back porches and parlor windows up and down Breed's Hill, uniting the Town for a few moments of obeisance to "God the Father Almighty, Creator of Heaven and Earth."

But even Gertie Kirk performed these rituals more by rote than by feeling. The religious center of the family was Alice's aunt Mary, whom the priests at St. Mary's liked to call "the most devout woman in the parish." Mary attended Mass daily—on weekdays, walking from her job at City Hall to a church in the North End, and on weekends, joining her family and neighbors at St. Mary's. From her modest salary, she contributed regularly to both parishes, but her favorite charity was missionary work among the American Indians. Bernie Kirk liked to say that his sister had "built half the tepees between here and the Rio Grande."

From these diverse strands, Alice wove her own tapestry of devotion. What stirred her most was the Catholic aesthetic—the ritual, the pageantry, the sensuous feel of faith. Her favorite ritual was the May Procession, in which the children of St. Mary's School marched through the Town's streets to honor the Virgin Mary—the boys as Swiss Guards carrying pikes; the girls in long white gowns and flowing headdresses. Religious devotions were as important to her childhood as hopscotch or jumping rope. Every day at St. Mary's School began and ended with prayer; and every Sunday morning the Kirk children trooped to the church for nine o'clock Mass. Never much of a Latin scholar, Alice couldn't follow the liturgy, but the sonorous phrases, the sweet smell of incense, the rumble of the organ as it swelled beneath the vaulted ceiling, the morning sunlight shimmering through the stained-glass windows filled her with a sense of peace and harmony.

Those were palmy days for the Church in Charlestown, its authority still largely unchallenged. Priests like Monsignor Allchin, pastor of St. Mary's from 1937 to 1955, brooked no disobedience from their parishioners. In 1951, when Allchin discovered that youngsters were sneaking out of his Masses to play street hockey, he ordered a curate named George Schlichte to stand guard at the door. Sure enough, as the Mass was only minutes old, a kid named Ryan scuttled down the aisle. "Where are you going, son?" asked Schlichte. "None of your business, Father," snapped the boy. When Schlichte recounted the story at lunch, the other curates laughed, but the pastor only nodded. Two months later, the boy came to the rectory looking for Schlichte. "Father," he implored, "please call my parents and get them off my back." It seemed that every morning for years, Allchin had walked by the family's home, invariably greeting them with a "Good morning, Mr. Ryan" or a "Fine day, Mrs. Ryan." But after the incident with their son, he had marched past without so much as a nod. The Ryans were deeply distressed, and when Mr. Ryan found out what had happened, he gave his son a beating, then told him, "Get up to the rectory and square us with the pastor."

The Kirks never kowtowed to the Church that way. When Alice was fourteen, she and some friends staged an epic snowball fight on the Training Field. Just then, Father John Fogarty of St. Mary's walked past. Ordering the children to halt their battle, he took their names, then called their homes to report them. Alice never forgot that incident. Over the years, it came to stand for the Church's determination to exercise authority outside its realm, and like her father, she bridled at such presumption. Some years later, when she married Danny McGoff, Father Fogarty presided at the ceremony, and remembering that snowy day on the Training Field, Alice took her vows through half-gritted teeth.

If Alice needed further evidence of the Church's inclination to meddle in temporal matters, she found it in the decision of Charlestown's priests to immerse themselves in the Town's urban renewal battles. It was a strategy born a few years earlier on the South Side of Chicago. When Saul Alinsky, the radical community organizer, sought to revive the deteriorating Woodlawn neighborhood, he struck a marriage of convenience with the Archdiocese of Chicago. Albert Cardinal Meyer knew that the Church had a heavy stake in neighborhoods like Woodlawn, whose Irish Catholic residents were departing faster than blacks could replace them. Alinsky and Meyer collaborated to halt the exodus and redevelop Woodlawn as an integrated community. Not only did the Cardinal order the neighborhood's nine pastors to provide $10,000 per parish toward Alinsky's efforts, he demanded wholehearted support for the redevelopment program, including endorsements from the pulpit. One pastor heatedly objected, warning that his white parishioners would never stand for it. "There'll be war, there'll be blood in the streets," he said. "Well, Father," replied the Cardinal, "prepare for war."

One of Alinsky's organizers in Woodlawn had been a Lithuanian Catholic named Joe Vilimas. In 1961, Ed Logue hired him away to organize community support for urban renewal in Charlestown. Not surprisingly, Vilimas made Woodlawn his model; once again, his campaign would be founded on an alliance with the Church.

Even before Vilimas arrived, Cardinal Cushing had signaled his support of Boston's renewal by delegating his most intimate associate, Monsignor Francis J. Lally, to serve as chairman of the new Boston Redevelopment Authority. Lally took up residence at St. Catherine's in Charlestown, where his very presence was a visible symbol of the Cardinal's commitment. Between them, Lally and Vilimas enlisted the three Charlestown pastors—Monsignors Flaherty, Shea, and Quirbach—in the renewal fight. The pastors didn't need much persuasion. Like Meyer in Chicago, they saw the steady drain of young Catholics to the suburbs as a dire threat to their parishes. Renewal, they believed, would stem that tide.

The clergy became particularly emphatic after the first Charlestown plan was howled down at a hearing on January 7, 1963. Five days after the hearing, Lally—as editor of the archdiocesan weekly, the *Pilot*—wrote an editorial condemning the plan's opponents. Three weeks later, the three Charlestown monsignori followed with a joint statement from their pulpits which went, in part: "Charlestown and its people are at a crossroad. The future of our district is mixed with uncertainty and fear. Amid the blight and decay and the ever-increasing commercial and industrial expansion, your home and your parish will vanish. Charlestown will be dead. . . . When another public hearing is called in Charlestown we hope that all the people of this district will attend and support the rebuilding of this town. Working together, in our own self-interest, we can achieve miracles."

When Logue decided that he was ready for another hearing—in March 1965—Cardinal Cushing set the stage with a statement assuring Charlestown that renewal offered "the most hopeful promise of the permanent rehabilitation of that beloved part of our great city." At the hearing itself, the Charlestown monsignori weighed in again with impassioned statements, concluding with Father Shea's abrupt call for a show of hands. When the plan was approved, some commentators credited the Church with carrying the day. But for every vote won over by the clergy, another was probably lost by their intervention. For Bernie Kirk was hardly alone in his submerged anticlericalism; many, Townies harbored a secret resentment of the Church, which at last it was permissible to voice. One opponent of renewal accused the priests of "selling the people of Charlestown for thirty pieces of silver." Others called for a boycott of the churches, particularly their collection plates. "If they won't support us," asked Joseph Catanzaro, "why should we support them?" Others took more direct action. One outraged parishioner punched Monsignor Shea in the stomach. And a businessman paid $800 to rent a huge billboard on the expressway which proclaimed: "Father Flaherty is a Judas."

The Charlestown churches never fully recovered. The extraordinary authority which priests had once enjoyed in the Town was irrevocably eroded. St. Mary's Parish, where Monsignor Flaherty had spearheaded the renewal crusade, was decimated by the BRA's bulldozers and years were to pass before new housing rose on the rubble-strewn lots. Opponents of renewal were convinced that the Church must have received some inducement, probably a secret share of the profits. Henceforth, many Townies—Alice McGoff among them—no longer regarded the Church as a spiritual body, but as a self-serving institution like any other, which wouldn't hesitate to ally itself with Charlestown's enemies if it envisioned some benefit for itself.

But Alice's mounting skepticism toward the Church had another, more private source. In her first five years of marriage, she gave birth to five children. When the fifth—Tommy—was born in 1962, the delivery took thirty-six hours and nearly killed her. At one point, the prognosis for mother and child was so grim that a priest was summoned to her room, standing by to administer the last rites. Although Alice and her baby both survived, the doctor warned her that she must never have another child; her body simply wasn't up to it.

The doctor's pronouncement was a terrible blow to Alice and Danny, both still in their mid-twenties. They couldn't imagine giving up sex with each other, but how could they continue, knowing it might cost Alice her life? Finally, Danny went to a priest at St. Catherine's, explained the situation, and asked for a special dispensation to use contraceptives. "No, my son," the priest replied. "Contraception is a mortal sin." All he could offer was the "rhythm method" of periodic abstinence. When Danny said that would never work for them, the priest said, "Well then, you and your wife must live as sister and brother." "Father," said Danny McGoff, "I had three sisters when I was growing up. I didn't marry Alice to have a fourth one." The priest said he was sorry, but there was nothing he could do for them.

When Danny told her what had happened, Alice wasn't very surprised. "What did you expect?" she asked him. "They have their rules." But the more she thought about it, the angrier she got. The priest had given her a terrible choice: celibacy or death. Clearly, he didn't much care whether she lived or died. But if her own life wasn't important, what about the five young children she would leave behind? Didn't the Church care about them?

Danny hadn't given up. Several months later, walking through the Boston Common, he passed the Paulist Center, headquarters of a priestly order which took a more liberal position on matters like birth control. On impulse, Danny consulted a Paulist father, who told him, "I can't give you any hard-and-fast rules on something like that. You have to follow your own conscience." Interpreting this as a special dispensation, Danny rushed home to tell his wife. But, by then, it was academic. Alice was already pregnant with twins, born prematurely—but safely—the following spring.

Even after the twins' birth, she never used contraceptives. The birth control prohibition had been hammered at her so long and hard she couldn't bring herself to violate it. She was like her father, who, once the Pope announced that you could eat meat on Friday, still insisted on fish. "What about all those people who are burning in hell for eating meat?" he would ask, only half in jest. The old dicta died hard.

Many of them did die, though. For just as Alice was confronting the Church's rigidity on birth control, the world's bishops were gathering in Rome for a conclave that was to change the face of modern Catholicism. The Second Vatican Council ushered in an *aggiornamento*—a spiritual renewal—which eradicated much that was negative and defensive in the Church's relations with society. Under Pope John XXIII, the Council approved historic declarations on religious freedom and the Jews, modernized the traditional liturgy, allowing

Mass to be celebrated in a country's mother tongue rather than in Latin, and permitted more informal administration of the sacraments.

For Alice, Vatican II was a mixed blessing. She approved its attitude toward other religions, a far cry from the Church's position when she was growing up. In those days, the priests at St. Mary's flatly prohibited their parishioners from entering a Protestant church or a Jewish synagogue. After all, Protestants and Jews were destined to fry in hell. She never knew a Protestant until she was an adult and even then she felt uncomfortable in their presence. That struck her as ridiculous now: everyone ought to be free to believe what he chose to. But the liturgical reforms were another matter. They came so swiftly, so abruptly, that she had no time to prepare. All of a sudden, one Sunday morning in October 1963, the priests at St. Mary's abandoned the Roman Mass as it had been celebrated for centuries. No longer did they turn their backs on the congregation as they mumbled the unintelligible mysteries of the Latin liturgy; now they faced their parishioners head on, speaking in the all too familiar accents of Irish America. The new style—democratic though it might be—blunted the aesthetics of Catholicism, long its principal attraction to Alice. The Church wasn't teaching religion anymore, it was teaching humanism, but she didn't need anyone to show her how to be human—she'd been granted that privilege when she was born; what she needed were priests to show her how to be truly Catholic. Instead, they were melting everyone together in one great religion.

Often it seemed as if Vatican II had opened the church door to all kinds of kookiness. Take the new breed of anti-war clergy—the Berrigan brothers plotting to kidnap Henry Kissinger, the priests offering sanctuary to war resisters, the Sisters in Maryland pouring sheep's blood over draft records. Her own feelings on the war were deeply conflicted: she wasn't sure what we were doing there in the first place, but once we were there, we ought to fight to win. Yet regardless of how you felt on the issue, what was the Church doing in the anti-war movement at all? Catholics had never been pacifists. Priests and Sisters should stop ridiculing the soldiers—Protestants, Jews, and Catholics—who were dying for their country. They should tend to the poor boys' souls. That's where the Church belonged—in your soul, not on a platform debating the issues.

Gradually, Alice noticed that the Church was beginning to take sides, too, in Boston's school wars. It was nothing very dramatic at first—a few statements by Cardinal Cushing supporting the Racial Imbalance Act, later echoed by his successor, Humberto Cardinal Medeiros. Such declarations didn't really bother Alice—they were the kind of pronouncements she'd come to expect from the Cardinal's office, high-minded expressions of brotherhood and racial equality which nobody took very seriously. But when Medeiros endorsed Judge Garrity's busing order in June 1974, Alice began to wonder just what this new Cardinal was up to. And when he ordered Catholic schools in the Archdiocese not to accept refugees from busing, she realized that Medeiros had thrown the full weight of her Church into the battle against her.

To Alice, the Cardinal's proclamations grossly violated Church dogma which had consistently put the rights of the family above the rights of the state. The anti-busing movement produced a pamphlet documenting the Church's statements on the question, most of them issued in the prolonged battle over the place of Catholic schools in a secular society. Alice found these statements clear and unequivocal. "Parents who have the primary and inalienable right and duty to educate their children must enjoy true liberty in their choice of schools," the Second Vatican Council had declared. And Pope Pius XI had written in 1929: "The family holds directly from the Creator the mission and hence the right to educate the offspring, a right anterior to any right whatever of civil society and the state and therefore inviolable on the part of any power on earth. This mission cannot be wrested from parents without grave violation of their rights." How could the Cardinal now defy these doctrines by ceding to a civil court the power to dictate where a Catholic family's children should be educated?

From the day in 1970 when Cardinal Medeiros had succeeded Cushing, she'd felt uncomfortable with this pious little Portuguese. Whatever you might say about Cushing, he was one of them, a Boston Irishman through and through. His very faults—his incessant politicking, his cronyism, his alliance with the Kennedys—were typically Irish failings. As a Cardinal he sometimes overreached himself, but as a man you had to respect him—a big strapping guy who wouldn't hesitate to toss a football around, or whack a kid when he got out of hand, or belly up to the bar with the rest of the fellas. Cushing was a regular guy. But Medeiros was something else—not only a foreigner, an outsider, but about as different from a Boston Irish priest as anything you could imagine. He was a holy little fellow, always bowing his head, wringing his hands, and praying in those whiny, singsong Mediterranean rhythms. Just like one of those Italian Popes. There was something about the new Cardinal, something *soft*, which made her profoundly uneasy.

Alice responded to the Cardinal's stand on busing by refusing to contribute to his annual Stewardship Appeal, a special archdiocesan fund drive designed to reduce the huge deficit which Medeiros had inherited from Cushing. She still contributed to the parish, but when the Stewardship envelope arrived, she simply scrawled across it "No Forced Busing" and mailed it back. Even her aunt Mary—who had never refused a Church cause—boycotted the Stewardship Appeal. If enough people did that, Alice thought, the Cardinal might eventually get the message.

The real truth was that no Cardinal Archbishop could make that much difference in the daily lives of Boston's Catholics. What mattered to them were their parish priests—the pastor and his two or three curates—who celebrated Mass on Sundays, heard their confessions, married them, visited them when they were sick, and gave them the last rites when they were dying.

Though crowded into one square mile, Charlestown's three parishes each represented a distinct slice of the Town. St. Francis de Sales' Church stood a bit haughtily at the crest of Bunker Hill, surrounded by the brown and gray three-deckers of its solid burghers; St. Mary's, the oldest Catholic church in town and once the most prestigious, now catered to a strange amalgam of the new gentry around Monument Square and older working-class families in the Valley; and St. Catherine's served primarily the social outcasts of the Bunker Hill housing project. Having grown up in St. Mary's Parish, attended its parochial school, been confirmed and married there, Alice would always think of herself as a St. Mary's girl, but now that she lived in the project, St. Catherine's was just a few steps from her door and it was there that she generally went for Mass or confession.

St. Catherine's pastor was William Anderson, an aging priest overwhelmed by project life and yearning for a quiet suburban parish. Many of his responsibilities fell on his pugnacious curate, Lawrence Buckley, a middle-aged Redemptorist priest who had served for twenty-two years in Puerto Rico and the Virgin Islands before returning to his native Roxbury in 1972. His long service in the Caribbean had left him with profound convictions about racial equality, and his two years in Roxbury only deepened that commitment. Arriving at St. Catherine's in 1974, Buckley resolved to confront his new parishioners' racial bias. In January 1975, he invited Pat Russell, the newly elected president of Powder Keg, to the rectory for a discussion of the gathering crisis. For nearly three hours they reviewed the history of Boston's school case and when Pat left shortly before midnight, Buckley was convinced that he had persuaded her to take a more "Christian" approach to the busing issue. A week later, he was dismayed when he saw her on television wearing a "Stop Forced Busing" T-shirt as she angrily confronted the Governor's Commission on the Status of Women.

Undeterred, he took his case into the pulpit. One Sunday in May 1975—a few weeks after the judge released his Phase II plan—Buckley delivered a sermon at St. Catherine's eleven o'clock Mass. Speaking of his experience on St. Thomas in the Virgin Islands, he called it "the happiest community I've ever lived in, a place where blacks and whites lived together, sharing what little they had with love and respect for each other's rights." Buckley urged his parishioners to abandon their racial preconceptions and work toward an integrated society in which all people were "free to come and go as they wish." Such integration was not only a "Christian principle," it was the law of the land. He warned them against politicians who tried to lead them down the "dead-end street" of resistance to the law, for such politicians wouldn't be around when they were ambushed on that street.

Many of his parishioners—who had never heard anything like that from the pulpit before—recoiled almost physically from Buckley's admonitions. After a few minutes, one man rose to his feet, moved to the back of the church, and stomped back and forth, muttering angrily under his breath. After Mass, Buckley was summoned to the rectory, where his agitated pastor was trying to mollify an elderly woman who was nearly speechless with rage. "Larry," said Father Anderson, "*you* answer Mrs. Gould." Later, on his way back to the church, he was assailed by three more women. "Nigger lover!"

they shouted. "You dirty little priest, why don't you go back to Roxbury! Go back to the Virgin Islands if you liked it so much!"

Alice McGoff hadn't attended Mass that morning, but within hours she'd heard four versions of what Father Buckley had said, each more horrifying than the last. She wasn't surprised—she'd already had one run-in with Buckley. When a friend at the housing project tried to enroll a child at St. Catherine's parochial school, she'd been turned down, ostensibly for violating the Cardinal's order against using the Catholic schools to escape busing. But one Sister at the school had disparaged her parish contributions, implying that she hadn't given enough to earn a place there. Outraged, Alice called Father Buckley to accuse the Church of "extortion." Buckley said that her friend was a "bigot" and that the Church wasn't going to be used as a "refuge for racists." Since that episode, there hadn't been much communication between them.

As Larry Buckley waged his crusade for racial justice at St. Catherine's, three priests in Charlestown's other parishes were mapping a different strategy. Bob Boyle, Bill Joy, and Jack Ward had known each other in the South End, where Boyle had been principal of Cathedral High School when Joy and Ward came to the Cathedral as young deacons straight out of the seminary. Their immersion in that district's social cauldron had lent them a sense of common purpose, a "mission" to the inner city. Largely by coincidence, all had found their way to Charlestown—Joy arriving first, in 1972, as a curate at St. Mary's; Ward, in 1973, as a curate at St. Francis'; and finally Bob Boyle, named pastor of St. Mary's in September 1974.

Pleased at being reunited, they met frequently—usually at St. Mary's rectory, where Boyle and Joy both lived—to share a meal, a drink, or simply the warmth of their friendship. But as Charlestown's busing crisis loomed nearer, their gatherings took on a more earnest tone. The three men felt a special responsibility, for they sensed that most of Charlestown's other priests wanted nothing to do with the racial crisis. That was confirmed at an abortive meeting of the Charlestown clergy called by Bishop Joseph Ruocco, the Cardinal's principal lieutenant on school desegregation matters. Ruocco, who had been touring Boston's neighborhoods to prepare for the fall, invited Charlestown's priests to meet with him at St. Mary's convent, but of the eleven priests stationed in Charlestown, only six showed up. Among the absent were the other two pastors, Anderson from St. Catherine's and Albert Cuttress from St. Francis'—both traditionalists who instinctively shunned such problems. Of the other curates, only Larry Buckley displayed real commitment on the issue.

Buckley had expressed interest in cooperating with the trio. Clearly disconcerted by the parishioners' anger at his sermon, and knowing that he could count on little help from his own pastor, he sought Boyle's assistance. "We can't do anything alone," Buckley said. "We've got to act together. The priests of Charlestown should issue a pastoral letter stating how we feel on school desegregation."

Boyle, Joy, and Ward did what they could to support Larry Buckley, but a pastoral letter didn't appeal to them any more than endorsements of busing from the pulpit. They admired Buckley's courage and honesty, but his head-on approach struck them as counterproductive; it reminded them of the Church's intervention in Charlestown's renewal—which may have produced a few victories, but ultimately lost the war, leaving a bitter residue of anticlericalism in the Town. Recognizing how deeply Charlestown resented the Garrity order, their strategy was precisely the reverse of Buckley's: rather than support busing as such, they focused on public safety, calling for measures to prevent violence and protect schoolchildren, both white and black; instead of confronting their parishioners' racial feelings head on, they tried to demonstrate their love and concern for the Townies, thus accumulating emotional capital to be spent in the difficult days ahead.

The three priests agreed on a division of labor. Joy and Ward took to the streets, developing what some called a new form of ministry, though they thought of it as a throwback to an earlier era in which the priest was a visible presence in every corner of his parish. Dressed informally, often without a clerical collar, they wandered up Breed's Hill, down Bunker Hill, and through the Valley, chatting with housewives on their stoops, teenagers in the playgrounds, men in drugstores and taverns. They didn't proselytize or preach, they listened, for they knew that half an hour across a kitchen table with most Townies was worth five hours in the pulpit.

Meanwhile, Bob Boyle dealt with the public sector—the Mayor's office, the police, courts, schools, and community groups like the Charlestown Education Committee. Though quietly paving the way for Charlestown's desegregation, he tried not to take formal positions which would limit his ability to work with Townies of all dispositions. When the Education Committee addressed its pleas to Judge Garrity, Boyle respectfully declined to sign them. And when summoned to testify in June 1975 before the United States Civil Rights Commission, he struggled for words to acknowledge the feelings on both sides. "I do not have any absolute answers to the dilemma of our beloved city," he told the commissioners. But he was certain of several things.

Of this I can be sure, that all of us must do what we do not like at times in order to guarantee the rights of others and thereby guarantee our own rights.

Of this I can be sure, that Boston and America are both diverse. That very diversity—if there is not deep, honest conversation and dialogue on all sides—can lead to misunderstanding. Misunderstanding can lead to hostility, hostility to destruction . . .

Of this I can be sure, we had better prepare for the fall. If ever we the people of Boston are to recite the Lord's Prayer together—not "my" Father, not "Dorchester's" Father, not "Roxbury's" Father, not "Charlestown's" Father, but "our" Father—then we better seek love as a solution, non-violence as a solution, quality education as a solution.

And of this I am also certain, that all of us here need the grace and wisdom of God. Our own wisdom has not been sufficient.

But even Boyle wasn't prepared for the ingenuity with which the mothers of Charlestown would solicit God's grace, nor for the exquisite bind in which he and his colleagues were to find themselves.

As the Powder Keg contingent advanced up High Street toward the waiting cordon of police on that second day of school, Boyle, Joy, and Ward stood ready on the sidewalk, anxious to prevent a bloody confrontation. But when the mothers knelt on the street, rosary beads in hand, reciting their "Our Fathers" and "Hail Marys," the three priests grew acutely uneasy. Then from the rows of bowed heads came a cry: "Father Boyle, come pray with us!"

Others chimed in: "Come join us, Father Joy!" "Here we are, Father Ward, lead us in our prayers!"

For one terrible moment the priests stood frozen, unable to move toward the mothers or away from them. How could they turn their backs on these women, how could they refuse to pray with their own parishioners? But how could they join them, knowing to what end their prayers were dedicated? Either option seemed intolerable.

When Superintendent Carpenter asked him to address the women through a bullhorn, Boyle was relieved. It gave him a chance to step out of his clerical role and urge the women to avoid a clash with the police. But the mothers wouldn't let him off so easily. One of them looked up at him with hurt and anger in her face and asked, "Oh, Father, why are you against us?"

Boyle felt tears welling in his eyes. Squatting on the street next to the woman, he placed his hand on her shoulder. "Madam, I'm not against you. How could I be against you?"

"Then why won't you pray with us?" she asked.

"I pray for you every day."

"No," the woman persisted, "I mean pray *with* us. Now. Here and now."

"Oh, God," Boyle said, "how I wish I could do that! But I simply can't. Please try to understand that."

Then, as the tears began to come, he turned away.

A few yards away, her throbbing neck encased in its protective collar, Alice McGoff looked on in mounting rage and incomprehension. Why couldn't the priests pray with them? After all, these were the men she confessed to; in them she confided her most secret thoughts, things she never told her husband, her father or mother. Yet here she was, at the most desperate moment in her life, fighting to protect her family, and her own priests wouldn't pray with her!

As the prayer marches went on day after day, the pressure on the priests grew more intense. Filing past St. Mary's rectory, the processions were a daily reproach, a challenge to the Church's relevance. After the first one, the priests learned to stay off the streets at that time of day, though they couldn't resist peering through the curtains. Once, as the marchers went by, a woman hurled her defiance at the rectory windows. "See," she shouted, "we don't need you anymore. We deal with God directly."

In late September, the mothers found still another way to provoke the priests. One day, Pat Russell fell into conversation with the Reverend Isaiah

Sears, minister of the First Baptist Church, one of Charlestown's three tiny Protestant congregations. Sears, whose legs were badly crippled from a childhood bout with polio, was a familiar—and cherished—figure in the Town as he hobbled up and down the hills on his aluminum crutches. When Pat complained that the Catholic priests wouldn't even show themselves on the streets during the prayer marches, Sears responded lightly, "I've prayed over a woman's new canary. I've prayed over an alcoholic too soused to know I was there. I've even blessed a Mother's Day present. If I can pray with a drunk, a bird, and a box of candy, I suppose I can pray with anyone."

"Do you mean it, Reverend?" asked Pat Russell. "Will you pray with us?"

Sears was startled. He'd never expected a good Catholic like Pat to ask help from a Baptist. "Oh no," he protested. "You don't want me." But Pat saw her opening and she took it. "Oh yes we do," she said. "We don't want to come into the church. We don't want your approval for what we're doing. Just say a prayer with us." Sears didn't see how he could turn them down. On September 26, several hundred Charlestown mothers marched around Monument Square to the Baptist church, only two doors from St. Mary's rectory. Hobbling onto the stone stoop, Sears delivered his prayer. Although they were of different faiths, he said, they were all children of God. Over the years, he'd come to know many of them and they were good, generous people. Now they were caught up in a desperate struggle. He prayed that God would show them a way through the darkness, so they could raise their families in peace and love.

Even with her head bowed in prayer, Alice McGoff had to smile at the abundant ironies. The priests of St. Mary's had raised her to fear and distrust Protestants, yet here was a Baptist minister blessing a group of Catholic women, while the priests cowered in their rectory.

The ceremony at the Baptist church didn't go unremarked at St. Mary's. The next day, Bill Joy suggested that the mothers might care to conclude their prayer marches in the small grotto behind St. Mary's Church. Some of the women wanted to reject the offer unless the priests promised to attend as well, but many appreciated the small gesture of reconciliation. A few days later, they made their regular loop around the Monument, then knelt in prayer before the statue of the Virgin in the grotto. Alice recognized it as the same statue she had helped to garland with spring flowers during the May Processions of her youth. Despite all her grievances, she felt at home there.

The prayer marches proved so effective that the mothers tried variations on the theme. Recalling that the Feast of Our Lady of the Rosary fell on October 7, someone suggested that, instead of merely reciting the prayers that day, they should act them out in a "Living Rosary." Rosary prayers are generally said while thumbing a set of beads. Working along the beads, the supplicant says the prayers in a prescribed order—an "Our Father," ten "Hail Marys," a "Glory Be to the Father," and a "Sorrowful Mystery," repeating the cycle until the last bead is reached. A "Living Rosary" would require seventy performers—five "Sorrowful Mysteries," six "Our Fathers," six "Glory Be to the Fathers," and fifty-three "Hail Marys."

Two elderly women, devout members of St. Catherine's, volunteered to organize the elaborate production, but as the feast day approached, few preparations had been made. At that point Alice McGoff and her friend Barbara Gillette assumed responsibility for the event. On the evening of October 7, the women, the children, and the few men taking part in the ceremony assembled in front of St. Catherine's Church, carrying flashlights covered with colored crepe paper to match their roles: white for "Sorrowful Mysteries," blue for "Our Fathers," yellow for "Glory Be to the Fathers," and red for "Hail Marys." Led by two choirboys with a cross, they marched up Bunker Hill Street to the Ryan Playground.

Alice and Barbara had agreed that the Rosary should be performed on the slanting wooden bleachers, so that spectators could plainly see the colors outlined against the night sky. As they marshaled their forces on the football field, out of the dark appeared the two women originally assigned to run the performance.

"Okay, girls," they said, "we'll take it from here."

"The hell you will," said Barbara, "we've got everything organized."

"But we've been appointed," the women protested.

Soon small bands of colored lights were marching here and there across the field under contradictory orders from two sets of generals.

"Okay, all the Our Fathers over here!" one of the women shouted. "Line up facing this way!"

"No, no, you Our Fathers," Alice yelled. "Stand fast until I tell you to move! Hail Marys over here!"

"What are you talking about?" the woman bellowed back. "I told the Glory Be's to stand over there!"

Alice grew red in the face. Barbara was so angry she could hardly speak. "In one more second," she said in a strangled voice, "I'm going to punch somebody in the nose." They looked at each other for a moment, then collapsed in laughter. "Come on," said Barbara, "let's get out of here." Turning their backs on the field of colored lights, they adjourned to the Cobblestone Bar and drank whiskey sours all through the Feast of Our Lady of the Rosary.

As Charlestown's crisis intensified that fall, St. Mary's rectory was frequently the tranquil eye in the hurricane. Located at the southeast corner of Monument Square diagonally across from the high school, it was an ideal retreat from the heat of battle. Bob Boyle and Bill Joy had resolved to make its somber, wood-paneled dining room a place where all parties, regardless of viewpoint, could find temporary sanctuary. A mug of steaming coffee, a sugar doughnut, and a sympathetic ear were available to anyone who rang the doorbell. It was where Frank Power went at dawn to share his private anguish; where Captain Bill MacDonald betrayed his doubts about police tactics; where Roberta Delaney, manager of the Little City Hall, despaired about the evaporation of Charlestown's "moderate middle"; where Moe Gillen wondered if he could any longer control the demons set loose in the Town. And on at least two occasions that fall, it was where Mayor Kevin White met with Charlestown's leaders, seeking to restore some semblance of order.

From midsummer on, the rectory also harbored a major actor in the drama. Father Michael Groden, the Cardinal's principal adviser on urban affairs, had lived at St. Mary's for several years, but on July 1, 1975, he was named director of the Citywide Coordinating Council, the body Judge Garrity had created to supervise desegregation. The judge hoped a priest's appointment to the post would help legitimize his order, much as Frank Lally had been used a decade earlier to sanctify urban renewal. But just as Lally's presence at St. Catherine's reminded Charlestown of the Church's stance on renewal, so Mike Groden's continuing residence at St. Mary's constituted further evidence to the Townies of the Church's support for desegregation. On occasion, demonstrators would shout epithets at the rectory. "Judas!" they chanted. "Traitor!" And when Father Groden failed to respond, they shouted, "We know you're in there, Groden, come down and defend yourself." More than once, when he emerged the next morning, he found the tires of his car slashed.

Sometimes invective was hurled at the other priests as well. Once, as Bob Boyle was crossing the Monument grounds, he passed a Powder Keg demonstration. "There's a Boyle on your ass!" shouted one man. Wheeling, the priest stared at his tormentor. "I hear you, Tom Johnson," he said.

Alice could never muster that kind of anger at the Church. As much as she might resent individual priests like Larry Buckley, she retained some degree of her reverence for the institution itself. And it was reinforced by her growing respect and affection for one priest in particular, the irrepressible Bill Joy.

Joy was Charlestown's favorite priest. His natural ebullience, gaiety, and wit made his name seem especially appropriate. Barely twenty-six, with a boyish grin and thick brown hair curling down his neck, he didn't look old enough to tend men's souls. Free of the ecclesiastical cant and sanctimony that had marked certain of his predecessors, he felt utterly at home with the Townies and they with him. Joy was particularly effective with the young, who treated him as a wise, yet playful older brother—a rapport all the more remarkable since Charlestown's youth had been rapidly drifting away from the Church. Once, the Town's families had prided themselves on giving a son or daughter to the Church, but those days were gone; between 1965 and 1975, only two Charlestown youths had become priests. And the decline in vocations was only one symptom of an underlying reality: religion was no longer a relevant consideration for most of Charlestown's young people.

Hoping to bring young Townies back to the Church, Bill Joy decided to begin with teenage girls. Male-oriented Charlestown bristled with clubs and sports programs for boys, but girls, more mature and self-reliant at that age, were generally left to their own devices. In late 1973, Joy set out to gain their confidence by forming a girls' basketball team in the Catholic Youth Organization league. Most of his players were tenth-graders at Charlestown High—among them, Lisa McGoff, Michele Barrett, and the others who later were to form the nucleus of Charlestown High's girls' team. They already had blue shorts, so Joy went looking for jerseys to match. Unsure what size to buy, he settled on small and medium boys' shirts, but when the girls tried them on, they were much too small. There was an awkward moment as Michele explained that even a teenage girl had physical characteristics which made it difficult to squeeze into a boy's T-shirt. The priest blushed a deep red, the girls giggled, and from then on they were the best of friends. A winning combination, they went all the way to the CYO finals, before losing to a team from the Cathedral. After the game, Joy took the girls back to his parents' house for sandwiches and Cokes. Sensing an air of regret at the party—not so much at the loss of the championship as because it was their final game—Joy said that they didn't have to break up just because the season was over; they could stick together because they liked each other.

So they did. On summer weekends, he would pile the girls into his car, spend a long day at the beach, then stop for pizza on the way home. That fall, they climbed Mount Monadnock, and that winter, Joy took them on their first skiing trip. They floundered and fell, but they loved it and loved him for bringing them. These trips with the young priest were the girls' one escape from Charlestown, their only glimpses of a wider world. They called them "Joy Rides."

Only after building this bridge of affection did Joy propose an overtly religious activity: a special Mass of their own. The girls readily agreed. Starting in October 1974, thirty girls assembled every Sunday evening at St. Mary's rectory, sitting cross-legged on the floor before a table draped with an altar cloth. Dressed in a plain black shirt and white collar, Joy would read a piece of scripture, play some recorded music, then deliver a brief sermon on issues which concerned them most: relationships with boys, tensions with parents, doubts about their futures. Afterwards, they went downstairs for pizza, Cokes, and discussion. Sometimes, Joy celebrated the Mass in one of the girls' own houses, lending the ritual an even more intimate air.

A dedicated member of Bill Joy's circle, Lisa McGoff rarely missed a Joy Ride or a Sunday-night Mass. She'd never thought of herself as a particularly religious person—the priests at St. Catherine's turned her off, and she rarely attended Mass there—but Joy was unlike any priest she'd ever known before. He was such a good guy, such a *sweet* guy. She found herself drawn more and more frequently over the hill to St. Mary's.

Bob Boyle and Bill Joy tried other innovations in the Mass, including a "lay lector" program in which members of the congregation read short selections from the liturgy, and Joy was delighted when Lisa volunteered to take part in the Good Friday services. Assigned the New Testament reading from Hebrews, Chapters 4–5, she practiced the difficult passage before the bathroom mirror at home. When the day arrived, she stood proudly before a huge holiday crowd and read: "Let us confidently approach the throne of Grace to receive mercy and favor and find help in time of need. In the days when he was in the flesh, Christ offered prayers and supplications with loud cries and tears to God . . .'"

Bill Joy's work with the girls paid dividends in the fall of 1975 when he found himself caught up in nightly skirmishes on Bunker Hill Street. More than once, as he and Jack Ward moved into the no-man's-land between the Tactical Patrol Force and crowds of rock-throwing youngsters, the kids turned their wrath on the young priests, accusing them of meddling in matters which were none of their business. "Get outta here, you fuckin' nigger lovers," they would cry. "Go back to your stinkin' church." But when Lisa McGoff and her girlfriends heard that, they would rally to Joy's defense. "You're wrong," Lisa would say indignantly. "He's okay. He's a Townie priest. Leave him alone."

Somewhat to her surprise, Alice found herself defending Joy too. At first, when Lisa had told her about the Masses in the rectory, she was suspicious. What was this young priest up to with her daughter? Was he brainwashing her for busing the way earlier priests had done for urban renewal? But Lisa kept insisting that nothing like that was going on. "He never even mentions busing, Ma," she'd say. "He's different from the others." Finally, Alice had to find out for herself, and she began crossing the hill to hear Mass in the grand old church of her youth, returning Sunday after Sunday. Soon she was nearly as pleased with Joy as her daughter was. Her friends in Powder Keg accused her of being naïve. "How can you like him, Alice?" they would ask. "He's a pro-buser." Maybe he was for busing—she didn't know and, frankly, she didn't want to find out; if he ever told her he was, if he made it explicit, she'd have to break with him as she had with the Cardinal. And she didn't want to do that. He was her last connection to the Church and she treasured him for it.

But Bill Joy derived little satisfaction from knowing that many Townies held him in high esteem while distrusting—even disliking—Cardinal Medeiros. For in the long run, he knew, the Church would thrive or wither as a single organism. Ecclesiastical authority was still rigidly hierarchical, and despite his remoteness from their daily lives, the only figure who could make the Church a powerful force for the spiritual and temporal well-being of Boston's Catholics was Medeiros himself. And as it happened, Joy knew the Cardinal better than most priests of his age and experience. As student council president at St. John's Seminary in 1970–71, it was he who issued the first invitation to Medeiros to address the student body and he who welcomed the Cardinal on his arrival. Although they were scarcely friends—the difference in age and rank precluded that—Joy felt a sympathy for the older man. He had discovered human qualities in Medeiros that many others had failed to detect.

But the Cardinal seemed unable or unwilling to show himself to the people of Charlestown. On several occasions through the preceding year, the priests at St. Mary's had urged him to make an appearance in the Town. When a sixteen-year-old girl was stabbed to death in May 1975 and two Chinese youths were arrested for the crime, Boyle suggested to the Cardinal's staff that this would be an ideal opportunity for Medeiros to demonstrate his concern

for Charlestown; by simply showing up at the wake, he could earn himself—
and the Church—great goodwill. But he didn't appear. The priests had also
hoped that he would attend the two hundredth anniversary of the Battle of
Bunker Hill, in June 1975, but again the Cardinal held back. During the first
week of school that fall, as the prayer marches wound past the rectory and the
priests struggled to retain some vestige of their former authority in the Town,
Medeiros telephoned St. Mary's nearly every day to keep abreast of developments. But he declined to come himself.

So when the Cardinal invited him to lunch in mid-September, Bill Joy
seized the opportunity. During the meal, conversation was light and inconse-
quential; but afterwards the Cardinal took the young priest into his study,
where they talked for more than an hour. Clearly dismayed by what was going
on in Charlestown—particularly the public attacks on the Church and on himself—he wanted a firsthand report from a priest at the scene.

Joy began by reassuring the Cardinal that things weren't nearly so bad as
they seemed from a distance. The people of Charlestown weren't all violent
racists. There were many open-minded moderates among them, but they
needed support and reassurance. And they particularly needed to feel that the
Church hadn't abandoned them. As for the Cardinal himself, the Townies
didn't hate him, they simply didn't know him. If only he would come to
Charlestown and meet the people face to face, Joy argued, he could begin to
break down the wall of mistrust erected against him. The meeting ended in-
conclusively, the Cardinal thanking Joy for his report but giving no assurance
that he would visit the Town anytime soon.

All through the winter and early spring of 1976, the Cardinal kept his
distance. Then, one Sunday morning in May, the Boston *Herald American*
published a major interview with Medeiros. "Cardinal Rejects City Leadership" read the page one headline. Asked about suggestions that he should play
a more prominent role in resolving the city's racial crisis—especially in heavily Catholic communities like South Boston and Charlestown—the Cardinal
had responded angrily.

"I am not colorful," he said. "I am not flamboyant—waving my red flag
before the bull. I am not going into South Boston to speak, to exhort, as so
many think I should. Why should I go? To get stoned? Is that what they'd like
to see? I am not afraid to get stones thrown at me. But I am afraid for Boston.
It does not need the opprobrium of national headlines saying that their Archbishop was stoned.

"I've been turned off in South Boston, anyhow. No one there is listening to
me. Eighty percent of the Catholics in South Boston do not attend Mass or go
to church. They wanted me to go to Charlestown, too. To get stoned. They're
looking for blood and they'd love to see me dead in the streets so they can sell
newspapers. Well, I don't think I will do that willingly. If it is true that I am
not accepted in Boston, then what could I do to stop it? They are not doing
what I tell them to do. I have appealed a thousand times. My priests appeal.
But there is no respect."

The Cardinal's interview reverberated through his Archdiocese. Many of the faithful reacted with disbelief. Could Medeiros really have said those things about his fellow Catholics? In South Boston and Charlestown, the reaction was even more intense. Catholics there stood accused of barbarism, of readiness to stone a prince of the Church much as twenty centuries before, ignorant heathens had abused and crucified the Lord. In Southie—which had borne the brunt of his scorn—the Cardinal was rebutted in the streets, in the taverns, and at public meetings. Louise Day Hicks said she had been "crushed" by the Cardinal's remarks. "South Boston has always boasted with pride that it has sent more young men and women to the religious life than any other community its size in the country," she said. "I respect Cardinal Medeiros the priest and invite him to walk in South Boston with me and preside at the holy sacrifice of the Mass in the community." Many of South Boston's priests felt personally impugned by the Cardinal's remarks. By the Saturday following publication of the interview, the uproar was so great that Medeiros met with twenty priests from the district and tendered an apology, which was read from South Boston pulpits over the weekend: "Your Archbishop reacted, after a long and anguished time, out of fatigue and anger. These, as you know, cloud the mind . . . Our Lord has proved once again that I am human and that we are all sinners."

Charlestown was equally offended. Never one of the Cardinal's admirers, Alice McGoff found in his remarks new justification of her low opinion. But whatever the Townies might think of him, they would never stone a holy man. It was unthinkable. What were they, Alice asked herself—animals? For the Cardinal even to hint at such a thing suggested how utterly out of touch he was. Powder Keg, in an official statement, admonished the Cardinal: "Forget not the ancient prophecy, 'Judge not and ye shall not be judged.'" And it expressed great regret that "a member of the organization which, for centuries, has been held in such high esteem and long-cherished honor would be reluctant to enter a town that was constructed with some of God's most valued tools." Moe Gillen, as chairman of the Charlestown Committee on Education, wrote to the Cardinal:

> On behalf of the people of Charlestown, I must take this opportunity to protest your reference to my community. . . . The widespread and deep-seated opposition to court-ordered busing in Charlestown has been overwhelmingly positive, constructive and non-violent. Under these circumstances, the impression created by your reference to Charlestown, however inadvertent, was unfortunate. . . . I would suggest the need for a greater sense of communication with the facts and feelings of the parents of Charlestown. . . . Towards this end, I would recommend for your consideration a meeting with representatives of the Charlestown Committee on Education.

The Cardinal agreed to the meeting and, on the afternoon of May 21, he received a Charlestown delegation in his Chancery office. The encounter between the Archdiocese and its aggrieved Charlestown parishes had the tone of a summit meeting. Seated with the Cardinal at the polished wood table were Chancellor Thomas Daily; Father John Boles, Archdiocesan Director of Education; and Bishop Ruocco. On the Townie side of the table were Moe Gillen; John Gardiner and Bob O'Brien of the Kennedy Center; Barbara Burns, a psychologist from the Bunker Hill Health Center; Mary Parker, treasurer of Powder Keg; and Fathers Boyle and Joy.

The Cardinal began with an apology. Though his remarks had looked harsher in the newspaper than he had intended, he now conceded that they were "unfortunate." He had only meant to explain why he felt his presence in South Boston or Charlestown would be counterproductive, in fact would only contribute to the tumult. "But if I have hurt any of you by my statements, I am humbly sorry for it."

If the people of Charlestown had been hurt, Moe Gillen replied, it was only because they had such deep respect for the Cardinal and for the Church he represented. Anything the Cardinal said naturally attracted a wide audience. For that very reason, they were eager to clear up any misunderstandings he might have. Charlestown was not as violent as it appeared. The Education Committee, of which he was chairman, and which was supported by a broad cross section of the Town, had worked hard to maintain peace and order in the community. They hadn't always succeeded, but surely there had never been— nor would there ever be—any danger to the Cardinal himself. If he would honor them with his presence, he would be received with the same devotion Charlestown had accorded all his predecessors.

If evidence for that was needed, it was there at his elbow. All through the hour-long meeting, Mary Parker fixed the Cardinal with a reverential gaze. Mary was the hard-liner in the Charlestown delegation—an officer of Powder Keg, an adamant opponent of busing, a determined foe of the Cardinal's position on the issue. Yet she was also a devout Catholic and never in her sixty-three years had she expected to be seated across the table from her Archbishop. When introduced to him, she inclined her head slightly as she would before an altar; when he spoke, she nodded in silent affirmation; and when she addressed him, it was in a voice filled with deference, if not awe. Whatever Medeiros had done to offend the people of Charlestown, it had barely diminished the power and mystery inherent in the office of Cardinal Archbishop of Boston.

20

The Cardinal

After the arid, mesquite-and-chaparral plains of mid-Texas, the lower Rio Grande Valley is a balm to the burning eye and scorched palate. Lush green fields run with the river, squared off by towering palms, and the air is sweet with oranges, lemons, and grapefruit. At Brownsville, where the café-au-lait Rio Grande empties into the aquamarine Gulf, the smell of freshly harvested fruit, waiting to be towed North, is overpowering. With some justification, the Chamber of Commerce calls Brownsville "the Citrus Garden of Eden."

In May 1970, Bishop Humberto Sousa Medeiros of Brownsville was at work in his office when he received a most important telephone call. Luigi Raimondi, Apostolic Delegate to the United States, the Pope's representative in America, required his presence in Washington at the first opportunity.

On June 1, Medeiros flew to the capital and met with Raimondi at his residence. Only then did the delegate inform him that Pope Paul VI wished to name him Archbishop of Boston.

The Bishop's first reaction was characteristic. "Your Excellency," he said, "would you mind if we prayed for a bit?" The two prelates went downstairs to the delegate's private chapel, where they knelt together in silent prayer. When they returned upstairs, Medeiros said that he was both honored and disconcerted by the appointment: the nation's second-largest diocese and perhaps its most prestigious, Boston was a staggering responsibility, its retiring Archbishop, Richard Cardinal Cushing, a legendary figure impossible to replace in Boston's affections. And there was something else worrying Medeiros. "Tell me," he asked, "does the Holy Father realize what he has done, appointing a Portuguese-American to be Archbishop of Boston?"

"Oh yes," said Raimondi, "I'm sure the Holy Father realizes what he has done."

"I mean," said the Bishop, "does he realize what it's equivalent to?"

"No," said the puzzled delegate. "What is it equivalent to?"

"Gethsemane," said the Bishop.

The garden to which Jesus withdrew on the evening before the Crucifixion and where Judas eventually betrayed him, "Gethsemane" is a chilling code word for Christ's agony, but it accurately reflected Medeiros' apprehensions about Boston. The son of immigrants from the Portuguese Azores, he had come of age in Fall River—fifty miles south of Boston—where he had got a taste of ethnic warfare, Massachusetts style. To many Fall River Irish, the Portuguese—or "Portogees," as they were invariably known—were only one step above the Negroes, and Humberto's schoolmates hadn't hesitated to remind him where he stood in the pecking order. Even as a parish priest and eventually as chancellor in the Fall River Diocese, he never won full acceptance from the Irish, who regarded the Church as their own domain. Frequent visits to Boston had convinced him that prejudice toward his people was, if anything, even greater there. From the Rio Grande's citrus garden—where he had become a hero to the Mexican-American farm workers—Boston must indeed have seemed like the garden of Gethsemane.

Medeiros' fears were not unfounded. When his appointment was announced, the city's Irish Catholics were stunned. For 124 years, the bishops of Boston had been men of Irish descent, and since the turn of the century, the hierarchy—from chancellor down through the lowliest parish priest—had been overwhelmingly Irish. Even the Italians, ever more numerous in the diocese, found it difficult to rise in Boston's Church. Now the faithful were being asked to accept as their new bishop not only a non-Irishman, but a Portuguese, one of the olive-skinned immigrants they had long regarded as third-class Catholics.

Shock waves from his appointment were felt first in rectories and convents throughout the diocese, where much of the Irish clergy saw it as a threat to their historic prerogatives. Though some of the younger priests welcomed the appointment of an outsider as a breath of fresh air, others expressed their dismay in unmistakable terms. In some rectories, the priests revived a ditty composed years before in a different context:

> *Hail Mary, full of grace,*
> *The Irish are in second place.*

The clergy's astonishment was echoed by their congregations. Grumbling could be heard, particularly in the city's working-class districts, about "that little Portogee" or the "spic Archbishop." And a few—a tiny handful, undoubtedly—took more direct action. In the weeks before he was to arrive, the Boston Chancery received several anonymous phone calls threatening Medeiros' life or Church property. On October 6, hours after he landed in Boston to take up his new responsibilities, a cross was burned on the Chancery lawn. The next evening, following his installation, intruders ransacked Newman House, the Catholic student center at Boston University, and shortly before midnight, a fire—clearly the work of arsonists—severely damaged the Archdiocesan Television Center and adjacent St. Jerome's Chapel. Later, a pipe bomb was discovered in the Chancery doorway. After the bomb squad disarmed it, police protection was redoubled there and around the Archbishop's residence.

These were disconcerting portents for Medeiros' tenure in Boston. But they were only one aspect of his reception, which was generally courteous, even enthusiastic. After 350 persons—among them Governor Sargent and Mayor White—greeted him at Logan Airport, state police escorted his motorcade to Cushing's residence, where he met privately with the desperately ill seventy-five-year-old Cardinal. Then the press was ushered into the room and Cushing spoke warmly of Medeiros: "He is a fine man, one of the finest members of the whole American hierarchy. I welcome him to the Archdiocese of Boston." Acknowledging the contrast in their temperaments—"we are two different types of men"—he put the most favorable construction on it: "He represents the higher type of man and he will lead our people closer to the Divine Master." Near tears, the Cardinal broke off and gazed sadly down at the floor. There was a long, awkward pause until someone asked Medeiros how it felt to be Cushing's successor.

"I will answer that," Medeiros replied, "by asking Cardinal Cushing for his blessing." He knelt on the floor before the Cardinal, who, rising unsteadily to his feet, intoned the ancient blessing of the Church in a half-audible whisper. Medeiros kissed Cushing's ring, and the old Cardinal, obviously moved, embraced him.

The next afternoon, after Boston's new Archbishop had been installed in solemn rites at the Cathedral of the Holy Cross, he spoke to the crowd of 2,500 faithful in humble tones which contrasted sharply with the splendor of the occasion. "I do not know how to serve you as your bishop, your shepherd, your father and your brother, with any show of oratory or philosophy," he said. "I cannot rely on any power of my own. Personally I feel too weak and too small for the task entrusted to me by the Holy Father. But I believe I can do all things in Him who is our strength and with your indispensable and loving cooperation."

Whatever he said that day would have been lost in a more powerful drama. Cushing was so consumed by cancer that few of his advisers had expected him to appear at the Cathedral, but he summoned his waning energies and hobbled painfully at the rear of the great procession, taking his place in the sanctuary, where he sat erect but haggard through the long ceremony. Finally a microphone was set before him, and the bishop who had presided over the Archdiocese for twenty-six years said goodbye in a voice drained of its once robust timbre. "Today we welcome—and warmly welcome—a new Archbishop. He is in the prime of his life, rich in character and ability, and full of promise for the years ahead. . . . I can assure our new bishop that nowhere in God's good world will he find more earnest collaborators, more willing hands and hearts to assist him, more fervent prayers in support of all his endeavors."

Then, his voice trembling with emotion, he bid farewell: "Whatever time is left for me, whatever pain or suffering, I offer joyfully for the Church that I have loved and tried to serve for three quarters of a century. Pray for me, as I pray for you—and God bless you all." At that, the vast throng surged to its feet and—with the new Archbishop now a neglected spectator—gave the aged Cardinal a five-minute ovation.

Even after the crozier of authority had changed hands, Medeiros was eclipsed by his predecessor. For three weeks the two bishops shared the episcopal residence on Commonwealth Avenue, Medeiros an uneasy guest in his own house, until Cushing drew his last breath on November 2. His passing provoked a massive outpouring of sorrow and affection. In four days of official mourning, more than half a million people filed past the burgundy-draped catafalque. Thousands more surrounded the Cathedral, standing ten deep along Washington Street, as eleven Cardinals and fifty bishops led the funeral procession. And once they had bid farewell to "this valiant newsmaker, this holy man, this zealous priest, this uncommon prelate," the Cardinal's broadbrimmed scarlet hat was hoisted high above the altar, where it hung beside Cardinal O'Connell's, there to cast its potent shadow on his successor for years to come.

If Humberto Medeiros was an alien graft on the sturdy frame of Boston's Irish Catholicism, so the first Massachusetts Catholics were loathsome eruptions in the Puritan body politic. To the "visible saints" who founded their communal life in compact with a fierce Protestant God, Roman Catholicism was the doctrine of the Antichrist, reeking with superstition, idolatry, and despotism. At first, this horror was largely visceral; straying into a Catholic service, John Adams found it "most awful and affecting; the poor wretches, fingering their beads, chanting Latin, not a word of which they understood; their Pater Nosters and Ave Marias; their holy water; their crossing themselves perpetually; their bowing and kneeling and genuflecting." This revulsion was reinforced by more palpable fears of French-Canadian Catholics, "who by their subtle insinuations industriously labor to debauch, seduce and withdraw the Indians from their due obedience unto his Majesty." For years, Guy Fawkes Day—the anniversary of a Catholic plot to blow up the Houses of Parliament—was celebrated in Boston as Pope Day, with rival gangs from the North End and the South End, each carrying horrible effigies of the Pope and the devil, doing battle on the Common. Revolutionary pamphleteers exploited Boston's antiCatholicism by equating British tyranny with popery. Only gratitude for France's assistance in the Revolution, and the need to neutralize Catholic Quebec, led Massachusetts to pass a statute of toleration in 1780.

By century's end, however, the excesses of France's own revolution—and fears that they would spread across the Atlantic—brought Boston's prosperous Federalists a new appreciation for the social discipline exercised by the Roman Church. Indeed, as Irish laborers came to outnumber French artisans in Boston's Catholic community, the Yankee ascendancy looked increasingly to the Church as a stabilizing force. By 1848, the Irish had appropriated the episcopal seat, not to relinquish it for a century and a quarter. But the first Irish bishops—John Fitzpatrick (1848–66) and John Williams (1866–1907)—were cautious men, intensely aware that they represented a scorned minority. Fitzpatrick was admitted to Yankee society—joining the Thursday Evening Club, becoming warmly known to Protestants and Catholics alike as "Bishop John." By contrast, John Williams was so austere that archdiocesan historians were "tempted to conclude that the chill of New England had frozen his Irish blood and turned a Celt into a somewhat extreme example of a well-known Yankee type." Yet so unsure was he of Yankee toleration that he never wore clerical garb and kept his churches off main thoroughfares. As for the indignities inflicted on his flock, the only remedy Williams could offer was relentless assimilation. Boston's Catholic journal took its cue from him when it admonished: "The good parish is remarkable for its orderly, well-dressed people, who take a pride in appearing decent, of being proper in their homes and conversation, and no brawls or tumults are ever heard within its walls."

Only with the advent of William Henry O'Connell in 1907 did the Archdiocese begin to exhibit the aggressive self-confidence already apparent in the politics of Honey Fitz and James Michael Curley. For too long, the new Archbishop believed, Boston's Church had been content to remain on the defensive, refuting the indictments brought against it by Protestant orthodoxy. Now, with the Irish triumphant in the temporal sphere, O'Connell proclaimed a new Church Militant. "The Puritan has passed," he declared in 1908. "The Catholic remains. The city where a century ago he came unwanted he has made his own!"

To the long-suffering Irish, his was a rousing message: no longer need you feel inferior, no longer need you model yourself after the Yankees, for you come from something older, deeper, and better—the Church of Rome. Educated at Rome's North American College, returning eleven years later to be its rector, O'Connell moved in the Vatican's inner circles. Impressed by the pageantry, pomp, and power of the Holy See, he henceforth took its lead in all matters, large and small. Enlisting in Leo XIII's crusade against "Americanism"—the heterodox notion that the American Church should adapt itself to native conditions and democratic practices—O'Connell became the country's principal advocate of papal supremacy. Particularly after he was elevated to Cardinal in 1911, he applied those same principles to Boston, centralizing all Church authority, becoming a miniature pope in his own realm. "When I ask you to do something," he once told the faithful, "trust me and do it."

He gave physical expression to this new confidence by taking Boston's Church "out of the Catacombs." Since the middle of the previous century, most of the city's Catholic institutions had huddled together in the South End. When the Cathedral of the Holy Cross was built on Washington Street in 1860, that neighborhood seemed about to become the city's most fashionable, yet even before the great Gothic structure was completed, the *haut monde* had drifted off into the Back Bay and the Cathedral was left standing in a dreary welter of dank saloons, livery stables, and dilapidated tenements. Nothing so reflected the contempt in which Yankee authorities then held the Irish community as their decision in 1898 to run the Elevated's trestle down the middle of Washington Street, where its dark latticework buried the Cathedral's broad façade in perpetual gloom. The trains thundered by every four to seven minutes, drowning out sections of the Mass, rattling the chalice on the altar, setting Irish teeth on edge.

The great Cathedral—larger than those of Strasbourg, Dublin, Venice, or Vienna—was too big an investment to abandon, so O'Connell left it where it was, but in recompense, he set out to build, on hilltops surrounding Boston, a little Rome such as he remembered from the hills of the Eternal City. First Boston College moved to an estate in Chestnut Hill; then the Passionist Monastery, the Cenacle Convent, and St. Elizabeth's Hospital to Nevin's Hill in Brighton. Finally, with a $2.2 million bequest from the theater magnate A. Paul Keith, O'Connell built himself an Italian Renaissance palazzo and a matching chancery on forty lushly landscaped acres in Brighton. In 1931, dedicating still another bucolic retreat, he declared: "On every hilltop now for miles around gleams the sacred sign of our redemption. Around and about the whole city, God has set up his fortresses of sacrifice and prayer."

Few could detect much sacrifice in the Cardinal's own imperial style. Relishing his role as Roman proconsul, he encouraged homage. On his return from investiture as Cardinal, twenty-five of the city's foremost businessmen—all of them Protestants—presented him with a gold casket containing an illuminated Latin address and a check for $25,000. The three-story mansion where he dwelled was one of Boston's most opulent houses, and when O'Connell moved in, he brought with him his houseman, Peppino; his coachman, Pio Zappa; and his music master, Pio DeLuca—all, like the terrazzo floors and tapestries, imported from Italy. The Cardinal entertained lavishly. At his dinner table, he discouraged the use of English, preferring Latin (the language of the Church) or French (the language of the Court). When he left his mansion—to spend Friday afternoons at the Boston Symphony, for example—it was in a giant Pierce-Arrow, accompanied by his black poodle, Moro. He summered in Marblehead, high on a hillside overlooking the harbor (after he ordered young picnickers off the rocks, a wag posted a sign which read: "The world is the Lord's and the fullness thereof, but the rocks belong to the Cardinal"). Each winter he embarked for his Bahamas estate, taking so many such holidays that he became known in certain Boston circles as "Gangplank Bill." Nor did O'Connell display any hesitation in sharing this wealth—and power—with his large family. He even made his nephew chancellor of the Archdiocese, an act of nepotism which backfired when the young priest secretly married. The information was leaked by O'Connell's enemies to Pope Benedict XV, who severely reprimanded the Cardinal for permitting such indiscretions.

O'Connell's sophistication contrasted sharply with the austere morality he demanded from most of his flock. Frankly elitist, he believed it was "monstrous for the masses to have an equal vote with men of property and education." The Catholics who filled his churches must be held to strict standards of behavior and shielded—through Boston's rigid censorship—from such immoral influences as Eugene O'Neill and D. H. Lawrence. Unable to analyze difficult issues, the poor required "thought ready-made." Only Catholics of wealth and breeding—"those who were running the world"—were entitled to a "high culture."

By then, of course, O'Connell had a hand in running not only Boston but the Commonwealth of Massachusetts. So complete was his control of Church machinery, so thorough his dominion over one million Catholics, that few politicians dared cross him. The most important question on any matter of public policy was "What does Lake Street think?"—a reference to the Cardinal's chancery address. In the corridors of the State House, O'Connell was known simply as "Number One."

The most resolutely conservative of America's bishops, O'Connell often voted Republican, a damnable heresy at that time in Boston's Irish neighborhoods. He adamantly opposed the Child Labor Amendment, labeling it "Soviet legislation" because it would infringe parental authority over child rearing (the amendment was soundly defeated at Massachusetts' polls). When Francisco Franco's planes killed a thousand civilians in Barcelona, O'Connell called the Generalissimo a fighter for "Christian civilization in Spain." A perfervid critic of the New Deal, he repeatedly spoke out against "atheistic Communism."

Yet, when it served his purposes, O'Connell could retreat behind his scarlet vestments. He resisted pressure to appeal for clemency in the Sacco-Vanzetti case, responding elliptically, "The justice of God is perfect and in the end, He and His Ways, mysterious as they are, are our hope and salvation." He assailed Father Charles Coughlin, ordering that radios in the rectories be turned off when the neo-fascist "radio priest" came on the air. But just as Pope Pius XII failed to condemn Hitler's concentration camps, so when bands of Irish youths ranged Blue Hill Avenue (they called it "Jew Hill Avenue"), harassing and beating Jews, the Cardinal was conspicuously silent.

Only rarely did the Cardinal intervene directly in electoral politics, but he made no secret of his distaste for the bumptious populist James Michael Curley. In 1937, Curley was running for mayor in a field of six, one of whom was School Committeeman Maurice J. Tobin. Curley was considered a shoo-in, but on election morning, the Boston *Post*—the favorite newspaper of Boston's Irish—replaced its normal front-page quote from Shakespeare or Goethe with something more topical. "Voters of Boston," read the notice prominently displayed above the masthead. "Cardinal O'Connell, in speaking to the Catholic Alumni Association, said, 'The walls are raised against honest men in civil life.' You can break down these walls by voting for an honest, clean, competent young man, MAURICE TOBIN, today. He will redeem the city and take it out of the hands of those who have been responsible for graft and corruption . . ." When the paper hit the streets, Curley's camp dispatched an emissary to the Cardinal's residence to explain that careless readers, not paying close attention to the punctuation, might conclude that His Eminence, in remarks delivered months before, was actually endorsing Tobin. The Curley forces requested a brief communiqué from the Cardinal disavowing any such intentions, but O'Connell kept the emissary waiting for nearly an hour before sending word that he was too busy to see anyone. Tobin beat Curley that day by an astonishing 25,250 votes.

Such was the awesome power which Richard J. Cushing inherited on September 28, 1944. But Cushing was a very different man from the refined and ruthless prince of the Church he succeeded. Born to a Cork blacksmith and a Waterford housemaid on Third Street in South Boston, he never lost the raffish air he had acquired on Southie's wharves and sidewalks. If not for World War I, Cushing might have followed O'Connell's road to Rome and there acquired a cosmopolitan patina. But never in Rome until after he became Archbishop, he remained a distinctively American churchman. Whereas O'Connell represented the Roman Catholic Church, imperial and imperious, hostile to much of the American experience, Cushing came to personify a native faith, consistent with the pragmatic, self-reliant, and democratic spirit of the New World.

Not long after assuming office, he pledged to refrain from "all argument with our non-Catholic neighbors and from all purely defensive talk about Catholicism." That position was tested early by a Jesuit priest named Leonard Feeney, who accused the Jesuits' own Boston College of heresy for teaching that salvation was possible outside the Catholic Church. Cushing withdrew Feeney's priestly authority, but the dissident only intensified his crusade, taking to the Boston Common, where he denounced Jews as "horrid, degenerate, hook-nosed perverts." Cushing had lived through the Christian Front's wartime xenophobia and had no intention of presiding over its revival. As a fund raiser, he had long cultivated wealthy Jews; moreover, his sister had married a Jew, whom the Cardinal called "the best Christian I know." Asked about Feeney, he would rasp impatiently, "Nobody can tell me that Christ died on Calvary for any select group!" In 1953, the Vatican upheld Cushing's stand by excommunicating the renegade priest.

But Cushing had a polemical streak too. He jousted peevishly with Protestant critics like Paul Blanshard, and on at least one issue—the menace of international Communism—he was as zealous as his predecessor. The anti-Communist crusade held a special appeal for American Catholics; intensely Catholic *and* American, it demonstrated at last the compatibility of faith and patriotism. As the cold war deepened, New York's Francis Cardinal Spellman and his assistant, Bishop Fulton J. Sheen, fulminated against "Satan-inspired Communists" and "anti-Christian minds drenched and drugged in the devil's cauldron." Cushing stood squarely in that tradition. After Yugoslavia's Archbishop Stepinac was imprisoned, Cushing denounced the "bloody and barbaric" behavior of the "Red Fascists." Soon he broadened his indictment to include "the parlor pinks, the fellow travelers, and out-and-out Communists who thrive in our midst." He formed a close friendship with J. Edgar Hoover, who often assigned FBI men to escort him on his travels. He once called

Robert Welch the most "dedicated anti-Communist in the country" and endorsed Welch's John Birch Society. As for Senator Joseph McCarthy—who enjoyed massive support among Boston's Irish Catholics—Cushing never explicitly backed him, but scrupulously avoided anything that might be taken for criticism. Asked for his opinion of the Senator, he once responded, "The whole thing depends on how you look at Communism. If you look upon it as one of the greatest evils that has attempted to undermine Western civilization, naturally you do everything you can to save our way of life from the inroads of evil."

During those early years, Cushing seemed torn by conflicting impulses—at times pulled toward a new ecumenical openness, at times toward an irascible ghetto Catholicism. What resolved that tension, putting a distinctive stamp on his regime, was the powerful influence of "the two Johns"—John Fitzgerald Kennedy and Pope John XXIII—the first redefining what it meant to be Catholic in America, the second what it meant to be Catholic at all.

When Cushing first met Joseph P. Kennedy in the mid-thirties, they didn't much care for each other. "The trouble with you two," a friend remarked, "is you're like peas in a pod." Soon the financier and the priest discovered some mutual interests—money, politics, and anti-Communism, in that order. In August 1946, during his first congressional campaign, Jack Kennedy presented Cushing with a family check for $650,000 to build the Joseph P. Kennedy, Jr., Memorial Hospital, the largest gift the Archdiocese had yet received and one calculated to please the district's Catholic voters. In years to come, the Kennedys added millions more for a whole array of hospitals, homes, and Catholic centers. According to one of Cushing's principal financial aides, the Cardinal worked out a cozy arrangement with the senior Kennedy: whenever the Ambassador wished, Cushing kicked back fifty cents on the dollar, "laundered" money available for any purpose the Kennedys might select, usually politics.

Cushing performed other services—raising campaign funds for Jack and bringing influence to bear on his behalf with the Catholic governor of Pennsylvania. But his most important contribution was his endorsement of Jack's political catechism. "I am not the Catholic candidate for President," Kennedy told Protestant ministers in Houston. "I am the Democratic Party's candidate for President who happens also to be a Catholic. . . . I believe in an America where the separation of Church and state is absolute—where no Catholic prelate would tell the President (should he be a Catholic) how to act." Cushing—the prelate everyone had in mind—emphatically agreed. "Senator Kennedy would resent absolutely having a Cardinal, a bishop, or a priest telling him how to act. I don't know anyone who would try to tell him." Jack rewarded his "spiritual adviser" with an invitation to deliver the inaugural invocation, which he did at stentorian volume and mind-boggling length.

While his celebrity grew from association with John Kennedy, Cushing owed his rise in the Church to Pope John. Pius XII had been in no hurry to elevate the outspoken American, but the rotund peasant's son who became John XXIII immediately recognized a kindred spirit and, within six weeks of mounting the Throne of Peter in November 1958, made Cushing a Cardinal. Boston's Archbishop knew little of John before he became Pope, "but when I saw him going to the prisoners, to old folks, to the laborers, even to the Communists, I said, 'Good God, that's my man!'" Later, Cushing called John "the only man who ever understood me" and "the best reproduction of Christ that I have ever met." Indeed, the Pope and his new Cardinal were remarkably alike—earthy, pragmatic, candid, and spontaneous. Few bishops anywhere were more likely than Cushing to accept John's judgment that humanity did not consist of friends and enemies of the Church but of a multitude of winnable souls. And few so enthusiastically welcomed his determination to "let fresh air into the Church" by calling an Ecumenical Council. But the sessions were conducted in Latin, a language Cushing had never mastered ("I didn't know whether it was Chinese or Eskimo," he admitted later), and he was largely indifferent to theology ("Do good and avoid evil was about as far as he went," one longtime aide recalls, "and even that was subject to interpretation"). The following year, Cushing led the fight for a Council declaration on religious freedom with an eloquent speech citing Thomas Jefferson on "a decent respect for the opinions of mankind," but the first Council session wasn't three weeks old before he was back in Boston, doing what he did best—raising money.

No less an authority than Jackson Martinelli, Pius XII's financial adviser, once observed, "There is not much difference between Standard Oil of New Jersey and the Catholic Church's operations. The only difference is that Standard produces oil and the Catholic Church produces a way of thought and life." Of necessity, Cushing devoted disproportionate energy to raising money. After World War II, Boston's Church followed its constituents into the suburbs, establishing eighty-five new parishes between Cape Cod and the New Hampshire border. In principle, each parish was responsible for raising or borrowing funds to build its own church, rectory, and parochial school, while the diocese concentrated on erecting seminaries, hospitals, regional high schools, and homes for the elderly. But Cushing was so impatient to get buildings underway that he often advanced a struggling parish the money out of diocesan funds; then, if its financial difficulties persisted, he forgave the principal, even the interest, for years to come. Meanwhile, he offered financial inducements to bring some sixty new Catholic orders into the diocese. His growing empire took staggering sums to build and maintain. Over and above the ordinary parish collections, the Cardinal needed $12 million a year, or about $30,000 a day.

Cushing was renowned for shameless—but folksy—fund raising. He'd go anywhere for a $1,000 fee and his speeches to communion breakfasts and Knights of Columbus dinners invariably ended: "Now we'll take up a collection." Even his table-hopping paid off as diners stuffed ten-dollar bills in the folds of his cassock. He got other things too. Once, when several nuns explained their needs, Cushing dipped into his pocket and came up with a handful of diamond rings. "Some of my little old ladies gave them to me," he said. "Here, why don't you raffle them off and see what you can get."

He rang every change on solicitation: at smokers, bazaars, lawn fetes, parish reunions, hockey games, theatricals, and spectacles at Blinstrub's Village, a South Boston nightclub which hosted so many of the Cardinal's charity events it became known as "Boston's Vatican." He raised even more money through a network of professional and business guilds—St. Luke's for physicians, St. Apollonia's for dentists, the Caritas Guild for liquor dealers. The telephone, gas, and electric companies and the big department stores were elaborately organized. Employees gave a quarter a week to their room captain, who passed it on to the floor captain, who gave it to the building captain, who took it directly to the Cardinal. And Cushing personally raised funds from major contributors like Middlesex County Sheriff Howard Fitzpatrick or former Governor Alvan Fuller, who each year invited the Cardinal to lunch, placing a $100,000 check under his plate. Cushing was preoccupied with finding new sources of cash. "I raise money," he told an aide. "What else am I good for?"

But as the years went by, and money began drying up, the Cardinal piled bank loans, bond issues, and personal advances ($5 million from the Kennedys alone) into a towering, but rickety, financial pyramid. For a time his credit was funneled through two small Catholic banks, which raised money from correspondent banks. Then Cushing struck a surprising deal with Boston's First National Bank, an unlikely partner for an Irish churchman. Not so many years before, Jim Curley had become so exasperated with the starchy First he had threatened to flood its vaults with water from a municipal main unless the bank advanced him funds to meet the city payroll. But Boston's bankers had come to terms with the Irish. It was the resourceful Ephron Catlin who persuaded Cushing to adopt a technique the First had employed to bail out Hollywood's troubled movie industry. The bank would loan money to the movie companies, then take its cut directly from the box office. Catlin proposed that its loans to the Archdiocese be recovered straight from the parish collection plates. "Cushing loved it," Catlin recalls. "For years he'd been looking for a way to get his hands on more of the parish money, although I don't think he liked it when I compared him to Sam Goldwyn." But soon even the First could no longer keep the Archdiocese afloat on its sea of debt. The Cardinal called on several New York banks, who refused him more credit. By 1967, his debt had reached an unprecedented $80 million. During his last decade, Cushing's obsession with money affected every diocesan activity, including efforts to grapple with the city's growing racial polarization.

Cushing had showed an early sympathy with blacks. In 1953, he paid $500 for a life membership in the NAACP and, three years later, he established St. Richard's Church in Roxbury for Boston's 1,000 black Catholics. Few dissenters questioned such ethnic segregation—then the pattern in most large dioceses—and the black community enthusiastically welcomed the gesture. Cushing gave the church his own name and frequently celebrated Mass there with the white Josephite priests. The Cardinal was genuinely popular in Roxbury at that time, responding with the same gracious patronage he bestowed on the infidels of Togo and Tanganyika (Catholic rectories in those days still displayed ceramic "tar babies" in which visitors stuck quarters for the African missions). "Open our hands and hearts to all the oppressed and afflicted," Cushing wrote in an early leaflet called "A Prayer for Brotherhood." On the cover was a photograph of the Archbishop beaming benevolently on a fetching little Negro girl as she kissed his ring.

But most Boston blacks never saw a priest, much less a Cardinal. They were Baptists, Methodists, or Pentecostals, which gave Protestant churches a greater purchase on black lives. Moreover, Boston's Irish had a legacy of hostility to abolitionism. Not surprisingly, as the sixties began, it was liberal white Protestants—heirs to Theodore Parker and William Lloyd Garrison—who took the lead in reaching out to the black community. In July 1960, a Protestant institute called Packard Manse—hitherto dedicated to ecumenical exchange with Catholics and Jews—opened a branch in Roxbury. "Suburban captivity is the greatest threat to Protestantism," it proclaimed. "It is time to reach out to the inner city." To head the new operation, it chose John Harmon, a white Episcopal priest already living in Roxbury. Later, Harmon persuaded his friend Harvey Cox, a professor at Andover-Newton Theological School, to move nearby as an act of "Christian witness." The Manse pioneered a series of "black-white dialogues" in Roxbury. Then, in November 1963—impelled to take more eye-catching action—Harmon, Cox, and twelve other Protestant clergymen from New England were arrested during a civil rights march in Williamston, North Carolina.

The arrests were big news back in Boston. After a week in jail—during which they sent a letter home saying, "We now know that in Christ there is no East or West, no South or North, no black or white. O Lord, gather together all separated brothers!"—the clergymen returned to a heroes' welcome. But for a few Catholic priests, the event was cause for chagrin. Father Shawn Sheehan, a professor at St. John's Seminary, wept bitterly—partly in sympathy for his brothers in Christ, but principally in shame because no Catholic priest had yet had the courage to put himself in jeopardy for racial justice.

Sheehan thereupon organized the first clerical demonstration in archdiocesan history. Through a driving rainstorm, thirty priests and a like number of Protestant clergymen walked silently in a "penitential procession" around the Boston School Committee, City Hall, and the State House. The demonstration took place just days after Louise Day Hicks had been resoundingly reelected, but the priests' spokesman maintained that it was not directed at Mrs. Hicks or any other politician. "In penance," he said, "the accusing finger is pointed only at self. We wish to silently bear witness and admit our guilt for all forms of segregation in the Boston area."

The activist priests felt particularly guilty about the Catholic stance toward the changing inner city, for as the Irish abandoned their old neighborhoods in the South End, Roxbury, and Dorchester, they left the Church's outposts there in profound disarray. Most of the blacks and Puerto Ricans who replaced the Irish were, at best, indifferent to priestly ministrations, at worst hostile (one church had to lock its doors during the day because intruders used the confessionals as urinals). Many older priests had difficulty coping with their new constituents. In Edwin O'Connor's *The Edge of Sadness,* Father Hugh Kennedy has given up on his polyglot South End parish until an acerbic colleague mocks his parochialism: "We all know what a real parish is . . . a fine, big, old-fashioned, well-kept church with—and here's the important thing—lots of Irish to put inside it! . . . The kind of people who can sing 'Ave Maria' inside the church, but can give you a chorus of 'There's a Little Devil Dancing in Your Laughing Eyes' on the way home. Those are the people the Church was really meant for, wouldn't you say, Hugh?"

In 1963, seven students at St. John's Seminary set out to change that mindset, to infuse the inner-city church with a new sense of mission. At first the group—sometimes known as "the Magnificent Seven"—met behind closed doors at the seminary, reading the pronouncements of Vatican II, pondering their implications for traditional Catholic theology and social action. That summer they spent two weeks in the loft of Roxbury's St. Richard's Church, taking a parish census during the day, talking with black activists at night. The next summer, they came back for a full month, and after their ordination, three of them obtained permanent assignments in Roxbury, determined to revitalize its moribund churches; but their ambitious scheme quickly foundered for lack of wholehearted support from the Cardinal.

Sympathetic though he might be with their goals, Cushing was uneasy with priestly activism, particularly with anything that smacked of civil disobedience. His discomfort surfaced in February 1964 during the second black boycott of the city's schools. In a television interview, Cushing called the boycott "a very, very dangerous thing. I am all for human rights—for every living, breathing human soul. But there is a better way of attaining these rights than by violating laws of society and by endangering the community by sending a number of children, emotionally upset, through the city's streets."

But two events in the spring of 1964 profoundly affected the Cardinal and his advisers. The first occurred on St. Patrick's Day. Distressed by the refusal of white working-class Bostonians to support its challenge of *de facto* segregation, the NAACP, for the first time, entered the South Boston parade. Its float bore a large portrait of the recently assassinated John Kennedy and beside it, in bold green letters: "From the Fight for Irish Freedom to the Fight for U.S. Equality." As it lumbered onto Dorchester Street near St. Augustine's Church, four teenagers leaped into the street brandishing their own homemade banner, decorated with shamrocks and reading: "Go home, nigger. Long live the spirit of independence in segregated Boston." Tomatoes, eggs, cherry bombs, bottles, and beer cans rained down on the float. A brick shattered the windshield and broke the driver's glasses. Police moved in, escorting the float to safety. The next day, the NAACP likened the incident to "the viciousness you would expect in New Orleans and the backwoods of Mississippi."

The second incident took place eight days later when two priests from St. Bridget's Church in Lexington—Father Tom MacLeod and Father John Fitzpatrick—were arrested trying to integrate a restaurant in Williamston, North Carolina. The Shamrock Cafe—the name rang ironically back in Boston—was just a few yards down the road from the spot where the Protestant clergymen had been arrested six months before. MacLeod and Fitzpatrick were the first American priests ever to be arrested for civil rights activity. MacLeod was the leader of the Lexington Civil Rights Committee who had once chastised CORE for demonstrating against housing discrimination on the Lexington Green; but like other priests of his generation, he had grown increasingly uncomfortable with his Church's passivity on the race issue. When the two priests arrived back at St. Bridget's after several nights in jail, their pastor, Monsignor George Casey—himself an ardent civil rights activist—welcomed them warmly: "You boys have a lot of spunk. You've brought us right back into the Ecumenical Movement." Cushing—annoyed because the pair hadn't consulted him—wasn't so pleased at first, but as congratulatory telegrams poured into the Chancery, the Cardinal came to see some merit in their action.

Widespread condemnation of the St. Patrick's Day incident and praise for the young priests encouraged the Cardinal to speak out. On Pentecost Sunday in April, he delivered his strongest statement yet on the race issue: "I call this city and its citizens to justice. I call them to see in their Negro neighbors the face of Christ himself. I call them to change their hearts and to raise their hands, before the evils that we are tolerating call down the wrath of God upon his forgetful people. . . . To every believer, I say love all men and especially love Negroes, because they have suffered so much from lack of love."

Only three months later, after rioting in Harlem and Rochester, Cushing sounded a more passionate note. Denouncing "the monstrous evil of racism," he said, "It is time we were disturbed, it is time we were shaken! We have been content to do things the easy way, to console with soft words and promises, to temporize and be patient in the face of inexcusable social evils. . . . In this hour, if the men of God are silent, the very stones will cry out!"

The voice was Cushing's, the sentiments largely his, but the passion, the commitment, the words themselves came from Monsignor Francis J. Lally, Cushing's ghostwriter and conscience on such matters. Lally was an unusual churchman: a Boston Irish priest who had risen from an insular background to serve on the executive board of the National Council of Christians and Jews and the national committee of UNESCO. Cushing made him editor of the *Pilot,* the archdiocesan newspaper, a pulpit from which he inveighed weekly against narrow parochialism and racial injustice. Later, he became chairman of the Boston Redevelopment Authority, a role in which he outraged Irish neighborhoods. To the Cardinal's more traditional advisers, Lally was anathema. Robert Welch, founder of the John Birch Society, dubbed him "the Red Monsignor" and urged Cushing to get rid of him, but Lally was custodian of one side of Cushing's nature and the Cardinal relied on him to give it expression.

To build a civil rights constituency, Lally formed a Boston unit of the Catholic Interracial Council, and on St. Patrick's Day 1965, a year after the

NAACP float had been attacked, some six hundred council members entered the South Boston parade. Just one week before, some of those same Catholics had marched with Martin Luther King in Selma, Alabama, when James Reeb, the Unitarian minister from Boston, was beaten to death by white segregationists. Moved now by evangelical zeal, they sought once again to equate the civil rights movement with Ireland's liberation struggle. The marchers—among them, 150 priests and nuns in clerical garb—carried banners stating: "The rights of every man are threatened when the rights of one man are threatened—John F. Kennedy" and "Beg Un Booah Ling," Gaelic for "We Shall Overcome." When they sang the civil rights anthem, they alternated it with lusty choruses of "When Irish Eyes Are Smiling." At first they were received with deference, even a spattering of applause, but rounding the corner onto Broadway, they were greeted by beer-drinking youths who pelted them with jeers and missiles. David Nelson, the council's president, was hit on the leg with a bottle; an ice-cream cone splattered a priest's shoulder; somebody spat a mouthful of beer in a black man's face. Prancing in front of the column, one kid yelled at the priests, "Hey, Father, you want your sister to marry one?" Father Ernest Serino, a husky Italian priest just back from Selma, had had enough. Lunging from the line of march, he grabbed the kid by the lapel, growling, "Shut your mouth or I'll shut it for you." The boy seemed ready to strike the priest before police rushed in to separate them.

Increasingly, Boston's Church found itself pincered between the newly aggressive black community and the angrily resisting white neighborhoods. By mid-1965, that struggle focused on the bruising tug-of-war between the NAACP and the Boston School Committee. Officially at least, the Archdiocese had thrown its weight behind the black community; Cushing himself was a member of the Kiernan Commission, which found in April that Boston's racially imbalanced schools represented a "serious conflict with the American creed of equal opportunity," and Lally in the *Pilot* warned: "We must pay for our wickedness as a people and do justice in the fullest sense to the Negro child." But some blacks believed that the Church could have done much more. Cushing's political clout was widely appreciated—legislators were still asking what "Lake Street" thought. When business interests wanted to redevelop the old New Haven Railroad yards as the Prudential Center, it was Cushing they asked to intervene with City Hall; when Boston University needed an exit from Storrow Drive, it was to Cushing they went for help. Why, blacks wondered, didn't the Cardinal do the same for them? When Louise Day Hicks won reelection that November with 64 percent of the vote, the NAACP charged that "neither bishops, priests, monsignors nor Cardinal Cushing have tried to do anything to improve the Negro's position."

There were those who believed that if Cushing had intervened behind the scenes he could have nipped Mrs. Hicks's crusade in the bud. The chairwoman was known to be a devout Catholic, a dutiful communicant; why, they asked, couldn't the Cardinal simply call her in and say, "Louise, I won't tolerate this in my Archdiocese. It has to stop"? (If that failed, they argued, he should excommunicate her as Archbishop Cody of New Orleans had once excommunicated the virulent segregationist Leander Perez.)

In fact, Cushing may have made one such effort. In the summer of 1965, he invited Mrs. Hicks to his residence. No one else was present and Cushing has left no account of what transpired. According to Mrs. Hicks, the Cardinal presented her with a crucifix, to which she responded, "You're giving me everything but your support, Your Eminence."

"Louise, my dear," the Cardinal is reported to have said, "you don't know what kind of pressure I'm under. The Negroes want me to go down to the School Committee and march with those demonstrators."

"Why don't you do that, Your Eminence," Louise says she answered. "Then come upstairs and receive my resignation."

"From the School Committee?"

"No, from the Church."

Some doubt Mrs. Hicks's version. But whatever happened that day, Cushing henceforth seemed wary of Mrs. Hicks. In 1966, under pressure from the Catholic Interracial Council, he established a Human Rights Commission to handle civil rights matters for the Archdiocese. Its director, Father Paul Rynne, went straight to Mrs. Hicks in an effort to moderate her stand. A few days later, he received a call from the Cardinal: "Let me give you some advice," Cushing said. "Don't bother that woman. I'm warning you, she's a tough bird."

What Cushing feared wasn't so much Mrs. Hicks herself as the effect of a public squabble with her on his financial deficit. Many of his biggest donors were traditional Irish Catholics who would deeply resent any effort to restrain the chairwoman. This danger was underlined by the Cardinal's coterie of conservative advisers who gathered in the pine-paneled basement of Cushing's chauffeur, Al Wasilauskas, for a few drinks at the end of the day. The Cardinal was getting out of touch with his constituency, they warned. By 1966, Cushing began cracking down on Catholic activists. After the Interracial Council objected to an ex-military man he had appointed as its chaplain, the Cardinal angrily withdrew the appointment but, along with it, his support for the council. Later that year, he announced that he was going to fire "that Communist" at Emmanuel College, an outspoken young nun named Marie Augusta Neal, who had been active in the black community. When Emmanuel's president intervened on her behalf, the Cardinal relented, but warned Sister Marie Augusta to "stay out of Roxbury."

Cushing's growing timidity was reinforced by his suspicions about Martin Luther King. The Cardinal felt most comfortable in a missionary relationship to the black community, in which the white Church was the benefactor to a largely powerless people; he was less easy as blacks began to assume control of their own destiny. Toward King, who personified that new aggressiveness, Cushing's attitude was largely defined by his friend J. Edgar Hoover, who showed him surveillance reports suggesting that King was both a Communist and a sexual degenerate. Cushing largely accepted that evidence and for more than a decade, while publicly permitting Lally to praise King in his name, he privately kept his distance. After King was assassinated, Lally put out the obligatory eulogy, but when the wife of the Democratic state chairman asked Cushing to request all Catholics to wear mourning bands for a week, he rasped, "Lady, why don't you go back to your kitchen!"

The Cardinal's retreat provoked an uprising in his own ranks. Some of "the Magnificent Seven" were still in Roxbury in June 1967 when blacks took to the streets in four nights of rioting. They rushed into the troubled district, eager to help, but angry blacks would have none of it. "Get off the street, Father," they said. "We don't want your Roman collars out here." Wounded by this rejection and impatient with Cushing's intransigence, twenty inner-city priests met at Shawn Sheehan's rectory to consider how the Church could be made more "relevant" to blacks. Eventually, they established an Association of Boston Urban Priests to push the Archdiocese into bolder positions. Their first step was unprecedented: open intervention in that fall's City Council election. Twenty-five association members endorsed Tom Atkins, the NAACP leader who only two years before had denounced the Archdiocese for failing to throw its moral weight against Louise Day Hicks's reelection. Warning that American cities could soon become "veritable concentration camps of the poor, the powerless and the voiceless," newspaper ads urged voters to "join us in working and voting for Tom Atkins."

Six months later, the association waded into even more troubled waters, condemning the Vietnam War and urging diversion of military spending into a "massive national effort" to solve the urban crisis. After Martin Luther King's death, the association grew still angrier, reflecting the Catholic radicalism then stirring across the country. This was the era when Daniel and Philip Berrigan became "criminals for peace," when young seminarians at Woodstock College destroyed Dow Chemical files, when the Catonsville Nine splattered blood on draft records. In Boston, Catholic activism continued to focus on the race issue. On April 4, 1969, the first anniversary of King's assassination, Faneuil Hall was filled for a memorial service. Abruptly, Father John White, one of the association's founders, rose to say: "I cannot remain here because the Church I represent has very little to do with the people and the causes which meant so much to Dr. King and for which he gave his life. The poor, the oppressed, the victims of war are not the priority of the Catholic Church in Boston." Then he walked out.

Two months later, the dissident priests took their boldest step yet. Normally a pastoral letter is the bishop's prerogative, an opportunity to speak over his priests' heads directly to the faithful. Now the association—representing barely 130 of the diocese's 2,500 priests—issued its own pastoral letter. The authors called it a "public criticism of the stance of the Church in Boston . . . an indictment not so much of individuals as of a theology and culture which, in our view, impede the preaching and living of the gospel." It concluded with eighteen recommendations to the Cardinal, among them a "substantially increased commitment of money and personnel for the urban ministry" and training of priests to make them "more sensitive to social responsibilities."

When the association submitted its letter to Cushing, he raised no objection; but, after its publication, he steadfastly refused to discuss the recommendations. Old and desperately ill by then, the Cardinal was either unwilling or unable to bring his enormous prestige to bear on the city's intensifying racial crisis. Many believed that the Church was the one institution which might have halted Boston's lurch toward race war, but by 1969 it was probably too late for that.

There is evidence that, before he died, the Cardinal had misgivings about his stance in this area. In August 1970, he met briefly with State Education Commissioner Neil Sullivan. The Cardinal acknowledged to Sullivan that many Boston Catholics "carried with them deep feelings of prejudice and distrust toward black people, and they trusted to too great an extent the leadership of bigoted and narrow-minded parish priests." According to Sullivan, Cushing was filled with remorse because he had done so little to change those attitudes.

Cushing's final years were troubled ones in almost every respect. Evidence of his deteriorating hold on the Archdiocese came in early 1966 when students at St. John's Seminary began agitating against its "dusty medievalism." Impatient with the spartan regime of their new rector, Lawrence Riley, the seminarians sought freedom to engage in ecumenical discussions, to take courses at secular universities, to express "reasoned opinions" in public, "in short, to be men of the sixties." When Riley refused to bend, 125 of the seminary's 375 students took a step which would have been unthinkable only a few years before: as the Cardinal addressed a group of pastors in the seminary library, they stood in silent vigil outside, demanding reform. The Cardinal met with student representatives, then promptly expelled the eight "ringleaders." But when other students went on a hunger strike, supported by hundreds of lay Catholics who picketed the Cardinal's residence all through Holy Week, Cushing partially backed down, dismissing Monsignor Riley and replacing him with a more flexible rector.

In July 1968, Pope Paul VI stunned much of the Catholic world with *Humanae Vitae,* his long-awaited encyclical on birth control. Ignoring a papal commission's recommendation for relaxation of the Church's stand, Paul reiterated the traditional position against all artificial contraception. That placed Cushing in a difficult position. Once a hard-liner himself—in 1948 he had blocked efforts to reform the state statute on contraception—Cushing had quietly modified his position. He maintained a surprising friendship with Dr. John Rock, a Catholic by birth, often known as "the Father of the Pill." When Rome denounced Rock, Cushing chortled, "My God, Johnny, you've got the whole Vatican pregnant!" At first, the Cardinal himself seemed to temporize on *Humanae Vitae.* His initial statement—"Rome has spoken. The matter is settled for now"—brought a stinging note from the Apostolic Delegate: "What do you mean, 'for now'?" But when the encyclical aroused a storm of protest among Catholics—including a statement by seven Boston theologians denouncing it as "neither biblical, theological, nor truly historical"—he retreated to orthodoxy, disciplining some of the rebels.

That was nothing compared to the furor the Cardinal stirred up that fall by condoning Jackie Kennedy's marriage to Aristotle Onassis. The Vatican held that by marrying a divorced man, the President's widow had "knowingly violated the law of the Church" and was ineligible to receive the sacraments. But Cushing staunchly defended her: "What a lot of nonsense! Only God knows who is a sinner and who is not. Why can't she marry whomever she wants?" That brought him an avalanche of abusive mail, apparently reflecting the covert resentment many Boston Catholics felt for the privileged Kennedys. In a moment of intense depression, Cushing talked of resigning. "If they don't understand me after thirty years," he said, "they'll never understand me."

He had long yearned to retire and devote his remaining years to missionary work in Latin America, but Pope Paul insisted that he clear up his crushing financial deficit before leaving office. Obediently, Cushing launched a Jubilee Fund to raise $50 million, almost three-fifths of the deficit, but even with the help of professional fund raisers, it collected only $28 million. Proud of his ability to wring "dollars out of Plymouth Rock," Cushing was devastated.

By 1969, the diseases which had gnawed at him for years—asthma, emphysema, bleeding ulcers, cancer of the prostate and kidneys—were taking a terrible toll. Gaunt, almost emaciated, he began drinking heavily to dull the pain. In his cups, he could be mawkishly self-pitying and abusive to priests (when a troubled young curate tried to consult him, Cushing snapped, "You don't have enough brains to lose your faith! Go back to your parish!"). Yet he still gave off flashes of the old "Cush": throwing out the first ball at Fenway Park; dancing a jig in an old folks' home on Thanksgiving Day; reciting "The Face on the Barroom Floor" to an ancient recluse; hot-dogging at communion breakfasts; striding across the room to stick out a big paw and bellow, "My name's Cushing—what's yours?"; riding the roller coaster at Revere Beach or the bumper cars at Nantasket as a covey of nuns, their habits flapping in the wind, giggled in delight at their antic Archbishop; trying on an endless assortment of hats—football helmets and yarmulkes, fireman's hats and straw boaters, baseball caps and Easter bonnets—symbols of his pragmatic, chameleon-like adaptation to a changing world.

But now his retirement was set—to coincide with his seventy-fifth birthday in August 1970—and speculation began to focus on his successor. Many names were mentioned—among them Bishop Bernard Flanagan of Worcester and Daniel Cronin, one of Boston's auxiliary bishops. The popular favorite was probably John Cardinal Wright. As prefect of the Congregation for the Clergy, Wright was the highest-ranking American in the Vatican, an intellectual known both for his progressive social stands and for his increasing theological conservatism. A former secretary to both O'Connell and Cushing, Wright had hoped to succeed his old mentors in Boston, but relations had rarely been smooth between Wright and Cushing (when told Wright had his eye on the episcopal throne, Cushing growled, "He may have his eye on it, but I've got my ass on it"). And Wright suffered from another major liability: among insiders he was believed to be a homosexual, a trait tolerated in cosmopolitan Rome, but a severe handicap in puritanical Boston.

Nevertheless, as a member of the powerful Congregation for the Bishops, Wright played a central role in selecting Cushing's successor. He had private scores to settle; if he couldn't have the job himself, he didn't want one of his enemies to have it. Like Pope Paul, Wright regarded Cushing as a maverick, unreliable on such critical issues as *Humanae Vitae*. Along with other conservatives—among them Apostolic Delegate Raimondi and New York's Terence Cardinal Cooke—he wanted Boston back in more orthodox hands. Humberto Medeiros was eminently safe in that regard.

Yet if conservatives found Medeiros convenient for their own reasons, so, ironically, did many liberals, who focused less on his theological orthodoxy than on his reputation as a social activist supporting Mexican farm workers in the Rio Grande Valley. Moreover, he was Portuguese, one of the Catholic nationalities long excluded from power in the American Church. For nearly a decade, the Vatican had been seeking to break up ethnic monopolies in American dioceses, and nowhere had one ethnic group dominated the Church so long and so thoroughly as in Boston. If O'Connell spoke for the lace-curtain Irish and Cushing for the Irish working class, so Boston's dissident priests and laymen hoped Medeiros would be Archbishop of the dispossessed non-Irish. Father Tom Corrigan, a founder of the Association of Boston Urban Priests, welcomed him as "a unique and exciting choice." The Catholic Interracial Council said Medeiros gave "every indication of being a spiritual leader of distinction."

But Cushing himself wasn't so sure. After sizing up his tiny, bespectacled successor, he began referring to him as "Birdy." One day, as he sat with an aide gazing out his residence windows toward the statue of Our Lady of Fatima, the dying Cardinal mused, "Birdy's going to take his rosary beads and trot around that statue out there saying his prayers. Then he'll come back and find his problems are still here."

Under the blazing Azorean sun, the whitewashed façade of Nossa Senhora de Saude Church dazzled his eyes until they ached. But the wooden pews, lit only by shafts of dusky light from the rose windows, were cool, tranquil, and consoling. That was Humberto Medeiros' favorite spot, a refuge from the stern austerity of home and school, an intimation of glories reserved for those who served Christ with all their hearts. When he was barely seven Humberto began attending Mass every day, perched beside his aged grandmother in her black shawl; and by the time he took his first communion there four years later, he knew he wanted to be a priest. The Church dominated the village of Arrifes on São Miguel, the largest island in the Portuguese Azores, where Humberto was born in 1915. His father, Antônio de Sousa Medeiros, raised vegetables on the rocky hillsides and ran a small variety store in the village. But by 1923 he had fallen deeply in debt and set off for America seeking more profitable labor. Between 1923 and 1928, Antônio Medeiros made three trips to America, working at a Fall River cotton mill, a nearby truck farm, a New York construction site, and a California ranch. When his family's turn arrived on the Portuguese immigration quota, he returned to Fall River, retrieved his job on the farm, and rented a tiny apartment on Davol Street.

In Arrifes, Maria Medeiros and her four children—Humberto, then fifteen; Leonel, thirteen; Manuel, eleven; and Natalie, eight—thought of America as a fairy-tale land, filled with incalculable riches. Arriving in April 1931, they were unprepared for the sour reality of Fall River's North End. A narrow spit of land wedged between the muddy Taunton River and the industrial wastes of Watuppa Pond, the North End was a fierce ethnic battleground. In its streets and alleys jostled three mutually hostile immigrant groups: the Irish, who had settled there first in the 1850s, gradually appropriating the best jobs and political control of the city; the French Canadians, who arrived a quarter century later and, after decades of discrimination, were just getting a toehold on respectability; and the Portuguese, now the bottom of the heap. When a Portuguese boy walked down Davol Street, the Irish and French kids would shout, "Portuguese stink fish," a gibe at the maritime stench which clung to his boots.

Although they lived virtually on top of each other, the three nationalities preserved separate institutional lives. There was St. Joseph's, the Irish Church, St. Mathieu's, the French church, and St. Michael's, the Portuguese church, each delivering sermons in its own language, an essential for many immigrants who—like Maria Medeiros—never learned English. At first, the Medeiros children spoke little English either. Soon they were installed at the Danforth Street School, widely known as "the dumbbell school," because it served children with learning disabilities, emotional problems, and records of minor delinquency. Although the Medeiros boys' only disability was their language, every morning as they walked to school they endured the taunts of neighborhood kids.

But his teachers soon discovered that Humberto was no dumbbell. Recognizing not only exceptional intelligence but artistic aptitude in the young immigrant, they helped him enroll in New Bedford's Swain School of Art. But that was a luxury the family could ill afford. By then the Depression was in full stride, cutting a terrible swath through Fall River's cotton industry. Soon the city which had boasted more spindles than Manchester, England, was filled with unemployed textile workers clamoring for relief.

The winter of 1932–33 was a bitter one for the Medeiroses. When his oldest son turned sixteen, Antônio insisted that he quit school and help support the family. In late 1932, Humberto became a sweeper at the Sagamore Mills, cleaning the alleys between the spinning frames for sixty-two cents a day. But his determination to receive an education never slackened; every evening after work and on weekends he studied French, Latin, algebra, and English. Only in January 1935, when his two brothers replaced him at the mill, could he return to school.

His preparations paid off handsomely. Admitted to Durfee High School as a sophomore, Humberto completed the four-year course in two and a half years, graduating first in his class of 651, compiling the best academic record in the school's history. He starred in the debating and drama societies. At graduation ceremonies in June 1937, he delivered a stirring oration, concluding with a challenge from Horace Mann: "Be ashamed to die until you have won some victory for humanity!" His classmates bestowed on him no fewer than seven superlatives: most brilliant, most original, most dignified, most studious, most talented, most interesting, and most promising.

Yet his years at Durfee weren't altogether happy ones. The school's oldest student, he was an awkward youth with no athletic prowess, a future priest who didn't drink, dance, or date, a "Portogee" in a school still dominated by the Irish, a figure so formidable his classmates held him in baffled, and uneasy, awe.

After the Fall River *News-Herald* lauded his academic record and described a mural of the Crucifixion he had painted for a Portuguese church, a wealthy Yankee widow named Florence Hutchinson offered to put him through Harvard. When Medeiros said he was going to be a priest, the Unitarian dowager decried the "terrible waste" of his talents, though she relented somewhat and contributed three hundred dollars toward his tuition at Washington's Catholic University.

Nine years later, Medeiros returned to Fall River as a priest, assigned to St. John of God Church, the parish where his mural hung behind the altar. The city's clergy were still rigidly Balkanized, grouped in Irish, French, and Portuguese "leagues," rarely crossing ethnic boundaries. For five years as a young curate Medeiros made the narrow circuit of Portuguese parishes. He had every reason to believe he would end his days as pastor of one of those churches.

What changed everything was the patronage of Bishop James Cassidy, an autocratic Irishman with a potent voice in Fall River politics. Cassidy knew that the Irish monopoly on his diocese couldn't last forever; one day soon a Portuguese priest would have to rise in the hierarchy. For years he had been watching Medeiros, and in 1950, when the young priest returned from a year of doctoral study in Rome, the Bishop took not one, but two unprecedented steps. He placed Medeiros at Holy Name Church, a lace-curtain Irish parish on the hill, and he named him assistant to the chancellor of the diocese. Under Cassidy's successor, James Connolly, his advancement was even more rapid: Vicar for Religious, vice-chancellor, and, soon, chancellor.

Those who knew Medeiros then detected little ambition for promotion. His thirst was for learning—already he had accumulated four degrees (including the prized doctorate in sacred theology) and nine languages (Greek, Latin, Hebrew, Italian, Portuguese, Spanish, German, French, and English). He often thought he would be happier teaching at a seminary or university. With his close friend Father John Driscoll, he wondered why any priest would accept the bishop's miter, with all its financial and administrative responsibilities.

But by then his advancement was inevitable. After Medeiros was named Bishop of Brownsville in June 1966, Driscoll rushed to his friend's rectory, where a celebration was underway. "Well?" he asked.

Medeiros looked up at him with a melancholy smile. "Like all the others," he said, "I took it."

Hardly an ecclesiastical plum, Brownsville was so remote that Medeiros had to look it up in an atlas. One of the nation's smallest dioceses, it had only 234,700 Catholics and 82 priests spread out over 4,226 square miles. Most of its communicants were desperately poor Mexican-American farm workers, earning eighty-five cents an hour in the fields, struggling to feed large families on twenty to thirty dollars a week. The nation's newest diocese, carved from the Corpus Christi region only eleven months before, Brownsville had been without a bishop since the first incumbent died in Germany on his way to take up the assignment. Medeiros was literally starting from scratch—with only the sparest of resources. Moreover, he was to arrive in Brownsville at a critical juncture in the valley's history. On June 1, Cesar Chavez's United Farm Workers had called fruit pickers out on strike at Starr County's melon farms, demanding a $1.25-an-hour minimum wage and union recognition. But the growers continued to harvest the crops with the help of Mexican "green-carders," so called because they had green permits authorizing them to cross the Rio Grande every day to work in the valley. The union, of course, regarded them as strikebreakers.

In the weeks between the start of the strike and Medeiros' arrival, the Church had already become deeply embroiled in the conflict. Clerical intervention came not from Brownsville, where the clergy was notoriously cautious, but from the Archdiocese of San Antonio, 250 miles to the north. San Antonio's Archbishop, Robert E. Lucey, was a fighting liberal, nationally known for his activism on behalf of the poor, minorities, and unions. Within days the Bishop's Committee for the Spanish-Speaking had dispatched food and clothing to the valley, followed quickly by three priests, who held rallies and Masses for the farm workers. One of them stood on the steps of the county courthouse and said, "These people are going to march and march until they have their rights and we're going to be marching with them every step of the way."

Priests in the Brownsville diocese—long dependent on wealthy landowners for their financial subsidies—resented the outsiders, who were soon augmented by more priests from Houston, Galveston, and Amarillo. It was one thing for these activists to play prophet for a few days, then return to their comfortable rectories in the big city; quite another for the resident priests to live with the consequences of their zeal. On June 19, Monsignor Don Laning of Mission, Texas, denounced the "intruders" and "impostors." Archbishop

Lucey struck back, attacking the valley priests as old-guard clerics indifferent to human suffering.

Into this wrangle, on June 26, stepped the new bishop. In his first public comment on the strike, Medeiros urged the farm workers and growers to settle their differences "in a Christian manner." Beyond that, he had no suggestions; the Church couldn't shirk its responsibilities in the secular realm, he said, but the solution to such disputes should be left to sociologists and economists. The Brownsville *Herald,* which had denounced Lucey as a left-wing meddler, praised the new bishop for his "judicious exercise of restraint."

In time, recognizing that he couldn't remain neutral, Medeiros supported the workers' demands for a living wage. "What they demand is theirs by natural right," he said. "We have no time to waste. We must hurry to bring about the needed reforms for situations whose injustice cries to heaven." He contributed $1,500 for use among the farm workers in Starr County, and when the strikers marched to the state capitol he met them at San Juan, offering Mass and defending their right to join a union and strike for "elemental human rights."

His position was more balanced than Lucey's. He stressed that employers had the right to defend themselves against unjust demands by labor unions, he urged laymen rather than priests to take an active role, and he discouraged outsiders from becoming further involved, emphasizing that the dispute had to be resolved locally. But he jousted openly with the growers, some of whom had apparently expected him to function as their private chaplain. He chastised them for their narrow perspective, warning that "fifty dollars in the collection box does not make you a Christian." When they denounced him for consorting with militant Chicanos such as the Mexican-American Youth Organization, or MAYOS, he stood his ground. "If Christ lived today," he once said, "do you think he would cut himself off from the MAYOS or the Black Panthers? He might not approve of everything they were doing, but he wouldn't isolate himself from them."

The valley's churches were segregated by class as well as by race. Medeiros' efforts to integrate them angered both Anglo and Chicano growers. The wife of one prosperous Chicano asked him, "Do you really expect me to go to church and kneel beside my servants?"

"Madam," Medeiros said, "I don't expect you to go to church. The way you are behaving, I expect you to go to hell."

Yet his critics in the union contend that Medeiros bent to the landowners' financial and political pressure, undercutting more militant support for the strike from forces surrounding Archbishop Lucey. Still, the Church can hardly be blamed for the collapse of the strike, which fell victim a year later to intransigent growers, tough Texas Rangers, persistent "green-carders," and hurricane Beulah, which swept through the valley, destroying 90 percent of the citrus crop and sharply reducing the demand for farm labor. In January 1968, Chavez called off the strike, resolving instead to establish a credit union, a legal-aid center, and a health clinic for farm workers. In this less polarized setting, Medeiros functioned effectively as an ally of the workers. For two weeks, in 1969 and 1970, he joined their migration north as they followed the crops, visiting their ramshackle camps, saying Mass in the fields. He dramatized his identification with the dispossessed by spending each Christmas and Easter in jail, explaining, "I want to be with the people who need me." To relieve the valley's acute housing shortage, he funneled money from Catholic charities into a housing scheme for low-income families. By the time he left in 1970, he had earned extraordinary devotion from the valley's Catholics.

From the start in Boston, Medeiros encouraged hopes that he would reach out to the underprivileged there as he had in Texas. "It is impossible to be a Christian without being concerned for every man, without being involved in the real-life situation of every brother," he said in his installation speech. Most of Boston's priests, whatever their ideological orientation, looked to the new Archbishop—still vigorous at fifty-five—as a man who could give Boston's Church a fresh sense of purpose.

For a while Medeiros assiduously made the rounds of bailiwick, often charming those he met along the way. He was at his best in a pastoral role, exuding warmth and simplicity. Once, on a visit to a school for retarded children, he preached a charming little sermon. Then five children rose and held up drawings of sheep.

"Who takes care of the sheep?" asked the school chaplain.

"The shepherd," replied the children.

"There's a shepherd in this room," said the chaplain. "Can anyone tell who he is?"

A little boy shouted, "Bishop Medeiros!"

"Thank you, children," the Archbishop replied, enfolding several of the grinning youngsters in a tight embrace. "Thank you, my little sheep."

Not everyone responded so warmly. Some older Irish pastors, in particular, resented Medeiros deeply and made no secret of their displeasure. In rectories throughout the diocese, priests vied with each other to imitate his lilting, singsong delivery. If Cushing had been known affectionately as "the Cush," now Medeiros became—in parody—"the Hum," and his residence, "Humberto's Hacienda."

Once, at a meeting of priests, someone said, "Your Archbishop has spoken on that issue."

"*My* Archbishop is six feet under," snapped a senior pastor.

And there were unconfirmed reports of much worse: priests turning their backs on the Archbishop and stalking from the room; racial epithets muttered under the breath and, on at least one occasion, spoken directly in his face.

Recognizing the depth of this resentment, Medeiros sought to ingratiate himself with Boston's Irish. On St. Patrick's Day eve in 1971, he dined with the Ancient Order of Hibernians, who endowed him with their customary regalia: a gnarled shillelagh, a green tam-o'-shanter, and a Probate Court decree authorizing him to change his name every St. Patrick's Day to "O'Medeiros." In turn, the Archbishop conveniently overlooked the ethnic skirmishing in Fall River's North End, the gibes at Durfee High, the careless snubs of Irish priests, not to mention more recent indignities. "I am very much at home among the Irish because they have shown such real love and devotion to me," he said with the trace of a brogue he attributed to "the saintly Miss Flanagan and the wonderful Miss Kerrigan." Then he sang snatches of his "favorite songs"—"Galway Bay" and "Danny Boy"—and rendered an uncanny impersonation of the actor Barry Fitzgerald (the elderly priest in that sentimental tintype of Irish Catholic life, *Going My Way*). Two years later—after his elevation to Cardinal—he even marched in the St. Patrick's Day parade, pumping hands and blessing babies along the route.

In his eagerness to please, Medeiros at times resorted to the kind of high jinks with which Cushing had long beguiled Bostonians. Honoring the ancient rituals, he took the nuns to Nantasket Beach, riding with them on the bumper cars, gnawing on a candied apple. He manfully posed for photographers in sailor caps, construction helmets, and Indian headdresses. Once, serving up a Thanksgiving dinner at an old folks' home, he even let the cameramen dress him in a chef's hat and apron. But he knew it wasn't working. "This isn't me," he plaintively exclaimed to a bystander.

Yet the real Medeiros—humble, righteous, intensely pious—was alien to many Bostonians. The Irish had always felt uncomfortable with public piety; it might be fitting in women, but in men it was somehow weak and prissy. Fall River's Portuguese and Brownsville's Chicanos might find Medeiros' religiosity entirely appropriate, but in Charlestown and South Boston his Mediterranean style—the melancholy brown eyes, the folded hands, the head bent forward and slightly to the left in a "papal tilt," the familiar "Jesus" instead of the straightforward "Christ," the humility ("Lord, I am your useless servant")—all reeked of incense and Byzantine rituals.

The cultural chasm was too deep. When Medeiros first attended an Irish wake in Boston, weeping by the bier, he was astonished to see several Irish priests laughing and joking nearby. The Irish liked a priest who treated his religion with a touch of irreverence: better still, a former halfback from Notre Dame or Boston College who could handle a pigskin as deftly as a chalice. Though Cushing never played football, he personified that muscular style. "I have tried to be a manly man and a priestly priest," he once said. Medeiros suffered badly in such comparisons. He'd never been any good at sports. In Fall River, when parish children asked him to play basketball, he didn't even know how to hold the ball. "I'm not too bad at shuttlecock," he laughingly told reporters on his arrival in Boston, then, sensing how important sports were to Bostonians, quickly added, "I'd like to see the Red Sox—and the Bruins too." But a few years later, when the *Globe*'s Irish columnist Mike Barnicle asked whether he'd seen any good hockey games lately, he said, "I like to see them skating and doing all that, but I don't like it when they start fighting. I walked out the last time. It was awful, right under my nose and the people carrying on. It looked like the old Romans in the arena—more blood—and I walked out."

Piety and personal example might suffice to govern a tiny rural diocese like Brownsville, with 40 parishes and 82 priests, but formidable political-administrative skills were required to manage a massive urban archdiocese such as Boston, with its two million Catholics, 406 parishes, and 2,500 priests. Almost from the start, Medeiros seemed overwhelmed by the task.

Within a year, he found himself at odds with the very forces which had most welcomed his appointment. The progressives in Boston's Church quickly realized they had misread Medeiros' record in Texas, perceiving him as a civil rights activist who would never hesitate to cast his lot with the poor and oppressed. Just a year after he took office, all sixteen members of the Archdiocesan Human Rights Commission threatened to resign unless he spoke out more forcefully on race and poverty. In a showdown at his residence, the Archbishop capitulated, agreeing to most of the commission's demands, including a pastoral letter on urban problems, which he issued the following year as "Man's Cities and God's Poor."

Still, in the bitter struggle over Boston's schools, Medeiros remained profoundly cautious, as if fearing to stir the fires of Irish resentment. In March 1972, when a legislative committee heard testimony on the proposed repeal of the Racial Imbalance Act, he declined to appear personally as some of his advisers had urged. Instead, he released a statement—read to the committee by an aide—composed largely of lengthy quotations from Cardinal Cushing. A year later, when the repeal motion surfaced again, he issued a revised version of the same statement. Only in April 1974—as the act's opponents mounted their last, most determined, campaign—did Medeiros take the stand himself and deliver an appeal for racial justice.

His temporizing disheartened the activists who had kept the pressure on Cushing during the sixties. Exhausted from their struggles, the Catholic Interracial Council and the Association of Boston Urban Priests gradually faded into oblivion. Repeatedly rebuffed, the Human Rights Commission—with the notable exception of its astute chairwoman, Pat Goler—became largely irrelevant. As some sixties firebrands left the priesthood in disillusionment and others retreated into routine parish work, the lobby for social commitment within the Church largely dissipated.

When Arthur Garrity issued his desegregation order in June 1974, Medeiros was notably silent. Protestant and Jewish leaders hailed the decision as "just" and "moral," but his secretary doubted the Cardinal would make a statement "any time soon." Only ten days later—in apparently offhand remarks after blessing the Gloucester fishing fleet—did Medeiros express measured satisfaction at the judge's order. "Busing may not be the most desirable way to integrate," he said, "but it's all we have right now. As long as people keep calm and quiet, all will be fine."

That set the tone for the Cardinal's future statements on the issue. Consistently endorsing the underlying goal of racial integration—because "it is morally right"—he called for peaceful compliance with the law. But he sought to distance himself from busing itself. At times—as on October 22, 1974—he said flatly, "I am opposed to busing and I always have been." At other times, he expressed himself more cautiously: "I didn't say I believed in forced busing or that I was against it. That's a means to an end. And how to plan the integration of the city, that's beyond me. I have no competence there."

With the Cardinal voicing such confusion, it was hardly surprising that priests throughout the diocese should have gone off in different directions. Some endorsed busing; many condemned violence; others rode the buses themselves to encourage peaceful implementation of the order. Still others—notably in South Boston—preached against the order, boldly encouraging their parishioners to resist it. There were those who wondered whether Cushing would ever have permitted the Church to speak with such disparate voices. Some suggested that the flamboyant Cardinal would have "put on the red" (dressed in his scarlet robes), taken a black child in one hand and a white child in the other, and marched up the steps of South Boston High, thus defining the Church's position once and for all.

But this is probably to sentimentalize Cushing, whose instincts on such matters were deeply mixed. In any case, the time had long since passed when any Archbishop of Boston could settle such questions by mere fiat. The Church no longer played a decisive role in most Bostonians' lives. Between 1960 and 1978, attendance at Mass declined from 75 percent to 55 percent of Greater Boston's Catholics. Only 5 percent of the same Catholics said they would turn to a priest for advice on an urgent personal problem. Some of this disaffection could be traced to the Church's teachings on birth control, which were markedly out of line with Catholic practices: one survey showed that 80 percent of married Catholics used some form of artificial contraception. Moreover, Vatican II had so democratized the Church that challenges to clerical authority were no longer scandalous. If the faithful could make their own conscientious decisions on many theological issues, how could they be denied liberty on questions like busing?

Though a bishop's proclamations were often ineffectual, his actions could sometimes be decisive. As early as 1973, many churchmen realized that Boston's Catholic schools might provide havens for refugees from busing, thus undermining desegregation. The parochial schools had good reasons to take what advantage they could from the situation. In Boston, as elsewhere, Catholic school enrollment had fallen off sharply since the mid-sixties—partly as a result of declining birth rates, partly because thousands of middle-class Catholics had moved to the suburbs, partly because Catholics were less committed to sectarian education than in years gone by, and partly because a shortage of teaching nuns compelled schools to hire lay teachers at substantial salaries and thus sharply increase tuitions. Between 1965 and 1973, archdiocesan enrollment fell from 151,582 to 86,469, while more than a hundred Catholic schools closed their doors. Pastors and Sisters, struggling to keep their schools afloat, would presumably take any students they could get.

In February 1974, the Archdiocesan Board of Education—which Medeiros headed—sought to stem the expected influx by prohibiting all but a few special transfers into the city's parochial schools. But this policy was deeply flawed, exempting 172 Catholic schools in the suburbs, many of which promptly admitted "refugees" from the city. During 1974–75, the sharp decline in parochial enrollment leveled off, while high school attendance even rose slightly.

This touched off a bitter struggle within the Church. Progressive priests and laymen demanded an airtight policy prohibiting all transfers, while Catholic schools warned that such a policy would put them out of business and Catholic parents asked how the Cardinal dared bar their children from schools built with their grandfathers' hard-earned dimes and nickels. Ultimately, the Archdiocese struck a curious compromise, closing the suburban escape hatch, but promptly opening another. Henceforth, schools throughout the diocese could admit any public school student—without examining his motives—so long as he filled an existing vacancy caused by another student's transfer or dropout. Thus, Catholic schools could exploit busing to stabilize—though, in theory, not to increase—their enrollments. Indeed, during 1975–76, nearly 4,200 students moved from Boston's public schools into the Catholic system (at least two-thirds of them apparent refugees from busing). Some schools took advantage of the situation to swell their enrollments, one such "haven" being Somerville's Little Flower School, which accepted dozens of students from adjacent Charlestown. Openly defying the Cardinal, Monsignor John Hogan said he would admit any Townie kid who applied, a stand which made him an overnight hero in Charlestown. As he marched in the Bunker Hill Day parade that June, parents rushed from the sidewalk to wring his hands in gratitude.

When evidence of such abuses surfaced in the fall of 1975, Medeiros announced that any priest or nun who had knowingly violated his policy would be "disciplined." Later that winter, the Archdiocese wrote to twenty-two schools, demanding an explanation for their suddenly inflated enrollments. That was the extent of the "discipline." Explaining the Cardinal's inaction, his aides noted that priests and Sisters enjoyed "substantial autonomy" in running their schools and, in any case, a rebellious pastor could only be removed through a rare and "unseemly" canonical trial.

By then, Medeiros was loath to challenge the traditional Irish ethos prevailing in most old-line parishes. He had felt the muscle of the anti-busing movement and it frightened him. Three emissaries from ROAR had called on him, imploring him to intervene on their behalf with Judge Garrity. When the Cardinal declined, ROAR launched demonstrations outside his house, with protesters brandishing placards reading: "Why does the Cardinal hate white children?" and "O Lord, why hast thou forsaken me?" Such activists were only a tiny fragment of the city's Catholics, but their presence outside his window seems to have awakened the Cardinal's old anxieties about the aggressive Irish. More and more, he retreated behind the Chancery walls, ceding his responsibilities in this area to others.

Characteristically, he let different priests speak to different constituencies. His conservative "urban coordinator," Father Paul Donovan, became the Cardinal's ambassador to the alienated Irish, meeting with Louise Day Hicks and her lieutenants, reassuring them that the Church wasn't their enemy. Later, Auxiliary Bishop Joseph Ruocco—a moderate, but the only Italian in the hierarchy and therefore something of an outsider—headed a committee to mobilize the clergy behind law and order. And a liberal, Father Michael Groden, was loaned to Arthur Garrity as staff director of the Citywide Coordinating Council, the judge's watchdog agency.

The Cardinal still spoke out from time to time—occasionally with surprising passion—but he rarely followed through on his pronouncements. "I'm not a judge," he would say. "I have no coercive powers. . . . All I can do is preach it, proclaim it, and let those who have ears to hear, hear. I can't crack your head and stick the Book in there." When critics questioned this narrow view of his authority, he asked gloomily, "What can I do? The more I say, the worse it gets."

This incapacity spread to other areas. For a decade the Archdiocese had built low- and moderate-income housing on Church-owned land in the suburbs. Hundreds of units were already occupied in Beverly, Lexington, and North Andover, but in the affluent South Shore town of Scituate—on "the Irish Riviera"—parishioners of St. Mary's of the Nativity Church blocked the development in a bitter court battle. When the Archdiocese finally prevailed in the Supreme Court, Medeiros surprisingly agreed to let eight parishioners sue him before the Church's own tribunal, normally restricted to marriage cases. After prolonged hearings, the three-priest panel ruled that the parish had not been adequately consulted. Ballots were distributed after Mass one Sunday and the parish voted overwhelmingly against the project (prompting one priest to remark bitterly, "At the Church of the Nativity there is still no room at the inn"). Ultimately Medeiros found another site in Scituate, but the surrender raised new doubts about his leadership.

Unfortunately for the Cardinal, his diffidence lent itself to satire. The most wicked foray in this genre was an article in *Boston Magazine,* consisting entirely of aphorisms, riddles, and parables:

"How can you tell Cardinal Medeiros from a marshmallow?" "He is the one without the corners."

"Why does Cardinal Medeiros carry pudding in his wallet?" "For identification."

Nobody at the magazine had anticipated what was to follow. After the *Pilot* and a popular radio priest denounced the "scurrilous" piece, hundreds of protest letters poured in, advertisers withdrew their ads, the magazine fired its editor, and the author—an Irish Catholic columnist for the *Herald American*—was dismissed by his newspaper. But all this may have been less a rallying around the Cardinal himself than an old Boston Irish reflex toward any slight to their Church.

One of Medeiros' liabilities was the massive debt he had inherited from his predecessor. Cushing had been a splendid benefactor, showering Boston's Catholics with schools, hospitals, colleges, and a dazzling array of human services. Not only was Medeiros unable to continue this largesse, he had to take some of it away, a practice not calculated to win him any friends. When he entered office, the debt had reached $42 million. Medeiros was uncomfortable raising money, temperamentally disinclined to put the bite on wealthy communicants, so in May 1971 he launched a bureaucratic substitute, the Archbishop's Stewardship Appeal. Reminding the faithful that "in this world we are only the stewards of the good things with which we are blessed," he assessed each parish a portion of the $7.2 million target. Its first year, the drive fell a million dollars short. By 1974, when the anti-busing movement organized a boycott, it produced only $5.1 million, and later did only slightly better. Determined to reduce the debt, the Cardinal had no alternative but to pare spending sharply. Between 1970 and 1977, he cut the budget by 40 percent, closed facilities, and curtailed activities of the Archdiocese's forty-three agencies. By 1977, the debt was down to a manageable $15 million, but clergy and parishioners alike bristled at the new austerity.

His social gospel stymied by Irish intransigence, his temporal programs crimped by budgetary restraints, the Cardinal increasingly devoted his energies to the defense of theological orthodoxy. Even before leaving Brownsville, he told an interviewer he supported the Pope "150 percent" on such critical questions as birth control, abortion, divorce, and clerical celibacy. And barely a month after reaching Boston, he bitterly excoriated the pro-abortion movement as "the new barbarism" which was "moving ruthlessly to upset the moral order established by God."

When Protestants, Jews, and Catholic liberals voiced dismay at the Cardinal's vehemence, Medeiros only intensified his campaign, labeling abortion "the murder of the innocents," ordering anti-abortion messages read from the pulpits of every parish, asking the faithful to sign "pro-life" pledges. In 1977, he mustered the Church's waning political influence to pass a bill banning the use of Medicaid funds for abortions in Massachusetts. Several years later, he helped force the political retirement of Congressman Robert Drinan, a Jesuit priest who had supported liberalized abortion laws. Then, five days before the election of Drinan's successor, Medeiros released a pastoral letter aimed at defeating Barney Frank, Kevin White's former majordomo, whom Drinan was actively backing. "Those who make abortions possible by law—such as legislators and those who promote, defend, and elect these same lawmakers—cannot separate themselves from that guilt which accompanies this horrendous crime," the Cardinal wrote. "It is imperative that Catholics realize the law of God extends into the polling booth." But the voters—about 40 percent of them Catholics—went decisively for Frank, prompting some commentators to wonder whether the Cardinal hadn't overstepped himself.

Medeiros showed little interest in the verdict of the Fourth Congressional District. On such matters, he had a constituency of one—the Pope. "I abide by the rules of the Church," he would say. "Those rules come from God and the Holy Father." A stickler for clerical tradition, Medeiros was rarely seen without his formal regalia—the crimson-edged black cassock, wide crimson sash, red skullcap, and ornate pectoral cross on a gold chain. While many Cardinals discouraged the formal address "Your Eminence" and kissing of the episcopal ring, Medeiros appreciated such acts of deference. His style was rarely authoritarian, but associates sometimes felt cold steel beneath his gentle piety. Once, speaking of a recalcitrant monsignor, he said, "The Jesus in me loves the Jesus in him, but frankly I don't much care for the rest of him." And there is the story of a young priest who had served as part-time speechwriter to Cushing and stayed on in the episcopal residence hoping to fill the same function for Medeiros. Each morning he came down to breakfast and looked hopefully at the new Archbishop, who didn't know what to do with him. If such a problem had confronted Cushing, the old Cardinal might have growled, "Father, get your ass out of here!" One morning, Medeiros said, "Father, I spoke with Jesus last night. Jesus needs you in Cohasset."

He could be tough indeed on those who violated his idea of clerical discipline. When no priest appeared to celebrate Mass at Boston University's Catholic Center in March 1974, Sister Gloria Fitzgerald conducted a "service of Christian community." Medeiros interpreted this as an attempt by an unordained person to celebrate Mass and forced Sister Gloria's resignation as cochaplain. Father Paul Shanley, a "street priest," had worked with Boston's gay community for several years, but in 1979 Medeiros denounced homosexuality as a "serious depravity" and told Father Shanley to find himself another job. Father Richard P. McBrien, a professor of theology at Boston College, had opposed the Vatican's positions on birth control, clerical celibacy, and ordination of women. In a confrontation, the Cardinal demanded that he stop attacking the Pope. Hardly a radical—he is now chairman of the Theology Department at Notre Dame—McBrien found Medeiros' position inexplicable. Medeiros ordered the *Pilot* to cancel McBrien's syndicated column and forced his resignation from the faculty at Pope John Seminary.

Though the Cardinal could still enforce his will within the Church, he was ill at ease in the secular realm, particularly dealing with public officials or politicians. "Politics is a noble science," he once declared, "the trouble is with those who abuse the science." In fact, Medeiros profoundly distrusted political entanglements. No longer did politicians care very much what "Lake Street" thought. In the old days, when the Mayor or Governor wanted to consult the Cardinal, they went to him; now he called on them. On the few occasions when Kevin White and Medeiros met at City Hall, they seemed to be talking different languages. "The Cardinal pontificated in his High Cathedral Prose, the Mayor muttered in his Ward Five Vernacular, and never the twain did meet," reported an eyewitness to one encounter.

Only once did the Mayor actually solicit Medeiros' help, seeking the

Church's support on a tax referendum. All he got in return was a pious lecture from Medeiros about the "two spheres" of church and state. Afterwards, White drove to an aide's house, downed two glasses of wine, and, pounding the table, shouted, "The bastards! The bastards!"

By the late seventies, the Cardinal felt unwelcome not only at City Hall but in many Boston neighborhoods. "I know I have hurt many people in this city," he said. "I did not intend to hurt them, but they've taken what I said as being against them." Increasingly, he shunned the city whenever he could, spending weeks on end in Alaska, Japan, Korea, the Philippines, Poland, Italy, and the Azores. "I'm not only Bishop of Boston, you know," he told one priest, "I'm a prince of the Church, and therefore I have responsibilities for the whole world." Sometimes he sought solace in Fall River, eating boiled clams in his brother's ample backyard, fishing with a handline off the rocks in nearby Newport. But, along with diabetes and high blood pressure, he suffered from increasingly dark depressions. "Years ago," he told friends, "I used to jump out of bed every morning, eager to get started on the day. Now I get up and think: O Lord, I wish I could hide under a tree on the top of a mountain!"

Above his bed in the residence hung a painting of outstretched hands, a souvenir of his fervent send-off from Brownsville, when a thousand Catholics ran across the tarmac to bid him farewell. It was perhaps the last time he had felt truly appreciated.

Across the room was another painting—a suffering Christ on the Cross—reminiscent of the mural he had painted years before in Fall River. At times Medeiros seemed obsessed with his own martyrdom. He often spoke of his "crown of thorns," his "torments," his "agony," his "cross." In 1976, asked in an interview whether he could ever win Boston's affections, he said, "I am not here to be loved, I am here to speak the word of God. Nor am I a leader. . . . If I were they would pay attention to me. . . . Our Lord was no leader to those who killed him, which was almost everybody at the time, who called for his death." Meanwhile, he refused to enter South Boston and Charlestown for fear of being stoned—the other biblical means of execution.

The Portuguese vision of Christ is a grim one: Christ humiliated, Christ scourged, Christ bloodied and pricked by thorns. In some Portuguese colonies, the faithful celebrate Good Friday by lashing themselves with bamboo-tipped whips, then dousing the cuts with vinegar to intensify the pain. At the great feast of Santo Christo in the Azores, statues of a tortured Christ, often in blood-soaked capes, are carried through the sorrowing crowds. Humberto Medeiros had always felt his priesthood as a painful burden, but in Boston his personal metaphor became explicitly Christ on the Cross. If years before he had feared to enter the Garden of Gethsemane, now he suffered in terrible isolation on the hill at Calvary.

21

Twymon

There was nothing otherworldly about Bobby McClain. No Negro preacher out of *Green Pastures* invoking a New Jerusalem to lead his people through the Vale of Tears, Union Methodist's zealous young minister concentrated on the here and now. "For too long we have overspiritualized the gospel," he told his congregation one Sunday. "We have been drilled in the virtues of poverty and patience. . . . We cannot leave the present injustices fatalistically for history to correct. The stimulus for our action can come from the future which God promises, but always we must call into question the present order of the world. Our future is not an opiate, but rather an active and militant one."

From her pew, Rachel Twymon stared at the figure in the pulpit, his sculptured Afro a dark halo against the altar. For years she'd listened to sermons and hymns admonishing her to endure this world's sorrows in expectation of a reward somewhere beyond the Pearly Gates. She was tired of enduring, weary of waiting for her just deserts. Bobby McClain's urgency swept her along. Let's get on with it, she thought, we got a bill here that's long overdue!

Since succeeding Gil Caldwell at Union Methodist in 1968, McClain had preached a theology in which Christ was not only the Son of God and Prince of Peace, but the "Great Liberator." The freedom he sought was temporal as well as spiritual, essential to the souls of his oppressed people, but also to "the physical needs and outer environment in which the body that houses the soul must live." Even before the first tenants moved into Methunion Manor in May 1971, McClain announced that his church would "fill another major void" in the South End. It had embarked on "a new and comprehensive Black Economic Development Program, designed to provide the black community of Boston with the needed services and facilities which it must have to survive." Union Methodist was "committing itself to getting Boston's black community into the American economic mainstream."

The program was less grand than it sounded, its principal resource 9,260 square feet of commercial space on the ground floor of 465 Columbus Avenue, one of Methunion Manor's four buildings. McClain proposed to develop that space as a "neighborhood shopping center" to meet the needs of Methunion's tenants and others nearby. But unlike conventional commercial ventures, Methunion's center would accept no applications from the whites—generally Jews, Lebanese, and Syrians—who ran most stores in Boston's black community; the church's project would be a prime example of the "black capitalism" then being promoted by the Nixon administration—black-conceived, black-owned, and black-operated for the benefit of black businessmen and their black customers.

The plan called for a "local development corporation" to funnel loans from the Small Business Administration to the six stores that would occupy the space. The corporation would also provide the stores with legal, financial, and management assistance, including a security system under which all cash would be whisked through vacuum tubes to an upstairs cashier/accountant who would make any necessary change, then enter the transaction in the company's books. In February 1972, two spaces were quickly allocated to church members wanting to operate a dry-cleaning establishment and a beauty parlor, and the corporation began seeking tenants for the four other units: a grocery, a women's boutique, a drugstore, and a restaurant.

For a time, the center's prospects looked promising, but the Small Business Administration required local corporations to provide 10 percent of development costs themselves. The money wasn't forthcoming and the project languished. Meanwhile, other potential tenants were turned away. In March 1973, a Montessori school wanted to lease the entire ground floor, but the board said no. A white congressman seeking a storefront for his campaign headquarters was also rejected. The Codman Company, Methunion's managing agent, repeatedly warned McClain that the housing project's deficits were growing, due in no small part to "the absence of income on the commercial space since inception of the project," yet firm in his commitment to "black economic development," the minister went on rejecting tenants he found unsuitable. The most persistent applicant was Melsha Blake, a black West Indian who wanted to open a restaurant, but for some reason McClain didn't approve him either. When the board rejected his application, Blake filed a complaint with the Massachusetts Commission Against Discrimination, alleging that he had been turned down because he was West Indian (the commission found no merit in his charge). When the cleaner and the beauty parlor failed, all 9,260 feet of commercial space remained vacant.

By then, Methunion Manor's financial crisis was of pressing concern to the Department of Housing and Urban Development (HUD), which had assumed the mortgage in May 1973 after Methunion defaulted on its payments. Union Methodist Church, through its housing corporation, retained control of the four buildings, but HUD grew increasingly impatient with the mounting deficits. In December 1973, it addressed the corporation in a stern letter: "The leasing of the commercial space has never been accomplished, which means that approximately $30,000 is being lost per year. We understand that a lot of businesses have expressed an interest in renting this space, but all have been refused. This commercial space must be rented. Without the income from that space, the project will be unable to operate and we will have no alternative but to foreclose." McClain conceded that only half his plan was now realizable; the other half of the space would now be rented conventionally. But it was too late. Lack of commercial revenue was only the final blow to a project already reeling from three years of deficit. In June 1974, the government went into Federal District Court seeking authority to foreclose Methunion's mortgage and sell the buildings to the highest bidder.

Methunion was by no means alone in confronting this fate. Across the country, hundreds of housing developments built under the subsidy programs of the sixties had been unable to meet their mortgage payments and had gone into default. Dozens had already been foreclosed, sold at auction to landlords who, deprived of government subsidies, had no choice but to raise rents, forcing all but the most affluent tenants into the streets. In Boston alone, seventy of seventy-three 221 (d) 3 projects were in default, many of them approaching foreclosure. Some Boston projects, locked deep in the black ghetto, might have difficulty finding buyers, but not Methunion Manor. Just across the railway tracks from the Back Bay, Methunion was convenient to downtown offices, stores, and restaurants; the sixty-floor John Hancock Tower soared overhead. Methunion Manor would win no architectural prize, but with a few structural changes, paint, air conditioning, wall-to-wall carpeting—and a new set of white tenants—it might soon take its place in the "New South End."

Faced with this prospect, Bobby McClain and his colleagues on the board of the Columbus Avenue Housing Corporation grew curiously passive. Discouraged by the collapse of their economic development scheme, daunted by massive debts, offended by persistent tenant complaints, they decided not to contest the government's position. The church's lawyer didn't even appear in court, and in January 1975, Judge Walter Skinner ordered Methunion sold to the highest bidder on February 25.

Methunion's tenants hadn't paid much attention to the legal maneuvering, but the newscasts of January 16 delivered a message so stark that few of them could ignore it: within a month or so, the project would have a new landlord who would almost certainly raise rents so high they would be forced to find new homes. Among those listening that night were Ray Diggs, a Boston bus driver; Adrian du Cille, a Welfare Department social worker; and Mark Manuel, an electrical engineering student. On February 2, they called a meeting in the church basement, attended by nearly a hundred other tenants. From this gathering grew the Methunion Tenants' Council, dedicated to preventing foreclosure at all costs.

At first they tried publicity. Assisted by several black professionals, they drafted a statement arguing that foreclosure was more than a fiscal strategy, it was a political decision reflecting the low priority America gave to housing for the poor: "The Department of Housing and Urban Development has completely surrendered to the betrayers of the people."

They tried the law. Aided by poverty lawyers, they went into federal court seeking a temporary injunction to halt foreclosure, arguing that if black and Hispanic tenants had to leave Methunion, they would be unable to find other suitable apartments in the South End. Forced out of that integrated community, they would be pushed deeper into the ghetto in search of affordable housing.

But before the suit could come to trial, they made the right political connections. Senator Edward Brooke, the only black in the Senate and the ranking Republican on the Banking, Housing, and Urban Affairs Committee, brought influence to bear on Vice-President Nelson Rockefeller, who virtually ordered HUD Secretary Carla Hills to put the foreclosure on ice. In June 1975, Diggs, du Cille, Manuel, and their professional advisers met in Washington with H. R. Crawford, HUD's Assistant Secretary, who granted them another six months' postponement. For the time being, at least, Methunion was safe. When she heard the news from Washington, Rachel Twymon crossed to the church and said a silent prayer. She thanked God for rewarding them in the flesh as well as in the spirit, for keeping a roof over their heads as well as a watch over their souls.

By 1975 Methunion was more to Rachel than a place to live. When the federal court took jurisdiction over the project, it appointed David Dretler, a Boston lawyer, as "receiver in bankruptcy." For a time, Dretler managed Methunion through a resident superintendent and a secretary, but in August 1975, convinced that the pair had been renting apartments for their own benefit, he fired them. Urgently needing a secretary who knew the ropes, he turned to Rachel, who had occasionally served as a volunteer for the old management company.

Rachel hadn't worked steadily since her specialty shop closed in May 1969. In 1972 she had joined a "work incentive" training program operated by the State Department of Employment Security, but once again her lupus forced her to drop out. Later, she enrolled in a real estate course, but gave that up too. For a few months she worked as a matron at the Charles Hayden Goodwill Inn for Boys. Through those years, she remained on welfare, receiving Aid to Families with Dependent Children as well as food stamps, but her funds often ran short. When Richard was about to graduate from Boston English, she bought him a black suit for the ceremonies, but her welfare check was late, the store refused to relinquish the suit until the down payment was made, and Rachel was distraught until Bobby McClain loaned her fifty dollars out of church funds. She resented her dependence on the welfare checks, which sometimes came on time and sometimes didn't. But her lupus wouldn't let her travel very far to a job, so she sat alone in her apartment, watering the plants, sewing clothes for the kids, and brooding on the lousy cards life had dealt her. She ached with unrealized possibilities. She could feel the potential within her, the energy which might have been harnessed to a thousand undertakings, but the world didn't want what she could give.

When Dretler offered to put her to work, it seemed like the perfect solution and, for a time, it was. The project office was just a few doors down the hall from her apartment, so she could leave a casserole in the oven and still get back to check on it. The office windows faced Columbus Avenue, so she could wave to friends while keeping an eye on her children. She brought in a few of her beloved plants to decorate the office and installed a television set so she could watch soap operas and quiz shows while she worked. Most of her duties were relatively easy: accepting rent payments, paying bills, keeping books, handling routine correspondence.

Unfortunately, she was also responsible for receiving tenant complaints. Dretler spent most of his time at his downtown law office, remote from the endless litany of tenant grievances. Rachel was readily accessible all day in the project office and even after hours tenants didn't hesitate to bang on her apartment door to report a faulty lock or a backed-up toilet. As lawsuits and bureaucratic infighting dragged on that year, she was besieged by inquiries: Was HUD really going to foreclose? Would rents be raised? By how much? If tenants had to move, would HUD find them a place to live? What was the church doing?

She mustered all the courtesy she could. When she knew the answer to a question, she gave it; when she didn't—and frequently she was as much in the dark as any tenant—she said she couldn't help. She processed complaints as quickly as possible, but with maintenance money nearly exhausted, broken windows and leaky roofs often went unrepaired for months. When tenants blamed her for the delays, she sometimes lost her temper, venting her anger on friends and neighbors—harsh words which stung. Soon tenants were grumbling, complaining that ever since Rachel took that job in the office she thought she was better than they were. Finally, the Tenants' Council filed a formal complaint, charging that she was "irreconcilably incompatible" with them.

Rachel's position at Methunion—halfway between the church and the tenants—had long been tinged with ambiguity. Now it was made even more difficult by the church's apparent lack of concern over Methunion's financial crisis. After the board of the Columbus Avenue Housing Corporation, composed entirely of church members, failed to respond to the government's suit, the Tenants' Council had angrily demanded that they be given a greater role in running the project. A senior board member replied, "We provided apartments for you people when you were homeless. We kept a roof over your heads all these years. Now you come in and berate us for what we haven't done. Well, I'll tell you this. I'd rather sell the project than let you have it."

Gradually the board relented and eventually six tenants—including Ray Diggs and Adrian du Cille—were elected to serve on it with five church members and Bobby McClain. But by then McClain seemed weary of Methunion and its troubles. For months, government agencies and community organizations tried to negotiate with him on Methunion's future, but he rebuffed their overtures. A high-ranking HUD official, in a memo to his superior, noted:

"Rev. McClain has been very uncooperative. He never returns any of our phone calls nor answers any of our letters. . . . It appears that Rev. McClain's uncooperativeness was a major reason for the default." Another HUD official wrote: "Rev. McClain has shown no interest at all in this project."

McClain was as much an enigma to his own congregation as to HUD. In the pulpit he was a dazzling orator who could wring shouts of joy and affirmation from his parishioners. In lay gatherings he was a forceful leader, a committed social activist who reminded some of his followers of Martin Luther King. But he was deeply suspicious of whites, which made it difficult for him to work with government agencies; in addition, he often seemed preoccupied with personal matters. In early 1978, the Pastor-Parish Relations Committee received an unsigned letter from a parishioner complaining about the pastor's lack of interest in his congregation. The committee had also heard rumors about the pastor's personal life, including the break-up of his marriage. All this had contributed to substantial defections from the congregation. After the committee met with Rev. McClain in April, he moved to the Methodist Board of Global Ministries in New York.

Before McClain left, however, the long-vacant commercial space was rented at last—part of it for a Head Start school, the rest to a black-owned grocery called the Bargain Store which in turn sublet part of its space to a combination record store and "bar-b-que" calling itself the Soul Center. Methunion's tenants found it ironic that all the brave talk of "black economic development" should have produced nothing but the Soul Center, for the record store quickly became one of their principal grievances. All day long and into the evening, rhythm and blues pulsed from a loudspeaker installed in the center's doorway, attracting kids from throughout the neighborhood. Inside they played pool and pinball, listened to records, and gnawed on ribs. But suspicions grew that someone in the store was dispensing something other than soul music and soul food—namely drugs (at least seven drug dealers were known to be operating in the Methunion complex, which came to be known, in some circles, as Methadone Manor). And the teenagers who hung out at the Soul Center were widely held responsible for a rash of crimes in and around the housing project.

Break-ins were continually reported throughout the four buildings, but particularly at 465 Columbus Avenue, which housed the Soul Center. More disconcerting still were the "walk-ins," burglaries for which no forced entry was required. One of the janitors or maintenance men had apparently sold the burglars a master key and, as a result, every lock in the building had to be changed. Handbag snatchings were common on the streets around the project. Several women reported that the thieves had fled into one of Methunion's buildings, and handbags were later discovered with the trash in the project's basements.

More violent crimes proliferated. One winter evening, Adrian du Cille was returning to his fifth-floor apartment at 465 Columbus Avenue with two large shopping bags in his arms. As usual, the elevator was out of order, so he began climbing the darkened stairwell. Reaching the third floor, he encountered three youths, who were drinking, smoking, and jiving to a transistor radio. When du Cille warned the boys to get out of the building, one of them brandished a shiny object and told him to hand over all his valuables. They took his wallet, containing ten dollars, his Timex watch, and a pocketknife. Running down the stairs, one of them hissed under his breath, "Better not call the police or we'll come back and kill you."

Du Cille did call the police, but none of his attackers was ever apprehended. Mindful of the boys' threat, du Cille began carrying a foot-long iron sash weight, which he wrapped in a piece of brown paper and tucked in his waistband. He carried it everywhere—to the store, to parties, or just out for a walk. One night, coming home from a friend's house, he encountered one of his attackers in the building lobby. The boy recognized du Cille and growled, "I hear you're accusing me of robbing you."

"Yeh," said du Cille, "you're a damn thief, and if I have anything to say about it, you'll be arrested."

The boy moved toward him, but when du Cille brandished the weight above his head, he turned and fled.

Du Cille wasn't satisfied with personal defense. A self-educated man, he had a gift for articulating his fellow tenants' anxieties, which he often did in the pages of Methunion Manor's Tenant Newsletter. A few weeks after the holdup, he wrote a passionate editorial, warning that Methunion was increasingly vulnerable to "gangs of rotten young degenerates— 'the young dead'— who congregate like vultures around it. Management has thus far made no effort to correct the situation, and the hapless tenants are left to the vile and ruthless elements, thieves and cutthroats, which pervade the area."

Under du Cille's prodding, the Tenants' Council made security a central issue in its continuing negotiations with HUD and HUD complied by granting the council authority to screen prospective tenants for troublemakers and criminals. Eventually, several tenants went a step further. Organizing a Methunion Tenants' Safety Patrol, they walked the project's hallways, stairwells, parking lots, and adjacent sidewalks, armed with little silver whistles called Acme Thunderers and, occasionally, more lethal weapons. Its leaders—including Adrian du Cille and Ray Diggs—were deadly serious. "You dope pushers, robbers, rip-off artists, vultures and your kind, beware!" Ray Diggs wrote in the project newsletter. Then, addressing himself to the tenants: "Security is a cause that should rally everyone. If you are lucky enough to have a color TV, we don't want you ripped off. If you are lucky enough to carry a few dollars in your pocket, we don't want you robbed. If you have children, we don't want them DOA because of an OD. In short, we plan to protect ourselves!"

But the patrol barely got started. In a project where single-parent families predominated, few men were available for such duties. Many of the male tenants held two jobs, which left them little time for walking the corridors.

Moreover, management, which had promised to provide badges and walkie-talkies, never came through. The patrol, which began with twenty men and women, quickly dwindled to four. After two months, it disbanded.

Another reason Methunion Manor never organized effectively may have been its recognition that much crime was directed elsewhere, largely against the affluent white world which increasingly hemmed the project in on all sides. Few tenants explicitly supported such forays into the white community, but, understandably enough, few were prepared to devote their evenings to patrolling dangerous streets in order to protect their white neighbors.

The issue of black crime was an explosive one in Boston throughout the seventies. Much of the resistance to busing was rooted in a fear of such crime, a conviction that young blacks were bent on mayhem and pillage against any whites who crossed their paths. Often that anxiety lurked behind elaborate rationalizations, but occasionally it surfaced, as in a document released by Louise Day Hicks and two other South Boston politicians in September 1974:

> Why is there resistance in South Boston? Simply stated, it is because it is against your children's interest to send them to schools in crime-infested Roxbury. . . . There are at least one hundred black people walking around in the black community who have killed white people during the past two years. . . . Any well-informed white suburban woman does not pass through that community alone even by automobile. Repairmen, utilities workers, taxi drivers, doctors, firemen, all have refused at one time or another to do what Judge Garrity demands of our children on an everyday basis.

Criminal statistics appended to the statement showed that, in the previous six months, there had been roughly twice as many murders, eight times as many rapes, and eighteen times as many armed robberies in Roxbury as in South Boston. The statement drew criticism from the black community and the liberal press, much of it focused on the claim that Roxbury harbored one hundred killers of whites. The critics produced police statistics showing that in 1973–74 some 223 murders had been committed in Boston, but that in only 181 cases was the race of the killer even known and, of those, only 23—or 13 percent—involved blacks killing whites.

For South Boston's indictment reflected a fundamental misconception about black crime. It was true that blacks committed violent crimes out of proportion to their share of the city's population (per capita arrests for murder were four times as common among blacks as among whites; 5.8 times for aggravated assault; 7.3 times for rape). But most of these crimes were committed by blacks against other blacks. Murder, rape, and assault generally occurred among people who knew each other, often stemming from arguments within families, between neighbors, among drinkers at a bar or kids on a streetcorner. Moreover, a black's assault on another black frequently received no publicity at all. For years, the Boston *Globe,* like other metropolitan dailies elsewhere in the country, routinely ignored murders in which blacks killed other blacks. In some cases, such crimes might even go unrecorded by police. An old police maxim went: "If a nigger kills a white man, that's murder. If a white man kills a nigger, that's justifiable homicide. If a nigger kills a nigger, that's one less nigger."

At least two crimes, however—robbery and burglary—didn't fit this pattern. For these were crimes, not of proximity or passion, but of profit. Whatever other circumstances might lead the offender to commit such crimes, the ostensible objective was pecuniary. In most American communities, it was whites who had the most money or goods for the taking.

There was still another reason why these crimes—particularly street muggings—tended to be black-on-white. Any mugger knew that his best chance of averting arrest was to rob someone he didn't know, indeed somebody from a different world; the single greatest inducement to street crime was a breakdown in social ties among neighbors. Holdups, muggings, and purse snatchings breed rapidly in an area whose residents are largely strangers to one another, best of all in a community where races or classes collide, so that the offender can commit his crime in one environment, then quickly find sanctuary in another. Not surprisingly, the South End had long been one of the city's most crime-ridden sections. A 1970 survey dividing the city into eighty-one neighborhoods showed that the slice of the South End on both sides of Columbus Avenue had the second-highest per capita rate of street crime in the city and the highest rate of residential burglaries.

By the early seventies, Columbus Avenue was a frontier separating two worlds. To the west, between the avenue and the railroad, descendants of the black railway workers who had settled there around the turn of the century still lived in sooty tenements, while newer black and Hispanic tenants occupied the grim slabs of Methunion Manor. To the east, between the avenue and Tremont Street, the young professionals had carved out their territory, graced by bow-front town houses, brick sidewalks, and spreading shade trees. A few aging white roomers still lived out their days in the last of the lodging houses by the tracks; a handful of black teachers and architects had purchased homes among the gentry. Otherwise, the broad cement ribbon, pitted with ruts and potholes, was a no-man's-land between white and black, prosperous and deprived.

Soon after the Twymons moved into Methunion Manor in June 1971, sixteen-year-old Richard began hanging out with a gang around the corner on Holyoke Street. Every evening they gathered on the steps of the Harriet Tubman House, a community center, to while away the night drinking Cokes, beer, or wine, smoking reefers, jiving to disco music from giant transistor radios, and exchanging invective. Soon they had devised more spirited entertainment—a strenuous version of hide-and-go-seek. The rules required all players to converge on Tubman House at precisely 7:30 p.m. The last two to arrive were "it" for the evening and were given fifteen minutes to conceal themselves somewhere in a six-block area. Prohibited from entering a building, they had to remain at street level—in a basement doorway, under a stoop, behind a parked vehicle, a fence, or a pile of trash. When the rest of the gang found them—as they almost always did—they beat them up.

One humid evening in early July, Richard and his friend were ambling down Holyoke Street, sipping 7-Ups, when they noticed the crowd around the Harriet Tubman House gleefully pointing in their direction.

"Oh shit!" his friend exclaimed. "Looks like it's our night."

By the time they reached the steps, the rest of the gang were shifting impatiently, eager for the chase.

"Hey!" cried Richard, playing for time. "Give me a chance to finish my soda."

"No way," said a kid named Ray, already consulting his watch. "You got fourteen minutes twenty seconds and counting."

Turning tail, the pair fled up Holyoke Street to Columbus Avenue, where they separated, his friend heading north toward the Hancock Tower, Richard south toward the brick spire of Union Methodist Church. Dodging right on West Newton Street, then right again on a narrow alley by the railroad tracks, Richard found a corrugated-tin shed containing two garbage cans. Pulling the pails apart, he wedged himself in between, and for nearly half an hour he squatted there, inhaling the stench of sour milk and rotting vegetables. When his legs cramped and none of his pursuers appeared, he decided to risk a different strategy. Part of Columbus Avenue had been blocked off that week for a street fair sponsored by "Summerthing," a mayoral program designed to keep the city cool through the long, hot summer. Under a canopy of colored lights, vendors sold ethnic food and soft drinks, while jugglers, clowns, and a black rock group called Soul on Ice provided entertainment. Seeking protective camouflage, Richard plunged into the youthful crowd around the bandstand.

As he was congratulating himself on his cunning, he felt a tap on his shoulder. Wheeling around, he confronted two grinning members of the gang. "Hi there, Rich," they chortled. "How ya doing, fella? Why don't you come along with us." Grabbing him by the elbows, they propelled him down Holyoke Street to Tubman House, where the rest of the gang quickly assembled. Pinning him against the building, his friends pummeled him on the arms, shoulders, and legs—hard knuckle chops which left painful bruises. Ray finished him off with a rabbit punch to the biceps.

The game was a grotesque parody of black aggression. As in the ghetto riots of the sixties, when blacks burned and pillaged their own communities, the gang members had been venting their rage on each other. But there was nothing to be gained from that, they realized, so gradually they turned their anger outward, seeking satisfaction—and profit—in the white world.

By then, Richard was at English High School, caught up in the turmoil of the Afro-American Society, seeking to extract reforms from the white administration, sometimes even coming to blows with white boys in the corridors. Often in those years he could feel a hatred for white people welling up within him, and every confrontation only heightened that feeling. One evening, coming home through the Boston Common, a gang of whites chased him all the way to Dartmouth Street, shouting racial epithets. There was something very wrong in America, he thought, if a black kid couldn't even walk the streets of his own city. If that's the way it was going to be, then maybe his street skills would come in handy, earning him a measure of revenge.

Richard had robbed white people long before that. When he was only twelve, growing up in the Orchard Park project, he began snatching purses on the Elevated. His friends took black and white women's purses indiscriminately, but even then Richard hadn't liked stealing from blacks—the money he took might be all they had to feed their children. It wasn't until he moved into Methunion Manor and joined the Holyoke Street gang that he began branching out, turning his talents to a skein of street "hustles." In the black world, "hustling" covered a multitude of minor crimes—from snatching purses and picking pockets to gambling and drug pushing—all informed by the hustler's conviction that he could get something for nothing.

Money remained scarce in the Twymon household. For some years, Rachel's Aid to Families with Dependent Children grant had averaged about $500 a month (supplemented monthly by $178 worth of food stamps, for which she paid $105). Even after she went to work full-time in Methunion's office, taking home $108.95 per week at the start, the family's economic situation scarcely improved, for her AFDC check was simultaneously reduced to $154.30 a month, leaving her about $580 a month to feed, house, and clothe herself and six children. The kids helped out now and then. One summer Richard worked on a *Globe* delivery truck, earning ten dollars a week. But well-paying jobs were virtually impossible for a black teenager to find. Any hustler with a modicum of skill and daring could do much better on the street.

That fall of 1971, the Holyoke Street gang adopted a song which encapsulated the hustler's ethos. On cassette decks and stereos, they played the O'Jays' "For the Love of Money" so often they knew it by heart and could sing it in unison:

> *For the love of money*
> *People will steal from their mother.*
> *For the love of money*
> *People will rob their own brother.*
> *For the love of money*
> *People can't even walk the streets.*
> *Because they never know who in the world*
> *They're gonna meet.*
>
> *For that mean, green, almighty dollar.*
>
> *For the love of money*
> *People will lie and they will cheat.*
> *For the love of money*
> *People don't care who they hurt or beat.*

For the love of money
A woman will sell her precious body.
For a small piece of paper
It carries a lot of weight.

For that mean, mean, green almighty dollar.

Money is the root of all evil.
Do funny things to some people.
Give me a nickel, brother.
Can you spare a dime?
Money can drive some people wild.

The mean green was all around them then, fluttering in the breeze, ripe for the plucking. It was over on Boylston and Newbury streets, where the rich folks did their shopping at those cute little boo-tiques. It was up at the Sheraton-Boston, where conventioneers waddled through the lobby, wallets bulging in their pockets. It was along Massachusetts Avenue, where white johns came looking for a little black action. And it was just across Columbus Avenue, where white couples had bought up the old rooming houses, pushed poor folks into the streets, then built their own little suburb in the heart of the city. Everywhere they looked, Richard and his friends saw money, white money, just waiting to be ripped off by bad dudes who knew how to hustle.

The gang which began on Holyoke Street and later hung out in the Soul Center was never closely knit. Around a core of four or five regulars assembled another dozen or so teenagers, from as far afield as the Castle Square housing project. Rarely operating as a unit, they split into two-man teams for their forays into the white community.

Richard and his partner prowled the white perimeter, seeking targets of opportunity. They might trail a likely looking mark for several blocks, waiting for a dark, deserted stretch, only to have him enter a crowded store or restaurant. Once, as they were about to strike, their target turned and glared at them as if he knew exactly what they were up to. Startled, they abandoned the chase.

One cold November evening on the Prudential Center plaza, they pulled off their first successful holdup. Lurking in the darkened shopping arcade, they noticed a white businessman gazing into a store window. They were so nervous they shouted simultaneously, "Give me your money!" Fortunately, the businessman was even more terrified than they were. His voice quavered as he begged them not to hurt him, his hands shook as he handed over a wallet containing eighty dollars. It was all so absurdly easy the boys had to laugh.

Once they got the hang of it, they realized they had everything working in their favor. Like the Vietnamese jungles to the Vietcong, the streets of the South End were their natural habitat, a tangled wilderness from which they could launch deadly ambushes, in which they could quickly take refuge. Fleeing from the Back Bay into the South End, for example, they knew which streets dead-ended at the railroad tracks, creating perilous cul-de-sacs, and which led to pedestrian footbridges, providing ideal escape hatches. Or, coming from the other direction, they knew which doors of Methunion Manor were usually left open, leading to a friendly apartment. They knew every corner and alley, fence and fire escape, for blocks around, while their white victims, like a clumsy army of occupation, stuck to the floodlit thoroughfares.

Again, like guerrillas, they kept their prospective targets under observation, learning their habits, and patterns of movement. Priding themselves on knowing far more about the interloper than he did about them, they cased the liquor and fancy food stores, watching the routes that whites took coming and going. They watched for men who drove foreign sports cars, wore suits, and carried briefcases, women with fur coats and gold bracelets. They kept an eye out for Chinese, who were said to carry lots of cash because they distrusted banks; they shunned Italians, who might be tied to the Mafia; they scoured the alleys for winos, whom they called "Irish," as in "Let's go rob Irish."

Of all the whites who strayed onto their turf, the wealthiest were the season ticket holders at the Boston Symphony. Every Tuesday, Thursday, and Saturday night during the winter season, they paraded through the Greek portico of Symphony Hall in their Chesterfield coats and pearl necklaces. Extra police patrolled Massachusetts and Huntington avenues on those occasions, but Richard and his pals learned to linger in the deserted side streets, waiting for the concertgoers to return to their cars. You could strike it rich back there, as Richard and David did one evening when they relieved an aging music lover of his elegant gold watch and a butter-soft calfskin billfold containing $350.

Richard didn't suffer greatly from remorse. Whites could always get more money, he reckoned; the guy he took $100 from probably had $50,000 stashed away in his safe-deposit box. Anyway, as every merchant knew, you couldn't afford to have a heart in business. If ripping off white folks was your business, that's what you did, you ripped off white folks.

The easiest targets of all were the white hunters who cruised Massachusetts Avenue looking for black prostitutes. Afraid to draw attention to themselves, they invariably surrendered their money with little protest. But the pimps on the avenue resented the holdup men, fearing they would drive away the white trade. One night, after Richard and his partner had moved in on a meek little hunter with a fat wallet, a pimp named Sweet Lou started hollering at them, "Hey, don't do that shit around here!"

"What the hell you talkin' about, man?" shouted Richard, who loathed pimps for selling black girls to white men. "Look at the stuff you're doing out here. Don't tell us what to do!"

"I'll kick your ass," blustered Sweet Lou.

"Kick whose ass?" Richard said, advancing on the pimp. "We do all the ass-kicking round here."

"Hey, brother," the pimp hollered, retreating down the sidewalk, "I didn't mean nothing. Okay? No offense."

Richard never carried a gun—that was for the professionals—but he often came armed with a fruit knife, a sharp little shiv that scared the hell out of his victims. Working the side streets off Columbus Avenue, his partner would grab the mark around the neck, yoking him with his elbow, while Richard advanced on him with the fruit knife, whispering, "Give it up, man, give it up." People usually complied with alacrity.

He had to be very careful, though. If the cops ever caught him with a weapon like that, his chances of a felony conviction would double or triple. One night, they'd held up a guy on Worcester Square and were sauntering down Massachusetts Avenue when a policeman yelled, "Hey you two, stop right there!"

With a reflexive jerk, Richard tossed the knife onto a grocery store roof.

The cop never noticed. "Okay," he bellowed. "You know what to do. Up against the car. Spread those goddamn legs."

Finding nothing, the cop let them go with a grudging apology. "Funny," he growled. "You look just like some guys we're out to get."

As they stalked the South End in search of appropriate targets, their attention was inevitably drawn to the town houses which had recently replaced the rooming houses along many of its side streets. From the darkened sidewalks on a winter's evening, their bay windows blazed with light, warmth, and unimagined luxury: chandeliers, oil paintings, African carvings, French tapestries, Chinese vases, ivory chess sets, leather couches, marble fireplaces topped with silver candelabra, all the insignia of the new urban middle class. Richard and his friends had never glimpsed such finery before, except in the movies. It stirred complicated feelings—envy, resentment, anger, and desire. Before long, they set out to get some of it for themselves.

Having graduated from purse snatching to mugging, Richard now specialized in burglary. The gang's best "B and E" man, he prided himself on his spiderlike agility and deft touch. Strictly a second-story man, he let the chumps have the first floor, where you ran the greatest risk of setting off a burglar alarm or being spotted from the street. He'd go up a fire escape or over a rooftop, jimmy a window or break through a skylight, and be in and out in five minutes, taking anything he could get into his canvas bag—cash, jewelry, silver, a television set, or radio. Occasionally, he and his friends pulled off something more ambitious. Once, they broke into a burned-out building and, with ropes and pulleys, removed an air conditioner from an upstairs window. Later, they even tried their hand at burglaries in the western suburbs. They'd borrow a friend's car, ride into a preselected neighborhood, and break into a house which looked promising. Occasionally, somebody would be home and they'd have to run for it. On the streets of such overwhelmingly white communities, their black faces often drew curious stares and once a motorcycle cop demanded their driver's license and registration. But, incredibly enough, Richard was never arrested.

His younger brother wasn't so fortunate. George had a talent for being in the wrong place at the wrong time. In July 1972, he was caught in a South

End riot triggered when police waded into a disturbance at the Puerto Rican Day celebration. Early that evening, he was standing with friends on Washington Street when a police car pulled to the curb. The rest of the crowd scattered, but the police arrested George, charging him with being a disorderly person and assault and battery with a dangerous weapon—for allegedly throwing a beer can at a policeman's chest. George insisted he'd never thrown anything, the officer failed to show up in court, and the charges were dismissed.

Quieter and more studious than his older brother, George had come under the influence of an extraordinary teacher. Harriet Schwartz, a veteran of the Boston public schools, had escaped the corrosive cynicism that afflicted many of her colleagues. Appalled by the fruitless treadmill of Boston's black schools, she was determined to find some way out for her most promising students. Every day after school, and all through one February vacation, she tutored six of them in math and English, helping to prepare them for private, suburban, or special city schools. In September 1970, George was admitted to West Roxbury's predominantly white Robert Gould Shaw School, named after the white colonel who had led Massachusetts' black regiment in the Civil War. From there he moved automatically into Roslindale High, another predominantly white school, where he compiled a satisfactory record in the college preparatory program.

But every day he came home from school to the raw realities of Methunion Manor, and soon he was hanging out with Richard's crowd. Before long, he too was a street hustler—snatching purses, picking pockets, later graduating to car theft and mugging. The brothers rarely pulled off a job together—Richard considered George unreliable, less committed to the street life, more likely to make a mistake. So George paired off with another kid, operating much as Richard and his friend did, waiting until their victim was alone on a deserted street, moving in from front and rear, grabbing a wallet, a handbag, or jewelry, then fleeing back to the refuge of Methunion Manor. Like Richard, George never used a gun, but, after several of his marks put up a struggle, he began brandishing a knife to great effect.

He might have gone on from there to more serious crimes had he not been arrested in October 1973. He was running that day with the best known of the South End hustlers, a hood named Anthony Black, who was *de facto* leader of the Soul Center gang. Anthony's father, Vernon, lived in Methunion Manor, where he ran a "trick pad," an apartment to which prostitutes took their customers. At an early age, when Vernon was running a similar establishment on Durham Street, Anthony had learned to prey on his father's customers. He'd watch as the prostitutes pulled up to the building in the customer's car, wait until they'd gone inside, then break into the car and take anything he could find. Afraid of being mugged, the white hunters invariably stashed their wallets under a seat or in the glove compartment and Anthony would make off with a fistful of bills. From that he graduated to mugging and armed robbery. Though barely five feet four and only a hundred pounds, he was a tough, cocky bantam, known to police as "the little Napoleon." Already a legend up and down Columbus Avenue, he had earned a faithful following among the neighborhood kids.

On October 21, 1973, one of Anthony's gang stole a pocketbook from a woman at the Midtown Motor Inn. In it they found the key to her car parked in the motel lot and they decided to take that too. As the oldest member along that day, George was delegated to drive. Rolling along Huntington Avenue near Copley Square, he failed to see a red light suspended high above the intersection and at once a police car pulled him over. George didn't have a license, but he was doing a pretty good job of bluffing when one of the policemen glanced in the back seat and spotted Anthony Black. "Oh, Mr. Black," he said. "We know Mr. Black quite well. Do you gentlemen mind stepping out here?" George was booked on auto theft. After the Reverend Bobby McClain testified on his behalf, the judge suspended sentence and gave him two years' probation.

By then, Rachel's third-oldest son, Freddie, was giving signs of becoming the family's most dedicated hustler. At the age of fifteen, he was already spending a lot of time around the Paradise Lounge on Tremont Street. The South End's most notorious bar, the Paradise was a hangout for drug pushers, gamblers, numbers runners, pimps, prostitutes, stickup men, enforcers, and fugitives of all sorts. Day and night, it was the place to get a fix, pick up a woman, make a bet, buy a weapon, fence some loot, exchange information on upcoming jobs, or get into a brawl. It was no place for a fifteen-year-old boy to be hanging out.

A social worker visiting Rachel in November 1973 reported that she had been "somewhat upset and depressed lately because her children are getting into all sorts of trouble."

If the boys were in trouble with the law, the girls were in trouble with boys. All through those teenage years, Cassandra and Little Rachel energetically experimented with sex. On spring and summer evenings, they hung out with a crowd of neighborhood kids at the corner of Carleton and Holyoke streets— smoking pot, drinking beer, "foolin' around." Night after night, Big Rachel angrily hauled them home.

On Thanksgiving Day 1974, after dinner at the home of Rachel's sister Alva, the family cleared the living room, put a stack of rhythm and blues on the stereo, and began to dance. As Big Rachel watched her daughters strut the floor, she noticed how heavy Little Rachel had grown. Suddenly she thought: That girl is pregnant, my thirteen-year-old daughter is pregnant! Rushing to Alva's room, she flung herself on the bed, where Alva found her an hour later. The sisters summoned Little Rachel, who reluctantly confessed her condition.

Big Rachel had often discussed sex and its consequences with her daughters and had cautioned them against fooling around, but knowing they would do it anyway, she also had instructed them in contraception and urged them to pay regular visits to a gynecologist. If, despite all these precautions, they got pregnant anyway, they'd better be ready to care for their baby. All that winter, a family debate raged over what to do with Little Rachel's child. The girl insisted she was ready and willing to raise it. Her mother dismissed that notion with scorn. "You're thirteen years old," she told her daughter. "You're a baby having a baby. And I can't take care of it for you. I got enough on my hands. We got to do something."

Little Rachel was already six months pregnant, too late for an abortion, so Big Rachel called the Boston Children's Service Association to arrange for adoption. When Alva heard that she rushed down to Methunion Manor to confront her sister. "You're giving away your own flesh and blood," she said. "Nobody in our family has ever done that before. It's a damn disgrace."

Big Rachel wasn't taking that. "You're not my mother," she said. "You're not my father. You're not my keeper. I don't have to tell you nothing."

Alva stormed out, but she was back a few weeks later. "Before you give that child away to strangers," she demanded, "I want you to give it to me." Rachel just stared at her. "You're not even going to answer me?" asked Alva.

"You mind everybody's business but your own," Rachel shot back. "I got nothing to say to you."

Little Rachel's baby was born in April 1975. For three days, she nursed her infant; then, with her reluctant permission, it was put up for adoption. For years to come, Little Rachel grieved for her child and never quite forgave her mother. And the quarrel left a legacy of bitterness between Rachel and Alva—never again were the sisters more than coldly civil toward each other.

Rachel was heartsick over her children's troubles. She'd done her best to make a good home for them, and God knew she loved them! They were all she had in life. They meant so much to her that maybe she loved them too much. But children couldn't live on love alone. They needed discipline. They needed a man around the house to provide a firm hand, even a razor strap if necessary. Her brother Arnold had tried to be a surrogate father to her kids, but he lacked the authority a real father would have had, and some of them had angrily repudiated him. Bobby McClain had helped too with advice and guidance, but increasingly he was preoccupied with his own problems. As the years went by, Rachel realized she would have to be both mother and father to her kids.

She became a rigid disciplinarian, setting tight curfews for them, insisting that they perform chores around the house before they went out, demanding that they tell her where they'd been and whom they'd been with. But the more she cracked down, the more they seemed to resent her. Nearly every evening there was some kind of shouting match in the Twymon household, Rachel accusing her children of being lazy and irresponsible, they denouncing her for being meddlesome and domineering. "Get off my back," George shouted at her one night. "Stop trying to run my life!" After his arrest for auto theft, George resolved to change his life, dropping out of the gang and setting his mind to school. But he and his mother remained temperamentally irreconcilable. Night after night they were at each other's throat. During one particularly bitter spat, Rachel hit him behind the ear with her cane. As soon as he graduated from Roslindale High, George left home, enrolling at Draughns Business College in Nashville, Tennessee.

One of the few adults at Methunion Manor who maintained any rapport with the street gang was a white Catholic priest, Father Walter Waldron. A founding member of the Association of Boston Urban Priests, Waldron had remained in the inner city long after most of his colleagues had retreated to suburban parishes or left the priesthood altogether. Assigned to the Cathedral of the Holy Cross, seat of Boston's Archdiocese, he chose not to live in its spacious rectory but to take an apartment in Methunion Manor, where he could make a real connection with alienated blacks in his parish.

Waldron developed a special relationship with the project's teenagers. Perhaps because he seemed less interested in judging them than in understanding how they perceived the world, many of them would visit him in his apartment to sip a soda, listen to records, and trade stories. And when they got in trouble, Waldron was always available with advice and assistance. He'd been before every judge in town urging clemency when he thought it was justified, or simply comforting young offenders and their families.

Detectives at the South End station house—most of them Irish Catholics— were angered by Father Waldron's activities, accusing him of making their job harder, of "protecting the troublemakers," of giving young criminals "sanctuary" in the bosom of the Church. "Those kids aren't even Catholics," they would grumble. "What's a priest doing with them anyway?" A priest's place, Waldron responded, was with the poor and dispossessed, no matter what their religion. In no way did he mean to underestimate the horror of crime, the hardship it worked on its victims, or the duty of police and courts to bring its perpetrators to justice. But, neither judge nor policeman, he was more interested in trying to understand what led these young people to commit such acts.

Most of them came from poor families, but Waldron doubted that profit was their principal motive. Easy money on the streets was certainly a lure, particularly when the potential rewards outweighed the risk of a long prison term. But only the real junkies—those with a voracious heroin habit—stole primarily for money.

An equally important motive, he concluded, was racial—and class—hostility. Some young blacks hated whites, convinced that they had enslaved, exploited, and misused black people so long that the gang was justified in taking whatever it could in return. Boston's school crisis had aggravated those feelings, while gentrification had laid bare the chasm between the white middle class and the black working/welfare class. Such indignities prompted some young blacks to lash out at whites in violent street crimes. For others, it provided a rhetorical justification, a rationalization for crimes they would have committed anyway.

Then there was the excitement, the thrill of danger. The kids told him repeatedly how bored they were. Yes, there were basketball courts, a swimming pool, and baseball diamonds within walking distance of Methunion Manor, and for several years Union Methodist Church had been operating a

"drop-in" youth center offering black history courses, a theater group, leatherwork and sewing instruction. Nevertheless, the kids still felt there was nothing to do but hang out on the corner, drink beer, and get high on reefers. Crime
lit up their bleak world.

Another significant factor, Waldron concluded, was pressure from their
peers on the street. For ghetto kids, street hustles and violent crimes were a
"rite of passage," demonstrations that one was no longer a kid, that one was
becoming a man. Risks must be run, rules broken, commandments violated.
In short, the boy who aspired to black manhood had to be a "bad nigger" first.
To shrink from that was to risk being labeled a momma's boy, a coward. "You
punked out on us, man," the others would say. "We were ripping the cat off
and you punked out on us. You're finished on this corner."

Their corner was the intersection of Braddock Park and Columbus Avenue.
To the right, as one faced Columbus, was the Soul Center, rhythm and blues
blaring from its doorway. On the left was Braddock Drugs, Hymie Krasnow's
place, where you could sometimes get a pint of liquor under the counter and
always a Ring-Ding or Moon Pie from the well-stocked display case. The gang
shuttled back and forth, generally spending midafternoon at the drugstore,
moving over to the Soul Center in the evening. Both stores were strategically
placed for the gang's purposes, each commanding a wide field of vision across
Columbus toward Rutland Square, Pembroke, West Brookline, and West
Newton streets. Lounging on either doorstep, they could watch the young
professionals coming home from work carrying their briefcases and evening
papers, or returning from the Sunnyhurst grocery and Cheese Cask liquor
store, their arms filled with shopping bags. As dusk fell over the South End,
the gang waited on the corner, poised for lightning strikes into the heartland
of the white gentry.

22

Diver

I like the slant of light at midday on a thousand chimney pots,"
intoned the poet David McCord.

"I remember as a small child being shown Boston through the eyes of my
grandfather, who was the first Irish Catholic mayor of this city," said Edward
Kennedy in that familiar twang. "Honey Fitz used to go down to the Old North
Church and stare at the marvelous steeple there and he would read to me the
Paul Revere poem."

"Boston baked beans start off with beans," chortled Julia Child. "According to *Mrs. Leland's Boston Cooking School Book,* copyrighted in 1883, you
start off by soaking one quart of pea beans in cold water overnight. In the
morning you put them into fresh cold water and simmer them until soft enough
to pierce with a pin."

The voices of Boston poured from quadriphonic speakers while forty slide
projectors threw images of the city across the auditorium's eight screens. In
barely an hour, the multimedia production *Where's Boston?* fashioned a dazzling urban kaleidoscope:

Italian vendors squeezing plump melons on their Haymarket stalls; Seiji
Ozawa leading the Boston Symphony in a fanfare from Berlioz's *Symphonie
Fantastique;* Hare Krishna acolytes, their saffron robes splendid against the
wintry Common; strings of colored lights at a North End street festival; the
jagged geometry of City Hall; the flash of militiamen's muskets on Patriots'
Day; the slash of silver skates on the Garden ice; a Mozart string quartet in
Mrs. Gardner's museum; the bleak austerity of Dorchester's triple-deckers;
Fred Lynn doubling off the green wall at Fenway Park; the throbbing beat of
jazz in a Back Bay nightclub; the great granite façade of the restored Quincy
Market; green tam-o'-shanters in the crowd on St. Patrick's Day; steamed

424

clams in a harborside restaurant; a runner crossing the finish line in the Boston Marathon.

When the last image had faded from the screen, Joan and Colin Diver turned to their out-of-town guests. "Well," asked Joan, "what do you think of our town?"

"Oh, Joan," said Patsy Shillingburg, "it's got to be the most exciting city in the country!"

The Divers were delighted. *Where's Boston?*, they knew, had been promoted by City Hall and financed by the Prudential Insurance Company to put the best face on Boston during the Bicentennial year. In focusing on the "urban renaissance," it embellished the old city a little, glossing over its racial and social problems. But it captured the grandeur of Boston's past, the diversity of its ethnic neighborhoods. This was the city Joan and Colin were helping to rebuild, and their pride was enhanced by the admiration they now sensed in their out-of-town visitors.

They had begun the evening with drinks at the Divers' house, then moved on to the *Where's Boston?* pavilion pitched in the Prudential Center. After a splendid meal at the Cafe Plaza in the Copley Plaza Hotel, they bid each other good night. It was 12:30 a.m.

The Shillingburgs caught a cab back to their hotel, but Colin took Joan by the arm. "It's such a beautiful evening," he said. "Let's walk."

"It's awful late to be out in these streets," said Joan.

"Don't worry," Colin joked. "I've got my umbrella."

Under a velvety autumn sky, they strolled down Dartmouth Street. Reaching Columbus Avenue, they turned right into the South End, their footsteps echoing across the deserted boulevard. At Holyoke Street, they could see, a block ahead, the usual cluster of young men lounging around the Soul Center. Exercising the caution which had become second nature to most white South Enders, Colin and Joan cut diagonally across the avenue, putting as much room as possible between themselves and the group on the corner.

Almost simultaneously, two of the black teenagers detached themselves from the crowd, drifting in their direction.

The Divers moved faster, heading toward the safe haven of West Newton Street, but their pursuers kept pace, one of them bouncing along the median strip, the other prowling a few steps behind on the sidewalk.

"Hey, whitey!" cried the first, a runty kid in a blue windbreaker, jeans, and ankle-high boots. "Where you going? You trying to avoid us? Don't you like us?"

Not answering, Colin and Joan hurried on.

"What's the matter?" said the other, a tall, wiry fellow in sweat pants and running shoes. "You folks afraid of us poor niggers?"

By then, the pair was blocking the sidewalk, cutting off their escape route.

"How come you don't say anything?" the tall kid said. "You too good to talk to us? Or you afraid we're going to steal your money?"

Colin was getting angry, but Joan kept her cool.

"We're not afraid of anything," she said lightly. "We live over here. Right around that corner."

"Is that right?" the boy said with a little grin. "Then you won't mind shaking hands with a nigger." He held out a long, snaky arm.

Was it a trick? Joan wondered. If she shook hands, would he assault her? Was he simply mocking her, calling her bluff? Or was it barely possible that he was making some awkward gesture, trying in his own hostile way to bridge the gulf of Columbus Avenue?

On an impulse, she stuck out her hand.

But Colin was taking no chances. Raising his furled umbrella, he shouted, "Don't you touch my wife!"

The boy wheeled on Colin. "You really think that umbrella's going to protect you?" he sneered. "If you point that damn thing at me again I'm going to take it away from you."

Now it was Joan's turn. Jumping between them, she hissed, "Don't you dare hurt my husband! Don't even put a hand on him. Just leave him alone."

For a moment, the four of them stood glowering at each other, frozen in a terrible tableau, until Colin noticed a car with a white driver moving in their direction. Grabbing Joan's arm, he leapt into the roadway, brandishing his umbrella over his head, shouting at the driver to stop. Alarmed by the strange group in the street, the motorist swerved to avoid them. Another car rushed past in the opposite direction as Colin shouted vainly at it too.

By now the blacks were getting jumpy, afraid that a motorist might actually stop and intervene. With a parting gibe or two, they edged toward Methunion Manor.

Colin half pushed, half pulled Joan down West Newton Street and through the basement door under their stoop. Not until the door was double-locked behind them and they were sitting in their kitchen with a stiff drink did they start breathing regularly again. Yet the two of them reacted very differently to the confrontation on Columbus Avenue. So long as it lasted, Joan had been terror-stricken. But once it was over she felt almost exhilarated. After all, they'd stood up to the danger, faced down their pursuers, and emerged unscathed. To her, the incident demonstrated that with a little will and character you could survive the South End's perils. Henceforth, she walked those streets with greater confidence.

Colin drew almost the opposite conclusion. While admiring Joan's composure, he was dismayed at his own reaction. He knew one should keep one's cool in such situations, but he'd felt a terrible anger welling up within him. Why should he have to stand there, a block from his own house, and take this shit from these kids? His instinct was to strike out and, if Joan hadn't intervened, he might well have hit one of them. God knows what mayhem might have ensued; they could have been seriously hurt, perhaps even killed. Yet precisely because he felt such anger himself, he could imagine the rage which boiled within Methunion Manor's young blacks. Columbus Avenue had become a no-man's-land, he realized—a frontier between two embattled communities whose interests were increasingly pitted against each other. For the first time, Colin began to wonder whether he really wanted to raise his family in the heart of a war zone.

For something had happened to the South End in the preceding decade. Despite its racial and ethnic diversity, the neighborhood had long enjoyed a rough social harmony. Even when young professionals began settling there during the sixties, they were rarely at odds with their less advantaged neighbors. Committed to equality and heterogeneity, often strapped for cash themselves, struggling to rehabilitate a gutted shell or shabby rooming house, those first "pioneers" generally felt a community of interest with blacks, Puerto Ricans, and poor whites.

But once the newcomers had established their South End beachhead, they were followed by a different breed of middle-class settlers, more affluent suburbanites with no particular commitment to heterogeneity and little interest in rehabilitating an old rooming house from scratch. Having bought already-restored town houses for $35,000 to $80,000, this second wave felt a greater stake in their investment, a deeper need for insulation from the poor, the black, and the unorthodox. The most mobile members of a mobile society, often with cultivated tastes, a desire for "gracious living" and pocketbooks to match, they were the quintessential urban consumers, prime targets for every "up-market" sales pitch ("Jack and Jill live in Boston. They moved here from someplace else. They're nice. They're young and fun. They live a life we understand at Jordan Marsh," advertised Boston's largest department store). Gradually, the blocks of restored town houses between Columbus Avenue and Tremont Street became a distinctive enclave, set apart—thanks to the Boston Redevelopment Authority—by brick sidewalks, ornamental streetlights, and ginkgo trees, as well as by its own standards, values, and social proprieties.

As early as October 1971, the *Globe* noted this phenomenon in an article headlined "South End Glows as Suburbanites Move In." Written by its society reporter, Marjorie Sherman, it announced that the South End was "on the comeback at last," beginning to rival "hippie-harried" Beacon Hill as "the place to have a townhouse." And it went on to list some of the latest arrivers. "Dr. and Mrs. Cesare Lombroso came in to Union Park from 'Pill Hill' in Brookline. They have done a fantastic job making a contemporary townhouse setting for their treasures out of a Victorian mansion and love the living they have. . . . University of Massachusetts Chancellor Frederick Broderick and his wife; architect Basil Alferieff; Colin Diver of the Mayor's Office; Polaroid Vice-President Mark Sewall; the Junior League Show House Lamplighter Mrs. Joseph Park, Jr., and her husband . . . are among the South Enders who love their thirteen-foot ceilings and 23 by 50 foot living rooms. The Roland Crowells, who have a superb townhouse on Union Park, bucked the traffic from Weston into town. 'Now we live in another world,' says Mrs. Crowell, whose duties at Wellesley College, and home in town, mean she can skim out with no traffic. Mr. Crowell nips downtown to Boit, Dalton and Church. No problem."

But others detected plenty of problems in the arrival of this new urban gentry. At first, the opposition to "gentrification" came principally from the South End's social work establishment. The neighborhood which Edward Everett Hale had once labeled "the most 'charitied' region in Christendom" and which later gave birth to Robert Woods's South End House continued to harbor an impressive array of social service agencies, settlement houses, missions, refuges, halfway houses, and homes for indigent men, women, and children. By the sixties, few who worked for such institutions regarded themselves as mere custodians for society's unfortunates; stirred by that era's activism, they had become advocates of a new social order. Social workers—who were closest to, and most sympathetic with, the South End's minority poor—were the first to speak out against the growing power of the white middle class. Their criticism may have reflected an element of self-interest. Those, like Mel King, who used social work as a springboard to politics had an interest in preserving their constituency. Those who remained in the "helping professions" could only function if their clientele was there to be helped. Spokesmen for the new gentry went a step further, accusing the settlement houses of "fighting to preserve the South End as an economic ghetto for the poor."

Before long, the advocate social workers found new allies: the student and ex-student radicals then breeding by the thousands in Boston's colleges and universities. With a Marxist perspective sharpened by their reading of Herbert Marcuse, Paul Goodman, and C. Wright Mills, these young men and women were particularly sensitive to conflict between the professional/technological/managerial bourgeoisie and the black/Puerto Rican/poor white proletariat. Nowhere in Boston did such class conflict seem closer to the surface than along the Columbus Avenue battlefront. Just as Massachusetts university graduates had once found an outlet for their idealism in Robert Woods's "scientific settlement work," so graduates of those same universities now enlisted in a struggle against "entrenched interests" in the New South End.

In the late sixties, a small group of radicals began publishing a fighting tabloid called the *South End People's News*. Frequently lapsing into street rhetoric like "Death to the Pigs!" and "All Power to the People!" the paper launched a heavy barrage against those who profited from gentrification. "There's a funeral procession slipping silently, a block at a time, through the South End," it declared:

The vile entourage of the real estate speculators, the land investors, the landlords and the rich in general continue to cast an ever-increasing shadow over what we know and love as the South End. . . . The housing projects, with all their ugliness, crampness and prison-like atmosphere, stand like concrete tombstones for the poor community. While just around the block from these projects are homes which could have been rehabbed for the people who live in them. Instead, these white culture clowns have paraded in with all their racism and capitalist greed, seeking to transform the South End community into a citadel of golden doorknobs and silver patios. . . . These large landlords, slumlords and investors must be threatened and harassed at every opportunity. We are talking about survival, so this would be a justified act of self-defense. The Man is standing on our neck and we have one last choice—allow him to continue until we are strangled to death or arise swiftly and strike this inhuman enemy.

Through the late sixties and early seventies, the radical–social worker alliance focused its agitation on landlords whose substandard buildings housed many of the South End's blacks and Puerto Ricans. In May 1968, a month after Martin Luther King's assassination, the activists decided to take direct action against the largest landlord of all. Under a variety of corporate names, three brothers—Joseph, Israel, and Raphael Mindick—owned some forty-four buildings in the South End housing from 700 to 800 tenants, most of them black. The Mindicks held another distinction: they were the neighborhood's most persistent violators of the housing code, yet activists had tried in vain to get effective code enforcement from the city. On May 5, the South End alliance organized a demonstration outside Israel Mindick's house in Mattapan. But Mindick wasn't home that day and, after picketing for several hours, the frustrated demonstrators reconvened to plan their next step. The consensus favored a demonstration the following Saturday outside Congregation Beth El in Dorchester, where Israel was a cantor.

That alarmed Rabbi Judea Miller, social action chairman of the Massachusetts Board of Rabbis, who had joined the demonstrators that day in an effort to deflect accusations of black anti-Semitism. Miller recognized that demonstrations at a temple were bound to prompt just such a charge, but, as he wrote a fellow rabbi, the Mindicks' activities were "terrible, scandalous," especially embarrassing to the Jewish community because Israel was known as "rabbi" to his black tenants. "That any pious Jew would make profit out of such degradation of other human beings is unthinkable," Miller wrote. To head off the planned protest, yet assure that conditions be corrected, he proposed that the tenants take their case before Boston's Rabbinical Court of Justice.

Rabbinical courts scattered through the United States deal with divorces, trusts, estates, and contractual disputes between Jews. Only rarely does a non-Jewish plaintiff bring a suit against a Jewish defendant and, on such occasions, the Jew is under no formal obligation to accept the rabbinical court's jurisdiction. However, Rabbi Miller believed that once the tenants filed their action, the Mindicks would find themselves under powerful moral duress to acknowledge the court's authority in the matter. As a cantor, Israel Mindick would be vulnerable to great pressure from the elders of his temple. Moreover, the whole family were Orthodox Jews who took their religion very seriously. As such, they could be embarrassed by the revelation that the dummy corporations under which they did business—Yiyu, Lirotzone, Imray, Fee, Vihegyone, Libee, Hashame, Lifonecho, Tsuri, Vigoali—spelled out in transliterated Hebrew a line from Psalm 19, "Let the words of my mouth, and the meditation of my heart, be acceptable in thy sight, O Lord, my strength, and my redeemer."

Miller's instinct was sound. The Mindicks accepted the challenge and, on May 8, they and the tenants' representatives appeared before five skullcapped rabbis in the downtown offices of the Associated Synagogues of Massachusetts. In subsequent hearings, the tenants argued that the Mindicks' buildings were rat- and roach-infested, unsanitary, hazardous, crime-ridden, and overpriced. In response, the Mindicks contended that they were not responsible for "abnormal conditions" in the South End, that they did their best to keep the buildings clean and safe, but that tenants threw garbage out the windows, broke furniture, and so vandalized the buildings that the family could no longer realize a profit from its South End properties.

The court heard testimony ten times during the next three months, but most of its work was conducted through an arbitration panel composed of members named by the tenants and landlords plus a neutral arbiter. Finally, on August 8, the rabbis promulgated a mutually acceptable agreement, binding in the city's courts. The Mindicks agreed to keep their properties clean and safe, to provide locks, hot water, and a minimum room temperature of 68 degrees, and to recognize the newly formed South End Tenants' Council as the tenants' sole bargaining agent. The tenants agreed to pay their rent promptly, care for their apartments, and make "reasonable efforts" to cooperate with the landlord. A complex arbitration and appeals process was established to resolve further differences.

In a memorandum on the law, the court cited Dr. Isaac Herzog's dictum that "the spirit of the law at times demands from man to conform to a loftier norm and standard than that which its letter can enforce." Applying that to the present case, the court held that "a landlord who would do business in a low-income area must accept the special hazards of such areas. . . . If his resources will not permit him, for example, to maintain the buildings in a non-hazardous condition, then he has no right to be a landlord. . . . The tenant, typically, has no financial reserve with which to fend off calamity; the landlord, typically, can accept temporary reverses. . . . Our aim is clear, it is—justice for all concerned. 'Justice, Justice, Justice, shalt thou pursue.'"

For a time it appeared that justice had indeed been achieved. But within months, the dispute erupted again. In February 1969, tenants of twenty Mindick buildings began a rent strike, arguing that the landlord had failed to live up to his part of the agreement. By then, the rabbinical court had concluded that the Mindicks were a liability to the Jewish community. Joseph "Inky" Mindick—invariably decked out in yellow polyester slacks, Hawaiian shirt, white shoes, and porkpie hat—was a caricature of the unscrupulous landlord. In March, the five rabbis fined the Mindicks $48,000. That May, worn down by the struggle with their tenants and wounded by the rabbis' reproof, the Mindicks sold thirty-four of their buildings to the Boston Redevelopment Authority, which, in turn, assigned them to the Tenants' Council for renovation and management.

Soon the council adopted another tactic for prying living space from South End landlords. On September 28, 1969, several council leaders appeared outside a brownstone at 22 Yarmouth Street, broke into a vacant apartment, and installed Genine Williams, a gypsy, and her three children. They offered the landlord, Stephen Wolfberg, $60 a month for the one-bedroom apartment he had planned to rent for $195. Wolfberg refused, got an eviction order, and put the woman out, only to have another "squatter" immediately take her place.

Steve Wolfberg had always regarded himself as a liberal and friend of the disadvantaged. A Harvard Law School graduate, he had worked briefly as a civil rights lawyer in the South before entering private practice in Boston. Soon after he and his wife Judith moved onto Rutland Square in 1968, Steve became active with a church-sponsored housing program known as Low Cost Housing, Inc., which bought up derelict buildings and rehabilitated them with volunteer labor. With Mel King as chairman and Steve as president, it quickly won a reputation for providing low-income tenants with decent housing at reasonable rents. Wolfberg also bought ten other properties on his own, renovating them with low-interest government loans, but soon he encountered financing difficulties and no longer felt able to make all the repairs his tenants demanded. After the Tenants' Council chose him as the first target of its squatters movement, his reputation as a social activist quickly dissipated. Tenants at another building launched a rent strike against him. His former colleague Mel King labeled him an "enemy of the community," and forced his resignation from Low Cost Housing. Wolfberg felt badly misused. "Here I am, one of the good guys," he told friends, "and I'm getting crapped on."

Two weeks after Wolfberg's building was occupied, the squatters movement spread to the property of another South End landlord, Ferdinand Arenella. On October 10, the council installed six black and Puerto Rican families in Arenella's recently renovated building at 694 Tremont Street. When the manager sought to serve eviction notices, police and Tenants' Council members became embroiled in a violent melee, during which a policeman was injured and four council members were arrested. One of those arrested, a black social worker named Ted Parrish, returned to the building and, standing beneath the squatters' motto, "Human Rights over Property Rights," told the crowd, "We're not moving, because nobody is coming in here to force us out of our community." Later, eighty tenants and their supporters converged on Arenella's home, where they chanted, "Poor people stay, Arenella go!" During the demonstration, one young man sprayed "Pig" in yellow paint on Arenella's car.

Ferd Arenella wasn't a man to take this kind of thing lying down. Like his neighbor Steve Wolfberg, Arenella was a lawyer who had drifted into real estate; now he earned most of his income from forty South End properties. A twenty-year veteran of the neighborhood, he had settled there before it became chic or idealistic to live in the inner city. Unhampered by ideological considerations, Arenella was determined to tough it out. But soon the confrontation got rougher than anyone had anticipated. Every day, the squatters at 694 Tremont Street collected their garbage—half-eaten pizzas, beer cans, eggshells, and rotting vegetables—and deposited it on the graceful steps of the Arenellas' town house at 11 Rutland Square.

Shortly after midnight on October 20, a mysterious fire broke out just down the block at 48 Rutland Square, causing $11,000 worth of damage. Eyewitnesses reported that the brick town house had flared up "like a tinderbox," strongly suggesting arson. Activists quickly noted that, although 48 Rutland Square was a private dwelling apparently unrelated to the tenant-landlord dispute, 48 Rutland Street—one block away—was an outpost of United South End Settlements, then serving as headquarters for the South End Tenants' Council and its squatters movement. Someone unfamiliar with the South End might easily have mistaken one "48" for the other.

At 2:00 a.m. the same night, another fire broke out a few doors away at the Arenellas'. Ferd, his wife, and child were awakened by flames racing across their rear deck. Police discovered two unexploded Molotov cocktails in the yard. A third firebomb had apparently ignited the deck, scorching the building's upper façade, causing $5,000 damage.

The dispute at 694 Tremont Street was ultimately resolved when Arenella and his partner agreed to let the squatters remain in the building, supported by leased housing grants from the Boston Housing Authority. But before long the Tenants' Council's battle with Arenella spread to a row of twenty-four tenements he owned on West Newton Street between Tremont Street and Shawmut Avenue. By 1969, these buildings were occupied principally by Puerto Ricans, the South End's most rapidly growing ethnic group. Assisted by Father William Dwyer of St. Stephen's Episcopal Church, they formed the Emergency Tenants' Council (ETC), which was soon locked in a bitter struggle for control of the properties.

On July 24, 1970—one week before Colin and Joan Diver moved in just down the street—black and Puerto Rican demonstrators blockaded the intersection of West Newton and Tremont streets to dramatize their grievances against the "pig landlord." Meanwhile, the *People's News* beat its tattoo on Arenella, denouncing him as "greedy, ruthless and dishonest," thundering, "We the community have had enough of you, Arenella. Cease and desist and leave this community!"

The pressures finally took their toll. In October 1970, at a news conference on West Newton Street, Mayor White announced that his administration had arranged for Arenella to sell the properties to a developer who would rehabilitate them, then sell them to the Boston Housing Authority, which, in turn, would contract with ETC to manage the buildings.

If the Mindicks were unreconstructed slumlords, Wolfberg and Arenella preferred whenever possible to exchange their low-income tenants for a classier clientele. But the new breed of South End landlord eschewed poor people altogether, developing properties explicitly for the "urban elite."

A graduate of Harvard College and Harvard Business School, Mark Goldweitz was ideally prepared for such an undertaking. When he rented a duplex apartment in the South End in 1969, he recognized at once the potential of those graceful old buildings. In 1971, he bought the town house in which he lived. Over the next three years—operating through nine limited partnerships financed by savings banks and wealthy investors—he accumulated forty-five buildings, renovating their 279 units as luxury apartments. Unlike many of his counterparts, Goldweitz was careful to retain his buildings' architectural character, restoring existing woodwork, plaster ceilings, and marble fireplaces. But he also added modern touches—stripping walls to the bare brick, installing recessed lighting, skylights, and roof decks. Sensitive to the wider environment, he provided free window boxes and, outside one building, even constructed a vest-pocket park, replete with sculptured sundial. The college professors, lawyers, and admen who rented his apartments—many of them gays, young singles, and couples without children—brought with them all the accouterments of urban chic: hanging ferns, butcher block furniture, Marimekko fabrics, Cuisinart food processors, and KLH sound systems. The curbs outside were lined with Volvos, Saabs, and BMWs. Goldweitz's buildings became the very essence of South End gentrification.

In part because of his personal style—he wore rep ties, sported gold cuff links, and drove a silver Mercedes-Benz 280 SL—he soon became the principal target of the social worker–radical alliance. In November 1973, a group calling itself the Committee for a South End for South Enders published a sixteen-page pamphlet denouncing Goldweitz's "greed and arrogance." His apartments, the committee noted, were far beyond the reach of low-income tenants: studios, $150–$200 a month; one bedroom, $200–$275; two bedrooms, $250–$300; three bedrooms, $325–$450. "The poorer members of the community, still a majority here, are forced to fight to get into a project," the committee said. Goldweitz vehemently denied that he had displaced anyone, since he purchased only vacant buildings, but the committee claimed that he routinely bought structures on condition that the old landlord evict the tenants. "The South End is not about to roll over and play dead," it warned. "Mark R. Goldweitz has built an empire here. But history teaches us that unless the needs of people are met, empires will eventually fall." To meet those needs, the committee demanded that Goldweitz rent all vacancies to low-income families at public housing rates until at least half of his units were occupied by such tenants—a proposal the landlord summarily rejected.

Opponents of gentrification soon broadened their indictment to embrace a whole "network" of mutually reinforcing parties: Boston banks—notably the Suffolk-Franklin Savings Bank, Workingmen's Cooperative Bank, and Home Savings Bank—which concentrated their mortgages in white middle-class sections of the South End while refusing loans in its blacker, poorer areas; real estate agents like A. E. Rondeau and Betty Gibson ("Specializing in the New South End") who steered affluent buyers and tenants into the community; government officials who funneled low-interest rehabilitation loans, intended for poor and moderate-income families, to prosperous owners who could have obtained conventional bank loans; the Boston Center for the Arts, a South End cultural center which took a big slice of the neighborhood's urban renewal funds to purchase and restore its sprawling, seven-building complex; chichi new boutiques, like one in the old Dover Street red-light district which began serving croissants in the shape of sailors and prostitutes; and the South End Historical Society ("Using the Past to Serve the Future"), which lobbied the South End onto the National Register of Historical Sites, then celebrated the community's faded elegance with a series of antiquarian lectures ("Taste and Attitudes in Victorian Window Gardens"), house tours, flea markets, musicales, and other "Victorian revels."

Every winter the Historical Society presented a "Victorian Champagne Ball" in one of the neighborhood's renowned edifices. In 1971, it took over the Back Bay Station, embellishing its shabby waiting room with potted palms, bouquets of gladiolas, little gilt chairs, and glossy shoeshine stands. The following year, it hired a private railroad car to bring guests from as far as Route 128. On January 26, 1974, the ball was held in the old Cyclorama on Tremont Street, built in 1884 to house Paul Philippoteaux's vast circular painting of the Battle of Gettysburg, later serving as a boxing arena, bicycle academy, wholesale flower mart, and, finally, headquarters of the Boston Center for the Arts. Under the high glass dome, the society installed a dozen department-store mannikins decked out in fanciful nineteenth-century costumes. The guests, who paid thirty dollars a couple, were encouraged to wear "Victorian furbelows and feathers" themselves or, failing that, black tie and evening gowns.

Many South Enders began the evening at small dinner parties scattered through the neighborhood, the Divers dining with their friends Dan and Mary Shannon. At the candlelit table, someone remarked that Joan's long green velvet gown and string of white pearls made her look uncannily like Mrs. Jack Gardner, the *grande dame* of Boston's Victorian art world. In his black tie and evening jacket, they all agreed, Colin looked less like "Mr. Jack" than a fresh-faced Jay Gatsby. Swept along by their table talk, the Shannons and their guests hardly noticed that it was 9:45 and that they were nearly an hour late for the ball. Bundling into warm coats and scarves, they hurried six blocks down Tremont Street to the floodlit Cyclorama—only to find that they had just missed a major demonstration by the newly formed South End for South Enders Committee.

On the sidewalk in front of the Cyclorama, and spilling out into Tremont Street, some 250 persons had milled about carrying signs which read: "Stop the Victorian Criminals," "South End Historical Society Is an Upper-Class KKK," and "Goldweitz Must Meet Our Demands." As the partygoers went by, the picketers thrust leaflets into their hands. "The luxury housing developers and others at this ball can be considered as nothing less than true enemies of the poor, the real South Enders. Extensive private development for the middle and upper class has the effect of creating another 'Georgetown'—an elite-oriented community. . . . So here this obscene 'Victorian ball' goes on and those who love our townhouses but don't want us to live in them sip their champagne and dance gaily. . . ."

Having scrutinized the demonstrators' message, Colin and Joan did their best to sip champagne and dance gaily, but they began to feel profoundly uneasy. They'd heard charges from South End social workers before, revolutionary rhetoric from the *People's News,* the outrage of black and Puerto Rican tenants against their landlords. But not until that night had they felt anger directed at them personally. Walking home past crumbling tenements and shabby rooming houses, they were acutely aware of the rage and resentment lurking in the darkened streets.

For by early 1974, the gentrification battle had left the South End more bitterly divided than ever. From the beginning, the South End's urban renewal plan contained an unresolved tension. On the one hand, it pledged to "protect and expand the city's tax base, arrest economic decline, and by stabilizing property values, protect private investment." On the other, it promised to ensure "the availability of standard housing at rentals that all displaced low-income residents wishing to remain in the South End could afford." Thus, while the BRA committed itself to bringing middle-class families back to the South End, it pledged to safeguard the interests of all low-income residents. By June 1973, many South Enders had plainly concluded that those two ends could not be pursued simultaneously. That month, social workers, radicals, and their tenant clients won control of the South End Project Area Committee (SEPAC), the elected citizen review board which held a veto over neighborhood renewal projects. For years, the board had been dominated by middle-class homeowners and realtors. After the "people's" slate took command, it adopted the "Zook Resolution"—named after its framer, the radical organizer Doug Zook—declaring that no further housing would be approved unless at least 25 percent of the units were reserved for low-income tenants.

Coming hard on the heels of the anti-Goldweitz campaign, the Zook Resolution stirred consternation among South End homeowners, who feared they were about to be overrun by the minority poor. Angriest of all was David Parker, a young carpenter and dedicated traditionalist who had meticulously restored his nineteenth-century town house to its original condition. High windows, ornate moldings, and pine floors framed a collection of hand-rubbed antiques: a Morris chair, a Boston rocker, a Connecticut clock. "Thomas Jefferson would have felt at home in this room," he said with evident satisfaction. But his house faced West Concord Street, a South End thoroughfare perilously close to the black "wilderness" and more vulnerable than the insulated blocks of Rutland Square, West Newton Street, and West Brookline Street. Parker deeply resented the "Gold Coast liberals," whom he accused of grabbing all the brick sidewalks, sculptured streetlights, and ginkgo trees for themselves while shrewdly maneuvering the subsidized housing they ostensibly favored into Parker's less privileged neighborhood.

Together with a neighbor—an architect named Herbert Zeller—and four-teen like-minded homeowners, Parker formed the Committee of Citizens for a Balanced South End, which sought to stem the influx of low-income housing by shifting the burden elsewhere in the city as well as to the suburbs. On December 11, 1973, it called for an "immediate moratorium" on further sub-sidized projects in the South End and designation of remaining renewal parcels for "responsible market-level housing." Two months later, committee members filed the first of several lawsuits to block low-income developments on the grounds that they would "perpetuate high-density ghettos of low-income blacks" and have a negative "environmental impact" on surrounding proper-ties. Later, they joined the battle against new halfway houses and detoxifica-tion and drug treatment centers, arguing that the South End had too long been a "wastebasket of American society."

Although many South End homeowners felt uncomfortable with the com-mittee's vehemence, its protest clearly reflected a widespread anxiety. Always sensitive to such ground swells, Kevin White's administration moved quickly to assuage it. In April 1974, the BRA announced that since it had exceeded its target of 3,300 low- and moderate-income units for the South End, it would no longer give priority to such housing. Henceforth, it would concentrate on "providing the ancillary amenities to make the South End a more attractive and liveable community." The BRA report stirred a predictable storm of pro-test and the Mayor retreated somewhat, calling for a neighborhood review. In May, SEPAC named an eleven-member committee, representing all the South End's factions and chaired by Joshua Young, the socially conscious banker from West Newton Street. After fourteen months of hearings, interviews, and statistical analysis, the committee released findings sharply at odds with the city's.

The BRA had found 6,015 subsidized units, or 46 percent of the South End's housing stock; the committee identified only 4,439 such units, 30 per-cent of available housing. Even that exceeded the BRA's goals, but the com-mittee argued that it fell at least 3,000 units short of the community's needs, largely because the trickle of young professionals had turned into a torrent, overrunning the South End's tenements and rooming houses. A single new family could displace as many as four or five old ones, forcing them into subsidized projects or out of the neighborhood altogether. The committee urged that the community reaffirm an "absolute responsibility" to provide housing for all South Enders who wished to remain there. To achieve that end, it struck a compromise between its competing factions—proposing that 25 percent of future units be reserved for low-income tenants, 25 percent be rented at market rates, with the remaining 50 percent left undetermined. But David Parker and Herb Zeller found even that intolerable and angrily resigned from the committee, denouncing it for capitulating to a "narrow sociopolitical ideology."

Far from mending the community's divisions, the report only exacerbated them. For housing in the South End had taken on heavy symbolic freight, beyond its function as shelter or even its value as real estate. It had become a tangible measure of class standing and of society's willingness to reward or ameliorate that standing. Though the South End struggle was frequently framed as "white" vs. "black," "majority" vs. "minority," "New South Enders" vs. "Old South Enders"—and, to some degree, it was all those—it was principally a class conflict, a battle between the "haves" and the "have-nots."

Its racial and ethnic dimensions were often misunderstood. Contrary to conventional wisdom, the worst victims of gentrification—those forced not only from their homes but out of the neighborhood altogether—were not overwhelmingly black and Puerto Rican. In absolute numbers, blacks declined as widespread demolition and rooming-house conversion cut the South End's population by more than a half within two decades, but the black share actually rose from 39 percent in 1960 to about 44 percent in 1975. During that same period, Hispanics grew from a negligible 1 percent to 9 percent, while Chinese and other minorities grew from 2 to 6 percent.

Meanwhile, despite the influx of thousands of young professionals, the white population sharply declined—from 58 to 40 percent. Many of the departing whites were aging "roomers" who, once their old lodgings had been appropriated, never found housing at rents they could afford. Others were remnants of the Irish, Italian, Jewish, Greek, Syrian, and Lebanese working-class communities who, as the South End became recognized as black and Hispanic "turf," abandoned their traditional enclaves (the new gentry may have tolerated physical proximity to blacks because they enjoyed a social distance; white workers, with no social buffer, required physical distance). Within fifteen years, the South End largely replaced its white population, exchanging the poor, tired, and aging for the young, prosperous, and energetic. Not surprisingly, between 1960 and 1970, the median income of South End whites more than doubled, from $3,771 to $7,792.

Nevertheless, affluent whites remained a small minority in the neighborhood. In 1970, three-quarters of all South End families still earned less than $10,000 a year. Whereas 45 percent of whites had incomes over $10,000, only 17 percent of blacks and 5 percent of Hispanics made that much, while 47 percent of blacks and 62 percent of Hispanics earned less than $5,000. The twin millstones of urban renewal and gentrification had ground away most of the South End's working class—both black and white—leaving the community deeply polarized between an overwhelmingly white middle class and a heavily black and Hispanic lower class.

Because racial and class categories largely overlapped, it was difficult to unravel the roots of South End hostilities. Most white conservatives steadfastly disclaimed any racial animosity, attributing their position to distaste for "lower-class behavior": noisy parties, blaring radios, squalid homes, littered streets, overflowing trash cans, vandalism, gangs, drugs, and violent crime. Those who sought to limit low-income housing projects ("publicly subsidized islands of crime and squalor") often argued that the South End was laboring under an impossible liability. Racial and ethnic integration was unexceptionable, the time-honored "melting pot" of American history. But class integra-tion, they contended, was something altogether different, a mixing of styles and standards which was "always a failure in American cities," destroying any neighborhood which persisted in that "ill-conceived experiment."

That position was anathema to the socially committed young professionals who had moved into the South End precisely because they sought a "truly mixed community," integrated by class as well as race. They weren't about to abandon that goal now. The struggle over subsidized housing divided the South End's new middle class against itself, pitting neighbor against neighbor, friend against friend, sometimes even husband against wife. Block association meetings frequently erupted in angry shouting matches. Two young mothers who had been stalwarts of the Bancroft Parents' Association stopped speaking to each other. A regular "boys' night out" poker game broke up because the four men could no longer stand the sight of each other across the table. A homeowner woke up one morning to find a neighbor's ax buried inches deep in the bright red veneer of his Victorian door.

No slice of the South End was so roiled by this conflict as the "Gold Coast" blocks of Rutland Square, Pembroke, West Newton, and West Brookline streets. Rutland Square, in particular, with its stately old houses surrounding a park, had been among the first blocks to attract young artists, architects, and social workers. For years it—and its extension on Rutland Street—was the heartland of the social worker–radical alliance. Old residents like Tristam Blake, administrator of the South End Community Health Center, architects Henry and Joan Wood, and Martin Gopen, a manpower specialist at United South End Settlements, were principal spokespeople for the neighborhood's poor and dispossessed. But Rutland Square's amenities attracted others who saw the situation rather differently—among them, the two embattled land-lords, Steve Wolfberg and Ferd Arenella. For years, they crossed to the other side of the square when they saw certain of their neighbors approaching. In-deed, Ferd Arenella suspected at least one of his neighbors of helping to fire-bomb his house.

West Newton Street, which adjoined Rutland Square on the north, enjoyed a similar vogue in the late sixties and early seventies. In one four-year period, no fewer than twenty-eight middle-class families bought houses on the Divers' block alone. And, like its neighbor to the south, it was sharply divided on social issues. At a 1974 hearing, one resident of the block cited Anthony Downs's dictum: "The fundamental problem of cities is that they have too many poor people in them"—while another quoted John Kenneth Galbraith's judgment: "The problem of the cities is capitalism and the only solution is socialism." Some residents vehemently supported the South End for South Enders Committee, while 102 residents of West Newton, Pembroke, and West Brookline streets signed a petition backing the Citizens for a Balanced South End in their stand against subsidized housing. David Sprogis, a prominent West Brookline Street realtor, wrote a series of letters to his neighbors angrily denouncing "liberals who do not know anything about city neighborhoods." A friend of long standing held a party at which he ceremonially burned the Sprogis letters.

Appalled by the savagery with which their neighbors had turned on one another, Kathleen Crampton, wife of the state's Commissioner of Community Affairs, Josh Young, and Joan Wood sought to defuse the situation. Forming the South End Citizens' Association—its name deliberately bland so as to offend no one—they groped for a middle ground to which "all South Enders of goodwill" might repair. But, by then, their constituency had largely fallen apart. After a few stormy meetings, the association disbanded.

Joan and Colin Diver watched the Citizens' Association experiment with dismay. They had hoped that a credible "middle" might emerge, one with which they could ally themselves, for neither extreme offered much hope of the varied, vital, but livable urban community they sought in the South End. Their friends were already arrayed on both sides. Whatever the Divers did, they risked alienating people they valued. But it was the opposing extremes which held them paralyzed, unable to enlist in either camp. One summer evening, sitting on their front stoop, Colin remarked sourly, "We're being asked to choose between the self-righteous and the self-interested. What kind of choice is that?"

He had no difficulty understanding the self-interest which drove Parker, Zeller, and their Balance Committee. Every cent the Divers had was sunk in their house and its costly rehabilitation. South End real estate had risen sharply since they had moved in, but the spread of subsidized housing and its pernicious by-products could threaten their investment. From his experience at City Hall, Colin knew how fierce was the resistance to subsidized housing in many Boston neighborhoods, not to mention the suburbs. Just as some suburbanites still drove their garbage downtown and dumped it on the South End's streets, so they were happy to have the region's social problems deposited there. But by taking the path of least resistance and concentrating so much low-income housing in the relatively liberal South End, the city was jeopardizing that neighborhood's stability.

Many South End projects struck Colin as disastrous failures of public policy, doomed from the start to bankruptcy, destined to spawn social problems. Methunion Manor was a striking example of everything he hated about such projects—mind-numbing ugliness, the social stigma of "poor people's housing," litter, noise, and crime. "No more Methunions!" had become a South End rallying cry, a sentiment to which the Divers subscribed.

Methunion wasn't the only subsidized project which concerned them. Nearby was a four-story building rehabilitated by the Tenants' Development Corporation, an outgrowth of the South End Tenants' Council. Intended for low- and moderate-income families, several of its apartments were leased to the Boston Housing Authority as "scatter site" public housing. Most of its tenants were sober and responsible, but one family was involved in all sorts of strange activities. Suspicious characters hung about their apartment day and night, apparently dealing drugs and soliciting for prostitution. Colin wished the TDC was more conscientious about tenant selection and, to that extent, he welcomed a suit the Balance Committee had brought against the corporation.

Yet he couldn't give the committee anything like wholehearted support. The argument about a target set seven years before struck him as beside the point. Thousands of poor people had been displaced by government action—the city had a moral obligation to see that they were adequately rehoused, as close as possible to their original homes. Moreover, he was unsettled by the committee's extremist rhetoric and meat-ax approach. Regarding all projects as slums in the making, it made no distinctions based on design, management, or tenant selection.

One evening in late 1974, the Divers' friend Sandra Perkins, the Balance Committee's treasurer, invited Colin and Ferd Arenella to meet with the committee's lawyer at her house. Sandra had begun to feel uneasy with her colleagues' head-on approach and she wanted Colin and Ferd, as neighborhood lawyers, to review the committee's lawsuit seeking to block a new project slated for Tremont Street. But from the plans Colin saw that night, Concord Homes struck him as infinitely preferable to Methunion Manor. Instead of trying to block it, he urged the committee to negotiate a deal for lower densities and a guaranteed number of market-level rents.

Whatever differences he had with the Balance Committee, he was even less impressed by the South End for South Enders Committee. After sitting through dozens of neighborhood meetings, he found the radicals' self-righteousness exasperating. At times, they could be downright demagogic. One week the *People's News* asked, "Have you seen the rear of the row house on Rutland Square that has a 'big-assed' picture window that covers the top two stories?" To Colin that was an open invitation to smash the window, outright incitement to violence. He was irritated, too, by his middle-class neighbors who talked so glibly about halting gentrification. Now that they had theirs, they wanted to be the last middle-class whites allowed in. He didn't understand how such hypocrisy served their interests, but of course they claimed to represent the "underprivileged." As time went by, Colin felt more comfortable with those who frankly represented their own interests than with those who spoke on behalf of "the people."

Joan shared Colin's irritation with radical rhetoric and liberal hypocrisy, but she remained more committed than he to public altruism. In part, that reflected her natural generosity; she couldn't parse the respective positions quite so methodically as Colin. In part, it reflected a professional disposition. Her experience at the Hyams Trust left her convinced that if institutional altruism was well conceived, adequately financed, and properly managed, it produced results. She was more sympathetic than Colin to the vast tribe of South End social workers. Though distrusting firebrands like Mel King, she respected many others who labored patiently and quietly on behalf of the poor, and during her tenure Hyams Trust had supported a host of agencies operating in the South End. Largely at Joan's urging, Hyams had made annual operating grants to the Emergency Tenants' Council since 1971. Despite her friendship with Ferd Arenella and her distaste for the way the council had wrested his properties from him, she admired its work in rehabilitating South End tenements for low-income housing. She was even more impressed when it began building a whole new community just across Tremont Street. Villa Victoria's attractive apartment towers and town houses were ranged around a graceful shopping arcade and plaza. Built primarily for the council's Hispanic clientele, it also housed blacks, Jews, Irish, Italians, Syrians, and Chinese, carefully selected and supervised by conscientious management. To Joan, Villa Victoria was subsidized housing at its best, tangible evidence that the poor could be housed humanely without injury to the neighborhood.

But the housing struggle cost Joan considerable anguish. She and Colin had settled in the South End so that their personal lives would echo their professional commitments to social justice; now their very presence was perceived as an assault on that ideal. She was reminded of an ecological principle: anytime you make one change in nature's equilibrium, you risk causing another change quite different from what you intended. They'd been so sure of themselves, so confident that they could help the poor and disadvantaged by living in their midst. Now the very people they'd come into the city to help regarded them with suspicion, if not outright enmity.

On more than one occasion, Joan tried to make human contact with those she was accused of exploiting. She had spearheaded the Bancroft's effort to make minority parents feel part of the school community, only to find that few blacks were eager to sit down with white mothers. It was even more difficult to make such connections outside the school. When Colin and Joan moved onto West Newton Street in 1970, their block had been at least half black, but as the white influx accelerated, many minority families moved elsewhere. The blacks who remained generally kept to themselves. Somehow, despite the best will on both sides, no social intercourse developed. Joan and Colin could count on the fingers of two hands the times they had been in a black neighbor's house or had entertained a black in theirs. The Divers and their white friends often reflected on the irony of their situation: they had moved to the South End because they valued racial and economic heterogeneity, but their lives remained disappointingly homogeneous.

So when Colin and Joan stumbled into a relationship with one low-income South Ender, they had special reason to value her friendship. Half Irish, half Penobscot Indian, Nicky Nickerson had lived for a while with a black gambling man, who had fathered her only child, Andrea. For nearly fifteen years, Nicky and Andrea shuttled back and forth across the South End, moving from one cold-water flat to another, a step ahead of the wrecker's ball and the gentrifier's paintbrush. Nicky drew Aid to Families with Dependent Children, food stamps, and other welfare grants, but, uncomfortable with her own dependency, she enlisted in every cause that came her way—demonstrating with the American Indian Movement, sitting in at the State House to demand welfare rights, squatting in slumlords' apartments to seek better housing, picketing with the South End for South Enders Committee at the Victorian

Champagne Ball, helping to publish the *South End People's News*. In her formidable capacity to protest, she personified the grievance of the minority poor against those who had suddenly "discovered" the neighborhood they had known all their lives.

By 1973, Nicky worked for a South End day-care center while living in a subsidized apartment on Columbus Avenue. Andrea, then fourteen, had begun babysitting for the Divers and other young professionals. One November evening on West Newton Street, Joan ran into Nicky, whom she knew only as Andrea's mother. Anxiously, Nicky reported that Andrea had dropped out of her "experimental" school, seemed unmotivated, and needed a stricter hand. Touched by her distress, Joan promised to do what she could. The only mid-year opening in the public schools was in South Boston, which hardly seemed the place for a troubled, half-black child. Eventually, Joan found Manter Hall, a private school in Cambridge known for dealing with learning disabilities. Manter cost $1,700, far beyond Nicky's resources, so Joan raised the money from friends, neighbors, and several trust funds. Andrea entered Manter that February, compiling an impressive record of A's and B's.

From that beginning grew a remarkable friendship. To a casual observer, Joan and Nicky would have seemed unlikely intimates. Then in her late forties, Nicky was nearly twice Joan's age. A high school dropout who took college courses at night, she couldn't match Joan's educational credentials. While Nicky eked out a meager living, Joan enjoyed the solid comforts of the urban bourgeoisie. An avowed socialist, Nicky had little in common with Joan's temperate liberalism. Yet those very contradictions, like poles of a battery, set up an electrical current, a spark which illuminated their relationship.

In the evenings or on lazy weekend afternoons, Nicky would wander by and they'd sit for hours in Joan's kitchen, sipping coffee and talking about children, neighbors, crime, politics, books, or movies. Sometimes Colin would join them and the conversation would turn to opera, a subject on which Nicky surprisingly knew more than he. Often she would tell stories—long, spellbinding sagas of randy Indians, high-rolling blacks, hard-drinking Irishmen, fancy women, double-dealing cops, and corrupt landlords. For Joan and Colin those were compelling moments, rare opportunities to penetrate the daunting barriers of race and class.

For Nicky, they were curious encounters. It seemed strange to be sitting there in that gorgeous house, surrounded by all those beautiful things, talking with the very people she'd been protesting against all those years. They often disagreed on urban development, on gentrification, on the respective rights of tenants and homeowners, but there was something about the Divers which transcended politics, which made everything else okay. They were *involved*— in the fate of their city, in the condition of their neighborhood, in the lives of people around them. When her radical friends asked why she spent so much time with those "rich honkies," she said, "I don't care whether they march with us or not. Their hearts are with us. They care."

"If something bugs Colin and me," Joan once told a friend, "we're the kind of people who have to do something about it." That, of course, was in the New England tradition. "If you know of any scandalous disorders in town," Cotton Mather admonished his parishioners, "do all you can to suppress them and redress them." Temperamentally, the Divers were Puritans, driven to right wrongs, to redress disorders. Practically, they had begun to shun the broader ideological issues, concentrating on concrete problems closer to home.

The first to engage them was traffic. Most South End streets dead-ended at the railroad, discouraging motorists; but West Newton rode a bridge over the tracks, creating a natural thoroughfare from the South End into the Back Bay. Each weekday, the street outside the Divers' home was clogged with some 4,000 cars, buses, and trucks, their engines shattering the calm, spewing noxious fumes, rattling windowpanes, cracking plaster, tormenting parents of small children.

In November 1971, Joan launched a one-woman campaign to rid the street of heavy trucks and buses. Responding to her protest, the police agreed to enforce posted regulations barring trucks over two and a half tons. She was less successful in preventing empty buses from "deadheading" across West Newton Street to Copley Square. After a year of her letters and phone calls, the Transit Authority finally selected a more circuitous route through nonresidential streets, but some drivers stuck to their familiar path until Joan reported them. One ignored the directive altogether until she flagged him down, personally ordering him off her block.

Meanwhile, as a member of the South End Committee on Transportation, Colin spent hours persuading city officials to establish an impenetrable maze of one-way streets to deflect commuters from the neighborhood. Most of West Newton Street had long been two-way; under the committee's plan, the Divers' block became one-way west, the adjacent block one-way east. The day the plan went into effect, Colin, Joan, and several neighbors manned the intersections at each end of the block, patiently explaining to irritated motorists why they couldn't use their accustomed route.

The street changes stirred unexpected discord in the neighborhood. Several popular merchants—a Lebanese greengrocer, a Chinese wine merchant, a black gas station owner—complained that their business had been severely eroded. An elderly woman who relied on taxis to get to work said she paid eighty cents more per day because the cab had to go around the block. Some residents claimed that crime had grown worse because there were fewer eyes on the street. These grievances, apparently legitimate, stirred misgivings in Colin. In his determination to reduce traffic, had he been imposing his own values on the South End rather than responding to its values? Were he and Joan trying to suburbanize the city rather than letting it urbanize them? With their reforming zeal, did they really belong in the city after all?

They couldn't help themselves: no sooner did a problem emerge than they set about solving it. In 1970, a South End branch of the Boston Public Library had been erected just across a small service alley from the Divers' house. The library and its adjacent playground were heavily patronized by neighborhood

children, including Brad and Ned Diver, but motorists seeking a shortcut frequently sped through that alley, posing a grave danger to young children. For
two years Joan waged relentless bureaucratic warfare against that traffic. After
dozens of letters and countless phone calls to four separate departments, she
finally persuaded the city to put "No Thru Way" and "Go Slow, Children"
signs at either end of the alley.

In the summer of 1974, a special problem developed in that alley. Prostitution had long been endemic to the South End. The first time Colin walked
home from work at City Hall, he was solicited on West Newton Street; the
Divers' dinner guests were sometimes approached on their way to the house;
the corner of West Newton and Shawmut Avenue was known for "nickel
broads," who sold their bodies for five dollars. Abruptly, in June 1974, the
problem became more acute. As police cracked down on prostitutes in the
Washington Street "Combat Zone," many returned to traditional haunts in
the South End. Because West Newton Street was heavily trafficked, the alley
by the library was particularly convenient for solicitation. By June, three or
four prostitutes could be found there every weekday afternoon. Construction
workers in panel trucks and suburban businessmen in late-model sports cars
cruised the alley, stopping to haggle over price, picking up the women of their
choice.

With her children in and out of the alley all day long, Joan was naturally
upset. Moreover, since most of the prostitutes were white or light-skinned
Hispanics, the men frequently made overtures to Joan and her neighbors.
(South End social workers suggested that middle-class whites were at last distressed about the problem because they were now subjected to the indignities
black women had suffered for years at the hands of white hunters.) Whatever
the reason, Joan and her close friend Linda Trum spent late afternoons and
early evenings on the Divers' stoop, taking down the license numbers of cars
in the alley, then forwarding them to the police for whatever action they cared
to take (johns were rarely arrested in Boston, though some years before police
had written such men at home, asking them to come into the station house for
a "conference").

Since the same women were in the alley almost every afternoon, Joan and
her friends got to know them by sight, sometimes even by name. There was a
Puerto Rican named Maria who was very small, surprisingly blond, and often
so strung out on dope she would stagger up to a customer's car and collapse
against it. There was a dark-haired woman who roamed the alley in blue jeans,
a halter top, and frequently, bare feet. Still another wore miniskirts and a blue
ribbon in her hair. Their pimp, a dumpy middle-aged black man, would sit on
the library steps surveying his stable. Between customers, the prostitutes
would go to the neighborhood grocery for pickles or popsicles, which they
consumed in the library yard.

Several of Joan's neighbors confronted the women, demanding that they
take their trade elsewhere. When Ellen Gordon told the dark-haired one, "I
don't want my children to see what you're doing," the prostitute broke into

tears, explaining that she had three children of her own, her husband was in prison, and she needed the money to support her family. But when Ellen warned another woman to get off the block, the prostitute hauled off and punched her in the face.

On the evening of June 17, Joan was leaving for the grocery store when another neighbor, Carol Feldman, ran over and grabbed her by the arm. Pointing toward a station wagon parked in the alley, she whispered, "There's a girl in that car giving a guy a blow job!"

"You've got to be kidding!" Joan exclaimed. When Carol shook her head, Joan went back inside and called the police.

The police arrested the prostitute and took the driver's name and address, but when Joan told Carol that both parties would be charged with committing an unnatural act in a public place, Carol refused to be the prosecution's witness. As a psychologist, she didn't believe fellatio was an unnatural act and feared that if she supported such a heresy she might be drummed out of the profession.

Moreover, she was then a Ph.D. candidate at Boston College, studying with Professor William Ryan, author of *Blaming the Victim,* an argument against the tendency to blame poverty, disease, and racial inequality on the victims themselves rather than on the victimizing forces in American society. To Carol, the john—who turned out to be a married man from working-class Somerville—was more victim than victimizer. A rich man could keep a mistress in a luxury apartment, but this poor guy had to do it in an alley and now faced up to twenty years in prison. She wanted no part in such a sentence. Carol couldn't work up much indignation about the prostitute either. Most streetwalkers were poor unfortunate women—classic victims.

Her refusal to testify became a *cause célèbre* in the South End that summer, exacerbating the community's ideological divisions. Joan Diver simply couldn't believe it. "You brought it to my attention!" she reminded Carol. "You were sufficiently outraged then. Your children play in that same alley. You've got some rights!"

Others felt even more strongly. Ellen Gordon angrily lectured Carol on the phone. The Arenellas stopped speaking to her altogether. But Rutland Square's radical/liberal community rallied behind her. When it seemed for a while as if Carol might be subpoenaed to testify, Jane Bowers offered to form a Carol Feldman Defense Fund.

When the case came to trial, Joan and Colin attended. Joan couldn't do much because she hadn't witnessed the sexual act, but she hoped to make enough fuss so that the case would attract notoriety, forcing police to remove prostitutes from residential neighborhoods. Without a prosecuting witness, the case quietly died. But eventually, the South End station house got the message. Late that summer, it sent plainclothesmen onto West Newton Street, arresting the prostitutes for soliciting an officer. By September, the women had moved their base of operations to Symphony Hall.

The street outside the Divers' door hadn't always been so disturbing. During their first years in the South End, when Joan was at home more, she spent hours at the window watching the street life unroll before her like an endlessly satisfying movie. After the monotony of Watertown and Brighton, the variety of West Newton Street fascinated and invigorated her; there was always something doing out there, something absurd, uncommon, and intriguing.

There was a neighborhood drunk named Freddy, a shambling black man who wandered the street all day long. Often he would appear with a broom, comically purporting to sweep the sidewalk and invariably trailed by small children who delighted in his antics. Joan had planted a small flower bed in their front yard, and it was routinely raided by passersby. When the doorbell rang one morning, there stood Freddy. "Please, ma'am," he said, "may I have one of your flowers?" Joan couldn't refuse him.

One Sunday, glancing out the window, Joan saw a taxi pull up across the street. A man got out, walked over to Dan Shannon's house, and urinated in his doorway. A Puerto Rican mechanic working on his car nearby grabbed a wrench and went after the man, bellowing, "Get out of here, you stinking pervert!" With that, a woman leapt from the taxi, wrenched a drainpipe off the Shannons' house, and advanced menacingly on the mechanic. She was about to hit him when two friends rushed to his assistance, sending the taxi and its occupants careering up the street.

When night fell, the street could be more forbidding. Once Joan was awakened by scraping noises from the house next door. Rushing to the window, she saw a man dragging a dishwasher into the street. Just then, Joan's neighbor Linda Trum yelled out her window, "That's not your dishwasher!" "It's not your dishwasher either, lady," the man responded. "I didn't get it from your apartment." With which he calmly resumed his task, interrupted only when an enraged Mike Trum burst from his doorway, driving the still-protesting burglar up the alley.

Anything that wasn't nailed down might disappear in the night. The Divers parked their blue Dodge Dart on the street in front of their house. On several occasions, vandals took the windshield wipers and hubcaps, adding random dents in the process. And one morning the car itself was gone. Several days later, the police found it, largely intact, in a black neighborhood.

Twice in those early years, the Divers' house was hit by burglars. While Joan was off taking a tennis lesson someone jimmied the street door and stole their stereo, TV set, camera, and electric typewriter. And one evening, while Colin was in the shower, Joan heard a noise in the front hall. Rushing to the head of the stairs, she saw two young black men rummaging through her purse on the vestibule table.

"What do you think you're doing?" she asked.

"We're looking for Mr. Jones," said one, a stock answer in such situations.

Then they walked out. When Joan examined her purse, she found her wallet gone.

Meanwhile, the Divers heard reports of much worse. A rash of violent street holdups, muggings, and assaults had broken out in the South End, concentrated in the no-man's-land along Columbus Avenue and the railway tracks. On October 31, 1974, an executive of the Polaroid Corporation named John Wolbarst was walking down Durham Street when a young black called out, "Hi." As Wolbarst turned, the youth plunged a large hunting knife into his stomach. Larry Pleas, a member of the Soul Center gang, was convicted of armed assault with intent to murder, and sentenced to twelve to eighteen years in prison.

Not surprisingly, all this took its toll on the Divers' benign view of city life. The pulsing streets which had once seemed so compelling, the bizarre characters who had made them smile, now seemed tinged with menace. They'd always thought of "crime in the streets" as a conservative issue, code words which Richard Nixon and George Wallace had used to pit the races and classes against each other. Now they saw it as a matter of urban survival. They became intensely security-conscious, locking and double-locking their doors, leaving lights on to deter burglars, using the car at night instead of walking. When they had to walk, they practiced street savvy, avoiding dark alleys, staying away from notorious bars, hovering like moths in the streetlight's glow.

Colin took special precautions. Years before, he had starred in Lexington's Little League, leading his Giants to the National League pennant in 1956. He was the team's top relief pitcher, but his greatest feats were performed at the plate, where he hit three home runs and knocked in nineteen. When the season was over, Colin kept his bat—a cracked and taped Louisville Slugger—stowing it with his basketball, tennis rackets, and soccer cleats at the back of the closet. As he grew older, he cleaned out most of that debris, but he held on to the bat, lugging it with him wherever he went. Now Colin rummaged in the basement, retrieved the Slugger, and installed it in a corner of the front hallway, ready for an emergency.

One evening, he was refinishing a bedroom floor when, out the window, he saw two old black men coming through the alley: a pensioner named Earl West who lived down the block and his friend from a housing project for the elderly. As Colin learned later, one of the men had just cashed his monthly social security check at Braddock Drugs, where he had evidently been spotted by the gang which hung outside the drugstore and the Soul Center. As Colin watched, two black youths trailed the men down the alley, then jumped them from behind. The victims, both in their late sixties, were too feeble to resist. They flailed about, but soon collapsed on their backs while the boys went through their pockets.

Colin raced downstairs, grabbed the Slugger from its niche by the door, and sprinted around the corner. When the muggers spotted him, they separated, one racing back up the alley, the other dodging between two cars, trying to slide past Colin. Coming at full tilt, Colin swung the bat in a wide arc, aiming for the second boy's shoulder. But the mugger saw the bat coming, jammed on the brakes, reversed direction, and easily made his getaway.

The old men hadn't been badly hurt, but one of them was in tears, terribly upset at losing his social security money ($160), his only means of support.

After the police took a quick report on the incident, Colin brought the men back to his house and served them a couple of whiskeys to calm them down. As he sat there soothing the victims, he felt himself trembling with rage. He couldn't forget the sight of those kids attacking helpless old men from behind. The more he thought about it, the angrier he got. He wanted to smash those kids in their ugly little faces. Finally he excused himself, got in his car, and, setting the Slugger on the seat beside him, drove around the South End for half an hour, searching for the attackers. He knew it was futile—surely by now they would have retreated to safety—but it made him feel better. At least he was doing something to protect his home, his family, and his neighborhood.

Some months later, as Colin left his house one morning, he became vaguely aware that something unusual was happening on West Newton Street. People were shouting. Somebody was running. A siren wailed. Suddenly he saw a black teenager running down the sidewalk toward him. A hundred yards behind came a police car in hot pursuit. Just then, the Puerto Rican mechanic jumped out and whacked the kid on the head with a bottle. The boy fell on his face, then got up and staggered down the street like a drunk. Colin and several passersby joined the chase, pursuing the boy for a block and a half until the police finally made the arrest.

As the West Newton Street contingent walked home together, Colin suddenly thought of the "hue and cry," an early Anglo-Saxon practice he had studied in law school. The victim of a crime, or the principal witness, would set up a cry, then all the neighbors would pour from their houses and give chase. According to Harvard, it was the most primitive form of law enforcement. Primitive it surely was, but Colin now suspected that it might prove more effective than the belated—and frequently futile—police response. Even if no thief was ever apprehended, it would put prospective criminals on warning that here was a neighborhood which cared for its own, which wouldn't sit by and watch innocent people being ripped off or assaulted.

One night later that winter, Joan asked Colin to go to the liquor store for a bottle of cooking sherry. Walking up the darkened sidewalk toward Columbus Avenue, he noticed a pair of black men coming toward him. When they were ten feet away, one jumped in front of him, the other moved to his side. Colin reacted quickly, darting between two cars and down the street toward the Tremont Street intersection. The pair followed him for a few steps, then turned and ran in the opposite direction.

Colin called the police, who, as usual, took a perfunctory report, then promised vaguely to "investigate." But this time Colin refused to be brushed off. He'd gotten a good look at the youth who'd blocked his path. The kid had a shaved skull, like a black Yul Brynner—a head so frightening Colin was sure he'd recognize him again. He telephoned Gordon Doerfer, a Rutland Square neighbor and Municipal Court judge, with whom he'd often discussed crime and the inadequacy of police response. Doerfer called a lieutenant at District 4. Later that night, two detectives showed up at Colin's house, bearing a notebook containing mug shots of every street criminal arrested in the South

End during the previous six months. For more than an hour, Colin pored over the celluloid pages, each of which held pictures of ten or twelve young men, photographed from the front, left, and right. There were hundreds of them and, except for a handful of Hispanics and a couple of whites, they were relentlessly black. He never found his Yul Brynner, but he saw more bleak and hopeless faces than he'd ever seen in one place before. The boys and young men who looked up from his dining-room table that night reflected such misery, such desperation, such malevolence that when Colin finally closed the book well past midnight he felt chilled to the bone. After the police had gone, he double-locked the door behind him, checking to make sure the Slugger was in its customary place. And when he went to bed he set a heavy shank of lead pipe on his night table.

23

McGoff

The New England town meeting, America's experiment in direct democracy, was also a celebration of community. At first it was merely the Puritan congregation reassembled to consider civil affairs, later the sturdy instrument by which the town charted its secular course. Farmers in muddy boots, blacksmiths fresh from the forge, teachers in chalk-smeared coats, carpenters, publicans, and ministers made their way to the meetinghouse on the hill, there to wrestle with the particulars of their common lives: repairs to the town bridge, grazing rights in the north field, a new road to the mill, raising the tax on rum, a fence to enclose stray animals. Debate was intense, petty rivalries and factionalism often intruded, but somehow a faith persisted that the meeting could resolve such differences, revealing the community's inherent consensus. Deep into the twentieth century—long after that accord had been eroded by diversity—the town meeting remained the ritual by which Massachusetts towns renewed their sense of harmony.

No town meeting had been held in Charlestown since 1874, when the Town was annexed by a burgeoning Boston. Yet, the more its fortunes declined, the more indignities it suffered at the hands of a careless world, the more the Town yearned for its lost identity. During the 1974 busing crisis—just a century after Charlestown surrendered its independence—Powder Keg laid claim to the town meeting tradition: every Tuesday evening at 7:30, it summoned all Charlestown citizens to the Harvard-Kent School. These "town meetings" rarely drew more than two hundred people, but in re-creating that time-honored rite, they invoked a simpler age when the New England village was sufficient unto itself, when the demands of community were proof against the call of equality.

Alice rarely missed a meeting. No matter how weary after a day at the telephone company, she grabbed a sandwich at home, then hurried down the street toward the little school. The neon lights of the auditorium beat down on cold linoleum, the wooden chairs felt like stone as speakers inveighed long into the night, but, surrounded by friends and neighbors, armed with common purpose, Alice knew that her town would prevail against all adversity. And that solidarity stemmed not just from defiant oratory, but from a welter of communal activity—rallies, processions, prayer marches, motorcades, dances, bake sales, raffles. All through the autumn of 1974, the town meetings sought to forge Charlestown into a "fighting team."

On the evening of January 21, 1975, Alice noticed that the tables which normally cluttered the stage had been pushed aside, replaced by a large white screen. "We have a treat for you tonight," announced Powder Keg's president, Pat Russell. "A film, called *Anarchy U.S.A.*, which should help us all understand what's happening to our city."

When the lights went off, the screen lit up with an excited young black shouting, "They're after the white man now, they're going to do him in!"

A typewriter rapped out: "Anarchy—the breakdown of law and order, a chaotic reign of terror," quickly followed by vivid images:

Blacks rioting and looting in Newark, Watts, Cleveland, and Chicago.

Leonard Patterson, a black educated in Moscow, warning that the Communists "use Negro people as cannon fodder in a violent and bloody revolution aimed at the establishment of an American Soviet dictatorship."

White segregationist J. B. Stoner declaring, "We shall not mix up with a bunch of savages."

Klansmen burning a cross while their robed leader pledged to "save the country from the onslaught of integration."

A huge red map of the "World Communist Empire," as Mao Zedong explained that the Chinese Communists were seeking "the same thing Lincoln fought for in the Civil War: the liberation of slaves."

What the hell was this? Alice wondered. Chinese Communists? Burning crosses? When Fidel Castro came on the screen with his arm around a black revolutionary, she could stand it no longer. Stomping into the lobby, Alice found a half dozen others already there, arguing about the film:

"It's Communist propaganda," someone said.

"It's the KKK, the Ku Klux Klan."

"Whatever it is," Alice concluded, "it stinks."

When the film ended, Pat Russell nervously took the stage, trying to calm the audience. "This isn't quite what we expected," she conceded. "They tell me we got this from a cop, a member of the John Birch Society. Maybe we should have looked at it first."

For two decades the Birchers had been quarantined as hatemongering extremists, but now Boston's busing turmoil seemed to offer them recruitment possibilities among the disaffected working class. From their headquarters in suburban Belmont they put out feelers to embattled white neighborhoods. A North End policeman supplied *Anarchy U.S.A.* to community groups throughout the city.

The film won few friends in Charlestown. Most of Powder Keg's nineteen-member executive committee—Alice among them—were horrified by its mix of alien ideology and homebred fanaticism. Seeking to mollify outraged Townies, the committee ordered a notice inserted in the "Powder Keg News" section of the Charlestown *Patriot* in which it apologized if the movie had "offended anyone in any way. We were under the impression it was an information movie on busing."

Several committee members strenuously disagreed. To them, the film was an appropriate warning of the way things would be if racial integration was imposed on white neighborhoods. Among these dissenters was Marie Goodrich, the committee secretary, who inserted another notice in the *Patriot* asserting that the organization "owed no one an apology." Marie was vigorously supported by her husband, Myron, and two other couples. During the next months, the split in Powder Keg's ranks widened.

The disaffection spread to Moe Gillen's Education Committee, on which Alice McGoff and other Powder Keggers had sought to mitigate Arthur Garrity's order. But two of them—a retired Air Force sergeant named Frank Van Gorder and his wife, Peggy—feared they were being inexorably drawn into collaboration with Garrity's court. On August 20, three weeks before the buses were due to roll, Frank submitted a stinging letter of resignation, countersigned by his wife. "I will not aid, sympathize or compromise with this committee for the smooth and successful implementation of Forced Busing," he wrote. "I will not in good conscience allow myself or this committee to dupe my friends and neighbors or the citizens of Charlestown. To them I can offer only one word of hope—RESIST!"

These intramural squabbles were echoes of a distant battle then beginning to divide the city's anti-busing movement.

When Elvira "Pixie" Palladino announced her candidacy for Boston's School Committee in 1975, the forty-three-year-old mother of two was little known outside her native East Boston. Part of a fiercely loyal Italian clan, she had gradually built a neighborhood fiefdom, becoming president of the East Boston Home and School Association, heading ROAR's East Boston branch (the One If by Land, Two If by Sea Civic Association), and representing East Boston on ROAR's executive board.

Pixie was often likened to Louise Day Hicks, but the two women were temperamentally at odds. The daughter of a powerful Irish judge, Louise had been raised a little lady. Born to an Italian shoemaker, the bottom of the heap in Depression Boston, Pixie confronted her world with gritty pugnacity. While Louise, a devout Catholic, deeply respected the clergy, Pixie tempered her devotion with a caustic anticlericalism. When Monsignor Mimie Pitaro, then a state legislator, opposed repeal of the Racial Imbalance Act, Pixie intercepted him outside the chamber and gave him "the Italian kiss of death"— three fingers taken to the lips, then quickly moved toward the target. Louise had mastered the art of indirection; Pixie rarely hesitated to say what was on her mind, often in explicit street language, which earned her the nickname "Garbage Mouth." Once, after denouncing a cop on the street, she boasted to reporters, "That's the worst Italian curse there is." (Roughly translated, it went, "May you vomit up your blood.")

She could be just as candid about her social views. In 1973, she told the *East Boston Community News,* "I don't believe in integration. God made people of different colors and once we lose our identity, we have nothing." Though she later denied making those remarks, her position on racial matters was certainly less equivocal than Louise's. Buoyed by her election to the School Committee in November 1975, Pixie became the spokesperson for those in the anti-busing movement who accused Louise of pulling her punches.

That view gained currency in the winter of 1975–76. Those who knew her well reported that Louise was deeply upset at the violence in her native South Boston, particularly at her own inability to restrain the extremists. A friend in the City Council frequently found her trembling on the verge of tears. But the grumbling that was now spreading through ROAR's rank and file focused on her relationship with Kevin White. A decade earlier, the two had seemed to be permanent antagonists, yet after White beat her for a second time in 1971, there were rumors of an accommodation. City Hall regulars noted that after Louise was elected to the City Council in 1973, she frequently threw her support behind the Mayor. Others pointed to the inordinate number of city jobs which had gone to Louise's supporters. After White won reelection in November 1975, some ROAR members openly wondered which side Louise Day Hicks was on.

Alice had heard the rumors, but for a long time she simply dismissed them. Louise was the mother of them all, the first public figure to challenge the liberal orthodoxy, for years the only one willing to risk black vituperation and media vilification. Alice had consistently supported her for the School Committee and the City Council—though not for mayor, a post for which she thought Kevin White better qualified. She simply couldn't believe that Louise would sell them out. But something happened that winter of 1975 to change her mind. Under Louise's auspices, ROAR had long held its weekly meetings and other functions at City Hall. In December, members were invited to a Christmas party there, then quietly advised to bring blankets, sleeping bags, and thermoses full of coffee. For once the party was over, ROAR was going to seize the building, holding it for the rest of the weekend to dramatize their grievances against the city administration.

Alice loved the idea. She'd voted for Kevin White, but she found his stand on busing distressingly wishy-washy. ROAR had held two other demonstrations against the Mayor—one at an East Boston speech, another a "sleep-in" at his hotel suite while he hosted the United States Conference of Mayors. He had shrugged off both episodes. But seizing City Hall was a stunt even Kevin White couldn't ignore.

On Saturday, December 13, Alice packed a blanket and pillow in a large shopping bag and set off downtown. From across the snowy plaza, City Hall glowed with warmth and light. Christmas trees strung with colored lights were scattered across the lobby. A lavish buffet lined one wall. Beer and mixed drinks flowed at two cash bars. An organist played carols over the sound system. Alice loved a good party and she knew she'd enjoy this one all the more in anticipation of what was to come.

Shortly before midnight, as five hundred revelers milled about the cavernous lobby, word circulated that the sit-in was off. Those who wanted to demonstrate should assemble for a motorcade to South Boston, where they would hold a vigil on the high school steps. Alice was stunned. Who had canceled the sit-in, and why? The vigil was ridiculous. Alice swallowed her anger and joined nearly four hundred other demonstrators in South Boston, but after an hour or so, she went home. Lying in bed, she began to understand what had happened. Only one person could possibly have called off the sit-in—ROAR was still Louise's organization. And only one person could have got her to do that—it was Kevin's City Hall. How long had this sort of footsie-wootsie been going on? How many cozy little games had been played out over their heads?

Mrs. Hicks's problems were soon complicated by skirmishing for the March 2 presidential primary. Pixie had thrown her support to Alabama's Governor George Wallace, whose racial animus appealed to many of Boston's embattled whites. Louise lined up with Senator Henry Jackson, a more moderate critic of busing. To ROAR's militants, that was a scandalous retreat. When Louise brought Jackson to an "Irish Rally" at Charlestown's Knights of Columbus Hall, Pixie's supporters set up such an outcry the Senator was unable to utter two successive sentences. After a frustrating half hour, he stalked out behind a phalanx of Secret Servicemen.

The disaffection grew after Louise endorsed Jackson's bill which would have brought Boston additional federal funds to pay certain indirect costs of busing. As the new City Council President, she insisted she had no choice but to seek relief for a city fast approaching a fiscal crisis. But that didn't mollify her critics. Indeed, so negative was the reaction among anti-busers that Pixie decided the time had come to challenge Louise's control of ROAR. Through February 1976, Pixie's supporters launched a bitter assault on Louise for betraying her own movement.

Sensing that her position was rapidly crumbling, Louise retaliated. On Sunday, February 29, the eighteen-member executive board was hastily convened in secret session at City Hall. (By then, Alice McGoff had assumed one of Charlestown's two seats on the board.) Rita Graul, Louise's chief lieutenant, presented them with a fifteen-point program, clearly designed to reassert Mrs. Hicks's waning control. Pixie would be removed from the board, ostensibly because she held an elected position on the School Committee. Three of her most vigorous supporters—Carol Stazinski of Dedham, Kay Flynn and Jean Fottler of Roslindale—would be banished from ROAR for "disruptive actions."

Alice had grown rather fond of the hot-blooded but warmhearted Pixie; she admired the outspoken Carol Stazinski; and, particularly after the abortive

City Hall sit-in, she harbored her own doubts about Louise. But bigger things were at stake: nothing less than the future of Boston's anti-busing movement. Alice sensed that Pixie was more of a hater than Louise, more likely to condone actions which would bring the movement into disrepute. Moreover, she didn't much care for some of Pixie's new allies, notably City Councilman John Kerrigan, a bigot if ever there was one. More practical considerations weighed against Pixie too. Tom Johnson had Louise—and the Mayor—to thank for his CETA position in the Public Works Department. Powder Keg had long been solidly in the Hicks camp and, somewhat reluctantly, Alice decided to stick with Louise.

In a stormy meeting at the Harvard-Kent School on March 8, Powder Keg ratified most of the fifteen points, approving Pixie's expulsion by a vote of 85–25. But by then Pixie's most determined supporters had already broken away, forming a rival Charlestown organization called the Defense Fund after its original purpose, the legal support of young Townies arrested for anti-busing activities. A few weeks later, the Defense Fund affiliated with United ROAR, a new citywide group representing the Palladino-Kerrigan-O'Neil faction, while Powder Keg retained its allegiance to Louise's ROAR.

The range of permissible dissent in Charlestown was limited. Powder Keg and the Defense Fund might differ as to means, but those who differed openly with the town's anti-busing orthodoxy—whether by speaking out in public, or by joining one of Garrity's parents' councils, or by actually putting their children on a bus to Roxbury—quickly discovered that the Town would not tolerate such heresy. Their windows were broken, their cars vandalized, excrement was smeared on doorknobs and knockers. One woman whose daughter was bused received a box in the mail one day. Inside was a large brown cat with its throat slit.

But so long as one held fast to central tenets of the faith, different styles of protest were acceptable. Powder Keg generally adopted Louise's more temperate tactics, while the Defense Fund took on Pixie's aggressiveness, attracting those whose appetite for protest could no longer be satisfied by prayer marches, living rosaries, and silent vigils. While Powder Keg remained essentially a women's organization, the Defense Fund was dominated by men. Like Powder Keg, the Fund sponsored a host of activities at its Bunker Hill Street headquarters—Easter egg hunts, raffles, and Friday-night dances—but its principal focus was on the streets, where many of its youthful adherents fought running battles with the police.

The growing schism coincided with some of the worst violence in modern Charlestown history. On Monday evening, February 16, a hundred youths assembled outside the Bunker Hill project, erecting barricades, pelting police cars with rocks, which shattered their windshields, sending six officers to the hospital. Similar clashes continued all week. On Tuesday night, a Molotov cocktail exploded on Polk Street. On Wednesday, a rock smashed a picture window at the Charlestown Library. On Thursday, a gang broke windows at the Meat Outlet, a butcher's shop on Bunker Hill Street, hauling away sides of beef. Somebody tampered with utility poles along Bunker Hill Street, causing the lights to spit fiery sparks in the night sky.

The week's events helped define the diverging viewpoints of Charlestown's two anti-busing organizations. In the next issue of the *Patriot,* Powder Keg clarified its position:

"We do not, nor have we ever, condoned the use of violence in anti-busing matters. We are appalled to see our community destroyed by our children who are being encouraged by certain unidentified adults who lack the maturity and guts to come forth and act for themselves. . . . We cannot submit to far-fetched, hell-raising doctrines of a handful of restless hoodlums who preach immediate, senseless, destructive action, as opposed to our way of meaning-ful, affirmative, carefully planned strategy."

The same issue carried a matching piece by Elaine Cormier, a moving force in the new Defense Fund.

". . . violence may have a different meaning to different people. Violence to me is the police that I saw attack a young man on the corner of Polk Street. . . . The police that told me to get the f—— off the street. . . . This is still my town. My children are fourth generation in this town and maybe the people that are dumping trash and causing commotion feel that this is the only way we can be heard. We lost in the courts and we lost at the polls. What is left? Put our kids on a bus??? Obey a law that to us is completely wrong? How do we change the law? How do we bring attention to ourselves? We're tired of marching, praying, demonstrating."

Within both groups there was intense disagreement on the efficacy of vio-lence. In Powder Keg, for example, Tom Johnson cultivated a florid bellicos-ity. "I'm not scared to throw a punch at someone who's throwing a punch at me," he would say. "I'm the bull of Powder Keg. I don't like marching with a permit. I'm for civil disobedience. All right, you take a rap on the head. Big deal. I've been arrested five times since we started. I'm the most violent mem-ber of Powder Keg." (All this was a trifle misleading. Owing his Public Works job to the Mayor, Johnson was amenable to suggestions from officials trying to keep Charlestown cool. One mayoral assistant noted: "You could say, 'Hey, Tom, up ahead at the corner there, it would be dangerous to take a right. Do yourself a favor and take a left.' He'd take a left. Pixie would reconstruct the street on you.")

But even Tom's rhetoric made Alice uncomfortable; it smacked too much of a personal animosity toward blacks that she didn't share. Adamantly op-posed to forced integration, she never regarded herself as personally preju-diced against blacks—after all, she'd lived side by side with them in the housing project for years. And now, as an information operator at the tele-phone company, she worked with many of them, and gradually she had be-come friendly with an outgoing young black woman named Betty Strickland. Betty was very worried about a brother who was being bused into Hyde Park High, one of Boston's most racially polarized schools. Alice told her how concerned she was about Lisa at Charlestown High. Somehow, through that terrible year, the two women maintained a tenuous rapport built in part on their mutual anxieties.

There were other blacks at the company, though, whom Alice couldn't stand. One in particular did nothing but complain about how "poor," "disadvantaged," and "misused" she was. Alice noticed that many of the blacks who talked this way were relatively recent migrants from the South, apparently drawn to Massachusetts by its liberal welfare policies. Such Southern blacks were simply different from the Boston-born Negroes she'd grown up with; they acted "as if they were still down on the plantation."

But though she had reservations about some of the city's blacks, she never felt comfortable with Tom Johnson's brand of belligerence. It condoned violence if not actually encouraging it, and it sent confused signals to the Town. On more than one occasion, she and Tom tangled openly at Powder Keg meetings. Once as he launched a harangue about "beating some heads out there," she told him he was talking dangerous nonsense. Tom called her a coward.

She was no Goody Two-shoes. She believed in aggressively asserting her rights, as she had in the September mothers' march when she pressed through police lines at the Bunker Hill Monument. But insisting on your rights was one thing, setting out to bust heads was another. In her opinion, violence only distracted people from the merits of the anti-busing case. They should take a leaf from Martin Luther King's book, making pests of themselves with sit-ins, boycotts, and marches but avoiding the hooliganism which had later tarred the black and radical causes.

Yet she realized how difficult it was to enforce such a policy. Powder Keg could condemn violence all it wanted, but lofty pronouncements did little to dampen the combustible atmosphere of the streets. As evening fell over Breed's Hill, a struggle was joined that had little to do with abstract issues or organizational strategies.

Alice knew the lure of that engagement. Fearing that one of her kids would be hurt or arrested, she implored them to stay off the streets at night. But her admonitions proved largely irrelevant, as each child followed his natural bent. Levelheaded and easygoing, Billy and Bobby had no taste for such skirmishing. Unable to resist the spectacle, Lisa, Robin, and Kevin were invariably drawn into the streets, though generally as non-combatants. A battle-scarred veteran of such contests, Danny, on weekends home from school, hung out with his old buddies and frequently got caught up in the fray. And his younger brother Tommy, a fresh recruit to the Green Store Gang, did frequent battle with the police.

If only because of their vantage point at Monument and Bunker Hill streets, the Green Store Gang was destined to be in the thick of things. For years they'd prided themselves on being the toughest "corner" in town, frequently the champs at football and halfball, not to mention rough-and-tumble street brawls. They could boast other achievements too: over the years, at least a dozen of the older boys had served time at Walpole or Concord Prison, while others awaited trials for assault or bank robbery. The Green Store Gang had a reputation to uphold.

The battles along Bunker Hill Street that first fall and winter were unfailing rituals, ceremonies as preordained as a Requiem Mass. As bleak afternoon faded to chilly dusk, the housing project disgorged its youthful battalions. Mustering by the Green Store, they pulled old two-by-fours, coils of chicken wire, corrugated boxes, and bunches of garbage into clumsy barricades. Fires blazed in drums of trash, casting an orange glow on the brick façades. Soon the first sirens whined over the hill; blue lights pulsed against the granite obelisk on the heights. As squad cars sped down the slope, screeching to a halt in the intersection, they were welcomed by a hail of rocks from youths waiting in ambush on the rooftops or clustered in the alleys. The missiles, some as large as grapefruit, shattered a windshield or two, showering the policemen inside with flying glass. Molotov cocktails exploded on the roadway, spewing jets of flaming gasoline. Here and there, a reckless youth dashed into the street, hurling a brick and a taunt. But when the police rallied for a charge, their assailants melted into the project, taking refuge in hidden courtyards, clammy basements, darkened apartments.

Tommy McGoff and his friends were particularly adept at the rooftop ambuscade. During daylight hours, the Green Store Gang heaped up mounds of rocks, bricks, bottles—even billiard balls—on the roofs. When the police advanced up the street, they looked like those chubby blue-and-white ducks at the shooting galleries down on Washington Street—easy targets for a well-aimed stone. Afer a while, the police began carrying plastic shields, posing a new challenge to the boys on the roof. One night, a friend of Tommy's dropped a bottle straight down, just missing an upraised shield, leaving an ugly gash on a cop's forehead.

Soon the Green Store Gang and its allies began stripping vacant apartments in the housing project for ammunition. Two buildings on Polk Street and two more on Bunker Hill Street were virtually gutted—sinks, shower heads, radiators, and toilets, even lath and plaster from the walls were ripped out and heaved at the cops. To many of those who lived in the project there was something fitting in this. The project was government property; busing was government policy; it was only just that one should be used as a weapon against the other.

When they went into the streets, the gang members frequently toted battered hockey sticks, convenient for many purposes. If they set up an ambush, leading a cop into a darkened hallway filled with kids, they could get in a jab with the taped shaft. Or when motorcycle cops gunned their big machines down the street, the kids could leap out and jam their sticks between the spokes of a spinning wheel, flipping the cyclist onto the pavement.

To Tommy and his friends, the police who came rolling up Bunker Hill Street those nights were an alien army of occupation. That was an old Charlestown reflex, rooted in the nineteenth century, when Boston's police were overwhelmingly Yankee (the city's first Irish cop, Barney McGinniskin, wasn't appointed until 1851 and lasted only three years before the nativist Know-Nothing Party sacked him). Yankee fear of an Irish-dominated police force was so intense that in 1885, when Hugh O'Brien became the city's first Irish mayor, the state legislature immediately gave the Governor control of Boston's police, a power the Mayor's office didn't retrieve until 1962. The Irish, of course, bristled at such slights, and especially those who had seen a bit of the "troubles" at home were quick to label Boston's police "the New England Black and Tans." Even after Irishmen joined the force in numbers, they often encountered resentment in Charlestown, which viewed them as cynical mercenaries, hired guns eager to turn on their own. A special loathing was reserved for the toughest cops, enforcers like the legendary "Dog Face" Jerome.

Eventually, many police assigned to Charlestown accommodated themselves to the Town, and as busing grew nearer, some Townies allowed themselves to believe the police would never enforce Garrity's dictates. After all, whatever differences they'd had in the past, most cops were Irishmen too, neighborhood guys imbued with the ethos of church, school, and family. These hopes were fanned when, days before the buses were to roll, the delegate body of the Police Patrolmen's Association resolved that police could refuse superiors' orders to arrest anti-busing demonstrators. But Garrity quickly summoned the union's attorney and sternly read him the penalties for such disobedience. A few police stayed home with the "blue flu," but the law was enforced.

Captain Bill MacDonald, the new District 15 commander, had worked hard the previous summer to establish rapport with Charlestown, but he made his position unmistakably clear: "Whatever any of us may think about busing," he told a town meeting in late August, "I can assure you, the buses will go through." Not surprisingly, MacDonald became a target for the demonstrators.

If the youths along Bunker Hill Street disdained the District 15 police, they loathed the TPF. From the start, Boston authorities had recognized that district police were ill qualified to handle violent anti-busing demonstrations. Most policemen were accustomed to operating alone or in pairs, rarely functioning in larger units. But riots could be contained only by coordinated maneuvers, rigorous discipline. Confronted during the mid-sixties with a pronounced increase in civil disorders, many American cities had formed elite riot squads. Boston's was the Tactical Patrol Force, seventy-five specially trained patrolmen augmented by specialists in the bomb squad and canine and mounted units. The TPF was blooded early in several black riots, scores of anti-war demonstrations, and other radical protests. Between riots, they functioned as decoys and undercover men, cultivating scruffy beards, fierce mustaches, matted hair, and nicknames to match ("Sewer Man," "Rat Man," "Frank the Snake," "Cement Head"). In their jumpsuits, leather jackets, combat boots, helmets, and plastic visors, they were a formidable outfit, bristling with pride and camaraderie.

But nothing in their experience had prepared them for the rigors—psychological as well as physical—of busing duty. They had no misgivings about doing battle with crazed blacks, foul-mouthed radicals, or long-haired hippies, no reluctance to wade in with truncheons swinging, teaching such people the perils of civil disobedience. But women and children from Southie and Charlestown—that was a different matter. With few exceptions, the members of the TPF were relentlessly anti-busing. Patrolman Robert Hayden spoke for most of his colleagues when, in an "open letter" to the people of South Boston, he discussed his feelings about such demonstrators: "They are fighting what almost everybody knows is a stupid law. I am one of many officers who wish them victory in their fight."

In deference to that cause, the TPF entered South Boston rather hesitantly at first. "But after the third or fourth rock," one patrolman explained, "you tend to forget the righteousness of their position." Relations deteriorated rapidly. The TPF took some of its worst abuse out of the beery taverns along Dorchester Avenue, especially a cramped and flyspecked bar called the Rabbit Inn. On Friday night of Columbus Day weekend in 1974, someone heaved a rock through the windshield of a TPF car parked outside the bar. When a lieutenant and two sergeants captured a suspect, a dozen patrons charged from the Rabbit Inn and assaulted the officers. The next night, the TPF returned en masse and, after removing their badges, went in to even the score. In a matter of minutes they reduced the cigarette machine and jukebox to twisted rubble, demolished several shelves of bottles and glasses, and sent twelve customers to the hospital with assorted head injuries. Henceforth, throughout the resisting white neighborhoods, "Rabbit Inn" was invoked to denounce the TPF as "mad dogs," "the goon squad," and "Garrity's Gestapo."

Such enmity posed special problems for patrolmen from the affected neighborhoods, forced to confront their own friends and neighbors. When the TPF was summoned into Charlestown on the first day of school in September 1975, a lieutenant approached Gene Simpson, the only Townie in the unit. "Gene," he suggested, "why don't you stay down here at the foot of the hill and watch the cars." It was a tempting offer. Gene hated the idea of marching up Breed's Hill to impose busing on other Townies. A disaffected Democrat who had voted for both Goldwater and Nixon, he regarded busing as a tragically misconceived policy which could only drive the races further apart. But he was a police officer; he enforced the law. Seven years before, he'd impassively accepted injury from a flying rock in the riots following Martin Luther King's death. Two years later, on the most memorable day of his life, he'd marched into Harvard Square to confront a bunch of berserk radicals. Surging up the avenue six abreast, the TPF had bellowed "God Bless America," telling the world how fervently they believed in what they were doing. But Gene knew it couldn't always be that easy. If you upheld the law against Communists and anarchists, you upheld it as well against God-fearing conservatives. "I appreciate what you're trying to do, Lieutenant," Gene said, "but I think I ought to go up there. I've got to face them sometime. It might as well be today."

The lieutenant agreed and Simpson took up his position in the skirmish line thrown across the top of Concord Street, only six doors from his house.

Among the demonstrators facing him were three women he'd known all his life.

"You're on the wrong side, Gene!" one of them shouted.

"Traitor!" hissed another.

Flushing red beneath his visor, he stood his ground, hoping the women wouldn't rush the line.

In the months to come, the same scene was repeated a dozen times, but Gene never grew accustomed to the anger in his neighbors' eyes. Once as he took a seat at his neighborhood tavern, a guy he'd known for years got up, grumbling, "I don't drink with the TPF." Later, his daughter reported that her best friend's father had forbidden them to play together because Gene was with "that damned bunch of goons."

Gene could understand why some Townies felt that way. The TPF weren't like other cops. They didn't perform routine police tasks such as walking beats, checking locks, making arrests. They were there for only one purpose: to intimidate people. Their very appearance had been carefully calculated to deter opposition: jumpsuits and combat boots reminiscent of the Green Berets, leather jackets and black gloves to hint of a Central European police state. They were trained to inspire dread with Grand Guignol theatrics: rapping their riot batons rhythmically on cars and light poles as they advanced, emitting guttural roars when they charged. Many a demonstrator had thought to himself: Oh my God, these guys are really nuts! And when sheer terror didn't do the trick, the TPF could swing their clubs with fierce resolve, reinforcing their fearsome reputations.

Alice had been raised to "respect the uniform." She had real affection for Nick Minichiello and a few other Charlestown detectives who'd kept a stern though kindly eye on her children over the years; she'd developed a sneaking respect for Captain MacDonald, whom she regarded as a tough but dedicated professional; she tolerated the Metropolitan District police, who, when they drew Charlestown busing duty, seemed to resent their distasteful task. But the TPF! They were the only ones who profited from this whole mess, many of them working thirty hours of overtime a week at ten dollars an hour. Alice had heard of one TPFer who built himself a home he called "Phase I," a boat he called "Phase II." No wonder they enjoyed their work so much!

On the streets they reminded her of wild animals. One night, as she was coming home from the Powder Keg office, the TPF charged up Bunker Hill Street, enforcing a 10:00 p.m. curfew. Alice ran for home, but two officers of the canine squad cornered her and several other women in a project courtyard. She didn't know which were more frightening, the German shepherds baring their fangs or the leather-jacketed cops growling obscenities. Even after the women ducked into a friend's apartment, the TPF kept their dogs at the door, potent reminders of their determination to control the streets.

If there was anyone worse than the TPF, Alice thought, it was the Mobile Operations Patrol, the motorcycle cops often employed, like cavalry, to charge unruly groups. One Saturday night, she was searching for her kids along

Bunker Hill Street when she heard the MOP squad gunning their motors in Hayes Square. First came a single cyclist, moving slowly to make sure the kids hadn't strung chicken wire across the roadway. Then a wedge of eight cycles swept up the street and through the protesting crowd. Watching from the sidewalk, Alice thought: It's as if we're Jews in the ghetto waiting for the storm troopers. All of a sudden, she couldn't stand there any longer, silently witnessing the violation of her town. Leveling her finger at the advancing motorcycles, she shouted, "Here come the Nazis! Here come the Gestapo! Heil Hitler!" At that, a helmeted cyclist veered from his course, jumped the curb, and came jouncing along the sidewalk toward her. She fled, but the cyclist pursued relentlessly, shouting as he came, "Garrity's whore! Get home, you goddamned trash! You're nothing but a white nigger!" Shaking with fear and rage, Alice finally took refuge in the Red Store.

Through the winter of 1975, the TPF—and, by extension, the MOP squad—became Charlestown's principal grievance. "The most brutal men I've ever seen," Pat Russell called them. "We've had it with the TPF. We want them out of our town." An ad hoc panel of community leaders denounced "excessive police presence and, in several instances, an overreaction on the part of the TPF. The TPF should be removed from Charlestown or, at least, held in reserve to be used only as a last resort."

But the TPF was already just that—a last resort, called into emergencies where ordinary police methods would not suffice. To those responsible for maintaining order, Charlestown that year seemed a permanent emergency, one which required extreme measures. The Town's protests were brusquely rejected, and the TPF's banshee yell went on echoing along Bunker Hill Street.

Feeling manhandled by the police, misused by City Hall, and oppressed by the courts, Charlestown now fell back on the process which in years past had often produced a redress of its grievances: an appeal to its United States congressman. Few American communities could boast the formidable array which had represented the Eleventh (now the Eighth) Congressional District—among them John F. "Honey Fitz" Fitzgerald, James Michael Curley, John F. Kennedy, and Thomas P. "Tip" O'Neill. Each was a Democratic sachem known for his savvy, clout, and capacity to collect and dispense favors. And none of them practiced the fine art of political *quid pro quo* more skillfully than the incumbent, the Majority Leader of the House of Representatives, Tip O'Neill.

For years, O'Neill had been widely regarded as just another Kennedy retainer. When John Kennedy advanced to the Senate in 1952, he helped to ensure that Tip, then Speaker of the Massachusetts House, would inherit his congressional seat, and O'Neill returned the favor by rallying House Democrats and big-city Catholics behind Jack's presidential campaign. Once Kennedy was in the White House, O'Neill faithfully supported his legislative program.

But theirs was never more than a marriage of convenience, for they had utterly different political styles. Raised in New York, accustomed to the cosmopolitan good life, Jack Kennedy early set his sights on a national constituency, assiduously avoiding entanglements with most Massachusetts politicians, for whom he harbored an undisguised contempt.

O'Neill was dedicated to the opposite proposition: "All politics is local." His was the ethos of the Corner—Barry's Corner on Rindge Avenue in heavily Irish North Cambridge, where he hung out from adolescence through early manhood with guys named Beefstew McDonough and Blubber Sheehan. That clapboard hutch served successively as a grocery, barbershop, pool hall, and eventually as a clubhouse called the Stumble Inn. For years, its worn wooden steps were the center of Tip's existence—a place to lounge on a hot summer's day gulping 3.2 beer; a table on which to play nickel-ante poker; ultimately a recruiting ground for his political organization. Long after he went to Congress, he remained deeply involved with Barry's Corner and the network it spawned. He was fond of quoting another political canon, attributed to Boston's celebrated boss Martin Lomasney: "The politician who thinks he can get away from the people who made him usually gets what is coming to him: a swift kick in his political pants."

For a quarter century, Tip stalked his district on Saturday afternoons, picking up his own laundry, pumping constituents' hands. Each tour produced a dozen appeals—to get a kid into college, push through a federal loan, or get an elderly woman into a housing project. Often pictured as a liberal dogmatist, O'Neill had little in common with the issue-oriented ideologues of the sixties. His was the politics of personal response, of care for individual constituents.

By late 1975, Tip was the second-ranking Democrat in the House, about to replace the ineffectual Carl Albert as Speaker. As he grew in stature, he became a familiar figure not just in Massachusetts but across the nation, a shambling bear of a man in rumpled suits, a shock of yellowing hair folded across his forehead, and a bulbous nose which lit up his jowly face like a neon tavern sign. He was an engaging raconteur, never better than when he launched in his gravelly voice into the story of Jake Bloom.

Jake ran a grocery store on Boston's Blossom Street. After his wife of forty years died, he got a hair transplant, lost fifty pounds, and took his new girlfriend to Miami Beach. But one afternoon, a lightning bolt rent the heavens and Jake was dead.

"Oh, God!" he cried. "I'm Jake Bloom from Blossom Street. Why did you do it?"

"Jake!" God replied. "I didn't recognize you."

This oft-repeated tale suggested that while others might change, Tip remained the same—an old-school politician, a man you could rely on.

Tip's district was an urban hodgepodge, embracing the state's third-largest city, Cambridge; comfortable suburbs like Arlington and Waltham; grimy working-class districts like Charlestown, Somerville, and East Boston; elegant enclaves like the Back Bay and Beacon Hill. But Charlestown held a special place in his affections, perhaps because the Townies had rallied strongly behind their fellow Irishman in his most difficult moment, the ferocious 1952 contest against East Boston's Mike LoPresti. In return he served up ample quantities of patronage, worked hard to provide federal subsidies for Charlestown's hard-pressed port facilities, and battled in vain to exempt the Navy Yard from Richard Nixon's vengeance against Massachusetts.

Long after Alice McGoff had lost faith in Ted Kennedy her confidence in Tip remained undiminished. He was a kitchen politician who got things done without all the Kennedys' posturing. She felt sure he could get the TPF off Charlestown's streets, eventually even lift the burden of busing from their shoulders.

In March 1975, O'Neill lent credence to these expectations when he told an anti-busing delegation he would ensure that a proposed constitutional amendment restricting court-ordered busing came to the House floor for a vote. Two days later, he went still further, pledging to vote for the amendment, although he had opposed similar measures in the previous session. His apparent reversal stirred consternation among blacks and liberals. By the end of the week, O'Neill was backpedaling, indicating that although he would vote for the amendment if it reached the floor, he would take no steps to get it there (a puzzling position since, without strong pressure from O'Neill, the amendment had little chance of emerging from the Judiciary Committee). By then, everyone was thoroughly confused. Some thought that was precisely what the canny Majority Leader intended. Others believed that the series of apparently contradictory statements indicated that O'Neill, trapped between liberal supporters in Cambridge and working-class whites in Charlestown, was genuinely ambivalent, susceptible to persuasion.

O'Neill's latest change of position came only two days before many of his constituents were to descend on the capital for a ROAR-sponsored March on Washington. Modeled on Martin Luther King's 1968 extravaganza, the march was attracting thousands of anti-busing activists from all over the country for an intensive round of workshops and lobbying, culminating in a massive rally on the Capitol steps at which ROAR planned to announce formation of a nationwide coalition to campaign for the constitutional amendment. Alice McGoff welcomed the event with undiluted enthusiasm: here was precisely the kind of dignified but forceful demonstration that would win them recognition. ROAR was developing into a white NAACP, a national alliance of white neighborhoods. She was so excited about the march that she took time off from the telephone company and sent a note up to Charlestown High so Lisa could accompany her. The trip cost them $57.50 apiece, but to Alice it would be well worth it if they could force Tip O'Neill off the fence.

In the dim pre-dawn hours of March 18, Powder Keg's delegation boarded three silver buses in City Square. The trip took twelve hours, but inside bus No. 62 the Townies were in a festival mood. Early in the evening, creeping through Washington's crowded streets, they let out a wild whoop as the Capitol's illuminated dome came into view. Pulling into the Quality Inn near the Pentagon, they were exhilarated to find the parking lot crammed with other buses, the lobby bursting with demonstrators. Some estimated that there were

10,000 marchers in town, others said 50,000. As Alice and Lisa collapsed on their beds, they felt caught up in a remarkable moment in American history, a gathering of oppressed people petitioning for restoration of their inalienable rights.

They awakened the next morning to a fierce thunderstorm lashing their windows. At breakfast in the motel dining room, a ROAR official announced that, because of the weather, those who wished to skip the march would be bused directly to the Capitol. "No busing for us!" shouted Powder Keg's Bobby Gillis. The Charlestown contingent cheered wildly.

Reaching the Washington Monument, they were dismayed to find barely 1,500 demonstrators—90 percent from Massachusetts—huddled on a grassy oval now reduced to a quagmire. Some marchers sheltered under umbrellas while others had improvised rainwear from green trash bags. But those who showed up that morning were determined to make their point despite the weather. Shortly after 10:00 a.m. they set off up the avenue, each neighborhood arrayed behind its own flag or emblem. The seventy Powder Keg representatives marched four abreast behind a huge banner reading: "Charlestown Against Forced Busing." Some wore tall Uncle Sam hats, others the revolutionary tricorns popularized by the Charlestown Militia. Many brandished small American flags.

Lisa didn't give a hoot about the weather. Snug in her hooded yellow slicker, she was grateful for a couple of days off from school, avid for her first look at Washington. Sloshing along beside her friend Beth Burton, she brandished a cardboard placard reading: "Here We Go, Boston!"

Alice was wearing her blue Powder Keg windbreaker and a green-and-white tam-o'-shanter, which soon felt like a sodden sponge around her ears. Within minutes the rain had destroyed her makeup. She was afraid she looked even worse than the hippie demonstrators who'd filled this same avenue through the sixties with their long hair and Vietcong flags. She'd dismissed them as a bunch of nuts. Who would have thought she'd be out here herself a few years later with mascara streaking her face like Apache war paint?

But, of course, there was nobody to see her—the rain had kept potential spectators away. The only others in the street that morning were the District of Columbia police, many of them black, who conscientiously patrolled their flanks. But it was too wet for violence. The only hint of it occurred outside the FBI Building when a South Boston parade marshal pointed at a car stopped at a traffic light. "That nigger gave us the finger!" he shouted. A few of the marchers turned menacingly and one of them yelled, "Hey, nigger, get out of the car and do that!" Just then the light turned green and the car sped off.

Reaching the Capitol at 11:00 a.m., they assembled on the glistening steps. Louise Day Hicks struck a lyrical note. "The tears of those affected by forced busing," she said, "have flowed just as hard as the rains that came today." But there was little consolation for the marchers that morning. Only one member of Congress showed up: Marjorie Holt of Maryland, author of the anti-busing amendment.

Where the hell were the guys from Massachusetts? Alice wondered. Where, in particular, was Tip O'Neill? Mrs. Hicks explained that a special meeting had been scheduled that afternoon between ROAR's executive committee and the Massachusetts congressmen; Tip would be there, she assured them. But when the meeting convened several hours later in a drafty hearing room, only four of the state's twelve representatives showed up, and when a dozen ROAR members sent an urgent note to Tip imploring him to join them, the Majority Leader declined to leave the House floor.

In the months that followed, Alice brooded over Tip's seeming indifference. Had all the power gone to his head? Had he finally lost touch with his working-class voters? Or had that little traitor Ted Kennedy gotten to him? Powder Keg's leaders renewed their request for a meeting with their congressman.

In October 1975, word came from O'Neill's office: he would be pleased to meet with a small Charlestown delegation. The group was carefully assembled to reflect all the Town's factions—Alice and Pat Russell from Powder Keg; Gloria Conway, editor of the *Patriot;* Jack "Sugar" Whalen, chairman of the Ward Two Democratic Committee; and Dennis Kearney, state representative from Charlestown. On the afternoon of October 10, the five were ushered into the Congressman's office in Boston's John F. Kennedy Federal Building and Tip courteously showed them to armchairs ranged in a semicircle around his desk.

Dennis Kearney led off, emphasizing that the delegation represented O'Neill's loyal supporters, stalwart Irish-Americans who had returned him to office year after year but who were now in trouble and needed his help. Pat Russell raised several grievances stemming from Arthur Garrity's order: the "terror tactics" of the TPF, the tight security at Charlestown High, the rule barring demonstrations within a hundred yards of any city school. O'Neill shook his head sympathetically, promising to do what he could.

Before long, they moved on to the central question: how did the Congressman stand on busing itself?

Ah, Tip said, he could understand exactly how Charlestown felt about busing. When his own kids were young, there was a parochial school just across the street in Cambridge, but it was all filled up and he and his wife, Millie, were terribly upset when they had to put their kids on a bus for another parochial school some miles away. Absolutely heartsick, Millie was. He had no difficulty understanding Charlestown's feelings.

Uh-oh, Alice said to herself, I think we're in trouble.

But what about the constitutional amendment? Jack Whalen wanted to know. Would the Majority Leader bring the amendment to the House floor?

Well now, Tip said, a constitutional amendment was a long-drawn-out process. Even after Congress approved it, it would have to be ratified by thirty-eight of the fifty states and that would take years, so it wouldn't really offer any relief for Charlestown.

But would the Congressman at least use his vast power to get the process started, so the people in the states could vote on it?

Ah well, he thought they were exaggerating his power a little; he didn't really have the kind of authority they were attributing to him.

"Oh, come on, Mr. Congressman," Alice interjected. "Everyone knows that, after the President, the Majority Leader is the most powerful man in Washington. If you really want to help the people of Charlestown, you can do it. The question is, do you want to help or don't you?"

A note of irritation crept into the Congressman's reply. He thought he'd done quite a good deal for the people of Charlestown over the years. He'd worked to get a ship into the Navy Yard so their men would have some badly needed jobs. He'd made sure that high schools like Charlestown's got a good hot-lunch program.

What was he talking about? Alice wondered. The Navy Yard was closed now, and Charlestown High didn't even have a cafeteria, much less a hot-lunch program. Long before their half hour was up, Alice was furious. All Tip had done was throw them a couple of well-gnawed bones. He was just like all the others.

Six weeks later, Powder Keg was back in Washington—this time to attend the House Democratic caucus, the forum in which Democratic members occasionally met to frame their party's position on pending issues. For the first time in history, the caucus was throwing its deliberations open to the public, and high on its agenda was a resolution instructing Democrats on the Judiciary Committee to report the anti-busing amendment to the floor within thirty days. It was a critical test for the measure, and ROAR had called out the troops for a last-minute bout of lobbying. This time they didn't bother with motel reservations, but rode through the night to reach the Capitol by 8:00 a.m., just in time for a couple of calls on the Massachusetts delegation before the caucus convened at ten. Tip was unavailable that morning, but a rumor raced through the corridors that the Majority Leader had at last decided to support the resolution. As Alice took her seat in the gallery, she was exhausted and rumpled but confident that this time their cause would prevail.

Her hopes were buoyed still further when the resolution quickly drew support from several Northern liberals, among them John Moakley, a Boston congressman known to be close to Tip. Moakley, whose district straddled South Boston and Roxbury, brought cheers from the gallery when he declared: "The parents of Boston deserve more than anguish, frustration, and uncertainty over their children's physical and educational well-being. The children of Boston deserve more than a life filled with metal detectors, riot squads, and racial tension. In Vietnam we saw the foolhardiness of destroying cities in order to save them. How much longer will we destroy school systems such as Boston's in the name of saving them?"

Then came the counterattack. First, Peter Rodino, the Judiciary Committee chairman, made it clear that he would not report the measure without a struggle. Then the Speaker of the House, Carl Albert, advanced to the podium. A frail figure, Albert spoke in a slow Oklahoma drawl, but Alice sensed that his words carried authority: "This [amendment] would be an attempt by the Congress, the legislative branch of government, to usurp that part of the Constitution which was allocated by the Founding Fathers to the Supreme Court."

Alice could see where the party's leaders were headed. Only one man could stop them. She glanced expectantly at Tip on the front bench, but the Majority Leader looked impassively ahead. Indeed, a few minutes later, when Albert's motion to table the resolution was put to a roll call, O'Neill voted "aye."

That was too much for Powder Keg. Jumping to their feet, Alice, Pat Russell, and the others booed and shouted. Tip looked anxiously over his shoulder, fixing them for a moment with a peevish eye, then stoically turned his back. Uniformed guards rushed the demonstrators, commanding them to be silent. When one young man objected loudly, two guards dragged him into the corridor. Alice and the others were quietly escorted from the gallery.

Later they learned that the motion to table had been carried 172–96, effectively dooming the anti-busing amendment for the session.

From then on, Powder Keg made no secret of its hostility toward Tip. On December 16, twelve Townies staged an hour-long sit-in at the Congressman's Boston office, refusing to leave until they read a list of demands on the phone to O'Neill in Washington. Throughout 1976, Powder Keg shadowed the Congressman wherever he went in the district, staging noisy protests in hotel ballrooms, American Legion posts, and church halls. Alice and Lisa took part in many of them, determined to wreak revenge for Tip's betrayal. "Dump Tip!" they shouted, a startling message in a district long known as "O'Neill Country." Not since his race in the fifties against Mike LoPresti had Tip faced more than token opposition in a primary. Now he had a serious challenger, a Belmont state representative named Edward F. Galotti. In most of the district, Galotti was a woeful underdog, but in Charlestown he drew fervent support from the anti-busing movement. So fierce was this opposition that O'Neill reluctantly heeded his advisers' warnings against campaigning in Charlestown. For months he couldn't even find a campaign manager in the Town. In the primary that September, the Majority Leader piled up substantial majorities elsewhere in the district, but lost Charlestown by an astonishing 3–2 margin. Even after easily winning reelection that November, O'Neill was reported to be stunned by the Townies' defection.

For Alice, Tip's betrayal was only the latest in a series of treacheries perpetrated by the very people who should have been her most zealous guardians—Irish-Americans like Arthur Garrity, Ted Kennedy, Kevin White, much of Boston's Irish Catholic clergy. If she asked herself whom she really detested in all this, it wasn't the blacks, who in many ways were as much victims as she was; it wasn't the Yankees from the suburbs, who were just as out of touch with urban reality as she'd always known they were; it was the Irish Catholic traitors, the people who should have known better but who had allowed wealth, comfort, power, or patronage to lure them from their basic allegiance to turf and tribe. Such betrayal seemed particularly shameful to a family like the Kirks, to whom loyalty and treason had been central issues for nearly three centuries.

The break with Tip severed a last, critical link with the Democratic Party. Alice no longer believed that the party of Honey Fitz and James Michael Curley, of Franklin Roosevelt and John Kennedy, cared very much about Charlestown. As time went on, Alice and her Powder Keg colleagues abandoned hope for prompt redress of their grievances. Their activism took on a ceremonial quality, rituals designed as much to express solidarity as to effect any substantial change in their environment. They displayed a nice feel for potent symbols—once they marched up Bunker Hill Street to hang Judge Garrity in effigy, led by two women dressed as the Statue of Liberty and the Blind Muse of Justice.

Most evocative of all was Powder Keg's annual minstrel show. No immigrant group had produced so many minstrel stars as the Irish, and well into the twentieth century minstrel shows remained a fixture of Boston's Irish neighborhoods. Although none had been presented in Charlestown in recent years, they remained part of its tribal memory, and not surprisingly, as Powder Keg searched for means of rallying the Town against hostile forces, the minstrel show, like the town meeting, seemed a natural candidate for revival.

Alice took up the idea enthusiastically, serving several years as the show's co-chairman with her friend Barbara Gillette, and also taking prominent roles on stage. Beginning each October, the Townies rehearsed several times a week, put through their paces by a professional director and often laboring late into the night to get the numbers just right.

On four consecutive evenings in March 1977, the Harvard-Kent School cafeteria was jammed for *Townies on Parade* The curtain rose on a gaggle of scruffy washerwomen, four white and one in blackface. Alice played "Pearl," who with "Sudsy," "Soapy," "Mopsy," and "Mafalda" desultorily scrubbed the stage while casting aspersions on the "high-muck-a-mucks" whose messes they were cleaning. Then their ruminations were interrupted by a pair of Keystone Kops in baggy pants, who began whaling them over the head with rubber truncheons. When the scrubwomen shouted, "Police brutality!" the audience applauded lustily.

The musical numbers were suffused with a nostalgia for better days: a medley of Irish tunes by the "Singing Fitzpatricks"; a "Tribute to Al Jolson"; a sing-along of "Put Your Arms Around Me, Baby, Hold Me Tight," with colored spotlights roving the audience while it swayed to and fro, arms linked.

When the songs were over, the spotlight picked up Alice McGoff, still dressed as Pearl the scrubwoman. "I love all that poetry and music," she said, "I got class." The audience roared derisively.

After intermission, the players returned in antebellum costumes for the "Show Boat Review," a tale about a Mississippi river town struggling to repel gamblers and hussies. The skit was studded with musical tributes to the Civil War era, among them Francis Fitzpatrick's remarkable rendition of "Ol' Man River."

Though his face was blacked and his inflection owed something to Paul Robeson, he rendered the familiar song with the same feeling he had brought earlier to "Danny Boy," seeming to remind his listeners that Charlestown, too, was a longshoreman's community and that Irishmen, as well as blacks, knew what it was to suffer. When the last verse echoed through the hall, the audience surged to their feet, calling him back for three bows.

The show ended with the entire cast on stage, dressed in red, white, and blue. Alice McGoff and Barbara Gillette stood on the apron as Barbara explained, "It's difficult to choose a last song. It has to represent the ideals of everybody who worked on the show. Don't let anybody kid you, we're united forever for liberty and justice for all."

Then, as a giant American flag unfurled behind them, the cast stepped forward and sang a rousing, teary finale.

> *My country is my cathedral*
> *The starry sky its dome*
> *They call it America*
> *But I call it home.*
> *From the Atlantic to the Pacific*
> *From the lakes to the Rio Grande*
> *We're one united brotherhood*
> *And united we will stand.*

But the more vehemently the Town proclaimed its unity, the more patent was its fragmentation.

The anti-busing movement itself was hopelessly splintered, with Louise and Pixie, ROAR and United ROAR, Powder Keg and the Defense Fund sparring acrimoniously with each other. And that was only the beginning of Charlestown's division. For busing had exacerbated the Town's ancient hostilities, setting parish against parish, hill against valley, the housing project against all comers.

Powder Keg and the Defense Fund drew their leadership and their most enthusiastic supporters from the project (even such activists as Tom Johnson and Barbara Gillette, who didn't live there, were closely identified with it by style and temperament). That was no coincidence. With their large families and crimped resources, the project dwellers were more directly affected by busing than other Townies. Too poor to pay parochial or private school tuitions, unable to escape to the suburbs, they were just as dependent on the public schools as their counterparts in the black community. The resentment which grew from this predicament detonated again and again in violent confrontations with the police.

Such disorders, in turn, simply confirmed the assessment the Town had long since made of the "project rats." Always ready to dismiss them as coarse vulgarians, the comfortable homeowners of Breed's and Bunker hills now concluded that they were vicious ruffians as well, hardly the sort of people with whom one wished to be associated. Moreover, property values were at last rising in the Town; the same young professionals who had flooded the South End were discovering the graceful old houses around Monument Square, and there was even talk of redeveloping the Navy Yard as a luxury apartment complex. Charlestown could only lose from further violence. At a secret meeting, some of the Town's leading citizens told Captain MacDonald that the police should "crack a few heads" down on Bunker Hill Street to teach "those people" a lesson. The middle-class Townies on the hills had no more use for busing than the project dwellers; they had simply opted out of the struggle. With most of their children safely squirreled away in parochial schools, the residents of St. Mary's and St. Francis de Sales' parishes increasingly shunned the town meetings, rallies, marches, and demonstrations concentrated along Bunker Hill Street in tormented old St. Catherine's Parish.

To a woman like Alice McGoff—who had grown up with such people on Monument Avenue—their reserve was particularly distressing, and it was all the more painful because among those holding themselves aloof from the busing struggle were her own family. By the mid-seventies, most of Alice's brothers and sisters had long since left Charlestown. Her sister Bernardine had moved to the suburbs as early as 1959, followed shortly by Donalda and Jim. When their father died in 1970, the other children had signed the Monument Avenue house over to the two youngest—Mary and Bobby—who lived there with their respective spouses through the early seventies. But neither couple had a child old enough for school, and neither became involved in Powder Keg. Sometimes they watched the marches and demonstrations on television and, spotting their sister in the ranks, they'd shout, "Atta girl, Alice!" They were with her—they really were; they just didn't care to get involved themselves. After a few years, the Monument Avenue house got a little cramped for two growing families, so they put it up for sale. Late in 1975, Mary and her husband left for Melrose. In July 1976, Bobby and his wife moved to Hingham, leaving Alice the last of the six Kirks still in Charlestown.

Alice could face facts as well as the next person: she was the poor Kirk, the widow with seven kids, the project dweller with limited resources; there was no way in the world she could move to the suburbs even if she wanted to. But even if she came into a lot of money she didn't think she'd ever leave Charlestown—she was rooted there, a Townie for life. And she couldn't understand how her brothers and sisters could remain so utterly aloof from the struggle which threatened to destroy their birthplace. When the family gathered for a holiday dinner at one of their comfortable suburban houses, Alice would invariably launch into a passionate tirade on the busing issue until eventually someone would say, "For Chrissake, Alice, give it a rest. Let's talk about the price of honey or anything, but let's enjoy the meal." That would only stir Alice up again and sometimes the meal broke up in bitter debate over the old Kirk issues of loyalty and betrayal.

As the tight little band of Powder Keg activists felt increasingly abandoned, their weekly notice in the *Patriot* struck a plaintive note. Urging a big turnout for a "unity march," it warned: "The only way to combat this foe is to unify for a common good. Remember the phrase 'divide and conquer,' for that is just what the bureaucratic dictators are striving to achieve in communities such as ours."

And soon its tone grew more querulous. After only thirty-eight people showed up for one town meeting, the column declared, "We had an anti-busing meeting last Tuesday and, believe me, if the British had walked in they would have laughed us off the battlefield. . . . Where are our patriots? Lying on Bunker Hill? Is this what your great-grandfather fought and died for?"

Ultimately, in a telling piece of guerrilla theater, Powder Keg held a funeral for the Town. One drizzly afternoon, Alice, Lisa, Robin, and Bobby McGoff joined 150 other Townies, most of them from St. Catherine's Parish, in a procession up Bunker Hill. Six pallbearers carried a casket containing likenesses of Arthur Garrity, a Catholic church, the Bunker Hill Monument, and Charlestown High School. Most of the mourners wore black, the women in veils, carrying white lilies and keening for the dead in that piercing wail traditional among the Irish. When they reached the Monument grounds, a high school bugler blew taps across the misty hillside. Pat Russell delivered a eulogy. Then they descended to that greasy stretch of black water dubbed Montego Bay, where the coffin was lowered into the sea. A death notice in the *Patriot* reported that the Town had died from a disease "perpetrated by Judge Garrity and Federal law." Members of the family were said to include "generations of loyal and abiding Townies."

24

The Editor

The lobster shift was a lonely one for the guard manning the marble lobby of the Boston *Globe*. In the dismal hours between midnight and dawn few employees came in or out, the phone on the reception desk stopped ringing, the only sound was the thump and swish of the giant presses. John McAuliffe would fortify himself with Styrofoam cups of muddy coffee while he waited for the freshly printed paper to come up from the loading dock. When the first edition arrived on the morning of October 7, 1974, he turned to the sports section, pleased to see that the Patriots had butchered the Baltimore Colts, 42–3. But the ink on the page was still wet and a black smudge came off on his fingers. He was reaching for a towel when he heard the first shot.

Dropping to his knees behind the desk, he could see the bullet hole, round and dark as a copper penny, drilled through the plate-glass window. Then he heard another volley crash into the pressroom.

At the newspaper's north entrance, guard Richard Cushing watched a beige sedan park by the median strip of Morrissey Boulevard. A man clambered out, rested a rifle on the hood, and pumped several shots into the building. Then the door slammed and the car fishtailed up the boulevard. When the police arrived at 12:47 a.m., they found three holes in the pressroom window and a fourth slug lodged in the lobby wall a few inches from where John McAuliffe had been reading his newspaper.

The next night, seven more shots slammed into the paper's rear yard, this time from a car speeding down the Southeast Expressway. A mechanic working on the engine of a *Globe* delivery truck reported a bullet humming past his shoulder; another bullet went through the windshield of a Volkswagen parked in the lot, a third into the wall of a newsprint warehouse.

The morning after the second attack *Globe* executives met with Joe Jordan, Boston's Police Superintendent. The cops had no hard evidence on who had fired the shots, but everyone knew that anti-busing forces, regarding the *Globe* as part of the liberal conspiracy, were mounting a major campaign against the paper. As busing began that September, bumper stickers had appeared all over town, reading: "We have had enough. Boycott the Boston *Globe*." On September 20, demonstrators picketed the paper's downtown business office. The next evening, a two-hundred-car motorcade blockaded the *Globe* plant as wailing mothers threw themselves in front of trucks, delaying distribution of the Sunday edition for three hours and setting off a melee in which a policeman and several *Globe* drivers were injured. A week later, youths slashed the tires on a truck delivering papers in South Boston and seized another truck at gunpoint, forcing the driver to dismount, then pushing his vehicle into ten feet of water in the Fort Point Channel.

With violence against the paper steadily escalating, publisher Davis Taylor, his son, the treasurer and heir apparent, William O. Taylor, business manager John Giuggio, and production director David Stanger, were in a grim mood as they gathered with Superintendent Jordan in the *Globe* boardroom. The five men quickly agreed on stringent new security measures: expansion of the paper's hired patrol force; stricter enforcement of the pass system; inspection of all packages and briefcases entering the building; installation of bulletproof glass on doors and windows; steel screens to shield the pressroom.

Then Joe Jordan spoke up again: for the time being, he wanted police snipers on the roof.

The executives were horrified. Absolutely not, they said. The *Globe* was a community newspaper which depended on rapport with its readers. If word ever got out that the paper had snipers on its roof, that trust would be shattered.

And what did they call eleven bullets in two nights? Joe Jordan wanted to know. If they wanted protection, they would have to let police take the necessary steps.

For the next few days, several sharpshooters with high-powered rifles and sniper scopes manned the newspaper's roof from dusk to dawn. *Globe* executives who held the closely guarded secret lived in constant fear of another rifle attack. If the police snipers fired back, they might easily kill one of the assailants. God only knew what might happen then!

But the next sally against the *Globe* came from a very different quarter.

The October 9 paper carried a story on page one headlined: "5 Black Juveniles Arraigned in Alleged Rape of White Girl," reporting that the five youths, aged fourteen to sixteen, had been charged with raping a fourteen-year-old Dorchester girl two nights before. According to the girl's sixteen-year-old boyfriend, they had been sitting on a stoop near their homes when the black kids approached and said, "Is this your old lady? She sure looks nice." Asked if they were from "Southie," the couple insisted they weren't, but the blacks said that was okay, they were white and that was "good enough." Police said the blacks then beat up the boyfriend and gang-raped the girl, leaving her on the Penn Central tracks bleeding and hysterical.

The story was an unusual one in several respects. Veteran *Globe* reporters couldn't recall the last time the newspaper had run a rape story on page one. But special circumstances were involved. The rape—if rape it was—had occurred only seven hours after the Haitian-born maintenance worker André Yvon Jean-Louis was badly beaten by a South Boston mob. The remarks attributed to the black youths suggested that the rape was intended, at least in part, as revenge for such assaults.

Still another factor figured in the prominent play given to the story. The editors made their judgment only hours after the first bullets crashed through the *Globe*'s windows, demonstrating again the fury some whites felt at the newspaper's allegedly "pro-black" bias. The Jean-Louis beating had already received extraordinary attention; to give the rape anything less than page one position would be to supply additional ammunition to the *Globe*'s critics. Robert Phelps, who had recently come from the New York *Times* to supervise the *Globe*'s busing coverage, felt that the paper had to put the rape story on page one, if only to demonstrate its impartiality on such matters. Tom Winship, the *Globe*'s editor, agreed.

But the paper's black reporters didn't. To them, the rape story was fresh evidence of the *Globe*'s effort to have it both ways on busing. Under Phelps's influence and with Winship's acquiescence, they believed, the *Globe* was in fact retreating from its earlier commitment to racial justice. How, they wanted to know, could you balance South Boston's blatant racism against blacks' demands for their constitutional rights? That was like equating right and wrong. The prominence given the rape story, they insisted, was a perfect example of the paper's moral confusion. And this, they held, was symptomatic of another problem: their exclusion from the *Globe*'s editorial process. Of the dozen blacks on the news staff, none had risen above the rank of reporter. In August, the blacks had met with Tom Winship to ask how a segregated group could make proper judgments on an integration story. Winship handled the protest calmly, reminding them that they were largely young and inexperienced, not yet ready to assume editorial responsibilities. Show me what you can do, he said, then we'll see about promotions.

Now, the rape story triggered further unrest among the black reporters. On the morning of October 9, eight of them signed a blunt letter to Winship: "Because of the ongoing school crisis and black/white racial turmoil in the city as a result of school desegregation the *Globe*'s black reporters feel an urgent need for permanent input into the *Globe*'s policy-making." Demanding a "black story editor to participate in news conferences and edit stories" and "black input into the editorial page," they nominated two of their number to fill these jobs. "We want both of these positions filled immediately and the nominees to begin work tomorrow."

Winship sought to deflect the demands with a coolly noncommittal reaction. In a return letter, he said there was an opening for an assistant metropolitan editor on the *Evening Globe*. "We invite applications from any of you or from any minority person working at the *Globe*." The paper could not hire an additional editorial writer, but it invited "any black person to participate in the daily 11 a.m. editorial page conference and/or submit written ideas and suggestions."

This only reinforced the blacks' determination. The next morning, ten black employees presented another letter to Winship. "We find it unusual and uncomfortable," they wrote, "to be working, in 1974, for a newspaper that has no black editor or editorial writer. . . . What we are demanding, therefore, is that the paper's editorial writing and editorship staffs be desegregated. This demand takes on particular importance against the background of present events in this city outside the *Globe* building. It is not at all clear that Boston will not be the place where the fabric of desegregation, woven over the past 20 years, begins to unravel. We want to make certain that inside the building this fabric continues to expand." With that, they resubmitted their demands of the day before.

When Winship failed to revise his position by evening, the black staffers informed him that "we cannot work until this grievance is resolved." Although their position fell short of a formal strike, they determined to withhold their services until their demands were met. By midday on the eleventh, a dozen blacks had assembled in the boardroom of Affiliated Publications, the *Globe*'s parent corporation. All through the afternoon, Winship, Phelps, and other editors shuttled in and out, bearing fresh bargaining positions.

Meanwhile, word of the black work stoppage spread through the newsroom, already ruffled by two nights of gunfire. A few white reporters and middle-level editors had long resented their black colleagues (one Halloween a picture of black Communist Angela Davis appeared in the afternoon paper with a headline, "Spooks Out Tonight," prompting one editor to warn: "Management must crush completely the anti-black cells at the paper"). These newsmen found it hard to believe that at the very moment the paper was being subjected to armed attack from whites, it was also being held hostage by its black employees.

"The disloyal bastards ought to be fired outright," said a veteran reporter known for his sympathy with ROAR.

"What are you talking about?" shouted a young white liberal. "It's your friends over in Southie who ought to be arrested for attempted murder!"

By evening, Tom Winship had acceded to the black demands. Carmen Fields, an outspoken young Oklahoman, was named an assistant metropolitan editor. The editorial writer's job went to John Robinson, a cool, discreet black who had been on vacation in Africa during the protest. The black employees returned to work the next day. But the struggle at the *Globe* was just beginning. Neither the militant whites nor the militant blacks knew that their countervailing pressures had opened a deep rift in the newspaper's executive ranks.

Not surprisingly, the business and editorial sides of the paper had different perspectives on the busing issue. To Tom Winship and his chief advisers—editorial page editor Charlie Whipple and executive editor Robert Healy—it was not only the biggest local story since John F. Kennedy's election to the presidency, it was a matter of principle, a test of the newspaper's long-standing commitment to racial justice and human dignity. To publisher Davis Taylor, his son Bill, and business manager Giuggio, the busing story was also a threat to the *Globe*'s high standing in the community, a challenge to its reputation for fairness and integrity, a threat to its increasing dominance of the Boston market. These differences had festered quietly for some time, but the attacks on the *Globe*'s building and trucks brought them to a head in that terrible first week of October.

Left to himself, Davis Taylor might not have intervened in Tom Winship's domain. In nineteen years as publisher, Taylor had steadfastly respected the division between publishing and editorial operations. But Bill Taylor and John Giuggio were less impressed by such niceties, more determined to curb the "knee-jerk" liberalism they detected across the aisle. Similar misgivings were harbored by the one front-office figure who could legitimately express them to Tom Winship.

Assistant to the publisher Crocker Snow had been brought back from the Tokyo bureau the previous June specifically to serve as liaison between editorial and business operations ("the *Globe*'s Cardinal Richelieu," Tom Winship called him). He seemed a perfect choice for that perilous undertaking. An able reporter and fluent writer, Snow had risen rapidly in the editorial ranks, where he was widely regarded as a possible successor to Winship. Well bred, well educated, and well connected, he enjoyed the publisher's full confidence. Surely if anyone could bridge the widening gap between the paper's two wings it was Crocker Snow.

As early as September 25—four days after ROAR's motorcade had delayed distribution of the Sunday paper—Snow outlined his views in a confidential memo to Davis Taylor. Noting that the Mayor's office might soon seek revisions in the court order, he wrote: "The *Globe* is in a precarious position on all this, being publicly identified with full implementation of the Garrity plan. . . . Should the plan change drastically, we, with our present stance and reputation, would not only lose face, but also credibility and influence. We would [look] like a lame duck editorial voice on this issue. This is not to say we should simply bend with the prevailing winds, that we should alter our stance if we think it is right. It does mean, however, that we should be aware of the dangers, and not go overboard in supporting a plan that we ourselves know to be a long way from perfect."

The memo echoed certain of Davis Taylor's private doubts and he encouraged Snow to pursue his attempt to modify the paper's editorial position. Then, on October 7, the first shots through the *Globe*'s windows confirmed the front office's worst fears: the *Globe* was no longer a passive observer; it was part of the story, one of the principal targets, out there alone "like Sally Rand." This was what happened when a newspaper got ahead of its readers. Something had to be done.

Hours after the first bullet smacked the wall above John McAuliffe's head, Snow issued another, more urgent, warning, this time directed to both Davis Taylor and Tom Winship:

"We are all getting deeper into the trench on this one. Trouble is rising, the boycott may be growing. . . . Yet Boston's leaders, the Mayor, the Archbishop, the Chamber [of Commerce], the Pols, are notably silent. . . . The *Globe*? We're firmly identified with the pro-busing, pro-Plan mentality. Few, if anyone, give us credit for being pro-court, first and foremost. Can we change this image? . . . The trouble with all this, of course, is that any change in Plan looks like a cave to the rock throwers. Similarly, a change in the *Globe*'s editorial stance could look like mere expediency. Bob Healy worries about this. He thinks we have to stand fast now on the matter of principle, then bend the practicality (the details of the Plan itself) once the principle is firmly established. I don't know. After all, we are worried about ultimate effects for the City and its people more than our own loss of face for altering our position."

Tom Winship was as worried about the gunshots as anyone else; he was concerned for the security of his reporters, as well as by prospects of a prolonged feud with the city's working-class Irish neighborhoods. But he wasn't about to retreat from the battlefield. On October 8, the morning after the second volley of shots, Winship rapped out a quick note to Crocker Snow.

"Thanks for the memo to me and Dave. It's a tight spot for all of us. But I'll be damned if I think we should cave in, as you put it yourself, and call for a change in the plan the court ordered. That is premature. . . . We would lose respect of friend and foe to twist and turn at this point when a federal law is being flouted. I agree with Bob Healy that we have to stand fast now on the matter of principle, the way the *Globe* did back in 1880."

The principle which Winship ascribed to his predecessors—defense of minority rights in a Yankee city—might have looked to others like enlightened self-interest, for the *Globe* of the 1880s had been a fragile enterprise, in dire need of a new constituency. Established in 1872 with lofty objectives, "the intelligent and dignified discussion of political and social ethics," it found Boston's aristocracy well served by the stately *Transcript* and indifferent to another quality journal. Only the persistence of merchant-prince Eben Jordan kept the foundering *Globe* afloat, and soon he launched a refitted version, shaped by his young general manager, Charles H. Taylor.

Abandoning the *Globe*'s carriage trade pretensions, Taylor turned to the city's burgeoning working class, most of it now Irish, Catholic, and Democratic. Such readers had long received cold comfort from the Republicans who monopolized Boston's editorial chairs. Taylor himself had been raised a Republican, serving for a time on the party's state committee, but now he wasted little time in shucking that allegiance, labeling the *Globe* a "progressive Democratic newspaper" and "advocate [of] all liberal measures which will advance the interests of the masses."

The *Globe*'s support for Irish rights—at home and abroad—was the natural corollary of its bid for a working-class audience. It gave lavish coverage to the Irish Land League's campaign for reform of the landlord system and ran a series on "rack rents." On a matter of more immediate interest to its Catholic audience, the *Globe* demanded that priests be permitted to administer last rites in Boston's hospitals. For years, dying immigrants had been forced to choose between hospital care and that ritual so critical to the repose of the Catholic soul. Ultimately most institutions capitulated, a famous victory long remembered by the paper's grateful readers.

In refashioning his journal for a broader audience, Taylor broke with other hidebound traditions. Most Boston papers were aimed exclusively at men, but the *Globe* introduced household hints, recipes, and serialized novels for women. News was whatever interested people, and that included generous helpings of sports. Such frivolities helped the *Globe* transcend its politics. "If I had my way, I wouldn't have a Democratic newspaper in the house," grumbled one Victorian Yankee, "but I can't keep the *Globe* out because my boy insists on reading the fool news about baseball."

Despite his ardent support for the Irish, Taylor managed to avoid the shrill partisanship of Pulitzer and Hearst. Fair play was the *Globe*'s watchword, encapsulated in Taylor's celebrated axioms which have been handed down through the years like stone tablets: "Try never to print a piece of news that would injure an innocent person"; "Always treat a man fairly in the *Globe* so you may meet him again and look him straight in the eye." He wasn't above pandering to the workingman's taste for mayhem: one week began with "An Awful Crime" and ended "More Bloody Work." But the grosser excesses of tabloid sensationalism were too sanguinary for his taste. He once suggested that Joseph Pulitzer would have "no appetite for breakfast if he did not find blood running down by the [New York *World*'s] column rules."

His was a sunnier disposition, summed up by a paragraph which became the *Globe*'s credo and still hangs on a bronze plaque in the newspaper's lobby:

> My aim has been to make the *Globe* a cheerful, attractive and useful newspaper that would enter the home as a kindly, helpful friend of the family. My temperament has always led me to dwell on the virtues of men and institutions rather than upon their faults and limitations. My disposition has always been to help build up rather than to join in tearing down. My ideal for the *Globe* has always been that it should help men, women and children to get some of the sunshine of life, to be better and happier because of the *Globe*.

For nearly two decades, this geniality paid off, helping the *Globe* become the region's dominant newspaper. Its symbol was now a beaming, rotund gentleman in a top hat with a broad sash around his middle proclaiming: "The Largest Circulation in New England." The Globe Man, as he became known, appeared daily on the front page and often elsewhere in the paper, shaking hands with friend and foe alike. Fat and prosperous, cheerful and complacent, the *Globe* grew increasingly disinclined to offend any segment of its hard-won readership. Taylor's sympathy for the Irish did not signify a lasting commitment to the underdog. Oswald Garrison Villard of *The Nation* described him as "a simple, sweet-natured person, undiscriminating, conventional, ignorant that there were such things as deep economic currents and terrible economic injustices." As the years went by, the *Globe*'s fairness descended into timidity, its benevolence into sanctimony.

A crescendo of circumspection was reached in 1896 as Western radicals were assailing the gold standard, much beloved of Eastern conservatives. When William Jennings Bryan rode the "free silver" stampede to the Democratic presidential nomination, he posed a dilemma for New Englanders that was particularly excruciating for the *Globe,* which had long stamped its approval on any full-blooded Democrat.

A perplexed Taylor cabled James Morgan, his editorial director, at the convention: "What do we say now?"

"Don't say anything," Morgan wired back.

All that fall the editors kept their opinions to themselves, a high-minded impartiality that soon became a habit. Not for three-quarters of a century did the *Globe* again endorse a political candidate.

Increasingly, Taylor and Morgan shunned unequivocal stands on any issue. The *Globe* began signing its main editorials "Uncle Dudley," after a popular tag line of the day, "Take it from your Uncle Dudley." Rambling, philosophical disquisitions, "Uncle Dudleys" expounded lofty principles, embroidered with classical esoterica.

A retreat to the high ground proved especially convenient as Boston politics were appropriated by pugnacious Irishmen. The *Globe*'s Yankee executives were repelled by Honey Fitz and James Michael Curley, but the voters who elected such demagogues were the heart of the paper's constituency, and for years the *Globe* went out of its way not to offend them. When a City Hall reporter exposed some of Curley's shenanigans in *The Nation*, the publisher sternly admonished him, "You'll lose all your following."

The *Globe* played it just as safe on the biggest story of the twenties, the Sacco-Vanzetti case. Its reporter, the former war correspondent Frank Sibley, concluded that the pair was innocent, but the *Globe* kept him on a tight leash; on execution day he was covering a flower show. Another reporter, Gardner Jackson, unable to find an outlet for his indignation at the *Globe,* quit to edit the official bulletin of the Defense Committee. Editorially, the paper was even more skittish. Uncle Dudley's only comment came the day the jury was impaneled, when he proclaimed that juries "work amazingly well. Human nature has a way of rising to unavoidable responsibilities." It remained for *The Atlantic Monthly* to publish Felix Frankfurter's trenchant analysis of the evidence, and for the conservative *Herald* to crystallize doubts about the verdict in a withering editorial that won the Pulitzer Prize. Through seven years of international debate, the *Globe* remained a timorous bystander.

The Great Depression only intensified the paper's caution. By then, Charles Taylor had given way to his son, William O., a pallid figure who had majored in biblical history at Harvard and who could produce a scrap of scripture for every occasion. In 1932—when the *Globe* came within $30,000 of going into the red—he blithely invoked Romans 8:18, "For I reckon that the sufferings of this present time are not worthy to be compared with the glory which shall be revealed in us."

But salvation was a long way off. By 1930, the *Globe* had to remove its pudgy symbol of preeminence, for no longer could it claim Boston's largest circulation, much less New England's. Both distinctions now belonged to the resurgent *Post*. Gaudy and flamboyant, it once gave away a motorcar a day, and won a Pulitzer Prize for exposing confidence man Charles Ponzi. Ultra-Democratic and super-Catholic, it unashamedly took up cudgels for the dispossessed as the *Globe* hadn't dared to do in sixty years. Mixing campaigns for free streetcar transfers and lower gas rates with stories of sexual aberration and outrageous felony, it rapidly replaced the *Globe* as Boston's working-class Irish newspaper.

The Hearst papers plied essentially the same trade, but somehow their enticements never matched the *Post*'s. For years, they gained much of their circulation by printing the daily Treasury number (known in Boston as the "nigger number"), an essential for those who played the policy game.

While the *Globe*'s old readership was eroded by the *Post* and Hearst, Boston's upper-class constituency was preempted by the *Christian Science Monitor, Transcript,* and *Herald*.

The voice of the Christian Science mother church—and free, therefore, from other papers' truckling to the Catholic Archdiocese—the *Monitor* consistently produced the city's best municipal reporting. But, never truly a Boston newspaper, it was read more assiduously in Washington and Los Angeles than it was in its own backyard. Its prissy abstention from crime, disease, death, alcohol, and tobacco denied it a popular audience.

While the *Monitor* never quite found its niche in the city, the *Transcript* was, if anything, too secure in its. Every evening just at teatime it was placed—never thrown—on the doorsteps of proper Bostonians. For a century it had been scrupulously edited for "our kind of people," offering departments like "The Churchmen Afield," and "Ripples," a yachting column which once expressed "the inability of the sailboat man to understand why anyone in his right mind should want to own a motorboat." Releases from the Anti-Vivisection Society were published verbatim, invariably concluding: "Tea was served. John Orth rendered several selections on the piano." Well into the thirties, the *Transcript* cherished the old traditions, publishing a football extra a half hour after the Harvard game ended, dismissing its managing editor for permitting the term "sexual intercourse" to creep into a story. But its blood was running perilously thin. By 1936, the paper's circulation was down to 31,000, barely enough to fill Harvard's stadium.

By then, the majority of the Anglo-Saxon audience had shifted to the meatier *Herald*. The voice of State Street's financial community and the Republican Party, it was owned by the First National Bank and the United States Shoe Machinery Corporation. Once linked to the anti-Catholic American Protective Association, the *Herald* was still anathema in Irish neighborhoods. But to old

Yankees, its prize-winning editorial page was the champion of fiscal responsibility and civic progress. Its more rambunctious evening companion, the *Traveler,* still sold well in the city, but the morning *Herald* increasingly found its readers in comfortable suburbs like Wellesley and Dover (while the *Herald* was delivered to the front door, the *Globe* often came through the back with the Irish help, becoming known in some circles as "the maid's paper").

Journalistic diversity is said to encourage aggressive reporting and bold advocacy. Yet in a city so fragmented by class, race, and ethnicity, competition often produced quite the opposite. With thirteen newspapers contending for Boston's market—five in the morning, four in the evening, and four on Sunday—there were only two ways to play the game: either batten on one class or ethnic bloc, pandering to its every preconception, or strike the lowest common denominator, placating all, offending none.

Squeezed between the patrician and the proletarian, the *Globe* struggled to keep a foot in each camp. "We're putting out a paper for the bottom half of the upper class, the middle class and the top half of the lower class," an editor of that era once explained. "We try to give everyone a chance to be heard in our pages. When I make up page one, I try to find a story for everybody: a crime story for Joe Blow, a woman's feature, something for the businessman, something for the kids."

The papers' commercial strategies revealed the same stratification. With its vast working-class audience, the *Post* monopolized national advertising—the cigarette, beer, and soap-flakes contracts from the big New York agencies. The *Transcript* and *Herald* took the fashionable retail trade. The *Globe,* on its broad middle course, cultivated classified advertising, a morsel for every want and need.

Demography and technology ultimately conspired to reduce this journalistic smorgasbord. As Boston's gentry decamped for the countryside, their traditional provisioners went out of business altogether or followed them to the new suburban shopping malls, so undermining the *Transcript*'s advertising that, in April 1941, it decorously expired. Then, as radio and television drew national advertising from the *Post,* its owners sold the paper to John Fox, a South Boston Irishman turned Wall Street wheeler-dealer, who wielded it as a bludgeon in his personal crusade against Communism. Through the mid-fifties, the paper beat a relentless tattoo ("Red Hordes Storm Dienbienphu," "Man Beaten by Red Gang"), relishing any opportunity to find an old Yankee enmeshed in the conspiracy ("Miss Anne P. Hale, 46, a social registerite, whose ancestors helped found the Massachusetts Bay Colony, was suspended tonight by the [Wayland] School Committee because of illegal Communist activities"). Fox himself contributed a series on the "Christ-like devotion" of Senator Joseph McCarthy.

In an Irish Catholic city then rabidly pro-McCarthy, it took courage for any newspaper to breast the tide. The *Globe* was more temperate than the *Post* but, aware that it shared the Senator's constituency, it did nothing to protest his behavior. James Morgan, still the *Globe*'s guiding spirit, concluded that a stand against McCarthy would lose the paper 100,000 readers. In private, he justified its silence by invoking a curious apologia called "The *Globe* Principle," first devised three decades earlier to explain the *Globe*'s reticence on E. Mitchell Palmer's anti-Communist raids: "The *Globe* policy is to uphold principles and not to tie itself up with personalities, necessarily transient. In fighting men, it would make too many enemies for the measures it advocates. . . . The *Globe* perseveres in a good-humored patience with each successive challenger of the American Way, in its faith that 'they, too, will pass away.'" (The *Globe* was more courageous when its own staffers ran afoul of the hysteria. Charlie Whipple, who covered McCarthy for the paper, had been a Communist at Harvard in the thirties. When State Senator John Powers threatened to subpoena Whipple, the *Globe* sent its political correspondent up Beacon Hill to warn Powers that it would not tolerate such harassment. The subpoena was quietly shelved.)

By transforming the *Post* into a strident broadsheet, John Fox may have won it some readers, but he alienated others. When he broke with the newspaper's Democratic heritage to support Eisenhower, the newsroom phones rang all night with outraged subscribers. Creditors' lawsuits brought the paper to its knees. In 1956, the 125-year-old war horse succumbed to mortal wounds.

With the journalistic spectrum thus shorn of its extremes and the *Monitor* and Hearst papers fading into insignificance, Boston's press wars were left with two principal contestants. Each brandishing the relics of ancient battles, each furnished in the full regalia of morning, evening, and Sunday editions, the *Globe* and *Herald* eyed each other uneasily from opposite ends of Washington Street.

Seeking to avert a costly war of attrition, the *Herald* pursued a shotgun marriage. Robert Choate, the *Herald*'s publisher, was a splenetic autocrat, model for the tyrannical Amos Force in *The Last Hurrah*. Having relentlessly urged merger on his *Globe* counterpart, William Taylor, he renewed his campaign after Taylor was succeeded by his son, Davis. When Davis went ahead with plans for a new *Globe* plant, capable of outprinting the *Herald*'s aging presses, Choate called on the John Hancock Insurance Company and the State Street Trust Company in a vain effort to block their loans for the building. Finally, in January 1956, he invited Davis Taylor to lunch at the Somerset Club on Beacon Hill. Choate was accompanied by Carl Gilbert, president of the Gillette Company and a *Herald* director; Taylor brought his cousin John, the *Globe*'s treasurer. The four men lunched in a private second-floor dining room, its walls lined with pale green silk. Over broiled scrod, Choate explained why further competition would do neither paper any good. "If you build, we'll build," he warned. "If you go to ninety-six pages in your first section, we'll go to ninety-six pages. It's like the arms race. For God's sake, let's stop it now. Let's put the two papers together."

Davis politely demurred—the Taylors cherished the *Globe*'s independence. As they finished lunch, Choate said coldly: "You fellows are stubborn.

Worse than that, you're arrogant. You better listen to us or we'll teach you a lesson. I'm going to get Channel 5, and with my television revenues I'll put you out of business."

For the time being, the Taylors didn't take Choate's threat very seriously. The *Herald* had been seeking Boston's third VHF channel since 1947, but on January 4, 1956—only three weeks before the lunch—a Federal Communications Commission hearing examiner had tentatively awarded the channel to Greater Boston Television, headed by Arthur Garrity's law partner, Richard Maguire. The ruling had been appealed to the full FCC, but the Taylors were confident the *Herald* wouldn't prevail, for the same reason the *Globe* hadn't applied in the first place: the commission's "diversification policy," which discouraged undue concentration of newspaper and television properties.

But "Beanie" Choate never gave up. All through 1956, he used every device in the lobbyist's repertoire to sway the FCC, including repeated calls on White House and congressional Republicans, and a critical lunch with Commission Chairman George McConnaughey. Shortly before Christmas the campaign paid off. In a preliminary vote, the commission instructed its staff to draft an opinion awarding Channel 5 to the *Herald*. Ruefully recalling Choate's parting words at the Somerset, Davis and his cousin John went to Washington for a frantic effort to reverse the decision. Within three days they visited every commission member as well as Massachusetts Senators John Kennedy and Leverett Saltonstall; New Hampshire Senator Styles Bridges; and Secretary of Commerce Sinclair Weeks. To each they delivered the same message: they had no interest in Channel 5 themselves, but they were determined to prevent the *Herald* from obtaining a weapon which could put the *Globe* out of business. The Taylors garnered little encouragement. House Minority Leader Joe Martin summed up the situation when he told them, "I'm afraid you fellas have just been outpoliticked."

They may have been outswapped as well. Joe Kennedy was determined to bring his son the 1957 Pulitzer Prize for *Profiles in Courage*, thus bestowing an extra dash of prestige on Jack's presidential campaign. But the biography judges didn't cooperate, nominating Alpheus Mason's *Harlan Fiske Stone: Pillar of the Law*, and seven runners-up. The senior Kennedy thereupon conferred with Arthur Krock, the New York *Times* Washington columnist and longtime Kennedy adviser. Together, they mapped a strategy to convert the Pulitzer Advisory Board, the thirteen editors and publishers who review the judges' nominations. Krock has confirmed that he "worked like hell" to get the prize for Jack, intervening with board members like fellow *Times* man Turner Catledge and Barry Bingham of the Louisville *Courier-Journal*.

But Joe Kennedy gave personal attention to the board's lone Bostonian—Robert Choate. According to one version of subsequent events, Joe sent his faithful retainer, Municipal Court Judge Francis Xavier Morrissey, to solicit Choate's vote. What's in it for me? the publisher replied. What do you want? asked Morrissey. To which Choate snapped: Channel 5.

Joe Kennedy had other reasons for proving useful to the *Herald*. He knew the Boston press could be bought—five years before, he had loaned John Fox $500,000 in exchange for the *Post*'s endorsement of Jack. Now JFK was seeking a massive reelection victory in 1958 to boost his presidential hopes and the *Herald*'s support could be critical. Still the city's largest daily, it was the Republican paper whose readers Kennedy needed for such a landslide (indeed, a year later, the *Herald* broke tradition by endorsing Kennedy, who won by a staggering 874,608 votes).

Moreover, Joe Kennedy had little affection for the *Globe*. In 1940, while Ambassador to the Court of St. James's, he had granted an interview to the *Globe*'s Louis Lyons. Already secretly sparring with FDR, Joe was about to stake out a carefully articulated isolationist position which he hoped would carry him to the White House in 1944. But relaxing in his suite at Boston's Ritz-Carlton Hotel, he indiscreetly shared his unexpurgated thoughts with Lyons: "Democracy is finished in England. It may be here. . . . If we got in [to the war], a bureaucracy would take over right off. Everything we hold dear would be gone." When the *Globe* spread the story over page one, Kennedy claimed he had been misquoted and insisted that the *Globe* fire Lyons. The newspaper stood firm (although once the furor cooled down, it shunted Lyons off to Harvard as director of the Nieman Fellowships for journalists). Meanwhile, Kennedy retaliated by withdrawing his liquor advertising—he then controlled all imports of Haig & Haig and Gordon's Gin—a boycott which cost the *Globe* two million dollars over six years. As late as 1961, days before his son's inauguration, Joe was still denouncing the *Globe*'s transgression.

Kennedy had ample motivation for a deal with the *Herald*, and he had the resources as well. At least two FCC members—Richard Mack and Robert E. Lee—were close to Kennedy. Whatever may have passed between Joe and the commissioners, the public record is intriguing:

In the last week of April 1957, the Pulitzer Advisory Board overrode its judges, leapt over eight distinguished nominees, and awarded its biography prize to *Profiles in Courage*. Robert Choate voted for Jack Kennedy's book.

On April 24, the FCC formally overrode its hearing examiner and awarded Channel 5 to the *Herald*. The vote was 4–2. Messrs. Mack and Lee voted with the majority.

Over the next fifteen years, the issue went back to the FCC twice, five times to the Court of Appeals, and three times to the Supreme Court, becoming the longest administrative case in American history. Though the *Herald* continued to operate the station, the license competition was ultimately reopened, and four contenders from every corner of Boston's ethnic and class map slugged it out in a bare-knuckled free-for-all. Yet the essential collision remained between the *Globe* and the *Herald,* a gritty war of survival that gradually transformed the Taylors and their somnolent newspaper. Like his father and grandfather, Davis Taylor had been a relentlessly conventional man—a lean, crew-cut sailing enthusiast and polite Episcopalian, who, as late as 1956, could write, "My social, political (independent), and religious convictions [are] normal, I hope, for a Harvard man." But perhaps for the first time in his placid existence, Taylor had been stung by Bob Choate's threats. The day after the *Herald* gained Channel 5, Uncle Dudley appeared with an uncharacteristically blunt editorial, concluding: "The *Globe* will continue to publish an independent newspaper as happily as it has for the past 85 years." It was a shot fired across the *Herald*'s bow, a warning that the *Globe* would not go down without a fight.

Not long thereafter, the paper appointed a new Washington correspondent, a young Irishman named Bob Healy. Healy's father had been a *Globe* mailer for fifty years, earning the Taylors' special affection and assuring that his sons would always have jobs at the paper. Bob parlayed his street savvy into the *Globe*'s top political beat, but he had other functions as well. If the Taylors stood aloof from Boston politics, they needed someone who could deal with the Irish pols, and Healy quickly became the family's principal pipeline to City Hall. Moving to Washington in 1957, he served as their special envoy on Channel 5, making sure the publisher was never "outpoliticked" again. By then, Washington was the front on which Boston's journalistic tong wars would be decided. An emissary from the *Herald* presented $50,000 in government bonds to Senator Styles Bridges. The *Globe* chased rumors linking a *Herald* stockholder to mob interests. But the biggest coup came from Healy, who obtained telephone company records documenting improper contacts between Choate and FCC Chairman McConnaughey.

The *Globe*'s new investigative zeal paid rich dividends. In 1961, Healy learned that Jack Kennedy intended to appoint his father's old gofer, Francis Xavier Morrissey, to the vacant seat on Boston's federal bench. The White House backed down when the *Globe* reported that Morrissey had twice failed the Massachusetts bar exam, then been admitted in Georgia under questionable circumstances. Four years later, Lyndon Johnson finally named Morrissey, but ex-Kennedy staffers like Kenny O'Donnell, fearing that the appointment would besmirch Jack's memory, fed Healy damaging new material which killed the nomination and won the paper its first Pulitzer Prize.

The Pulitzer was particularly welcome because it put an official stamp of approval on the *Globe*'s new editorial leadership. In September 1965—the very month the paper launched its final assault on Morrissey—Tom Winship became the *Globe*'s editor.

The appointment stirred some talk of nepotism because "young Tom"— then forty-five—succeeded his father as the paper's principal news executive. Cheerful, tractable Larry Winship had been an appropriate editor for the *Globe* of the forties and fifties. A protégé of the circumspect James Morgan, he began on the Sunday paper and remained a "soft news" man, inclined toward the inoffensive feature story (he once assigned a piece on what people keep in the backs of cars). Even his close friend Felix Frankfurter, who once called Winship "a really wise New Englander," conceded that he was "not much concerned with general ideas or causes." Boston's most pressing problems— rampant McCarthyism, endemic corruption, stagnant industries, decaying neighborhoods, ethnic strife, racial segregation—did not engage him.

Nothing in Tom Winship's youth promised more involvement with the troubled city. Raised in exurban Sudbury, a truck-farming community sixteen miles west of Boston, he received an education anachronistic even in that part of the world. In nearby Sterling, the industrialist Henry Ford had discovered the one-room schoolhouse linked by legend to Mary and her little lamb. Installing it on a Sudbury hillside, he furnished it with nineteenth-century desks and a potbellied stove, then recruited a teacher and sixteen Sudbury children. For six years, Tom Winship played his appointed role in Henry Ford's tableau. When Ford produced a movie about Mary and her lamb, Tom's job was to hide the animal under his desk until the director was ready for it. As he gamely hugged its woolly neck, the lamb shat all over his new shoes.

This was not, perhaps, the best place to acquire a thirst for learning. Entering Harvard in 1938, Tom concentrated in cultural anthropology. But the ruling passion of his young life was skiing. With his Norwegian roommate, he founded Harvard's first ski club and led the ski team to fourth place in the Dartmouth Carnival.

Graduation left him at loose ends. As his classmates went off to war, Tom—his eyes damaged at birth—was classified 4F. No civilian career seemed attractive, least of all newspapering. Twice a month during college he'd gone downtown for lunch with his father, but nothing he had glimpsed in the *Globe*'s musty offices or at journalistic watering holes like the Bell and Hand had ever stirred his imagination. He was damned if he was going to spend the rest of his days in a green eyeshade huddled over a stack of greasy copy paper. When nothing else presented itself, Tom enrolled as a management trainee in a sanitary napkin factory. But quickly tiring of Kotex, he memorized the eye chart and found a berth in the Coast Guard recruiting office, a job which included peddling press releases to the Boston papers. Pleasantly surprised when his name opened editors' doors all over town, Tom wangled a combat correspondent's assignment aboard a transport ferrying troops onto Omaha Beach. The invasion of Europe was heady stuff for a young reporter. All about him as he prowled the French coast were the most renowned names in wartime journalism: Ernie Pyle, Don Whitehead, Wes Gallagher. Winship was hooked.

Reassigned to Washington as chief of correspondents, he had plenty of time on his hands. Coast Guard headquarters was directly across the street from the Washington *Post*. With his father's introduction, he got a nighttime job writing obituaries for the *Post* and, after his discharge, a full-time position covering police headquarters. Weightier events left him strangely indifferent. If pressed, he called himself a Wendell Willkie Republican; in fact, he was largely apolitical. So Tom was caught by surprise when Leverett Saltonstall, Massachusetts' Republican senator, asked him to serve as his press secretary. The appointment would obviously benefit the Senator—though the *Globe* still gave no political endorsements, favorable coverage in its news pages would lend a Republican credibility in Democratic Boston, and a Winship on his staff would help assure that. On Tom's part, it was a rare opportunity to see Washington from the inside out, and *Post* publisher Phil Graham urged him to "get up there on the Hill and learn where the men's rooms are." For two years he immersed himself in congressional politics, an apprenticeship which left its lasting imprint. Despite his personal admiration for Saltonstall, Tom was dismayed by the Grand Old Party's unrelenting negativism. By the time he returned to the *Post* in 1948, he was a political junkie—and a Democrat— for life.

At Phil Graham's suggestion, Tom took the redevelopment beat, an important assignment as Washington began to tackle the fetid slums which had crept to within blocks of the Capitol. Graham was crusading for a bold slum-clearance program and Tom became one of his principal agents, writing dozens of stories on the renewal of Southwest Washington. For a young man raised among Sudbury's tomato patches, it was an abrupt exposure to the ills of urban America. Until then he had known only one Negro well enough for conversation: a carefully groomed Harvard classmate. Suddenly, he found himself in a brick wasteland, interviewing Georgia and Mississippi blacks who had trekked north during the war in search of work and stayed on seeking a piece of the American Dream. Their blasted hopes kindled the first spark of Tom Winship's social conscience.

Later he was drafted for another crusade much favored by Graham and the liberal Georgetown set—the mounting demand for District of Columbia home rule. That too was largely a racial issue, for the House and Senate committees which governed the district were traditionally dominated by reactionary Southerners, while the city itself was increasingly black. Not surprisingly, Tom identified closely with Graham, Felix Frankfurter's elegant protégé who had taken Washington by storm and become perhaps its most influential private citizen. He particularly admired the publisher's determined use of the *Post* to champion liberal causes.

Ben Bradlee, another *Post* reporter, later to become the paper's editor, got a revealing glimpse of the way Graham operated. In the summer of 1950, an ugly race riot erupted over the integration of a public swimming pool. After hours on the street, Bradlee returned to the *Post* offices to find his story cut to the bone and buried on an inside page. When he exploded, Graham dragged him into a meeting with Clark Clifford of the White House and two Justice Department officials, all in black tie. When Bradlee recounted what he had seen, Graham warned his guests that the *Post* would print the full story unless they closed all municipal pools and agreed to open them the next summer fully integrated. The officials agreed. Graham's insistence on being a prime mover, not just an observer, may sometimes have compromised his newspaper's integrity, but Tom Winship seemed not to notice. Years later he credited Graham's example with convincing him that "a newspaper must put itself on the line to help its city through the great crises."

Returning Tom's attention, Graham moved him rapidly up the ladder: a stint on the paper's promotional staff, national political reporting, then assistant city editor. Some thought he might have risen much further, but in 1956 came an offer he couldn't refuse.

With Bob Choate's hot breath on his neck, Davis Taylor knew he had to strengthen the *Globe*'s editorial staff. Tom's name had often cropped up, but his father was leery of the nepotism issue. "I can't ask him," he'd tell Davis, "you can." One evening, Davis called to invite him to join the *Globe* as Washington correspondent (which would presumably lead to an editorial position). Tom consulted a colleague, who told him, "If you want a scrap, take it. Boston's the last good newspaper fight left in the country." Tom welcomed the challenge. Weary of derisive cracks about the tired old *Globe*, he wanted to redeem his father's name; resentful of Choate's bulldozer tactics, he itched for a counterattack. Within twenty-four hours, he accepted Taylor's offer.

Taking over the Washington bureau shortly before the 1956 Democratic convention, at which Jack Kennedy made his bid for the vice-presidential nomination, Winship talked his way into the candidate's suite at the Stockyards Inn, perching on the toilet while Kennedy soaked in the tub and watched the roll call on TV. When he came within a whisker of winning, the rest of the press corps nearly beat down the door, but Tom was already inside with a nifty exclusive. Over the next two years, he got a lot of good stories out of Kennedy. It was a mutually beneficial relationship: Jack, a Massachusetts politician in pursuit of the presidency; Tom, a Massachusetts reporter in pursuit of an editorship. Happily for both, an Irish Catholic's rise to the highest office in the land was a blockbuster story back in Boston. Unlike his father, Jack harbored no animus toward the *Globe*, pragmatically using its pages whenever he could. Thus was born a natural alliance which lasted for years.

At times the *Globe* grew perilously close to the Kennedys, as in 1962 when, just as Ted announced for Jack's old Senate seat, Bob Healy heard rumors that the young candidate had once been expelled from Harvard for cheating on a Spanish exam. In three extraordinary meetings in the Oval Office, the President himself negotiated with Healy to provide material if the story was played "below the fold." Eventually it did appear just below the fold, written not as a sensational disclosure but as a low-key confession. If the story had to surface—and eventually it would have—that was surely the most acceptable format for Ted and his brother.

By then Winship was back in Boston as metropolitan editor, a new post designed to deal with an ironic turn of events. For eighty years, the *Globe* had been struggling for supremacy in Boston's crowded marketplace. Finally, in 1957, it had reached that goal, only to find it a prize not worth the contest. For Boston's inner-city population was beginning to decline, growing older, poorer, and blacker. As the *Globe* mastered that arena, the *Herald* was consolidating its hold on the exploding suburbs, then in the first fine flush of postwar prosperity. So long as Bob Choate's newspaper ruled that affluent sphere it would hold a decisive edge in advertising—and the potential for delivering on its publisher's baleful threat to the *Globe*.

Commissioned to lead the paper out of its urban captivity, Tom Winship now mounted a double-pronged assault on the *Herald*'s suburban stronghold. Under his prodding, the paper at last transcended garden club chitchat and Little League line scores to start examining the substance of suburban life. Meanwhile, he beefed up coverage of science, medicine, education, and the arts, a blandishment to the educated men and women then flocking to Massachusetts' universities, research labs, and high-technology companies.

This new perspective also gave Tom an excuse for some muckraking: examinations of the troubled state university and Boston's archaic public schools, even some long-overdue attention to municipal corruption. Such innovations provoked resistance from *Globe* veterans who had done well under the old order, notably Andy Dazzi, the classified advertising director. For years the paper's principal ambassador to politicians downtown—he had actually managed two mayoral campaigns—Dazzi and advertising manager John Reid had long kept a powerful grip on the editorial product, maintaining a blowsy spatter of nightclub and racetrack ads across the bottom of page one and ordering up puff pieces on influential advertisers. The front-page ads were a particular embarrassment to Tom Winship and he waged a relentless campaign for their removal.

In the early sixties, as he advanced through the hierarchy, Tom carried on a private dialogue with his father, still the *Globe*'s top editor. In brief communiqués, they debated news policy, headlines, and editorials. Leavened with sly family jokes and the affection of father and son, the exchange was nonetheless a contest between the old *Globe*, battling for survival, and the new *Globe*, struggling to be born. When Tom applied for assistance in getting rid of front-page ads, his father responded: "Sorry. Advts. very interesting part of Page One." When the paper began to reflect Tom's political interests, Larry warned: "You'll have to watch now that we don't give space to politics at cost of other material. Only 13 percent read politics as against 79 percent who read human interest, women's stuff and sports." And when Tom sought to drop Barry Goldwater's column, his father warned: "My feeling is that we are underestimating the circulation value of the right wing audience. Bigger than most places here, except the Bible belt." But the old man's grip was loosening. In late 1964, he scribbled: "Don't bother to call me evenings. Do what you think right and I will take the responsibility." The baton was ready to be passed.

Tom's assumption of command in 1965 coincided with another *Globe* watershed: at long last it overtook the *Herald* in suburban circulation. Soon that new balance of power was graphically revealed. The 1966 campaign for State Attorney General pitted Elliot Richardson, a Brahmin Republican, against Francis X. Bellotti, an Italian Democrat. Richardson was a Harvard skiing pal of Tom Winship's, a liberal reformer who echoed the editor's own politics—a candidate, in other words, congenial to the *Globe*'s new suburban constituency. Still bound by its self-imposed ban on political endorsements, the *Globe* nevertheless made little secret that fall where its sympathies lay. In the past, Richardson could have counted on automatic endorsement from the

Republican *Herald,* but Bob Choate was dead by then, and his successors, in their struggle for survival, had struck an alliance with Bellotti. On election morning, the *Herald* ran a front-page editorial denouncing Richardson as a "manicured Senator McCarthy" and throwing its weight behind his Democratic opponent. Two *Herald* editorial writers immediately defected to the *Globe.* Almost overnight, Boston's journalistic gladiators had reversed positions: the establishment *Herald* became the spokesman for Boston's aggrieved inner city; the shabby old *Globe,* the voice of Massachusetts' academic, technological, and social elite.

The capital of that world was across the river in Cambridge, whose dinner parties and salons Tom now frequented, forging friendships with John Kenneth Galbraith, Arthur Schlesinger, Jr., and others. Cambridge was the Massachusetts equivalent of Georgetown, where, ever since his days on the *Post,* Tom had hobnobbed with journalists like Ben Bradlee and Mary McGrory. All through the Kennedy and Johnson years, liberal intellectuals, politicians, and newsmen shuttled along the Cambridge-Georgetown axis and, increasingly, it was to those red brick enclaves that Tom Winship looked for his closest friends, his social values, his political commitments. Whatever he collected on that circuit was scrupulously recorded on a reminder pad, then scattered through the newsroom in a blizzard of story suggestions.

The Cambridge-Georgetown influence was reinforced by his four children, three of them true exemplars of the sixties, caught up in most of the demonstrations and lifestyle experiments of that tumultuous decade. Some of his kids' unorthodoxy may have come down through the maternal line, for their mother was the daughter of A. Sprague Coolidge, ardent civil libertarian, defender of Sacco and Vanzetti, a onetime candidate on the Socialist ticket. Elizabeth Coolidge, a strong-minded woman with liberal convictions, had married Tom Winship right out of college, eventually becoming a popular *Globe* columnist on teenage problems. The Winships' home in suburban Lincoln was a freewheeling place. The children had wide latitude to express themselves: in his front hallway Tom kept a photographic gallery of his kids in irreverent poses.

Tom was determined to inject some of this youthful iconoclasm into his own staff. For decades the *Globe* had been like a pudding, with a thin crust of Yankee editors, a thick custard of veteran Irish subeditors and reporters, and here and there a few raisins—an Italian, an Armenian, a Jew or two. Many of the reporters were sons of printers and mailers, for the *Globe* was a benevolent institution: the Taylors never fired anyone, and although they had fended off the Newspaper Guild, they always paid above Guild scale, with usually "a little something extra" at Christmas. It was a warm bath nobody wanted to get out of. Much of the staff Tom inherited had been soaking in it for years.

Seeking a different breed, he recruited young reporters at the *Harvard Crimson* and *Yale Daily News.* Soon the newsroom was filling up with earnest young men and women, bristling with mid-sixties visions. Tom was a quarter century their senior, his pink cheeks, sandy hair, and clear-rimmed glasses reminiscent of McGeorge Bundy, C. Douglas Dillon, and all those other scions of the Yankee establishment. But his flowered ties, red suspenders, and ankle-high boots, reinforced by the breezy idiom of an Irish politician ("Whadya say, pa? Howya doing?"), proclaimed: *I am not one of them*. Quickly establishing an easy rapport with his "city-room Weathermen," he encouraged them when they produced (with "tiger notes," beginning: "Terrific job, tiger!"), defended them at editors' conventions ("These young people still think the newspaper is one of the most effective instruments for social change; they are not in the business in order to become stenographers"), and rallied around them when they got in trouble. When one flamboyant reporter was arrested for accompa-nying—and allegedly abetting—an airdrop of supplies to militant Indians at Wounded Knee, Winship proudly asserted that the *Globe* man had been "cov-ering a legitimate news story for the paper; we are defending his right to do so." One Labor Day weekend, another young reporter was arrested by state troopers for growing marijuana in his New Hampshire backyard. The reporter called Winship at home, and the editor, wearing his favorite lounging clothes—a bright orange jumpsuit—leapt into his car, drove to the jail, and delivered a personal check for the $4,000 bail.

Winship's enthusiasm for youth occasionally got him in trouble with his own staff. Once, in a *Globe* advertisement, he declared, "All of a sudden everybody over 26 is middle-aged." That was too much for several veterans banished to the evening paper's rewrite desk. At their insistence, the publisher yanked the ad after the first edition and Winship had to sit through a grueling session with a delegation of "old-timers" demanding equal rights. Tom sol-emnly promised to mend his ways, then went right on promoting the youth movement.

By 1967, he had made the newspaper his own. Two telling blows at tradi-tion announced Winship's new *Globe:* ads were at last banished from page one, and Uncle Dudley was evicted from the editorial page. For years, Win-ship kept on his desk a small marble tombstone embossed: "Uncle Dudley, Died January 4, 1966." The first move was more dramatic, clearing the way for a bright new makeup, but the second was more significant, for Uncle Dud-ley's passing allowed the *Globe,* at last, to begin taking unequivocal stands on important issues—starting with Vietnam.

For months Winship had been hearing about Vietnam—from his kids, his Cambridge friends, the city-room Weathermen. In April 1967 he gathered all the material he could find on the messy little war and sent editorial page editor Charlie Whipple off to Vermont to read it. The result was a series of six edi-torials urging the government to bank the fires of war and seek a negotiated peace. For years to come, the *Globe* was at the cutting edge of American opinion on Vietnam: in 1968, it launched a "Draft Counselor" column to ad-vise young men on their rights; in March 1969, it devoted the entire op-ed page to an anti-war speech by Nobel Prize winner George Wald; that October it became the second major American paper to call for unilateral withdrawal; in May 1970, during the Cambodian invasion, Winship joined a delegation of

Elliot Richardson's Harvard contemporaries which called on the Under Secretary of State to express their horror at the incursion, a visit which contributed to a pronounced cooling in relations between Tom and his former skiing partner.

Not many Americans, however, were aware of the *Globe*'s trailblazing. Winship suffered from the paper's relative obscurity, feeling particular distress in 1971 after Cambridge's own Daniel Ellsberg presented the Pentagon Papers to the New York *Times* and the Washington *Post*. Three months before, the *Globe* had run a story about the still-secret report, and now Winship implored the author of that article, Tom Oliphant, to somehow get part of the Papers. Oliphant's entreaties finally reached Ellsberg. On June 21, a caller identifying himself only as "Bosbin" told Winship that if he sent one staffer to a Harvard Square phone booth, another to a booth in Newton, one of them would receive a delivery. Late that afternoon, a news editor walked into the office with a package containing 1,700 pages. After the *Globe* rushed the first installment into print, Winship received a call from Attorney General John Mitchell, who rasped, "Well, Tom, I see you're in the act too." Although the Justice Department moved to block further publication, Winship was exultant. At long last the *Globe* was, indeed, *in the act*.

It was there to stay. Richard Nixon was the perfect foil for a liberal Massachusetts newspaper, and so long as he clung to office, the *Globe* was one of his most determined antagonists. Cartoonist Paul Szep mercilessly lampooned the President as a raving paranoid with drooping jowls and sunken eyes. The Washington bureau, though breaking little of the Nixon epic, produced such aggressive coverage that the White House excluded it from the President's 1972 trip to China. The *Globe* brought special gusto to Watergate (three of its staffers were on the Enemies List), and the Monday after the Saturday Night Massacre it became the first major newspaper to demand Nixon's resignation.

But Vietnam and Watergate were relatively easy issues for the *Globe*. More perilous were political, social, and racial questions which cut to the heart of ancient Boston resentments. For decades the newspaper had scrupulously protected Catholic sensibilities, fawning on the Cardinal, even finding a job in the pressroom for Cushing's nephew. Now it campaigned for liberalization of Massachusetts' antiquated birth control law, a stand which might not offend Cushing, but surely alienated more orthodox Catholics. While once it had printed only fluffy encomiums to the city's neighborhoods, now it enlisted in Boston's urban renewal wars, backing Ed Logue in his confrontations with various ethnic interests.

But boldest of all was the *Globe*'s decision to give its first political endorsement in seventy-two years. The occasion: the daunting prospect of Louise Day Hicks as mayor of Boston. Davis Taylor and many of his Yankee editors were New England "abolitionists," quick to support the Southern civil rights movement. Although slow to act on the same principles in Boston, the *Globe* soon threw its full weight behind the struggle for school desegregation, fair housing, and equal employment practices. But its reaction to Mrs. Hicks's 1967 candidacy grew from something more than a passion for racial justice. In part it was a matter of class. The huge marshmallow of a woman in her tentlike dresses was patently from a different social order—the frumpy world of the Irish middle class that the *Globe* had only recently left behind. Her election would make Boston look like a goofy city. Ben Bradlee would say, "Hey, who's that idiot mayor you've got up there." The *Globe,* at last on its way to national recognition, would be just another bush newspaper in a bush town.

Tom Winship had no great enthusiasm for Kevin White; his personal choice for the job had been Ed Logue, an old friend from Washington days. But when Logue lost the preliminary election and the choice came down to White and Hicks, Winship decided that the *Globe* had to intervene. Charlie Whipple and Bob Healy agreed, and Davis Taylor consented on one condition. Fearing a backlash from Irish readers, he ordered that the editorial include a reference to the *Globe*'s nineteenth-century campaign to permit Catholic priests to administer last rites in Boston's hospitals, evidence that the newspaper supported "equal opportunity for all," regardless of race, religion, or ethnic background.

Meanwhile, Winship's young tigers were shattering icons right and left. For years the *Globe* had enjoyed a relationship with Harvard approximating that of *Osservatore Romano* to the Vatican. Each June, it dispatched squadrons of reporters to cover the university's commencement, scrupulously documenting how grounds keepers raised the candy-striped pavilions, what drinks alumni favored at the bars. Then, in April 1969, the Students for a Democratic Society led a strike demanding that the university sever all ties with the Pentagon and the CIA. Covering the story for the *Globe* were two young Harvard graduates who displayed sympathy for the students and skepticism toward President Nathan Pusey. Their coverage made life acutely uncomfortable for Davis Taylor, then serving on the university's Board of Overseers. Although other board members—notably journalist Teddy White—angrily demanded that he crack down on the pair, Taylor gritted his teeth and declined to interfere with Winship's news operation.

Now the *Globe* was breaking new ground daily, rapidly becoming the most countercultural of major American newspapers. One Sunday it appeared with the word—WOMEN—stripped across page one, proclaiming a special edition on feminist concerns. The Sunday magazine produced an issue on the fiftieth anniversary of the Soviet Revolution (with contributions from Communist writers), a sympathetic piece on Gay Liberation, an article on the youth culture so daring it was published by the *East Village Other* with a note: "This story is reprinted from the Boston *Globe,* not an underground newspaper." When an article about singer Janis Ian quoted lyrics from her song "New Christ Cardiac Hero," the front office warned that such blasphemy could cost the paper heavily in Catholic neighborhoods.

Any consternation the Taylors may have felt at Winship's innovations was ameliorated for the time being by the paper's new prosperity and prestige. The *Globe* had opened an impressive lead in circulation when in March 1972 came the decisive stroke it had sought for so long: completing fifteen years of litigation, the FCC found the *Herald* guilty of improper lobbying, revoked its license for Channel 5, and awarded it to a competitor. Stripped of its principal revenue producer, the *Herald* stumbled on for three more months, then sold out to Hearst, which merged the empty shell with its own daily to create the Boston *Herald American*. This left the *Globe* virtually unchallenged as New England's dominant newspaper. Meanwhile, Winship's staff embellished its reputation with two more Pulitzers: for Szep's cartooning and for a series on corruption in suburban Somerville. In January 1974, *Time* magazine named the *Globe* to its list of the nation's ten best newspapers.

Not everyone applauded the selection, for by then the *Globe* was a highly personal institution, mirroring Tom Winship's weaknesses as well as his strengths. Like him, it was obsessively political, providing superb coverage of local, state, and national campaigns, though less impressive on the performance of government, less still on foreign affairs, business, and finance. It cultivated a stable of provocative columnists—Ellen Goodman, Diane White, Martin Nolan, George Frazier—but consistently overvalued opinion and undervalued fact (at one count it ran well over a hundred columnists—syndicated and local). It developed a tough-minded investigative unit, the Spotlight Team, which uncovered judicial impropriety, "no-show" public employees, and slipshod trade schools; yet much of the paper's valuable news space was squandered on huge photographs of sandy dunes and honking geese, and a regular front-page feature called "In This Corner," devoted to such nonsense as a reporter who looked like John Denver or another who hated umbrellas. It boasted the nation's best sports pages, an unalloyed joy to fans of Carl Yastrzemski or Jim Plunkett, but if one sought to follow the work of George Balanchine or Jasper Johns, it could be maddeningly inattentive. In short, the *Globe* was erratic and capricious. But it was also ebullient, inventive, surprising, and almost never boring. Even its detractors conceded that less than a decade after assuming full control, Tom Winship had transformed the *Globe* from one of the nation's worst metropolitan newspapers into one of its best.

But even as the paper rode this crest of approbation, a powerful undertow was tugging at it from within. Most of its employees—particularly in the advertising, circulation, and mechanical departments—were conservative, working-class Catholics with no taste for Winship's bold adventures. Once, as George Wallace arrived for lunch with *Globe* editors, a crowd of printers gathered in the lobby to applaud him. "I only hope I get as good a reception upstairs," said the Alabama Governor. "Don't count on it, George," said a husky linotypist. On several occasions, printers and mailers refused to handle stories they found objectionable. Even middle-level editors and veteran reporters rankled at Winship's alarums and excursions, which they labeled "Tomfoolery." The newsroom was split down the middle, as much by style as by politics. Dismayed at their sudden obsolescence, the old-timers nipped on pints of scotch stowed in their bottom drawers while Winship's "hippie reporters" smoked pot in the men's rooms, banana peels on the roof. The *Kultur-*

kampf claimed its first casualties when an editor was discovered to have had an affair with a reporter who worked for him, which resulted in her pregnancy. Reaching the limits of their toleration, the Taylors fired the editor. The reporter says that when she insisted on having her child out of wedlock, she was "fired" too (the *Globe* says she resigned).

Soon word percolated through the paper that Tom Winship himself was in trouble with the front office. More orderly and politically conservative than his father, young Bill Taylor was dismayed by Tom's ostentatious nonconformity and slapdash administration. Insiders believed that once Bill became publisher he would look for a new editor, but that may have been averted through some unusual mediation. Bill's cousin Charles Taylor had been provost of Yale before abruptly abandoning academia to become a Jungian analyst in New York. Now the call went out for Charlie, who commuted to Boston for several years, serving as a kind of "court psychiatrist," helping his cousin and Tom Winship move from mutual suspicion to tenuous accommodation.

Eventually both men concluded that Winship's tendency to spontaneous combustion needed to be balanced by a new sense of rigor and discipline. This seemed particularly imperative as Boston's approaching school desegregation crisis confronted the *Globe* with a complex story which would make heavy demands on its professionalism. Fortuitously, in that winter of 1973–74 an editor was available who possessed precisely the qualities the *Globe* was looking for. Bob Phelps had been with the New York *Times* for more than nineteen years, the past eight as deputy chief of its Washington bureau. A meticulous editor, scrupulously attentive to detail, he was particularly adept at communicating his seasoned judgment to young reporters. But this very circumspection could prove a liability in the helter-skelter of a breaking story, and Phelps became a scapegoat for the *Times*'s disappointing performance on Watergate. Passed over for bureau chief, he concluded that the time had come to look elsewhere. Christopher Lydon, a former *Globe* reporter then with the *Times*, alerted Winship, who scribbled a note to Phelps: "I'm told I'd be a damned fool if I didn't see you. Why don't you come up and talk with me?" After prolonged negotiations, Phelps received the title of assistant managing editor for metropolitan news. Yet it occurred to him that the *Globe* wasn't so much hiring Bob Phelps as it was hiring the New York *Times*, that what it wanted was the *Times*'s reputation for objectivity imprinted on the busing story.

The *Globe* had ample reason for concern. For more than a decade its coverage of Boston's racial turmoil had been skewed toward the black community. When a black child was confined in a school cloakroom with tape over her mouth, the *Globe* kept the story alive for more than a week, using it to dramatize the plight of minority pupils in a white system. But when young Negroes disrupted a School Committee meeting, black leaders objected to the front-page coverage and the paper beat a hasty retreat. Unlike many papers which strictly separated news and editorial page operations, the *Globe* kept them united under Tom Winship. "We were pretty shameless in using the news columns to show how we felt," recalls one reporter. "The *Globe* was on the side of the angels then, and all the angels were black."

This sympathy found unusual institutional expression. After blacks hooted Louise Day Hicks off the stage of Campbell Junior High in June 1966, one Boston television station ran film of the episode narrated by Mrs. Hicks herself. This so alarmed black leaders that they turned to their one sure ally in the white media, meeting for three hours with the Taylors and Tom Winship. Assured of *Globe* support, they dispatched telegrams to every newspaper and television and radio station in town, over the signature of Celtics star Bill Russell, warning that Boston risked a ghetto uprising like those in Watts and Harlem. On June 24, forty editors and news executives met for breakfast at Russell's restaurant. The blacks had good reason to complain, for most Boston papers barely covered the ghetto (for years, when a legman called the Hearst city desk with a juicy crime, a rewriteman would ask, "Is it dark out there?"— meaning "Is the victim black?" If the answer was yes, the reporter was told to forget it). Now the blacks demanded some far-reaching changes: the hiring of staff reporters to cover all phases of black life; more attention to the "positive side" of the community; increased employment of blacks in the press; and a media-community committee "so that we can get to know you and have you know us before the crises develop." When the editors concurred, Tom Winship enthusiastically accepted election as co-chairman of the new Boston Community Media Committee.

For two years the committee limped along with modest results. Then in early 1968 two events lent it a fresh sense of purpose. One was the Kerner Report, which condemned reporters and editors for failing to communicate "the degradation, misery and hopelessness of life in the ghetto." The other was the assassination of Martin Luther King, with its violent echo in Boston's streets. Shortly after King's death, the council convened 120 black and media representatives for a weekend conference in New Hampshire. In an apocalyptic mood, accentuated by Robert Kennedy's assassination, they met virtually nonstop for three days, descending from their green hillside with a new zeal to confront Boston's racial crisis.

Nowhere was that sense of urgency more acute than at the *Globe*. After King's assassination, Davis Taylor pleaded with downtown department stores to underwrite the emergency telecast of James Brown's concert, "if only for your plate-glass windows." Meanwhile, the *Globe* took a hard look at its news staff—then employing just two blacks above the rank of clerk—and immediately recruited four Negro interns from the University of Massachusetts. Desperate for seasoned black hands, Winship reached into the *Globe*'s own circulation department for a former NAACP public relations man named Dexter Eure to write the paper's first black column, "Tell It Like It Is." Soon after the New Hampshire conference, Winship loaned Eure to the media council as its temporary executive director.

In years to come, the committee proved an uneasy alliance. Blacks expressed dismay because Boston's press continued to reflect "the biases, paternalism and indifference of white middle-class America." Media members bridled at the "excessive demands and overheated rhetoric" of black leaders. Although the *Globe* developed doubts about the undertaking, it stuck with it through the early seventies, dispatching senior editors to meetings, supplying a lion's share of the budget, remaining publicly identified with what one editor called "the press's effort to atone for 200 years of injustice to black Americans."

The newspaper's position was further revealed in its attitude toward the Irish working class. When Charlestown demonstrators staged a noisy demonstration at City Council hearings on the urban renewal plan, the *Globe* ran a column in the form of a letter from a Townie woman named "Daisy" to her sister "Mazie" in the suburbs. "Wow [it went in part], what a ball we had! Wish you were there. Us loyal Townies almost tore the roof off City Hall. You'd have been proud of us, Mazie, only Ma says it was terrible the way we booed the priests and ministers. But that was our strategy—keep the other side bottled up. Boo them. Yell them down and don't give them a chance to talk. Ma is old-fashioned, you know. She doesn't know anything about democracy in action—ha, ha."

Now and then, the *Globe* made a gesture toward inner-city ethnics. In the late sixties, it joined City Hall in a sudden rediscovery of Boston's neighborhoods, establishing an "Urban Team," running series on white communities like East Boston and Charlestown, lending reportorial—if not always editorial—support to the battles against airport expansion and highway construction, though giving no ground on racial issues.

As the busing crisis neared, the *Globe* invoked its nineteenth-century support of Irish rights with increasing frequency. "We have decried the double standard at every turn," it said in a 1973 editorial supporting the racial imbalance law. "It's wrong when used to exclude blacks from certain schools now, just as it was wrong in our early days when job advertisements carried the tag N.I.N.A., meaning No Irish Need Apply. We refused all ads from businesses which used that label." But this recital of favors past only intensified current resentments. Like the Catholic Church, the Democratic Party, and the Kennedys, the *Globe* seemed to have deserted Boston's Irish in their hour of need.

By the time Bob Phelps arrived in April 1974, white backlash already was threatening to swamp the *Globe* in a tide of indignation. Determined to wrest the paper off its perilous course, Phelps wasted no time in shifting direction. At a *Globe* "think tank" that May he asserted that the paper was going to be "fair" and "balanced," that it would present "all sides" of every issue. In line with the *Times*'s traditional separation of news and opinion, Phelps said he never read editorials. "I don't want to know what the *Globe* thinks about the news," he said. "I just want the news."

Those who chafed at Tom Winship's unbridled enthusiasms were delighted by Phelps's advocacy of professionalism; those thriving under Winship's loose rein were dismayed by the specter of oppressive editing. One of those whom Phelps made uneasy was Dexter Eure, by then the *Globe*'s director of community relations and its principal liaison with black leadership. In the discussion that followed Phelps's speech, Eure asked him how he could direct the *Globe*'s busing coverage if he didn't know anything about the minority community. It was both a question and an accusation, and Phelps tried to defuse it with a quip. "Don't tell me about minorities," he said. "I'm more of a minority than you are. I'm part American Indian."

In fact, Phelps did have some Seneca blood in his veins. But the quip failed to reassure—or amuse—blacks on the staff. Once at a staff meeting Phelps suggested that everyone choose an Indian name. Most of the writers went along, but when it was Carmen Fields's turn, the young black woman glared up the table at Phelps. "Black Foot," she said. "And Black Arms. And Black Legs. And Black Head. And Black Neck."

In the face of such misgivings, Phelps made several structural changes in the editorial operation. He established a "story editor" system to compensate for the *Globe*'s notoriously weak copy desk. In June 1974, every reporter was assigned to one of four story editors, who closely supervised his articles from inception to publication. And he stopped reporters from doubling as columnists, covering a news event one day, coming back the next with subjective commentary. Most of the reporters were not pleased; they saw Phelps's innovations as a shift from what had long been a "writer's paper" to a more rigidly controlled "editor's paper."

Winship himself was unimpressed by Phelps's punctilio—he had never been one to sacrifice excitement for order—but he let the new man have his way. For Tom was more worried than he acknowledged about the *Globe*'s capacity to cover the impending busing confrontation. That spring he dispatched Bob Healy to newspapers in four cities—Denver, Detroit, San Francisco, and Riverside, California—which had experienced school desegregation. On his return, Healy produced a confidential memo describing what each paper had learned. Among other things, he concluded: "It is important that someone, other than the newspaper, play a leadership role in support of school integration. . . . Make sure that black attitudes on busing are known. No one should get too far ahead of the black position. . . . As the time for implementation of the system approaches, anticipated violence and the statements of violence should be carefully avoided in the news columns. . . . Finally, it might be a good idea for a *Globe* editor to live in Boston."

The last point particularly worried Winship. Of the paper's top twenty editors, all but two lived in the suburbs. Chris Lydon had urged his friend Bob Phelps to live in the city, where he could learn its ethnic and class attitudes firsthand, but, ardent ornithologists, the Phelpses bought a home not far from Winship in Lincoln. Even Irish reporters generally settled at one remove from the inner city in enclaves like Scituate and Hingham. The *Globe*'s prevailing voice was that of a Harvard-educated lawyer from the suburbs—affable, humane, and well intentioned, but no longer entirely comfortable in the city of his youth.

Irish politicians loved to twit the *Globe* about its suburban orientation.

State Senator Billy Bulger, an acerbic wit from South Boston, regaled audiences with an apocryphal anecdote: "I was talking with Tom Winship not long ago. I said, 'Mr. Winship, how do you know so much about Boston?' He said, 'Well, we have an Urban Team.' I said, 'How can I get in touch with them?' And he said, 'You just call the regular number during the day, and in the evening you dial long-distance.'"

Such gibes cost Tom some sleepless nights. The critics had a legitimate beef, he thought. Originally he had favored a metropolitan plan under which city children would be bused to the suburbs and vice versa, but once the Supreme Court barred such "cross-district" busing in the Detroit case and the *Globe* began lecturing city dwellers about their obligations under Garrity's order, Winship wondered whether he ought to be living in a rambling farmhouse at the end of a wooded lane in Lincoln. (What fun the Irish pols would have if they knew that the two Vermont Morgans grazing in Tom's pasture were named Seamus and Clancy.) During that summer of 1974, riding the 7:52 train to work each morning, he toyed with the idea of buying a house in the city, but his wife was more committed to country living, less afflicted by liberal guilt. They stayed where they were.

The *Globe*'s anxiety was aggravated that summer by pressure from a newly aroused Boston Community Media Committee. At an all-day meeting on July 10, black members demanded that the press commit itself to "implementation of the law," express its commitment through both "advocacy journalism and straight reporting," and "use its awesome power to influence leaders in the private sector." The press agreed to work toward these ends. That summer president John I. Taylor represented the *Globe* at a series of meetings designed to assure that the press play a "positive role" in the fall's events.

An ad hoc committee went to work with indisputable vigor, consulting other "opinion leaders," distributing 50,000 bumper stickers which read: "Take it easy, for the kids' sake," cooperating with Boston's Advertising Club in the production of radio-TV spots on which sports heroes like Bobby Orr and Carl Yastrzemski drawled, "It's not going to be easy, but that never stopped Boston."

Meanwhile, black demands were reinforced by pressure from Mayor White, who had both institutional and political reasons to play down any violence that might develop in the autumn. In two meetings with media representatives and two more with "on-air talent"—none of which was publicly reported—White and his aides urged the press to handle racial incidents judiciously, avoid any language or pictures which might exacerbate tensions, and put the best possible face on desegregation.

These proposals found their readiest acceptance among radio and television executives, who viewed the committee as a convenient means of satisfying FCC requirements that they respond to community needs. Not burdened by such considerations, newspapermen were more wary of "pack journalism," more alive to the dangers of "news management." By midsummer, several *Globe* representatives had raised warnings about the process. But the Ad Hoc Committee—with John Taylor's participation—plunged ahead with its most controversial project, a "Boston Media Statement" proclaiming the press's own commitment to the court order. Early that summer, it drafted a declaration which said, in part, "We shall spare no effort, nor overlook any resource at our disposal, to ensure that everything possible is done to make integration work . . . because the law tells us it is right and necessary." Eventually cooler heads prevailed, settling on more modest language: "We need all Bostonians to help make school opening this September safe and quiet. We have a mandate from the federal court to desegregate our schools. Some of us agree with that decision; some of us don't. But there is one thing we can all agree with; we love our children and we want no harm to come to them. We all must come together to that end, because it is our kids that count." Signed by twenty newspaper, television, and radio executives—John Taylor for the *Globe*—it was released on August 25, just two weeks before the first buses rolled.

Later, press critics would submit that statement as evidence that Boston's media had compromised their credibility by engaging in cooperative efforts verging on self-censorship. There could be little doubt that some institutions temporarily abandoned objectivity. The *Herald American*'s lead story on the morning school opened read like a sermon: "The safety of 94,000 children and the salvation of Boston's historic standing as a community of reasonable and law-abiding families are at stake today as the city reopens its public schools." Lovell Dyett, operations manager of the NBC outlet, put it most explicitly when he said, "We are going to use television to create an atmosphere of compliance with Judge Garrity's order."

The *Globe*'s position was more complicated. Bob Phelps, with his *Times*-ian sense of propriety, had no use for either the Media Committee's or the Mayor's exhortations, assiduously keeping his distance from both. When *Time* magazine later suggested that the *Globe* had been part of a civic conspiracy to "play it cool" and "downplay any incidents of violence," Phelps and Winship were furious.

But the *Globe* needed no conspiracy for it to treat the busing story with special care. For generations the Taylors had never doubted they were citizens of Boston first and newspapermen second. In Tom Winship that tradition was reinforced by Phil Graham's brand of liberal activism. Since the early sixties, when it lobbied for Ed Logue's appointment as Redevelopment director, then got him the resources he needed, the *Globe* had rarely hesitated to put its muscle behind objectives it regarded as salutary. Uninhibited by traditional journalistic objectivity, which he once described as "a code word for playing it safe," Tom Winship periodically mobilized his news pages for crusades to control handguns or prohibit the sale of beverages in non-returnable bottles. Behind the scenes, Winship and Healy cooperated with Kevin White, Frank Sargent, and other officeholders on projects to advance the public weal. Prospective candidates, zealous legislators, advocates of every stripe danced attendance on the *Globe,* seeking its patronage. If power-conscious Bostonians had once asked, "What does Lake Street think?", now they wondered, "What does Morrissey Boulevard say?"

To Davis Taylor and Tom Winship alike, the *Globe*'s responsibility in that fall of 1974 was clear: to guide Boston through its travail with the least possible injury to all parties. In mid-August, Phelps drafted and Winship issued an extraordinary document, a "Memo to All Hands" containing thirteen "guidelines" for busing coverage. Taken one by one, most were journalistic platitudes: "We talk to all sources dispassionately, keeping our views to ourselves," "We check out rumors and tips, not print[ing] them unless substantiated." But some reflected unusual anxiety: "In such a delicate situation, it is imperative that headlines be scrupulously accurate, that headline words be chosen with delicacy . . ." "The editing of stories regarding the integration situation also should be done with utmost care." And some seemed significant precisely because Phelps and Winship felt it necessary to say them out loud: "We print an accurate record of what our reporting finds. If there is violence, we say so. . . . We do not suppress news because it doesn't fit our views of what we hope happens. . . . Above all, we must remember that the Boston *Globe*'s credibility is at stake. Our news columns must be believed—not just by those who agree with our editorial policy, but by those who disagree. Our aim is to convince all that the *Globe* is committed to the goal of seeking out the truth."

A few days later, when assignments for the opening day of school were handed out, veteran *Globe* staffers were flabbergasted at the battle plan Phelps had devised: a small army of reporters—sixty in all—was to be deployed across the city, manning every site of potential trouble. "You almost got the feeling that by covering every base, we were covering our own asses," one reporter recalled. "We were suffering one of the most massive cases of corporate angst in history."

Despite this meticulous preparation—or perhaps precisely because of it—the *Globe*'s opening-day coverage set off acrimonious debate both within and outside the newspaper. Although angry crowds had stoned black children in South Boston, injuring nine and leading the Mayor to prohibit gatherings of three or more persons, the *Globe* appeared the next morning with a reassuring headline: "Boston Schools Desegregated, Opening Day Generally Peaceful." The lead story emphasized "a minimum of confusion and disruption throughout the city," saving South Boston's troubles for the third paragraph. Page one was dominated by a large picture of black and white elementary students bathed in ethereal light as they got acquainted in a school yard, while the *Globe*'s lead editorial, headlined "A Fine Beginning," suggested that the day's events "had to be regarded as a plus." The *Herald American* took a similar tack, as did most local television and radio stations.

This contrasted sharply with the national media, most of which focused relentlessly on the disruptions. "Violence Mars Busing in Boston," headlined the New York *Times* over a story by its Boston correspondent, John Kifner, who opened with "Rock throwing, jeering crowds in South Boston," waiting for the second paragraph to report that "other parts of the city were calm."

Soon recriminations were flying back and forth, the national press accusing the locals of cover-up, Bostonians charging out-of-towners with yellow journalism. One confrontation took place at Harvard, where *Globe* editors and national reporters gathered to discuss busing coverage. Late in the evening, after several drinks had been consumed, Bob Phelps got into a heated altercation with the *Times*'s Kifner.

"You covered that first day like a police reporter," Phelps chided. "The real story was that seventy-nine out of eighty schools were completely peaceful, but you focused on the one that had trouble."

"Sure," Kifner shot back. "If 3,000 jets take off on a given day and all but one land safely, you don't write, '2,999 Airliners Arrive at Destinations,' you write 'Jet Crash Kills 200.'"

"But airliners land safely every day," Phelps retorted. "This wasn't a routine event, it was an important test. If you test 100 missiles and 99 of them perform adequately, you don't write, 'One Missile Crashes,' you write, '99 Percent Hit Targets.'"

There was something to be said for each position. But nothing could exonerate the *Globe* in the eyes of Boston's embattled Celts. A decade of liberal causes—civil rights, Vietnam, the youth culture, women's liberation—had irrevocably eroded the Irish neighborhoods' faith in the newspaper they had once called their own. The paper's positions on birth control, abortion, gay rights, pornography, and the like eventually led the Massachusetts Council of the Knights of Columbus to condemn its "irreligious attitude toward all things Catholic." And now *Globe* editorials were hammering relentlessly at the resisting white parents, warning them that their anti-busing position was not only illegal but immoral. Tom Winship had the final word on editorial policy, but most of these dissertations were the work of a determined Yankee named Anne C. Wyman. The *Globe*'s one true Brahmin (her *C* stood for Cabot), she lived on a Cambridge hillside from which she viewed the busing issue in starkly moral terms. Hers was the "Cotton Mather position," by which she meant, "If it's right, it's right. Once you embark on the course, there's no turning back."

But it was less the paper's editorials that nettled South Boston and Charlestown than the abstraction with which the *Globe* covered such communities, rarely capturing their gritty intensity, their sense of turf, their smoldering resentment. Traditionally, the *Globe* approached its fragmented city through a corps of emissaries. Eager that every racial and ethnic community feel represented in its pages, it used society writer Alison Arnold to address the Yankees, Leo Shapiro the Jews, Dexter Eure the blacks, Bob Healy the Irish. For years Healy took this responsibility seriously, arguing that the *Globe*'s essential constituency was "Joe Six-pack," the Irish Catholic father of six who lived in a Dorchester three-decker, attended his parish church, drank at the neighborhood tavern. But once Healy got a Nieman Fellowship, began lecturing at the Institute of Politics and playing squash at the Harvard Club, he eagerly shouldered all the liberal banners. Nobody could be as tough on his co-religionists: "If they don't like integration," he'd say, "we'll shove it down their throats." Joe Six-pack might find solace in the *Globe*'s more conventional micks—Dave Farrell, a shrewd practitioner of clubhouse politics, and Jeremiah Murphy, a sentimental raconteur of Gaelic legend—but most of the street-wise Irishmen left on the paper were aging veterans shunted aside by Winship's youth movement. The young Ivy Leaguers who now filled the newsroom were ill at ease in the Irish neighborhoods, unable to belly up to the bar with longshoremen and truck drivers. The handful of reporters who still lived in the city had long since removed their children from the public schools and could feel little connection to families still trapped by those dismal institutions. Desperate for someone to cover the thankless "anti-busing" beat, Phelps had turned that summer of 1974 to a New York Jew named Bob Sales, widely regarded as one of the paper's savviest reporters. But Phelps and Sales were temperamentally incompatible. By September the *Globe* had nobody assigned full-time to cover ROAR and its allies.

One of the few staffers at home in Southie's taverns was columnist Mike Barnicle, an engaging young Irishman hired directly off the political circuit, where he had written speeches for John Tunney and Ed Muskie. On the first day of busing, Barnicle stationed himself across the street from South Boston High, blending easily with a crowd of angry whites, some of them brandishing sticks and bottles. That afternoon he wrote a vivid column filled with quotes like "Goddamned niggers! Why don't you go to school in Africa!" Fearing that such unvarnished realism would only inflame the situation, Winship killed the column. Later he dropped three more commentaries and two Szep cartoons in an effort to stem the angry tide lapping at the *Globe*'s doorstep.

But it was too late. Anti-busing leaders kept the movement's wrath focused on the *Globe*, State Senator Billy Bulger denouncing its "paternalism" and "contempt for the Boston resident," School Committeeman John Kerrigan labeling it "a corrupt and immoral newspaper," its reporters "maggots of the media." After several reporters covering South Boston were threatened by angry crowds, the *Globe* removed the paper's name from the side of staff cars and developed a special SOS—"Bulldog!"—which could be shouted across its walkie-talkie network. Though editors did not sanction subterfuge, some reporters when challenged said they worked for the *Christian Science Monitor*. But no stratagem could deflect Southie's rage. For weeks the *Globe* received bomb threats almost nightly, causing lengthy searches and evacuations. Other callers threatened to kidnap several Taylor children, to break one reporter's kneecaps, to kill both Phelps and Winship.

ROAR sought to harness this anger to a citywide boycott of the *Globe*. In mid-October, three men made the rounds of South Boston newsdealers warning that if they continued to carry the paper, their stores would be firebombed. A police investigation produced no arrests, but several dealers refused to stock the *Globe* and newsstand sales in the neighborhood fell off sharply. Meanwhile, anti-*Globe* graffiti sprouted on walls and roadways: "Print the Truth," "Mash the Maggots." Over the next few months the paper's circulation in the city declined by 15,000, about 12 percent of its Boston readership, though barely 3 percent of total sales. Although some of this decline stemmed from a simultaneous rise in subscription prices, the boycott probably cost the *Globe* 7,000 readers. A modest loss, scarcely threatening the paper's preeminence, it might have been larger were it not for the immense popularity of the *Globe* sports pages in the very neighborhoods most angered by its busing coverage.

The boycott, the gunshots, the hijackings and threats were alarming evidence that the *Globe* was terribly out of touch with part of its community. That fall Bob Phelps submitted a memo to Davis Taylor analyzing the newspaper's dilemma. "The *Globe* does not know the people and the neighborhoods of Boston the way it should," he wrote. "We are part of the establishment that has lost close touch with the people that we used to have. There are others in Boston who have also lost that close touch—the business and professional community. It's time for all of us to learn more about our neighbors."

Soon readers got their first intimation of the debate splitting the *Globe*'s executive ranks. On October 12, Crocker Snow expressed in a column some of the doubts he had voiced in memos to Winship and Davis Taylor. Opening with a lyrical description of ducks silhouetted against a scarlet sunset near his North Shore home, he noted that "twenty miles south as a duck flies, the same setting sun glints off the hoods of burning cars at Mission Hill and the blue plastic riot helmets of the TPF. . . . It is all in the nature of a self-fulfilling prophecy, like a horrible quicksand drawing the city down." His portrait of a city straining in the yoke of an unworkable court order was hardly calculated to ingratiate him with Tom Winship. Placed in the front office as an advocate for the editorial outlook, Crocker seemed now to be lining up with the business side. That evening Winship wrote him a note: "I thought the first thing you learned in journalism school was to substantiate your charges. The kind of patent generality included here is worse than nothing."

One line in Crocker's column which particularly irritated Winship was a suggestion that opponents of busing were appealing to a "higher moral calling, a personal one, like the war resisters and draft evaders [whom the liberals] cheered all the way to Sweden." That was a persistent theme in the *Globe*'s painful reappraisal that fall: how—some in-house critics asked—could a newspaper which so enthusiastically supported civil disobedience against Southern segregation and the Vietnam War condemn Boston's mothers for using similar techniques against a court order they considered unjust? As the staff debated, Bob Phelps had a reporter put the question to sixties activists, who proved similarly divided. "God, it's terribly hard to judge these women," replied Mrs. Malcolm Peabody, who had spent two nights in a St. Augustine jail in 1964. "I still think that what Martin Luther King said was right—that you could disobey the laws of the land if you had to, if you did so openly, and were prepared to take the punishment." But Jonathan Kozol, who had gained national attention in 1967 with his indictment of Boston's schools, said,

"We're seeing today not civil disobedience in its classic sense—moral action taken by choice, driven by love, devoid of fear—but mob terror and decades of miseducation, stirred by demagogues, preplanned by those who feed on hate."

This, in turn, raised the troubling issue of class. Some critics contended that in passionately supporting middle-class draft resisters, the *Globe* had failed to note that it was working-class youths who fought—and died—in Vietnam. Now those same observers argued that, in vehemently backing Garrity's busing order, the paper was once more putting the burden on those least prepared to bear it.

One *Globe* man who rarely overlooked class was Mike Barnicle. Cultivating a Breslinesque rhetoric ("He was of politics, this Patrick J. McDonough. He was Irish. He was Catholic. He was Democrat. He was human") and his own brand of pugnacity, Barnicle loved to attack the establishment, particularly such symbols of Yankee privilege as Harvard, the First National Bank, orange Volvos, Earth Shoes, and wine lists. There was a certain irony in all this, for Barnicle himself was anything but proletarian—for years he lived in the suburbs, drove foreign cars, hobnobbed with Cambridge literati. But one of his suburban friends was Robert Coles, the psychiatrist and author, who had been pondering the class dimensions of busing. In mid-October, Barnicle did a lengthy interview with Coles, who boldly defied liberal orthodoxy. "The busing is a scandal," Coles said. "I do not think that busing should be imposed like this on working-class people exclusively. It should cross these lines and people in the suburbs should share it. . . . The ultimate reality is the reality of class. And to talk about [busing] only in terms of racism is to miss the point. . . . [Working-class whites and blacks] are both competing for a very limited piece of the pie, the limits of which are being set by the larger limits of class which allow them damn little, if anything."

Tom Winship—who agonized over his paper's suburban orientation and supported the notion of metropolitan busing—devoted the entire op-ed page to Coles's interview, stirring up a storm of protest in liberal circles. Yet, regarding the city through thick panes of bulletproof glass, *Globe* editors saw little choice but to seek an understanding with the white working class. In mid-October, a curious item began appearing regularly: "The Boston *Globe* wants to receive suggestions and ideas as well as information about events and incidents related to the city's wide-ranging school busing program. . . . All letters will be read by a *Globe* editor. The information will be considered in the paper's coverage of this complex and controversial subject." Bob Phelps and assistant executive editor Jack Driscoll visited South Boston, Charlestown, and Dorchester for "coffee klatches" with parents, while Tom Winship invited ROAR's Virginia Sheehy to lunch, then published two of her fiesty pronouncements on the op-ed page.

In the following months, the *Globe* intervened still more directly, using its power in a determined effort to ease the city's agony. Bob Phelps and Tom Winship held off-the-record sessions with Judge Garrity. Healy and Winship called on Cardinal Medeiros, urging him to mobilize the "moderate Catholic middle." Winship lunched with attorneys for the black plaintiffs, suggesting that they accept the Masters' Plan. And at one critical juncture, Winship telephoned Kevin White to propose a city-sponsored Procession Against Violence. When the Mayor accepted the suggestion, the *Globe*—without disclosing its own role in the matter—urged Bostonians to turn out for what "could be the most important show of faith and unity this city has ever witnessed." Two days later, the Mayor appointed Davis Taylor to a thirteen-member Committee on Violence "to delve into the causes of racial violence and find ways to reduce the hostility."

Despite the *Globe*'s best efforts, the violence only intensified, drawing the paper further into the contradictions of its "balance" policy. Once, when a white man was dragged from his car and severely beaten by a gang of black youths, the *Globe* buried its three-paragraph account on an inside page. Almost immediately, the switchboard lit up with outraged calls, many of them noting that, two weeks before, the *Globe* had given banner headlines to a similar attack by white youths on a black man. The *Globe* responded with severity, demoting the responsible editor, publishing an abject *mea culpa* on page one: "The *Globe*'s policy is to report the news as fully and fairly as possible, without manipulating or slanting of any kind. But there can be many a slip between policy and practice. And this is what happened here. Poor judgment prevailed . . . and it cannot be excused." Yet this merely drew a salvo from the other camp, which charged the *Globe* with "exaggerating black violence."

In its frantic efforts to offend no one, the *Globe* somehow managed to offend everyone. Gradually the clamor from all sides took its toll. Skittish and defensive, the paper retreated to a mechanical evenhandedness, keeping a running count of column inches devoted to "pro-black" and "pro-white" stories, trying to keep them approximately equal. Afraid that its news judgment wouldn't be trusted, it no longer sought to reach a consensus on each day's events, relying instead on a thorough recapitulation of the police blotter. Diligent in its collection of data, meticulous about covering all angles, it trusted that somehow the truth would emerge from the welter of fact.

On May 5, 1975, the *Globe* was rewarded with the most prestigious of all journalism awards, the Pulitzer Prize Gold Medal for Meritorious Public Service, given for "massive and balanced coverage of the Boston school desegregation conflict in a bitterly emotional climate." The jurors concluded that the *Globe* had "withstood pressures from both pro- and anti-busing forces to put the issue into perspective and inform the public impartially." To Tom Winship and Bob Phelps, the prize came as splendid vindication, an exquisite compensation for months of anguish. But there was no celebration in the newsroom that afternoon. Editors and reporters alike agreed that the *Globe* must not seem to be profiting from the city's ordeal. As Davis Taylor issued a sober statement acknowledging Boston's travail, the newspaper did everything but apologize for its award.

That evening, several of the *Globe*'s unreconstructed Irishmen, victims of the youth movement and utterly cynical about the Winship regime, adjourned to their favorite watering hole, a noisy Italian restaurant called the Venetian Gardens. After numerous drinks and irreverent toasts, one of the newsmen, gazing deep into his shot glass, pronounced a private epitaph on the day's events. "That's not a Pulitzer Prize," he concluded, "it's a goddamn Purple Heart."

25

Twymon

When Alva Walker was nine years old, a brother took her Raggedy Ann and stuffed it in a pot of greens simmering on the stove. By suppertime, the doll was a shriveled crone.

Growing up in a family of eight children, Alva had to watch her playthings carefully. She begged her parents for a dollhouse in which to keep her treasured possessions, and her father, who could do almost anything with his hands, hinted that he might build her one. Her mother said she'd try to get one from the Cooper Community Center. But Christmases and birthdays passed without a dollhouse.

When she was fifteen and had outgrown such childish things, Alva went off to spend a year with her uncle Moses Baker in New Haven. A meticulous man who maintained a spick-and-span establishment near the Yale campus, Moses insisted on having his plates warmed before each meal, his pictures hanging just so on the walls. From him, Alva learned to appreciate the good life.

Gradually her childhood yearning for a dollhouse gave way to an adult obsession with a house of her own. In her dreams, it was a white clapboard cottage with green shutters, a big elm tree on the front lawn, and a white picket fence; in such a house, she would be secure from the vicissitudes of city life. But Alva realized that she would have to labor for such rewards. When she was sixteen, she quit high school to work at Schrafft's candy factory in Charlestown, remaining there for eighteen months until she married Vernon Kinch and went off with him to Waterbury, Connecticut. But the marriage didn't last; in 1959, while Alva was pregnant with her second child, Vernon left her.

Back in Boston, she went to work at the Goddess Bra Company, where her mother and sister had also been employed. But Alva had no intention of getting trapped in a subsistence-level job. Determined to break into "high tech," where the real money was, she began wiring computers at an RCA plant in suburban Needham while studying computer programming and getting her high school diploma at night. Meanwhile, she had begun seeing an amiable North Carolinian named Otis Debnam. In 1962, Alva and Otis set up housekeeping in a five-room apartment on Calder Street. In 1965, they had a child, Otis Jr., and when Alva's divorce became final in 1973, they were married.

Relentless in their pursuit of better things, the Debnams worked around the clock, each holding two jobs. Otis worked as a bank courier during the day and for a rubber company in Newton at night. In 1974, Alva became a computer operator at Gillette, while doing data processing at night for the Boston School Department.

For Alva, in particular, it was an arduous schedule. Gillette was headquartered in South Boston, hostile territory for blacks, requiring vigilance as she came and went. She was the first black as well as the first woman ever to work in the company's computer room. The white men who sat all around her were predictably resentful, most of them refusing to show her the ropes, even to speak with her. But it was a good job, with a decent salary. Alva had plans for that money.

Her co-workers weren't the only ones who resented Alva's ambition. Her sister Rachel Twymon took each of Alva's advances as a personal affront. Ever since they were children, the Walker girls had sniffed at each other's pretensions. To Rachel, Alva was "Miss Astor," living well above her means; to Alva, Rachel was "Miss Rich Bitch," going to theaters and fancy restaurants while living off her welfare check. Alva kept noting that Rachel made her daughters' clothes, until Cassandra and Little Rachel were ashamed of their "mammy-made" dresses. Rachel asked Alva's daughters how their mother could afford to buy so many new clothes from Lerner's and Filene's; what man was she getting the money from now? Any affinity that remained between the two women was snuffed out by the bitter wrangle over Little Rachel's baby. By the mid-seventies, Big Rachel was barely speaking to her "highfalutin sister."

That didn't faze Alva, who was ready to make her next move. The Calder Street apartment had grown cramped for two adults and three school-age children. With Alva and Otis each bringing in two salaries and paying a hefty share to Uncle Sam, they needed tax deductions. Everything pointed toward the house Alva had always wanted. In July 1975, they began their search, concentrating on that part of Southeast Boston from Dorchester through Mattapan into which the black ghetto had been expanding for more than a decade.

Alva did the looking, most of it through a realtor named Charlie Butts, who had extensive listings in the area. Several mornings a week, someone from the Butts agency took her around to examine houses. She began in Mattapan, the nicest of the neighborhoods now opening up to blacks, but most properties there were single-family homes, well out of the Debnams' price range. They needed a two-family house, so that income from the second unit could help pay their mortgage.

One morning in August, Alva visited 185 Centre Street in the Codman Square section of Dorchester. A three-story frame house painted battleship gray with white trim around doors and windows, it had a sloping shingle roof, a small front porch, a patch of grass and shrubs surrounded by a neat picket fence. The owners, a white couple named Jim and Bertha McKenna, lived in seven rooms on the top two floors, renting the ground unit to an elderly white couple. They were asking $25,000.

Alva knew this was the one she wanted. When Otis saw the house a few days later, he agreed. They put $900 down, getting an FHA-insured loan for the rest. The Debnams moved into their new home on January 24, 1976.

On Sunday evening, February 1, Alva and Otis entertained their first guests—Mike Davis, a cousin of Alva's first husband, and Charlie Lane, Mike's brother-in-law. After supper the four sat down at the kitchen table for a bout of whist, a game long popular in the Walker family. Just as Mike and Otis ran an impressive streak of diamond trumps, there was an excited knock at the door. It was Frank Leonard, the downstairs tenant, shouting, "Mrs. Debnam, someone just tossed a rock through our window!"

As the men examined the debris on the Leonards' floor, Alva summoned the police, but when two cops arrived a half hour later, they weren't very impressed. "Kids," they said. "Happens all the time around here." The Debnams and their guests returned to the whist table.

The next evening, as Alva was fixing dinner, she heard a crash in the next room. A large beer bottle had hurtled through the window, dashing shards of glass across their bed. The whole family raced down two flights and into the backyard just in time to see three hazy figures behind a high mesh fence in the macadam playground of St. Mark's School.

"Did you kids throw that bottle?" Alva demanded.

"Yeh, nigger," said one of the figures. "Wanna make something of it?"

"No," said Alva. "I just want you to stop it."

"I'll tell you what we want," said another figure. "We want you niggers out of here."

"You've got until Wednesday," said the third figure. "Or else."

Once again Alva called the police. Once again two cops showed up, took a report, and promised to investigate.

The next evening, just at dusk, Alva was fixing her daughter Charlene's hair while Maria, her other daughter, and young Otis watched television. Suddenly one of the kitchen windows exploded as a huge rock clattered across the linoleum. From the school yard Alva heard a cheer and someone yelled, "Two more nights, nigger. Get out if you know what's good for you."

This time Alva summoned not only the police but much of the family: Mike Davis, Charlie Lane, her brother Jo-Jo, her sister Helen. Someone suggested it was time to bring in the press, so Charlie called Gary Armstrong, a black reporter for Channel 7, who arrived to tape an interview with Alva in her glass-strewn kitchen.

Did they have any idea why they were being attacked? Armstrong asked.

No, said Alva. They hadn't harmed anyone. All they'd done was to move into their new home.

Well, said Armstrong, the neighbors seemed to feel they'd moved into white territory, that they had crossed an invisible line.

Invisible line? asked Alva. What invisible line?

The boundary the Debnams had violated was a legacy of B-BURG, the effort by Boston savings banks following Martin Luther King's assassination to provide mortgages for the city's low-income blacks. Restricting such loans to a narrow corridor abandoned by retreating Jews, the banks had carefully skirted Irish neighborhoods, leaving a *de facto* racial border zigzagging across the city. Part of that "B-BURG line" followed Washington Street through Codman Square, slicing Dorchester in two, leaving everything to the west heavily black, everything to the east overwhelmingly white.

That many homes purchased with such mortgages were vastly overpriced and soon retaken by the banks only aggravated the social ravages of that policy. As the original "B-BURG families" moved out, their houses were often resold to other blacks less ready to assume the responsibilities of home ownership. Hundreds of Haitian refugees flooded the area, bringing with them the reggae beat, a Caribbean-French patois, and exotic new foods like coconut bread and barbecued goat. Between 1970 and 1975 the population turnover in the western sector, fueled by blockbusting and speculation, was so explosive that it ripped the community to shreds. Codman Square—once a graceful colonial crossroads marked by the spire of the Second Church in Dorchester—was transformed almost overnight into a black rendezvous where bands of boisterous youths flocked around funky new enterprises like Brother Lord's Music Sounds. After two white men were killed in the square during 1975, it was shunned, especially at night, by all but the most adventurous whites.

By then the sharp boundary had begun to crumble. A few blacks ventured across Washington Street, cautiously staking their claims in the white domain which stretched from there toward Dorchester Bay. The first pioneers were so rare that they posed no threat to their neighbors and encountered little hostility. But the advent of citywide busing in 1975 aggravated the situation, as black children from the western sector were bused across Washington Street and whites were moved in the other direction, raising fears that no racial boundaries were secure. Meanwhile, the new black homeowners had begun to approach Dorchester Avenue, the main street of Irish Catholic Dorchester. "Dot Av," as it was known to its denizens, was a breezy jumble of laundromats, luncheonettes, and variety stores, interspersed with taverns called the Emerald Isle, the Blarney Stone, and the Irish Rover, which still sold Guinness stout and McCardle's ale on draft. As blacks edged closer to that Gaelic stronghold, many whites feared that the B-BURG barrier was giving way for good, that one day soon the deluge would come sweeping through their neighborhood, destroying property values, eradicating community life as they knew it.

Much of this anxiety focused on Centre Street, a pleasant, tree-shaded thoroughfare which stretched a mile from Washington Street to Dorchester Avenue. By 1975 the black advance had reached about halfway between those two ethnic bastions. When the Debnams bought No. 185, they knew nothing of the nervous standoff. Neither the McKennas, who were eager to sell their house, nor Charlie Butts, well known for his aggressive brokerage in changing neighborhoods, had ever mentioned it. Nor were the Debnams aware of the rumors racing along Centre Street that week: that the NAACP had bought the house to "crack" the community; that a white man had served as an intermediary; that the McKennas' own daughter had wanted to buy the house but was outbid by the blacks; that the Debnams were on welfare. Not until rocks and bottles began crashing through their windows did Alva and Otis realize they had jumped two blocks beyond the nearest black family, ratcheting the level of apprehension another notch.

Alva's interview on the eleven o'clock news found a receptive audience around the corner. Eileen Bisson, twenty-seven, and Janet Connors, twenty-six, shared a Clementine Park three-decker. Both women also belonged to Racial Unity Now (RUN), a small group of Dorchester whites devoted to curbing racial violence and forging an alliance between whites and blacks.

RUN had grown from an unusual effort by Cambridge radicals to organize Dorchester's white working class. The experiment shrewdly focused on Municipal Court Judge Jerome Troy, who had long dispensed his special brand of justice: acquittal for those with money or influence, jail or military service for those who lacked such resources. Accumulating 10,000 signatures on a petition for his removal, the insurgents later took their case to the Massachusetts Supreme Court, which ultimately barred Troy from the bench. But even this famous victory couldn't hold the alliance of middle-class radicals and working-class recruits together. As more young ideologues arrived to test their Marxist principles on a proletarian community, the Dorchester contingent kicked over the traces, expelling many of the outsiders. The organization gradually collapsed, leaving a residue of politically conscious young people eager for new forms of community action.

When a dark-skinned Colombian named Mario Munez was severely beaten by whites outside a Dorchester Avenue tavern in January 1975, a feminist collective, whose members had been active in the Troy campaign, organized a fund-raiser to pay his hospital costs. That, in turn, led to formation of Racial Unity Now—an amalgam of Dorchester's working-class activists and remnants of the New Left belonging to the Communist Labor Party, the October League, and the Revolutionary Union. Over the next year, RUN helped defend several black families harassed by white youths. Soon they evolved sophisticated techniques, including a "phone chain," which could put several dozen members on the streets within minutes, and a "house-sitting" procedure which provided round-the-clock protection for embattled blacks.

When they heard of the Debnams' plight just before midnight on February 3, Eileen and Janet went directly to their assistance. Rushing down Clementine

Park, turning the corner onto Centre Street, they saw that all the lights at No. 185 were out, with no movement behind the curtains. Approaching cautiously along the far sidewalk, they noticed two black women seated in a car directly across the street from the Debnams' house. Assuming the women had fled from the attack, Eileen and Janet rapped lightly on the car window.

After three assaults in three nights, the Debnams had responded as best they could: turning off the lights to wait for another attack, hoping to identify their assailants. Alva and Helen had stationed themselves across the street in the Debnams' red Oldsmobile, where they were still sitting when the two white women knocked on the windows. Convinced that the newcomers were part of some fresh assault, they shrank back in terror. Only gradually, as the women smiled and gestured, did the sisters roll down their windows a few inches and eventually invite them into the back seat. For half an hour the women whispered to each other, Alva and Helen recounting what had happened at the house, Eileen and Janet explaining RUN's objectives. Later they entered the darkened house together. Mike Davis appeared from the shadows, Janet summoned her husband, Larry Turner, and soon the gathering became a full-fledged council of war. Sleepless for nearly forty-eight hours, Alva and Otis were on the brink of nervous exhaustion, but once they realized that these white people really intended to help them, they babbled their gratitude. When they finally staggered off to bed, Eileen and Larry sat in the car until dawn, keeping watch on the house.

In succeeding days, RUN's twenty-five members mapped strategy for the Debnams' defense. In similar situations their role had been limited to guarding an embattled house, but now conditions were clearly deteriorating. Apparently provoked by the busing crisis and by rapid neighborhood change, racial harassment was spreading through Dorchester. The week the Debnams moved onto Centre Street, a black woman named Ruby Bradley and her seven children had fled their apartment on nearby Templeton Street after eight nights of attack by white youths—the fourth black family forced off that street in less than a year. Convinced that the situation could be brought under control only with wide neighborhood support, RUN called a community meeting.

For several evenings that week, members passed out leaflets. "EMER-GENCY," the flyers proclaimed. "Some of our neighborhood's young people have been throwing rocks, bricks and bottles at some of our new neighbors on Centre Street every night since February 1. We don't think this is right. After working hard for years to buy a home, they chose our neighborhood. We welcome them and want to put an end to these attacks. Come to the community meeting to welcome them and to discuss what to do. St. Mark's School. February 13, 7–8:30 p.m."

Some seventy people showed up at the school's basement auditorium that night to hear the Debnams and RUN explain what had happened. One of Otis' co-workers at the rubber company—a recent immigrant from Ireland—delivered a brief testimonial, calling Otis "a damned good man who ought to be our ally, not our enemy." Alva told of the attacks on her family, concluding: "Nobody's going to tell me where I can live and where I can't. Hard as I had to work to get this house, nobody's going to take it away from me." Her speech drew sympathetic applause and several expressions of outrage from white homeowners who recalled their own encounters with neighborhood vandals. A dozen people volunteered to defend the Debnams. Another thirty-five signed a petition urging District 11 to station a police car outside their house.

Responding to community pressure, Captain William V. McCormack gave orders for a blue-and-white cruiser to guard the Debnams during evening hours. As long as the car was there the youths kept their distance, but no sooner did it leave at midnight than they reappeared, pelting the house with renewed vigor. The police insisted there was nothing much they could do unless the Debnams provided them with names, addresses, or—at the very least—detailed descriptions of their assailants.

Meanwhile, the vandals stepped up their assaults. On February 20, a particularly determined attack shattered three rear windows. And later that week, youths attacked Jim and Bertha McKenna's new home in Quincy, breaking four windows and cracking their car windshield, in apparent revenge for their sale of the Centre Street house to the Debnams.

On February 25, RUN distributed another flyer. "Vandalism has long been a problem in the neighborhood," it said, "but attacks on the Debnam family are by far the worst we've seen. It's up to us to deal with this—no one else will do it for us. . . . Neighbor after neighbor, young and old, say the attacks must end. We have to put all our heads together to figure out how. The last meeting ended with a call for another. It's scheduled for St. Mark's School, Sunday, February 29. 7–10."

On the lawn of St. Mark's Church, a giant statue of Christ stretched its arms toward a row of shabby three-deckers. Carved in its granite base was the legend "Come Follow Me."

A monument to Catholic power in the O'Connell-Cushing era, St. Mark's vast compound just off Centre Street embraced not only the red brick Gothic church, but a rectory with four priests; St. Mark's School, with an enrollment of seven hundred; and a convent of the Sisters of Notre Dame de Namur, housing twenty nuns. Francis Cardinal Spellman once called St. Mark's "the finest parish in the country" and, indeed, some of Boston's most eminent communicants once lived there. Among them was Honey Fitz, who brought his family to Welles Avenue in 1903. Elected Mayor of Boston three years later, Fitzgerald became a benefactor of St. Mark's, where his daughter, the future Rose Kennedy, often attended Mass with the family. In those years, the parish frequently led the Archdiocese in per capita contributions. Through the twenties and thirties, the Irish middle class settling Codman Square were proud to say they came from St. Mark's, and even when they moved to the suburbs, they often left instructions that they were to be buried back in the old ground.

Later, as the neighborhood's tone declined, St. Mark's lost much of its glamour, but the extravagant dimensions of church, school, and convent still recalled its most potent era.

The priests who manned St. Mark's knew that times had changed, that their Church no longer played a dominant role in its parishioners' lives. Attendance at Mass was sharply down, increasingly limited to the halt and the aged. On racial issues, in particular, the priests moved with great circumspection. Pastor Tom Mooney was a cautious man, disinclined to challenge the beliefs of his flock. Among his three curates, only Father Joe Greer showed any impulse to address delicate issues. When Humberto Medeiros established a Cardinal's Coordinating Committee to mobilize priests and nuns behind Garrity's order, Greer was one of only two Dorchester clergymen willing to enlist, helping to coordinate a program for priests to ride school buses into South Boston and, on several occasions, preaching on the subject. But after several parishioners called him a Communist and a woman in a neighborhood restaurant threw a salad in his face, even Greer trod more carefully.

The Debnam situation posed a particularly acute problem for St. Mark's because the family's house was flanked on two sides by the parish school and its playground. Most of the attacks came from the playground itself, boys heaving rocks and bottles over a ten-foot mesh fence, then fleeing toward the convent at the rear of the compound. On several occasions, the Debnams and their allies approached Father Greer, urging him to use the Church's moral authority to stop the attacks. "I think you're exaggerating our power," Greer told them. "The young people don't listen to us anymore. Our school has had several hundred windows broken. I've been held up myself. My car's been stolen. What can we do?" When Mike Davis wondered why the neighborhood kids were so hostile to blacks, Greer recalled that when he was growing up in Roxbury, black kids beat him up almost every day. "Unfortunately," he said, "that's the way things are in Boston." When Otis Debnam complained that vandals used the school yard as a privileged sanctuary for attacks on the house, Greer said, "I sympathize, Mr. Debnam, but there's not much we can do about that. For centuries the Church has offered sanctuary to outlaws."

Greer had gladly authorized the first community meeting in the school auditorium, but after receiving heated complaints from neighborhood youths, he was reluctant to make it available again.

"Don't you think you're moving a little fast?" he asked a RUN delegation. "It takes a while to undress the human being and put new clothes on him. You have to have education, you have to have environmental change, you have to have theological change. It takes a long time."

"We don't have time, Father," said Eileen Bisson. "We've got to change this neighborhood now."

"Okay," Greer said, "you can have the hall. But let me warn you, people are getting a little upset. I think you should be very cautious."

Impatient with Greer's equivocation, RUN invited Father Bill Mullin of adjacent St. Ambrose's Parish to address the meeting. The other Dorchester priest on the Cardinal's Coordinating Committee, Mullin was a leader of the Association of Boston Urban Priests, an ardent advocate of black rights. Church etiquette required that he inform St. Mark's priests that he would be speaking in their parish, but Joe Greer hardly put out the welcome mat. "You don't know the neighborhood," he said. "It'd be better if you didn't come." Never one to shrink from confrontation, Mullin resolved to come anyway.

Perhaps because an outside priest was expected, Father Tom Mooney, St. Mark's pastor, made a point of appearing at the school hall that Sunday evening. Seventy neighbors filled the front rows as Mooney—standing beneath an American flag and a picture of Jesus Christ—delivered a brief invocation, then excused himself to attend a wake.

Paul Couming of RUN introduced Bill Mullin, who spoke briefly on the Church's concern for racial equality, citing the Catholic Bishops' declaration that "segregation cannot be reconciled with the Christian view of our fellow man." As he moved on to the Debnams' plight, eight young men carrying beer cans drifted into the rear of the hall, where they struck up a loud conversation with Father Greer. When Mullin tried to make himself heard over their banter, they shouted derisively at him.

"Who are you?" yelled a man in an orange T-shirt. "Where the hell were you when I was growing up around here?"

"I'm Bill Mullin from St. Ambrose."

"We don't need any outsiders around here," yelled a man in a "Spaceman Bill Lee" T-shirt.

The heckling continued as Otis Debnam spoke of his family's experience. "We came here looking for a new house," he said. "We weren't looking for any trouble."

"Oh yeh?" shouted a man in a green football jersey. "What about that white girl who got burned to death in Roxbury? Who did that? The niggers, that's who."

The shouting grew still louder as Tom Couming, Paul's brother, described the ravages of blockbusting in Mattapan. When Tom appealed for quiet, he met fresh abuse.

"We don't have to shut up," said the man in the T-shirt. "This is our hall."

Paul Couming tried to regain control. "If anybody wants to say anything," he urged, "ask the chair for recognition."

"Recognition, shit!" shouted the man in the football jersey, moving down the aisle toward the speakers' table. "I don't recognize you!"

Suddenly the T-shirted man grabbed the table and flipped it on its side, sending Father Mullin, Paul Couming, and others sprawling backwards. Wading through the debris, he threw a wild roundhouse at Tom Couming, then wheeled on Otis Debnam. "We don't want any fucking niggers in this neighborhood," he shouted. "We're not going to break your windows anymore. We're going to burn your house professionally." With that, he punched Otis in the gut. Otis countered with an overhand right.

Similar fights broke out all over the auditorium. Someone knocked Tom Couming down, then pummeled him about the head. Someone else jumped on Paul Couming's back, dragging him to the floor. Another man advanced on Sandy McCleary of RUN, bellowing, "You fucking white bitch," then threw a chair at her.

Most of the audience ran from the hall, several of the women sobbing. One screamed, "For God's sake, somebody call the police!"

In fact, a plainclothes policeman had been present for most of the meeting. Roy Covell, community relations officer from District 11, had been assigned to monitor the proceedings. Just before the attack on the speakers' table, he had realized things were getting out of hand and rushed out to summon reinforcements. After the fighting had raged for five minutes, a half dozen police cruisers converged on St. Mark's. When the police burst into the hall, several skirmishes were still underway.

"Clear the hall!" a sergeant bellowed. The eight young men rushed out the door, heading toward Dorchester Avenue. "That's them!" RUN chorused. "Those are the guys who broke up the meeting."

But the police made no arrests. Later, at an angry meeting in the Debnams' living room, Roy Covell explained that in neighborhood disputes, it was up to the aggrieved parties to bring their own complaints. The Debnams and their supporters should swear out warrants against the eight men. But when the Debnams and Coumings went to Dorchester Municipal Court the next morning, the clerk refused to issue warrants without the men's full names and addresses. John Doe warrants were available only to police officers, not private citizens, he said. Although RUN didn't know who the men were, it had taken the precaution of having a photographer present in the school hall, and came to court that morning armed with pictures showing some of the men's faces, but the clerk adamantly refused to accept the photographs as identification.

After several hours of fruitless argument, Alva Debnam called the Boston office of the FBI, where she eventually reached Otis Cox, a black agent serving as its civil rights coordinator. Only after Cox called the clerk did the Dorchester court finally issue John Doe and Richard Roe warrants for two men whom the photographs showed assaulting Tom and Paul Couming. When police at District 11 saw the pictures they immediately recognized one of the men as Stephen Mulrey, a twenty-one-year-old former resident of the area who had moved to South Boston but still hung out with his buddies at a private Dorchester Avenue bar called the Shawmut Club.

Once the Shawmut had been an important neighborhood institution. Through the fifties and sixties, the men who congregated there were public-spirited citizens who held Christmas parties and Las Vegas nights, often donating the proceeds to charity. But gradually the club was appropriated by a younger crowd who used it as an after-hours spot for heavy drinking and pool and card games. Many of its members no longer lived in the neighborhood, but returned there regularly, seeking the camaraderie of their youth. And as blacks drew closer to Dorchester Avenue, the Shawmut became a rallying

ground for those who wanted an eleventh-hour stand along the "Irish Magi-
not Line."

After police put the word out on the street, Mulrey's lawyer brought him
in. The second man was quickly identified as William J. Flaherty, twenty-two,
of Dorchester, also a Shawmut Club habitué. The pair claimed that RUN's
radicals had refused to let them speak and then attacked them, forcing them to
strike back in self-defense. The authorities did not believe them. Mulrey was
charged with assault and battery with a dangerous weapon (to wit, a steel
chair), assault with a fist, and threats to commit a crime. Flaherty was charged
with assault and battery and threats to commit a crime. The case was assigned
to a young district judge named James W. Dolan.

Appointed to the Dorchester Municipal Court in 1974, Jim Dolan set out to
restore some measure of authority to a bench badly tarnished by Jerome Troy's
malfeasance. But he soon discovered that his limited powers made it difficult
to dispense anything remotely approaching justice. For one thing, district
judges couldn't sentence a juvenile to prison. Any offender under the age of
seventeen could be committed only to the Department of Youth Services,
which had sole discretion as to how long—if at all—he should remain in
custody. It was by no means unusual for the department to release a young
person in less than twenty-four hours. Since many crimes which came before
district judges—vandalism, malicious destruction of property, larceny, simple
assault—were commonly committed by juveniles, Dolan found himself relatively powerless in these areas.

Moreover, under Massachusetts' *de novo* system, any defendant convicted
by a district judge had the right to an entirely new trial in Superior Court.
Because of the heavy volume of criminal cases passing through Boston's
courts, it was hoped that defendants facing relatively trivial charges would
accept disposition by a district judge; yet since every American had a constitutional right to a trial by his peers, they could exercise that right by calling
for a jury trial in Superior Court. In practice, many defendants convicted at
the district level, and virtually anyone sentenced to prison, demanded a new
trial, which, because of the heavy backlog, often was delayed as long as a
year. During this time the defendant was on the streets under no supervision,
and when the case finally came to trial, it frequently led—because witnesses
or police were unavailable or because other events had intervened—to a sharp
reduction, even dismissal, of charges.

To keep control of such cases, Judge Dolan often gave a suspended sentence. This put the offender under the Municipal Court's own probation department and allowed the judge to sentence him directly to jail—with no right
of appeal—if he violated the terms of probation. When civic associations
complained that Dolan was "soft" on crime, he tried to explain that, whatever
sentence he might feel a defendant deserved, he was compelled to make a
trade-off between the abstract demands of justice and the realities of an imperfect judicial system.

Dolan had another way of keeping such cases in his jurisdiction, for he had at his disposal a federally subsidized mediation unit called the Urban Court Program. Such operations had cropped up throughout the country, grounded in the notion that many "crimes" which came before local courts were in fact disputes between relatives, friends, and neighbors, better handled through non-punitive mediation. To facilitate that process, the Dorchester Urban Court trained community residents to sit on "mediation panels" which sought to resolve conflicts and "disposition panels" which advised judges on what sentence to impose.

When the Mulrey-Flaherty case came before him on April 1, 1976, Dolan saw it as a perfect opportunity for community mediation. Deep-seated racial hostilities, he believed, could not be corrected by a stretch in prison but might prove amenable to more subtle techniques. That afternoon, Dolan referred the case to the Urban Court.

Leaders of the mediation program disagreed. Mulrey and Flaherty had no prior relationship with the Debnams, they noted; Mulrey didn't even live in the neighborhood. The case didn't lend itself to mediation. But in referring the matter back to Dolan for trial, the Urban Court suggested that it tackle the larger issue of the Debnams' right to peaceful enjoyment of their new home. White youths in the neighborhood must be shown that the Debnams were human beings too, that they had the same rights as other Americans. The Debnams and RUN might benefit from confronting their antagonists across a table, from seeing that they were real people with their own quotient of fears and anxieties. Dolan agreed. On April 3, he authorized the Urban Court to mediate the increasingly violent confrontation on Centre Street.

To Alva, Otis, and their defenders, the situation had long since passed the mediation stage. Between February 29 and April 3, hardly a day had gone by without some sort of attack by whites, whom the Debnams had taken to calling "the Pilgrims." All through the long winter nights, the family could hear the clatter of missiles on the gray clapboards. Every morning, the three Debnam children—Charlene, Maria, and young Otis—patrolled the yards, collecting rocks, bottles, and beer cans. By March 7, the Hughes Glass Company had replaced seventeen windows at a cost of $302.75. Over the next month, the vandals claimed another nine windows. Eventually the Debnams installed Lexon, a shatterproof plastic, at thirty-three dollars a pane. Even with their double salaries, the cost strained the family budget.

The strain on their nerves was even harder to bear. It was eerie, never feeling secure in their own house. They couldn't walk past a window without casting an apprehensive glance at the school playground. They couldn't concentrate on a book or card game for fear the room would explode with flying glass. A simple walk to the grocery was a perilous mission. The children had to be watched at all times. Sleep came hard, every sound a reminder that there were enemies out there in the dark who had threatened to burn the house down. Often, after they finally fell asleep, they were awakened by revelers from the Irish Rover or Emerald Isle roaring past the house, honking their horns and shouting, "Niggers suck!"

The ordeal was even more onerous for Frank Leonard, the Debnams' white downstairs tenant, who wore a pacemaker to control a serious heart ailment. Not realizing that No. 185 was a two-family house, the assailants tossed almost as many rocks through the Leonards' windows as they did through the Debnams'. Doctors warned that the constant barrage was aggravating Mr. Leonard's heart condition.

The Debnams quickly learned they couldn't depend on the police for protection. Almost from the start, their relations with District 11 had been thorny. Patrol cars frequently took twenty minutes to respond to a call. When they showed up, the cops usually asked if the Debnams could identify their attackers. When they said they couldn't, the police often shrugged their shoulders as though to say: If you don't know who attacked you, what do you want us to do about it?

There was something to be said for the police position. If they stationed a patrol car out front, the kids stayed away—but the car couldn't remain there all night. As soon as it left, the kids returned, heaving rocks and bottles out of the school yard, then retreating into the night. By the time the police responded to a call, the kids were probably sitting in their living rooms watching television. It wasn't a situation the ordinary patrolman was equipped to handle, but when the Debnams asked for detectives, they were told the district's eight plainclothesmen had their hands full with murders, rapes, aggravated assaults, and burglaries. Did they really expect detectives to be pulled off such life-and-death matters to track down a bunch of rock-throwing kids?

Yet the police attitude had other roots as well. Like most Boston police stations, District 11 was overwhelmingly white and largely Irish Catholic; many of the policemen sympathized with their co-religionists' struggle to preserve a white community along Dorchester Avenue. The Debnams were by no means the only people to complain that Dorchester's police were inattentive to racial harassment. George Lincoln, the white landlord of a Templeton Street building, had often considered inserting a warning in his rental ads: "People of minority races are advised not to apply as there is no adequate police protection in this hostile neighborhood where only whites are acceptable."

Some cops regarded the Debnams as troublemakers, intruding where they weren't welcome, then complaining loudly when they didn't get the protection they thought they deserved. If anything, RUN was worse, a bunch of radicals who had driven old Judge Troy off the bench. The police particularly resented the Debnams' appeals to the press. One detective warned Alva: "All this publicity is doing you more harm than good. If you'd just keep your mouths shut for a year, you'd be able to live here in peace."

By April, relations with District 11 had deteriorated so far that Deborah Anker, a lawyer representing the Debnams, arranged a meeting with Boston's Police Commissioner, Robert DiGrazia, Superintendent Joe Jordan, and

Deputy Superintendent Lawrence Quinlan. After the Debnams laid out their grievances against the police, the Commissioner and his aides explained their problems. They sympathized with the Debnams—this kind of racial attack was a nasty business, and District 11 was doing everything humanly possible to stop it. But the law was the law. The police couldn't arrest people simply because they looked suspicious. To make an arrest, the police either had to see someone commit a crime or obtain positive identification of the culprit. The family should try to identify their attackers.

The Debnams had heard all that before. The meeting merely reinforced their conviction that they could expect little from the police. Alva quit her second job with the School Department so that she could stay home every night with the children. That put the breadwinning burden on Otis, who continued to hold two jobs, which kept him away from the house between 6:00 a.m. and midnight. To fill that gap, Alva turned to her family—to her brothers John and Jo-Jo, to her sister Helen, to Charlie Lane, and particularly to Mike Davis, who spent virtually every night at the house for weeks on end. Later, as the attacks persisted, the Debnams appealed to virtually anyone in authority—to Ted Kennedy, Kevin White, Deputy Mayor Jeep Jones, Governor Michael Dukakis, State Attorney General Frank Bellotti, Cardinal Medeiros, the NAACP—with meager results.

For a brief time, both federal and state investigators became interested in the Debnam affair. The FBI's Otis Cox assigned two agents to look into the matter. Robert Cook, a Justice Department official from Washington, also spent several weeks on the case (once, when the Debnams heard rumors that someone planned to firebomb their house, Cook went up and down Dorchester Avenue, warning service stations not to sell gasoline in containers). Officials briefly considered summoning federal and state grand juries, but later abandoned the notion.

In mid-spring, several Black Muslim and Black Nationalist groups from Roxbury approached the Debnams. If nobody else was going to defend the family, they would be happy to oblige. And one of them went further. What the Debnams needed, he said, was a little muscle; smash up a few of those white neighbors' houses and the assault on the Debnams would stop.

No, thanks, said Alva and Otis. We don't need any of that stuff.

So, as the stones came through their windows night after night, they depended more and more heavily on RUN. When the organization first volunteered to defend the Debnams, it hadn't expected a protracted siege. As late as March 11, RUN was still reaching out to the community, hoping to mobilize white neighbors with a conciliatory leaflet. But as the assaults continued, RUN gradually developed a paramilitary battle plan. Dividing the night into three shifts—eight to midnight, midnight to three, three to six—it assigned four defenders to each period. Through trial and error, it devised four "battle stations": two defenders on the top floor, one watching the front, one the rear;

someone on the second floor, keeping the troublesome school yard under constant observation; a fourth behind the front door, watching Centre Street.

The attackers proved remarkably resourceful, however. Noting when the defenders changed shifts, when they seemed to relax their guard, the youths varied their tactics to exploit these moments of vulnerability. RUN then shifted its strategy too, relying increasingly on advanced technology. By April, it had two small vans stationed in the neighborhood, one behind St. Mark's Church, the other on nearby Nixon Street. From a citizens band "base unit" on the third floor of the Debnams' house, a "radio coordinator" maintained contact through walkie-talkies with defenders in the vans. With the defense team in constant communication, the vans warned the house of any attacks forming in their sectors, while the base informed the vans when youths were retreating in their direction.

Just what RUN should do if it cornered one or more of the attackers was a matter of some dispute. From the start, the organization had been split by ideological differences, leading to the resignation of several members who favored a more determined campaign against the "forces of racism." Similar disputes developed over the Debnam case. RUN's defenders often carried baseball bats in their cars, potent weapons for self-defense that were easily explainable as innocent sports equipment. A few of the most zealous activists yearned to use their bats on the attackers. Others hoped to capture the youths and place them under citizen's arrest. But lawyers associated with RUN sternly warned against such "vigilantism," fearing it could lead to civil suits by aggrieved parties. RUN therefore concentrated on photographic identification of the attackers. Several defenders in the house and one in each van were equipped at all times with a camera and flash equipment. When an attacker got close enough, the defender would leap out and snap his picture. Any shots that came out were turned over to the police, in hopes that they would provide sufficient evidence for prosecution.

In practice, the picture taking only exacerbated tensions in the neighborhood. Since it was difficult to distinguish attacking youths from innocent passersby, RUN snapped pictures of everyone who went by the house, often provoking strenuous objections. One night, after they had photographed a green Chevrolet making its third pass at the house, six white youths jumped out of the car and angrily confronted the picture takers. From the house burst six defenders, led by a black man carrying a double-barreled shotgun. "Give me those car keys," he told the driver. "This is the third time you guys have been past here. You aren't getting these keys back tonight and you aren't leaving until the Man comes." When the police arrived, the black gave them the keys and said, "Get these guys out of here. I don't want to see them again."

On March 16, RUN's strategy provided fresh ammunition to its critics. When a rock went through the Debnams' living-room window, a RUN sentinel in the front hall spotted several youths scattering down Centre Street. He gave chase, accompanied by Alva's brother Jo-Jo, while the base unit alerted other defenders in cars and vans. A RUN member named Kathy Navin, cruising the streets in her Toyota sedan, saw a white youth in flight. Drawing alongside, she asked if something was wrong. The boy said two men were chasing him. Eventually he got in the car—whether at his suggestion or hers was a matter of some dispute—and they drove away. A minute later, Kathy picked up Jo-Jo Walker, who identified the boy as one of those he had seen in the street. Kathy then drove to the Debnams', where RUN photographed the boy, then told him to go away and not come back. The next day, the police charged Kathy Navin with kidnapping Michael McKeon, a fourteen-year-old student at St. Mark's School. Judge Dolan quickly dismissed the charge, but the incident damaged RUN's reputation in the community, contributing to a widespread suspicion that something ominous was going on at 185 Centre Street.

In the wake of such incidents, RUN became increasingly alienated from the neighborhood. Its determined defense of the Debnams had turned 185 Centre Street into a fortress against the outside world. RUN's most ideological members increasingly saw the white neighbors as unalloyed racists, a hostile force which could not be bargained with, only repelled. This proved a self-fulfilling prophecy. Some previously sympathetic adults were put off by the armed-camp atmosphere. Rumors that RUN was "a bunch of Communists" made rapprochement still more difficult.

A handful of white neighbors, sensing that things were getting out of hand, made one last effort to mobilize the community behind the Debnams. In late March, a college professor named David Stratman, who lived around the corner on Samoset Street, invited Alva and Otis—but not RUN—to meet with him and a few sympathetic neighbors. Stratman believed that both RUN and ROAR, for their own reasons, were seeking to make race the central issue in the city. Only by defusing the racial question, he believed, by embedding situations like the Debnams' in a nexus of common concerns, could the community's polarization be halted. That meant relying on the best instincts of the neighborhood—not on radical missionaries from Cambridge—to restore a sense of decency and perspective. At the meeting, several participants volunteered to help. One woman active at St. Mark's said she would speak with the priests, urging them to get more involved. Paul Tafe and Marie Garrett, the youngest members of the group, volunteered to seek out the vandals themselves.

District 11 maintained a list of 147 locations—street corners, parks, school yards, and drugstores—where Dorchester's youth gangs customarily hung out. Some 2,580 young people between the ages of ten and twenty-five were said to belong to such gangs, but police cautioned that the word "gang" should be construed loosely to mean any group of youths who hung together for any purpose—from street hockey to smoking dope to merely "messing around." Few of them bore the colorful names, the bizarre regalia or lethal weapons popularized by *West Side Story*. Few were regularly involved in overt criminal activity, though many engaged in random vandalism against public buildings or private homes.

But rapid change in Dorchester's neighborhoods and the city's tense racial climate had begun to alter that. The gangs, which generally carried the names of the street or corner on which they hung out, became more aware than ever of their turf. Their members often spoke of themselves as "protectors" of the neighborhood. Those who could remember the days when their parents lived west of Washington Street would say: We didn't defend ourselves then, we let the colored push us out; now we're going to fight for our territory. Some gang members no longer lived in Dorchester at all but returned from South Shore communities on weekends or evenings to help defend a turf that was no longer their own. It didn't take much to move the gangs to action; the slightest alteration in territorial patterns—as simple as blacks hanging a basketball net on a new light pole, or taking their clothes to a new laundromat—could ignite fears of fresh incursions, triggering a racial explosion.

The Debnams' house was boxed by four such groups—the Roseland Street gang, which took its name from the street just behind St. Mark's Church; the Shawmut Station gang, which hung out at the subway station on Clementine Park; the Mather Street gang, which met on a corner just across Centre Street; and the Wainwright Park gang, named after a grassy rectangle two blocks from the Debnams'.

One night in late March, Paul Tafe and Marie Garrett strolled across the school yard to the stoop where the Roseland Street gang usually congregated after supper. Only a few years older than the gang members, who ranged from fifteen to twenty, Paul and Marie easily struck up a conversation. As a sociology student at the University of Massachusetts, Paul was interested in what motivated these youngsters, and as the leader of a rock group called Ashmont, he enjoyed a certain prestige in the neighborhood. He told them he'd been up at the Debnams' recently, where he had seen the ruin caused by their stones. It must be a terrible thing to have rocks crashing through your windows night after night, he said. Why did they do it?

We don't like niggers, the kids said. We want them out of our neighborhood. If we throw rocks through their windows night after night, eventually they'll get the message and move out.

But didn't they see what havoc they were wreaking in the neighborhood? asked Marie. Weren't they destroying the very community their parents had worked so hard to develop?

No, said the kids. Their parents wished they could do the same thing. But grown-ups couldn't throw rocks, so the kids were doing it for them.

By April 3, David Stratman's moderate caucus conceded that it could do little to halt the confrontation on Centre Street. The initiative now passed to the Urban Court, which, under Judge Dolan's auspices, launched its mediation effort. On April 24, the community was summoned to a meeting at Our Saviour's Lutheran Church, where Urban Court officials explained the undertaking. The plan called for a negotiating panel of ten persons: Alva and Otis Debnam, four white adults, and representatives from the four street gangs. The community selected a student, a retired fireman, a traffic policewoman, and a housewife as the adult representatives. Two Urban Court mediators, Kathy Grant and Barbara Sullivan, spent hours making the rounds of the gang hangouts, until each contingent chose someone to attend the mediation sessions.

On May 1, the participants gathered at Urban Court headquarters for the first session, which went surprisingly well. All parties showed such willingness to talk that Kathy and Barbara called another session for May 8. But, from the start, the second meeting was a disaster. The Roseland Street gang hadn't attended the first meeting. This time it sent two youths who began shouting at Alva Debnam, "There isn't any point in talking, because sooner or later we're going to get you niggers!" Alva told them, "You better not try. You come anywhere near me or my children, I'll kick your asses down the avenue!" After an hour of mutual recriminations, the meeting broke up in disarray. A third session was never called.

As long as mediation held any hope of success, Judge Dolan reserved judgment on the Mulrey-Flaherty case, so as not to jeopardize the delicate negotiations. Once those efforts collapsed, he came under heavy pressure from the Debnams' supporters to give the men prison terms as an object lesson to the community. On June 14, twenty neighbors wrote to Dolan, urging him to "act swiftly" in the case. "Unless the Court makes it known that it will not tolerate actions such as those that occurred February 29," they wrote, "then not only the Debnams but the entire community will continue to be victimized."

A week later, Dolan responded by finding both men guilty on all charges. Still seeking to keep jurisdiction over the matter and to involve the community in its resolution, he sent the case to an Urban Court "disposition panel" for a recommended sentence. The panel proposed that the cases be continued without a finding for six months as a means of assuring the men's good behavior. Dolan agreed, provided the defendants agreed to pay for all windows broken at the Debnams' house during that period. But Mulrey and Flaherty flatly refused that condition. Reluctantly, Dolan then sentenced Mulrey to twenty days in prison, Flaherty to ten days, suspending both sentences and putting the men on probation for six months. Just as the judge had feared, Mulrey and Flaherty immediately sought new trials in Superior Court, where several months later charges against both were dropped.

The failure of police and courts to deliver a stern warning may have paved the way for a fresh outburst of violence, or perhaps it was only the onset of summer weather which sent the gangs into action. On the evening of June 13, white teenagers drinking beer and watching a softball game at Town Field became embroiled with a group of Puerto Ricans from nearby Geneva Avenue. Before the melee was over, Jackie Pembroke, a seventeen-year-old high school student, lay bleeding to death from a knife wound in the chest. Later in June, three more youths were stabbed and four policemen injured in three nights of bitter street fighting between roving gangs of whites and blacks.

The renewed racial combat proved particularly discomfiting to organizers of Boston's Bicentennial celebration. Ever since the elaborate municipal festivities got underway in April 1975, there had been a certain irony in commemorating Boston's eighteenth-century struggle for the Rights of Man against the background of Boston's contemporary collision over human rights. But now the celebration was about to culminate in the Bicentennial Moment itself— July 4, 1976—to be marked in Boston by a parade led by the Ancient and Honorable Artillery, a reading of the Declaration of Independence from the State House balcony, a patriotic oration at Faneuil Hall, and, finally, a mammoth concert on the banks of the Charles. Just as thousands of dignitaries, tourists, and newspeople were about to descend on the city, Dorchester's racial warfare threatened to preempt the headlines. As the great day approached, Mayor White ordered police officials to do everything in their power to halt the violence.

Perhaps because the troubles had spread to other parts of Dorchester, Centre Street was relatively peaceful in those last days of June, and Alva and Otis decided to celebrate the nation's two hundredth birthday—as well as their own survival—with a giant barbecue in their backyard. "There hasn't been much reason to party around here these past few months," Alva told Mike Davis. "We're going to make up for lost time. It's going to be a blast!"

For days in advance, the Debnams, their family and friends prepared in earnest. Alva's mother baked a big chocolate cake. Brother Tommy and his girlfriend bought the bread and rolls. Brother Fred took responsibility for the liquor and beer. Sister Helen got the ice cream. For two straight nights, Alva was in the kitchen nearly nonstop, baking sweet potato pie, white potato pie, coconut pie, and frying up a huge batch of chicken. Early on July 4, brother John—still a soul food cook at Bob the Chef—put coals on the grill and started turning out his succulent barbecued ribs, along with T-bone steaks, hamburgers, and hot dogs. Charlene and Maria set up the stereo system in a window of their parents' room. Young Otis put on a big stack of disco and rhythm-and-blues records, which were soon resounding through the neighborhood.

By late morning the yard filled up with celebrators. Most of the family was there, with the notable exception of Rachel Twymon, who was in Nashville, Tennessee, with her son, George. (Alva's troubles on Centre Street had done nothing to improve relations between the sisters. As far as Rachel was concerned, Alva had brought the problems down on her own head by her insistence on buying a house in white Dorchester.) But four of Rachel's children were present: Cassandra, Rachel, Wayne, and Fred. Blacks from the South End and Roxbury mixed easily with white defenders like Eileen Bisson, Sandy McCleary, Janet Connors, and Paul Couming, neighbors like David and Sally

Stratman, David and Ellen Rome, Paul Tafe and Marie Garrett. Two neighbor-hood kids, Jim Sorenson and Steve Youmans, scampered through the yard with young Otis, setting off Roman candles, shaking up Coke bottles and spraying each other with the brown fizz. Seventy blacks and thirty whites filled the backyard all through the long, lazy afternoon, eating, drinking, talking, and singing, savoring that special moment in American history.

Late in the day, most of the partygoers drifted off, many of them headed for the Boston Pops concert on the Charles. The family and a few friends settled down at three card tables, set up in the shade of a spreading oak, for the Walkers' traditional round of whist. When the mosquitoes began biting around eight o'clock, they moved the card game up to the kitchen while the kids took the stereo unit into the empty room for a disco party.

The Debnams' cookout hadn't gone unnoticed on Centre Street. All through the neighborhood, bedecked that day with American flags and patriotic bunt-ing, whites had grumbled at the commotion around No. 185. Never had any-one at that end of Centre Street seen so many "colored" so close at hand. Their cars were parked in every available spot for blocks around. The music from their stereo could be heard a hundred yards away. Some of the neighbors, busy with their own celebrations, hardly noticed. Others shrugged and said, "Well, it's a holiday." But more than a few were furious. "They're rubbing our noses in it," one mother told her daughter as they sat in beach chairs on the front lawn. "They're showing us what it's going to be like when they take over."

Two blocks away, in Wainwright Park, a hundred white youths had gathered for another traditional July 4 event. Every year for as long as anyone could remember, the Wainwright Park gang and its friends had celebrated the holiday with a huge bonfire. Early in the afternoon, they began assembling in the park, playing basketball on a court at one end, softball on a rough diamond at the other, drinking beer and smoking dope on a stretch of macadam scrawled with graffiti: "Gays Suck, Liberals Suck, Brits Suck, Niggers Suck." At dusk, they stacked their wood in a ten-foot pyramid just behind second base, where, doused with gasoline, it ignited with a great rush, the flames leaping fifteen feet in the air, lighting up the severe façades of the three-deckers around the park. Well into the night, the kids cavorted about the blazing pyre, celebrating the day much as colonial youths two hundred years before had marked such occasions.

As Dorchester's blacks and whites each observed the Bicentennial in their own fashion, more than 400,000 others had gathered on the banks of the Charles for the Boston Pops' 47th Annual July Fourth Concert. It was an astonishing throng which jammed the esplanade that evening, spreading out on blankets and beach chairs from the Hatch Shell down Storrow Drive and spilling onto the Cambridge shore. More than 25,000 watched from sailboats and motor launches anchored in the river; hundreds more perched in trees up and down the shore. It was the largest crowd ever to attend a live concert anywhere in the world, the largest assembled for any purpose in Boston history—but an overwhelmingly white middle-class crowd, with nary a black in sight. At 8:30 p.m., to a standing ovation, eighty-two-year-old Arthur Fiedler stepped onto the podium, raised his baton, and launched into Weber's "Jubilee Overture," followed by Tchaikovsky's Concerto No. 1 in B flat minor.

About 9:00 p.m., the bonfire in Wainwright Park had begun to die down and a foraging party was dispatched for more wood. Two neighborhood teenagers, Bill Thomason and Jim McCarthy, found their way up Melbourne Street to Centre, then east one block to the Debnams' house. The yard was deserted by then, the only sounds the disco beat from the front room, the card players' chatter from the kitchen. Thomason and McCarthy crept along the white picket fence which squared off the front yard. Planting their feet, hauling on the rail, they ripped up an eight-foot section, then raced down Centre Street bearing their prize.

At 9:05, the orchestra in the Hatch Shell brought the Tchaikovsky concerto to a triumphant conclusion and broke for intermission. The vast audience stirred, people reaching into wicker hampers for a sandwich or a deviled egg, grabbing a beer from the cooler, smoking a cigarette. Low murmurs of satisfaction rumbled along the river.

From the windows of the empty room where the young folks were dancing, Cassandra Twymon caught a glimpse of the picket fence being yanked from the lawn. "Somebody's messing with the fence," she yelled.

Rushing to the window just in time to see Thomason and McCarthy in flight down Centre Street, the young blacks bolted to the door. As they passed the kitchen, where the adults were still at the whist table, somebody shouted, "Pilgrims outside!"

With instincts honed from months of such alarms, Alva, Otis, Fred, John, Jo-Jo, Tommy, Helen, Mike, and a half dozen others dropped their cards and rushed down the stairs. Soon, some thirty blacks were thundering along Centre Street in hot pursuit of the missing fence.

At 9:22, his snow-white hair and mustache blazing in the arc lights, Arthur Fiedler returned to the podium and, poised before a great mound of white chrysanthemums and red carnations, crashed into "The Star-Spangled Banner." All along the esplanade and across the river on the Cambridge shore, the crowd rose to their feet. When the last strains of the anthem had washed across the water, Fiedler invited his listeners to "sing the patriotic songs with us, would you, please."

Consulting printed lyrics distributed earlier, the throng raised its collective voice, first hesitatingly in "America" and "America the Beautiful," then more confidently in "Yankee Doodle Dandy," "Columbia the Gem of the Ocean," "You're a Grand Old Flag," and "The Battle Hymn of the Republic."

Wheeling from Centre Street onto Melbourne Street, the blacks could see a crowd of whites gathered around the bonfire in the center of the park. As the first wave of black teenagers reached the chain link fence around the basketball court, someone shouted, "Here come the niggers!" With that, the Wainwright Park gang and its friends surged from the park, chasing the blacks back toward Centre Street. Before long, thirty blacks and fifty whites were at war with rocks, bricks, bottles, beer cans, two-by-fours, and porch railings.

At 9:34, Fiedler raised his baton once more and led the eighty white-jacketed musicians into their traditional finale, "The 1812 Overture." As Tchaikovsky's heroic phrases swelled toward a climax, they were joined by sixteen cannon shots from a battery of 105-mm. howitzers on the riverbank, a tintinnabulation of bells from the Church of the Advent, geysers of red, white, and blue water from a fireboat behind the band shell, and a shower of feathery white fire-works. As puffs of gray smoke drifted into the black sky, the crowd cheered ecstatically. Long-haired girls perched on their boyfriends' shoulders, fathers held children aloft, a priest from South Boston waved a huge American flag. From the roof of a nearby building, where a CBS crew was concluding the network's Bicentennial coverage, correspondent Charles Collingwood said, "Boston has never seen anything like this and probably never will again." In New York, Walter Cronkite nodded his assent. "In a day marked by crescen-dos," he said, "this is perhaps the high point."

As the donnybrook on Melbourne Street reached *its* crescendo, Alva's brother Tommy raced back to the Debnam house, where he had parked his brown Buick sedan. Jumping behind the wheel, he gunned the car down Centre Street and swerved through the melee into Melbourne Street. Misjudging the turn, he crashed into the far curb, coming to rest with one wheel on the sidewalk. Almost immediately the car was surrounded by a swarm of angry whites, pounding on the windows with fists and sticks. When Tommy wrenched open a door and jumped out, one youth heaved a trash barrel at him, while another aimed a porch railing at his head. He ducked back inside.

Tommy "Mugger" Walker had a nasty temper. As a child he had proved so willful he was sent off to the Lyman School, an institution for troubled youths. As a teenager, hanging around the Carter Playground, he was a tough lineman on the Panthers, an even tougher street fighter with the Emperors. Relentless with bat, brick, and knife, he could really hurt you. As a young man, he was in constant trouble with the law, receiving two suspended sentences for assault.

Later, he channeled his anger into more positive enterprises. Since following his father onto a construction site at the age of eighteen, Tommy had worked in the building trades. But the construction unions and the contractors both resisted black workers. Once, when Tommy approached an Italian builder for a job, the man said, "I already got a minority."

"What do you mean?" asked Tommy. "I don't see anybody else around here."

"Him."

"He's a Puerto Rican."

"Right," said the builder. "He's my minority."

Eventually, Tommy and several friends helped organize the United Community Construction Workers, which picketed building sites demanding that contractors hire black workers and pressured government to guarantee blacks their share of work on publicly funded projects. A determined organizer, he was elected to the UCCW's board of directors, becoming a familiar figure at job negotiations.

But the Walker clan remained wary of Tommy. They knew things were either right or wrong with him, that he wasn't strong on subtle shades of gray, and they had tried to keep him away from the situation on Centre Street. Most of Alva's other brothers had been around the house all spring, but Tommy didn't turn up there until a couple of weeks before July 4, when Arnold said, "Come on, Tommy. Ma didn't want you up here, but this is something you ought to see." Some months later, Tommy said, "Maybe Ma was right. She knew I wouldn't have much understanding of white folks telling my sister where she could or couldn't live."

Slamming the car into reverse, Tommy backed through the intersection, then accelerated into Melbourne Street. Zigzagging down the hill toward Wainwright Park, the car veered to the left, striking sixteen-year-old Richard Moore, tossing him high in the air and catapulting him onto a nearby stoop. Next in the car's path, Janice Mulkern, nineteen, was hit so hard she landed on the automobile's hood with both legs mashed against a blue Chevrolet parked at the curb. Finally, the onrushing vehicle struck the Chevrolet with such force that it hit Bill Thomason—one of the youths who had ripped up the Debnams' fence—crushing his right leg against a light pole.

Somehow eluding the whites milling around the car, Tommy made his way back to the Debnams' house, where dozens of police and a large contingent of angry neighbors had quickly converged. Scuffles broke out. When a white youth began hassling Alva's daughter Maria, her cousin Cassandra Twymon knocked the boy off his bike. But when Alva's brother Fred Walker became embroiled with seventeen-year-old Richard Manning, police arrested both men, charging them with "participating in an affray." An hour later, Tommy Walker and several other blacks from the Debnam house went to District 11 to bail Fred out. As Tommy stood in the station-house lobby, a white youth pointed him out to police as the driver of the car on Melbourne Street. He was charged with assault and battery with a dangerous weapon (to wit, an automobile) and held on $50,000 bail.

Tommy's arrest did nothing to assuage the white neighbors. For the news from Carney Hospital wasn't good: Richard Moore had a broken cheekbone and a fractured right leg; both of Janice Mulkern's legs were broken in several places; and, eighteen hours later, Bill Thomason's crushed right leg was amputated just above the knee.

As word of the amputation raced through the neighborhood, a protest rally was scheduled for Wainwright Park on Friday, July 16. At eight that evening some 125 whites ranging in age from ten to forty gathered by the scorched circle in the park. After a spate of angry speeches, the crowd marched three abreast up Melbourne Street, past the scene of the crash, toward the Debnams' house. The procession was led by two patrol cars, the rear brought up by four helmeted policemen on motorcycles. Drawing abreast of 185 Centre Street, the marchers raised their fists and chanted, "No more niggers!"

As the Wainwright Park gang passed the house, they added a more pointed epithet. "Give us a leg," they shouted. "We want a leg!"

From the Debnams' porch, Alva, Otis, Mike, Jo-Jo, and others responded with a few choice epithets of their own. Several shook baseball bats at the marchers. A rock soared out of the darkness. The blacks on the porch tossed something back. In a minute, rocks and bottles were flying in both directions. It took the police nearly half an hour to restore order.

From his window on Samoset Street, Paul Tafe watched the march with mounting distress. This had gone too far, he thought. Perhaps if he talked with the kids again he could persuade them to back off. Walking to the basketball court, he found a dozen members of the Wainwright Park and Roseland Street gangs drinking beer in the moonlight. They were getting quite a reputation, he told them, but three people had been injured already. If they weren't careful, somebody was going to get killed. Why didn't they let things cool down a while? The kids sipped their beer and nodded.

Uneasy, Paul went off to visit his girlfriend. Returning home at 1:00 a.m., he found two members of the Roseland Street gang camped on his doorstep.

"We want to talk to you," said one.

"Sure," said Paul.

"Which side are you on?"

"I'm on your side. I'm on the side of that boy who lost his leg. I'm on the Debnams' side. I'm on the side of anybody who gets hurt in this thing."

When one of the youths moved menacingly toward him, Paul leapt for the haven of his doorway, but the other kid caught him with a right to the jaw. Trying to put the storm door between himself and his assailants, Paul took another blow in the gut, which doubled him over. He struck out, putting his fist through the glass panel. Only after the two youths had fled did Paul find he was bleeding not only from the hand but from a deep knife wound in his leg. A friend rushed him to the hospital, where doctors, after giving him a pint of blood, said the knife had severed a large vein. If he hadn't reached the hospital so quickly, they said, he might have bled to death.

That month's events provoked a new responsiveness from District 11. Deputy Superintendent Lawrence Quinlan had had enough. Summoning two detectives, Frank Olbrys and Ed Kennealey, he told them, "We need a racial squad. You're the racial squad. Get up on Centre Street and put a lid on this thing."

Veteran members of the district's "juvenile" unit, Olbrys and Kennealey knew many of the gang members and the gangs knew them. Conventional Boston detectives, they decorated their office with signs reading: "This is our flag. Be proud of it" and "Kindness to the guilty is cruelty to the innocent." Both found Alva Debnam a bit loud and aggressive for their tastes, and they regarded RUN as "Cambridge-type people out to give the system a good kick in the teeth." But, once deputized by their superior, they did their job. Instead of sitting outside the Debnams' house in a conspicuous police car, they stood in the shadows of St. Mark's school yard or around the corner on Nixon Street, waiting for the youths to strike.

Over the next two months, Olbrys and Kennealey made more than a dozen arrests around the house. On one occasion, lurking behind a tree, Kennealey saw a youth cock his arm as if to throw. The detective seized the kid's hand, extracted a rock, and placed him under arrest. Some nights later, after a black Plymouth circled the Debnams' house with three youths shouting, "No more fucking niggers!" Olbrys stopped the car and arrested its occupants. That weekend, he apprehended four kids who had thrown beer bottles against the front porch.

But despite the detectives' diligence, the culprits rarely received much of a sentence. None of them ever spent a night in jail. The most celebrated incident occurred on September 10, a lively night around the Debnams' home. Shortly before 1:00 a.m., a firebomb exploded in the driveway, scorching the family car. Three hours later, two figures were seen prowling the yard with a pistol, shouting racial epithets and ultimately firing one shot toward the house. The detectives arrested Fred Gavin, nineteen, and his brother John, eighteen. Originally, both boys were charged with assault with a deadly weapon, and Fred with illegal possession of a gun. But the assault charges were quickly reduced to disorderly conduct. Finding John guilty, Judge Dolan gave him a three-month suspended sentence. He found Fred Gavin guilty of disorderly conduct and illegal possession, which carried a mandatory sentence of one year in prison. But on appeal in Superior Court he was acquitted of both.

By autumn, Tommy Walker's approaching trial became the focus of attention in the neighborhood. With three of their children still nursing serious injuries, many white neighbors demanded vengeance. Others hoped a guilty verdict would seal the Debnams' fate, forcing them off Centre Street. The Walker clan and their supporters—endorsing Tommy's version that the car had been stolen just before the incident—protested his innocence with equal vehemence.

Some RUN activists had formed the Thomas Walker Defense Committee, raising money to pay his lawyer and distributing a flyer in Dorchester which announced: "Thomas Walker is innocent. Bias and prejudice could put him in jail, despite the testimony that doesn't identify him. Demand equality and justice for Thomas Walker before you or your own are victimized! Educate yourself and your children on racism—your life may one day depend on it!"

But other RUN members weren't so sure. All fall, debate raged within the tiny organization, splitting it along class and ideological lines. Many of RUN's working-class members strongly suspected that Tommy had, indeed, been driving the car on July 4. Others simply didn't know. Most of those with deep roots in Dorchester argued that to proclaim Tommy's innocence in that angry neighborhood without being sure of the facts was political suicide. But the Cambridge radicals contended that a determined campaign on Tommy's behalf was a political imperative. After all, even if Tommy was guilty, none of the whites who had attacked the Debnams for months had gone to jail. Why should he? Moreover, if Tommy was legally responsible for injuring three white youths, he had been morally justified in defending his sister and her family. How long were the Debnams supposed to suffer persecution? they asked. Wasn't there a natural right of self-defense?

On May 17, 1977, Tommy's trial opened before Superior Court Judge James P. McGuire. After a prolonged wrangle over jury selection, a panel of ten whites and two blacks was chosen. Prosecutor Tim O'Neill opened his case with the victims. Janice Mulkern, steel braces glinting on both legs, testified that she had seen Tommy Walker deliberately cut the wheel toward her. William Thomason, after hobbling to the witness stand on crutches, said he had seen the car hurtling toward him at great speed. Under cross-examination, Thomason conceded that he and other youths from Wainwright Park had thrown rocks at the Debnams' house on several occasions. Asked whether he had intended to force the family out of Dorchester, he replied, "In a way." But Judge McGuire would not let defense attorney Winston Kendell explore the background of attacks on the Debnam house, holding that such testimony was irrelevant to the case at hand. Kendell concentrated instead on demonstrating that Tommy wasn't driving the car on July 4, presenting several relatives and friends who testified that a white youth had stolen the car minutes before the crash. Tommy himself did not take the stand.

With impassioned pleas for justice from both sides, the jury retired on the morning of May 27. Four hours later it was back with a question: "Is intent necessary to prove assault and battery?" Yes, Judge McGuire told them, "to commit an assault and battery you've got to have in your mind the intent to do so." But, he said, "one cannot read in the mind of another what he intends

. . . a man is presumed in the law to have intended to do that which he does, and to have intended its ordinary and natural consequences."

At eleven the next morning, the jury returned a verdict of guilty, and Judge McGuire sentenced Tommy Walker to not less than four and not more than seven years in Walpole Prison.

Well before Tommy went to jail, the attacks on the Debnams' house had begun to subside. Perhaps it was the sudden police diligence, perhaps the alarm of white adults at the rash of injuries, perhaps simply the boredom of youths tiring of their long campaign. By the end of 1976, Olbrys and Kennealey returned to other duties and RUN withdrew its defenders.

But the siege had taken its toll on 185 Centre Street. In midsummer, Frank Leonard, the Debnams' white tenant, died of a heart attack brought on, his physician suspected, by the constant turmoil surrounding the house. Meanwhile, the ordeal had helped to blight the Debnams' marriage. Unable to forgive Otis' prolonged absences during the worst violence, Alva suspected that he was running around with other women. Otis vehemently denied this, insisting he had been working night and day to support the family. But their differences proved insurmountable. Before long they were separated.

Alva and her children remained on Centre Street. Once every six weeks or so, a rock or bottle came through a window. Occasionally a late drinker on his way home from the Irish Rover or the Emerald Isle would stop outside the house to shout a slurred epithet or two. But, after a time, most of the neighbors learned to ignore the intruders in their midst.

26

McGoff

Watch out, dearie," a male voice muttered. "I've got your number." "Who's this?" asked Lisa McGoff. "Never mind," said the voice. "You just be careful." Confused, Lisa hung up.

The next night the voice was back, warning: "You're a little girl with a big mouth. If I were you, I'd keep it shut." "Who *is* this?" Lisa cried. He hung up.

All that evening in March 1976 the McGoffs debated the mysterious phone calls. At the telephone company, Alice had dealt with her share of cranks, most of them obscene or abusive. But, neither dirty nor angry, Lisa's caller delivered his warnings in a feathery whisper which lent them a special terror.

His admonitions seemed directed at Lisa's role in the White Caucus. That spring of her junior year she had led repeated demonstrations downtown to protest conditions at Charlestown High. Her name appeared in the paper, her picture on TV; anyone could look up her number. At first Lisa suspected one of the blacks at school, but the caller sounded more like a white adult. The McGoffs couldn't understand what he was up to.

Several nights later, he called with an explicit threat. "I've got your girl-friend," he warned. "If you don't stop talking, I'm going to kill her."

Panicked, Lisa called all her best friends, who were safe and accounted for. The caller was apparently bluffing, but the McGoffs took no chances. The next morning, they reported the threat to Captain MacDonald at District 15, and on MacDonald's advice, Lisa stopped answering the telephone. Her mother and brothers screened all calls, accepting only those from friends. Eventually the mystery caller abandoned his campaign. But for weeks to come Lisa dreaded retaliation. Afraid to walk to and from school alone, she begged her brothers and classmates to accompany her. Particularly fearful at night, she remained home evening after evening rather than risk assault from a dark alley.

Just as she began to regain her composure, the April 5 march on City Hall concluded with the attack on Ted Landsmark. Crouched by a wall at the edge of the plaza, Lisa watched the fists and feet flailing at the black lawyer, the American flag leveled at his chest. Sobbing with terror, she buried her head in her hands, trying to disappear.

It wasn't so much the racial confrontation which horrified her—she suspected Landsmark of provoking the incident—as the fury of the assault. For weeks she relived the episode in her nightmares. Always the dream was the same: huddled by the wall, burrowing into a corner, she shrank from the menacing creatures which thrashed about her. Each time she woke clammy with sweat, shivering with apprehension.

That spring ended on a sour note. The Last White Class felt particularly close to a teacher named John Brennan, another former Dallas Cowboy drafted by Frank Power to keep order at the school. John was a Townie through and through. His marriage to a Connecticut girl had broken up in part because she didn't like the Town and he couldn't imagine living anywhere else. Lonely after she left him in 1975, he spent much of his time with the school's embattled seniors, encouraging their resistance to busing. As class adviser, he was more of an older brother than a teacher. Billy McGoff and many of his classmates would go down to Big John's house in the evenings and sit around for hours playing records.

John Brennan's favorite song was "I'll Always Love My Mama," a disco number by a black group called the Intruders, about a black man's love for his mama.

> *I'll always love my mama*
> *She's my favorite girl*
> *I'll always love my mama*
> *She born me in this world*
>
> *Sometimes I feel so bad*
> *When I think of all the things I used to do*
> *My mama used to clean somebody else's house*
> *Just to buy me a new pair of shoes*
> *I never understood how mama made it through the week*
> *When she never ever got a good night's sleep*
>
> *Remember when we used to run around there*
> *Steal the hubcaps off the cars*
> *And take the batteries too*
> *We was lucky we ain't got busted, man*

Hypnotized by its driving rhythm-and-blues beat, Billy and his friends couldn't hear enough of the song. At the senior prom that spring, they made the band play it twelve straight times. When it came time for the seniors to choose a song to sing at graduation, there was no contest.

But to the Minority Students' Council and some black parents, this was a blatant effort to slip racial innuendo into the graduation ceremony. To them, "I'll Always Love My Mama"—with its focus on a black scrubwoman and her ne'er-do-well son—had clear racial overtones. Besides, James Howard, the black music teacher, had plans of his own—he'd been preparing his predominantly black Glee Club, of which Cassandra Twymon was a member, to sing at graduation, and the song he'd chosen was "We've Only Just Begun," a ballad about young people starting off in life together.

> *We've only just begun*
> *White lace and promises*
> *A kiss for luck and we're on our way*
> *And yes we've just begun.*

In May, the debate grew angrier. The blacks formally protested "I'll Always Love My Mama." The Last White Class didn't want Howard's black Glee Club singing at their graduation. Moreover, the whites contended that "We've Only Just Begun" was black propaganda, a way of saying, "We've only just begun to take over your school."

Bob Murphy had to make the decision, and he chose to omit both "I'll Always Love My Mama" and the Glee Club. James Howard at the piano would play—and the seniors would sing—"We've Only Just Begun." But when The Last White Class gathered at Hynes Auditorium on June 2, Billy McGoff and his classmates stood silent all through the song. To Lisa it was, indeed, as if some alien force had taken over their school. After Billy's graduation, she decided she didn't want to return to Charlestown High in the fall.

It was a wrenching decision. All her young life she'd looked forward to being a senior there. To most young Townies, that was the Big Moment: for one brief year, before starting to earn a living or raise a family, they were Kings and Queens of the Hill, masters of all they surveyed. But for Lisa busing had changed all that. Her junior year had been one long succession of boycotts, walkouts, sit-ins, and demonstrations. To be sure, she had helped orchestrate some of that unrest, but she had had enough. She couldn't take another year.

When Lisa told several teachers of her decision, they were distressed. A solid B student and born leader, she was a prime candidate for a college scholarship. She mustn't sacrifice all that. Alice took a different tack. Lisa didn't have to return to school if she didn't want to—Alice would support whatever decision she made. But why decide right then? Perhaps she'd feel differently in the fall.

Through most of that Bicentennial summer, hanging out at the Harvard-Kent gym, playing basketball and volleyball with her friends, Lisa tried to put the high school and its problems out of her mind. Then in mid-August she spent a rare week away from Charlestown. Boston University sponsored an "adventure-challenge camp" in New Hampshire for underprivileged city youths. Modeled in part on the Outward Bound program, it was designed to teach young people about the natural environment, encourage them to take prudent risks, and help youths from different social backgrounds function as a team. In the group which arrived in the foothills of Mount Monadnock on August 8 were nine young Townies, Lisa among them.

Lodged in Robert Frost House—a large cabin flanked by huts named after Ralph Waldo Emerson and Henry David Thoreau—the campers followed an exacting regimen. Rising at 6:45, they ran a half mile, did thirty minutes of calisthenics, took a plunge in Halfmoon Pond, then breakfasted on flapjacks and bacon before embarking on a rigorous schedule of organized recreation. At first, they concentrated on games intended to promote cooperation and interdependence: the "human knot," a spider's web of arms and legs which had to be untangled without anyone letting go, or the "trust fall," in which each camper fell backward from a ladder into his colleagues' arms. At midweek, they set off on a three-day bivouac: canoeing along Lake Spoonwood, climbing Mount Skatutakee, pitching two-man tents on the summit. By Friday they were ready for the climactic tests: a steep slide along a nylon cable into the icy waters of the Nubanusit River, and the "high traverse," in which they climbed a sixty-foot rope ladder, then inched their way along cables suspended between two trees, while someone on the ground held a safety rope looped over a cable and attached to their waists.

Of the forty campers in Lisa's group, seventeen were blacks from Roxbury and the South End. She came to know three of them—Tony, Nelson, and Herb—reasonably well. On the bivouac she shared a campfire with Nelson, who proved a skillful short-order cook. When she did the high traverse, it was Herb who held the safety line, assuring her against a fall.

When the week was over and the camp bus brought them back to the city, Lisa found the leave-taking more difficult than she'd expected. Those days in the mountains had been so intense, the feelings of mutual dependence so keen, that bidding goodbye to kids she barely knew, she was surprised to find her eyes brimming with tears.

In September, Lisa resolved to go back to Charlestown High. To leave now, she realized, would be the coward's way out. Why should she let a bunch of black kids ruin what could be the best year of her life? She still didn't care for most blacks—they were too loud, too raunchy, too alien. But her brief experiences with a few classmates the year before and those vivid moments in New Hampshire had dissipated the fear she once felt. No longer did she see most blacks as potential rapists or assailants; she could live with them if she had to.

But if she went back to school she was determined to have a traditional Townie senior year; Garrity and the black kids weren't going to take that away from her. She was going to have a yearbook, a prom, a banquet, a formal graduation just like everyone else. And to make sure that things turned out as she planned, she would be senior class president.

The family often joked about a McGoff "dynasty" at the high school. Danny had been senior class president in 1974. The following year Billy narrowly lost his race, settling for Student Council vice-president. Both Alice and her sister Donnie had been class treasurers, while Uncle Steve Texeira had been president. Lisa was determined to follow in that succession.

She faced a formidable opponent: Eddie Irvin, the "shop mug" convicted of kicking Ted Landsmark on City Hall Plaza that spring. A lively wisecracker and practical joker, Eddie had long been a popular figure in the electrical shop. His role in the Landsmark affair, far from discrediting him with most of his classmates, had only fortified his reputation. For weeks he'd been in the papers and on TV, making him the closest thing the school had to a genuine celebrity. Class vice-president the year before and still supported by a solid bloc of shop votes, Eddie was the odds-on favorite to move up to president.

Some teachers and administrators found that prospect dismaying, fearing it would be viewed as fresh evidence of Charlestown's racism; despite Lisa's aggressive leadership of the White Caucus, she struck them as the lesser of two evils. One teacher was so determined to block Eddie Irvin's path that he borrowed a time-honored technique from Boston's electoral wars, persuading a third candidate to enter the lists. Since football captain Jim "Chippa" Godding also came from the electrical shop, his candidacy was calculated to split Eddie's natural constituency.

Lisa didn't see the race as an ideological contest. She liked Eddie and stood by him after his arrest. But while she hadn't sought to profit from his conviction, she was prepared to accept any support the issue might bring her. Campaigning that fall with fierce resolution, she plastered the school walls and bulletin boards with brightly lettered posters proclaiming: "Don't Goof Off— Vote McGoff!" And while Eddie ran alone, Lisa put together a slate of popular girls: Carolyn Wrenn for vice-president, Kelly Gamby for treasurer, and Joan Smith for secretary.

When the votes were tallied on September 27, Eddie Irvin had built up a heavy margin in the electrical shop, but Chippa Godding drew off just enough of the shop mugs for Lisa to squeak through by twelve votes, carrying her running mates with her. At dinner that night, the McGoffs hailed the latest member of the dynasty.

In the following weeks Lisa took on a number of other functions: secretary of the Student Council, editor in chief of the yearbook, staff editor of *Chip*, the student paper, and seats on the Senior Activities, Senior Banquet, and Prom committees. With a hand in virtually every class activity, she was now in a position to work toward the traditional Townie year she craved. Her classmates were weary and perplexed, eager for someone to show them the way; underclassmen traditionally followed the seniors' lead. If she played her cards right and carried her supporters with her, she might help restore some semblance of the good old days at Charlestown High.

But there were other influences at work. Determined to keep busing at the forefront of Townies' attention, Powder Keg went on agitating. Alice McGoff attended every rally and demonstration she could, and when school opened in

September, Alice and other Charlestown mothers resumed their prayer marches up the hill. On October 4, Powder Keg called a major boycott at the high school, urging all students to walk out in protest against "the second year of judicial tyranny on Bunker Hill."

For the first time in many months, Lisa failed to join a boycott. The night before, she told her mother, "I just can't do it, Ma. I'm class president now. I have to set an example." For both mother and daughter it was a difficult situation—others would surely notice that Lisa had failed to follow her own mother's lead. But except for refusing to put her kids on a bus, Alice had never insisted that her children fall in line behind her. If they were old enough to go to high school, they were old enough to make their own decisions. "Don't worry about it, Lisa," she said that night. "I'll do my thing, you do yours."

In part, Lisa's new attitude reflected urgings from the new senior class adviser. The class of '76 had drawn much of its militancy from its adviser, John Brennan. So great was Brennan's influence on The Last White Class that Headmaster Bob Murphy suspected him of fomenting many of Charlestown High's troubles and allowed his contract to lapse.

Lisa and her classmates turned instead to an exuberant math teacher named Pat Greatorex. In a town known for vivid personalities, Pat was an original— a squat fireplug who played ferocious linebacker for the Townie team, a wild man off the field as well as on. Once he had a few drinks in him, he would swallow everything in sight—a handful of change, a lighted candle, a dozen roses—earning himself the title of "Geek," a carnival performer who bites the heads off live chickens. He was equally renowned for other antics. Once, after the Townies had beaten a team called Billy's Cowboys, Pat showed up at the 520 Club dressed only in red bikini underwear, boots, a ten-gallon hat, and a belt of six-shooters, winning him his second moniker, "the Rhinestone Cowboy." His special blend of muscular virility and raffish derangement made him a legendary figure in the Town.

When Lisa asked him that fall to be senior class adviser, Pat said, "I'd like to help you guys, but I'm not interested in all that sit-in and walkout garbage. If that's what you're into, count me out." Lisa assured him she was tired of it too, that all she wanted was an old-fashioned senior year. "Okay," said Pat. "I'm your man."

Not everyone appreciated Pat's approach. He got more than a few anonymous phone calls warning him to stop playing Garrity's game. And up at the barbershop his friends told him that Bobby Davidson of the Defense Fund had been going around town saying that Greatorex was a "nigger lover." A few days later, outside the high school, Pat braced Bobby against the fence and told him that if he mentioned his name once more he'd punch him in the nose.

One obstacle to the kind of year both Pat and Lisa wanted was money. The prom, the senior banquet, the class trip were all expensive, so Pat and Lisa devised a scheme to raise the necessary funds. Pat bought candy wholesale; Lisa organized a cadre of senior girls to sell it during lunch hour. They called their plan Project Zit, after the pimple which often accompanies a sweet tooth; they posted signs in the corridors reading: "Fat is beautiful. Eat more candy." The school's hunger for sweets was insatiable. The class raised $4,000, earning Pat Greatorex still another nickname, "the Candy Man."

Greatorex enlisted several colleagues to help him minister to the class of '77. One was Dick Glennon, a civil service instructor, who served as adviser to the yearbook staff. Since Lisa was yearbook editor, she and Glennon worked closely together, and that was fine with her, because she had a powerful crush on him. The principal romantic interest in Lisa's life remained Chuckie Hayes, a Townie hockey star who played for Don Bosco High. He was everything she'd always wanted: blond, blue-eyed, a superb athlete. They had dated all through high school, and the summer before her senior year he gave her a friendship ring, which Lisa assumed was the first step toward their engagement. But that didn't stop her from mooning over Dick Glennon.

Lisa cherished Pat Greatorex and pined for Dick Glennon, but she revered Jerry Sullivan, widely regarded as the school's best teacher. Jerry had unusual credentials for a public high school. His father, an executive in Joseph P. Kennedy's film empire, sometimes ran movies down to Hyannis Port, where he established cordial relations with the future President. Jerry grew up in suburban Wellesley, went to private school, then on to Harvard. Arriving at Charlestown High in 1970, he quickly displayed formidable teaching skills and, after a year off for a master's at Harvard's School of Education, returned to become chairman of the Social Studies Department as well as president of the short-lived Faculty Senate. A dedicated liberal, he hung out with the faculty's other social activists, who regularly gathered for "Thank God It's Friday" sessions at the Warren Tavern.

But through the early seventies, Jerry forged a close friendship with that quintessential Townie, John Brennan. At first, the improbable pair confronted each other across a chasm of class and culture. Yet each was huge—John six feet three and 240 pounds, Jerry six feet six and 290 pounds—generating that special affinity of men who tower over the rest of the world. Somehow even their polarities—Wellesley vs. Charlestown, Harvard vs. Boston College, suburban liberal vs. ethnic conservative—drew them together, each strangely attracted by the world he didn't know. If Jerry taught John to acknowledge the saving graces of the two-toilet Irish, so John gave Jerry a quick course in Charlestown's festering resentments. The first year of busing brought them even closer together, as Jerry came to question some of his most cherished assumptions about schools and race.

His teaching career had been grounded in an old-fashioned American faith in the efficacy of education. He had chosen the public schools because he wanted to bring the blessings of knowledge to the poor and disadvantaged. And he shared the liberal conviction that if only blacks could be guaranteed an equal—which meant integrated—education, they could claim their share of the American Dream.

But recent years had shaken these assumptions. Charlestown High had always been a school of last resort, but the buses had brought blacks who were even less prepared than Charlestown's whites. What benefit, Jerry wondered, could possibly derive from mixing the poor with the impoverished, the disadvantaged with the handicapped?

When the students were asked to write capsule autobiographies, it was often difficult to tell whether the authors were white or black.

"I live in a wore-down, dilapidated neighborhood," wrote a kid from Lower Roxbury. "Run-down houses, run-down streets in a run-down neighborhood, full of a lot of run-down people. So obviously, if the people are run-down, they're the ones who run down the neighborhood. You see, my community at one time was junkie-infested. But it isn't now. The junkie population has decreased and the wino and reefer addicts have increased and now all we have is a bunch of delinquent juveniles in the neighborhood. . . . The neighborhood is messed up or degrading to me and others with morals. . . . Urban living stinks."

"I got up late," wrote a white youth. "I'd been late six times already and didn't want to get suspended, so I just stayed out of school and fooled around all day. Me and my friend snuck on the train and went over to the [Boston] Garden. We tried to sneak into the movie theaters, but they kept chasing us out. . . . So we went back to Charlestown and just hung around, and then we got a ride over to the junkie to sell the copper piping we lifted last night. We stopped at McDonald's, stayed there for a while, and then we came back up the corner and hanged around until it got dark. . . . Everyone had money, so we got loaded. We brought all our stuff behind the V.F.W. and we stayed there all night. I left to go down to the store and the kid I was with stole a cassette player out of a car. He was loaded and the cops came and we had to dig. I wasn't even in on it, but they still would of pinched me. . . ."

Once brimming with enthusiasm, Jerry was now overcome by the futility of it all. It was hard to get his students—white or black—to read a book. The school's library held 3,000 volumes and was hung with inspirational signs like "Knowledge is the key to the future" and "The only thing necessary for the triumph of evil is for good minds to do nothing." But the librarian complained that few students ever took her wares home. The only book checked out five times over the past year was *Orr on Ice,* by Bruins star Bobby Orr. If Jerry Sullivan assigned his students to write a book report, they often did little more than plagiarize the blurbs on the cover. If he called on them to discuss their reading in class, they would say, "It was boring," or simply sit there tongue-tied. How did you teach kids like that?

But even a dispirited Jerry Sullivan was a better teacher than most of his colleagues. In his senior elective on twentieth-century world history, he searched for new ways to make Fascism, the cold war, the atom bomb, and the United Nations relevant to kids who'd never been twenty miles from their doorsteps.

One morning, as Lisa and her classmates settled behind the scarred wooden desks of Room 438, Jerry said, "I assume you've all read the selection from Alvin Toffler's *Future Shock*. Can you give me some examples of the problems which will affect you in the years ahead?"

"Kids smoking dope?" a white kid suggested.

"Okay," said Jerry. "Drugs are a problem."

"Houses that are falling down," offered a Puerto Rican girl.

"Sure," said Jerry. "Shelter is a problem for all of us."

Soon the blackboard was filled with an extensive catalogue of contemporary social problems: drugs, shelter, pollution, food supply, declining family life, the crisis of religion, unemployment, threats to world peace, racial tensions, energy shortage, crime, disasters, disease.

"That's quite a string of predicaments," Jerry said. "But many of them have been with us since the beginning. Which is really new?"

"Racial tensions," suggested a white youth.

"Really?" said Jerry. "Haven't we always had tensions between groups?"

"Not in the early days, when whites were superior and the colored were inferior."

"You mean before the Civil War?"

"Yeh, like in slavery days."

"Well," Jerry said. "Now that slavery has been abolished, we're trying to sort out legal rights and obligations. Of course, not everyone agrees on things like busing and affirmative action."

Lisa raised her hand. "The racial stuff isn't that new," she said. "We've always had it. What's new is the governmental interference. Governments are getting more power."

"More than Hitler and Stalin?" Jerry asked.

"Well, no," said Lisa, "but in its own way it's worse, because it pretends to be democratic. Democracy is slipping away. The federal government is taking over the power of the states, the state is taking over what the city should have, the city is taking what the family should have."

Jerry smiled, recognizing the rhetoric from Powder Keg's literature. But he had to admit that Lisa delivered it well. She was nimble, alert, never afraid to speak her mind, though she tended to exaggerate.

"Would you say you're suffering from Present Shock?" he asked.

"Yeh, Mr. Sullivan," Lisa said, "I got it bad."

But that shock was beginning—very slowly—to recede. One bit of evidence was the pleasure she got from her psychology course, presided over by her only black teacher, Steve Grace. The former football coach at Roxbury High, Grace had transferred to Charlestown the previous summer, becoming one of four blacks on its faculty of fifty-two. He wasn't altogether happy there. To compensate for his football job, Charlestown offered to make him assistant basketball coach, an insufficient recompense which he ruefully declined. He'd been assigned the school's smallest classroom, a narrow space barely large enough for its twelve desks and chairs. And from the beginning several white teachers and many white kids made it clear that he wasn't welcome.

Gradually Steve overcame such resentment by simply ignoring it. Instead of bristling at the slights, he displayed an aggressive friendliness which first astonished, then beguiled the Townies. In the hallways he greeted even the most hostile whites with a cheery "Good morning, Tommy," "How you doing, Sharon?" In class, he went out of his way to show he wasn't favoring blacks. Once when he stopped a black boy from hassling a white girl, the boy shouted, "Hey, Mr. Grace, you're black. How come you're on my case?"

"You think just because you've got a black teacher you can do anything you want?" snapped Steve. "Well, there isn't any Black Power in this room. And there isn't any White Power. There's only the power of Amazin' Grace."

On St. Patrick's Day, Steve bought fifty stickum shamrocks to paste all over his classroom, even sticking one on his collar. The Townies were astonished. "Hey, Mr. Grace," one boy said, "are you Irish?"

"Do I look Irish?"

"No."

"Well, you don't have to be Irish to celebrate St. Patrick's Day. Like you don't have to be black to appreciate Abdul Jabbar or Aretha Franklin."

Soon, white kids he'd never seen before were poking their heads through the door to ask for a shamrock, and several blacks used them to decorate their school books.

White teachers warned him that he mustn't, under any circumstances, discuss racial issues in class. That struck him as ridiculous. Surely race was the one subject uppermost in everybody's mind. Why not bring it out in the open?

One day a Townie hockey player complained that suburban teams thought everybody from Charlestown carried a knife in his back pocket. Steve explained that that was what psychologists called a stereotype; everybody was afflicted with them, particularly on subjects and people they didn't know much about. In his junior and senior classes, he asked each race for their stereotypes of one another. In Lisa's class, some of the answers were surprising.

"Blacks can't dance," one white kid said. "When they try to rock 'n' roll, they look silly."

"That's a relief!" quipped Steve. "All these years I've been told I had rhythm."

"White folks smell," said a black.

"That's interesting," said Steve. "How many of you white folks think blacks smell?"

When a forest of white hands reached for the ceiling, the classroom erupted in nervous laughter. It was the first time Lisa could remember whites and blacks at Charlestown High laughing together.

Such moments were rare indeed. The school was largely free of the brawls and boycotts which had kept it in constant turmoil the year before, but blacks and whites held rigidly aloof from one another. In class they sat separately—whites generally in front, blacks in the rear. At lunch hour the division was still more pronounced, whites holding center stage around the teacher's desk while blacks clustered in a corner. Hurrying through the hallways or up and down the crowded stairwells, they bumped and jostled, rarely exchanging more than a careless epithet.

Lisa still felt uncomfortable with most blacks. Two boys made her particularly nervous because they wouldn't leave her alone. When they passed in the hallways they held their hands over their hearts and crooned, "Look how fine!" or "Isn't she foxy!" She realized that those were supposed to be compliments, but she refused to acknowledge them for fear the boys would take further liberties. She felt equally estranged from most black girls in her class, especially those, like Cassandra Twymon and Anita Anderson, whom she found loud and aggressive. Most blacks still seemed alien creatures from another world.

In years gone by, the two races might have encountered each other in the Glee Club, Chess Club, Science Club, Camera Club, or Candy Stripers. But with teachers and students now unwilling to stay at school any longer than necessary, most extracurricular activities had atrophied during the busing era. The third-floor auditorium, once humming with assemblies, rallies, and theatricals, now stood vacant because Bob Murphy regarded such gatherings as a foolhardy invitation to further disorders.

Though blacks and whites didn't traffic with each other, a few mavericks moved uneasily between the two camps. Among them were Janeth and Enrique Rivas, who had emigrated to the South End in 1975, just in time to board the first buses for Charlestown. Now seniors, they were light-skinned, middle-class Colombians easily distinguished from the school's working-class Puerto Ricans, who were often regarded as black. The Rivases occupied a no-man's-land which afforded them an unusual vantage point for observing the opposing forces.

An avid reader of novels and poetry, sixteen-year-old Janeth kept a diary which recorded her bemusement at both whites and blacks.

She examined the Townies: "Since I haven't made many friends, I have a lot of time to analyze them and sure feel sorry for them. They might have a great deal going, you know, but they don't seem to take advantage of this. . . . They don't push, they don't get out of their own town. They are born, raised and die without knowing that there are thousands of people that would give them a helping hand."

Black behavior: "In the area designated for lockers, this morning there was a group of black girls yelling at each other so loud that the building seemed to disintegrate. . . . 'Individualized behavior,' perhaps!"

Dropouts: "A guy in my homeroom who is eighteen or nineteen and wasted a year already because he 'hates niggers way down to his guts,' decided to leave school again."

The final bell: "It's incredible how in tenths of a second the school is empty. But it's a sad feeling, though, to see a lot of empty heads and pea-sized brains walking out, with an even smaller future ahead."

Lisa McGoff wouldn't have put it quite that way, but she too was dismayed by the sluggishness that seemed to beset the school that year. As autumn descended into winter, Lisa sought some means of rallying her classmates. A teacher suggested that the class of '77 sponsor a Christmas tree in the school's front lobby. Lisa loved the idea—Christmas was her favorite time of year, standing as it did for warmth, closeness, and good cheer, all the traditional Townie virtues which she hoped to restore at Charlestown High. But Bob Murphy was dubious: it seemed extraneous to his central task of keeping blacks and whites from each other's throats. When Lisa persisted, he relented, but with one condition: she must try to involve black students, so nobody could claim the Townies had expropriated Christmas.

Lisa readily agreed, but when she approached several blacks on the Senior Activities Committee—Cassandra Twymon among them—they weren't interested. To decorate and light the tree meant staying several hours after school, then returning home after dark through hostile Charlestown. It seemed more trouble—perhaps more danger—than it was worth.

Even so, Lisa pressed ahead. Her next problem was finding a tree. Pat Greatorex was reluctant to take money allocated for the senior prom or banquet, so several security aides took matters into their own hands. Downtown in the Haymarket shopping district, where Italian merchants had a huge selection of trees, they picked out a towering fir with graceful boughs. While one of them distracted the vendor with football talk, two others hustled the tree into their pickup and made for Charlestown. Creaking up Breed's Hill, they were dismayed to see a police car nudging them to the curb. But it was only a friend who exclaimed, "That's the biggest damn tree I ever saw! I been looking for one like that." He seemed disappointed when they told him they'd chopped it in the New Hampshire woods.

They installed the tree in the marble lobby, embraced by the curving stairways where the winter before Charlestown whites had staged so many bitter demonstrations. One evening, a half dozen senior girls joined Lisa for the tree-dressing ceremony. For hours they draped the boughs with red, blue, and yellow bulbs, golden balls, shimmering spangles, peppermint canes, artificial snow, and, at the very pinnacle, a dazzling silver star. When their work was done and the tree lit up with dozens of winking lights, the girls sang a chorus of "Silent Night."

The response to the tree was electric. As students filed through the metal detectors the next morning, they exclaimed over the first touch of gaiety the school had permitted itself in more than sixteen months. Soon there was a clamor for more—anything—to break the dismal routine. With the basketball team about to play its traditional rival, South Boston High, and the hockey squad entering a critical tournament, someone suggested a pep rally.

Like many of the school's extracurricular activities, pep rallies had been allowed to lapse. Once busing began they had fallen under Bob Murphy's strict prohibition on any gathering that might provoke violence. Now Lisa implored the headmaster to show some confidence in the class of '77. Murphy was reluctant—pep rallies were notoriously raucous affairs, designed to stir not only school pride but a territorial chauvinism which could easily slip into racial hostility. Nevertheless, he consented.

For sports was the one arena in which whites and blacks had managed to collaborate at Charlestown High. The few blacks who gained anything but grudging toleration were invariably those who displayed prowess on court or field. One was Sandra Payne, a high-scoring forward on the girls' basketball team. At first she encountered only distrust from her white teammates, but soon her one-handed jump shot claimed their applause, her kooky merriment their affection, and she became known to one and all as "Spacey." Another was Joe Strickland, an acknowledged star at both football and basketball, now rewarded with a co-captaincy of the basketball team. His uncanny grace, the sheer ebullience with which he played, reminded several white teachers of a young Willie Mays. Those coltish good spirits proved irresistible to his teammates and captivating to many of the senior girls (among them a blond cheerleader named Diane Nadeau, with whom Joe joked—*but only joked*—about going to the prom). Lisa and her friends loved to kid around with Joe because he never took offense at their gibes, invariably responding in kind. "A real good nigger," his classmates called him, or "the only good nigger I ever met."

As they organized the pep rally, Lisa and her friends cast about for an appropriate theme. When seven of them gathered after school one day, Carolyn Wrenn said, "How about the Seven Dwarfs?"

"Who'd be Snow White?"

"Joe Strickland," someone suggested.

They all laughed. But Lisa sensed an opportunity. This time Mr. Murphy would surely insist that blacks be included in the show, yet some whites were bound to take offense. It'd be better if they could make a joke of the whole thing, and who could pull that off better than loose and breezy Joe? When they approached him, he readily agreed.

On Friday, December 17, some three hundred students crowded into the third-floor auditorium. Blacks and whites automatically found their way to separate sections of the hall, from which they regarded each other with glum apprehension. Husky security aides and male teachers ringed the walls, watching for the first sign of trouble. Outside in the corridors, a dozen policemen stood at the ready.

Chippa Godding as MC welcomed the audience to "the first pep rally we've had in more than five years." Thanking Mr. Murphy for "his faith in us," he admonished the students to be "worthy of that trust."

Three cheerleaders, in blue Charlestown High sweaters, pranced onstage to lead the crowd in a desultory cheer: "Right on, Townies, right on."

Then came the Seven Dwarfs, clad in sloppy denim overalls, T-shirts, striped socks, and white sneakers, trudging across the stage as they chanted:

Hi ho, hi ho,
It's off to work we go

We keep on working all day long.
Hi ho, hi ho, hi ho, hi ho.

Every few feet one of them would fall, the others tumbling over her, landing in a heap, then untangling themselves and marching off in another
direction.

Eventually, they assembled at center stage to introduce themselves: Carolyn Wrenn as Sneezy, waving a big white handkerchief; Maureen McDougall
as Happy, with oversize teeth; Kelly Gamby as Doc, with black spectacles and
knit cap; Rebecca Miller as Bashful, hiding behind her fluttery hands; Jean
Smith as Sleepy, with drooping eyelids; Joan Smith as Dopey, with a pointed
dunce cap; and Lisa as Grumpy, her face crumpled in a doleful grimace.

Then, turning toward the wings, they called, "Whitey!" "Hey, Snowy!"
"Come here, Snow White!"

Out leapt Joe Strickland in a Charlestown High T-shirt, a long green skirt,
a Hawaiian lei around his neck, a yellow flower in his hair, dashes of white
paint on his ebony cheeks.

The auditorium rocked with laughter as Joe, striking a girlish pose, yelled,
"Give me a T."

"You got your T," the crowd responded.

"Give me an O."

"You got your O."

"Give me a W."

"You got your W."

And so on until Joe demanded, "What have you got?" and the crowd thundered, "TOWNIES!"

Then the Dwarfs advanced toward the apron, spread their hands wide, and
launched into a ragged rendition of "I'm Dreaming of a White Christmas."
Every time they reached the word "white" they paused to let Joe deliver it in
his off-key baritone. The kids seemed to love it, and when the rally ended
several minutes later, they rewarded the performers with a standing ovation.

The long-run reaction was mixed. Bob Murphy was so pleased with the
rally's decorum that he took to the public address system to congratulate his
charges on their good behavior. Several teachers found the Seven Dwarfs skit
"charming." But others weren't so sure. One young liberal said he had
"cringed in embarrassment" all the way through. And several black students
berated Joe Strickland for playing "Stepin Fetchit for the white folks."

Gradually Murphy relaxed his rigorous regime. Soon he authorized another schoolwide event, a "Gong Show" to be produced by the Student Council on March 4. Once again the senior girls did most of the organizing, and
Mr. Grace and two other teachers agreed to serve as judges. Several blacks—
among them Cassandra Twymon—were enlisted to dance or sing. Lisa and
Carolyn Wrenn dressed up as "fifties persons" in plaid skirts, fluffy sweaters,
pearls, and penny loafers to sing a golden oldie called "Bobby's Girl." But the
grand prize was taken by Pat Greatorex and another brawny teacher named

Jimmy Kent, decked out as "special ballerinas of the Boston Ballet" in flowing wigs, red leotards, and gauzy tutus. Their improbable pirouettes and arabesques brought down the house.

But though such diversions eased tensions at Charlestown High, they did nothing to defuse the underlying confrontation. In case anyone was inclined to forget it, the race issue had a way of cropping up just when it was least expected.

The school day began with a homeroom period, during which teachers took attendance, made announcements, and presided over the weekly Pledge of Allegiance, long a matter of contention at Charlestown High.

One morning in March 1977, as Assistant Headmaster Bob Jarvis came on the public address system to say, "All please stand for the Pledge of Allegiance to the Flag," most of the students in Lisa's room stumbled to their feet. But Nancy Green, a black senior who had been absent for much of the winter, remained sitting in the front row. As thirteen youthful voices intoned the familiar litany—"I pledge allegiance to the flag of the United States of America and to the Republic for which it stands"—John Humphrey, a hockey star who had recently scored three goals in Charlestown's victory over South Boston, turned on Nancy Green.

"What's the matter with you?" he shouted. "You too good to stand up?"

Nancy stared straight ahead, giving no sign that she had heard him.

Humphrey persisted. "Don't you people respect the flag?" he asked. "Don't you respect your country?"

Standing nearby, Lisa was surprised by the anger in his voice. She sort of liked Nancy Green, a gentle, dignified girl who never came on strong like Cassandra Twymon or Anita Anderson. And Lisa knew something John Humphrey didn't know: that Nancy was a Jehovah's Witness, which prohibited her from taking oaths or pledges of any sort. Whatever other reservations Nancy may have had about such patriotic observations, her religion prevented her from taking part.

When Humphrey went on denouncing the girl, Nina Wright—their homeroom teacher—ordered him into the hallway. There the argument raged on. Nina explained that no student was required to stand against the dictates of his or her conscience, but Humphrey continued to inveigh against busing, blacks, and Nancy Green in particular. When his teacher asked him to apologize, he said he would offer an explanation of his behavior to the class but never to "that girl." Eventually, the hockey star was suspended for five days. On his way out of school that afternoon he put his fist through a glass door panel, leaving a jagged hole that went unrepaired for weeks, a tangible reminder of Charlestown's persistent resentments.

It was scarcely surprising that when the class of '77 issued invitations to the senior banquet on March 24, few blacks chose to attend. Pat Greatorex worked hard to get them there, promising that two of his most formidable friends from the Townie team—defensive tackle "Ditso" Doherty and linebacker Jerry McCormick—would maintain order. But the banquet was scheduled for 7:00 p.m. at the Cobblestone Restaurant on Medford Street, a section of Charlestown considered perilous for blacks even during the daytime. Ultimately, only four of the class's eleven blacks showed up: Eddie Dykes, Curt Shepherd, Sandra Payne, and Joe Strickland.

The Townies turned out in force, the boys in formal suits and ties, the girls in bright party dresses or slacks. The Cobblestone's Charlestown Room was "colonial"—brass chandeliers, yellow bulbs molded to look like candles, the stucco walls bedecked with American eagles, fifes, drums, and musketry. Formica tables formed a square, leaving room for a dance floor, and by 7:15 a student d.j. had a thick stack of disco records spinning on the phonograph. But the party got off to a slow start as boys sat with boys, girls with girls, whites with whites, blacks with blacks.

Suddenly a dark-haired senior named Julie Finn dragged a reluctant shop mug out to dance. Soon they were joined by others, and for nearly an hour the floor was filled with writhing bodies. Only one minor incident marred the festivities. When Eddie Dykes asked a blond girl to dance, a white boy told him to move on. For a moment a scuffle seemed certain to erupt, but Ditso Doherty muscled in between the boys and the party resumed.

When everyone had finished supper, Lisa rapped her spoon on her glass and someone yelled, "Let's hear it for the class president," triggering heavy applause.

"Aw shucks," said Lisa. "I don't deserve that."

"You're right," yelled Patti Rooney. Everybody laughed and clapped still harder.

"But I'll take it," Lisa said. "And there are lots of other people who deserve our thanks. During our three years at Charlestown High we've had the privilege of working with some of the finest people in the Town. We can offer them nothing but respect."

Polite applause.

"But how," Lisa asked, "can you respect Mr. Greatorex, the Geek?"

Laughter and boos.

"Page 943 of Webster's Unabridged Dictionary defines a geek as 'a carnival performer.' I ask you, how do you respect a man like that?"

Wild hilarity.

"Mr. Greatorex, the Geek, the Rhinestone Cowboy. We the senior class of Charlestown High say, it's been a pleasure knowing you."

A tumult of glass rapping, table pounding, foot stomping, and hand clapping until a beet-red Pat Greatorex stumbled forward to accept their tribute.

Then Joan Smith, the class secretary, rose to read the Prophecy: "Here we are, ladies and gentlemen, at the social event of the year. This is your big-mouth reporter, talking to you live from Charlestown High's Class of '77 Twentieth Reunion. I will be giving you a minute-to-minute update on some of our famous classmates as they come in. Some are arriving now, and the first one in the door is the former Miss Carolyn Wrenn. Apparently she couldn't find a babysitter because there are twelve little ones tailing her. . . . Floating in behind them is Sandy Payne, famous woman astronaut, better known as Space Woman. . . . I don't believe my eyes, our next guest is Lisa McGoff, without Charlie or the other angels. . . . Speaking of famous couples, here comes NAACP Couple of the Year, Diane and Joe Strickland."

Finally Kelly Gamby read the Class Will.

"To Susan Cooney, we leave a six-pack of Michelob and Mike Dolaher— and, on weekends, Frankie Kelly.

"To Joe Strickland, we leave a Snow White costume and a full-length mirror.

"To Stan Caiczynski, we leave his own version of the Polish national anthem."

Most clauses were received with snickers or ribald laughter.

But when Kelly reached the next item, she turned to Eddie Irvin and said, "I hope you don't take this as an insult."

Dapper in a blue pants suit, Eddie smiled reassuringly.

"To Eddie Irvin," Kelly said, "we leave a full-size mural of City Hall Plaza and his own American flag."

With that, the class of '77 rose nearly as one to give Eddie a prolonged ovation. Only a handful of seniors—among them the Rivases and the four blacks—remained sitting at their tables.

For weeks the ovation provoked intense debate in the faculty lounge. The small liberal coterie saw it as evidence that anti-black feeling was as strong as ever at Charlestown High, simply awaiting a new pretext to erupt. Others dismissed such fears, regarding the applause as noisy affection for the class joker who had gone through a trying year. Still others contended that it had little to do with Eddie at all, that it was a ritual expression of Townie solidarity, of Charlestown armed against the world.

Lisa had mixed feelings about it. Still fond of Eddie, she was glad to pay tribute to him, but she felt bad if the ovation had embarrassed Joe Strickland and the other blacks. For Lisa was beginning to gain some perspective on her situation, to understand how others saw her. For the first time, she was expressing interest in the world beyond her town. Only a few days after the senior banquet, Lisa and three classmates embarked on a week-long visit to Washington, D.C. Sponsored by a nationwide program called Close-Up, the trip was designed to acquaint high school students with the workings of their national government. Jerry Sullivan escorted the Townies, who converged on Washington with a hundred other youths from the Boston area, joining delegations from Detroit and Atlanta.

Most of the participants had never been in their nation's capital before, but Lisa's two Powder Keg expeditions had left her feeling like an old Washington hand. Her mood was markedly different this time. Storming Capitol Hill with her mother, she'd been consumed by righteous indignation at unresponsive legislators and their bureaucratic allies. Since then, much of her anger had dissipated. Although she still regarded busing as an abomination, she was more interested now in understanding how such policies came into being and what could be done to reverse them.

For six days, the Close-Up delegations quizzed public figures all over town. The hundreds of students were divided into groups of seven, each with a secretary to pose questions and record the answers. Lisa became her group's secretary and took an active role in questioning Massachusetts Congressmen John Moakley and Paul Tsongas, Hugh Wilhere, chairman of the National Commission on Law Enforcement and Social Justice, and Ralph Alvarez of the Environmental Policy Center.

To Lisa, the most interesting session was with William White, Jr., a black man who was assistant staff director of the Civil Rights Commission. A year earlier, she would have found it difficult to sit in the same room with such a man. Now she listened intently as he declared that school desegregation was "an indisputable national goal." In some cities busing had been bitterly resisted, but it wasn't going away. "Your fellow citizens across this land have showed that it can work. Even where it's been difficult at first, desegregation sets off a process which leaves a strong, united people."

Lisa raised her hand. "Isn't busing the main reason that thousands of white families have deserted Boston's public schools?" she asked.

Such considerations were irrelevant when basic constitutional rights were at stake, White insisted. But Lisa bored in. "You haven't mentioned the word 'forced,'" she said. "Don't you realize that in most cases it isn't racism, but the idea that government can force you out of your own school, out of your own town? There has to be some other way to get desegregation." But Lisa noticed that the suburban kids seemed bored by the subject. It didn't apply to them. They seemed so carefree, it made her mad to think that they were enjoying themselves while kids in the city—black and white—were going through all this racial crap.

It was time to move on, she thought, time to attend to other things. The first was college. Despite her extracurricular responsibilities, Lisa's grades had held up well—A in biology, B+ in psychology, B+ in economics, C+ in English, C's in algebra and physical education. But the college boards frightened her. Most teachers were so preoccupied with maintaining order in their classrooms they had little time to prepare seniors for the critical exams. Lisa was particularly worried about math, always her weakest subject. Luckily Pat Greatorex provided some last-minute tutorials and Lisa slipped by with respectable scores. In April she was accepted at Bunker Hill Community College, a new two-year institution across town.

The last month of school passed in a blur. On May 5, the seniors held their prom at Montvale Plaza, Lisa arriving on the arm of a dashing Chuckie Hayes (only four blacks showed up, led by Joe Strickland in a rented Rolls-Royce). A week later, all the Townie seniors—except the blacks—spent the day swimming and playing softball at a resort in the Berkshires. There was a party somewhere in town every night, the boys drinking too heavily, the girls laughing a little too gaily, the class of '77 trying hard to mask its nervousness.

As graduation day approached, Alice McGoff was torn by seemingly irreconcilable emotions. For years she had channeled her waking energies into the crusade against Arthur Garrity's order. Morning after morning, she had trudged up Breed's Hill, chanting her "Hail Marys" and "Our Fathers," flinging imprecations at the forces which occupied the heights. For Alice and her colleagues in Powder Keg, the high school which straddled the hill had become a potent symbol in their struggle, as much an emblem of the fight for self-determination as the granite obelisk which towered above it. At all costs, they urged, Charlestown High must resist judicial tyranny. Yet Alice had watched with mounting admiration as Lisa assumed leadership at the school, managing through force of personality to restore some vestige of solidarity and tradition. Her child was a determined young woman now, armed with the courage of her convictions. Some Powder Keg members might complain about Lisa's role at the school, suggesting she had somehow sold out to the "probusers," but Alice defended her, proclaiming a mother's pride.

Then on June 2—five days before graduation—Alice woke up just after midnight with sharp pains in her chest. Billy drove her to Massachusetts General Hospital, where doctors concluded that she was suffering a gallbladder attack. The offending organ had to come out, they said, and the operation was scheduled for the morning of June 8, only hours after Lisa was to graduate.

"Okay," said Alice, "take the damn thing out. On one condition: I'm going to my daughter's graduation the night before."

"Out of the question," said the doctor.

"Listen," Alice shot back. "My daughter has just gone through two years of busing. She's the president of her class. She runs the show up there. I'm going to be at her graduation. I'm not asking you, I'm telling you!"

Finally the doctor shrugged. "It's against every medical principle," he said, "but do as you like."

At 6:30 p.m. on June 7, Alice got dressed, signed out of the hospital, and hitched a ride with Billy to Hynes Auditorium in the Back Bay. When mother and daughter embraced in the lobby, Alice handed Lisa a single red rose, tied with a silver ribbon. "Anybody who graduates from high school under these circumstances," she said, "deserves a rose."

Lisa turned, tears glistening in her eyes, and led the class of '77 up the aisle. She held the rose before her, a splash of magenta against her white gown. Taking her seat in the front row, she listened as Assistant Headmaster Bob Jarvis opened the school's 129th graduation with a backward glance at the 35th. A brisk young administrator, often critical of Charlestown's low standards, Jarvis struck a rueful note as he recalled that the 1873 ceremonies had included a Greek declaration entitled "Demosthenes and the Crown," a Latin dialogue called "Aeneas and the Sibyl," the song "Wake, Gentle Zephyr," and a valedictory address on "The Value of Purpose in Life."

Pragmatic as ever, Headmaster Bob Murphy recited the cautionary tale of Mary Ellen Barry, a Townie lass who had dropped out of high school in 1913. Now seventy-eight, she deeply regretted her childhood indiscretion. One day her daughter-in-law called to inquire if there was some way Mary Ellen could get her diploma. When the School Committee consented, Murphy and the Superintendent journeyed to her house in Braintree, "where that seventy-eight-year-old lady sat on her porch, enjoying one of the happiest and proudest moments of her life. I mention this to show you the value of a diploma. So when you receive yours today, cherish it and use it to the fullest of your ability."

School Committeewoman Pixie Palladino, always the politician, paid handsome tribute to Charlestown's "great tradition, exemplified by your Bunker Hill Day parade on Sunday next, which I will be pleased to attend."

Patti Rooney, the valedictorian, spoke of her class's tumultuous experience at Charlestown High, marked by "helicopters, newsmen, policemen, and buses, by fear and confusion."

Finally it was Lisa's turn. For more than a week she had labored over her speech, trying to distill the essence of her years at Charlestown High. Now, after Bob Jarvis introduced her as "a fine young lady, a very active young lady, a very responsible president of her class," she scrambled up the steps toward the stage. Stumbling for a moment over her long rayon gown, she righted herself and lurched on toward the microphone, as applause crashed about her.

"Mrs. Palladino, Mr. Murphy, faculty, fellow graduates, parents and friends," she began, her mouth so dry she could hardly get her tongue around the words.

"Tonight as I stand on this stage, looking out at all of you, memories of our years here seem unavoidable. As sophomores: the memory of coming to a new school, meeting new people, making new plans. As juniors, the memory of junior day, of class rings. Now as seniors, the memory of getting committees going, preparing for college."

Lisa could see her mother, Billy, Danny, Kevin, and three of her aunts seated together in the family section. Alice smiled up at her, clearly fighting back her tears, as Lisa plunged on.

"We were having fun with all our activities—like the yearbook, the prom, the senior banquet. But we were also maturing, learning and growing. Now as graduates we still have far to go. We must take our places in society, and as adults we can no longer rely totally on parents and teachers to make our decisions.

"High school was more than fun. It was learning about life. It was learning to keep on going in spite of everything that happened. We will always have this knowledge as well as our memories to use as we venture into the world, into society filled with different people, different problems, and the great unknown."

27

Twymon

In the quiet moments before the first bell, Cassandra felt almost at home at Charlestown High. It was a tranquil time, that quarter hour after the buses arrived but before the Townies rushed up the stairs; a blessed respite in which to marshal her strength for the day ahead.

Room 415 was a narrow chamber, looking out through a row of cloudy windows toward the docks and cranes of the Mystic River shore. With its drab walls, cracked blackboard, and scarred wooden desks, it was hardly attractive. But in those early-morning hours, as the smoky light filtered off the river, bathing the desk where Jerry Sullivan sat sipping coffee from a chipped mug, it seemed a cozy enclave in a hostile world.

The only blacks assigned to Jerry's homeroom, Cassandra and Curt Shepherd took quickly to the shambling teacher in his tweed jackets, button-down shirts, and shiny cordovans. As he swabbed the blackboard, beat clouds of chalky dust from the erasers, and thumbed his index cards, he kept up a stream of chatter with the two youngsters hunched before him. Spinning tales about the Harvard football team or the movie theater he managed in the summer on Martha's Vineyard, he gentled them into the daily routine. And his rumbling voice, crooked smile, and prodigious bulk were profoundly reassuring to Cassandra.

But once the clock struck eight and a dozen Townies tumbled through the door, the climate in Room 415 changed markedly. Under other circumstances, some of those very whites made cautious overtures across the racial gulf, but together in a classroom, under the appraising eyes of their colleagues, none dared such a gesture. Only the most outgoing blacks could thaw that icy front, and neither Curt nor Cassandra boasted the necessary self-assurance. Even Jerry Sullivan's bluff geniality couldn't crack the rigid demarcation which kept the whites massed on one side of the room, the two blacks sheltered in the lee of the teacher's desk.

Curt and Cassandra barely knew each other, rarely exchanging more than perfunctory greetings, but they found solace in each other's presence. Sometimes, as the whites gibed at them from across the room, Curt turned in the second row to give Cassandra a sardonic little grin, to which she responded with a barely perceptible nod. But Curt was there only three hours a day. When the bell rang at 11:06, he gathered up his books and headed for the Occupational Resource Center across town, where he took vocational courses. For the next twenty minutes, as the students downed box lunches at their desks, Cassandra was the only black left in the room. With a dozen Townies whooping around her, she bowed her head and concentrated on her baloney sandwich. Sometimes when she finished eating, Jerry Sullivan stopped by to ask how she was doing, but that did little to relieve her loneliness. As the weeks passed, Cassandra felt acutely uncomfortable in Room 415.

Increasingly, she sought out her one true friend at the school, a lively, high-strung girl named Desiree Johnson. Cassandra and Desiree shared a first-floor locker, where they met every morning to deposit their coats, pick up their books, and exchange the latest gossip before walking arm in arm to their homerooms. As Cassandra grew more disturbed by her isolation, she implored Jerry Sullivan to let her eat lunch, at least occasionally, in Desiree's room. That was strictly against the rules, but realizing how lonely Cassandra was, Jerry reluctantly acceded.

Others proved less sympathetic. Exasperated by Cassandra and Desiree, civil service instructor Dick Glennon dubbed them "Frick and Frack," a phrase the girls found vaguely insulting ("If we called him something like that," Cassandra complained, "we'd be in trouble"). One morning, when she and Desiree lingered in the corridor through the opening minutes of his class, Glennon ordered Cassandra to stay half an hour after school. Afraid of staying in Charlestown after the other blacks had gone home, she refused. Punished with a one-day suspension, Cassandra conceived a burning resentment of Glennon, whom she labeled a "prejudiced person."

Uncomfortable in most classes, she was sometimes careless in attendance. When the librarian complained that Richard Wright's *Native Son* was two weeks overdue, Cassandra insisted that she'd returned the book. Their dispute dragged on through Cassandra's third-period class, earning her another one-day suspension.

Her favorite subject was English, partly because her teacher, Maryann Mathews, took special pains to involve blacks in the class. Most Charlestown teachers regarded Shakespeare as too complex for their students but Maryann refused to believe that. That fall she had her students read *Othello*—with Joe Strickland as the noble Moor. At first, Joe mouthed his lines with little apparent comprehension. "Ay," he mumbled, "let her rot and perish, and be damned tonight; for she shall not live: no, my heart is turned to stone; I strike it, and it hurts my hand."

"Joe," Maryann interrupted, "do you know what this is all about?"

"I'm not sure," he conceded.

So Maryann translated Iago's treachery into sporting terms. Suppose, she suggested, that Clarence Jefferson had tried to grab Strickland's place on the basketball team by arousing jealousy in Maryann's husband, basketball coach Larry Mathews.

Joe began to read his lines with new conviction. "O monstrous, monstrous!" he cried.

Even Maryann hesitated when, working their way through a new anthology, they came on a story called "The Boy Who Painted Christ Black," about a Georgia youth who stirred a furor by depicting the Savior as a black man. "There'll be a lot of fuss in this world," says one character, "if you start people thinking that Christ was a nigger!"

Knowing the Church's importance in Charlestown, Maryann feared that the story might offend some Townies, but eager to give her black students a sense of belonging, she decided to take the chance. After they'd read it aloud, one girl from a devout Bunker Hill family exclaimed, "Miss, I'm surprised you'd teach something like that!" But Cassandra was quietly pleased. She'd always pictured Christ as brown—like the gaunt and bearded beggar who panhandled on Columbus Avenue.

Maryann spotted unrealized potential in Cassandra—a lively intelligence, a quick if caustic wit, a vivid flair for self-expression, tools which were rarely put to work. (Tests that year showed that Cassandra read at a tenth-grade level, spelled at a ninth-grade level, calculated as a sixth-grader.) Maryann was particularly dismayed by Cassandra's reluctance to read, her dismissal of book after book as "boring," "stupid," or "dumb." When Maryann assigned her *Julius Caesar,* Cassandra called it "a lot of 'Thou are beautiful, Juliet' or some mess like that"; *The Glass Menagerie* was "a bunch of dumb little animals"; *Seven Days in May,* a "stupid war story." Every time Cassandra picked up a book, she went to sleep after ten pages or so. "They're all so boring," she complained. Once, in a counseling session, Maryann told her, "I'd like to punch you in the nose. You think so well, Cassandra; you write wonderfully. If you'd just do a little work, you'd be getting an A. But you get C's. I want to grab you by the shoulders and shake you." Cassandra shrugged.

Larry Mathews, who had her in his economics class, found Cassandra even more exasperating. She was clearly brighter than most of his students, but sometimes she didn't bring the most basic materials to school. "I need a pencil," she'd tell him. "Do you have any paper?" And frequently she simply put her head down on the desk and closed her eyes.

"Are you ill, Cassandra?" he'd ask. "Do you want to go to the nurse?"

"No," she'd say. "I'm okay. I'm just tired."

Much of that fall, Cassandra was simply exhausted, worn out by her nightly rounds. For she and her sister Rachel had ripened into handsome young women, captivating the dudes who hung out at the bars and nightclubs near the corner of Massachusetts and Columbus avenues.

Ever since Little Rachel became pregnant at age thirteen, her mother had known the girls were "messing around." At first she sought to restrain their sexuality with strict pronouncements about where they could hang out, whom they could see, what they could do. But the girls displayed a knack for threading their way through their mother's most elaborate obstacle course. Just when Rachel thought she had them hemmed in, they found some loophole through which to crawl. If she dispatched them to the corner for ribs and fries, they'd return hours later with Kentucky Fried Chicken, saying they'd misunderstood her and gone all the way to Shawmut Avenue. One night a neighbor spotted them at the Venice, a dark, noisy tavern just up the avenue from Methunion Manor. In months to come, whenever the girls disappeared for a couple of hours, Rachel could invariably find them around the pinball machines at the rear of that dusky bar. She never caught them with a drink in their hands— they were clearly underage—but she always suspected that the men they met there slipped them drinks or drugs under the table.

When she taxed them with their transgressions, they were flatly unrepentant. At fifteen and sixteen, they regarded themselves as emancipated young women, ready to taste forbidden pleasures. Their bravado only drove Rachel to new strictures: before they left the house at night or on weekends, they had to clean their rooms, wash the dishes, scrub the bathtub. When the girls protested that none of their friends did such onerous housework, Rachel would fly into a rage. "What am I?" she'd cry. "The jolly black mammy who cleans up after everyone around here?" Sometimes after the girls did their chores, Rachel would find some small deficiency and order them to spend the rest of the night correcting it.

Their arguments grew louder and angrier, mother and daughters confronting each other in a pitiless test of wills, neither side about to back off. Sometimes the scenes ended with one or both girls stomping out of the apartment while their mother stood in the hallway shouting after them, "If you go this time, you don't need to come back!"

Aware that the girls were fooling around with men, Rachel urged them to be careful—to choose their sexual partners with some discretion, use birth control devices, make regular visits to the gynecologist. As in other matters, the girls often ignored these warnings.

In mid-September 1976, Cassandra got sick. The doctor prescribed daily medication, but she often forgot to take it. One evening, Rachel entered her daughter's room to ask if she had taken the medicine. "I ain't taking those stupid pills," said Cassandra. "Oh, yes, you are!" "No, I ain't. Now get off my case!" Something in Cassandra's response ignited the flashpan of Rachel's anger. In a moment, mother and daughter were flailing at each other with fists and nails. The squall was over in thirty seconds, but it left Rachel spent with rage. Later that night, when her friend Daisy Voight called from New York, she poured out the story of her recalcitrant daughters.

Daisy had grown up on Hammond Street, just a block from the Walkers' house on Ball Street. Leaving Boston at the age of nineteen, she had gone to New York, where she raised two children, entered public relations, and made something of a name for herself in Harlem's cultural and political worlds. But for nearly two decades she had stayed in touch with the Walker clan, especially with Rachel. A curious blend of sophistication and earthiness, Daisy provided a perfect sounding board for Rachel's mounting desperation.

So affected was she that evening by Rachel's tears that the next morning she wrote the girls a seven-page letter.

Dear Cassandra and Rachel [she said in part]. Your mom is one of my dearest friends and she is a person for whom I'd put my hand in the fire. I don't play letting nobody mess with my friends and there's plenty of hurt niggers around Boston and New York to prove my point. I'm writing to tell you that if you continue to fuck with my personal friend, Rachel, I will kick your asses. . . .

You think that there is some kind of dumb generation gap, that your mom is out of touch with what's going on, that if she was in touch she wouldn't be able to get over and hang out anyway cause she's too old. You think just cause she don't smoke pot she's square. Well let me tell you something about your mother that you don't know and that she probably won't tell you and may not thank me for telling you. When I met your mom she was hanging out, raising all sorts of hell. . . . Your mom had two children before she got married which don't seem to me to indicate that she curled up nights with a good book. My understanding of that scenario was that the gentleman dug your mother and wanted to give her the Great American Dream—2.2 children, a little bungalow, and one husband all her own. She objected to the kind of personal freedom that she would have to give up and declined. In other words, she could have if she had wanted to, but elected not to. Subsequently she married your Pops, who was a real drag. Your mother takes a long time to move but when she does it is with great finality. You see I would have put the tired nigger out long before either of you came along. But your mother is basically a softy, but she ain't no fool and she ain't no square.

I myself do not agree with all the things your mother believes in and we have great long-distance and face-to-face arguments to prove it. . . . I don't have to go for her shit cause I'm not dependent on her, but you are and as long as you are dependent on somebody you got to go for their shit no matter how bad the shit. . . . She got the power over you cause she got the money. If your momma got as cold and as icy as she could you all would be in a trick, but she ain't ready to do that yet. Unfortunately— cause if I was her I'd move and let you little monsters go for your- selves. . . . I am icy and I am going to encourage your mom to be the same. Forewarned is forearmed. . . .

But your momma is a poor black woman, the most oppressed animal in this society. We, you, me, her are way down at the bottom of the totem pole and ain't nobody gonna give us any slack. . . . And this is the whole point of the letter I think. You all is out in the street chasing the Great American Dream—a big dick—just like I was, just like your mom was, just like most American women are. And there ain't no soothing big dick out there—it don't exist—the dick that can take away all the pain of being poor, black, ugly and a woman in this society. . . .

Look, ladies, I love you both. Shit, I dangled you on my knees and changed your funky diapers and I know what I'm talking about. You all are getting ready to fuck up in a grand manner. You all going to be out there barefoot in the snow if you don't check yourselves. There is no American dream for poor black girls from Boston. Only nightmares. The folks you are running with now cannot take care of you. They can barely take care of themselves. . . . Look around you again and look at the numbers of women you can see that have children by themselves that they are taking care of and look at how many of the women have any kind of positive relationship going on. The men in Boston is jive and you all let them get away with it. Remember it takes two. You broads up there are very trifling. Why don't you decide to break out of that dumb pattern and get some real power for yourselves. Cause pussy power ain't shit. The only power that matters is money power. . . .

You all trying to be bad bitches before you have the basics together. Both your momma and I could have given bad bitches classes for Survival 101. Just think about it. Could you have survived 40 years with what you know now and have brought six crazy little monsters to adulthood? Tell the truth. Seriously, one last thing. A bad bitch is a woman, black or white, who knows who she is, knows how to get what she wants, can be sweet or evil depending on the situation, who can take care of herself without begging nobody for nothing. If you don't pass that test then you need to slow down and take a look at yourself, then get yourself some bad bitch lessons. Cause let me tell you honey, being a woman is a bitch and if you ain't got your shit together you gonna blow and blow big. Like they say in the street, ask your momma. Love, Daisy.

P.S. If there is any part of this letter you don't understand or if you want to cuss me out or if you want some bad bitch lessons, you may call me collect.

The girls got a charge out of Daisy, relishing her earth-mother style and street lingo. But she was their mother's friend, a middle-aged woman with middle-aged notions, an authority figure bound to support other authority figures. They never called for "bad bitch" lessons.

In the weeks that followed, Cassandra and Rachel plunged deeper into the South End's street life. Gradually they shifted their base from the dim recesses of the Venice to the brighter lights and faster pace of Massachusetts Avenue. Long known as "the Great Black Way" or "Black Broadway," that thoroughfare had once boasted some of the country's premier jazz clubs. But Kelly's, the Wig-Wam, and the Savoy had gone the way of all flesh. Wally's Paradise lingered on, but surrounded now by a dingy array of bars, luncheonettes, pool halls, video arcades, fast-food joints, and massage parlors. Only at night did the street retrieve some of its old glamour. Then arc lights cast an orange glow over the sooty façades; disco sounds washed from the doorways, backed by the click of billiard balls; and dudes in wide-brimmed hats paraded their fancy ladies up the boulevard.

Habitués of "the Avenue" were always on the lookout for fresh talent. Not surprisingly, the Twymon girls quickly took up with older men: Cassandra with Ricky, a thirty-nine-year-old married guy she encountered in a South End fish market; Rachel with Horace, a twenty-seven-year-old sport she met through mutual friends. Soon the girls were spending every available hour with their lovers. Often they skipped school, leaving home in the morning as if to board the bus, then slipping off to meet their friends. When their mother discovered what they were up to, she cracked the whip. Every morning for several weeks she walked the girls down the street to make sure they got on the bus. And she proclaimed a tough new curfew: ten on weeknights, eleven on Fridays and Saturdays. But these strict measures only intensified family tensions.

On the evening of November 16, Mrs. Twymon accompanied her friend Teresa Saunders to Channel 7, where Teresa was to sing and play the piano on the NAACP's weekly program, *Lift Every Voice*. Cassandra was out that night, but as the two women left for the station they asked young Rachel if she wanted to go along. She said no, and her mother found that a little peculiar. Like most teenagers, Rachel was fascinated by television, spending endless hours in front of the set. Why wouldn't she seize the chance to look behind the scenes?

Later, as she listened to Teresa soaring through the spirituals, Mrs. Twymon felt a premonition. Try as she might to focus on the music, she was nagged by a suspicion that something was terribly wrong at home. After the taping, the producer took the two women to the Playboy Club for dinner, and when they returned to Methunion Manor at about eleven, neither Cassandra nor Rachel was there. Taking a hurried look around, Mrs. Twymon noticed a suitcase missing from the hall closet, some of Rachel's clothes gone from her room. "Oh my God," she told Teresa, "I think Rachel's run away."

About midnight Cassandra returned from a late date with Ricky. Her mother said nothing, hoping she would drop some clue to Rachel's whereabouts, but Cassandra went straight to bed. For hours, Mrs. Twymon lay awake, listening for the door, hoping her fears would prove exaggerated, but at dawn Rachel's bed was still empty.

That morning, she asked Cassandra where Rachel was. Cassandra clearly knew, but wasn't telling. "She's doing what she wants to do," she said. "What's wrong with that?" Her mother flew into a rage, demanding an answer and suggesting that if Cassandra didn't cooperate, she could leave too.

Over the next few days she kept her daughter's flight a secret, telling only her brother Arnold, who said, "Rachel left on her own. She packed her bags and took off. The best thing we can do is wait. One day she's going to get tired out there on her own. She'll come home."

Instead, on the evening of November 19, Cassandra left too.

Mrs. Twymon was numb with disbelief. Every day she put in her time at the project office, but so preoccupied was she with her daughters' disappearance that when night fell she could scarcely remember what she'd done all day. By then Thanksgiving was drawing near, always a festive but tumultuous time for the Walkers. Appropriately for a family which felt so deeply rooted in the New England experience, the Walkers had long celebrated that most colonial of all holidays with a gathering of the clan. Even in years when they had little to be grateful for, grandparents, parents, aunts, uncles, brothers, and sisters assembled that day—usually at Alva's house—for a marathon of eating, drinking, dancing, talking, and card playing. In their childhood it had been a joyous occasion, but as family misunderstandings proliferated, the dinner's geniality frequently unraveled in bitter squabbles. The quarreling usually began at the evening whist game when one player accused another of cheating, provoking a bout of mutual recriminations which invariably ended with a couple of guests walking out. Nonetheless, Thanksgiving retained a powerful hold on the Walker imagination.

This year's gathering was to be a special reunion, for Daisy Voight, her new boyfriend, Ron, and her teenage children, Eric and Madeleine, were due in from New York to spend the weekend at Alva's house. A popular figure with the Walker clan, Daisy was a powerful attraction, her visit a topic of conversation for weeks in advance. Cassandra—who was particularly close to Eric and Madeleine—had eagerly looked forward to their arrival. Now, growing lonely in her self-imposed exile, she yearned for their company. Indeed, the longer she stayed away from home, the more her thoughts turned toward Thanksgiving and the friends and family who would be descending on Alva's house that day.

Since November 19, Cassandra had been living with her friend Barbara in an apartment on Ruthven Street while spending most of her time with her lover, Ricky. That arrangement provided romance and adventure, but little of the security she'd taken for granted at Methunion Manor. Every morning she talked on the telephone with her sister Rachel, ensconced in another friend's apartment on Massachusetts Avenue. Often they talked for hours, exchanging intimate revelations, making plans for their fugitive existence, speculating on what their mother was doing to get them back. But disembodied conversations were no substitute for the palpable warmth of friends and family.

On Thanksgiving morning, Cassandra took the bus up Blue Hill Avenue to Alva's house. When she encountered her friend Madeleine, the two girls fell into each other's arms. When Daisy saw Cassandra, she rushed to call Methunion Manor. "Rachel!" she cried. "There's one daughter you don't have to worry about. Cassandra just walked through the door."

"Oh my God!" Rachel exclaimed. "At least I've got something to be thankful for today."

"Why don't you come out and see her?"

"You know I can't do that. Alva and I aren't speaking."

Alva's feud with her sister—which had begun over Little Rachel's baby three years before—had steadily intensified. All through the siege of Centre Street the previous spring and summer, as other family members rallied to Alva's defense, Big Rachel resolutely kept her distance. She had never set foot in her sister's embattled house.

"I'm not coming out there," she told Daisy that morning. "If Cassandra wants to see me, tell her to come over here."

Once she hung up, Rachel was swept by alternating waves of relief and rage. At least Cassandra was safe. And if she was all right, then Little Rachel might be okay too. But what was Cassandra doing at Alva's? The notion that Cassandra might feel more comfortable with Alva than with her own mother drilled a painful spike through Rachel's chest.

In midmorning, Teresa Saunders stopped by to see if Rachel wanted to go to the Ministerial Alliance's Thanksgiving Day service. Rachel rarely missed a church service of any kind, but that day she didn't think she could sit still for an hour. Later her son Wayne urged her to come out to Alva's, but Rachel refused, so Wayne went by himself, arriving just as twenty-three people sat down to dinner where only months before the sentries of Racial Unity Now had stood guard with clubs, cameras, and walkie-talkies.

Alva had roasted a magnificent goose. There was pungent stuffing, sweet potato pie, rice, peas, mince pie, pumpkin pie, ice cream, fruit, and cookies, all washed down with prodigious quantities of soda and beer. By dusk the dinner dishes had been cleared away, whiskey and brandy began flowing, and the adults sat down to play whist. They didn't have to wait long for the traditional fight to break out, this time between Alva's brothers Tommy and Frederick. Nobody quite knew what triggered it, but suddenly there was Tommy weaving unsteadily in the middle of the living room, brandishing a silver-plated revolver at Frederick. Two other brothers—Arnold and Walter—crept across the floor, murmuring soothing words, until they persuaded Tommy to set the revolver down next to his pony glass, filled with thirty-year-old brandy.

With things getting out of hand, Alva drove her mother home. That was the opportunity Daisy had been waiting for. Somehow, she thought, mother and daughter had to be reconciled. Walter Walker drove Daisy down to Methunion Manor, where eventually she persuaded Teresa, Rachel, and Freddie to return with her to Centre Street. "Okay," said Rachel, "as long as Alva isn't there." But when they arrived at about 8:00 p.m., Cassandra wouldn't talk with her mother. She nodded perfunctorily, promising only to visit Methunion Manor in a couple of days.

Gradually the conversation at Centre Street turned to a party many of the Walkers were planning to attend that evening. Susan Page was a formidable black woman who had bought a house in nearby Hyde Park. About the time that Alva's house had come under attack, Ms. Page and her three children became similar targets of neighborhood youths. Soon Susan and Alva were appearing together on platforms throughout the city, appealing for action to halt racial harassment, so when Susan summoned her friends and supporters to a Thanksgiving-night party, she invited not only Alva but the rest of the Walker clan.

As Rachel stood in her sister's living room, talking uneasily with friends and family, Tommy—who always enjoyed baiting his "churchy sister"—harangued her about the party. "Hey, Rach," he said, "we're going to have everything over there—liquor, dancing—you'll love it."

Rachel gave him a cold stare. "No, thank you, Thomas," she said. "That's not my kind of party."

Of her three children planning to attend—Cassandra, Wayne, and Freddie—Rachel worried most about Freddie, who had his problems with the law and shouldn't be hanging around that kind of party. "Frederick," she said, "I don't think you ought to go. You won't have any way of getting back, you know. There's no public transportation from Hyde Park at that time of night."

"There you go again, Rachel," said Tommy. "Trying to run everybody's life. Freddie's a man. He can do anything he wants."

"Frederick," said Rachel. "You going with them or with us? Because we're leaving. Now."

"I'll go with them," said Freddie.

"Fine," snapped Rachel. "Goodbye."

At about 9:30, the remaining guests piled into two cars and went off to Susan Page's party. When they arrived, about seventy-five people—two-thirds black and one-third white—were milling around the house. On the ground floor, folks were eating and drinking, while in the basement rec room, under a flashing strobe light, the young people were dancing to disco sounds from a record player. It was such a good party nobody wanted to leave. Not until nearly 2:00 a.m. did the Walker family return to Alva's house—everyone, that is, except Freddie, who had wandered off earlier in the evening.

The next morning Alva had her first opportunity to ask Cassandra why she'd run away. "I was tired of the hassle," she said. "I just wanted to be on my own." What about Rachel? Did Cassandra know where she was? Yes. But she wasn't saying. She and Rachel had promised never to disclose each other's whereabouts.

"But, Cassandra," Alva pleaded, "your sister's only fifteen. She can't manage by herself. And she's too damn young to be messin' around with some dude twice her age. Now tell me where she is!"

Cassandra refused. All Friday morning they worked on her in relays, wheedling, cajoling, and threatening. The most Cassandra would do was to call Rachel and invite her out to the house. She showed up late that afternoon. Alva told her she could stay there if she promised to stop seeing Horace. Rachel agreed and went off to get her clothes, but she never returned.

On Sunday morning, Alva decided to take Cassandra home. Calling her mother, she said, "Rachel, I know you're a big-time Christian, but don't go to church this morning. I'm coming down to see you."

"What we got to talk about?" Rachel asked.

"It's important. I'll be right there."

Only in the car on the way to Methunion Manor did Cassandra finally relent, agreeing to point out where Little Rachel was staying. As they passed a crumbling tenement near Wally's Paradise, Cassandra said, "She's in there."

When Alva buzzed the fourth-floor apartment, Rachel was still in bed with Horace. Stumbling to the squawk box, she asked, "Who is it?"

"Rachel!" Alva shouted. "This is your aunt. Get your ass down here."

"Shit!" said Rachel. Pulling on her nightgown, she hurried downstairs.

"Okay, baby," Alva said. "The game's up. Let's get your stuff and get out of here." Following Rachel back upstairs, she confronted a sleepy-eyed Horace sprawled on a mattress in the middle of the living-room floor. He never said a word as Rachel quickly threw her stuff into a suitcase and left.

Driving to Methunion Manor, Alva herded the girls into their mother's apartment. "Here are your daughters, Rachel," she said. "The wandering ladies return."

Once again, Rachel was assaulted by conflicting emotions. The girls were back at last. But it was Alva who had brought them. "What am I supposed to do?" she asked, her voice heavy with sarcasm. "Throw my arms around them and say all is forgiven?" She paused, staring at the girls sitting side by side on the couch across the room. They seemed so young and vulnerable. "Rachel, baby," she asked. "What made you run away?"

"All those rules and stuff," Rachel said. "Wash this. Dry this. Do that. Do this. I couldn't stand no more of that shit."

"Well, nothing's going to change, you know. The same rules are still here. I work all day and I'm not coming home and clean up behind you all. You understand that?"

The girls stared back at her. Neither said a thing.

"Oh, Rachel," Alva said. "Why don't you ease up a bit? Give them a little slack."

That did it. "Why don't you mind your own business?" Rachel said. "Just butt out!"

"Rachel, your daughters have been out on the street, living with older men. What should I do? Close my eyes?"

That stung. "I never asked you to do anything, Miss Know-it-all."

"Tell me something, Rach," Alva said. "What would you do if you found my daughters in the street?"

"Step over 'em," Rachel snapped. Then, wheeling on her own daughters, she said, "Look, it's up to you. You can come home, but you're coming back to the same rules you left. If not, you can go right out the door with your nosy aunt."

"You're putting them out?" Alva cried.

"No, they got a choice. They can do what they're told to do here. Or they can go with you. What's it going to be, girls?"

They said they'd go with Alva and, a moment later, they did.

That afternoon Rachel wept as she rarely had before. After years of holding her family together by sheer force of will, now it was disintegrating before her eyes. One after another, her children were deserting her. What else could possibly go wrong?

At about 1:30 the next afternoon, Rachel was working on Methunion's accounts when she had an official visitor. Detective John Farrell of the District 4 plainclothes squad was looking for a young man believed to live in Methunion Manor. The police had a description: nineteen or twenty years old, short-cropped black hair, very narrow shoulders, approximately 150 pounds, last seen wearing a beige suit, a white scarf, and a silver chain with a five-pointed star.

A terrible weariness washed over Rachel.

"He got a name?" she asked.

"All we know is 'Freddie.'"

Just then Farrell's partner, Eddie Twohig, rushed in, followed by a distraught young woman. "She thinks she saw him in the hallway," Twohig said.

The two detectives and the woman hurried down the corridor. As they stood outside apartment 105, the door opened and a young man stood framed in the light, a five-pointed star glistening on a chain around his neck.

"That's him," shouted the woman.

Displaying his badge, Farrell asked the man's name.

"Frederick Twymon."

"Were you at a party in Hyde Park on Thanksgiving?"

"Yeh."

"Jack!" said Twohig. "That's enough!"

"All right," said Farrell. "Mr. Twymon, I'm placing you under arrest." Then he took out his Miranda Card and read the suspect his rights.

When Freddie Twymon was nine years old, he was named Roxbury's "Tom Sawyer of 1967." The annual contest, sponsored by the Roxbury Boys' Club, sought out the local youth who most closely resembled Mark Twain's hero. Thirty boys, decked out in straw hats and patched dungarees, competed in wood-chopping, apple-dunking, and fence-painting contests, and when Freddie emerged victorious, his beaming face appeared on page three of the Boston *Record-American*, making him something of a neighborhood celebrity.

When he was a child, Freddie's ebullience and spunk were irresistible. He'd try anything once. Daisy Voight snapped a picture of him standing on his head in a massive snowbank, his mischievous smile beguiling even upside down. Many inner-city blacks were terrified of water, but Freddie took to it readily, becoming a star of the Boys' Club swimming team. When others in the club science program shrank from a twenty-three-foot python, Freddie posed with the giant creature draped around his neck.

But somehow adolescence seemed to drain that formidable energy. When he was fifteen or so, Freddie stopped going to the Boys' Club, preferring to spend his afternoons on the Boston Common with a gang of vagabonds. Those who saw him there in the summer of 1973 were astonished by the change in his appearance. Once a spiffy dresser, he now looked more like a hippie, disheveled in ragged T-shirts and droopy jeans. His eyes bloodshot, his face impassive, he was drinking a lot of wine, smoking a lot of reefers. Coming home drunk night after night, he struck his brother George as "the spitting image of his father."

About that time Freddie started stealing from the family. At night, while his mother slept, he'd sneak into her room and snitch a couple of dollars from her purse. Later he grew still bolder, taking money and clothing from his brothers; when caught, he invariably insisted he was "borrowing" the stuff for a few days. Richard and George warned him to stay away from their things, and finally, when he lifted an expensive tape deck from their room, they took him down to the boiler room and beat the hell out of him.

Nothing could turn Freddie around as he drifted deeper into trouble. For a time in 1973–74, he hung with the gang outside the Soul Center and Braddock Drugs, preying on the gentry across Columbus Avenue. But soon he found more professional company, spending his nights at the Rainbow Lounge on Tremont Street, a notorious hangout for South End stickup men, drug dealers, numbers runners, and prostitutes.

In the fall of 1974, Freddie was going with a girl from Chelsea. One night he stayed late at her house, then came home by subway. At the City Square Station in Charlestown, never a comfortable place for black passengers, he was arrested by two transit policemen for attempting to break into a safe in the change booth. Although he loudly protested his innocence, he was arraigned the next morning in Charlestown District Court, charged with breaking and entry (and later received a suspended sentence).

Not surprisingly, his nightly dissipation took a heavy toll of Freddie's schoolwork. In elementary school he had shown considerable promise, often winning gold stars for achievement and deportment, but now he lagged badly in both English and math, failing to complete ninth grade at East Boston's Barnes School. In the fall of 1974, as busing got underway in South Boston and Roxbury, his mother arranged for him to repeat that grade at the relatively tranquil Jamaica Plain High.

On September 12—two days after his arrest in Charlestown and with the case still pending—Freddie started at Jamaica Plain. A few days later he got into a fistfight with a white boy, was suspended for three days and told he couldn't return unless escorted by his mother. On the appointed day, Rachel and Freddie were walking toward the subway when she noticed a knife sticking out of his pocket.

"What's that for?" she asked.

"If one of those white bastards messes with me today," he said, "I'm going to kill him."

"Freddie," she said, "I'm not taking you anywhere with that knife."

"Well, I ain't going to school without it."

He never returned to school and some weeks later he left home, moving in with a pal on Tremont Street. Over the next year, Freddie engaged in a series of petty crimes: car theft, burglaries, and robberies. Occasionally he was arrested—for attempted auto theft in March 1975, for receiving stolen property in July—but he never got more than a suspended sentence, often committing his next crime while out on probation from the last one. His family grew increasingly impatient with him. Once, after he failed to appear in court for a hearing, his mother made him turn himself in to police. As the charges piled up, Freddie talked about leaving town altogether, running off to see his father in Alabama, but when he called to ask permission, Haywood Twymon said he had no place for his son to stay.

On August 18, 1975, Freddie crossed a critical boundary. Having spent the day hanging out with friends on the Boston Common, he was standing on Arlington Street just across from the Ritz-Carlton Hotel when he noticed an attractive young white woman parking her red Vega, then searching for change to put in the meter. When he offered her two dimes, the woman—a twenty-three-year-old vocational counselor named Gail Rockmore—thanked him profusely. They fell into conversation. Gail liked Freddie's open face and ready smile; he seemed like "a nice, harmless kid." When she went to get a hamburger at McDonald's he tagged along, and they talked for another quarter hour at a table overlooking the Public Gardens. Then Gail left for her evening lesson at the Evelyn Wood Reading Dynamics Institute a few doors away.

When she emerged at 9:30, Freddie was still standing on the corner, talking with a white youth. They asked for a ride up Beacon Hill. When the white boy got out on Charles Street, Freddie said he lived a few blocks away. Gail drove four blocks and stopped.

"No," Freddie said. "It's a little further."

She drove another block. When her passenger made no move, she said, "I'm sorry. This is it. Please get out."

"Just turn in there," Freddie said, indicating an adjacent alley.

Starting to panic, Gail said, "No! I'd like you to get out now!"

Freddie leaned across the gap between the bucket seats and grabbed her by the neck.

"Stop!" Gail shouted. "I'll do anything you want." But as soon as he relaxed his grip, she pushed open her door and jumped out.

"If you leave," he said, "I'll take your car."

"You can have it!" she shrieked.

Running back down Charles Street, she flagged a car and told the driver, "Some guy just tried to kill me."

Seeing her enter the other vehicle, Freddie gunned the red Vega up Cambridge Street. Gail and her companion gave chase, alerting two policemen in a cruiser, who chased the Vega onto Tremont Street, where it jumped a red light, swerved right, and hit a utility pole. Freddie leapt out and ran down Winter Street, ducking into Locke-Ober, Boston's most elegant restaurant. Taking refuge in its basement men's room, he was arrested there a few minutes later by Patrolman John O'Brien. Convicted of larceny of a motor vehicle, assault and battery, operating a car without a license, and leaving the scene of an accident, Freddie was sentenced on September 8, 1975, to up to two and a half years in Concord Prison.

The Massachusetts Correctional Institution at Concord, as it was officially known, was a grim bastion of penal servitude not far from the Old North Bridge and hard by the graves of Ralph Waldo Emerson and Henry David Thoreau. The Commonwealth's younger, more malleable offenders usually ended up at Concord, while more seasoned criminals went to the maximum-security prison at Walpole. But there was nothing easygoing about Concord. Those who had served there called it "tough time," a severe, unrelenting regime.

Freddie—henceforth Prisoner No. 49471—shared a two-man cell with a succession of short-timers. Put to work varnishing park benches in the wood-working shop, he was later transferred to the kitchen, where he washed pots and milk trays.

From the moment he walked through the gates, Freddie drew ardent attention from the prison "queens," always on the lookout for good-looking young "punks." One husky pederast—known to guards and prisoners alike as "Diane"—showed a special interest in Freddie. "Here's a pack of cigarettes," he'd say. "Come up to my room." Terrified by these advances, Freddie did his best to rebuff them, but Diane didn't give up. Gradually his importunings became more urgent, laced with not so subtle threats of violence. Finally one day, when Freddie rejected him again, Diane forced him to his knees and was about to sodomize him when a sympathetic guard intervened. Frantic to escape Diane's energetic courtship, Freddie sought some means of hurrying his parole. Strictly speaking, the Parole Board wouldn't release a prisoner until he had guarantees of a home and a job; but such assurances were so difficult to obtain inside prison that a private organization, called the Self-Development Group, had received the board's approval for an experimental "release and support program" in which the group began working with prisoners before their release and continued to provide assistance once they were out.

On November 8, 1975, Freddie scrawled a note to the Self-Development Group: "I would like to talk to you about your program. I think I'll be interested in getting into it. I see the Parole Board in January." Some days later, in a formal application, he listed his skills as "electrical, repair radio, TV," his job interests as "help kids stay away from where I've been (jail)," his occupational goals, "teaching, swimming."

Once he was accepted, he began working with Eddie Collins, the group's Concord representative, a hip young black man who knew his way around Boston's streets. Through that winter, Freddie attended Ed's counseling sessions, learning to set "short- and long-term goals," "establish a realistic budget," and make a good impression at job interviews. When Freddie decided he wanted to be an electrician, Ed enrolled him in the Recruitment Training Program that provided released prisoners with thirty hours of instruction in a construction trade, then guaranteed them a job. It was a sweet deal and Freddie wanted it badly. But all depended on his being paroled by February, when the training got underway.

On January 13, the day of his scheduled appearance before the Parole Board, Freddie had a particularly unpleasant run-in with Diane, in which the older man warned him: "Punk, you better come across pretty soon if you know what's good for you." The confrontation left him shaken, in no shape for a crucial showdown with the board. And when he walked into the hearing room later that morning, he was further unnerved to find that he recognized one of the two board members serving on the panel that day. The Reverend Michael Haynes, minister of the Twelfth Baptist Church and Martin Luther King's longtime ally in Boston, had grown up around the corner from the Walkers and had known them all their lives. He didn't know Freddie well, but recognizing the name on the file before him, he began by asking, "Mr. Twymon, do you know me?"

"Yes, sir," said Freddie, "I do."

Then Haynes launched his formal interrogation: why had Freddie dropped out of school, whom had he been hanging out with, was he on dope or alcohol, how had he gotten into trouble in the first place?

As the questions poured out, Freddie grew angry. Here was this big-shot minister, a friend of his mother's, interrogating him as though he were a member of the family. What right did he have to ask questions like that?

Then Haynes got to more personal matters. "Frederick," he said, "I know your mother very well. As you know, she's a very sick woman. She's suffered a great deal. I know that having you in here has caused her more pain . . ."

Before he could finish, Freddie leapt to his feet and slammed both hands down on the kidney-shaped table separating him from the panel. Tears welling in his eyes, rage rising in his throat, he felt like grabbing the table and flipping it over on Haynes, but somehow he restrained the impulse, spun around, and rushed from the room. For a minute or so, he stood in the corridor, tears streaming down his face. When Haynes sent for him, Freddie said, "You were playing with my mind."

"I wasn't playing with you, Frederick," said the minister. "I was trying to get the information we need to make a determination. I'm sorry you walked out and under the circumstances I think we'd better put your case over to next month."

Three days later, the board's administrative assistant wrote to Freddie: "It appeared that you were emotionally unable to deal with a hearing this month. Hopefully by February you will have enough impulse control to present yourself in a more positive light." Realizing he'd blown his chance at the electrical training program, Freddie sank into a depression. In February and March the board took no action on his parole. He thought he'd never get out.

Then, abruptly, things turned for the better. In late March, he was transferred to the farm dormitory just beyond the walls. In April, he passed his high school equivalency test, an essential step toward a decent job outside. Finally, on April 27, the board approved his parole. On May 7, 1976, after eight months behind bars, he left Concord.

Family and friends offered encouragement. "You can change your life," his brother George said on the phone from Nashville. "You've got what it takes," said Eddie Collins. "Now use it!"

Rachel gave him his old room at Methunion Manor, but as yet he had no job. On May 14, the Self-Development Group set up an interview with Inner City, Inc., a subsidiary of the Polaroid Corporation. The job provided electronics training, good pay, opportunities for advancement. Freddie got through the interview and the physical, then missed several appointments and was dropped from consideration. Instead, through a family friend, he got a municipal job, manning the Alewife Brook Sewerage Pumping Station. When that lasted barely a month, he took another dead-end position, raking leaves and sweeping walkways in Blackstone Park. For a time in midsummer he worked as a busboy in the Pavilion Room of the Sheraton-Boston Hotel, but lost that after three weeks when he violated a rule against hanging around the hotel on his day off. The Self-Development Group referred him to jobs as a radio-TV repairman and a pantry steward at the Harvard Medical School, but neither panned out. Through late summer and early fall Freddie was unemployed.

He didn't care for his parole officer, a Latino named Juan Snowden, whom he called "the wrong kind of dude." At first, Freddie reported regularly, but as the months went by he often remained out of touch for weeks on end. After he missed several appointments, Snowden tried in vain to reach him at home. Things came to a head on November 23, when he failed to appear once again. The next morning Freddie called in an agitated state. Snowden confronted him with his missed appointment, saying he was "tired of excuses." Freddie explained that he was deeply upset about his sisters' disappearance and asked Snowden to give him a lift to a place he'd heard one sister was hiding out. Sensing that his client was losing control, the parole officer told him to wait right there, he'd be over in a minute. But when Snowden got to Methunion Manor, Freddie was gone.

Distraught over Little Rachel's alliance with Horace, Freddie had decided to take matters into his own hands. From behind the housing project he dug up a .22 caliber pistol he'd buried three months before and told a friend he was going up to Massachusetts Avenue to "get my sister back from the dude." At the last moment, he thought better of this plan.

The next day—Thanksgiving—Freddie spent the afternoon at Alva's house enjoying the goose and sweet potato pie. Then he joined the other guests at Susan Page's party. Downstairs in the recreation room he met a young white woman named Marianne.

Marianne was a thirty-one-year-old graduate student and college teacher with impressive credentials. A 1969 graduate of the University of Maryland, she had a master's degree from the London School of Economics, had completed all her requirements, except the dissertation, for a Ph.D. in economics from Yale, and had spent a year as a visiting scholar at the Bangladesh Institute of Economic Research. After returning to the United States in 1975, she began teaching economic principles and international economics at Boston State College, while continuing her research at Harvard.

But Marianne had another life—as a dedicated Marxist. Her experience in Bangladesh had left her with the conviction that former colonial powers were systematically exploiting Third World peoples; back home she saw countless parallels in the treatment white America accorded its black, Hispanic, and other minorities. With little prior experience in political organization, she determined to enlist in the "socialist struggle," and began scanning Boston's radical spectrum for a group to which she could devote her formidable energies.

Her search ended in February 1976 when she attended a lecture by E. P. Thompson, the celebrated British Marxist. His address was followed by commentaries from several Boston Marxists, among them Michael Hirsch, organizer of the Boston branch of a tiny Trotskyist sect called International Socialists. IS, as it was known, concentrated its activity in the industrial realm, working to establish "opposition caucuses" within labor unions. At the time of the Thompson lecture, the branch had only eleven members, most of them young and working-class, all of them white. In early March, Marianne joined up.

Marianne's passion was the race issue. That was fine with her new comrades, who had long sought some way for the organization to grapple with America's racial crisis. Seeking principally to recruit white workers, it found issues like busing and affirmative action potentially divisive. Not surprisingly, it had concentrated on "Third World" causes as remote as possible from Boston: leading a campaign to expose the South African investments of the First National Bank of Boston, collecting clothing to send to guerrillas in Zimbabwe, and working to free Gary Tyler, a black teenager serving a life sentence for the 1974 killing of a white youth in Louisiana.

In the spring of 1976, Marianne was named the branch's "black coordinator," a position she took very seriously. Teaching only part-time at Boston State, she could devote plenty of time to IS business, seeking to rally Boston blacks to her agenda. One IS member recalls, "She put in a lot of time, but it just wasn't working. Boston blacks didn't give a damn about some kid in Louisiana or guerrillas in Zimbabwe. Moreover, Marianne, like the rest of us, was white. We were viewed with suspicion, and rightfully so."

Marianne carried this commitment into her personal life. That summer she fell in love with a thirty-three-year-old black man who claimed to be a Panther fugitive. When he told Marianne that he needed $2,000, she gave it to him. Warning that the guy was a "con artist," Mike Hirsch ordered her not to give him any more.

In her capacity as "black coordinator," Marianne became involved with

Alva Debnam's struggle on Centre Street. That spring she sat in several times at the Debnam house, and later she met Susan Page, who invited IS members to her Thanksgiving-night party. Marianne planned to go with Rob, who headed the branch's work on the Gary Tyler campaign.

On Thursday, Mike Hirsch had Rob and several other branch members to his house for Thanksgiving dinner. With plenty of wine and grass, they were all high as kites by nightfall. Rob didn't feel like going all the way across town to the party, so he called Marianne to beg off. Then Mike got on the phone to tell Marianne she didn't have to go—it wasn't an official duty, it was just a party. Of course, the branch needed all the black contacts it could get, so it wouldn't be a bad idea.

Marianne said she'd go. She'd already baked a pecan pie to take with her. Moreover, it was part of her job; she ought to be there.

Dressed in a heavy red sweater, blue maxi-skirt, and high leather boots, Marianne drove her 1968 van into Hyde Park, arriving at the Page house at about 10:00 p.m. At around midnight, Freddie Twymon asked her to dance, and for about forty-five minutes they moved together to the disco beat. Onlookers later testified in court that they seemed to be getting along very well.

At about 1:00 a.m. Marianne was ready to leave. "Anybody need a lift to Cambridge?" she asked. "I do," said Freddie, explaining that he lived in Cambridgeport, an enclave on the Charles River. Unfamiliar with Hyde Park, Marianne wasn't sure which route to take, but Freddie said he was a cabdriver and would show her the way.

Twenty minutes later, as they turned onto Shawmut Avenue in the South End, Marianne asked, "Are you sure you know where you're going?"

"Oh yeah," he said. "Just do what I tell you."

Freddie directed her into a darkened parking lot. Suddenly, he reached over and grabbed the keys. Opening the driver's door, he pushed her out. Then he jumped out and grabbed her around the neck.

"Freddie!" she cried. "Don't do it!"

"Shut up," he said. "Do what I tell you."

She tried to get away, but he tightened his grip around her throat, pushing her through narrow alleys and darkened playgrounds. At one point she spotted a car with its motor running and two shadowy figures inside. Hoping to attract the occupants' attention, she jerked away from Freddie, but he quickly corralled her again, grasping her harshly across the shoulder. "If you had cooperated," he growled, "it could all be over by now."

At the front door to Methunion Manor, Freddie let them in with a key. Then—as Marianne later testified in court—he pulled her into the elevator, took her to the basement laundry room, and ordered her to get undressed. Once she'd removed her skirt, sweater, green tights, panties, and boots, he told her to lie down on the laundry table and had intercourse with her.

Then he made her get dressed again, pulled her back onto the elevator, and rode to the sixth floor, where he directed her onto a stairwell landing. There he licked her vagina, had her take his penis in her mouth, had intercourse with her once again, then smeared his own excrement on his buttocks and made her lick it off.

After that, he took her across the sixth-floor hallway to the other landing and raped her on the cement floor.

Next he took her back down to the laundry room and made her lie down on the floor, where he raped her again, then forced her to masturbate while he masturbated.

"You didn't come yet," he said. "Why haven't you come?"

"You do a good job," she reassured him. "Sometimes I don't come."

Abruptly he told her to kneel against the wall while he urinated across her breasts.

Next he took her out into an alley behind the building and raped her on a car fender.

Leading her back into the laundry room, he had her lie down on the table and shoved a fabric-softener bottle up her vagina until she cried out in pain.

"What do you want me to do?" she exclaimed. "What else do you want to do?"

"You're going to stay here until you have an orgasm," Freddie said.

But a few minutes later he changed his mind. "I'm going to let you go," he said. Opening the basement door, he told her to walk straight ahead. Threading her way through an alley, she found her van in the parking lot and drove back to Cambridge.

Reaching her apartment near Harvard Square at about 6:00 a.m., she stripped off her soiled clothing, took a hot shower, and applied contraceptive jelly around the diaphragm she'd worn all night. Then she collapsed into bed. When she woke several hours later, she went to the Harvard Community Health Plan for a physical. The next day, she and her roommate drove through the South End until they identified the building where the rape had taken place. But perhaps out of a woman's reluctance to discuss her experience with male officers, perhaps out of a Trotskyist's distaste for mobilizing the powers of the capitalist state against a poor black man, Marianne waited until noon Monday before going to the police. Later that afternoon she accompanied Detectives Farrell and Twohig to Methunion Manor.

Arraigned on November 30, Freddie was held at Charles Street Jail until his family came up with the $2,500 cash bail.

It was a terrible week for Rachel. A great sorrow and a great rage surged within her and she couldn't quite tell them apart. Frederick's arrest was bad enough, but the crime with which he was accused was more than she could bear. To a woman who prided herself on her church attendance and bourgeois respectability, rape seemed the most horrible of all offenses. To a lifelong integrationist and follower of Martin Luther King, rape of a white woman was a repudiation of everything she believed. At moments she wondered whether Freddie hadn't done this just to humiliate her.

Yet her anger at Little Rachel and Cassandra was, if anything, more powerful than her distress over Freddie's arrest. For the girls had openly defied, even humiliated, her by choosing to live with Alva. After consulting her boss, David Dretler, Rachel filed an application that week with the Boston Juvenile Court asking that she be relieved of all responsibility for her daughters. The application—under Massachusetts' "Child in Need of Services" law—would give the court authority to remove the girls from their mother's home and place them in a setting where they could receive the services and discipline they required.

The court sent each girl a notice, announcing that her mother was seeking to designate her a "stubborn" child—namely, "a child below the age of seventeen who persistently refuses to obey the lawful and reasonable commands of his parents or legal guardian, thereby resulting in said parents' or guardian's inability to adequately care for and protect the child." The court appointed a public defender—Sandy Brushart—to represent the girls' interest.

Several days later, Cassandra and Little Rachel appeared for scheduled interviews at the court's probation department. Late for their appointments with Philippa Myers, the probation officer assigned to the case, they were seen by two student workers. Both girls complained that their mother made "unreasonable demands" on them for errands, household work, and other tasks. Both said that she often beat them with an electrical extension cord or a belt with a metal buckle. Cassandra showed the student worker scars which she said came from these beatings. Both girls said they were unwilling to return to their mother's house and wanted to remain with Alva.

When their mother saw Mrs. Myers a week later, she said the girls flagrantly disobeyed her orders both in and out of the house, coming and going as they wished, spending much of their time with older men. But she vehemently denied that she beat the girls, claiming that her lupus didn't leave her the stamina for such exertions. She no longer wanted the girls in her home, she said, but she didn't want them with Alva either. She wanted them committed to the Department of Public Welfare for placement in an appropriate setting. The girls should come to the house and take everything that belonged to them, so they would know that a "clean break" had been made.

At a preliminary hearing before Judge George W. Cashman on December 13, Mrs. Myers reported that commitment to the Welfare Department seemed the only workable solution. Mrs. Twymon told the court she'd always insisted on obedience from her daughters; since they now refused to heed her, she had no alternative but to expel them from the house. Ruth Lewis of the Welfare Department said that a prolonged clinical evaluation was required before permanent placements could be made, and meanwhile the girls should remain with their aunt. After Sandy Brushart confirmed that the girls had no objection, Judge Cashman ordered them committed to the Welfare Department, with temporary custody to Alva. But when he admonished them to obey their aunt, Cassandra angrily denied that they'd ever been rebellious. It was impossible to obey their mother, she claimed, because whatever you did, another task was always waiting. Well, let's see how it goes with your aunt, the judge said, setting another hearing to review his order in six weeks.

Two weeks later, Cassandra entered the hospital for repair to her ovaries. The surgery revived her mother's protective instincts, for almost immediately she began backing away from her position at the hearing, telling Mrs. Myers she hoped Cassandra would spend her convalescence at Methunion Manor. Once again she was wounded, as Cassandra decided to recuperate at Alva's.

On December 28, Mrs. Twymon called the Welfare Department to have Cassandra and Rachel removed from her Aid to Families with Dependent Children budget, reducing the biweekly grant from $122.30 to $42.60, paving the way for the department to shift those monies to Alva. Yet on January 5 came further evidence of a softening in her position toward her daughters. In a letter to Ruth Lewis of the Welfare Department, she noted that on January 3 Little Rachel had paid an unexpected visit to Methunion Manor and expressed a desire to return home. "I explained to Rachel that she must speak to either yourself or Mrs. Myers before she could come home," she wrote. Requesting that the department conduct a "suitability investigation" of Alva's home, she said, "At the end of the six-week trial period I would hope that this case will be reviewed by the judge and all concerned parties. I would hope at that time the girls will be able to see where they are going and, perhaps more importantly, where they have been."

Mrs. Twymon shifted ground several times that winter. To Mrs. Myers she seemed "so ambivalent about her daughters, it was difficult to get a consistent position from her." One day she dropped hints that she wanted the girls back; the next she would talk again of a "clean break." Not long after telling one social worker, "My door is open," she changed the locks on her apartment so the girls couldn't slip in and out undetected.

The one constant was implacable hostility between Mrs. Twymon and her sister. In conversation with third parties, each accused the other of breaking up the family and of setting a bad example to the girls. Alva denounced her sister as "a mean and evil person" who didn't understand teenagers' need for freedom. Rachel suggested that Alva led a dissolute life and was an inappropriate model for her daughters. While Little Rachel went on paying weekly visits to Methunion Manor, Cassandra kept her distance. Mrs. Twymon accused Alva of encouraging Cassandra's hostility, while Alva claimed that her sister wouldn't even let Cassandra collect her clothes and school books.

Through January and early February, mother and daughters were examined by social workers and psychologists who prepared evaluations for the court. Mrs. Twymon, one social worker wrote, "is a very depressed, angry and rigid woman who has been deprived and experienced losses because of her illnesses. She is unable to understand the adolescent needs of her children. . . ."

Mrs. Twymon's inability to discuss her pain with us and her overwhelming hostility and resistance preclude the development of a therapeutic relationship through which the girls might be returned to her."

The girls' anger, the same social worker concluded, stemmed from "early separation anxiety" associated with their long stay in foster homes.

One psychiatrist described Cassandra as "distressed and petulant . . . rather surly and quick to take offense," though "later friendly and spontaneous." She concluded that Cassandra was "a rather defensive young lady who has strongly rebelled against an overly controlling mother."

A psychologist described Little Rachel in much the same terms, as "a sullen, angry and somewhat depressed adolescent."

On February 9, Judge Cashman held a second hearing to review the case. Alva and the two girls were not present, so Mrs. Twymon would have a full opportunity to make a case against her sister. Addressing the court that morning, she urged that the girls be removed from Alva's house immediately. It was a "hostile home," she said, where the girls were being encouraged to defy her. Moreover, she contended, Alva was living with a man not her husband (a reference to Alva's new boyfriend, Sam Jones, who had moved in with her that winter).

Then Carol Cullen, a Welfare Department social worker, reported on her visit to the Debnam house. Ms. Cullen said she found no evidence of a man living in the house. Nor did she detect any reluctance on Alva's part to let the girls see their mother. "Mrs. Debnam told the worker that the mother was welcome to call or visit her daughters in her home at any time and the girls may do the same if they wish." In short, she found the Debnam home "most appropriate" for the two girls.

After hearing Ms. Cullen's report, Judge Cashman turned to Rachel and asked if she considered her sister a "bad woman."

"I go to church," Rachel said. "But my sister leads a different kind of life. She has undermined my relationship with my girls."

"Is there any other member of your family able and ready to take the children?" Judge Cashman asked.

"No," she said.

The judge told Rachel he wasn't going to involve himself in her dispute with her sister. His role was to serve "the best interests of the children." After the girls' attorney assured him they wished to remain with their aunt, the judge continued his December 13 order for three more months.

Alva accepted her foster-mother role with cheerful resignation. The house was overcrowded, but after months of living with vandals outside and sentinels inside, the Debnams found two teenage girls a minor inconvenience. But they *were* expensive. Even after Mrs. Twymon informed Welfare that the girls were no longer at home, Alva had difficulty getting the AFDC grant transferred to her. It took three official interviews before a check for $120 began arriving every two weeks. Meanwhile, she made room for the newcomers by moving out of her own room, sleeping with Sam Jones on the fold-down couch in the living room. Young Otis took her room; Cassandra and Rachel moved into Otis' room. For a time at least, the girls got along well with Alva's daughters—Charlene and Maria—and the household settled into a pleasant routine.

The move to Alva's did complicate the daily commute to school. Rachel had a relatively simple bus trip to Boston Tech, but Cassandra had to take the subway downtown to Park Street, then change for the South End, where she boarded a bus for Charlestown High. The tumultuous events of fall and winter took a toll on Cassandra's scholastic performance. In the September-October marking period she did remarkably well (five B's and one C+), but in November and December, as she ran away, went to court, and moved to Alva's, her grades fell off precipitously (one B+, one B, two C's, two C−'s, and a D). Only in art—where a talented teacher had captured her attention—did she consistently get good grades.

Outside class she found even less to engage her. Elected that fall as an alternate on the new Student Council, she attended only one meeting, when the white girl she backed up fell sick. All fall her friend Sandy Payne urged her to come out for girls' basketball, but that meant staying late for practice. Cassandra had no intention of sticking around Charlestown any longer than she had to.

Only once that year did she join in a school activity. Even classmates who barely knew her had admired Cassandra's strong voice. She never missed an opportunity to exercise it: in the corridors, in the ladies' room, on the bus to and from school, she belted out rhythm-and-blues tunes from groups like Wild Cherry and Tavares. When the Student Council began organizing the March 4 "Gong Show," Lisa McGoff urged her to enter. Afraid that the whites would ridicule her, Cassandra resisted for weeks, and only when Joe Strickland and Sandy Payne added their pressure did she capitulate. To her astonishment, her lively rendition of the Tavares song "You Are My Shining Star" brought her a round of applause and honorable mention in the show. Her prize: a foot-long green toothbrush, which a delighted Cassandra hung on her bedroom wall at Alva's.

But one such achievement did little to ease the loneliness which ate at her all through that winter. Every day she spent in Room 415, its unremitting whiteness seemed more oppressive. There was nobody to jive with, nobody who knew what she was going through, nobody to give her back a sweet, warm communion. And when she sought out other blacks in the corridor or the ladies' room, she was pulled up short by white administrators determined to avert racial collisions: no talking, no lingering, get out of the halls, go to your homeroom.

The more she was frustrated in other encounters, the more desperately she craved her friend Desiree's company. In the morning the two girls talked in the corridors well past the final bell, at each class break they somehow found each other, and at lunch Cassandra invariably persuaded Jerry Sullivan to let her spend those twenty minutes with Desiree.

Then in early March, Desiree's homeroom teacher told Jerry that too many kids were drifting into her room at lunchtime. She'd appreciate it if he would keep Cassandra with him. When Jerry told this to Cassandra, she grew distraught. Those twenty minutes huddled alone on her side of the room were agony. She missed Desiree desperately, and she blamed Jerry Sullivan for this abrupt turnabout, a betrayal of their old relationship.

On March 21, Cassandra and Desiree came to school with tin whistles clamped between their teeth, emitting high-pitched trills that could be heard all through the school. Bob Jarvis, the school's chief disciplinarian, stuck his head out his door and told the girls to shut up. Later, he told Jerry Sullivan, "Cassandra Twymon's running a little wild. Every time I look up, she and this Desiree are out in the halls. I want you to get that girl under control. Keep her in the homeroom where she belongs."

The next morning, as Cassandra and Desiree idled in the fourth-floor hallway, Sullivan hurried up to them. "That's enough, Cassandra," he said. "Let's get in the room."

"I've got plenty of time, Mr. Sullivan," she said.

"No, you don't. Let's go."

When Cassandra declined to move, Jerry became so exasperated he stuck out a giant hand to nudge her toward the classroom door—a violation of school regulations prohibiting teachers from touching students except to break up violent confrontations.

"Get your hands off me!" Cassandra shouted, as she and Desiree flounced downstairs, ignoring the teacher's remonstrances.

Jerry summoned Bob Jarvis, who commanded Cassandra to "get up those stairs!" When she entered Room 415, Jerry told her, "You know, I really don't care what you do. But as long as Jarvis is on my back, I'm going to be on yours. If you'd just be where you're supposed to be for once, maybe we could get on to other things." But Cassandra put her head down on her desk, refusing to say a word.

Suddenly, all Jerry Sullivan's frustration at court-ordered busing, at ill-prepared or insolent students, exploded in a torrent of emotion. "Okay, Cassandra," he said. "If you're going to treat me like a dog, I'll treat you like a dog. So don't look to me for favors anymore. No more passes to the lav. No more permission to see Desiree. I'm not bending the rules for you anymore."

At lunch the next day, Cassandra asked for a pass to the lav. Jerry said no. She asked for a pass to the office. Jerry said no. So Cassandra simply walked to the office, where she asked to see Headmaster Murphy. An outraged Jerry Sullivan immediately reported the incident to Jarvis, who came to the doorway of his cubicle and called, "Cassandra, may I see you, please?"

Cassandra stood with arms folded, refusing to acknowledge him. Twice more he called. Twice more she refused to respond. "Okay," snapped Jarvis. "That'll be a five-day suspension."

Eventually Murphy received Cassandra in his office, condemned her behavior, and told her to come back the next day with her mother. Mrs. Twymon was spending the week at a church conference in Arkansas, so Cassandra promised to bring someone else, and the next morning she returned with her brother Richard, a shrewd negotiator. After an hour-long meeting with Murphy and Jarvis, the administrators agreed to reduce Cassandra's suspension to one day if she would make a new effort to abide by school regulations. Cassandra, who still felt more victim than culprit, grudgingly agreed.

But her sense of grievance persisted; she'd had it with Charlestown High. Beginning that last week in March, Cassandra was absent from school two out of every three days. Morning after morning she set off for Shawmut Station as if on her way to Charlestown, then headed for Roxbury to see her friends. Rachel began skipping Boston Tech as well: she let Alva drive her to Codman Square, waited until her aunt's car was out of sight, then boarded a bus for Massachusetts Avenue. They ran the same games at night, telling Alva that they were visiting their mother while staying with their boyfriends till well past midnight.

For though Alva's house had once been a welcome refuge from the rigid regime at home, now it seemed less hospitable. Overt attacks on 185 Centre Street had largely ceased, but neighborhood youths kept watch, venting their anger on blacks who came and went. Whenever Cassandra or Rachel strayed very far from the front door, whites threw snowballs at them and chanted, "We'll get you, nigger!" Inside, the Debnams and their guests, at close quarters all through that long winter, had begun to turn on each other. Rachel and Cassandra grated on Charlene's and Maria's nerves. There were constant arguments about bathroom rights, squabbles about household chores. One evening after Rachel refused to wash the dishes, she and Charlene got into a shouting match which ended with them rolling about on the kitchen floor. Alva, too, had grown impatient with her charges. She suspected Rachel of disobeying her orders to stop seeing Horace, and she accused Cassandra of flirting with Sam Jones, while Cassandra suggested that Sam was making passes at her.

Things came to a head on April 19, when Alva called Philippa Myers to complain that the girls were up to their old tricks. The probation officer ordered the girls to report to her on April 21 and, when they did, she warned them that unless they obeyed their aunt, the judge might be forced to place them somewhere else. But Cassandra knew that so far as she was concerned such warnings were largely bluff. On March 16 she'd turned seventeen, putting her beyond the Juvenile Court's reach. With her high school years coming to an end, she'd thought about going to work. On an earlier visit to Mrs. Myers she'd talked about applying for an assembly-line job at the General Motors plant in Framingham, or a secretarial position with the John Hancock Insurance Company. In any case, she'd come of age: she didn't have to take orders from her mother, her aunt, the judge, or the probation officer any longer.

On Tuesday, April 26, for the first time in months, Cassandra spent the whole night with Ricky. It was nice, and Ricky liked it too. Why couldn't they do it all the time? he asked. Why not? Cassandra wondered. Later that morning, she consulted her friend Barbara, who invited Cassandra to share her apartment for only twenty-five dollars a month, some help with her kids, and a hand with the housework. That afternoon, while Alva was at work, Cassandra went back to Centre Street, gathered up her clothes, and took them to Barbara's place on Ruthven Street.

On April 28, Alva called Mrs. Myers to report that Cassandra had disappeared. The probation officer told her to call the police, track Cassandra down, and have her in court for the scheduled case review on May 4. But Alva never spoke to the police. Instead, a few days later, she called Carol Cullen at the Welfare Department to say that, even if Cassandra was found, she didn't want her at the house anymore. Nor Rachel either. She'd had it with both girls.

On May 4, despite the misgivings of social workers and psychologists, Judge Cashman ordered Little Rachel returned to her mother (although he required her to attend a summer work and counseling program supervised by the court). With Cassandra still missing, he issued a default warrant in her name.

In early May, Cassandra got a job at the Morgan Laundry on Massachusetts Avenue, ironing sheets for seventy dollars a week. She rarely went to Charlestown High anymore. When she missed her appointment for a yearbook photo, Lisa McGoff asked her for a short poem to fill the space. Cassandra wrote "Because," which she dedicated to Ricky.

> *Because you are sweet*
> *Because you are so sweet*
> *Because is why*
> *I Love You.*
> *Because you are fine*
> *And because you are mine*
> *Because is why*
> *I Love You.*
> *Because you are you.*

For a while it was fine indeed: good sex at night, long, lazy weekends in bed, Chinese food and beer while Ricky watched the Red Sox on TV, Cassandra curled against his knee. Then her idyll turned bad around the edges. She got strung out on dope, stayed out a little too late a little too often, wasn't eating or sleeping right. She and Ricky had a fight and one night she found herself standing on the corner of Massachusetts and Columbus avenues, a notorious haunt of black hookers serving the white hunter trade. As it happened, her uncle Arnold drove by that night. Pulling to the curb, he drawled, "Well, Cassandra, it looks like you're a midnight social worker." At first she didn't understand what he meant. Then it hit her. Oh, *please!* That had never entered her mind! And if she was going to hook, would she do it just a couple of blocks from home, where her own family could see her? She wished they'd give her a little more credit. But the incident unsettled her and she stayed off the corner for a while.

Then in early June she lost her job at the laundry and, short on cash, she had trouble coming up with the rent. Tired of minding Barbara's kids and cleaning the cluttered apartment, she wanted out. A dozen times that month she felt like calling her mother to say hello, but she knew that if she did there'd be a huge hassle. Then on Sunday, July 24, a freak storm hit Boston. For hours that afternoon a thick layer of sooty clouds hung over the city, shutting out the sun, turning the streets as dark as midnight. Cassandra was frightened—and feeling terribly homesick. Almost before she knew it, she was knocking on her mother's door.

Little Rachel opened it and said, "Well, damn!"

Big Rachel was still in bed when Cassandra popped in to say, "Hello, Mother."

"Hello, Cassandra," her mother replied.

On July 29, Big Rachel told Philippa Myers that she was "quite satisfied" to have Cassandra and Rachel at home as long as they wanted to be there.

A week later, Philippa met Rachel on the street outside Methunion Manor, reporting later that she "seemed much more relaxed and less rigid than the last time I spoke with her. The problems [with Cassandra and Little Rachel] seem to have diminished. The mother's attitude has softened quite a bit."

Cassandra had feared her mother would be furious with her for failing to graduate from Charlestown High, but to her astonishment, she discovered that she *had* graduated. Her repeated absences in the fourth marking period should have ensured an unbroken string of failing marks, but Murphy and Jarvis decided to overlook that. Although nobody responded when Cassandra's name was called at the graduation ceremonies, her mother had gone to Charlestown High a few days later to pick up the parchment in its blue leatherette folder. She hung it on the wall near her favorite Martin Luther King memorial plate and a plaque embossed: "There are no limits on God's ability to make things right in my life."

It had been a terrible year, culminating on June 21, when Freddie was found guilty on four counts of rape—he was acquitted of four others—and sentenced to six to ten years in Concord Prison. But Rachel gave thanks that God had made some things right in her life. Her daughters were home at last, eager for reconciliation. Richard, still running an elevator at Massachusetts General Hospital, was planning to enroll in pharmaceutical school. George was at Tennessee State College working toward his BA. Wayne, completing his college preparatory program, planned to become a cadet in the Boston Police Department.

Of all her children, Wayne best exemplified the bourgeois values Rachel had sought to instill in her family. Every Saturday he worked as a busboy in the Bird Cage Restaurant at Lord and Taylor's. All morning, expensive cars deposited well-groomed suburbanites at the exclusive Back Bay store, and by noon the restaurant was filled with women chatting about their children in college, their trips to Europe, their houses on the Cape. Another black youth—searching in vain for a black face among the elegantly dressed ladies—might have bristled at all that wealth and privilege, but Wayne found it "a whole new trip. I've seen things like that on TV, but now I see them in real life. I don't resent those ladies. I just want to figure out a way to make some of that money too.

"I like the ideal," Wayne confided. "Like, what's that show on TV, *The Brady Bunch?* That's an ideal, you know, where they've got lots of money and they've got lots of kids—three boys and three girls—and everything's kosher. Something happens, but it always comes out straight. And people, they're always happy. They never have to get mad and, you know, have fights and things. They're always happy. That's a good show, a good family show."

28

The Mayor

In his penthouse suite overlooking the Miami Beach skyline, George McGovern is eating Total with bananas and cream. Across the room on the 25-inch screen comes word from the convention floor: Delaware puts him a little closer. Two minutes before midnight, Dick Wall of Illinois rises to cast 10.5 votes for "Scoop" Jackson and "119 resounding voices for a great humanitarian . . ." McGovern is the Democratic nominee for President.

The candidate huddles with press secretary Dick Dougherty and aide Fred Dutton on the vice-presidential nomination. A survey by McGovern pollster Pat Caddell shows that Ted Kennedy would be the strongest running mate; a McGovern-Kennedy "super-ticket" would begin the race only two percentage points behind the incumbent Nixon and Agnew. Just after midnight, McGovern calls Kennedy in Hyannis Port. Ted listens attentively, but declines.

McGovern instructs campaign director Frank Mankiewicz to convene the high command that morning and give him half a dozen names by noon. Traditionally a presidential candidate relies on a few old cronies to help him select a running mate, but McGovern is committed to participatory democracy. At 8:30 a.m., twenty of his senior aides assemble in the Doral Hotel's executive conference room. Most of those at the table are suffering from a lethal combination of overwork, undernourishment, late-night celebration, and little sleep. Some confess to nasty hangovers, several have hurled themselves into the surf in a vain effort to revive their clouded senses, but nobody is quite up to par when Mankiewicz raps his glass and announces: "We have three hours to choose the deputy commander of the civilized world." Reminding his colleagues that the McGovern campaign has blazed new trails across the American political landscape, he urges them to show the same imagination in their search for a Vice-President. "Let's not limit ourselves to a few tired old faces," he says. "Let's bring up every name we can think of, including people in the private sector."

Over the next hour, thirty-seven names are mentioned. Despite Mankie-
wicz's admonitions, no fewer than seventeen are McGovern's colleagues in the
United States Senate. Another six come from the nation's state houses. Three
are congressmen. Three are mayors: Moon Landrieu, John Lindsay, and Kevin
White. Eight are from the "private sector," ranging from Walter Cronkite to
Father Theodore Hesburgh.

In that first hour, the mood is light, almost frivolous—"like a group of
fraternity boys who had spent most of the night successfully stealing the other
school's mascot," Gary Hart recalls. But, after a coffee break, the atmosphere
grows more earnest. Each name must be supported by a sponsor and at least
one second. Heated debate ensues. At 11:40, only seven names remain: Walter
Mondale (the group's "pie in the sky" choice; most participants believe he will
refuse); Sargent Shriver (Pierre Salinger's candidate); Larry O'Brien (Rick
Stearns's man); Pat Lucey (the candidate of South Dakota's Lieutenant Governor Bill Dougherty); Abe Ribicoff (believed to be high on the candidate's
own list); Tom Eagleton (a long shot); and Kevin White (the group's "realistic"
choice, backed by a solid consensus).

Just before noon, Mankiewicz, Hart, Salinger, and Jean Westwood take
the names to McGovern's suite. For the next hour, he reviews the list with
representatives of four of his principal constituencies—women, blacks, Chicanos, and mayors. Then, joined by more advisers, he decides to offer the
nomination to Mondale, but just as expected, the Minnesotan declines, unwilling to jeopardize his reelection to the Senate that fall.

Campaign coordinator Hart, who sponsored Kevin White at the morning
meeting, renews his advocacy. Hart has met the Mayor only twice but finds
him attractive and articulate, with "a sense of what America is all about." Now
he reminds the candidate that White would be an ideal ticket balancer, strong
in precisely those areas where McGovern is weak: urban, Catholic, a New
Englander, a proven administrator, with strong ties to organized labor and
traditional powers in the party, notably the redoubtable Richard Daley. Moreover, no one can think of anything substantially wrong with him. McGovern
barely knows White. But his first two choices—Kennedy and Mondale—are
out of the running. Shriver is in Moscow. O'Brien is too much the "old pol."
Pat Lucey's wife is too outspoken. Time is running short. At about 1:40 p.m.,
the candidate picks up the phone to speak with the Mayor of Boston.

His call does not altogether surprise Kevin White—though, two hours earlier, it would have seemed highly unlikely. Like most of Massachusetts' prominent Democrats, White had chosen that spring to run for delegate-at-large on
Ed Muskie's primary slate and, like all his colleagues, he was easily routed by
McGovern's insurgents. Although he had met secretly with McGovern the
Saturday before the primary, he saw that as a routine courtesy call, designed
to keep channels open to an important big-city mayor. With little hope of
playing a prominent role in the fall campaign, he hadn't even bothered to go
to Miami, dispatching three aides as observers. As the balloting began on

Wednesday, July 12, the Mayor joined his wife, Kathryn, and their five children at his summer place near Bourne on Cape Cod.

At 11:15 Thursday morning, he put down a book to play tennis with his wife, but after twenty minutes it began to rain and they returned to the rambling, brown-shingled house overlooking Monument Beach. At 11:45, the phone rang in the upstairs bedroom. It was Ted Kennedy calling from Hyannis Port, just fifteen miles to the east.

"Hi, how are you?" said the Mayor. "Why don't we form a third party. I'll be your campaign manager."

Just alerted by a phone call from a McGovern staffer, Kennedy told White that he was on the "short list" for Vice-President. White didn't take the call very seriously, but soon thereafter the pace quickened. Pierre Salinger reached Ira Jackson, an assistant to the Mayor, at his parents' home, where he was recuperating from an operation. McGovern needed a full biography of White, copies of his most important speeches, eight-by-ten glossies of the Mayor and his family right away. An incredulous Jackson, groggy with Valium, raced to City Hall, running every red light he encountered ("I figured I had a papal dispensation"). In the Mayor's office, he found aides Bob Kiley and Frank Tivnan besieged by calls from across the country. Soon John Chancellor of NBC and an assistant to Walter Cronkite at CBS were on the line, inquiring about rumors sweeping Miami Beach that White was about to become McGovern's running mate.

Finally, at 1:40 p.m., the phone rings in Bourne, and White, still in tennis shorts and a blue cable-knit sweater, answers.

"Hi, Kevin, this is George McGovern."

"Hi, George! You did a superb job. I watched you last night."

McGovern asks White if he would like to run with him. The Mayor would be delighted. For a few moments they discuss the "issues"—McGovern's preoccupation with the Vietnam War, White's focus on the urban crisis—and find they are not far apart.

"I'd like to have you with me," McGovern says. He wants to make a couple of "routine" phone checks and promises to call back in a few minutes to complete the deal.

When White hangs up and tells his wife, she puts her hand to her mouth and murmurs, "Oh, Lord, Lord, Lord."

Things are moving very fast now. Mankiewicz and Salinger are on the phone to Bourne and to Boston, seeking more information. Kiley and Tivnan rifle the files for the requested materials. With dozens of newsmen descending on City Hall, Tivnan orders the Mayor's office sealed. Ira Jackson, bearing a bulging portfolio, races to Bourne, a sixty-mile trip he makes in barely forty-five minutes.

In Miami Beach, Salinger asks aide Milton Gwirtzman to draft nominating and seconding speeches for White. Gwirtzman calls a disbelieving Barney Frank in Boston to get background on the Mayor, then raps out several speeches, which he rushes to McGovern's suite. Gary Hart leaves the suite, goes to the "situation room," and asks Rick Stearns how long it will take to prepare nominating petitions (the new McGovern-inspired rules require signatures from 200 delegates to be submitted to the Democratic National Committee headquarters in the Fontainebleau Hotel by 4:00 p.m.). Stearns says the petitions have already been circulated in blank; all he has to do is to insert the candidate's name. Hart tells him to insert the name of Kevin White.

The Mayor calls his old friends Harvard professor Sam Huntington and his wife, Nancy, who are vacationing on Martha's Vineyard. Reaching Nancy as she mops her kitchen floor, White whispers, "McGovern wants me on the ticket. Get ready for a flight to Miami."

But the Mayor doesn't know how he's going to get himself and his entourage to Miami in time to accept the nomination that evening. Then comes another phone call from Ted Kennedy, offering to solve the problem. George Steinbrenner is flying in from Cleveland to pick Kennedy up in Hyannis and take him to Miami. Why doesn't the Mayor hitch a ride. White agrees. There is even talk of a helicopter to ferry the Mayor's party from Bourne to Hyannis, an intimation of executive privilege which flutters more than a few breasts.

Shortly after 2:00 p.m., Secret Service agents in McGovern's party pass the word: protection should now be extended to White.

In McGovern's suite, Frank Mankiewicz turns to George McGovern and asks whether he has checked with Ted Kennedy. McGovern says that, as a courtesy, he has asked someone to inform Kennedy that White is high on the list, but Kennedy's response was inconclusive. "I think you ought to speak to him yourself," Mankiewicz advises. After all, Teddy may not welcome another Irish Catholic from his home state gaining a position that could make him the heir presumptive to the presidency.

McGovern goes into his bedroom to place the call. A few minutes later he emerges.

"What'd he say?" Mankiewicz asks.

"He said, 'Okay.'"

"No, George," he persists. "What'd he *say?*"

"He said, 'Okay, if that's the way you want it.'"

Silence.

"That means 'no,' George."

McGovern calls Kennedy back. This time Ted is more explicit. He can't campaign for the ticket with any enthusiasm if White is on it. He suggests Wilbur Mills, Abe Ribicoff, or Tom Eagleton. So strongly does he feel about White that he might reconsider his own refusal. McGovern picks up on that. If Kennedy will reconsider, the spot is his. Ted says he'll think about it and call back in half an hour.

While McGovern waits for Kennedy's final answer, a call comes in from John Kenneth Galbraith, a Kennedy ally and delegate-at-large from Massachusetts. Galbraith tells McGovern that the Massachusetts delegation is "up in arms" at White's selection. White had fought the McGovern forces tooth and nail in the spring primary, and many members of the delegation, including Chairman Robert Drinan, have no use for the Mayor. If McGovern persists in his selection, 70 percent of the 102-member delegation will walk off the floor.

McGovern remembers Senator Kenneth Keating of New York stalking out of the 1964 Republican convention to protest Barry Goldwater's nomination. He shudders at Galbraith's prediction, but it is Ted Kennedy's opposition that really worries him. How can he campaign for President without Kennedy's enthusiastic support?

At 3:00 p.m., Frank Wilson, Kevin White's driver, arrives at the Bourne house with three films for the Mayor's weekend viewing: *The Yearling, Beckett,* and *The Man with No Name.*

"Don't leave, Frank," says White. "I may have to go to Hyannis. I may need a plane."

At 3:15, Ted Kennedy calls McGovern back. He won't run himself, but he still opposes White and urges consideration of the other names.

McGovern assures him White will be dropped.

He calls Abe Ribicoff, who is disinclined to run. The candidate then tracks down his closest friend in the Senate, Gaylord Nelson, who also begs off.

It is 3:45, fifteen minutes before the deadline. "I think I'll go with Tom," he says.

After McGovern has talked to the enthusiastic Eagleton, Mankiewicz takes the phone. "Now, Tom," he says, "is there anything in your background that we ought to know—any problems, you know, like dames, or a loan that went bad . . ."

At 4:05 p.m., McGovern finally calls White back. "Kevin," he says, "I have to apologize to you. I couldn't put it together. For reasons that I can't explain to you—and may never be able to explain to you—I've just offered the vice-presidency to Tom Eagleton."

The Mayor watches on television as McGovern delivers a rousing acceptance speech ("Come home to the affirmation that we have a dream!") and accepts the convention's tribute with a glowing Tom Eagleton at his side.

Kathryn White weeps that evening. His arm around her shoulders, Kevin stares moodily at the surf rolling off the black water of Buzzards Bay.

If ever a man was bred for politics it was Kevin White, the product of a remarkable union in which two diverse strains of Boston history were uneasily woven.

His mother's people were Hagans, emigrants from Ireland to Nova Scotia during the Great Famine. By the time they reached Massachusetts several decades later, they had taken on the protective coloration of the Maritime Provinces, a sober rectitude which gained them quick acceptance among Boston's Yankees. Opening a fashionable shoe store downtown, Henry Hagan joined the Citizens' Municipal League, became president of the Chamber of Commerce, and eventually won election to the City Council as a candidate of the Good Government Association, that band of municipal reformers known colloquially as the "Goo-Goos." Serving on the Council for eight years, one term as President, Hagan was a bitter critic of James Michael Curley, and Curley's forces lashed back, labeling him "a haughty turncoat, in whose veins ice water substitutes for the warm blood of his ancestral land."

In 1928, Hagan's daughter Patricia married a different kind of Boston politician. The gregarious son of a Galway-born brewer, star quarterback at Boston College and later for the semipro Providence Steamrollers, Joe White took to politics with particular gusto. He held virtually every office accessible to a Boston politician: four terms in the State House of Representatives, four in the State Senate, fourteen years on the Boston School Committee (four as chairman), ten years on the City Council (two as President). In 1945 he announced for mayor, but Governor Maurice Tobin preferred his old friend Fire Commissioner Bill Reilly and urged White to drop out. Wary of bucking the Governor, he retired from the field, for Joe White was nothing if not prudent. All through his decades in politics he kept a cushy state job as director of the Telephone and Telegraph Division in the Department of Public Utilities. In addition, he was said to have an interest in an oil distributorship run by his brother-in-law, State Senator Jim Scanlon. So many irons did White have in the public smithy that when he ran for lieutenant governor his opponents hired a sound truck to tour the city's streets with a little parody called "Joe White and His Seven Jobs."

But White wasn't simply a reincarnation of James Michael Curley. Like many Irish-Americans of his era, he was intensely proud of his hard-won respectability. His electoral strength was concentrated in the "upper wards," the southern reaches of the city now largely inhabited by second- and third-generation Irish families advancing rapidly into the middle class (while Curley always drew best among the working-class denizens of the "lower wards"). His name, not readily identifiable as Irish, helped attract voters in the Yankee and Jewish districts. So secure was his reputation as a "high type" Boston politician that when the New Boston Committee assembled its "reform slate" in 1951, White was the only incumbent councilman included. Declining to feed off ethnic rivalries, he served for a time as regional chairman of the National Conference of Christians and Jews. An accomplished storyteller and witty performer—reminding his sons of Maurice Chevalier—he never stooped to Curley's demagoguery.

But the White household suffered strains. Joe thrived on his eternal round of banquets, rallies, torchlight parades, and Irish wakes; a congenital handshaker and backslapper, it took him half an hour to walk the quarter mile from the State House to City Hall. Patricia loathed that kind of politicking; there was something demeaning about it. When Joe went off to one of his dreary testimonials at the Parker House, she preferred staying home in West Roxbury reading Tolstoy or Willa Cather. A former public school teacher, she read deeply in the European Catholic intellectuals like Newman, Chesterton, and Teilhard de Chardin, and subscribed to the liberal Catholic journal *Commonweal*. Though deeply religious, she was plainly outside the American Catholic mainstream as represented by Richard Cardinal Cushing and Senator Joe McCarthy. A Stevensonian liberal, she staked out advanced positions on political and social issues. Determined that her children bear the stamp of culture, she insisted that, even though none of them had any real feeling for music, they all gather around the radio on Saturday afternoons to listen to the Metropolitan Opera.

It was Patricia who chose her sons' rather literary Christian names— Kevin, Terrence, and Brendan—unusual for a time when most Irish-American boys were called Patrick, James, or Francis. Joe White didn't much care for any of them, but he was particularly distressed by his eldest son's. "Jesus," he'd grouse, "how do you expect a kid named Kevin to get on the ballot?" Joe's State House friends would smirk as they asked, "How's Kelvinator?" Indeed, Kevin wasn't his father's favorite child—a distinction reserved for the second son, Terrence. From childhood, Terry had identified with Joe, soaking up his clubhouse lore and tactical cunning, while Kevin gravitated toward his mother. For years Patricia took her son's part in his endless running battles with Joe.

Young Kevin was a chronic hell-raiser, a natural leader always chosen to captain the neighborhood boys in their sporting contests, as well as in less wholesome pursuits. More than once the future mayor barely escaped the long arm of the law, though not that of his father. Unbeknownst to most of his constituents, Joe White was a heavy drinker. In deference to his teetotal wife, he did his boozing outside the house, but when he came home drunk, he often took a belt or razor strap to his recalcitrant son. Relations between father and son got so bad that even when Joe hadn't been drinking he'd haul off and knock Kevin down.

At Cranwell, a Jesuit preparatory school in western Massachusetts, Kevin disrupted classes so repeatedly he was asked to leave. Moving on to Tabor Academy, he compiled another dismal record. In part because of reading problems stemming from a dyslexic condition, he graduated eighty-third in a class of eighty-five. Only the intervention of Headmaster James Wickenden persuaded Williams College to admit him as one of its "ten-percenters"—students with low grades but other indicators of potential. Nor did he distinguish himself at Williams, where he played a little football and served as vice-president of the Newman Club.

Despite bad relations between father and son, Joe White was a potent influence. Nobody was surprised when Kevin majored in political science, then went on to Boston College Law School, the traditional breeding ground of Irish politicians. In 1956, he reinforced those credentials by marrying into another famous political family, the Galvins of Charlestown. "Mother" Galvin's seven daughters were the pride of the Town, one prettier than the next, each educated at the best Catholic institutions, polished with elocution and ballet lessons. None was a more perfect lady than slim, ash-blond Kathryn, who graduated from Newton College of the Sacred Heart in 1956, just as Kevin signed on as assistant to Suffolk County District Attorney Garrett

Byrne. Kathryn and Kevin were married that June, moving into a cramped apartment at 122 Bowdoin Street. For the next four years, Kevin divided his time between the DA's office—where he specialized in the criminal side of paternity suits—and a private law practice with another assistant DA, Larry Cameron.

That summer of 1956, Joe White was caught in the most ill-conceived venture of his career. For years he'd supported Suffolk County Sheriff Fred Sullivan, who, in turn, plied him with patronage. But when the two had a bitter falling-out, some of those whom Joe had placed as court officers feared that they would lose their jobs and urged him to run for sheriff himself. Against his better judgment, Joe acceded. By the time Kevin returned from his honeymoon, his father was headed for a debacle. Determined to spare him that humiliation, Kevin and Terry worked around the clock to pump life into the moribund campaign.

In those days, all Boston newspapers ran political ads on the front page, often piling them one upon another. The brothers waited until the last moment, then descended on the newspaper office with a new ad, which would be stacked above the rest, pushing it into the enviable position "above the fold." Meanwhile, Mother Galvin mobilized his strength in the "lower wards." The campaign came alive. In late summer, the White boys asked Galvin to assess their prospects. "You'll always know if you're going to lose," the old campaigner noted. "You'll be able to smell defeat."

The Saturday before the Democratic primary, the brothers were crossing the Boston Common when Kevin asked, "You smell anything?"

"Yes," Terry said, "I do."

The next Tuesday, Joe carried Boston but lost the county's outlying reaches, falling 1,000 votes short of the nomination. But his sons had survived their baptism by fire.

Through the late fifties, Kevin White watched another Boston Irishman move to the very doorstep of the White House. Not surprisingly, Jack Kennedy had a profound influence on the young assistant DA. To a young man in White's position, Jack Kennedy's cool diffidence seemed the standard by which to measure himself. When Honey Fitz's grandson declined to kiss babies or try on Indian headdresses, Mother Galvin's son-in-law nodded in instant recognition. For JFK's example merely reinforced the lesson Kevin had absorbed at his mother's knee: not for him the boozy bonhomie of the traditional Boston pol; rather, the dignified mien of the public servant. It was perhaps not entirely coincidental that when Kevin White left his father's West Roxbury base for Beacon Hill in 1956, he settled in the very apartment block where Jack Kennedy had established his voting address a decade before, and that when he opened the law office of Cameron & White that fall, it was in the building which had harbored Kennedy's first campaign headquarters.

By early 1960, as Jack Kennedy advanced on the presidency, Kevin White joined a band of Yankee and Jewish liberals intent on bringing the spirit of the era to Boston's heartland. For years, the Ward Five Democratic Committee, representing Beacon Hill and the Back Bay, had been controlled by a veteran named Charlie McGlue. Now Beacon Hill attorney Carl Sapers, assembling a reform slate, thought Kevin would add ethnic balance. Backed by a cadre of energetic young gentry, the ticket swept to a decisive victory.

While politics was becoming Kevin's vocation, it remained an avocation for Terry, who had married at eighteen, quickly fathered five children, and required a substantial income. In 1955, he founded a company which took advantage of his political connections as well as his name. White Lines, Inc., did just what its title suggested: it painted white lines down the center of streets. Soon his firm had won contracts in Boston and many other New England cities. The business minted money, leaving Terry plenty of time for his favorite hobby, politics. To many, his seemed the best political mind in the family.

After Kevin was elected to the Ward Five Committee, Terry spotted an unusual opportunity. A veteran pol named Joe Ward, then serving as Massachusetts Secretary of State, was running for governor, leaving the Secretary of State's job up for grabs. So far the race had drawn a lackluster field and Terry believed Kevin could make a good showing. But he had to sell the idea. Patricia was dead set against it. She'd never wanted her father or husband in politics, and she certainly didn't want that life for Kevin, whom she regarded as too refined for the hustings. Joe White didn't think his eldest son was up to it. But Terry persuaded them both. Then he and his father went to work on Kevin, who was particularly reluctant when he discovered that he'd have to resign his $5,000-a-year job in the DA's office. At length Terry convinced him, promising to help bankroll his campaign.

Once Joe White had enlisted in the campaign, he was in it all the way, but he still couldn't communicate with Kevin, so Terry was the conduit between them.

Behind the scenes, Joe and Terry sought to clear Kevin's path. A few days before the convention, they called on State Senate President Johnny Powers, a tough-talking pol from South Boston who would share the convention chair. A spokesman for the city's "lower wards," Powers wasn't the Whites' kind of guy and Patricia had been aghast the previous year when Joe supported him for mayor. In return, Powers had promised that if elected he would appoint Kevin City Treasurer. But he'd lost the mayoral race and now the Whites were there to claim a different return on their investment.

Cornering Powers outside the Senate chamber, Joe reminded him that Kevin was running for Secretary of State. "Can you give him a little help?" he asked.

"Well, sure," said Powers, "but I don't know what I can do. He has to prove himself."

At that, Terry moved in. "Suppose Kevin could finish second on an early ballot? Could we count on you then?"

"Of course," said Powers, clearly annoyed at being pressed so hard.

On June 19, the balloting began at the Boston Arena, an ancient hockey and wrestling emporium. The superannuated structure had no air conditioning and temperatures hovered in the nineties. It took nearly twelve hours to nominate the top of the ticket, so the balloting for Secretary of State didn't begin until 9 p.m.

All evening, Joe White and Mother Galvin prowled the floor, calling in chits from a combined sixty-five years in politics. As the voting began, Joe went to work on John Regan, a power in Joe's own West Roxbury, but Regan was pledged to the front-runner, Francis X. Ahearn. Finally, Joe stationed himself in front of the West Roxbury delegation and stared directly at Regan, who did everything to avoid his eye. When he did look up, he saw Joe still there, silently mouthing, "My boy, John. My boy."

West Roxbury went for Kevin White, as did a surprising number of other delegates. Although Ahearn headed the first ballot with 432 votes, Kevin was second with 352, narrowly edging out Governor's Councilor Edward J. Cronin. In an office beneath the stands, the gubernatorial nominee Joe Ward and his powerful ally, House Speaker John "Iron Duke" Thompson, watched the tally, debating where to throw their strength. After the first ballot, Owen Brock, one of Ward's campaign managers and a cousin of Joe White's, urged them to support Kevin, arguing that Joe and Mother Galvin would be valuable assets in the campaign. When Thompson and Ward concurred, they summoned their supporters—already celebrating at the hotels—to vote for Kevin White.

Frank Ahearn and Eddie Cronin knew that their only hope of survival was an adjournment until morning. There were legitimate arguments for one—the convention had been in session for thirteen straight hours and the heat was so oppressive that one Lynn delegate had been rushed to the hospital. So many delegates had left the floor that delegation chairmen now stood alone by their microphones, casting hundreds of absentee votes—a practice permitted so long as no delegate demanded a poll of those present.

Toward 11 p.m., rumors swept the floor that Cronin was about to address the convention to throw his votes to Ahearn or demand adjournment. Terry White rushed to the podium, telling Johnny Powers, "Now's the time. We need you!" When Cronin approached, Powers refused to let him speak.

On the second ballot, Kevin White jumped ahead with 481 votes to Ahearn's 339 and Cronin's 293. Ahearn was desperate now. Standing on a chair, he complained loudly that he was being "jobbed." Pounding his gavel, Powers noted that only a delegate could challenge a count. Ahearn's supporters howled with rage. Fistfights broke out on the floor. Fearing that a riot might force an adjournment after all, Joe White dashed to the podium, gesturing frantically for his people to calm down. But Ahearn's forces kept up their clamor until Powers ordered uniformed police to clear the floor of all non-delegates. At 11:25 p.m.—with police standing guard in the aisles—Powers proclaimed Kevin White the winner on the third ballot.

The young candidate was so unknown that fall that Jack Kennedy introduced him to a rally as "Calvin Witt." But White went on to beat another promising newcomer, Republican Ed Brooke, and didn't relinquish the Secretary's office for seven years. The responsibilities were hardly onerous—his bailiwick included the State Archives, State Elections, Vital Statistics, Public Documents, Trademarks, and Notaries Public. His principal accomplishment was sponsorship of the Corrupt Practices Act, requiring that all candidates for statewide office disclose their campaign contributions and expenditures. The second such law in the nation, it drew wide attention, launching Kevin's reputation as a progressive. Compared to later legislation, the statute was shot with loopholes, but it almost provoked a blowout with the Kennedy clan.

By autumn 1962, White had already declared limited independence from the Kennedys. When Ted announced that spring for his brother's old Senate seat, Kevin endorsed his opponent, Eddie McCormack. He did that in part out of gratitude to Eddie's uncle, the former Speaker, who had done Kevin's ailing father a crucial favor; in part because he harbored some personal animosity toward Ted (once when Ted was busy he asked Kevin to take his wife to a reception, prompting Kevin to ask indignantly, "What does he think I am? A driver?"). White respected Jack Kennedy, but he resented the way the First Family threw its weight around in Massachusetts politics, handpicking "Chub" Peabody as governor, reserving the senatorial plum for Ted. Perhaps because he owed his advancement so heavily to his own father, Kevin was particularly sensitive to the nepotism issue. Barely a year older than Ted, he regarded him as direct competition; he was damned if he'd climb on the Kennedy bandwagon.

Even without White's endorsement, Ted won handily. A few days after the election, an underling in the Secretary's office showed his boss clear discrepancies in Ted's campaign finance report. Since that was the first year candidates had been required to file under the new law, many reports contained such errors, but Kevin jumped at the chance to embarrass the Senator-elect, ordering his staff to prepare a news conference. Only when Terry White warned that challenging the brother of a sitting President was sure political suicide did Kevin reluctantly cancel the announcement.

It isn't clear how much Ted knew about these events, but White's relations with the Kennedys were strained from then on (one aide remembers Ted nervously disposing of cigarette ashes in his cuff rather than ask White for an ashtray). The roots of the McGovern imbroglio were sunk deep in their mutual suspicions.

The office of Secretary of State offers its incumbent one striking opportunity. Since all town clerks report to him, the Secretary has ample reason to stay in touch with these influential politicos. Early in his first term, White pledged to visit each of the Commonwealth's 351 towns and cities. Relentlessly over the next few years, he and general counsel Dick Dray climbed into Dray's red Mustang and headed off for some remote community. In May 1964, he flew by seaplane into Gosnold, a tiny island village in Buzzards Bay, dramatically completing the tour.

After he was reelected with the largest plurality ever received by a statewide Democratic candidate, his thoughts turned to the governorship, but his advisers were sharply divided on the best route, so in May 1966 White convened his brain trust at the airport motel. Associates like Dick Dray and Jackie Mulhern urged that he run first for mayor of Boston, but Kevin was repelled by the grubby minutiae of city government as well as by his father's brand of urban politics (no longer much of an influence, Joe White had suffered a stroke and would die the following year). Preferring the loftier realm of state government, Kevin wanted to run for Attorney General. Terry concurred. But to seek a new state position Kevin would have to sacrifice his old one and, if he lost, he would be out of office altogether. Abandoning that notion, he announced for a fourth term as Secretary of State.

Jackie Mulhern, one of Kevin's oldest friends, continued to brood about the mayoral race. The city was the quintessential arena of the sixties, he concluded, the laboratory in which an ambitious politician could make his mark. One day in November 1966, he invited Terry White out to Newton's Woodland Golf Club and made his argument in detail. After four hours, Terry summoned Kevin. Over dinner in the club's dining room, his brother and his old friend persuaded Kevin to run for mayor.

Terry signed on as campaign manager and all through that winter he shrewdly orchestrated a public relations effort to frighten Mayor John Collins out of the race. Full-page ads gave the false impression that White was lushly financed; friendly columnists suggested that powerful forces were coalescing behind him. In mid-spring Collins dropped out, throwing his support to Redevelopment Director Ed Logue, a nationally known figure with impeccable liberal credentials and influential friends in the media, among them Tom Winship. Although the *Globe* was still bound by its self-imposed prohibition on political endorsements, Winship did little that summer to disguise his enthusiasm for Logue.

When White proved stronger than anticipated, the Collins-Logue forces landed what looked at first like a knockout blow. A challenger turned up enough errors in White's nominating papers to threaten a disqualification. Fighting for his survival, Kevin charged that Logue was behind the challenge; intent on preserving his "non-political" image, Logue disclaimed any role in the matter. Meanwhile, Terry White led an espionage operation designed to prove his brother's claim. The challenge had been filed by one Richard Iantosca, a name utterly unknown in Boston politics, and the mystery deepened when Iantosca disappeared from home and job. But White's amateur sleuths ransacked barrooms and staked out hotels, eventually locating the intermediary between Logue and Iantosca. His disclaimers now discredited, Logue withdrew the challenge, and several weeks later finished fourth in the preliminary, setting the stage for a runoff between Kevin White and Louise Day Hicks.

Once the race narrowed, its character altered radically. Mrs. Hicks's reputation as the "Bull Connor of the North" attracted a torrent of media attention. When *Newsweek* caricatured her on its cover and the *Globe* abandoned a century of neutrality to endorse White, they transformed the contest into a political morality play: Good arrayed against Evil in a succession of stark tableaus. If Louise was never quite the racist her enemies conjured up, Kevin was never quite the righteous crusader (betraying no recognizable ideology through his early years, he'd often been called "light as a feather"). But once the drama was cast, the candidates played out their appointed roles. By early autumn liberals from near and far had rallied to Kevin, among them Barney Frank, fresh from Harvard. Signing on as a researcher, the irrepressible Barney was soon playing a major role behind the scenes, stamping the campaign with his own convictions on social and racial issues.

All this left Terry White deeply disconcerted. Very much his father's son, a pragmatic nuts-and-bolts campaigner, Terry warned Kevin that he had lost touch with his roots. As Terry saw it, the new ideological war could only repel the working-class ethnics on whom his brother would ultimately depend. Indeed, the more fashionable Kevin's cause became in Cambridge, the less appeal it had in Andrews Square and Field's Corner. Late in the campaign, polls showed a perilous erosion of White's once substantial lead; in November his victory margin was barely 12,000.

Through the following weeks Barney's influence continued to grow. One after another, senior posts in the new administration went to *his* nominees, most of whom—like Hale Champion, Sam Merrick, Bill Cowin, Dave Davis, and Colin Diver—had no roots in the city. Though Terry regarded himself as a New Deal–Fair Deal progressive, he had little patience with Barney's self-conscious liberalism. In turn, the Mayor's liberal advisers saw something vaguely sinister in Terry, whom they dubbed "Raoul" after Fidel Castro's *éminence grise* brother. But Terry found himself in an increasingly difficult position, unable to deliver jobs for the ward-based faithful or to control the course of his brother's administration. Exhausted and embittered, he sent word on the eve of the inaugural that he would not attend the ceremony. Kevin locked his bedroom door and wept.

Yet the next day he demonstrated again his determination to break with the past. For the first time in living memory, the inauguration was held in Bullfinch's classic Faneuil Hall. After a string quartet played Haydn, White delivered a brief but eloquent discourse, the work of Kennedy speechwriter Richard Goodwin. Instead of the time-honored luncheon at the musty Parker House, the Mayor and his guests adjourned for baked capon and vintage Riesling at the elegant Ritz-Carlton Hotel. And that afternoon, White pointedly omitted the traditional hand-pumping tour of City Hall, initiated in the regime of James Michael Curley.

So as Terry went back to painting lines on streets, his brother blazed his own audacious trail that was to lead him four years later to the brink of the second-highest office in the land.

The morning after George McGovern and Tom Eagleton took their bows in Miami Beach, a reporter found the Mayor still morose but struggling to regain his equanimity. "All I want is to get up a family tennis tournament," he said, "enjoy the rest of the weekend, and get back to work."

Returning to Boston on Sunday evening, he was confronted by a crisis. As the city sweltered through a heat wave, a scuffle broke out at the Puerto Rican Day festival in the South End. When police waded into the crowd, ten policemen and thirteen civilians were injured. There was further street fighting the next night, with several stores firebombed and looted. As dusk fell on Tuesday evening, the Mayor decided to visit the troubled neighborhood. Slinging his jacket over his shoulder, he set off on a walk through the riot area. Hundreds of youths followed him down rubble-strewn streets to the Cathedral housing project, where he "deputized" fifty of them to keep the peace. His arms draped around two grinning boys, the Mayor then led a curbside colloquium on the South End's future. When it was over the kids cheered.

Yet almost immediately White faced another problem. The Rolling Stones, completing an American tour, were scheduled to perform that evening at Boston Garden. Diverted by bad weather, their plane had landed at Warwick, Rhode Island, where Mick Jagger and Keith Richard were arrested after an altercation with a policeman. Fifteen thousand young people were at the Garden impatiently awaiting the Stones while their idols were behind bars fifty miles away. If the South End had temporarily settled down, the kids in the Garden were edging toward a riot of their own. Wheeling into action on this second front, the Mayor telephoned the Governor of Rhode Island and the Mayor of Warwick. Within an hour, Jagger and Richard were released on Kevin White's personal recognizance. Two limousines pulled up to the jailhouse door and, with Rhode Island police leading the way, sped the parolees toward Boston.

While they were on their way, fresh troubles broke out in the South End: more stores on fire, two squad cars overturned. Pressed for reinforcements, the Mayor diverted most of the police detail from the concert, leaving the Garden acutely vulnerable. He then decided to appeal directly to the crowd milling angrily about the arena, still unaware of what had happened to the Stones. But when he advanced to the microphone, most of the audience seemed in no mood to listen to some damned politician. "Get lost, stiff," they shouted. "No speeches tonight!"

Suddenly announcer Chip Monck grabbed the mike and bellowed, "Shut the fuck up!" They shut up.

"You want to know why I'm here?" the Mayor asked. "The Rolling Stones were busted in Rhode Island about two hours ago. But I've called the Governor and gotten them out and they're on the way here now."

"Right on, Kevin!" someone shouted.

"But now I need you to do something for me. As I stand here talking, half my city is in flames. I'm taking some of the police away from here and I want you to do me a favor. Just cool it, will you? Cool it for me. Cool it for the city. And after the concert ends, just go home. We're keeping the subways open until after the show. But don't go down to the South End. Just go home.

I appreciate it. Thank you." With a great roar, the crowd rose to their feet and 15,000 kids, many of them stoned, gave the Mayor of Boston a standing ovation. While the Tactical Patrol Force brought the South End under control, there wasn't a single arrest at the Garden that night.

That evening had shown Kevin White at his best: spontaneous, courageous, resourceful, and articulate, at ease with his diverse constituencies, ready to put himself on the line for the city he governed. When the Mayor's personal appeal switched on, it was palpable—like a radioactive isotope, it quickly registered on any political Geiger counter. My God, his aides would exclaim, it's working! They could feel it—and so could he. That evening, as he waited to go onstage at the Boston Garden, he thought back to the night of Martin Luther King's assassination four years before, when he had made a similar appeal from that very stage to James Brown's black audience. It had worked then and it worked now. The Mayor knew he was good. If only others would recognize just *how* good, and give him a larger stage on which to exercise those powers!

That night in mid-July left Kevin White on a sustained high which the next few weeks did nothing to dispel. For as Tom Eagleton was compelled to reveal his medical history and to withdraw from the ticket, White's name surfaced once again. Mayor Wes Uhlman of Seattle forwarded his candidacy in an open telegram to McGovern: "Urban problems will be America's greatest challenge for the next four years. Kevin H. White is the man with unparalleled background in dealing with our urban crisis: he would make a strong addition to your ticket and would be a truly great Vice-President." For days in early August, White believed that McGovern might, indeed, turn back to him. And by the time Sargent Shriver received the nod on August 8, the Mayor was ready to read even that as a favorable omen.

Concluding that the Democratic ticket was doomed, he believed its defeat would end McGovern's and Shriver's hopes of ever occupying the White House. As for the party's other presidential aspirants—Humphrey, Muskie, Jackson, Lindsay, et al.—they had all trooped through Kevin's office that year looking for support and the Mayor had taken their measure. He knew he was their equal, if not their superior. White believed that anyone who succeeded in Massachusetts politics could make it in Washington. After all, Massachusetts was the only state where politics was a full-time occupation for adults—he called it the "Stillman's Gym of American Politics." So who had a better claim on the Democratic Party's shattered leadership than the latest star on the Massachusetts horizon, the consensus choice of McGovern's advisers?

Such considerations were still on his mind when, in early September, White left for his first trip to Europe. When he joined his friends Sam and Nancy Huntington in Woodstock, England, the three of them began talking of a White-for-President campaign in 1976. The more they discussed it, the more entranced they were by the idea.

That autumn a small group of the Mayor's closest advisers—the Huntingtons, Bob Kiley, Frank Tivnan, and pollster Tully Plesser—began meeting to lay the groundwork. Early the next year the circle was widened to include Ira Jackson, a young Harvard graduate who joined White's staff in 1972; Ann Lewis, Barney Frank's sister, who in her brother's absence had quickly become one of the Mayor's principal operatives; Jackie Walsh, a street-wise political organizer; Shelly Cohen, former Massachusetts director of Americans for Democratic Action; and Curtis Gans, a veteran of Eugene McCarthy's presidential campaign. The meetings were super-secret, shielded not only from the press but from most city officials as well. Sometimes the group met at the Huntingtons' town house on Brimmer Street, sometimes at the Colonnade Hotel, a Back Bay establishment conveniently out of the political mainstream.

All agreed that White began with formidable liabilities. First, there was Ted Kennedy, *de facto* chief of the Massachusetts party, no great friend of Kevin's and not about to be eclipsed by another Boston Irish Catholic. Then there was the mayoralty itself, hardly a launching pad for the presidency (no one had ever jumped directly from a City Hall to the White House). Finally, there was White's need to run for reelection in 1975, a year in which his national campaign should be shifting into high gear.

Yet these debits might be converted into assets. Although White couldn't risk an overt assault on the Kennedy establishment, he might quietly build a counter-establishment, capitalizing on latent anti-Kennedy sentiment within the party, much of it generated by the Chappaquiddick affair. He could use his mayoralty to demonstrate leadership in a city which mirrored the ethnic diversity and multifarious problems of the nation at large. Finally, reelection by an impressive margin in 1975 could help set the stage for a national bid the following year.

Through the winter of 1972–73, his brain trust elaborated its strategy. The Mayor would be portrayed as the answer to the Democrats' post-McGovern dilemma: how to bring the party "home" to its traditional constituency without alienating new recruits among the young, women, and minorities. Kevin White, his aides argued, was the only prominent Democrat able to bridge that gap. Relatively young (he was forty-two at the time), well educated, attractive, he had strong credentials with blacks, Jews, academia, and the liberal media. Yet he was also enough of a traditional Irish politician to enjoy excellent relations with old-liners like Dick Daley of Chicago and Pat Cunningham of the Bronx. In an era when many Democrats had emancipated themselves from big labor, he remained on good terms with George Meany of the AFL-CIO and even with the hard hats of the Building Trades Council. At a time when many candidates were posturing legislators, White was a big-city administrator accustomed to dealing with the bread-and-butter issues of urban life. In sum—as the Mayor often claimed on his own behalf—he was the best of both worlds, a street-savvy pol at home in the seminar rooms of Harvard, a splendid hybrid who could achieve John Lindsay's ends with Richard Daley's means.

There remained the problem of how to give the Mayor the national exposure he needed while permitting him to spend most of his time at home running the city and preparing for reelection. The three-pronged solution was ingenious.

First, White should claim a leading role in remaking the Democratic Party. The party's new chairman, Robert Strauss, secretly detested Ted Kennedy and was glad to do what he could for White. What the Mayor wanted was a place on the Democratic National Committee's prestigious Executive Committee; what he got was the co-chairmanship of the 1974 Democratic National Campaign Committee, a job he shared with an ambitious former governor of Georgia named Jimmy Carter. White and his people were bitterly disappointed, but when Ira Jackson called Strauss to complain, the chairman drawled, "Boy, the difference between the Executive Committee and the Campaign Committee is the difference between chicken shit and chicken salad. I'm doing all I can for you, boy." Indeed, the campaign post offered an ambitious politician rich opportunities to befriend candidates around the country and thus to store up IOUs which could be cashed in two years later. The problem was that both Jimmy Carter and Kevin White had the same idea. From the beginning, each sensed the other's secret agenda. In months to come, as both men sought to milk political advantage from the committee, they regarded each other with ill-disguised hostility.

Carter held one obvious advantage: no longer an incumbent, he was free to roam the country, using his campaign position to make direct contact with candidates. Largely confined to City Hall, White couldn't do that, so his game plan called for others to travel for him. These were the "ambassadors"—six or eight people in and out of city government who could appeal on White's behalf to interest groups around the country. They were led by Gerry Pleshaw, a special assistant to the Mayor for women's affairs and chairwoman of the Massachusetts Women's Political Caucus, who had good ties with elected officials in many states. There were Bob Holland with labor, Jackie Walsh with other mayors, Paul Parks and Jim Loving with blacks, Teri Weidner and Ann Munster with women and community organizations. All through 1974, the ambassadors crisscrossed the country—to South Carolina and Arizona, Wisconsin and California—sometimes on "vacation time," sometimes on city time, generally funded by private sources, wherever possible piggybacking on city assignments. Only rarely did they explicitly sell Kevin White. Instead, they plugged into political networks, tried to make themselves indispensable, and developed obligations which they could cash in on when the overt campaign got underway. But in the long run there was no substitute for direct contact between the candidate and those he sought to woo, especially when the candidate was as magnetically charming as Kevin White. It was here that the Mayor and his advisers came up with their most innovative ideas, designed to exploit not only White's own appeal but the grace and grandeur of his city.

High on Beacon Hill was an elegant brick-and-granite mansion once owned by the historian George Francis Parkman. At Parkman's death in 1908 he bequeathed the mansion to the city, and for the next sixty years it had served as the headquarters of Boston's Parks Department, but Kevin White had never set foot in the building until he attended a cocktail party there after the 1968 Harvard-Yale game. Struck by the classic proportions of its Empire-style drawing room, its marbled hallways and soaring staircase, he immediately moved the Parks Department into City Hall and refurbished the sixteen-room mansion with $366,000 in city funds and $250,000 in private contributions. First it served as an Urban Affairs Center, later as Boston's official guest house. By 1973, as the Mayor's advisers mapped his national campaign, it seemed the perfect setting in which to display the candidate himself.

That October, gold-embossed invitations went out to a formidable roster of politicians, academicians, and journalists across the country, summoning them to a series of dinners with the Mayor of Boston. Those who accepted over the next year ranged from Bob Strauss, Walter Mondale, and Jay Rockefeller to Leonard Woodcock, John Kenneth Galbraith, and Tom Brokaw.

The dinners followed a rigid agenda. Some twenty guests would gather for cocktails among the apricot-striped sofas in the downstairs reception room, move to dinner beneath the great chandelier in the second-floor dining room, then adjourn for brandy, cigars, and conversation in the restored carriage house. Whether the subject was "Women in Politics" or "Ethnicity as a Coalition Builder," its focus was Kevin White—always at his best in small groups— flashing wit, irony, and deft little riffs of political philosophy.

Quickly the strategy paid off with increased national exposure. Marianne Means in her syndicated column called White "ambitious, healthy, intelligent, stylish, articulate." Tom Wicker wrote that "an articulate man like Kevin White, given some success in office and a little money and luck, might do well for himself in a presidential primary campaign." Jimmy Breslin, Jack Germond, and David Broder all put White on their lists of legitimate candidates.

By early 1974, the campaign shifted into second gear, with the Mayor himself venturing onto the hustings. In a January blitzkrieg through nine Western and Midwestern cities, he addressed political gatherings, met newspaper editors, huddled with party chiefs. In February he toured North Carolina. In May he spoke to New York's Lexington Democratic Club, lunched with an editor in Atlanta, and watched the Kentucky Derby with Louisville's mayor. In June he made another major Western swing.

That spring America was caught up in the final throes of Watergate, and everywhere White went he called for "a new integrity and decency in government," a "rededication of party politics to public service." Then he warned: "We must greatly expand our presidential candidates for 1976; never again must we allow those candidates to come exclusively from the U.S. Senate. We must ensure that new faces have ample opportunity for wide exposure, pressure under fire, extensive debate and the test of public scrutiny." Few listeners missed his message. Growing still bolder, he twitted Ted Kennedy for doing a "disservice to the party" by delaying a decision on whether to seek the presidency in 1976. When Kennedy bowed out, White noted that the Senator's decision had "made it possible for other Democratic candidates to seek support."

His aides began briefing him on macro-economics, defense, and foreign policy. Ira Jackson scheduled a series of foreign trips: to Israel, to Ireland, to Rome for an audience with the Pope. In August 1974, eighteen advisers met at the Huntingtons' Martha's Vineyard home for a weekend of strategizing. Ira brought elaborate organizational charts; Tully Plesser brought stacks of polling data. There was talk of campaign finance and mass mailings, state chairmen and delegate counts. Late one afternoon as the Mayor sprawled on the veranda poring over a map of primary states, a young aide crept up behind him and played "Hail to the Chief" on the harmonica.

But that summer's euphoria was built on shifting sands, for even as White and his aides charted a bold course toward the White House, they knew that events were underway that could foreclose any chance for the presidency and even jeopardize his reelection as mayor.

Arthur Garrity's desegregation order in June had posed an excruciating dilemma for Kevin White. Through his early years in office he had lent a sympathetic ear to minority needs, earning himself the resentment of white neighborhoods. But even in his days as "Mayor Black," White had recognized the danger of aligning himself with a remedy as unpopular as busing. When Louise Day Hicks campaigned to repeal the state's Racial Imbalance Act, White defended it while stubbornly insisting that it didn't require busing. In 1971, when the NAACP first filed suit in federal court, White said that school desegregation was a "noble objective, but I must disagree strongly with the method they suggest of achieving it. I have long been, and still am, opposed to forced busing." When asked if he would put his own children on a bus, he said, "Probably not" (an academic question since, for most of this period, he kept his five children in private schools, only belatedly sending his youngest into the public system). At one juncture, he even stooped to an unequivocal pledge he surely knew he couldn't redeem: "There will be no busing in this city as long as I am mayor."

Through the early seventies, the Mayor had skirted the issue by having as little as possible to do with the schools. Acting on the sound political principle that if you can't control a situation, you shouldn't take responsibility for it, he had referred all educational questions to the largely autonomous School Committee. Only under heavy pressure from his staff had he ultimately hired specialist Robert Schwartz to develop a schools policy for him. In April 1973 he revealed the fruit of Schwartz's labors—a position paper that sought to shift the focus from busing to the larger question of how to achieve "equal educational opportunity" for every schoolchild in the Boston metropolitan area. Schwartz argued persuasively that racial integration improved student achievement only if accompanied by class integration. He urged a mixture of "magnet" schools and "voluntary transportation" to and from the suburbs to give poor people, both white and black, the same access to quality education as was enjoyed by the rich.

But it was too late for such ambitious reforms. As state and federal courts drew ever closer to their inevitable edicts, racial tensions in the city had begun to escalate. Robert Coles may once have admired Kevin White's ability to "win the confidence of both blacks and whites . . . without stirring either of them to more envy and more bitterness," but the Mayor knew he could no longer work such legerdemain. When René Wagler's immolation set off racial skirmishing throughout the city in October 1973, the Mayor had exclaimed, "I'm a demolitions expert trying to defuse a bomb. If I make an error, I will become a paraplegic, both politically and otherwise." White's sense of imminent apocalypse was echoed by many of his aides, who argued that the busing turmoil would surely abort his presidential effort. But Ira Jackson, now that campaign's principal architect, disagreed. "The eyes of the nation will be on you," he told the Mayor. "If you can hold the city together, you'll look even better than ever."

Even before Arthur Garrity ruled in June, the Mayor had resolved to confront Boston's anti-busing forces head on. From mid-April through the blistering summer, he conducted a series of 11:00 a.m. "coffee klatches" and 5:00 p.m. "sunset hours," trekking three or four times a week into the far reaches of Hyde Park or West Roxbury to sit in somebody's pine-paneled basement and talk busing with a score of parents. By letting them blow off steam directly to him, he hoped to ease some of their rage, and though he made no speeches, his remarks were laced with one consistent theme: he opposed busing and supported efforts to test Garrity's order in the Supreme Court, but as long as it was the law of the land, it had to be obeyed. However one felt about the substantive issue, the safety of Boston's schoolchildren came first.

But the Mayor didn't entrust his political future solely to solemn exhortations; he took out insurance by making clandestine overtures to his old adversary, Louise Day Hicks. Although White and Hicks had twice opposed each other for mayor and were widely believed to occupy opposite ends of the ideological spectrum, there had never been personal acrimony between them. Indeed, when Mrs. Hicks had returned to the City Council in January 1974, chairing the Ways and Means Committee, they recognized certain common interests. She needed to nurture her organization, which fed on jobs. For his part, the Mayor needed a majority in the nine-member Council, no easy matter when faced with such obstructionists as "Dapper" O'Neil and Chris Iannella. Moreover, the Mayor's probable opponent a year hence was former State Senator Joe Timilty, whom Mrs. Hicks detested. All the elements of a deal were at hand and, beginning that winter, the rivals edged toward an accommodation—through the good offices of a mutual friend, the Mayor's veteran lobbyist, Larry Quealy.

But with Boston on the brink of serious racial strife, the timetable for the rapprochement was accelerated. Six days after Garrity's order in June, the Mayor stayed late in his office, waiting for his assistants and secretaries to leave. At 6:45 p.m., a car drew up to the rear of City Hall and Quealy ushered Mrs. Hicks into the Mayor's private elevator, which whisked her to his fifth-floor office. When White and his guest emerged ninety minutes later, the broad outlines of a deal were in place. Louise would support the Mayor in the Council whenever possible; she would help "cool" the city during the busing crisis; and she would keep ROAR neutral in the 1975 mayoral race. In return, the Mayor would open the patronage spigot for her supporters.

The Mayor kept his promise, finding places on his payroll for a dozen Hicks loyalists or their relatives. One became a deputy sealer in the Department of Weights and Measures; another a motor equipment operator in the Public Works Department; still others were squirreled away in the Employment and Economic Policy Administration and the Economic Development and Industrial Commission. So generous was the Mayor's allocation that Louise told a colleague half jokingly, "I don't have enough names for the jobs he gives me."

Mrs. Hicks delivered too, so far as she was able. The day before the buses rolled in September, she called a news conference to declare: "There must be peace in the city tomorrow. I pray that no harm will come to any child. I abhor violence." Privately, she urged her lieutenants to curb troublemakers. But it was too late. The movement Mrs. Hicks had presided over now had a perverse momentum of its own. She asked a friend if federal investigators might hold her responsible if someone were killed in the riots. To assuage her conscience—and perhaps to hedge against a federal indictment—she began feeding the Mayor's office intelligence on when and where trouble might be expected, and on occasion these warnings helped avert more serious violence.

For months the White-Hicks détente remained a closely guarded secret, surfacing only after Pixie Palladino's faction charged Louise with "selling out" to the Mayor. Many rank-and-filers were outraged to discover that while posing as a hard-liner, Louise had helped White muffle their protests. Eventually, Pixie's faction broke away to form a rival and more militant ROAR.

One of the Mayor's assistants recalls: "Kevin was like a child that summer before busing began, like a kid so terrified of the future he won't step on the cracks in the sidewalk. He persuaded himself that if he was very good, if he stepped right in the middle of all the squares, he'd somehow avoid the awful thing that was lying in wait for him."

It didn't work, and Boston reaped its whirlwind. Just what lay ahead for the city became clear that first day when rocks and bottles shattered against the buses carrying black students home from South Boston High. When the Mayor arrived at a Roxbury community center that evening, he found three hundred black parents enraged at the day's events, especially at the city's failure to maintain order. As the parents demanded immediate arrests in South Boston and a call-up of the National Guard, White nervously temporized. A hefty woman in the front row rose to her feet, leveled an accusing arm in his direction, and shouted, "I trusted you! I believed in you and you let me down!" As others echoed her charge, the hall erupted in fury, several of the parents advancing menacingly toward the stage. Shaken and sweating, the Mayor pleaded for more time. "It's not the Lord's guarantee," he said, "but I'm asking you for another chance and then, if I can't produce, I'll fight alongside you." Escaping through a side door, he ducked into his car, looking as frightened as any of his aides had ever seen him. "Wow," he exclaimed, "I could have been slaughtered in there!"

Within hours, the Mayor had grown even more concerned about militant whites. On Saturday, September 14, reports reached the "busing operations center" in the City Hall basement (known colloquially as "the Bunker") that South Boston's notorious Mullens might soon enter the struggle. The Mullens took their name from John Joseph Mullen Square at E and O streets, where they had long hung out. Many Mullens were hardworking longshoremen, truck drivers and firemen, but others were involved in less admirable activities: loan-sharking, bookmaking, hijacking, and enforcing. The police called them the "Irish Mafia." Now reliable informants said the Mullens would join a scheduled anti-busing march on Monday, and if police attempted to halt the march, the "wise guys" were ready for a shoot-out.

According to fresh reports on Sunday, the Mullens were supplying Southie youths with guns. Convinced that the next day's march might be the critical moment in the entire busing saga, the Mayor and his advisers assembled at the Parkman House on Sunday afternoon. "We can't screw around," the Mayor said. "We gotta call in the feds." Bob Kiley telephoned FBI Director Clarence Kelley, once Kevin White's choice for Boston Police Commissioner and always ready to help the Mayor out. At once Kelley ordered his Boston agents to knock on the wise guys' doors, just to let them know the Bureau was watching. Meanwhile, the Mayor reached Tip O'Neill on the Cape, asking him to alert President Gerald Ford that federal troops might soon be required.

The next step was to persuade Judge Garrity to prohibit Monday's march. When Ira Jackson called the judge at home, Mrs. Garrity answered. She seemed nonplussed by the call, and after a long pause—apparently to consult her husband—she came back on the line to say the call was "inappropriate" and perhaps "contemptuous." The judge wouldn't speak to the Mayor. When Ira relayed Garrity's message, Kevin White was stunned. Here they were, dealing with the President of the United States and the Director of the FBI, but they couldn't reach some damn judge out in Wellesley. "That stupid son of a bitch," White railed. "That arrogant ass! He issues his damn order, then retires to his suburban estate and refuses to talk with the only guy who can make it work!"

Later that night, after consulting with his top police commanders, White banned the march himself. The next day a massive police presence contained roving bands of men and boys in Southie. Although nine persons were injured and twenty-one arrested, the Mayor's worst fears never came to pass. But the more Kevin White brooded about the judge's slight, the angrier he got. In his darkest moments, White harbored a suspicion about Garrity. He knew the judge had been trained by Jack Kennedy, nominated by Ted, supported by the whole clan. Was this arrogance of his just another Kennedy tactic to undermine the Mayor?

On Sunday, September 22, White made a second effort to reach Garrity at home. This time he received a return call from Hayden Gregory of the Community Relations Service, relaying a stern lecture from the judge. The Mayor shouldn't try to call him again; if he had anything to say, he should say it in court. Six days later—as if to underline his rebuke—Garrity made White a party to the case.

The Mayor was furious. "What the hell does he think?" White thundered to his staff. "He's bigger than the Mayor of this city? What does he think— we're a bunch of clerks? I'm gonna give him a goddamn lesson."

Many of White's aides shared his contempt for the judge. To blow off steam that week, they chanted an impromptu ditty:

> *There was a man named Garrity*
> *Who refused to give people parity.*
> *He was a Kennedy man,*
> *A flash in the pan,*
> *Created by an act of charity.*

On October 4, with the city apparently slipping into sullen torpor, White took off for a weekend's rest in Florida. While he was away, the Tactical Patrol Force went on its rampage through South Boston's Rabbit Inn. The day he got back, a Southie mob trapped and severely beat the Haitian handyman, André Yvon Jean-Louis. Hours later, an exasperated Mayor resolved to throw the whole mess back in Arthur Garrity's lap. The Rabbit Inn affair indicated that his police were at the end of their tether; the daylight attack on Jean-Louis suggested that Southie mobs no longer heeded Boston's police. But White suspected that a kid who heaved rocks at an Irish cop might think twice before tangling with a federal marshal who could haul his ass into Garrity's court to face a stiff prison sentence. White particularly liked the marshals' symbolism: they would demonstrate for everyone to see that this was the work of a federal judge, dependent for its enforcement on federal power. The Mayor would be off the hook. Moreover, the marshals would have another advantage: they would stave off the National Guard, ill-trained, trigger-happy fellows from the countryside who could only exacerbate the Mayor's problems. That very afternoon, he asked the judge for 125 marshals.

At 2:30 the next afternoon, Kevin White entered Arthur Garrity's crowded courtroom and took a seat on a folding chair in the aisle. Peering over his stack of papers, the judge appreciated "the benefits of the Mayor's presence," then went on questioning Assistant Corporation Counsel Kevin Maloney about the city's request for marshals.

A moment later, the Mayor rose. "I don't mean to be presumptuous, your honor, but . . ."

"I would like to hear from you," the judge said somewhat frostily, "but if you'll just let me finish my question."

As Garrity continued, White slipped to the table where the city attorney was standing. "Let me take over," he whispered. Maloney sat down.

"Your honor," the Mayor began, "this city is under great emotional strain. What we have in this city is hysteria. Hysteria breeds violence. The question before us is whether the federal government is willing to step in after the city has given a maximum effort but before a collapse"—he paused for emphasis—"a holocaust."

Garrity said his court didn't have 125 marshals. He had only 23, and they were functionaries who served subpoenas and stopped spectators from smoking in the courtroom. White said he'd accept 23; it was important to establish a "federal presence" in the city and the marshals would be *symbols* of that presence.

The judge, who believed that White had failed to provide adequate police protection for the buses, now fixed the Mayor with a stern regard. "This isn't a case that needs symbolism," he said. "This is a case that needs security."

"With all due respect," said White, "I believe your understanding is only eighty percent accurate."

A mayoral aide who sat nearby recalls: "It was like a Greek drama. Here were two great institutions, the Executive and the Judiciary, confronting each other head on. Each had profoundly different values: a Mayor, the supreme politician, for whom everything was ultimately negotiable, and a Judge, the supreme moralist, for whom constitutional rights were simply not negotiable. Sitting there, one realized that there was no way these two could accommodate their differences. A collision was inevitable, as predestined as Oedipus sleeping with his mother and murdering his father."

As the Mayor jousted with the judge, an aide handed him a message. White glanced at it and stuffed it in his pocket, then read it again, glowering. When Garrity called a ten-minute recess, the Mayor shared the message with those around him. President Ford had just held a Rose Garden news conference. Asked for his reaction to White's request for marshals, the President said that it was up to the court; he had no plans to intervene. "I would like to add this," he said. "The court decision in that case, in my judgment, was not the best solution to quality education in Boston. I have consistently opposed forced busing to achieve racial balance as a solution to quality education. And, therefore, I respectfully disagree with the judge's order."

White was dismayed. As he struggled to maintain order in his city, the President of the United States not only refused assistance but lent public support to opponents of the court order. A moment later, Arthur Garrity returned to further deepen the Mayor's distress. The law was clear, he said; no marshals could be ordered into Boston's streets until all local and state resources had been exhausted (that is, police from surrounding communities, the state police, and the National Guard). He had every confidence that "integration in the schools can be achieved by community efforts."

The Mayor was wild with anger. Everybody had covered their ass, everybody but Kevin White, who was stuck with the blame for anything that might go wrong. Well, no more! From now on he was looking out for Number One. Summoning a news conference the following noon, he struggled for words to express his sense of grievance. "The President and Judge Garrity, by their decisions and statements, in my opinion have abandoned their commitment to the use of federal resources to implement the federal court order." Therefore, he warned, unless and until he got more federal aid, guarantees of safety for Boston's schoolchildren, and unspecified changes in the desegregation plan, he would "not publicly support on my own volition the implementation of the second phase of the plan."

His remarks stirred a tumult in the pressroom. Just what did he mean? reporters wanted to know. Was he refusing to enforce the law?

No, said the Mayor, he'd obey all the judge's orders. But he would refuse all "voluntary acts," all employment of "my imagination, my skills, my talent." Unless you play it my way, he seemed to be saying, I'll let my city go down the drain. A few minutes later, alone with aides in his office, the Mayor realized he'd mangled his statement. "I should never have gotten into this," he moaned. "I'm going to be seen as a George Wallace with a striped tie."

He'd done all he could for the moment; maybe if he stuck the parties together in a room, they could thrash things out for themselves. That Friday, aides assembled five whites and five blacks for a secret negotiating session at City Hall. The Mayor stopped in to wish them well, then left for Dorchester, turning the chair over to Erwin Canham, the distinguished editor emeritus of the *Christian Science Monitor*.

The meeting began amicably enough, but soon got out of hand when Melnea Cass, a seventy-eight-year-old matriarch from Roxbury, spoke of the Jean-Louis beating in South Boston. "I don't blame whites for their prejudices," she said. "You can't help the way you feel, because you got it from your parents."

"Nobody calls me a bigot," replied ROAR's Rita Graul. "I'm a God-fearing Christian." And pointing a finger at Mrs. Cass, Pixie Palladino disowned any guilt for the Haitian's beating: "My first reaction, from the pit of my stomach, was that he deserved exactly what he got. He had no business being over there in the first place."

Pandemonium erupted. One black slammed her notebook to the floor. Another turned on Mrs. Palladino, shouting, "You think everybody's a nigger! You don't see people as human beings!" Another stormed from the room in tears.

Arriving in Dorchester, the Mayor got an urgent call on his car phone, an aide demanding, "You better get back here. This place has gone berserk!" By the time he returned to City Hall his peace talks were in shambles. Surveying the wreckage, the Mayor ruefully conceded that there was no way for him to abdicate management of the crisis.

By mid-October he turned his attention back to the court; somehow he had to get Garrity to listen to reason. One of his problems, he thought, was his representation in the courtroom. Corporation Counsel Herb Gleason and his assistant, Kevin Maloney, were hardly Clarence Darrows. What he needed was a heavyweight, someone of such stature the judge would have to listen. The first name to be suggested was Cyrus Vance, the former Secretary of the Army and a veteran presidential troubleshooter. An aide noted that Vance could be particularly helpful in handling the issue of federal marshals and eventually federal troops. He had been Lyndon Johnson's special representative during the Detroit riots, deftly negotiating with Detroit's Democratic mayor, Jerome Cavanaugh, and Michigan's Republican governor, George Romney, arranging for the 82nd and 101st Airborne to replace the undisciplined Guard. If anybody could sort out Boston's security mess, it was Vance. In any case, he would look awfully good in court.

When Bob Kiley called him in New York, Vance was willing to consult but dubious about any ongoing role. He was serving that year as president of the Bar Association of the City of New York, a consuming job that left him little time. Vance suggested that they bring in Burke Marshall, Jack Kennedy's Assistant Attorney General for Civil Rights, now a professor of law at Yale.

Late in October, Vance and Marshall spent a day in Kevin White's office, suggesting ways to alleviate his problems, but neither man was willing to represent the city in court. They tried former Watergate Special Prosecutor Archibald Cox, then recuperating at Cambridge University in England, but Cox turned them down. The meeting eventually produced another strategy. Rather than seeking a high-priced lawyer, White might persuade Garrity to accept a master in the case, then point him in the direction of someone well tuned to the Mayor's problems. Vance and Marshall suggested Paul Ylvisaker, a former Ford Foundation executive with ample political credentials, who was then serving as dean of Harvard's School of Education. A few days later, Kevin White rode across the Charles to talk to Harvard's president, Derek Bok. Explaining the city's desperate situation, he asked Bok to make the dean available. Ylvisaker spoke to Garrity, who offered him the job. The Mayor's elaborate plan seemed to have worked, until Ylvisaker withdrew because of a technical conflict of interest.

Eventually Garrity chose his panel of four masters, led by Eddie Mc-Cormack, who got on famously with White, and indeed the Masters' Plan reflected much of the Mayor's thinking. When the plaintiffs objected, contending that the plan fell short of "root and branch" desegregation, White invited their lead lawyer, Nick Flannery, to City Hall to discuss the matter. Painting a portrait of a city on the brink of anarchy, he urged Flannery to compromise.

"Mr. Mayor," Flannery said, "the plaintiffs will do anything we can to alleviate your problems, except curtail desegregation."

The Mayor moved to his huge office window overlooking the Quincy Market shopping mall. "Sometimes when I look out this window," he said, "I see Belfast out there."

"Oh, I don't know," said Flannery. "It looks like Quincy Market to me."

The Mayor scowled.

When the judge finally rejected much of the Masters' Plan, White expressed "bitter disappointment." Garrity, he said, had "virtually guaranteed a continuation of the present level of tension and hostility throughout the city." With that, the Mayor's efforts to influence the court's orders largely ceased. He learned, most reluctantly, to live with them. Privately he continued to denounce Garrity's "callous disregard for the city's delicate psyche." He had equal contempt for those on the other side. (When the newly appointed School Superintendent, Marion Fahey, briefed him on her plans, the Mayor took elaborate notes on a yellow legal pad. An aide who saw the pad later reported that White actually wrote—over and over—"Holy shit! Holy shit! Holy shit!") He reserved his greatest disdain for those Massachusetts politicians—Ted Kennedy among them—who remained aloof from the battle while occasionally giving him the benefit of their advice. "I feel like a field commander in the middle of a war," he once remarked. "Every so often some general walks out on the field and says, 'Tsk, tsk, this is awful. How about flanking the right?' I say, 'Okay, I'll flank to the right with you.' I look around and he's back at the old HQ."

White's own pronouncements remained deeply equivocal: adamant opposition to "forced busing" matched by eloquent appeals for law and order. His critics accused him of carrying water on both shoulders. Why, they asked, couldn't he simply declare busing right, legally and morally? That, his defenders argued, would be politically suicidal and strategically self-defeating. "Eighty percent of the people in Boston are against busing," White told an interviewer. "If Boston were a sovereign state, busing would be cause for revolution." Only a leader who condemned it outright had a prayer of persuading Bostonians to heed his admonitions for law and order.

Unfortunately for the Mayor, his exhortations were only sporadically observed. Night after night, the TV networks ran lurid footage of disorders in Boston's streets, scenes which reminded older viewers of confrontations in Little Rock, Nashville, and Birmingham. The Mayor needed no prompting to recognize what all this was doing to his presidential aspirations. If he couldn't control his own city, people were certain to ask, how could he run the nation? For a while, White did his best to refute the bad press. "It is insulting that Boston is demeaned by grossly oversimplified images," he wrote on the New York *Times* op-ed page. "The picture of Boston as a city torn apart, rife with violence and hatred, has never been true. The vast majority of our population is law-abiding and peaceful, and has remained so throughout the busing crisis." But it was too late for such palliatives. By late 1974, the White-for-President campaign was reeling. The Mayor drew back, fearful of looking ridiculous.

On November 12, 1974, White held a Parkman House dinner for his rival, Jimmy Carter ("We've got to do something for the little asshole," Ira Jackson confided to a friend). Chris Lydon, the former *Globe* staffer who had moved on to report national politics for the New York *Times,* wangled an invitation, then blew the cover on White's dinner-table strategy. The next day, Jack Cole of WBZ-TV tried to get into the mansion with a film crew and, when his way was barred, did an icy commentary asking why any reporter, much less any taxpayer, should be refused entry to public property. The Mayor was furious, demanding to know who had leaked to the press. Soon afterwards, he fired three political operatives, in part to plug the leaks, in part to signal that the grand enterprise was winding down. By February 1975 Ira Jackson had found a job at Harvard.

The Mayor still allowed himself to dream. In September 1975, on his way to a White House conference, White and press secretary Barry Brooks were stopped at the gate and asked for identification. The Mayor, who never carried a wallet, shrugged helplessly, but the quick-thinking Brooks produced a Boston newspaper with Kevin's picture on the front page.

"Okay," the guard told White, "you're in"; then, pointing at Brooks, "You're out."

"Fuck him," said Brooks. "When we come back here to live, I'm in, he's out."

The Mayor loved it. As late as fall he was still toying with entering the 1976 New Hampshire primary. But in his gut, White knew these were fantasies, for by then he was in the toughest political fight of his life. Twice he had faced "that fat, dumb broad," who, whatever fervor she might generate among the faithful, never developed a citywide following. Now he confronted the more formidable Joe Timilty, a lean, handsome ex-Marine, a hard-liner on crime, an unequivocal anti-buser, a candidate who could ignite the tinder of accumulated grievances without looking like a kook.

The Mayor's polls showed him comfortably ahead. Then in April the *Globe*'s Spotlight Team charged that Fire Commissioner James Kelly had pressured firemen into contributing to White's campaigns, threatening unfavorable assignments for those who didn't cooperate. After Kelly resigned, he and his deputy were indicted—though ultimately acquitted—on illegal fund-raising charges.

Hard on the heels of this came a more bizarre revelation. For years Kevin White had lived in dread of a scandal which would stain his administration just as Water Commissioner James Marcus' 1967 indictment for Mafia-connected kickbacks had grievously damaged New York's Mayor John Lindsay. White had often warned his aides that they couldn't afford a "Marcus thing" in Boston. Halfway through the 1975 campaign, the New York-based magazine *New Times* revealed that, in fact, Boston had already had its "Marcus thing"—five years before—but that White had successfully covered it up.

John D. Warner was, in many respects, a carbon copy of Jim Marcus: a boyish, charming Ivy Leaguer, with an air of forthright rectitude. As White's first Parks Commissioner, Warner quickly became a confidant and companion of the Mayor's. So close did the two men become that, as White prepared to run for governor in 1970, he often mentioned Warner—by then director of the Boston Redevelopment Authority—as his probable successor at City Hall. A coolness crept into the relationship after White lost his bid for higher office but Warner wouldn't surrender his mayoral ambitions. Then, in late 1970,

White learned that Warner had apparently pocketed $15,000—either by diverting an illegal contribution intended for White's gubernatorial campaign or by soliciting a bribe. In White's version, he asked Boston contractor David Nassif for a contribution and Nassif replied that he'd already given. When the Mayor said that he had no record of such a gift, Nassif insisted that he'd passed $15,000—five times the legal limit—through Warner. But Warner denied receiving the money. White then summoned Nassif to a suite at the Parker House Hotel and, with a tape recorder covered by an Oriental rug, recorded the contractor's story. When he played the tape for Warner, demanding his resignation, the BRA director refused.

The Mayor had a problem. His evidence wasn't strong enough to take to the District Attorney, and White didn't relish the notion of publicizing his administration's transgressions. Yet if he was forced to fire Warner, or if the commissioner challenged him for mayor, White wanted the press immunized against Warner's charm (White had never forgotten Tom Winship's infatuation with an earlier BRA director, Ed Logue, and knew that even then Warner was wooing Winship). On Sunday, December 20, the Mayor visited *Globe* publisher Davis Taylor at his house in suburban Westwood and told him the story. The Yankee publisher wasn't comfortable with the machinations of Irish politicians and turned to his emissary on such matters, Bob Healy. White and Healy met that afternoon in an interrogation room at the Quincy police station. After gaining the editor's assurance that it was off the record, the Mayor played his tape. According to Healy, the recording was "worse than the Nixon tapes," muffled by the rug and by the Fire Department Band as it passed the Parker House playing "Santa Claus Is Coming to Town." Healy says he couldn't make out how much money had passed hands, or who the contractor was, but White's purpose had been accomplished. Sending word through intermediaries that the *Globe* knew all, the Mayor forced Warner's resignation the very next day. Not a word appeared in print until *New Times* broke the story five years later.

Not surprisingly, this saga of surreptitious taping, apparently illegal campaign contributions, and cover-up soon became known as "Warnergate," prompting a spate of other revelations about White's use of his incumbency to raise campaign money. During the last two weeks of October, Boston's suddenly aroused press produced an astonishing array of charges about the Mayor's fund-raising techniques: forced contributions from businessmen and city employees, contributions solicited in exchange for city contracts, CETA jobs used as payoffs for contributions, a mayoral suite maintained in the Parker House to receive large donors bearing cash. Seizing on these disclosures, Joe Timilty spoke of "a climate of corruption" at City Hall.

The Mayor responded with a curious amalgam of candor and obfuscation. Of his demand for one hundred dollars from each city employee, he said that was "only twenty-five dollars for each year in my term," likening it to the *Globe*'s annual Christmas charity appeal. To one reporter he replied—off the record—with the tale of the Southern politician who, when charged with similar depredations, declared, "Some of you will see me as your next governor, you'll give a lot, and when I become governor you'll get a lot. Some of you are going to wait a little, then you're going to give me a little, and you will get a little from me in due time. The rest of you, you're not going to contribute to my campaign, and to you I say, you will get good government."

Later he broadened his rebuttal, arguing that reporters were "applying post-Watergate morality to pre-Watergate events." Did they expect politicians to be "conceived immaculately"? Indeed, most of the offenses laid at White's door that fall were time-honored practices in Boston—and elsewhere in urban America. Certainly, the Mayor fully exploited his control of real estate assessments, tax abatements, permits, licenses, inspections, change orders, architectural and engineering contracts to put the arm on those doing business with the city. But what the press had uncovered was more a corrupt system of campaign financing than an example of personal malfeasance. In failing to provide that context, the newspapers sometimes seemed to be suggesting that Kevin White had created the system, when the real problem was that the system compelled many politicians to act that way.

Moreover, White's complaint that Boston reporters were engaged in "a cross between the McCarthy era, the Reformation and the minor witch hunts" may have been hyperbolic, but it contained a grain of truth. For something happened to the city's normally compliant press corps that autumn. Fired by the Watergate exploits of Dan Rather, Seymour Hersh, Woodward and Bernstein, Boston's young reporters had begun to scour the landscape for iniquity. Some stories—notably those by the *Globe*'s Mary Thornton and Curt Wilkie—were the products of dogged probing into City Hall's nether regions. A striking departure from the paper's usual veneration of White, the Thornton-Wilkie pieces triggered a bitter war at the *Globe,* pitting White's old ally, Bob Healy, against the new mandarin of objectivity, Bob Phelps. On more than one occasion, Healy tried to kill or water down a Thornton-Wilkie exposé, while Phelps—who believed the paper had been far too committed to the Mayor— stood by his reporters. The city's alternative papers, the *Phoenix* and the *Real Paper,* also contributed some valuable reporting and analysis. But radio and television, with their lust for the quick fix, were frequently superficial, sometimes irresponsible. And the *Herald American* plumbed new depths of unprofessionalism when, in mid-October, it abruptly abandoned its loyalty to the Mayor and became Timilty's overwrought champion. In the campaign's closing week, the *Herald* launched a series of front-page attacks on the Mayor, some of them only thinly disguised as news stories—a blatant vendetta unlike anything Boston had witnessed since the worst excesses of John Fox's *Post.*

White lashed back at his tormentors, trotting out police officials who charged that "organized crime" was using the press to discredit him and Police Commissioner DiGrazia. His press secretary followed with calls to WNAC-TV, alleging that one particularly aggressive reporter was a "close associate" of mob figures. Later the same reporter had his car impounded for $1,100 in parking fines. Several enterprising newsmen were barred from mayoral news conferences, and White tried repeatedly—but unsuccessfully—to get the *Globe*'s Mary Thornton removed from City Hall. Finally Jack Cole—the most persistent of the Mayor's critics—was fired by WBZ-TV. Cole sued, charging that the station had caved in to mayoral pressure; he won a $100,000 judgment, which was later overturned by an appeals court.

The Mayor's political consultant, John Marttila, called the 1975 campaign "the most brutal election I've ever been in." The *Herald American* termed it "a nasty, negative free-for-all." The *Globe* likened it to "a carnival spectacle, two wrestlers writhing in a muddy pit." To Kevin White it seemed "a run on the corporation," a raid on his psychic capital which left him wasted and spent. From mid-October on, White behaved erratically—retreating from the campaign for days on end; flying into rages at his subordinates; sinking into bleak moods from which nobody could rouse him; making phone calls to friends in the middle of the night; prowling the city's streets in his station wagon. One night, as two reporters grilled him again on the corruption charges, he nearly wept on the air, pleading with the interviewers to understand his position. Fearing that the Mayor was nearing a nervous breakdown, the very aides who had been trying to get him out on the campaign trail now did everything they could to keep him from public view.

As in his father's race for sheriff two decades before, Kevin could smell defeat—its stench was in his nostrils. On election night, he took his family to dinner to prepare them for the loss he knew was coming; appearing at his headquarters several hours later, he looked "positively stricken." By then, his aides knew he was going to win, but the Mayor simply couldn't accept it. Noting that Timilty hadn't yet conceded, he believed his rival was preparing to "steal" the election. "Get me the Police Commissioner," he shouted. "I want all the machines impounded." Bob Kiley calmed him down, persuading him to give his victory speech. By dawn the Mayor had come through with a margin of 4.8 percent.

But even such vindication did nothing to exorcise the demons which rode Kevin White all that winter and spring. Like Winston Churchill, renounced by Britain's voters after World War II, White felt betrayed by the very constituencies which had once been his most ardent supporters—blacks, liberals, and the *Globe*. "We're the first liberation army in history to be stoned by the people we freed," he told one aide. Most of the city's black elected leadership, dismayed by White's performance on busing, had endorsed Timilty, and even though the black electorate rallied to the Mayor, he resented their leaders for abandoning him. Likewise the liberals, who he felt had fled his camp at the first breath of scandal. The *Globe* had finally endorsed the Mayor for a third straight time, but White couldn't forgive Tom Winship for letting Mary Thornton and Curt Wilkie flog him daily on page one.

White's relationship with Winship was complex and ambivalent. In many respects the two men were alike: creative, imaginative, and perceptive, yet impulsive and inconsistent; given to bursts of productive energy, but also to wild alarums and excursions. Both owed their advancement in part to their fathers and were sensitive to suggestions of nepotism. Both had risen as far as they could in Boston's parochial arena and yearned to succeed in the big time. Each fed the other's national ambitions because it reflected well on himself. Winship would tell Dave Broder or Mary McGrory, "You ought to take a look at our mayor. He's a comer," while White would tell Henry Jackson, "You ought to cultivate the *Globe*. It's got clout." Whatever tensions might prevail in public, there was often an accommodation behind the scenes. When the Spotlight Team did a tough series on the Assessing Department—a principal focus of corruption charges at City Hall—it reached the Mayor in advance to make sure that it evoked a statesmanlike response. One of the Mayor's former press aides recalls, "It was as though they'd said, 'Kevin, we're going to fire four bullets. We'll kill three, wound one. Then we're going to send the ambulance. Have the goddamn good sense to get on board!'"

But at times it seemed as if White and Winship had been put on earth to drive each other crazy. The day the Mayor hired Bob Kiley, he gave him a lecture on the *Globe*, his text drawn from Edwin O'Connor's *The Last Hurrah*. With wry hyperbole, he claimed to be Frank Skeffington, the pol patterned after James Michael Curley, while Winship was Amos Force, the Yankee publisher ("a miserable, vindictive, bastardly figure," wrote O'Connor). His lesson: on Boston's ethnic battlefield there could be no permanent alliance between two such disparate characters. Whatever relationship one might imagine one had with Winship, one shouldn't count on it, because "he'll throw you off the bridge at the critical moment."

Yet no mayor of Boston could ignore Tom Winship and his newspaper, and vice versa. Somehow they lived with each other—flattering, cajoling, prodding. White loved to gibe at Winship for his suburban perspective. When the rifle shots went through the *Globe*'s windows in the fall of 1974, a City Hall aide recalls, White suggested that Winship "call the constabulary out in Lincoln." And after White showed signs of cracking during the 1975 election, Winship asked him, "Kevin, have you ever thought of seeing a psychiatrist?"

But by the spring of 1976, White didn't need a shrink to tell him what to do. He was mayor for four more years, and this time he was going to consolidate his position so that never again would he be humiliated; never again would he have to worry about Tom Winship's moral posturing, the *Herald American*'s vindictiveness, the blacks, the liberals, or any of his other critics. He'd spent his first eight years in office trying to do what was right—and what had that got him? Nothing but carping and irresponsible attacks. Well, maybe he'd never be President, but if he had to be mayor for the rest of his life he was damn well going to do it on his own terms.

Some who watched the Mayor's evolution over the next few years would say he had gone from John Lindsay North to Richard Daley East. But the equation with Lindsay had always been superficial. The similarity in style—tousled hair, necktie askew, coat over shoulder—disguised profound temperamental differences. Lindsay was a poised WASP, White a mercurial black Irishman. Like his idol, lawyer-statesman Henry Stimson, Lindsay was content to drift in and out of politics, trying his hand at the law, writing, television; perceiving no such options for himself, White was a politician for life, consumed by the process. Lindsay was a Protestant moralist, dedicated to making politics "more wholesome"; White was an Irish pragmatist who could chuckle knowingly when an aide said Lindsay was "giving good intentions a bad name."

White came to echo Daley's classic verdict on Lindsay's New York: "I get the feelin' nobody's in charge here." And he could sympathize with Seth Cropsey's judgment on Daley's Chicago: "It is not a grand vision, but American cities do not need a grand vision. What they need is to work." As early as the late sixties, White had encountered Daley at national mayors' conferences. In 1972, he read Mike Royko's *Boss,* an acid portrait by Daley's most rigorous critic, but drew the opposite conclusion from the one Royko intended: for all his crudeness, Daley was in charge. Their close relationship dated from July 1975, when, playing host to the U.S. Conference of Mayors, White lavished special attention on his senior colleague. Escorting him around the city, White talked with pride about his Little City Halls, the keystone of his early years. If there was a pothole on your street, White explained, you went to your Little City Hall to get it filled. Daley was incredulous. Could anybody do that— whether they'd been *for* White or *against* him in the last election? *Why,* for God's sake? Soon White sent an aide to Chicago to see how things were done out there, and before long he brought a University of Illinois authority on Daley to lecture Boston city employees on the master's technique.

But White was as different from Daley as he was from Lindsay: volatile where the Chicagoan was stolid, impatient where Daley was meticulous, melodramatic where Daley was self-effacing. White was too eclectic, too confident of his own uniqueness, to pattern himself on *any* paragon. He borrowed many people's ideas, taking community schools from Lindsay, "Summerthing" from Milwaukee's Henry Maier, redevelopment schemes from Montreal's Jean Drapeau. For a time he borrowed avidly from a fifty-year-old book—*The Great Game of Politics* by Frank Kent—which explained how the bosses of the past had dominated their cities. Always juggling the formula, he groped toward a synthesis of his own. For years he'd talked about combining the best of Lindsay with the best of Daley (his staff gibed, "You've got Lindsay's political savvy and Daley's compassion"). In early 1976—still reeling from the one-two punch of busing and the ferocious campaign—he altered the mix again, stirring in a big dose of Daley's *Realpolitik.*

Beginning that March, the Mayor held a series of secret Parkman House breakfasts to brief campaign workers and city employees on his new political organization. At the peak of the pyramid was a "Committee of Five," composed of five trusted political lieutenants (all full-time city employees). Under them would come 22 "ward coordinators" supervising 252 precinct captains, who, in turn, would direct the activities of 2,000 block workers. Each block worker would be responsible for 25 citizens, soliciting their votes and acting as their intermediaries with Kevin White's regime.

White told the breakfasters that the new organization would gradually replace his Little City Halls, which had "failed to deliver" politically. Henceforth, strict political criteria would prevail for the delivery of most city services. If you were a "KHW Positive" (a term from the previous fall's polling operation, meaning a Kevin Hagan White supporter), you'd get your pothole fixed; if you were a "KHW Negative," you'd bust an axle.

In the months that followed, city employees were drafted wholesale into the new organization, compelled to attend weekly planning sessions, required to canvass voters, distribute literature, or work the telephones—often on city time. Even the highest-ranking officials weren't exempt: the City Auditor was spotted one afternoon holding a sign for a White-endorsed candidate on Columbus Avenue. A few balked. When an assistant press secretary declined such "demeaning" tasks, her precinct captain warned: "You better look out! You're among ten or twelve people who are being watched." Such pressures intensified when the Mayor used a referendum on property tax assessments as a training exercise for his troops. Those who "put out" during the purely political effort were rewarded with promotions and raises; those who merely performed their municipal duties received no such favors. Pressed to justify this fusion of political and governmental service, the Mayor seemed to echo his brother's judgment of years before. His bright young advisers, he said, "had no roots. They were not out in the neighborhoods. So I said, let them have twenty-five people each. They should know what it's like to try to get a favor done for each of the twenty-five. . . . I did it more to develop them than to save me."

Although Richard Daley had provided the model for this operation, several City Hall officials detected more than a trace of Richard Nixon in the Mayor's new style. One evening in April 1976, White attended the Boston premiere of *All the President's Men*. The next morning, at a meeting of his senior staff, someone asked how he'd liked the film, triggering a fifteen-minute tirade on the lessons of Watergate. The President, White said, had been brought down by "a pair of young punks" who didn't know their ass from their elbow about government (one listener was certain that the Mayor was thinking as much of Curt Wilkie and Mary Thornton as of Woodward and Bernstein). Nixon hadn't deserved to be hounded out of office; he hadn't done much more than they'd done right there in Boston—except get caught. At that, several aides felt like crawling under the table.

White had always been fascinated by the exercise of power. For years he played a game with his staff. He'd ask whom they regarded as the most powerful man in Boston, by which he meant "the guy who can do whatever he wants to you, but you can't do anything back to him." They would tease him by tossing out names—Cardinal Cushing, Tom Winship, mob leader Gerry Angiulo, longshoremen's boss "Red" Moran—but sooner or later they'd say, "Oh, you, Kevin," and he'd beam. He always said there were only three political jobs worth having—mayor, governor, and President—because they were the only ones in which you could get anything done. When Tully Plesser tried to interest him in a cabinet post, White said, "You mean sit at a table and when you speak you hold up your hand and they say, 'No, we'll tell you when you can speak'? You got to be kidding!"

In late 1976, White made an audacious bid to consolidate his power by tacking a proposal for partisan elections onto a charter reform package. Since 1909, Bostonians had chosen their mayor through a non-partisan contest, with the two highest vote getters in the preliminary facing each other in a runoff. Reintroducing partisan elections, the Mayor claimed, would increase voter participation and "revitalize the two-party system." But critics contended that the principal beneficiary would be Kevin White himself. With the prerogatives of incumbency and his new political organization, White would almost certainly win a partisan primary; then, since the city was overwhelmingly Democratic, he would be the odds-on favorite to swamp any Republican opponent. If the proposal succeeded, Kevin White might be Boston's mayor-for-life. In public, White vehemently denied such considerations. In private he was blunt: "Don't you see," he told skeptical aides. "This is the Congress of Vienna! Afterwards it'll be a breeze." At the last moment, the plan was killed in the state legislature.

Only momentarily fazed by this setback, the Mayor worked out a full theory of executive power. "There is a growing timidity of chief executives in the exercise of authority, influence, and command," he told any audience which would listen. "Born of an overreaction to Vietnam and Watergate, political reformists are tying the hands of elected officials as the Lilliputians tied Gulliver, in an effort to prescribe good government by imposing restraints. If the presidency is in trouble as an institution it is not so much because it has become too powerful as because it has become increasingly dysfunctional. Power is to be exercised, not husbanded."

Increasingly he insisted on the trappings of power as well. No longer did the Mayor appear in public with coat over shoulder and sleeves rolled up ("It became a mannerism," he told one interviewer. "I consciously keep my coat on these days"). Years before, he had refused to use the massive limousine inherited from John Collins, buying a Ford station wagon instead, and often riding up front with the driver. But by the mid-seventies he was back in a limo (which, by tradition, bore the numbers 576, the number of letters in the names James Michael Curley). Although he earned only $40,000 a year—the legacy of a bitter standoff with the City Council—he traveled in style at city expense. On one trip to Washington seeking financial assistance from the Carter administration, he and his party were met at National Airport by a caravan of chauffeured limousines (the Admiral Limousine Service charged Boston $1,567.50 for two days). On a trip to New York, the Mayor stayed in a $250-a-night suite at the Hotel Pierre. The press dubbed him "Kevin de Luxe."

He justified such expenditures by calling Boston "a world-class city" which required "a certain level of dignity" from its chief executive. "When

I'm in Washington I'm not treated like some kind of donkey. I do it by knowing my place, without trying to strut. I know the President is the President, Tip is Tip, Teddy is Teddy. They can kick the shit out of me in private. But publicly, no. I think that adds to the city." When told that New York's Mayor Ed Koch had taken a city bus to his own inauguration, White hissed with contempt, "One of these days some guy is going to do something like crawl. I will never crawl. I will stand and kick, but I will not crawl."

He worked in handsome surroundings, a sumptuous suite looking out through tinted windows at Quincy Market ("You don't need to run for President," Ed Muskie told him. "You already have the nicest office of any public official in America"). But he wasn't satisfied. Soon he outraged the City Council by announcing plans for a $90,000 dining room and kitchen. Meanwhile, with every passing year, he spent more time at the Parkman House. For an Irish boy, born in lower-middle-class Jamaica Plain, reared in lace-curtain West Roxbury, and settled at the shabbily genteel base of Beacon Hill, the great mansion on the hilltop was the consummation of his fantasies, a house from which he could actually look *down* on the Brahmins. In the spacious dining room lined with eighteenth-century Chinese wallpaper of pink-red birds and butterflies, he served his guests—at city expense—such specialties as Strawberry Gantoise and Chicken Vallée d'Auge. Sometimes as he strolled the cornflower-blue rug, warmed his feet by the American Empire fireplace, or dashed off a note at the mahogany secretary, he couldn't believe his good fortune. Completing an interview with a Philadelphia newsman, he paused at the door, gazed up at the graceful, curving stairway, and said, "It's got to be the loveliest staircase in America!" One spring evening another reporter was driving along Beacon Street when he spied the Mayor on the wrought-iron balcony surveying his city. When the reporter saluted, the Mayor responded with a papal blessing.

In all of this, his mother's patrician tastes were evident. At a reception in his City Hall office, an Irish commissioner examined the volumes of history and literature and rasped, "Nice books. Who chose them for you?" To which Patricia Hagan White responded imperiously, "I did, Commissioner." Patricia also had a hand in selecting the Gilbert Stuart portrait of George Washington—on loan from the Boston Museum of Fine Arts—that graced one wall, the Beethoven sonatas that played softly on the stereo system. With Joe White dead and Terry in self-imposed exile, Patricia was often her son's principal adviser. He showed her his speeches, sought her advice on books and journals, consulted her about the broad lines of public policy. He named his three successive cocker spaniels after her political heroes—Jeff (for Thomas Jefferson), Andy (for Andrew Jackson), and Adlai (for Adlai Stevenson). When he presented gold medals to seven "Grand Bostonians," her sensibility informed the selection: poets Archibald MacLeish and David McCord; historian Samuel Eliot Morison; conductor Arthur Fiedler; banker Ralph Lowell; physician Paul Dudley White; and only one politician—and one Irishman—former Speaker of the House John McCormack.

Like his mother, Kevin was determined to cast off the image of music-hall Irishman worn by the departed husband and father. When an opponent called Kevin a "Boston pol," he said that was "the worst thing anybody ever said about me." When a black aide asked whether he planned to march in the St. Patrick's Day parade, he said, "I feel about that the way you do about a minstrel show." Mindful of his father's thralldom to the bottle, Kevin was a virtual teetotaler who occasionally took a glass of chilled white wine. He never joined the Knights of Columbus and kept his distance from the Church, declining to kiss the ring of the aging Cardinal Cushing, offering little more than civility to Humberto Medeiros.

He demanded deference from the WASP world. And never had he seemed so happy as on the summer day in 1976 when Queen Elizabeth visited Bicentennial Boston. Escorting her about his domain, he positively preened, as if to say: Here's the Queen of England with a thousand years of imperial history behind her paying a call on the grandson of Irish immigrants! He loved to quote Mayor Thomas Lynch's remark, made at his 1836 inauguration, that the Irish were "a race that never will be infused into our own, but on the contrary will always remain distinct and hostile." Well, the Mayor seemed to say, smoothing his gray flannels and blue blazer, do I really look so different?

But he *was* different. Beneath his J. Press wardrobe, Kevin White was anything but a tight-lipped, buttoned-down Yankee. A cauldron of insecurities and resentments, of black Irish rages and Celtic depressions, he personalized everything—*my* city, *my* police chief, *my* tax rate. That left him immensely vulnerable, unable to differentiate between a glancing blow and a fatal wound. No matter how he might aspire to the accouterments of the upper class, he was most at ease with landsmen like Vice-Mayor Eddie Sullivan, State Treasurer Bobby Cranc, Speaker Tip O'Neill. At eleven o'clock at night, when you kick off your shoes, you do it with men who share your cadence, not your concepts.

In truth, White privately detested the Brahmin bankers and businessmen with whom he was compelled to traffic during the day. Through all his years in office, he never established cordial relations with the powerful Vault. For a time he chose to deal with his own counter-Vault, a handpicked coterie of pliant merchants. His only intimate friend in Boston's commercial world wasn't a Yankee at all, but a Canadian-born Jew named Mort Zuckerman, who made a fortune in Boston real estate before buying *The Atlantic Monthly*. Like White, Zuckerman was an outsider, the object of Yankee condescension and obstruction. And, like the Mayor, he had beat the Yankees at their own game.

As the seventies drew to a close, Kevin White won his fourth consecutive term—an unprecedented feat in Boston, rare anywhere in the nation. Except for six-term Henry Maier in Milwaukee, he had served longer than any other mayor of a major American city. His substantive achievements were not inconsiderable: innovations like Little City Halls, "Summerthing," and community schools; the halting of superfluous highway construction and airport expansion; a massive capital improvements program, producing dozens of new schools, libraries, parks, fire and police stations; recruitment of superior public servants; a new reputation for Boston as one of the most vibrant and livable cities in the land.

But that reputation was derived from a narrow swatch of the city—a square mile of new office towers, hotels, restaurants, and shops along the fashionable fringes of the Boston Common. The longer the Mayor remained in office, the more he betrayed what aides called his "edifice complex," a craving for monuments to memorialize the Kevin White era. No place so symbolized this imperial Boston as the development which the Mayor admired through his tinted office windows. The handsome granite warehouses of Quincy Market had been converted into a massive cornucopia of America's consumer culture, brimming with crystal, china, books, records, stereos, and tape recorders, not to mention shrimp, oysters, kebobs, crepes, bockwurst, pepper Brie, spinach pâté, salad Niçoise, popovers, Häagen-Dazs ice cream, and chocolate-chip cookies. Among the multitudes which surged along its corridors and piazzas, one searched hard for a black face, even a stray visitor from nearby Charlestown or South Boston. The market was an incongruous memorial to a mayor who had come into office promising to reverse his predecessor's emphasis on downtown development in favor of the long-neglected neighborhoods. In his first term White had done just that—but problems of the neighborhoods were systemic, rooted in intractable dilemmas of race and class, while downtown could be treated with quick infusions of cash and chic. Gradually, the Mayor took the easy way out.

Nowhere was his retreat from the tough issues more evident than in the area of race. Once he had failed in his initial efforts to "broker" the busing crisis, he largely abandoned his attempts to resolve Boston's chronic racial tension. Periodically—as in his 1979 inaugural address—he proclaimed some new crusade on the matter, but before long it would grind to a halt for lack of leadership. When blacks complained of his vacillation, the Mayor accused them of ingratitude. After he told one group, "You wouldn't even be in this room if it weren't for me," neighborhood activist Percy Wilson snapped, "Don't give us this master-slave thing." Such exchanges made it difficult for blacks to function in the White administration. Year by year, the highest-ranking black at City Hall, Deputy Mayor Jeep Jones, found his influence further circumscribed. After a series of racial incidents in Dorchester and East Boston, he exploded during a meeting with the Mayor, demanding that White take vigorous steps to halt such attacks. "Black people must be able to move about this city without fear of assault," he shouted. "We are taxpayers, voters, human beings. When is all this going to change?" The Mayor shouted back, charging Jeep with disloyalty. Soon afterwards, Jones resigned.

By then the commitment to social change which had characterized Kevin White's early years in office had largely ebbed away. That commitment had coalesced over the issue of race in the aftermath of Martin Luther King's assassination, and it dissolved over the issue of race in the busing crisis of 1974–75. No longer very interested in such matters, the Mayor seemed increasingly obsessed with his own political survival.

He dreaded the prospect of losing public office. For more than two decades he hadn't had to worry about finding a parking space or getting tickets to Fenway Park. Looking out his office window at the forest of anonymous skyscrapers, he shrank from the idea of renting space in one of those towers and practicing law for a living. One day, as the Mayor was walking down the street, a guy in a windbreaker yelled at him, "We'll get you, Kevin, the way we got the Governor." Wheeling on his tormentor, White shouted, "Shut up, you son of a bitch. I'm going to survive because I'm going to beat the shit out of you!"

But the political organization designed to ensure his survival suffered from the same liabilities that beset most of his public programs: his moodiness and short attention span. The Mayor could be eloquent when enunciating grand philosophical principles, but he was terrible on the details. He just couldn't be bothered. One day, somebody asked him what the city budget was, and, unable to remember whether it was $50 million or $500 million, he just made up a figure. But a political machine requires infinite attention to detail. Richard Daley thrived on such painstaking diligence; Kevin White did not. "You run the machine," Daley used to warn, "or the machine runs you." As time passed, it often seemed as if White's machine was running him.

For years he had boasted that none of his people had ever gone to jail. Then, in a matter of months, two senior operatives—his Ward Thirteen coordinator and a ranking redevelopment official—pleaded guilty to extortion charges and received substantial prison terms.

At about the same time, some 1,500 members of his organization were invited to a birthday party for the Mayor's wife at the Boston Museum of Fine Arts. The workers were informed by their superiors that a "gift" of at least fifty dollars was expected from each. Coming just when many municipal employees were being laid off in an "economy" drive, the request had teeth. In the end, 401 persons contributed a total of $122,000. Investigators later determined that many of these people had deposited cash in their personal accounts in the same amount as their "gifts." This suggested that the event may have been designed, in part, to launder illegally raised money (although one of the party's organizers was later acquitted of that charge).

Twenty-four hours before the party was to take place—as municipal employees were threatening a demonstration outside the museum—Joe White's son prudently canceled the party and promised to return the money.

A reporter asked why.

"The museum," explained Patricia Hagan's son. "There was going to be a situation where beautiful pictures would be ruined."

29

Diver

The South End had its own Judge Garrity, sometimes known as "the other Garrity," "the good Garrity," or "the real Garrity," to distinguish him from W. Arthur Garrity of Wellesley and the Federal District Court. Their black robes notwithstanding, nobody was likely to confuse the two jurists. Arthur was circumspect, exacting, and meticulous; Paul was hot-tempered, impatient, informal in the extreme: he had been known to look down from the bench and say, "Hey, guys, I've been up here all morning and I'm getting tired. Why don't we take a break so I can have a cup of coffee." Paul Garrity was as street-wise as the defendants who appeared before him. Born to an Irish trolley worker and his French-Canadian wife, he went to Boston College and BC Law School and worked as a poverty lawyer before becoming the first judge of Boston's new Housing Court. When Boston judges were required to live in the city, Garrity and his wife moved from suburban Dedham to the South End, buying a bow-front town house at 22 Rutland Square, just a block from the Divers.

One evening in the spring of 1975, Paul heard a scream from outside his house. Rushing onto the sidewalk, he found a young woman bleeding from a stab wound in the side. The judge took her into his kitchen and called an ambulance, but when the victim was rushed to the hospital she left behind a yellow plastic umbrella smeared with blood. Paul stuck it in the hall closet, but every time he went to get his tennis racket he saw the little parasol with its telltale streak of red. After a month or so, the damn thing bothered him so much he took it downstairs and burned it in his furnace.

That summer, burglars broke into Garrity's house and stole a coin collection which had belonged to his great-grandfather. A few weeks later his friend Dick Bluestein, associate director of the Boston Legal Assistance Project, was mugged on West Newton Street on his way to a meeting at Garrity's house.

Then that fall a rash of violent crimes broke over Rutland Square—eight muggings in November alone. Convinced that the neighborhood was becoming "a damned Dodge City" and unencumbered by the liberal philosophy which inhibited some of his neighbors, he was determined to do something about it.

One of Paul's closest friends was Municipal Court Judge Gordon Doerfer, who lived just a couple of doors away. As the holdups continued that winter, other homeowners on Rutland Square approached the two judges for help. Garrity and Doerfer would normally have been reluctant to use their special influence with the police, but feeling that their own families'—and their neighbors'—security was at stake, they asked Captain Al Flattery of District 4 for greater police vigilance.

Embracing the South End and the Back Bay, District 4 reported more serious crime than any other subdivision in the city. As many as twenty holdups could occur on its streets during a single summer night; gambling, prostitution, and drug dealing were rampant. A beleaguered commander, Al Flattery struggled to please a dozen vociferous constituencies, but when Garrity and Doerfer approached him that fall, he responded as most police officials would: he assigned four officers to keep nightly watch on the judges' houses. For several weeks, the uniformed patrolmen took turns sitting in parked cars in the alley by the South End library sipping coffee from Styrofoam cups and watching the Garrity and Doerfer residences.

So obvious were the cars and their passengers that no mugger or break-in artist dared approach while they were there. But since the patrolmen never got out of their cars, the criminals were free to pursue their activities nearby. And this, of course, stirred resentment among the judges' neighbors, who suspected that Garrity and Doerfer had sought special protection while letting the square's other residents fend for themselves. Embarrassed and exasperated, the judges went over Flattery's head to Deputy Superintendent Walter Rachalski. To strengthen their case and repair relations with their neighbors, they brought along three people who they knew were equally concerned with the crime situation: Dick Bluestein, community activist Holly Young, and Joan Diver.

The conversation that evening in the deputy's office was not encouraging to his visitors. Rachalski explained that his division's resources were already stretched to the breaking point. Policemen from all over the city had been mobilized for the busing crisis. At night, his men were on call for South Boston, Hyde Park, or Charlestown, wherever the trouble was, then had to be at Madison Park High at 6:30 the next morning. That left little manpower to handle break-ins and muggings; it was impossible to maintain the kind of intense surveillance which might deter such offenses, and with only eleven plainclothes detectives, it was difficult to mount more than perfunctory investigations after the crimes had been committed. In any given case, the chance of arresting a "perpetrator" was negligible. Nevertheless, sensitive to his visitors' political clout, Rachalski ordered the two stationary cars replaced by an eight-man foot patrol on four parallel streets: West Brookline, Pembroke, West Newton, and Rutland Square.

The cops of District 4 had little sympathy for the South End's embattled gentry. Third-generation Irish and Italians who had followed their compatriots to the suburbs, they couldn't understand why any young professional would choose to live in a troubled inner-city neighborhood. Responding to a burglary or holdup on West Newton Street, they often told the victims, "Well, if you live in an area like the South End, you have to expect this sort of thing."

For a time, the foot patrols could be seen every evening on West Newton Street. Then they disappeared altogether, not a blue uniform to be seen for hours on end. When residents complained, a rash of traffic tickets started appearing on cars along the four streets. Many were for the most minor of violations—parking more than a foot from the curb—something which was difficult to avoid when the streets were lined with snowbanks. To those hit with such summonses, it seemed that the police were taking revenge for being called out on foot patrol in the middle of a harsh New England winter.

Nobody was angrier than Colin Diver. Six years with the Mayor and Governor had left him with rigorous standards for public service. After running Bill Cowin's abortive campaign for lieutenant governor in 1974, he had reluctantly moved into the private sector, accepting a joint appointment in the Law School and the School of Public Management at Boston University. His new focus there on the particulars of management technique gave him even more exacting criteria for assessing governmental performance. By any standards, the Boston police didn't measure up.

As parking tickets settled like wet snowflakes along West Newton Street, Colin called Deputy Superintendent Rachalski. "Look," he said, "we'd be better off if you pulled your men off the street and let the muggers do their work. That way my neighbors and I might lose, say, thirty dollars a night, and people could protect themselves by not carrying cash. This way we're getting ripped off with two hundred dollars in parking tickets every night. You may call that police protection. I don't."

From Rachalski's apologies it became clear that the ticket blitz wasn't the work of resentful patrolmen. District 4 clearly didn't trust its own men to walk their assigned beats in the heart of winter. Suspecting that the patrolmen would hole up in a bar or some other cozy retreat, their superiors had ordered the ticketing to assure that their men were at least out on the street where they might deter, if not actually apprehend, a criminal. Meanwhile the Divers and their neighbors were paying the price.

Impelled by the same sense of responsibility which had led them to confront truck traffic, commuter congestion, substandard housing, and rampant prostitution, Colin and Joan gradually assumed command of the war on crime. They kept a careful list of every crime committed in their corner of the South End. Friends and neighbors called at all hours to report incidents, which Joan inscribed in a loose-leaf notebook. In neat schoolgirl's script she recorded the informant's name, the location, date, and time of the crime, the number and description of the assailants, their weapons (if any), the victim's name, the goods or money taken, and whether or not the crime had been reported to the police.

The level of criminal activity remained fairly constant through the Christmas season, but as 1975 ended, the situation on the Divers' block deteriorated radically.

It started on Tuesday, December 30, when a man up the street was mugged in the alley behind his house.

At 5:00 p.m. the next day—New Year's Eve—a gang of boys with sticks stopped an elderly man on the sidewalk and took his wallet.

Half an hour later the same gang grabbed an old woman's purse.

At 5:45 on January 6 the Divers' next-door neighbor, Linda Trum, was returning home with her three-year-old daughter when two young men came up behind her. One of them put his arm around her neck and, as she struggled, her assailant said, "Don't scream. Just give us your money." She said she wasn't carrying any. The men rifled her pockets, then ran off down the block.

At 9:45 that same night, Colin and Joan were watching television when they heard a scream from the alley behind the house. Colin grabbed the Slugger, the bat with which he had once helped win the Lexington Little League championship, and ran into the alley. There he found a woman named Terry Baksun, whose purse had been snatched. Colin looked up the alley, but the mugger had fled.

After dinner the next night the Divers had an appointment to look at a new Kirby vacuum cleaner. The salesman—a college student named Bobby Jacobs—was aggressive but charming, and Colin and Joan smiled to themselves as he ran the machine up and down their dining room, demonstrating a bewildering array of tubes and brushes.

At 8:20 p.m., their elder son, Brad, hollered down the stairs, "I think I heard a scream outside."

Colin gestured to Jacobs to turn off the vacuum cleaner.

"Are you sure, Brad?"

"I think so."

Colin ran to the door, grabbed the Slugger from its niche, and dashed out onto the sidewalk, where he found a twenty-five-year-old black woman named LeSola Morgan.

"What's the matter?" Colin asked.

"He took my pocketbook."

"Who did?"

"Some guy. He hit me in the face and grabbed my purse."

"Which way'd he go?"

"Down there," she said, pointing toward Tremont Street.

As Colin started off in that direction, he saw a man run out of the alley by the library carrying a large black handbag.

"That's my pocketbook," yelled LeSola Morgan.

"Stop!" Colin hollered. "Stop! Thief!"

The man ran harder, thundering past the library.

Taking up the chase, as he had so often in the past, Colin noticed something unusual about his quarry. Most of the others he'd pursued through these streets were kids who ran like NFL ends, gone before he got anywhere near them. But this one was different: a man in his late twenties or thirties, lumbering down the sidewalk like a rogue elephant. And Colin was actually gaining on him!

At Tremont Street, the man dodged a screeching taxi, darted past a honking panel truck, and charged across the busy thoroughfare. Colin hesitated for a moment. Tremont was a significant boundary to his world, the southern border of the gentrified South End. Beyond it stretched a row of tenements, occupied principally by Puerto Ricans, Dominicans, and Cubans. The O'Day Playground halfway down the block was the center of the South End's heroin trade, a dangerous place at any time of the day or night. On other chases in months past Colin had always stopped at Tremont, unwilling to carry his pursuit into alien territory. But he was fed up. After six crimes of violence on his block in barely a week, he had to catch one of these bastards! Without further reflection, he hurtled across Tremont and sprinted after the fleeing figure.

It was a dismal night, cloudy and cold. Streetlights glowed in the fog. A fine drizzle lay an icy slick along the pavement, but Colin kept his footing, quickly making up the ground he'd lost. The mugger was running down the middle of West Newton Street. Gaining steadily on his man, Colin thought: I'm actually going to catch this guy! He could feel the smooth, round handle of the Slugger in his right hand. Raising the bat, he thought: Am I really going to hit this guy? Can I? Should I? Before he could deliberate further, he came abreast of his target and swung the Slugger in a short, powerful arc against the man's head.

As if he'd pulled some hidden trigger, the scene erupted in a clutter of disjointed images.

The mugger collapsed in a heap on the street.

Tripping over the body, Colin tumbled to his knees, sliding six feet along the ice.

The purse flew from the man's grasp, coming to rest in a puddle.

The Slugger broke in two, the barrel sailing onto a nearby stoop, the jagged handle still clenched in Colin's hand.

Struggling to his feet, Colin turned to confront his antagonist, who was hauling himself upright. For a moment, the two men stood in the middle of the street, staring at each other. The mugger shook his head slowly, as if to clear the mist before his eyes, and suddenly lurched forward.

My God, Colin thought, he must have a knife or a gun!

But either the man didn't see him or wanted nothing more to do with him, for he began staggering—half running, half walking—up the sidewalk.

Colin picked up the pocketbook. Once more he hesitated. He'd retrieved the woman's money, he'd given the guy a good thwack on the head—maybe he should just forget about him.

At that moment, Bobby Jacobs, the vacuum cleaner salesman, came steaming up the street, yelling, "What's going on?" Emboldened, Colin pushed the pocketbook into Jacobs' hands. "Hold this," he said. "I'm going after the guy."

Retrieving the Slugger's heavy barrel from the stoop, he ran up the sidewalk, nearly colliding with two black men dressed to the nines for an evening on the town. "Hey," yelled Colin. "Help me out, will you? See that guy down there? He just robbed a girl. Grabbed her pocketbook."

"Aw, man," said one of the men. "You *got* to be kidding."

"Come on," Colin said. "He smashed a black woman in the face."

"All right," said the second man.

Colin and his new ally resumed the chase. Just short of Shawmut Avenue they corralled the mugger, who was too groggy to put up much resistance. Colin grabbed him by one arm, the black guy by the other, and together they propelled him onto Shawmut, where a police car was advancing majestically up the avenue. Colin jumped into the roadway and rushed directly into the squad car's path, forcing it to a halt.

Alighting from his car in amazement, Patrolman Gerald Abban asked, "What the hell's going on here?" Still out of breath from the pursuit, Colin did his best to explain. Finally Abban took custody of the mugger—who turned out to be Ruberto Caban, a thirty-year-old Puerto Rican from nearby West Concord Street.

After other police came to the house to take his story, Colin was left ruefully contemplating the evening's events. Only gradually did the implications of what he'd done begin to sink in—he'd clobbered a guy over the head with a baseball bat. Not since boyhood scuffles had he inflicted injury on another human being. It was one thing to bluster, as many of his neighbors did, "If I ever get my hands on one of those bastards . . ." It was something else to actually do it. And with a weapon as lethal as a baseball bat, there was always the possibility of serious injury. Ruberto Caban had looked a little wide-eyed out there, like a prizefighter who'd been hit once too often. If anything was wrong with him, a zealous lawyer could sue Colin for thousands in medical bills. For his own sake, as well as Caban's, he hoped he hadn't inflicted any real damage.

The broader implications were even more disturbing. Nearly a decade before, he'd moved into the city to help bring racial justice to Boston. Now he was rushing out of his house to hit dark-skinned people over the head. Before him on the kitchen table lay his boyhood bat, splintered beyond all further use. Some of his cherished assumptions were in smithereens as well.

The next morning, Colin and Joan went to Municipal Court for Caban's arraignment on a charge of unarmed robbery. All through the hearing, Caban glowered at the Divers, who were somewhat relieved when he was held on $1,500 bail. After the hearing, Colin left for Boston University and Joan for the Hyams Trust, where she tried to concentrate on foundation business. But her mind kept returning to what had happened the previous evening—and the previous week. The nightly routine of crime was taking its toll. That afternoon she wrote a letter to Kevin White:

> Dear Mayor White,
>
> The South End has become an unlivable neighborhood. In the last week there have been six muggings on our block of West Newton Street alone, three within a 24-hour period within ten yards of our house. Colin himself apprehended a mugger last night. This follows a steady increase of incidents since the summer.
>
> I am bringing this to your attention because people are now considering moving out. You have taken a great interest in this area and supported requests by residents for streetlights, trees, traffic changes and other improvements. But unfortunately, we are now faced with a situation with which we cannot live. A dirty street can be tolerated for some period, but threats to our lives cannot.
>
> This is not just a problem of our block or our economic class. In fact, one block with subsidized housing has hired a police detail of their own. The Police Department seems totally immobilized. It appears that the police need to consider different ways of patrolling and must be accountable to the area they serve.
>
> We are fully aware that increasing crime is a national problem and there are complex social, police and court problems involved. But this fantastic city is going to be done in if the situation cannot be controlled.

Eight days later, the Mayor responded:

> Dear Joan:
>
> Thank you for your letter of January 8 concerning the crime problem in your area. Colin is to be congratulated for apprehending a mugger. There are not many people who would do such a thing. Give him my regards and admiration for his action.
>
> You may be sure that I want to see the South End restored to its pristine condition. It was once the most beautiful section of Boston and I intend to do all in my power to see it made one of the better sections of the city. It already is in many respects.
>
> I have sent your letter to Commissioner DiGrazia and he has made Deputy Walter Rachalski aware of your concern and has sent your letter to him for appropriate action. The Deputy will have his Community Service Officer visit you to discuss the problem areas of your neighborhood and of the entire South End.
>
> Best wishes to you and Colin for 1976.

The Mayor's intervention brought modest results. In mid-January, Kirk O'Donnell, the Mayor's principal political lieutenant, called Richie Hall, his chief operative in the South End, and read him the letter. "What the hell's going on down there?" he asked. "If things are that bad, why haven't you said something?"

"Yeh, it's bad," said Hall. "But what are you going to do? We haven't got enough police to watch every block around the clock."

"Well," said O'Donnell, "Kevin wants something done about it."

Not a great deal happened. John Sacco, the District 4 Community Service Officer, and Robert Mullane, the district's Patrol Supervisor, called the Divers to express their concern, but in weeks to come, patrolmen were as scarce as ever on West Newton Street.

After his capture of the mugger, Colin became a controversial figure in the neighborhood. To some of his neighbors he was a hero, a bold and fearless defender of the community. To others, he was a reckless vigilante, a hothead who had set a dangerous example. Among his critics were the police. "Your husband is really crazy," a patrolman told Joan one day. "He should never have gone after that guy. I've seen a lot of people killed or badly hurt tangling with a robber that way."

Colin knew they were right. He couldn't wage a personal war against South End criminals; individual acts of retribution weren't the answer. A friend of the Divers on Rutland Square kept a loaded revolver in his night table. Colin had argued with him about it, noting all the dangers involved in private use of firearms. But, obsessed with street crime, his friend was adamant, and Colin feared that one day he would use that gun. Something had to be done to institutionalize people's anger, to harness their indignation in a cooperative effort with real prospects of success.

Three blocks away on West Canton Street a group of homeowners had tried something which caught Colin's attention. In November 1974, led by a community activist named Chris Hayes, they had formed a street patrol to mount guard on their block through the late afternoon and early evening, and crime had declined significantly. In mid-January, Colin invited Hayes to a meeting in Paul Garrity's living room, where he left his audience favorably disposed.

For a few weeks they temporized. Then, on January 24, West Newton Street was alarmed by two particularly brutal crimes. Early that morning an elderly Greek was hit on the head during a holdup in the alley behind the Divers' house; hours later he died of a heart attack, the first fatality of that winter's crime wave. That very afternoon, on adjacent Pembroke Street, a twenty-three-year-old pharmacist named John Poirer returned to his apartment and found the front door jimmied. As he dialed the police, the burglar emerged from a bedroom and ordered him to hang up and empty his pockets. Poirer complied, then bolted from the room and began desperately ringing nearby doorbells. The burglar followed him into the hall and shot him in the back. Doctors said the young pharmacist would be paralyzed from the waist down.

Horrified by the savagery of these attacks, the Divers decided to move quickly toward a West Newton Street patrol. Joan suggested that they call in another specialist in such matters—Dain Perry, director of the Crime and Justice Foundation, a citizens' organization which promoted reform of the criminal justice system. Joan knew Perry through the Hyams Trust, which had supported part of his foundation's work, and on several occasions she had consulted him about crime in the South End. Dain Perry had recently become a convert to "community crime prevention," the idea that a community must take responsibility for its own crime rather than delegating it to the police. Perry suggested that the Divers call a meeting of area residents, which he would be happy to address.

On January 11, some twenty-five West Newton Street and Rutland Square residents assembled at the South End library. Colin Diver opened with a summary of crime statistics and efforts to improve police protection, then turned the meeting over to Perry, who lost no time in making his case. "The first thing you have to realize," he said, "is that police resources are terribly limited. They can't give continuous special treatment to any single neighborhood, because there are simply too many neighborhoods with these problems. The police can't be everywhere at the same time.

"You can go out and hire guards to do the job for you, but that only shows you're scared. Worse yet, it's the ultimate rip-off because the criminals are making you shell out your hard-earned money to keep them away. Even if the guards succeed in driving off the criminals, as soon as the guards leave the wise guys will be right back.

"The most important ingredient in protecting your neighborhood is to show that the community takes care of its own. You must demonstrate that you will not tolerate crime in your midst. You've got to organize. You've got to communicate. Ultimately, you've got to get your own eyes and ears out there on the block. You've got to form some kind of citizens' patrol to show those who would do you harm that you don't intend to sit idly by and let them push you around."

Perry's advice alarmed some in the audience. To the Rutland Square contingent in particular, it smacked of vigilantism, lynch parties, frontier justice. But to most in the room, it seemed the only way out, the last resort for a community with its back to the wall. The group agreed to recruit their neighbors and reconvene the following week.

On February 7, Perry returned with more detailed information about citizens' patrols. He also brought a Freon horn, a gas-powered unit about the size of a small aerosol can which emitted a shrill blast that could be heard for blocks around. "This little thing should frighten off any attacker," Perry said. "It'll also bring your neighbors to their windows and any passing policeman to your assistance. When you hear one of these on the block, the first thing you should do is call 911, the police emergency number. If four or five people make the same call at the same time, don't worry—better too many than no one at all. The next thing is to grab your own horn, run out on the street, and sound it. That kind of ruckus is guaranteed to scare off even the most hardened criminal."

The second meeting ended with agreement that West Newton Street should form such a patrol as soon as possible. Not surprisingly, Colin was designated its captain and principal organizer. But he had one serious misgiving. Unless they were very careful, he feared, the patrol could take on racist overtones. The twenty-five homeowners gathered at the library that morning were overwhelmingly white, while their antagonists on the street were largely black and Hispanic. The dark-on-light nature of most South End crime was a reality which even the most committed South End liberal could not gainsay.

Such polarization was bringing out a latent racism in Colin—something he'd never felt before. Whenever he saw a couple of black kids bopping along West Newton Street, the muscles in his neck and shoulders would tense up. He knew it was grossly unfair to assume that such young people were up to no good; of 5,000 black kids roaming the South End and Roxbury on any given day, only a tiny fraction were committing crimes. He realized that many of the "criminals" were only children, striking back at the sorry hand life had dealt them. Nevertheless, he responded as if it were "us vs. them." It frightened him.

The Divers' dream of an urban neighborhood integrated by both race and class was receding before the relentless advance of gentrification. Rising rents and condominium conversions had forced many blacks out of the community, while those who managed to hang on had little contact with their white neighbors. Crime only aggravated this social isolation, herding the white middle class into a fearful ghetto of its own.

Colin knew that this was counterproductive. Not only were blacks more often victims of violent crime, but those with a stake in society were frequently more sensitive to the issue than their white counterparts, precisely because their struggle for property and position had been more arduous. At community meetings, Colin had met several black South Enders determined to resist the rising tide of lawlessness, notably Adrian du Cille, chairman of the Methunion Manor Tenants' Council. Determined to protect the block patrol from charges of racism, Colin asked one of his black neighbors, a former Army sergeant named Willie Mandrell, to serve as the patrol's co-captain. Once Willie agreed, he and Colin together recruited half a dozen more blacks. The patrol was still overwhelmingly white, but there were just enough blacks in the ranks to defuse the racial issue somewhat.

Eventually, Colin enlisted nearly fifty neighbors—both men and women—for regular turns on patrol, devising a three-week rotation so that nobody served more than ninety minutes every twenty-one days. Two patrol members were assigned to walk the block weekdays from late afternoon through early evening. Women generally got the early shift (5:30–7:00), while men took the later hours (7:00–8:30). Colin bought a case of seventy-five Freon horns wholesale, selling them to other members at $1.70 apiece.

Once the patrol began operation in mid-February, Colin would rush home from Boston University every evening to make sure his troops were properly deployed. In the gathering dusk he surveyed the block from the top of his stoop or strolled the sidewalks until it was time for dinner. If one of his people failed to show up, he arranged for a substitute or filled the empty slot himself.

Every third Wednesday at 7:00 p.m. he walked his own shift with Horace Graham, while every third Friday Joan took the early turn with a black woman named Mary McFarling.

The patrol proved an effective deterrent. Those who preyed on West Newton Street evidently learned to recognize the patrols and stayed off the block so long as they were visible. That first month, only three incidents were reported during patrol hours. But later at night or on weekends the crimes continued unabated. By then, the block's residents had developed a certain street sense. They learned that most crimes occurred in the dark and isolated middle of the block, in the alleys behind their houses, or on footbridges over the railroad tracks. They learned to look both ways when leaving the house or getting out of a car; to use the door at the top of the stoop rather than the entrance beneath the stairs; to have their key ready when they approached home; and, whenever possible, to avoid carrying a purse or wallet. Joan devised a ruse of her own. Leaving home each morning, she waved to a vacant window, hoping to persuade anyone who might be watching that the house was occupied.

Meanwhile, Colin kept pushing the police for more protection, and under his prodding, District 4 zeroed in on the gang operating out of Methunion Manor. The police grew especially suspicious of the Soul Center, the record store and "bar-b-que" where the gang was known to hang out. Night detectives Frank Sheehan and Tom Connolly watched the place closely, using undercover men to seek evidence of drug dealing and fencing stolen goods. But the investigation failed to turn up conclusive evidence.

Colin refused to give up. Over and over he called Al Flattery, Walter Rachalski, and any other police official who would listen, demanding more attention for West Newton Street. The breakthrough came in early February when Colin learned that his next-door neighbor, Mike Trum, had a daughter in school with a child of Gary Hayes, an assistant to the Police Commissioner. Trum talked to Hayes, who called Colin at the university. "I know exactly what you're going through," Hayes began. "I've already checked the data. The crime rate in your area is out of hand. I'm going to get some people from the Tactical Patrol Force on it right away."

The very next morning the TPF's commander, Captain Fred Conley, and Patrolman Billy Dwyer were in the Divers' kitchen drinking coffee and explaining what they might do to help. That winter of 1975–76, the TPF still had heavy responsibilities for enforcing busing in South Boston, Charlestown, and Hyde Park. But, under explicit orders from Hayes to clean up the South End, Conley said, "We'll just have to get people on overtime. We'll come down here for three or four hours in the evenings and see what we can do."

The principal vehicle would be the TPF's Anti-Crime Squad, a thirty-man unit trained for use in high-crime areas. The unit specialized in "decoy" operations, in which several members posed as helpless drunks or frail young women while their colleagues lurked nearby, ready to grab anyone who molested them. Such operations had worked well in honky-tonk districts downtown, which the TPF preferred because they offered opportunities for quick and easy arrests. But Gary Hayes, among others, had long been urging the squad to get away from downtown and address the grievances of high-crime neighborhoods. Colin's complaint had provided a convenient opportunity for such an experiment.

Billy Dwyer, an ingenious young anti-crime officer, was placed in charge of the South End operation. Dwyer devised an elaborate scheme built around two decoys, policewomen Kathy Fitzpatrick and Marie Ann Donohue. Establishing a command post at radio station WEEI, on the forty-fourth floor of the Prudential Center, he installed a high-powered telescope to track the two "sitting ducks," as he called them, along their route. A transmitter would beam signals to receivers concealed under the policewomen's wigs, and each woman had a tiny microphone hidden in the index finger of her right glove, so that by scratching her nose, she could communicate with the command post. Finally, three plainclothesmen equipped with walkie-talkies cordoned the women in a moving wedge: one twenty paces ahead, one twenty paces behind, the third across the street.

Beginning in mid-February, Kathy and Marie took turns simulating a South End career woman returning from work. Emerging at about 6:00 p.m. from the Huntington Avenue subway stop, the decoy of the evening would turn right on West Newton, cross the railroad tracks and Columbus Avenue, then stroll toward the Divers' house. There she would sit at the kitchen table, sipping coffee and swapping stories with Colin and Joan, until it was time to go out and try it all over again. For nearly two weeks the women trolled that route many times. On every passage, they saw young blacks clustered in the doorways of the Soul Center and Braddock Drugs. The boys whistled and made suggestive remarks, but not once did anyone make a hostile move in their direction.

Colin and Joan were baffled. They knew that as soon as the Anti-Crime Squad left, the muggings would resume. Billy Dwyer was sure of it too. Convinced that his decoys had somehow been spotted, he abandoned that operation and launched another. This time he put his men in unmarked cars, vans, and station wagons, instructing them to cruise the South End's streets at irregular intervals.

The new plan paid off with six arrests in barely three weeks. The most important break came on February 18, when Dwyer himself, riding down St. Botolph Street, spotted a young woman holding a bloody towel to her head. The woman told him that she'd been walking along St. Botolph Street when she heard footsteps behind her. Turning, she saw a young man drinking from a green bottle. As she went on her way, she heard a bottle crashing into the bushes, then felt a heavy blow to her head as someone grabbed her purse.

After putting her in an ambulance, Dwyer searched the bushes, examining half a dozen old bottles until he finally found a fresh one—a green Fanta ginger ale—still ice cold. Back at the crime lab, the bottle yielded a clear set of fingerprints.

On February 20, two other crime squad members were cruising by the railroad tracks when they saw someone snatch a woman's handbag. Running up West Newton Street toward Columbus Avenue, the mugger tried to hide in a darkened doorway at the top of a stoop. The two cops arrested the youth, and when they compared his prints with those on the Fanta bottle, they proved to be identical. The youth was Anthony Black, the acknowledged leader of the Soul Center gang. Tried on both counts, Black was sentenced to five to seven years in prison.

But the very night Black was arrested, another incident took place a few blocks away which would have profound repercussions in the neighborhood. Shortly after midnight, two young blacks scaled the rear wall of a house on Pembroke Street, popped the lock on a window, and climbed into the home of stockbroker Chip Huhta and his wife, Marie. At gunpoint, they roused the Huhtas and Ginger Brown, a teenager from suburban Sudbury who was staying with them for an "urban experience" semester. While one of the youths held Chip and Ginger in the study, the other put his arm around Marie's neck, held a screwdriver to her throat, and demanded that she show him where the valuables were. He took a ring off her finger, sixty dollars from a drawer, and the children's collection of silver dollars (but never disturbed the three children, asleep on an upper floor). The intruders then bound Chip, Marie, and Ginger with lamp cords and ripped the telephone from the wall.

The smaller, more easygoing of the pair was almost apologetic. "We do this all the time," he explained. "You gotta understand. This is our job. You go to work every day. We go to work every night." But his larger, more menacing partner seemed consumed by rage at the white world. "Shall we kill them?" he asked. Without waiting for an answer, he turned to the Huhtas and shouted, "It's all your fault! Why do you come to our area? You honkies should be in South Boston with all the other racists! You don't belong around here!" Fortunately, after further invective, the pair simply walked out the front door. Numb with terror, the Huhtas managed to rouse their tenants on the fourth floor, who summoned the police. Within twenty-four hours, word of the events on Pembroke Street had raced through the South End, seeming to confirm the neighborhood's worst fears. Colin and Joan, who were old friends of the Huhtas, got a blow-by-blow description of what had happened.

In truth, the police offensive—even the arrests—had done little to curtail crime in the area. All through late winter and early spring, fresh bulletins poured into the Divers' house. As Joan meticulously recorded them in her notebook—page after page of muggings, holdups, assaults, and burglaries—Colin went on pressuring the police for better protection. By now the policemen of District 4 had grown accustomed to the Divers. They knew Colin and Joan had powerful friends at City Hall and police headquarters, but they were also impressed by the couple's determination to protect themselves and their friends. Some of them even seemed abashed at the department's failure to provide better service to the neighborhood, although others defended their performance, laying the blame on other sectors of the criminal justice system.

One night, Detective Sergeant Frank Coleman turned in exasperation to Joan and said, "Look, Mrs. Diver, maybe we didn't do too well by you for a while. But you've got a lot of help now—the TPF, the decoys, special patrols. We're getting arrests. The trouble is, we're getting the same people over and over." As evidence, he pulled out Anthony Black's record—a dozen arrests beginning at the age of fifteen. "We pull him in," Coleman said, "the courts release him. We pull him in again, the courts let him go again. What do you want us to do? Your real beef now is with the courts. You ought to go down there and get a meeting with the judges."

Coleman's remarks echoed much of the Divers' own experience with the courts, much they had heard from the neighborhood judges, Doerfer and Garrity. In late February, Colin drafted a letter to Judge Jacob Lewitton, chief justice of the Boston Municipal Court. To buttress his position, he had the letter co-signed by six other South End activists, among them two blacks—Adrian du Cille and Willie Mandrell.

> *Dear Judge Lewitton [the letter began],*
>
> *We are writing to request your help in ending the reign of terror which exists in the South End. . . . Today the South End is under siege. It is engulfed in an epidemic of crime that threatens to destroy it as a community. . . . The people of this area have been literally terrorized—imprisoned in their homes—by gangs of young hoodlums who roam the South End casually attacking, threatening, robbing and raping with impunity. . . .*
>
> *In recent months, we and many of our neighbors have expended enormous amounts of time and taken often considerable personal risk to combat this menace. The residents of several streets have organized street patrols in early evening hours to help their neighbors return home from work safely. Several residents have personally chased and in at least two cases apprehended muggers. . . . In the past three weeks, the Police Department has assigned teams of decoys, male and female, and expanded patrols, marked and unmarked, in a search for solutions. Now, at last, these efforts have begun to result in arrests.*
>
> *We are now concerned that the familiar patterns of the past will be repeated, whereby many of those who have been arrested and convicted have been returned to the streets only to victimize us further. Too often, we feel, individual criminal acts, perhaps committed unarmed or by persons not previously convicted or by juveniles, are not considered seriously. Low bail is set, cases are continued freely, sentences are suspended, and the wave of terror in our streets and homes continues unabated in spite of these arrests.*
>
> *We firmly believe that the Court should see these individual acts of violence in the context of the utter and widespread lawlessness which is destroying our community. . . . We most earnestly request an opportunity to meet with you and other members of the Court, in order to present the*

*facts and impressions gathered by us during the course of months of ded-
icated citizen crime fighting.*

In March, Colin and his co-signers met with the judge in his chambers.
Lewitton heard them out politely, then launched into an elaborate explanation
of the court's problems in dealing with crime. But Colin was ready with a
vigorous rebuttal. Based on his own survey of Massachusetts statutes as well
as practices in other communities, he urged that the court tighten bail procedures to keep dangerous criminals off the streets while awaiting trial; his own
preference would have been a preventive detention system similar to that recently enacted in the District of Columbia. A few years earlier, Colin couldn't
have imagined himself taking that position, and even now it was widely regarded as heresy for liberals to support such tough measures against crime.
But after months of battling the South End's hoodlums, Colin had lost patience
with procedures that set habitual criminals loose on the community to commit
one or more additional crimes before being brought to trial on the original
charge. Some escaped trial altogether. Take Ruberto Caban, the man he'd
chased and captured in January—that was the most open-and-shut case he
could imagine. Colin had taken up the chase within seconds of the mugging
and had recovered LeSola Morgan's purse from the man's grip. Yet Caban had
been released on bail and had never shown up for trial in Superior Court. God
knew where he was now.

In a state like Massachusetts, Colin conceded, outright preventive detention wasn't politically feasible. But given existing statutes, he argued, the
courts could do a much better job of protecting the public, while still preserving the constitutional rights of defendants. "It's a jungle out there," he warned
the judge. "If you don't do something quickly, we're going to lose the war
against crime. Then we might as well get gun permits and barricade our
doors." Lewitton promised to consider Colin's point of view, but the South
Enders left the judge's chambers with modest expectations.

By then, Joan was in a better position than her husband to promote some
measure of judicial reform. That January, Governor Michael Dukakis had
named former Watergate Special Prosecutor Archibald Cox to head a blue-
ribbon committee on Massachusetts' antiquated court system. Convinced that
judicial unaccountability was aggravating Boston's crime situation, eager to
find a forum for her views, Joan had called Dan Taylor, an old friend then
serving as the Governor's counsel, to ask if Dukakis planned to include on the
committee any consumers—rather than dispensers—of justice. Taylor didn't
know but said he'd find out. Barely an hour later he called back to say that the
Governor would be delighted to have Joan on the panel.

On February 4, the Select Committee on Judicial Needs met for the first
time at the State Office Building. A formidable group, its twenty members
included State Attorney General Frank Bellotti, Supreme Judicial Court Justice Edward Hennessey, and former Senate Judiciary Chairman John Conte.

All were lawyers, except Florence Rubin, president of the Massachusetts League of Women Voters, and Joan.

The committee's principal assignment was to find ways of reducing the massive backlog of cases in state courts. A survey showed that of the ten slowest courts in the nation, five were in Massachusetts. Suburban Middlesex County was the slowest of all, with a five-year delay before a civil jury trial could be held. "Justice is being denied with each passing day in Massachusetts," the Governor had said.

The committee zeroed in on administrative measures to alleviate overcrowding of the dockets: a new chief administrative judge to manage the entire state court system; greater flexibility in assignments, permitting judges to transfer from court to court; and consolidation of court budgets.

Joan was more interested in strengthening the criminal justice system. She was particularly concerned with lenient bail policies and excessive continuances. In Boston, she knew, one out of every four defendants failed to appear for trial, while the probability of a defendant defaulting increased 10 percent for every month a case was continued. But neither Cox nor his staff was eager to grapple with such divisive issues, afraid that they would make it more difficult to reach a consensus on administrative reforms. Nevertheless, Joan persisted, submitting several lengthy memoranda to the committee which argued, among other things, that the courts should be stricter in granting continuances; that judges should more carefully consider a defendant's previous arrests, releases, and defaults before setting bail; and that defendants who failed to appear for trial should be more aggressively prosecuted. When Archibald Cox suggested that she favored preventive detention, Joan—like her husband—insisted that she wasn't going that far. She emphasized that any bail system "must take into account the individual rights of the defendants, such that the imposition of bail is not used as punishment." But, like Colin, she argued that "the courts must take into account the legitimate demands of the public for accountability and should ensure that the bail system is adequately administered and enforced." The committee's report, written by Cox himself, included Joan's recommendation on continuances, but only a pallid paragraph on bail.

Joan had other worries that winter and spring of 1976. The Bancroft School, where both her sons were now enrolled, was in greater turmoil than ever. The spring before, parents had prevailed in their effort to preserve the Bancroft as a unique enclave of open education in a sea of traditional scholasticism. But theirs had been a Pyrrhic victory. Forced to choose between a "district" school, to which students would be rigidly assigned by "geocode," and a "magnet" school, offering special programs and drawing applicants from throughout the city, the parents had opted for district status to guarantee that the Bancroft remain a South End institution. But in June they learned that the geocodes from which the Bancroft would draw had been significantly altered, retaining most of the school's white students but transferring many of its original blacks and enrolling other blacks whose parents neither sought nor wanted open education for their children. Moreover, the School Department had somehow miscalculated the Bancroft's enrollment. By opening day, 253 students were assigned to a building with a capacity of barely 200.

The result was total chaos. With the large new enrollment crammed into seven classrooms, anything approaching organized instruction—much less the Bancroft's innovative program—proved impossible. Teachers struggled to maintain acceptable levels of noise and discipline. Books and materials were in desperately short supply. To alleviate overcrowding, one teacher gave her classes in a former supply closet.

These conditions proved especially difficult for Lois Varney, the young primary-grades teacher whose imaginative techniques had drawn Joan Diver to the Bancroft in the first place. Lois had thrived in the old Bancroft, where she could offer her abundant talents to twenty-five children, all of them there because their parents had selected this alternative form of education. It was something quite different to preside over forty youngsters, half of them utterly new to the Bancroft and there against their families' wishes. It took months to show such children that the unstructured and spontaneous atmosphere carried with it corresponding responsibilities. Meanwhile, Lois was compelled to give the newcomers a disproportionate share of her time, diverting energy from the more settled students who knew what was expected of them. Among these was Brad Diver, at eight years of age a comparative veteran of the Bancroft.

As always when the Bancroft was in danger, articulate and well-connected South Enders bombarded school officials with demands that the program be preserved. This time, they urged the School Committee to give them part of the Rice Building, barely a hundred feet across the playground. In 1971, determined Bancroft parents seeking space for a junior high component had "liberated" a Rice classroom and held it against all comers. Later, the Bancroft gained a second room at the Rice, moving its two kindergarten classes there. But sixteen Rice classrooms remained occupied by the English-Language Center, Boston's school for newly arrived immigrants. Contending that such a school could be located anywhere in the city, Bancroft parents now argued that they needed still more of the Rice. Not surprisingly, the English-Language Center vigorously resisted their contention.

On October 29, 1975, the School Committee met to hear both sides. Dorothy Berman, the Bancroft's teacher-in-charge, presented her school's argument. "We are unique," she said. "That's why you should consider our problems." Committeewoman Kathleen Sullivan conceded that the Bancroft was "crowded to the gills." But Bernie Magooby of the English-Language Center invoked the seizure of the first classroom ("They came and they sat there. Then they took another room. This year they want two more rooms. A few years from now the whole school they will want") and teacher Mary Duplain pleaded the rights of the immigrants ("Do you wish to prove to the students that democracy and quality of education is for all, or do you wish to prove that might is right?"). Well, thought Joan Diver, she couldn't blame them for fighting back—she'd do the same in their position. She felt bad about grabbing their space, but the Bancroft's needs were even more compelling than theirs.

The School Committee eventually granted the Bancroft two more Rice classrooms, not then being used for English instruction. Lois Varney volunteered to occupy one of them. In mid-December, her class was installed in a jerry-built room carved from a third-floor auditorium judged unsafe for larger groups. A slab of plywood fifteen feet high had been erected down the center aisle, dividing the auditorium into two rectangular spaces, but the ceiling was thirty feet high and sounds from both classrooms mixed in a great hubbub. In the corridors, Lois' pupils were sometimes harassed by older immigrant youths who resented their presence. It was a terrible atmosphere for learning.

Arthur Garrity's order had created such overcrowding and confusion that it led to measures at odds with the school's founding principles. Even Lois Varney found herself resorting to the very kind of discipline she abhorred in the traditional Boston classroom. In adapting itself to the new exigencies, the Bancroft had sacrificed much of the warmth and spontaneity which had once made it so distinctive.

Finally, by 1976 many Bancroft students were in academic difficulties, with reading scores a particular focus of concern. Joan and Colin were dismayed to learn that Brad's scores had actually declined. As a second-grader he had tested as "Third Grade, 7–9 Months"; as a third-grader, he registered only "Third Grade, 2–4 Months." For a child of Brad's promise, that was plainly unacceptable. Joan and Colin wondered once again whether they were sacrificing their children's future on the altar of their social principles.

Colin had already played with the notion of leaving the South End. All through that grim fall and winter he felt trapped in the city. In November, he and Joan took a half measure, making an offer on a vacation house in Gloucester. Many South Enders owned second homes on the North Shore, Cape Cod, or Martha's Vineyard to which they retreated on weekends and summer vacations. Somehow just knowing that the clapboard cottage was waiting there by the sea made the daily abrasions of urban life more bearable. At the last moment, the Divers' deal fell through, and Colin's dissatisfaction with the South End grew as the winter wore on. It wasn't only the crime; suddenly, he was less tolerant of all the minor annoyances he'd come to take for granted—the garbage piled in the alleys and backyards, the filth littering the gutters, the graffiti scrawled on the walls of the South End library, the drunks staggering up Tremont Street, the abandoned buildings on Columbus Avenue, the music blaring from a window in Methunion Manor, worst of all, the unresponsiveness of the city and its institutions. He could no longer tolerate this feeling of always fighting his surroundings. He felt that he was shoveling back the ocean with a teaspoon. He wanted out.

Colin wasn't the only South Ender with such feelings. Ever since Dick Bluestein had been mugged the previous September, he'd felt uneasy on the South End's streets, and in February he and his wife, Kate, moved across the railroad tracks into the Back Bay. Other friends of the Divers were contemplating a move as well—Gordon and Jane Doerfer had looked at houses in Ipswich and Newburyport, Steve and Judy Wolfberg were making the rounds in Brookline, Julian and Barbara Cherubini were looking in Newton—but none of them talked about it very much. The rebirth of the South End had been a joint enterprise, an experiment which depended on mutual reinforcement and communal solidarity. Nothing would sap the community's morale more quickly than word that people were beginning to move out. So until a decision was actually made, nobody said a thing.

And the Divers were far from reaching a decision. For whatever her husband and her neighbors were thinking, Joan Diver stubbornly held such misgivings at bay. Despite everything, she couldn't imagine living anywhere but the South End. Where else could she hold a responsible job yet be within fifteen minutes of home and school in case her children needed her? Where else could she walk to the symphony, a ball game, a dozen good restaurants? Most important, where could she find the kind of friends she'd made there in the past six years? Yes, there was a lot of dirt, a lot of noise, a lot of crime, but there was a real community as well. If you had troubles, your neighbors were always there to help; if you sounded your Freon horn, there'd be fifty people on the sidewalk within moments. People griped together, organized together, played together. In the summertime, they sat around on their front stoops drinking lemonade and swapping gossip. In the fall, they all pitched in to mount their traditional street fair. Every winter, fifty South Enders trooped off to New Hampshire for a weekend of skiing and skating. How could they give up all of that?

For months Joan held firm, but eventually the daily assaults, muggings, and purse snatchings on West Newton Street wore her down. During an anguished evening in late February, Colin persuaded her to "examine the alternatives" outside the city. They told themselves they weren't setting out to buy a house, they just wanted to see what was available, to find out what they could afford.

Like most self-conscious South Enders, the Divers had long painted the suburbs with broad strokes of opprobrium. Now they had to make some distinctions, narrowing their search to Brookline and Newton, the most accessible of the outlying districts, the most liberal and heterogeneous. Each had good schools and relatively low crime rates; each was densely populated with people much like themselves—lawyers, doctors, academicians, and artists; each had a cultural and intellectual life of its own.

The Divers called realtors and pored over newspaper ads, examining any house that sounded promising. But their standards were high. They weren't going to settle for some ticky-tacky Cape Codder or brick colonial in a modern subdivision; accustomed to their handsome old town house, they were determined to find another Victorian, certainly nothing built after 1900. But weeks of looking produced nothing suitable, and in mid-March they temporarily abandoned the search.

Then a realtor called to tell them about a house on Church Street in Newton Corner and they drove out to see it. At first glance, it was just what they wanted: a sprawling Greek Revival built around 1850, it had a lot of charm plus many architectural details crying out for restoration. But as they tramped through fourteen rooms on three floors, the Divers thought: It's simply too big; a family of four would rattle around in a place like that, and it needs too much work. It just isn't practical.

That night Joan woke around midnight. For nearly an hour, as she watched the headlights stippling her bedroom ceiling, she thought about what they'd seen that afternoon. If the house was so close to what they wanted, why had they backed away at the last moment? At breakfast the next morning, she said to Colin, "You know that house we saw yesterday? If it's unacceptable to you, it's not because there's something wrong with it, it's because you don't want to move. Maybe we ought to come to terms with that right now. We could start by going back to take another look."

Now it was Colin who hung back. He didn't have time, he said; he'd set that afternoon aside to work on their taxes and listen to the opera. So Joan arranged to see the house again by herself. Before going, she prepared a detailed list of all their questions. The house—and the neighborhood—met every one of their qualifications. When she got home at dusk, she urged Colin to make a bid. "Okay," he sighed. "Let's do it."

That evening, the Divers were scheduled to attend a benefit for "Summerthing," the city's annual summer festival. Dining with three other couples, they sorted through the neighborhood gossip, some of it hair-raising, much of it absurd— that bittersweet gallows humor which gave life in the South End part of its special flavor. But Colin and Joan were in no mood for laughter. Behind their forced smiles they were hiding a nasty little secret: very soon they might no longer be South Enders. After dinner, the four couples drove to the Commonwealth Armory, where Buddy Rich and his band, Gerry Mulligan, and Melba Moore were entertaining some 2,000 Bostonians. A large South End contingent was there, dancing, drinking, having a fine time, but the Divers couldn't get in the mood. Pleading fatigue, they left early.

The next day, they bid $65,000 on the house. The realtor said they'd probably hear within twenty-four hours, but no reply came on Monday, or Tuesday, or Wednesday. The realtor assured them there was no problem; it was a very good bid, and the owners were just checking with their accountants. But there was still no answer on Thursday or Friday.

The Divers were growing impatient. Colin wanted to get their South End house on the market as soon as possible; Joan wanted to get the whole thing over with—she couldn't stand the daily deception of her friends and neighbors. Finally, on Saturday morning, their bid was accepted. That afternoon, Joan went next door and told her closest friend, Linda Trum, "I wanted you to be the first to know," she said. "I didn't want you to hear it on the street."

It was as if someone had ripped out a wall of Linda's house. For six years the Divers and the Trums had lived side by side, sharing the pains and pleasures of life on West Newton Street; Linda couldn't imagine the South End without Joan. An hour later, Anne Dodson stopped by the Divers' house, and on an impulse, Joan told her too. For a moment Anne was speechless. Then she said, "You know, whenever I think about leaving the South End, I can't do it because of the people. People like you and Colin. All the efforts you put into the street patrol. I just couldn't leave people like you." Joan ached with guilt.

Later that afternoon, Colin called Doe Sprogis, a South End friend who happened to be a realtor. "I've got some bad news and some good news," he said. "The bad news is we're leaving the South End. The good news is we're giving you an exclusive on the house." Doe was just as ambivalent as the Divers. She was glad to have the listing, but Colin and Joan were South End stalwarts; it would be a less vigorous neighborhood without them.

Now that the deed was done, Colin wanted to make their old house as attractive as possible to prospective buyers. On the parquet floor in the back parlor was a Ping-Pong table which belonged to their friends the Moriartys from Rutland Square. That very afternoon Colin called Marshall Moriarty and together the two old friends carried the table back across the alley. As Joan watched from an upstairs window her eyes filled with tears.

Within hours, word of the Divers' decision reverberated through the bow-front houses. No news could have been more disconcerting to homeowners along West Newton Street and Rutland Square. The Divers were the most active couple in the neighborhood, the most effective manipulators of the city's bureaucracies. Their defection was widely regarded as evidence that something had gone terribly wrong in the South End, that this brave experiment in city living was foundering on the shoals of urban reality.

Across the street, Dr. Dan Shannon, a prominent pediatrician at Massachusetts General Hospital, asked himself: What do the Divers know that we don't know? Colin and Joan traveled in political circles inaccessible to most of their neighbors. Maybe the Mayor was abandoning the South End; maybe a whole new slug of subsidized housing was destined for Tremont Street; maybe the Divers were getting out before housing values began to plummet. The Shannons had left suburban Dedham because they found life there unbearably "sterile." For seven years they had labored to rehabilitate a gutted shell they dubbed "Daniel's Dream." They loved the South End and refused to face the prospect of moving back to the suburbs. On Monday morning, Dan Shannon met Joan at the Tremont Street bus stop. "When you get out to Newton, Joni," he said, "you're not going to need your Freon horn, because if you blow it, there won't be anybody there to help you. They're too busy taking care of their swimming pools." Joan was devastated. It seemed a terrible thing for a close friend to say.

In weeks to come, other neighbors made cutting remarks. One said that the Divers' move was "the equivalent of blockbusting," implying that it could trigger a massive exodus from the neighborhood. Another old friend avoided the Divers for many weeks. Joan began wearing sunglasses, because whenever she saw friends on the street, whether they were sympathetic or critical, her eyes would tear up.

Colin wouldn't tolerate suggestions that they were "abandoning" their friends and neighbors. When Paul Garrity suggested as much, Colin snapped, "People who make remarks like that obviously aren't comfortable with their own neighborhood. If you can't see people moving in and out as a normal process, if you need other people as crutches to keep you here, then maybe you ought to get out too. Why don't you examine your own motives instead of criticizing mine?"

The Divers' most difficult discussion was with eight-year-old Brad, who had come to love the Bancroft, where he had many close friends. When his parents told him they were moving, he threw a terrible tantrum, weeping, stomping through the hallways, calling them names, insisting that he wouldn't live anywhere else. Colin said to him, "Brad, you know that we love you very much and wouldn't let anything bad happen to you. You've liked all the decisions we've made for you until now—like deciding to send you to the Bancroft—and you're just going to have to trust us that we're making the right decision for you now."

At first, six-year-old Ned didn't know what to make of the move. Then, barely a week after the Divers signed an agreement on the Newton house, Ned had an experience which resolved his ambivalence. The boys had a set of keys with which to let themselves in when they got home from school. One afternoon Brad quickly went out again, leaving the door ajar. Seizing the opportunity, a black teenager entered, telling Ned he wanted a glass of water. Instead, he raced through the house grabbing change off bureau tops and tables. Returning from work, Joan heard Ned yell, "Mommy, a robber's stealing all Daddy's money." The youth fled, with Joan in vain pursuit. When she got back, she found Ned at the top of the stairs weeping hysterically. He took days to regain his equanimity.

Barely $1.50 was taken that day, but it was one of the few times that the sanctity of the Divers' house had been violated, and it only heightened their anxiety.

That same week in early April, high school students from Charlestown and South Boston kicked and beat black lawyer Ted Landsmark as he hurried to his meeting at City Hall. Barely two weeks later a gang of black teenagers dragged a white auto mechanic named Richard Poleet from his car in Roxbury and beat him senseless. With tensions reaching an intolerable pitch, Boston seemed poised on the brink of a race war.

When Kevin White, at the *Globe*'s prompting, summoned Bostonians to a Procession Against Violence on April 23, Joan had to be there. That Friday morning she left the Hyams Trust, joining the huge throng which swept from the business district across the Boston Common to the assembly point at Charles and Beacon streets. At 11:40, the marchers headed ten abreast up the broad flank of Beacon Hill, past the gleaming State House dome, past the sooty Saint-Gaudens monument to Colonel Robert Gould Shaw and his black soldiers who had died together in 1863. Led by the Mayor, Senators Ted Kennedy and Ed Brooke, Governor Mike Dukakis, and other notables, they walked in silence, without banners and placards save for one small sign which hung from the neck of a black man: "Bless the Peacemakers." Once the marchers had assembled on the red brick of City Hall Plaza, police estimated them at 50,000, the largest such gathering in Boston since the 1969 Vietnam Moratorium. As Joan gazed about her at the salesclerks and bankers, waitresses and housewives, barbers and professors standing solemnly in the April sunshine, she was deeply moved. The procession seemed an expression of all that was brave and beautiful in the city she loved.

But it wasn't enough. Within forty-eight hours, the violence resumed, a spattering of racial incidents across the anguished neighborhoods. As the spring wore on, the city's agony seemed a magnified echo of Joan's own desperation. She felt an acute sense of loss, as if she were in mourning for someone near and dear. Her grief was relentless, embracing the South End community which had nurtured her these past six years as well as Boston itself, the city to which she and Colin had dedicated their young lives. Joan had never lost a close relative, but she supposed it would feel much like this hollow ache in her chest. By May the ache had grown into a sharp pain, aggravated by a rasping cough. Joan's doctor told her, "You must be very nervous about something. You're swallowing a lot of air. That's what's giving you the pain."

On May 11, she flew to Atlanta for the annual meeting of the Council on Foundations, a league of 793 philanthropies from across the nation. The four-day conference was marked by a heated debate on the position that foundations should take in the racial arena. A study by the Human Resources Corporation concluded that a "woefully inadequate" share of foundation funds went to minority groups. In response, Council directors had framed a resolution on "Foundations and Social Justice," which read in part: "Whereas, the signers of the Declaration of Independence found to be self-evident these truths: that all men are created equal and that each of us has the right to life, liberty and the pursuit of happiness . . . Be it resolved that organized philanthropy should recognize the urgent obligation to help bring about constructive social change. . ."

The Hyams Trust had only one vote on the resolution, to be cast by its secretary, Bill Swift, so Joan wasn't called upon to take a formal position. But the resolution left her ambivalent. Its principles were impeccable—the very notions which had drawn her to philanthropy in the first place. Inside Hyams and elsewhere in Boston's charitable community she had urged foundations to become agents for constructive change. Yet the violent crime and social disintegration of the South End had shaken her faith in traditional liberal nostrums. Though she remained committed to equal opportunity and social justice, she was no longer sure that New Frontier–Great Society programs such as public housing, model cities, affirmative action, and court-ordered busing were well-conceived means to those ends. All during the conference, she felt like standing up and shouting, "Isn't anybody going to say that things aren't working very well?"

She was sure of only one thing: that nobody had all the answers. That week, she spent as much time as she could riding around the city, observing how Atlanta had confronted its racial and social problems. Here was a predominantly black city with a black mayor, yet somehow it seemed less tense than Boston, blacks and whites mingling in its stores and public transportation with little apparent friction. She knew there was a large black middle class, boasting its own insurance company and bank, giving blacks the clout to deal with the white power structure. And deal they had—in the famous 1973 school settlement, which created a pattern sharply different from Boston's. Confronted with a school system already overwhelmingly black, Atlanta's NAACP had chosen not to press for massive cross-city busing, which in any case would have produced relatively little integration. Instead, it had hammered out a settlement—roundly condemned by national NAACP leaders—which sacrificed integration for black control of the city's schools (by 1976 there was a black superintendent, a black majority on the school board, and a black board president).

Atlanta's trade-off had stirred the old debate between integration and community control. Joan could recognize assets and debits on both sides, but at least here was another approach, free from the conventional liberal pieties. Was black power and self-confidence sufficient compensation for the lost goal of integration? All that week she debated such questions with two friends, a white Atlantan named Linda Copeland, whom she had met years before as a student at Wheaton, and a black woman named Anna Jones, assistant director of Boston's Permanent Charity Fund, with whom Joan shared a hotel room. Linda, who lived in a handsome white neighborhood not far from downtown, thought the settlement had paved the way for relatively peaceful coexistence between Atlanta's whites and blacks. Anna—the daughter of Mordecai Johnson, the late president of Howard University—feared that Atlanta was headed for a "separate but equal" solution.

On the final day of the conference, Joan and Anna took a guided bus tour through the city. Late in the afternoon, they rode past Southview Cemetery, where Martin Luther King had been laid to rest after his assassination. As the bus glided beneath a canopy of giant oaks, Joan made out the eternal flame by King's headstone. Suddenly her throat throbbed with the loss of so many dreams buried there in the red Georgia clay.

All through that spring and early summer, Colin felt some of the same remorse. Walking to and from his office at the Boston University Law School, he passed Marsh Chapel, where he and Joan had been married, where their friend Howard Thurman had presided as chaplain, where Martin Luther King had worshipped as a divinity student. In front of the chapel the university had erected a monument to King, a cluster of cast-iron shapes, turned reddish brown by rust, which resembled a flight of birds soaring skyward. On three sides were chiseled passages from his writings. It was a provocative reminder of the man and the event which had brought Colin into Boston nearly a decade before. Passing the monument twice a day, he recalled that time when moral imperatives had seemed so clear and compelling and he caught himself yearning for that old certitude, for that sense of high purpose which had swept him through the late sixties and early seventies.

All that spring and early summer, the South End house stayed on the market, with no buyer willing to pay the asking price. But the Divers decided to move into the Newton house on August 1 so that the boys could get acclimated before school began and Colin and Joan would have a midsummer respite in which to recover from the emotional cyclone of the spring, a time in which to consider where they had come from and where they were going.

Since the baseball bat incident, some of his critics in the South End had dismissed Colin as a hypocrite whose liberal convictions had melted away as soon as they confronted his self-interest. They were fond of quoting such dicta as "A conservative is a liberal who just got mugged" or "A conservative is a liberal whose kid just got bused." Colin conceded that, of late, he was paying less attention to the needs of society and more to his own, his wife's, and his children's. Not long ago he would have apologized for that; now he saw no reason to. What was wrong with wanting to live in a community where he could walk the streets without fear, where he could leave his family at home without worrying about their safety, where he could send his children to public school with confidence that they were getting a sound education? What was wrong with demanding effective police protection, efficient courts, clean streets, well-maintained parks, good lighting, adequate garbage collection?

Yet he liked to think that the changes in his social and political outlook were grounded in something more than narrow self-interest—namely, in his years of government service and his life in a troubled urban neighborhood. For if the central tenet of liberal faith was the efficacy of governmental intervention, Colin's experience had made him something of an apostate. Eight years before, as he entered Kevin White's administration, he had thought the city was very much like a poor person who suffered from dirt, disease, poverty, hunger, and crime. The first priority was to devise programs addressed to those human needs. One should hire a staff of bright, committed young people, turn them loose on such problems, and come up with fresh solutions. What happened to those ideas, how they were put into practice, hadn't concerned Colin very deeply.

Four years with Kevin White and two with Frank Sargent had taught him that ideas alone were virtually useless, that government couldn't define people's needs for them, that "solutions" worked only if they were perceived as such by a substantial constituency and implemented by skilled managers. Moreover, unless such programs were shrewdly calculated, they were often ineffective, even counterproductive, producing consequences quite opposite from those the reformers had intended.

By late 1976, Colin was dividing his time equally between Boston University's Law School and its School of Public Management. The study of law dealt with rights, management with procedures; law with what should be, management with what worked. These two approaches to the world were naturally in tension. Shuttling between them, Colin increasingly saw himself as an intermediary, giving managers a better appreciation of constitutional rights, showing lawyers how to implement such norms.

He was particularly concerned with the growing role of judges in managing public institutions. For governmental intervention was especially hazardous when it came not from politicians, who were responsible to a popular constituency, but from judges guided only by their reading of the United States Constitution, centuries of common law, and judicial precedent. Eight years before, just completing his stint as the *Harvard Law Review*'s Supreme Court Note Editor, Colin had been especially sensitive to constitutional imperatives, looking to the judiciary for affirmation of rights flouted by callous legislators and arrogant executives. Not surprisingly then, he had welcomed Arthur Garrity's decision in the Boston schools case. But gradually he came to wonder whether Garrity's remedy—massive cross-city busing—was appropriate to the violation he had found, and whether this example of judicial activism hadn't finally set back the very cause it was designed to advance.

Unlike legislators directly accountable to the electorate, and executives with substantial resources at their disposal, judges depended heavily on society's respect for their adjudicatory role. They could prevail only with the co-operation of other governmental bodies and, ultimately, with assent from the people themselves. But Garrity's sweeping remedy so affronted the conventions of white Boston that he never got that cooperation. Instead, thousands of whites found an effective means of subverting his order.

In September 1972, the year Garrity first heard testimony on the NAACP suit, some 90,000 students were enrolled in Boston's public schools, roughly 54,000—or 60 percent—white. By 1974, when the judge issued his long-anticipated order, the system's total enrollment had slipped to 82,000, about 55 percent white. By 1976, only 71,000 students were left in the system, barely 44 percent of them white. In just four years Boston's schools had lost nearly 20,000 white students—to parochial schools, private academies, the streets, or because their families had left the city altogether.

This precipitous decline had set off a vigorous debate in legal and academic circles. Some critics saw it as indisputable evidence that massive numbers of white families had pulled their children out of the public schools to protest Garrity's order. Others were less certain. They noted that white enrollment had been eroding for more than a decade before Garrity even received the case, in part because of the declining white birth rate, in part as a result of the long-term migration of middle-income families from city to suburb. Even those, like the Divers, who left the city during the initial busing years were often reacting to many conditions simultaneously—as much to crime, dirt, noise, and the unresponsive bureaucracy as to the disruptive effects of the busing order.

But whatever share of the white exodus could be directly attributed to Garrity's rulings, there could be little doubt that the goal of effective school desegregation had been substantially undercut by the steady drain of white students. By the end of 1976, blacks, Hispanics, and other "minorities" were already a majority of the school population, and before long blacks themselves became a majority. With that "tipping point" passed, most authorities agreed, the system would grow increasingly black year by year. More important, with middle-income parents of all races pulling their children out of the system, the remaining students increasingly came from the lowest economic and social strata of the city's population. More and more, Boston's busing program consisted of mixing the black poor with the white poor, the deprived with the deprived.

What might have been done—or still could be done—to prevent this deplorable outcome was a thornier issue. From a purely juridical standpoint, Garrity had probably been correct in declining to consider warnings of white opposition to his order; the Supreme Court had held that judges could not permit a "heckler's veto" by tailoring their findings to fear of white violence or flight from the schools. On the other hand, many critics contended, it made no sense to launch a profound upheaval in a city's social and racial fabric in order to produce a result diametrically opposite that which was intended. Surely, they argued, there must be some way, while preserving the plaintiffs' constitutional rights, to prevent Boston's schools from becoming the preserve of the black and the poor.

Colin was particularly troubled by the class dimensions of this situation. Years before, in the wake of King's assassination, he and Joan had addressed their professional careers and personal lives to the racial crisis, in particular to the Kerner Commission's solemn warning that we were becoming two societies, one white and one black. As the decade wore on, Colin came to perceive the "American dilemma" less in purely racial and legal terms, more in class and economic terms. Wherever he looked he saw legal remedies undercut by social and economic realities. Eventually, he believed, the fundamental solution to the problems of a city like Boston lay in economic development. Only by providing jobs and other economic opportunities for the deprived—black and white alike—could the city reduce the deep sense of grievance harbored by both communities, alleviate some of the antisocial behavior grounded in such resentments, and begin to close the terrible gap between the rich and the poor, the suburb and the city, the hopeful and the hopeless.

Yet here, Colin was painfully aware, his social analysis collided head on with his self-interest. Though he was convinced that Boston's inner city could thrive only if it held on to its white middle class, he simply couldn't live there any longer. Professionally, the Divers remained committed to Boston—Joan through her work at the Hyams Trust, Colin through teaching and consulting at the university. But their personal lives turned inward, focusing on friends, family, and home.

Colin had always drawn special pleasure from shaping the space in which they lived. In the South End, some of his sweetest hours had been spent on a scaffold following the whorls and scallops of the ceiling plaster. Now, in that first summer of self-imposed exile from the city, he found solace in beginning work on their new home.

The sprawling white clapboard house with its green shutters and slate roof was an architectural hybrid: it had been built in the Greek Revival style of the mid-nineteenth century, with its ornamental pilasters and triangular pediments, but half a century later, during the Colonial Revival, it had been remodeled with an open porch at one end, a new doorway at the other. Lately the house had fallen into disrepair. First, Colin redid the kitchen, tearing down a cheap plasterboard ceiling and restoring the original scale of the room. Then he converted a fifth bedroom into a combination bath and laundry, opening a door through a walk-in closet into the master bedroom. He removed another bathroom which blocked light from an arched Palladian window in front. He rewired, laid new tile, replastered, and repainted throughout.

The most distinctively Colonial feature of the house was a white picket fence which flanked it on both sides. Constructed at the turn of the century, the fence was built in the seventeenth-century style without a single nail, its balusters and rails fitted together with mortise and tenon, a square peg in a square hole; but with years of neglect, it had sagged and buckled for yards at a stretch. Colin set out to rebuild it. All that winter in his basement workshop he cut hundreds of new balusters, 1⅜ inches square, topped by an ornamental molding. Then he ripped dozens of new rails, three inches high and nine feet long. With saw and file he cut the mortises, keeping them ¹⁄₃₂ of an inch smaller than the tenons to guarantee a snug joint. When spring came, he spent evenings and weekends fitting the pieces together, then laying on three coats of white paint. In early June the job was done, the intricate junction of peg and hole sealing off the Divers' perimeter, rearing its ivory spine against the world.

Epilogue

Colin Diver still teaches law and public management at Boston University, where he was promoted to full professor in 1981. In 1983, he was named chairman of the State Ethics Commission, which combats corruption and conflict of interest in state and local government.

Joan Diver remains executive director of the Hyams Trust. In 1982, she was named chairman of the Board of Trustees of the Mutual Bank Foundation and in 1984 of the Horace Cousens Industrial Fund, which helps needy individuals in the city of Newton.

Brad and *Ned Diver* attend Newton North High School, from which they will be graduated in 1985 and 1987, respectively. Brad is an accomplished jazz guitarist, while Ned plays the trombone in several ensembles.

Arthur and *Heather Makechnie* returned to Boston in 1979. Abandoning his Ph.D. thesis, Arthur became director of food services at the Cambridge School of Weston. He and Heather devote much of their time to assisting Vietnamese refugees. They have taken four Vietnamese children into their home and have sponsored an annual Thanksgiving dinner for refugees.

George Makechnie, Dean Emeritus of Sargent College, is a consultant for development planning to the dean of that college. Working to increase public appreciation of the life and thought of the late Howard Thurman, he is a trustee of the Howard Thurman Educational Trust, and a liaison between the Trust and Boston University.

Anne Makechnie died on September 12, 1980, after a nine-month battle with cancer. Until her illness, she had remained one of the most active real estate brokers in Lexington.

Ethleen Diver still maintains a small law practice in Lexington. She celebrated her eighty-first birthday in 1984.

Benjamin Diver died on March 12, 1981, of cancer at the age of eighty-six. To the end he maintained a love of classical music and all things British.

Rachel Twymon has been a medical assistant in the trauma area of the MIT Medical Department since January 1979. She continues to live at Methunion Manor.

Cassandra Twymon lives in Atlanta. She is enrolled at the Bryman School, studying to be a medical assistant.

Rachel Twymon (daughter) lives with her three-year-old son, Michael, in a South End apartment.

Richard Walker (Twymon) works as a cook at a private school in Nashville, Tennessee. He was married in 1983 and has a one-year-old daughter.

Wayne Twymon, after training as a cadet in the Boston Police Department, became a cook at an MIT dormitory. He was married in 1984.

George Walker (Twymon) graduated from Tennessee State in 1981. He is now at the Interdenominational Theological Center in Atlanta, studying to become a minister of the United Methodist Church.

Frederick Twymon, after serving five years at Concord Reformatory, was transferred to a Boston pre-release center and works during the week at Charlie's Eating and Drinking Saloon.

Helen Walker lives in a housing-for-the-elderly project on Tremont Street. She is eighty years old.

Hasan Sharif (Arnold Walker) has been an administrative supervisor in the State Department of Social Services since June 1980. He also teaches in the faculty of continuing education at Roxbury Community College.

Tommy Walker was released from Walpole Prison in 1979 and has resumed construction work in Boston.

Alva Debnam is a computer operator for Stone and Webster Engineering Co. and takes night courses at Northeastern University. She has left her embattled house on Centre Street, settling ten blocks north in a primarily black neighborhood.

Alice McGoff is still with the New England Telephone Company, working in the corporate services department. She and her three youngest children live together in Charlestown.

Lisa McGoff married John Collins on September 26, 1981. John works as a maintenance man at the Boston Garden. Lisa is in the billing department of H. P. Hood, a milk company in Charlestown.

Danny McGoff is employment officer at the John F. Kennedy Human Service Center in Charlestown and coaches basketball at Christopher Columbus High School in the North End.

Billy McGoff is an electrician. He was married in October 1984 to Taryn Muise.

Kevin McGoff works as a stagehand at the Boston Garden and as a disk jockey at Shaun's, a Quincy Market discotheque.

Tommy McGoff is completing a tour as a chef in the United States Coast Guard.

Robin McGoff is a hairdresser at Sheer Delight, a Charlestown beauty salon.

Bobby McGoff is in his junior year in the liberal arts program at Boston University.

Louise Day Hicks was narrowly defeated for the City Council in November 1979. Suffering from a serious eye condition, she temporarily retired to private life, but a year later Kevin White appointed her to the Boston Retirement Board, which supervises the city's pension system. When she left the board in 1982, the Mayor found her yet another job: a part-time position with the city's Public Facilities Department, at fifty-five dollars an hour.

W. Arthur Garrity is still on Boston's Federal District bench, where he retains ultimate authority in the Boston schools case. But in December 1982, as part of a progressive "disengagement" from the case, he gave the State Board of Education primary responsibility for monitoring compliance with his rulings.

Humberto Cardinal Medeiros died on September 17, 1983, after surgery to repair a badly damaged heart. Six months later, he was replaced by Bernard F. Law, a Harvard-educated priest of Irish-German descent, known for his efforts to facilitate desegregation in Mississippi during the sixties.

Thomas Winship retired as editor of the *Globe* on January 1, 1985, and became the first Senior Fellow at the Gannett Center for Media Studies at Columbia University. He was replaced by Michael Janeway, a former managing editor of *The Atlantic Monthly* who joined the *Globe* in 1978.

Kevin White, under federal investigation for campaign finance irregularities, announced on May 26, 1983, that he would not seek a fifth term as mayor. Taking a teaching and consulting job at Boston University, he was succeeded at City Hall by former City Councilman Raymond L. Flynn, described in his campaign literature as an "urban populist."

The Bancroft School has been converted to luxury condominiums.

Acknowledgments

In the course of seven years on this project, I have received more than my ration of assistance, support, advice, and encouragement.

My work was underwritten, in part, by the John Simon Guggenheim Memorial Foundation, which awarded me a fellowship in 1978–79; the Institute of Politics at Harvard University, where I was a fellow in 1976–77; the John F. Kennedy School of Government, where I was an adjunct lecturer in 1979–80; and the School of Public Communications at Boston University, where I was an adjunct professor in 1977–78. I am grateful for their help.

For research assistance, I thank Richard Doherty, Karen Falkenstein, Kevin Murphy, Elaine Makovska, Chris Landry, Toby Wertheim, Alice Richmond, Richard Henderson, and Drina Archer.

I am grateful to the staffs of the Boston *Globe*'s library (particularly David Beveridge), the Boston *Herald*'s library (particularly John Cronin), the Widener Library of Harvard University, and the John F. Kennedy Library.

In 1977–78, I served in the Study Group on Urban School Desegregation sponsored by the American Academy of Arts and Sciences. I learned much from its participants and am especially grateful to Diane Ravitch for her insights into the complex relationship between community and equality.

I thank my editors at Alfred A. Knopf, Inc.—Robert Gottlieb and Charles Elliott—for the critical intelligence, infinite care, and consummate professionalism they have lavished on this book.

I thank my wife, Linda Healey, for her many shrewd judgments and her tenacity in defending them against my prickly pride of authorship.

Anyone who has read the preceding pages will recognize the enormous debt I owe to the Divers, the Twymons, and the McGoffs. Each of these families has spent hundreds of hours with me—in formal, tape-recorded interviews, in casual talk over a meal or drink, in countless phone calls to fill holes or check facts. They have opened their homes to me; suffered me to read their correspondence and pore through confidential records; introduced me to their friends, neighbors, and professional colleagues. They have, in sum, opened their lives to me with a candor and magnanimity for which I am deeply grateful.

Among the hundreds of others who have helped me on this book, there is one I must single out for special thanks: Thomas N. Brown, professor of history at the University of Massachusetts in Boston. Wise scholar, matchless teacher, gracious and gentle man, Tom has provoked me with subtle and Socratic dialogue to a deeper understanding of his city.

In the lists that follow—one for each group of family chapters and one for all others—I have tried to thank everyone by name. If I have omitted anyone, I beg his or her indulgence.

DIVER

Mary Rose Allen, Michael Ambrosino, Sheldon Appel, Ferdinand and Diane Arenella, Norman Asher, Tom Atkins, Ellen Baker, Dorothy Berman, Joel Bernard, Dick Bluestein, Jane Bowers, Phil Bradley, Marnell Bubar, Ken and Sue Campbell, Richard Card, John Coakley, Frazier Cocks, Frank Coleman, Leonard Colwell, Patricia Corcoran, Bill Cowin, Albie Davis, Ben Diver, Brad Diver, Colin Diver, Ethleen Diver, Joan Diver, Ned Diver, Peter and Anne Dodson, Gordon and Jane Doerfer, Anthony Douin, Adrian du Cille, Billy Dwyer, Rev. William Dwyer, Mr. and Mrs. Edward Ellms, Leonard Fein, Ruth Fein, Carol Feldman, Kathy Fitzpatrick, Bob Foster, Barney Frank, Marion Fremont-Smith, Henry J. Friendly, Tom Gaffney, Lola Garland, Paul Garrity, Alan Gartner, Fred Glimp, Mark Goldweitz, Martin Gopen, Richie Hall, Chris and Clare Hayes, Gary Hayes, Herb and Anne Hershfang, Ralph and Molly Hoagland, Cyril Joly, Anna Jones, Nathan Kaganoff, Stanley Katz, Gordon Kershaw, Mel and Joyce King, James Leamon, Priscilla Lee, P. A. Lenk, Michael Lerner, Theodore Levitt, Lance Liebman, Linda MacGregor, Rev. Thomas MacLeod, Anne Makechnie, Arthur Makechnie, George Makechnie, Heather Makechnie, Norman Makechnie, David Mann, Daniel Mayers, Priscilla McKapplip, Edwin McKechnie, Horace McKechnie, Sam Merrick, Sally Merry, Nina Meyer, Mary Morrison, Michael and Arline Morrison, Theresa Morse, Charles Mulcahy, Nicky Nickerson, Andy Olins, Paul Oosterhuis, David Parker, James Parker, Sandra Perkins, Dain Perry, Barbara and Henry Petschek, Lillian Radlo, Dorothy Reichard, Frank Rich, Royden Richardson, Ed Richmond, Larry Robbins, Bill Roeder, Homer Russell, Timothy Saasta, Joan Saklad, Fred Salvucci, Muriel Sanford, Dan and Mary Shannon, Frank Sheehan, Pat and Ed Shillingburg, Gracelaw Simmons, Danny D. Smith, David Horton Smith, Mason Smith, Peggy Smith, Jeff Steingarten, Rabbi Malcolm Stern, William N. Swift, Alan Taylor, Janet Taylor, George and Susan Thomas, Howard Thurman, Iris Tolbert, Mike and Linda Trum, Jack T. Turner, Bob Underhill, Lois Varney, James Vickery, Judy Watkins, Bob Weinberg, Jack White, Bettina Willey, John Wolbarst, Steve Wolfberg, Paul and Judy Wright, Josh and Holly Young.

TWYMON

Emily Achtenberg, Deborah Anker, John Barclay, Ruth Batson, Ira Berlin, Eileen Bisson, Phyllis Blakely, Bea Boves, Bill Brackman, Rev. James Breeden, Dave Brown, Marilyn Brown, Charles A. Broxton, Rev. William M. Bussy, Walter Byars, Edmund Byne, Rev. Gilbert Caldwell, Brian Callery, William Canty, Bishop Edward G. Carroll, Porter Carswell, Michael Chesson, Albert Chipman, Eddie Collins, Melody Cook, Mrs. C. L. Cousins, Joel Crenshaw, Mrs. Edith Cromwell, Ed Crotty, Lee Daniels, Lois Dauway, Mike Davis, Alva Debnam, Otis Debnam, Otis Debnam, Jr., John Demeter, Roger Dewey, Janetta Dexter, Ray Diggs, James Dolan, Michael Donahue, David Donald, David Dretler, Kevin Earls, Stan Edelman, Robert F. Engs, Sandige Evans, Ada Focer, Laura Foner, Gerald Fraser, Evelyn Ward Gay, Lizzie Graham, Kathy Grant, Rev. Joseph Greer, Phil Gresham, Deidre Griswold, R. U. Harden, Scott Harney, Rev. Charles Harper, Rev. Mike Haynes, Charles Hill, Dr. A. M. Hillhouse, Michael Hirsch, Mary Holman, Brady Hughes, Charlayne Hunter, Sarah Jackson, Dr. J. Warren Jacobs, Hugh M. Jenkins, Clarence "Jeep" Jones, John J. Jones, Maria Jones, Wendy Kaplan, Edwin J. Kennealey, Charlene Kinch, Maria

Acknowledgments / 657

Kinch, Edythe Lewis, Frank Lewis, Ed Logue, Mrs. Archie Lowe, Arthur Lycett, Reginald Mack, Janice MacPherson, Peter Mancusi, Margaret Johnson Mansfield, Calley Mathis, H. R. Mathis, Carl McCall, Sandy McCleary, Wayne McEwing, Jean McGuire, Elizabeth McNeil, Fritz Melval, Bill Morrison, Walter Morrison, Emery Mosher, Leticia Mosher, Steve Moss, David Mugar, Rev. Bill Mullin, Philippa Myers, Arthur Neily, Ingram Neily, Carl Nickerson, Frank J. Olbrys, Mrs. W. P. Oliver, Gordon Oppenheim, Lois Osborne, Ashley Padgett, Peter Parham, Mrs. Andrew Pennington, Elizabeth Pleck, Frank Power, Seymour Rainey, Jack Regan, Dan Richardson, David and Ellen Rome, Elliot Rothman, Robert Royster, Wiley Ruggles, Byron Rushing, Kenneth Salk, Harriet Schwartz, Hasan Sharif (a.k.a. Arnold Walker), Robert Siflinger, John Sills, Nathan Spivey, Dighton Spooner, Alice R. Stewart, Rev. Charles Stith, Mattie Stone, Ben Story, Lois Story, David Stratman, Joe Strickland, Gerald Sullivan, Paul Tafe, Jean Tibbs, Chuck Turner, Cassandra Twymon, Frederick Twymon, Haywood Twymon, Rachel Twymon, Rachel Twymon (daughter), Wayne Twymon, Daisy Voight, Mrs. Marguerite Wagner, Rev. Walter Waldron, Audrey Walker, George Walker, Helen Walker, James Walker, John Walker, Richard Walker, Tommy Walker, Mrs. John Ward, Mamie Lee Washington, Magnolia Williams, Robin Winks, Richard Wolfe.

McGOFF

Ann and Peter Anderson, Sam Barnes, Ann Blackham, James Blaine, Frank and Joan Boucher, Rev. Robert Boyle, Bruce Brand, Carol Bratley, Jim Breay, John Brennan, Eileen Brigandi, Rev. Lawrence Buckley, Ruth Butler, John Caddigan, Chris Callahan, Jock Callan, Katherine Carroll, P. J. Carroll, Daniel J. Casey, Rick Cash, Ann Castro, Brendan Mac Giolla Choille, Jim "Shorty" Connolly, Jim and Gloria Conway, David Craig, Roberta Delaney, Robert Dinsmore, Jerry Doherty, Lynn Doherty, Michael Donovan, Peg Donovan, Edward and Mary Evers, Pamela Fairbanks, Kathleen Field, Richard Fisher, Billy Galvin, William "Mother" Galvin, John Gardiner, Kay Gibbs, Hunna Gillen, Mary Gillen, Maurice Gillen, Barbara Gillette, Steven Grace, John Grady, Pat Greatorex, John Green, Rev. Thomas Hamill, Joan Hansen, Cindy Hayes, Robert Jarvis, Tom Johnson, Rev. William Joy, Dennis Kearney, John V. Kelleher, Frank and Barbara Kelly, Jim Kerrigan, Mary Killoran, Bryan Kirk, James Kirk, John Kirk, Joe Kirk, Robert and Chris Kirk, Anton Lahnston, Ted Landsmark, Peter Lynch, Capt. William MacDonald, Alf MacLochlainn, Louis Maples, Larry and Maryann Mathews, Oren McCleary, Gordon and Helen McClung, Peter McClure, Alice McGoff, Billy McGoff, Bobby McGoff, Danny McGoff, Kevin McGoff, Lisa McGoff, Robin McGoff, Tommy McGoff, Charles McGonagle, Pat and Barbara McGonagle, Thomas C. McNally, Peter Meade, Rev. John Mulgrew, Mike Mullan, Robert Murphy, Ann Neary, Bob O'Brien, Donalda O'Brien, Leon O'Brion, John O'Connor, Rev. John O'Leary, Mon O'Shea, David Overly, Joe Owens, Mary Parker, Frankie Perreault, Peg Pigott, Ernest and Ethel Pothier, Enrique Rivas, Janeth Rivas, Patti Rooney, Tom Rose, Alice Rosikas, Noel Ross, Michael Ruddy, Pat Russell, Rev. Ernest Serino, Elizabeth Shannon, James Shannon, Brian Sheehan, Jack Sheehan, Mike Sheeran, Gene Simpson, Lewis H. Spence, Eliot Stanley, W. Scott Stanley, Joe Vilimas, Martin Walsh, Rev. Jack Ward, Diane White, Virginia Winters, Carolyn Wrenn, Nina Wright.

OTHER

William Alonso, Alan Altshuler, Michael Ansara, Robert Sam Anson, John Borden Armstrong, Ken Auletta, Richard Ballou, Martha Bayles, Samuel Beer, Derrick Bell, Gary Bellow, Michael Beschloss, Steve Bing, John Bok, Earl Bolt, Clark Booth, Charles Bourke, Jim Brann, Owen Brock, Frank Broderick, Barry Brooks, Emmet H. Buell, Jr., Bernice Buresh, Constance Burns, Maria Burwell, Al Carderelli, Thomas J. Carens, Eve Carey, Kenneth Carey, George Carroll, James Carroll, Turner Catledge, Ephron Catlin, Robert Caulfield, Hale Champion, Paul Chapman, Susan Cheever, Karen Clark, Marie Clark, Muriel Cohen, Shelly Cohen, Steve Cohen, Jack Cole, Jean Cole, Robert Coles, Bud Collins, George Collins, John Collins, Rev. Peter Conley, James Michael Connolly, Janet Connors, Elizabeth Cooke, Tom Corrigan, John and Helen Cort, Robert Cover, Harvey Cox, Peter Cowen, Rayleen Craig, Herbert Crimlisk, Timothy Crouse, John T. Day, Reuben Dawkins, John Deedy, Margaret del Guidice, Robert Dentler, Alan Dershowitz, Edwin Diamond, Larry DiCara, Diane Divoky, Karen Dobkin, Francis J. Doherty, Jr., Parker Donham, Jim Doyle, Richard Dray, Rev. John Driscoll, John P. Driscoll, Ron Edmunds, Ann Eldridge, Gordon Emerson, Steven Erlanger, Dexter Eure, Marion Fahey, David Farrell, Steve Farrell, Joseph Featherstone, Joseph Feeney, Bob Fichter, Carmen Fields, Owen Fiss, John Flaherty, Lisa Flanagan, J. Harold Flannery, Thomas Fleming, William Foley, Eric Foner, Mo Ford, Ian Forman, Ron Formisano, Don Forst, Badi Foster, James L. Franklin, Hirsh Freed, Bernard Frieden, Richard Gaines, John Kenneth Galbraith, John Galvin, Peter Gammons, Curtis Gans, Alex Ganz, Joseph Garrity, John Garrity, W. Arthur Garrity, Arthur Gartland, George Gendron, Tom Gerber, K. Dun Gifford, Nathan Glazer, Herb Gleason, Charles Glenn, Rolf Goetze, Stan Goldsboro, Frank Goodman, Joyce Grant, James Green, David Greenway, Gary Griffith, Charles Grigsby, Rev. Michael Groden, Paul Grogan, Herbert Gutman, Milton Gwirtzman, Dennis Hale, Robert W. Hallgring, Herbert Hambleton, Frank Harris, Joseph Harsh, Ken Hartnett, Kenneth Haskins, Bob Hayden, Robert Healy, Rev. Brian Hehir, William Henry, Burton Hersh, Seymour Hersh, Louise Day Hicks, George Higgins, Fred Holborn, Rob Hollister, Harold Howe, Sam and Nancy Huntington, Howard Husock, Lester and Helen Hyman, Harold Isaacs, Ira Jackson, Michael Janeway, Christopher Jencks, Donald Jensen, Nicholas Johnson, Arthur Jones, Austin Jones, Frank N. Jones, Robert Jordan, Ward Just, Katherine Kane, Jon Katz, Godfrey Kauffmann, Herb Kenney, Larry Kessler, Langley Keyes, John Kifner, Martin Kilson, Ed King, David L. Kirp, Donald Klein, Joe Klein, Michael Knight, Ken Kobre, Msgr. Francis Lally, Al Larkin, Austin H. Lawrence, William Leary, Brian LeClaire, Charles Leftwich, Tim Leland, Robert Lenzner, Terry Lenzner, John Leubsdorf, Bob Levey, Ann Lewis, John V. Lindsay, Martin Linsky, John Livingston, William Looney, Eugene Lothery, Peter Lucas, Alan Lupo, Christopher Lydon, Sandra Lynch, Paula Lyons, Elaine Maddox, Richard Maguire, John Maher, Pauline Maier, Phyllis Malamud, J. Joseph Maloney, Michael Mandelbaum, Robert Manning, Burke Marshall, Kim Marshall, Ed Martin, Gordon Martin, John Marttila, Anna Mays, Richard P. McBrien, Nina McCain, Edward McCormack, John McCormack, Wendell McDonald, Vic McElheny, George McGrath, Kate McMahon, Jack McManus, Charles McMillan, Timothy Meagher, Humberto Cardinal Medeiros, Manuel Medeiros, Natalie Medeiros, Herman Mello, Jim Menno, Ian Menzies, Phil Meyer, Frank Michelman, Bill Miller, Rabbi Judea Miller, Nancy Mitchell, Marilyn Monteiro, Frank Morgan, Tim Murphy, Msgr. Edward G. Murray, James M. Nabrit III, Marie Augusta Neal, Gloria Negri, David Nelson, Mary Perot Nichols, Martin Nolan, Eric Nordlinger, Dave

Jean Paul Tremblay

O'Brian, David O'Brian, Jr., John O'Bryant, Vince O'Donnell, Tom Oliphant, Gary Orren, Paul Parks, Herbert Parmet, Orlando Patterson, Thomas Pettigrew, Robert Phelps, Gerry Pleshaw, Tully Plesser, J. Stanley Pottinger, John Powers, Lloyd Prentice, Bob Pressman, James Purdy, Lee Rainwater, Diane Ravitch, Perri Reeder, George Regan, Robin Reisig, Arnie Reisman, Elliot Richardson, David Riesman, Caryl Rivers, Eleanor Roberts, John Robinson, Rev. Edward Rodman, David Rogers, Steve Rosenfeld, Robert Rosenthal, Roy Rosenzweig, Michael Ross, Richard Rowland, Michael Ryan, Rev. Paul Rynne, Bob Sales, Janet Savage, Kirk Scharfenberg, Arthur Schlesinger, Jr., George Schlichte, Rhoda Schneider, Stanley K. Schultz, Robert Schwartz, Janet Scott, Marvin Scott, Rev. Isaiah Sears, Terry Philip Segal, Terry Seligmann, Mark Seltzer, William Shannon, Margaret Garrity Shea, Rev. Shawn Sheehan, Tom Sheehan, Virginia Sheehy, Mark Siegel, Harvey Silverglate, Joseph Slavet, Mary Ellen Smith, Mel Smith, Paul Smith, Crocker Snow, Paul Solmon, Barbara Solomon, Margaret Spengler, John Spiegel, Micho Spring, David Stanger, Rich Stearns, David Steinberg, Elizabeth Stevens, George Stoney, Leonard P. Strickman, Edward Sullivan, Rev. Eugene Sullivan, Carol Surkin, Laurence Susskind, Charles Taylor, Davis Taylor, John Taylor, Stephan Thernstrom, Mary Thornton, John W. Tierney, Frank Tivnan, Cyrus Vance, Eric van Loon, Jack Walsh, Robert Walsh, Sam Bass Warner, Isabel Gates Webster, John Weis, Sara Wermiel, Steven Wermiel, Charles Whipple, Kevin White, Terrence White, Enoch Whitehouse, Curtis Wilkie, Roger Wilkins, Charles Willie, John Wilpers, Thomas Winship, Ed Winter, Jane Wishner, Jerry Wishnow, Jules Witcover, William Wolbach, Robert Wood, Virgil Wood, Anne Wyman, Jerry Wynegar, Paul Ylvisaker.

Several books and unpublished dissertations have been especially useful to me in preparing this work. They are: Jan Hart Cohen, "To See Christ in Our Brothers: The Role of the Texas Roman Catholic Church in the Rio Grande Valley Farm Workers' Movement" (Master's Thesis, University of Texas at Austin, December 1974); Donald Norman Jensen, "School Desegregation in Boston: The Courts and Public Policy" (Ph.D. Thesis, Harvard University, June 1979); Gordon E. Kershaw, *The Kennebec Proprietors* (Somersworth: New Hampshire Publishing Co., 1975); Langley C. Keyes, *The Rehabilitation Planning Game: A Study in Neighborhood Diversity* (Massachusetts Institute of Technology, Boston, 1969); Jonathan Kozol, *Death at an Early Age* (Houghton Mifflin, Boston, 1967); Alan Lupo, *Liberty's Chosen Home: The Politics of Violence in Boston* (Little, Brown & Co., Boston, 1977); James Vincent Menno, "The Urban Priest and the Ministry of Justice: A Study of Clergy Response to Desegregation in Boston" (undergraduate paper at Boston College); Douglas O'Connor, "Remembering Roxbury," *Boston Magazine* (April, 1977); Kenneth P. O'Donnell and David Powers, with Joe McCarthy, *Johnny, We Hardly Knew Ye: Memories of John Fitzgerald Kennedy* (Little, Brown & Co., Boston, 1972); Herbert S. Parmet, *Jack: The Struggle of John F. Kennedy* (The Dial Press, New York, 1980); Elizabeth Hafkin Pleck, *Black Migration and Poverty: Boston 1865–1900* (New York: Academic Press, 1979); Peter Milo Shane, "The Origins of Educational Control: Class, Ethnicity and School Reform in Boston, 1875–1920" (Honors Thesis, Harvard College, March 1974).

A Note on the Type

The text of this book was set in a digitized version of a type-face called Times Roman, designed by Stanley Morison (1889–1967) for *The Times* (London) and first introduced by that newspaper in 1932.

Among typographers and designers of the twentieth century, Stanley Morison was a strong forming influence as a typographical advisor to The Monotype Corporation, as a director of two distinguished English publishing houses, and as a writer of sensibility, erudition, and keen practical sense.

Composed by Graphic Composition, Inc.,
Athens, Georgia.
Printed and bound by Fairfield Graphics,
Fairfield, Pennsylvania.
Designed by Iris Weinstein.

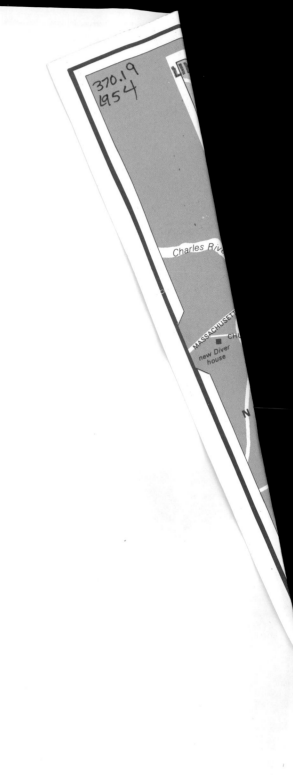